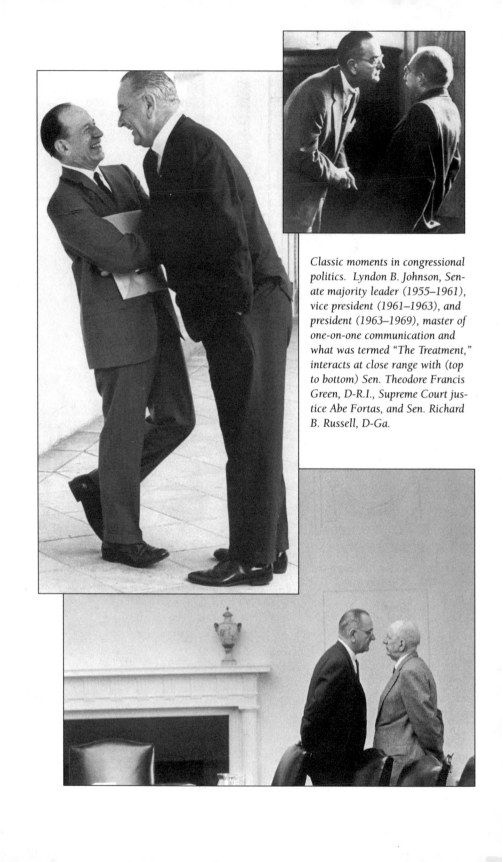

Classic moments in congressional politics. Lyndon B. Johnson, Senate majority leader (1955–1961), vice president (1961–1963), and president (1963–1969), master of one-on-one communication and what was termed "The Treatment," interacts at close range with (top to bottom) Sen. Theodore Francis Green, D-R.I., Supreme Court justice Abe Fortas, and Sen. Richard B. Russell, D-Ga.

Congress
and Its Members

Ninth Edition

Roger H. Davidson
University of Maryland

Walter J. Oleszek
Congressional Research Service

CQ PRESS

A Division of Congressional Quarterly Inc.
Washington, D.C.

CQ Press
1255 22nd Street, N.W., Suite 400
Washington, D.C. 20037

(202) 729-1900; toll-free, 1-866-4CQ-PRESS (1-866-427-7737)

www.cqpress.com

⊚ The paper used in this publication exceeds the requirements of the American National Standard for Information Sciences—Permanence of Paper for Printed Library Materials, ANSI Z39.48-1992.

Printed and bound in the United States of America

07 06 05 04 03   5 4 3 2 1

Photo credits: Agence France-Presse, 419 (middle); AP/Wide World, 2 (bottom), 80 (top right, bottom left, bottom right), 150 (top left, middle), 291 (bottom), 319 (top), 345 (bottom), 419 (bottom); Scott J. Ferrell, Congressional Quarterly, 2 (middle), 12 (bottom), 118 (bottom), 192 (middle, bottom), 228, 260 (top, bottom), 291 (top), 319 (bottom), 345 (top, middle), 367 (top, middle, bottom), 391 (middle, bottom), 447; Franks for Senate, Inc., Smith & Haroff, 80 (top left); *The Hill,* 118 (top); LBJ Library, frontispiece (middle, bottom); Library of Congress, 12 (top); *New York Times,* frontispiece (top); Reuters, 2 (top), 38 (bottom), 150 (bottom), 192 (top), 291 (middle), 319 (middle), 391 (top); Hung Liu/U.S. Bureau of the Census, 38 (top); U.S. Navy, 419 (top).

Library of Congress Cataloging-in-Publication Data

ISBN: 1-56802-816-4
ISSN: 1539-1779

For Nancy; Douglas, Victoria, Elizabeth, Thomas, James;
Alexander, Chris, Teddy, Emily, and Olivia
R. H. D.

For Janet, Mark, and Eric
W .J .O.

Contents

Part 4   Policy Making and Change in the Two Congresses

10   Congress and the President   291

11   Congress and the Bureaucracy   319

12   Congress and the Courts   345

13   Congress and Organized Interests   367

14   Congress, Budgets, and Domestic Policy Making   391

Preface

As authors of the ninth edition of a book that first appeared in 1981, we are perforce believers in the maxim that in politics six months is a long time and four years practically a lifetime. Events of recent years surely bear out this wisdom.

The presidency of Bill Clinton took Congress and the American people on a wild roller-coaster ride of success and disappointment. George W. Bush, Clinton's successor, emerged from the 2000 presidential contest that ended in the political equivalent of a tied score resolved by a judicial coin toss. Thus Bush faced the daunting task of governing in the absence of a clear electoral mandate. But his moderately successful presidency was dramatically transformed by the terrorist attacks of September 11, 2001, which enabled him to reinvent himself into a wartime leader.

Political forces on Capitol Hill reflected a recent partisan realignment. The new century found the two parties in a state of virtual parity. The Republicans began the 108th Congress (2001–2003) with 229 House seats, a sufficient but not overwhelming majority. In the Senate the GOP edge was a 51–48 (with one Independent who tended to side with the minority Democrats)—by no means a comfortable majority in a chamber that values independence and often requires supermajorities to conduct business.

The fluctuating fortunes of Presidents Clinton and George W. Bush and the Republican congressional majorities remind us of the pervasive pluralism of our political system, with its diversity of viewpoints and interests. What presidents and congressional majorities see as their mandates soon bump against the Founders' intricate "auxiliary precautions" for preventing majorities from winning quick or total victories. Not the least of the system's qualities is what we call the "two Congresses" dilemma: Congress is a conduit for localized interests and concerns as well as a maker of national policy.

In this edition we discuss new developments and fresh research findings regarding nearly every aspect of Congress. The impact of the September 11, 2001, attacks cannot be minimized. A wartime environment—thus far embracing two fighting wars in the Middle East and an ongoing war on terrorism—places extreme pressures on Congress. Deliberative legislative processes may seem out of place when people demand immediate, concerted actions. But hasty actions invariably are regretted, and sober reflections may demand legislative oversight and reconsideration.

The strength of partisanship and party leadership—perhaps the biggest Capitol Hill "story"—has at last gained serious attention from analysts. Party competition—the so-called permanent campaign— pervades nearly every aspect of legislative life. We record changes in the committee system, floor procedures, and the Capitol Hill "establishment." Congress's shifting relationships with presidents illustrate the centrality of the White House–Capitol Hill connection and raise once again fundamental questions about the results of unified versus divided party control.

Amid all these global and political changes, there are underlying constants in Congress's character and behavior. Most important is the dual nature of Congress as a collection of career-minded politicians and at the same time a forum for shaping and refining national policy. We employ the "two Congresses" theme to explain the details of congressional life as well as the scholarly findings about legislators' behavior. Colorful personalities and practical examples illustrate the enduring topics essential for understanding Capitol Hill. We strive to describe recent events and trends precisely and perceptively; more than that, we try to place these developments in the broader historical and conceptual frameworks necessary for understanding how Congress and its members function.

For congressional experts, these are the best of times and the worst of times. On the one hand, we have witnessed an era of astonishing change on Capitol Hill—dramatic shifts in congressional membership, partisan control, structural and procedural arrangements, and policy agenda. Congress ought to validate its position as an initiator of national policy making. Yet, at the same time, executive decision makers, federal judges, and elite opinion makers profess widespread distrust of Congress. In our judgment, and that of most careful observers, this skepticism far outruns the institution's actual defects and shortcomings—a paradox that is manifested in our new edition of *Congress and Its Members*.

This edition, like its predecessors, is addressed to general readers seeking an introduction to the modern Congress as well as to college or university students taking courses on the legislative process or national policy making. We have tried to provide our readers with the most accurate, timely, and readable information possible, along with the most important and thoughtful insights from scholars and practitioners alike. Although wrapped around our core theme and a number of subthemes, the book's chapters are long on analysis. For this we do not apologize. Lawmaking is a complicated business that demands special skills; those who would understand it must encounter its details and nuances. At the same time, we trust we have conveyed something of the energy and excitement of the place. After all, our journalist friends are right: Capitol Hill is the best "beat" in town.

Anyone who has prepared nine editions of a book has incurred more debts to friends and fellow scholars than could ever be recounted. Authors are primarily indebted to their readers, in this case the students and teachers at the hundreds of colleges and universities here and abroad where our book has been adopted. We have benefited from a large number of scholars and, for this edition, several outstanding young scholars.

We acknowledge our colleagues at the Congressional Research Service and elsewhere: Mildred Amer, Stanley Bach, Richard Beth, Sarah A. Binder, Colton Campbell, Joe Cantor, Kevin Coleman, Royce Crocker, Paul E. Dwyer, C. Lawrence Evans, Louis Fisher, Gary Galemore, Kevin Gates, William Heniff, Henry Hogue, David Huckabee, Frederick Kaiser, Robert Keith, Johnny H. Killian, Mike Kolakowski, Forrest Maltzman, Ronald Moe, John S. Pontius, Harold Relyea, Sula P. Richardson, Paul Rundquist, Steve Rutkus, Elizabeth Rybicki, Richard Sachs, Judy Schneider, Eric R. A. N. Smith, Sean M. Theriault, and Donald Wolfensberger.

Our friends at CQ Press deserve special appreciation. Brenda Carter, director of the college division, patiently encouraged us at every step. Charisse Kiino, our editor, proved once again the exceptional quality of CQ's editorial work. Colleen McGuiness provided skilled and probing editorial assistance. Christopher Karlsten coordinated the entire effort and tried to hold us to our deadlines. Belinda Josey kept the trains running on time. Talia Greenberg gave invaluable advice on photo research. Deborah Ismond fashioned fresh graphics throughout the book and implemented our concept of congressional time lines.

Our deep appreciation for our families, for their love and support, cannot be fully expressed in words. As a measure of our affection, this book is dedicated to them.

Roger H. Davidson, Santa Barbara, California
Walter J. Oleszek, Fairfax, Virginia
June 2003

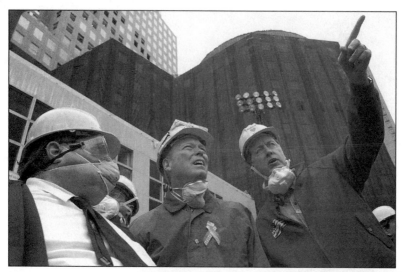

Rep. Jerrold Nadler, D-N.Y., and the "two Congresses" after disaster strikes the World Trade Center in his Eighth District. Above, Nadler (left, in mask) and Democratic leader Dick Gephardt, Mo., are shown areas of devastation as lawmakers tour Ground Zero. Nadler (left) and fellow New York Democrats Joseph Crowley and Carolyn B. Maloney attend an Appropriations Committee markup to lobby for New York City aid. Below, Nadler talks with New York mayor Michael Bloomberg.

1

The Two Congresses

A U.S. representative rarely gets to see a part of his constituency attacked and destroyed. But Rep. Jerrold Nadler, D-N.Y., did on the morning of September 11, 2001. Nadler, who represents Wall Street, the Upper West Side of Manhattan, and portions of Brooklyn, was watching television in his Washington, D.C., apartment when the second jetliner hit the World Trade Center, his district's most prominent landmark.

"Holy God, this is a terrorist act," Nadler exclaimed. "I immediately decided I had to get back to my district." [1] With a steadily fading cell phone his only link to the outside world, he and his wife coped with several disrupted train rides, reaching the Hudson River eight hours later. Meanwhile, his staff members—in Washington, Brooklyn, and lower Manhattan—struggled to keep abreast of developments and to respond to field inquiries from frantic constituents.

"What's amazing is when you come up to New York on the train, you can normally see the twin towers from [northern New Jersey]," Nadler recalled. "All we could see was a plume of smoke. I can't tell you how empty I felt. I felt violated. This is my New York I'm coming home to." [2]

Nadler spent the next few days talking to constituents and surveying the disaster site. His Web site featured a new page with phone numbers and links for those in need of disaster relief services. Lawmakers from districts affected by the disaster quickly formed a bipartisan task force to develop legislative responses.

Nadler's experiences illustrate the themes in this book. The work of Congress is conducted not only on Capitol Hill but also in states and districts hundreds or thousands of miles away. Nadler has lived all his life in or near his district: born in Brooklyn, educated at Columbia University and Fordham Law School, worked as an attorney, served sixteen years in the New York State Assembly. Like most of his colleagues, his career is enmeshed in partisan politics. A liberal Democrat, he worked for local and national candidates, including the Eighth District's Rep. Ted Weiss. When Weiss died in 1992, Nadler's close ties with insiders in the heavily Democratic area won him the party's nomination.

Nadler's Capitol Hill role is an extension of his district's character—with its large concentration of liberal Jewish voters and gay and lesbian activists. As a member of the Judiciary Committee, he defended President Bill Clinton in the impeachment imbroglio and upheld his party's positions on such issues as gun control, abortion, crime, consumer issues, and civil liberties. His liberal voting record (AFL-CIO, Americans for Democratic Action) is 100 percent;

conservative groups rank him in the single digits.[3] In 2002 he was reelected by three quarters of the Eighth District's votes.

The Dual Nature of Congress

The crisis in New York's Eighth District underscores the dual nature of Congress. Like all members of Congress, Nadler inhabits two very different but closely linked worlds. Nadler's activities highlight integral aspects of the national legislature—Congress as a lawmaking institution and as an assembly of local representatives. The question is how can these disparate elements be reconciled?

The answer is that there are two Congresses. One is the Congress of textbooks, of "how a bill becomes a law." It is Congress acting as a collegial body, performing constitutional duties and debating legislative issues. And it is an intriguing subject. To tourists and Cable Satellite Public Affairs Network (C-SPAN) viewers no less than to veteran analysts, Capitol Hill is a fascinating arena where many of the forces of American political life converge—ambitious politicians, cabinet members, lowly bureaucrats, and lobbyists both powerful and weak. The issues they voice on Capitol Hill, to invoke a timeworn sentiment, affect the well-being of all.

This Congress is more than a collection of its members at any given time. It is a mature institution with a complex network of rules, structures, and traditions. These norms mark the boundaries of the legislative playing field and define the rules by which the game is played. Individual members generally must accept Congress on its own terms and conform to its established ways of doing things. Paradoxically, the institution at once both resists change and invites change.

A second Congress also exists, glimpsed in New York's Eighth District, that is every bit as important as the Congress of the textbooks. This is the representative assembly of 540 individuals (100 senators, 435 representatives, 4 delegates, and 1 resident commissioner). It is composed of men and women of diverse ages, backgrounds, and routes to office. The electoral fortunes of its members depend less upon what Congress produces as an institution than upon the support and goodwill of voters hundreds or thousands of miles away. "As locally elected officials who make national policy," asserts Paul S. Herrnson, "members of Congress almost lead double lives." [4]

The two Congresses are in some ways widely separated. The tight-knit, complex world of Capitol Hill is a long way from New York's Eighth District, in perspective and outlook as well as in miles. Moreover, the two Congresses are analytically distinct. Studies suggest that public officials and citizens view the twin functions of elected assemblies—lawmaking and representing—as separate, definable tasks.

Yet these two Congresses are closely bound together. What affects one sooner or later affects the other. Nadler has fashioned his own representational style. His language and his brash liberalism speak in the accents of his hometown.

The Historical Basis

The dual character of Congress is rooted in history. Congress's mandate to write the nation's laws is found in Article I of the U.S. Constitution, which details the powers of government as set forth by the founders in 1787. It was no accident that the Constitution's drafters devoted the first article to the legislature nor that here were enumerated most of the government's powers. Familiar with the British Parliament's prolonged struggles with the Crown, these authors assumed the legislature would be the chief policy-making body and the bulwark against arbitrary executives. ("In republican government, the legislative authority necessarily predominates," observed James Madison in *The Federalist Papers*.)[5] Although in the ensuing years the initiative for policy making shifted many times between the legislative and executive branches, the U.S. Congress remains virtually the only national assembly in the world that drafts in detail the laws it passes, instead of simply debating and ratifying measures prepared by the government in power.

As a representative body, Congress must respond to the insistent demands of voters and constituents. Although not specifically spelled out in the Constitution, these duties inevitably flow from constitutional provisions for electing representatives and senators.

The House of Representatives was intended to be the most representative element of the U.S. government. Representatives are elected directly by the people for two-year terms to ensure that they do not stray too far from popular opinion. As Madison explained, the House should have "an immediate dependence on, and an intimate sympathy with, the people." [6] For most members of the House, this two-year cycle means nonstop campaigning, visiting, looking after constituents, and errand running. For some the job is simpler than for others; yet no elected official is immune to electoral defeat.

The Senate originally was intended to be one step removed from popular voting to temper the House's popular passions: State legislatures selected senators. But the founders ultimately were overruled. In 1913 the people's voice was assured with the ratification of the Seventeenth Amendment, which provided for direct election of senators. Although elected for six-year terms, senators must stay in close touch with the electorate. Like their House colleagues, senators typically regard themselves as servants of their constituents. Most have transformed their office staffs into veritable cottage industries for generating publicity and handling constituents' inquiries.

Thus the Constitution and subsequent historical developments affirm Congress's dual functions of lawmaker and representative assembly. Although the roles are tightly bound together, they nonetheless impose separate duties and functions.

Legislators' Tasks

The dualism between institutional and individual duties surfaces in legislators' daily activities and roles. As Speaker Sam Rayburn, D-Texas, once remarked: "A congressman has two constituencies—he has his constituents at home, and his colleagues here in the House. To serve his constituents at home, he must also serve his colleagues here in the House." [7]

Senators and representatives suffer from a lack of time to accomplish what others expect of them. No problem vexes members more than that of juggling constituency and legislative tasks. Despite scheduled recesses for constituency business (called "district work periods" by the House, "nonlegislative periods" by the Senate), the pull of constituency business is relentless. The average representative spends 120 days a year in the home constituency; the average senator, 80 days.[8] Even in Washington, legislative and constituency demands clash. According to one study, less than 40 percent of a representative's Washington time is allotted to lawmaking duties on the floor of the House or in committee.[9]

Members of Congress, when asked to describe the functions they should perform in office, stress the twin roles of legislator and representative. Legislators vary in how they balance these roles, not to mention what time and resources they devote to them. With their longer terms, senators can stress voter outreach and fence mending during the year or so before reelection and focus on legislative activities at other times. Yet senatorial contests normally are more competitive and costly than House races, and many senators now run flat out for reelection all the time—like most of their House colleagues.[10]

Legislators must choose between the demands of these two roles. A congressionally sponsored survey asked members about how they spent their time and what they would like to do ideally as a member of Congress. By a wide margin the senators and representatives said they would devote extra time to lawmaking and other Capitol Hill duties instead of to constituency demands.[11]

Congress's dual nature—the unresolved dichotomy between its lawmaking and representative functions—is dictated by the Constitution, validated by historical experience, and reinforced by the inclinations of voters and legislators alike. Yet Congress is one body, not two. The same members who shape bills in committee and vote on the floor must rush to catch planes back to their districts, where they are plunged into a different world, one of local problems and personalities. And the same candidates who must sell themselves at shopping center rallies must in the nation's capital help shape the federal budget or military weapons systems. The unique character of Congress arises directly from its dual role as a representative assembly and a lawmaking body.

Popular Images

The notion of the two Congresses also conforms with the perceptions of the average citizen. Opinion studies reveal that people view the U.S. Congress through lenses different from those through which they see their individual senators and representatives. Congress as an institution is perceived primarily as a lawmaking body. It is judged mainly on the basis of citizens' overall attitudes about politics, policies, and the state of the union. Do people like the way things are going, or do they not? Are they optimistic or pessimistic about the nation's future? Do they subscribe to Mark Twain's cynical view that Congress is "a distinctly native criminal class"?

By contrast, citizens view their own legislators as agents of local concerns. People judge their legislators by such yardsticks as service to the district, communication with constituents, and home style (the way officeholders deal with the home folks). In judging their senators or representative, voters are likely to ponder questions such as these: Is the legislator trustworthy? Does the legislator communicate well with the state (or district) by answering mail promptly and offering timely help to constituents? Does the legislator listen to the state (or district) and its concerns?[12]

The public's divergent expectations of Congress and its members often send conflicting signals to senators and representatives. Congress as a whole is judged by policies and results, however vaguely these are understood by voters. Individual legislators are more apt to be elected, and returned to office, because of personal qualities and constituent service. For many legislators, this incongruity dictates a strategy of opening as much space as possible between themselves and "those other politicians" back in Washington—including their party's leaders.

Back to Burke

On November 3, 1774, in Bristol, England, the British statesman and philosopher Edmund Burke set forth for his constituents the dual character of a national legislature. The constituent-oriented parliament, or Congress, he described as

> a Congress of ambassadors from different and hostile interests, which interests each must maintain, as an agent and advocate, against other agents and advocates.

The parliament of substantive lawmaking he portrayed in different terms. It is

> a deliberative assembly of one nation, with one interest, that of the whole—where not local purposes, not local prejudices, ought to guide, but the general good, resulting from the general reason of the whole.[13]

Burke preferred the second concept and did not hesitate to let his voters know it. He would give local opinion a hearing, but his judgment and conscience would prevail in all cases. "Your faithful friend, your devoted servant, I shall be to the end of my life," he declared; "flatterer you do not wish for." [14]

Burke's Bristol speech is an enduring statement of the dilemma confronting members of representative assemblies. Burke was an inspired lawmaker. (He even sympathized with the cause of the American colonists.) But, as might be said today, he suffered from an inept home style. His candor earned him no thanks from his constituents, who turned him out of office at the first opportunity.

Burke's dilemma applies equally on this side of the Atlantic. From colonial times to the present, American voters have tended to prefer their lawmakers to be delegates, who listen carefully to constituents and follow their guidance. During an encounter in Borger, Texas, an irate Baptist minister shouted at then-representative Bill Sarpalius, D-Texas, "We didn't send you to Washington to make intelligent decisions. We sent you to represent us." [15] Sarpalius subsequently was defeated for reelection. The authors of the Constitution expected intimate bonds between voters and lawmakers (at least in the House), ensuring them by providing frequent elections.

So it does no violence on constitutional theory to assume that election, or reelection, is the paramount operational goal of individual office seekers. As a former representative put it: "All members of Congress have a primary interest in getting reelected. Some members have no other interest." [16] After all, politicians are (like other people) self-interested, and winning elections is the prerequisite for achieving long-range political goals. "[Reelection] has to be the *proximate* goal of everyone, the goal that must be achieved over and over if other ends are to be entertained" writes David R. Mayhew in his noted essay *Congress: The Electoral Connection*.[17] (Mayhew's essay is a classic exercise in "If, then" reasoning: If reelection is assumed as the goal of all members, then what can this reveal about the institution? Quite a lot, as Mayhew demonstrates.)

The reelection imperative is by no means the whole story. Burke's idea that legislators are trustees of the nation's common good is still extolled. In a 1995 decision, U.S. Supreme Court justice John Paul Stevens noted that, once elected, members of Congress become "servants of the people of the United States. They are not merely delegates appointed by separate, sovereign states; they occupy offices that are integral and essential components of a single national Government." [18]

Furthermore, legislators do not always engage in self-interested bidding for local constituents' votes. Politicians harbor a range of ultimate goals (health, wealth, fame, family, religious faith). Among the most prominent is promoting what they view as the public interest. It is reasonable, therefore, to assume that elected officials "make an honest effort to achieve good public policy." [19]

Burke posed the tension between the two Congresses so vividly that we have adopted his language to describe the conceptual distinction that forms the crux of this book. From Burke, we have also drawn the titles for Part 2, "A Congress of Ambassadors," and Part 3, "A Deliberative Assembly of One Nation." Every legislator sooner or later must come to terms with Burke's dichotomous Congress; citizens and voters will have to form their own answers.

Divergent Views of Congress

Congress has been the subject of a huge array of books, monographs, and articles. Many of its features make Congress a favorite object of scholarly scrutiny. It is open and accessible. It can be approached by traditional means—journalistic stories, case studies, and normative or historical accounts. It is amenable to scientific analysis, whether empirical, mathematical, or theoretical. Its work can be measured by statistical indicators (floor votes, for example) that permit elaborate comparative analyses. And Congress is, above all, a fascinating place—the very best site from which to view the varied actors in the American political drama.

Writers of an interpretive book on the U.S. Congress thus can draw on a multitude of sources, an embarrassment of riches. Studies of Congress constitute a vast body of political literature. This is a mixed blessing because all this information must be integrated into something resembling a coherent whole. Moreover, much of the writing is highly specialized, technical, or theoretical. We have tried to put such material into perspective, make it understandable to interested nonspecialists, and use illustrative examples wherever possible.

A gaping chasm exists between this rich literature and the caricature of Congress often prevalent in the popular culture. Pundits and humorists from Mark Twain and Will Rogers to Jay Leno and David Letterman have found Congress an inexhaustible source of raw material. The other branches of government have nothing like the cartoon image of lawmakers as corrupt, pompous windbags. Citizens tend to share this disdain toward the legislative branch—especially at moments of furor over, say, congressional pay raises or ethics scandals.

The picture of Congress conveyed in the media is scarcely more flattering. Journalistic hit-and-run specialists, especially news magazines, editorial writers, and talk-show hosts, perpetuate a cartoonish stereotype: an irresponsible and somewhat sleazy gang resembling Woodrow Wilson's caustic description of the House as "a disintegrated mass of jarring elements." [20] Legislators in their home states or districts often contribute to Congress's poor image by portraying themselves as escapees from the funny farm on Capitol Hill. As Richard F. Fenno Jr. puts it, they "run *for* Congress by running *against* Congress." [21]

Citizens' ambivalence toward the popular branch of government—which, by the way, goes back to the beginnings of the Republic—says something of the milieu in which public policy is made. To comprehend how the two Congresses function—both the institution and individual members—popular stereotypes must be abandoned and the complex realities examined. This book is intended to fill in the details left unexamined in popular accounts. We believe we know our subject well enough to appreciate Congress's foibles and understand why it works the way it does. Yet we try to maintain a professional—yes, scholarly—distance from it.

According to an old saying, two things should never be viewed up close: making sausage and making laws. "I don't think I'd want to tell the public how laws are made around here," confessed Sen. Peter Fitzgerald, R-Ill. "It's not a pretty process." [22] Despite this warning, we urge readers to take a good look and form their own opinions about Congress's effectiveness. Some may recoil from what they discover. Numerous flaws can be identified in members' personal or public behavior, in their priorities (incentive structures), and in their lawmaking practices. But careful observers also will discover much behavior in Congress that is purposeful and principled, many policies that are reasonable and workable. We invite students and colleagues to examine with us what Congress has done thus far and consider what prospects lie ahead.

"A woman's place is in the House—and the Senate." Above, the seven women members of the 71st Congress (1929–1931), a decade after women won the right to vote nationwide. In January 2003, below, all fourteen women senators met at a "power coffee" to greet two new members. They join sixty-two women serving in the House during the 108th Congress (2003–2005).

2

Evolution of the Modern Congress

The first Congress met in New York City, the seat of government, in the spring of 1789. Business was delayed until a majority of members arrived to make a quorum. On April 1 the thirtieth of the fifty-nine elected representatives reached New York; Frederick A. C. Muhlenberg of Pennsylvania was chosen Speaker of the House. Five days later the Senate achieved its quorum, although its presiding officer, Vice President John Adams, did not arrive for another two weeks.

New York City was then a bustling port on the southern tip of Manhattan Island. Congress met in Federal Hall at the corner of Broad and Wall Streets. The House occupied a large chamber on the first floor and the Senate a more intimate chamber upstairs. The new chief executive, George Washington, was still en route from his home at Mount Vernon, his trip having become a triumphal procession with crowds and celebrations at every stop. To most of his countrymen, Washington—austere, dignified, the soul of propriety—embodied a government that was otherwise no more than a plan on paper.

The two houses of Congress did not wait for Washington's arrival. The House began debating tariffs, a perennially popular legislative topic. In the Senate, Vice President Adams, a brilliant but self-important man, prodded his colleagues to decide upon proper titles for addressing the president and himself. Adams was dubbed "His Rotundity" by a colleague who thought the whole discussion absurd.

On inaugural day, April 30, Adams was still worrying about how to address the president. The issue was discarded when the representatives, led by Speaker Muhlenberg, burst into the Senate chamber and seated themselves. Meanwhile, a special committee was dispatched to escort Washington to the chamber for the ceremony. The swearing-in was conducted on an outside balcony in front of thousands of assembled citizens. The nervous Washington haltingly read his speech. Then everyone adjourned to St. Paul's Chapel for a special prayer service. Thus the U.S. Congress became part of a functioning government.[1]

Antecedents of Congress

The legislative branch of the new government was untried and unknown, searching for procedures and precedents. And yet it grew out of a rich history of development—stretching back more than five hundred years in Great Britain, no less than a century and a half in North America. If the architects of the Constitution of 1787 were unsure how well their new design would work, they had firm ideas about what they intended.

The English Heritage

From the time of the English king Edward the Confessor in the eleventh century, the central problem of political theory and practice was the relationship of the Crown to its subjects. Out of prolonged struggles, a strong, representative parliament emerged that rivaled and eventually eclipsed the power of the Crown. The evolution of representative institutions on a national scale began in medieval Europe. Monarchs gained power over large territories where inhabitants were divided into social groupings—among them the nobility, clergy, landed gentry, and town officials. The monarchs brought together leaders of these groupings, or estates of the realm, not to create representative government but to fill the royal coffers. As Charles A. Beard and John P. Lewis observed, "Even the most despotic medieval monarch could not tax and exploit his subjects without limits; as a matter of expediency, he had also to consider ways and means." [2]

These groups—parliaments, they came to be called—evolved over the centuries into the representative assemblies of today. Four distinct stages of their development have been identified. At first the parliaments, representing the various estates, met to vote taxes for the royal treasury, engaging in little discussion. Next, these tax-voting bodies evolved into lawmaking bodies that presented the king with petitions for redressing grievances. Third, by a gradual process that culminated in the revolutions of the seventeenth and eighteenth centuries, parliaments wrested lawmaking and tax-voting powers from the king, transforming themselves into truly sovereign bodies. In the nineteenth century, finally, parliamentary representation expanded beyond the older privileged groups to embrace the masses, eventually every adult man and woman. [3]

By the time the New World colonies were founded in the 1600s, the struggle for parliamentary rights was well advanced into the third stage, at least in England. Bloody conflicts, culminating in the beheading of Charles I in 1649 and the dethroning of James II in 1688 (the Glorious Revolution), established parliamentary influence over the Crown. Out of such struggles flowed a remarkable body of political and philosophic writings. By the eighteenth century, works by James Harrington (1611–1677), John Locke (1632–1704), and others were the common heritage of educated people—including the leaders of the American Revolution.

The Colonial Experience

This tradition of representative government migrated to the New World. As early as 1619 the thousand or so Virginia colonists elected twenty-two burgesses, or delegates, to a General Assembly. In 1630 the Massachusetts Bay Company established itself as the governing body for the Bay Colony, subject to annual elections. The other colonies, some of them virtually self-governing, followed suit.

Representative government took firm root in the colonies. The broad expanse of ocean shielding America fostered self-reliance and autonomy on the part of colonial assemblies. Claiming prerogatives similar to those of the British House of Commons, these assemblies exercised the full range of law-making powers—levying taxes, issuing money, and providing for colonial defense. Legislation could be vetoed by colonial governors (appointed by the Crown in the eight royal colonies), but the governors, cut off from the home government and depending on local assemblies for revenues and even for their own salaries, usually preferred to reach agreement with the locals. Royal vetoes could emanate from London, but these took time and were infrequent.[4]

Other elements nourished the tree of liberty. Many of the colonists were free spirits, dissidents set on resisting all authority, especially that of the Crown. Readily available land, harsh frontier life, and—by the eighteenth century—a robust economy fed the colonists' self-confidence. The town meeting form of government in New England and the separatists' church assemblies helped cultivate habits of self-government. Newspapers, unfettered by royal licenses or government taxes, stimulated lively exchanges of opinions.

When Britain decided in the 1760s to tighten its rein upon the American colonies, the restraint was met, not surprisingly, with stubborn opposition. Did not the colonists enjoy the same rights as Englishmen? Were not the colonial assemblies the legitimate governments, with authority derived from popular elections? As British enactments grew increasingly unpopular, along with the governors who tried to enforce them, the locally based colonial legislatures took up the cause of their constituents.

The colonists especially resented the Stamp Act of 1765 (later repealed) and the import duties imposed in 1767. From these inflated customs receipts the home government began paying the salaries of royal governors and other officials, thus freeing those officials from the grasp of colonial assemblies. The crisis worsened in the winter of 1773–1774, when a group of colonists staged a revolt, the Boston Tea Party, to protest the Tea Act. In retaliation, the House of Commons closed the port of Boston and passed a series of Intolerable Acts, further tightening royal control.

National representative assemblies in America were born on September 5, 1774, when the First Continental Congress convened in Philadelphia. Every colony except Georgia sent delegates, a varied group that included peaceable loyalists, moderates such as John Dickinson, and firebrands such as Samuel Adams and Paul Revere. Gradually anti–British sentiment congealed, and Congress passed a series of declarations and resolutions (each colony casting one vote) amounting to a declaration of war against the mother country.[5] After Congress adjourned on October 22, King George III declared that the colonies were "now in a state of rebellion; blows must decide whether they are to be subject to this country or independent." [6]

The First Continental Congress gave colonists a taste of collective decision making, and the Second Continental Congress proclaimed their independence from Britain. When the Second Continental Congress convened on May 10, 1775, many still thought war might be avoided. A petition to King George asking for "happy and permanent reconciliation" was even approved. The British responded by proclaiming a state of rebellion and launching efforts to crush it. Sentiment in the colonies swung increasingly toward independence, and by the middle of 1776 Congress was debating Thomas Jefferson's draft resolution that "these united colonies are, and of right ought to be, free and independent states." [7]

The two Continental Congresses gave birth to national politics in America. Riding the wave of patriotism unleashed by the British indignities of 1773–1774, the Congresses succeeded in pushing the sentiments of leaders and the general public toward confrontation and away from accommodation with the mother country. They did so by defining issues one by one and by reaching compromises acceptable to both moderates and radicals—no small accomplishment. Shared legislative experience, in other words, moved the delegates to the threshold of independence. Their achievement was all the more remarkable in light of what historian Jack N. Rakove describes as the "peculiar status" of the Continental Congress, "an extra-legal body whose authority would obviously depend on its ability to maintain a broad range of support." [8]

More than five years of bloody conflict ensued before the colonies won their independence. Meanwhile, the former colonies hastened to form new governments and draft constitutions. Unlike the English constitution, these charters were written documents. All included some sort of bill of rights, and all paid tribute to the doctrine of separating powers among legislative, executive, and judicial branches of government. Equal branches were not created, however. Nearly all the constitutions gave the bulk of powers to their legislatures. Earlier conflicts with the Crown and the royal governors had instilled a fear of executive authority. "In actual operation," a historian wrote, "these first state constitutions produced what was tantamount to legislative omnipotence." [9]

The national government was likewise, as James Sterling Young put it, "born with a legislative body and no head." [10] Strictly speaking, no national executive existed between 1776 and 1789—the years of the Revolutionary War and the Articles of Confederation (adopted in 1781). On its own, Congress struggled to wage war against the world's most powerful nation, enlist diplomatic allies, and manage internal affairs. As the war progressed and legislative direction proved unwieldy, Congress tended to delegate authority to its own committees and to permanent (executive) agencies. Strictly military affairs were placed in the hands of a designated leader: George Washington, who at the war's end returned his commission to Congress in a public ceremony. Considering the obstacles it faced, congressional government was far from a failure. Yet the mounting inability of all-powerful legislative bodies, state and national, to deal with postwar problems spurred demands for change.

At the state level, Massachusetts and New York rewrote their constitutions, adding provisions for potentially strong executives. At the national level, the Confederation's frailty led many to advocate a more energetic government—one with enough authority to implement laws, control currency, levy taxes, dispose of war debts, and, if necessary, put down rebellion. Legislative prerogatives, it was argued, should be counterbalanced with a vigorous, independent executive.

In this spirit, delegates from the states convened in Philadelphia on May 25, 1787, intending to strengthen the Articles of Confederation. Instead, they drew up a wholly new governmental charter.

Congress in the Constitution

The structure and powers of Congress formed the core of the Constitutional Convention's deliberations. On these questions, the fifty-five delegates at the Philadelphia convention were divided, and more than three months passed before they completed their work. A tripartite governmental system was outlined, with Congress named first in the Constitution. The plan, agreed upon and signed September 17, 1787, was a bundle of compromises. Nationalist and states' rights interests—large and small states, northern and southern states—had to be placated. The result was a singular blend of national and federal features based on republican principles of representation and limited government. The Constitution served the nationalists' goal of an energetic central government that could function independently of the states. It also conceded the states' rights principle of limited powers shared by the various branches.

Powers of Congress

The federal government's powers are shared by three branches: legislative, executive, and judicial. Although considered one of the Constitution's most innovative features, separation of powers arose from English and colonial experience, which argued for dispersing governmental functions. It was advocated by philosophers Harrington, Locke, and the baron de Montesquieu. The Articles of Confederation's failure to separate these functions was widely regarded as a mistake.

Legislators have unfettered authority to organize the chambers as they see fit and are accorded latitude in performing their duties. To prevent intimidation, they cannot be arrested during sessions or while traveling to and from sessions (except for treason, felony, or breach of the peace). Members in their deliberations enjoy immunity from any punitive action: In speech and debate, "they shall not be questioned in any other place" (Article I, Section 6).

Despite their worries over all-powerful legislatures, the founders laid down an expansive mandate for the new Congress. Mindful of the achievements of

New World assemblies, not to mention the British Parliament's age-long struggles with the Crown, they viewed the legislature as the chief repository of governmental powers. Locke had observed that "the legislative is not only the supreme power, but is sacred and unalterable in the hands where the community have placed it." [11] Locke's doctrine found expression in Article I, Section 8, which enumerates Congress's impressive array of powers. Here is laid out virtually the entire scope of governmental authority as the eighteenth-century founders understood it. This portion of the Constitution reflects the founders' vision of a vigorous legislature as the engine of an energetic government.

Raising and spending money for governmental purposes lies at the heart of Congress's prerogatives. The power of the purse was the lever by which parliaments historically gained bargaining advantages over kings and queens. The Constitution's authors, well aware of this, gave Congress full powers over taxing and spending.

Financing the government is carried out under a broad mandate in Article I, Section 8: "The Congress shall have power to lay and collect taxes, duties, imposts and excises, to pay the debts and provide for the common defense and general welfare of the United States." Although this wording covered almost all known forms of taxing, there were limitations. Taxes had to be uniform throughout the country; duties were prohibited on goods traveling between states; and "capitation . . . or other direct" taxes were prohibited, unless levied according to population (Article I, Section 9). This last provision proved troublesome when the U.S. Supreme Court held in 1895 (*Pollock v. Farmers' Loan and Trust Co.*) that it applied to taxes on incomes. To overcome this confusion, the Sixteenth Amendment, ratified eighteen years later, explicitly conferred the power to levy income taxes.

Congressional power over government spending is no less sweeping. Congress is to provide for the "common defense and general welfare" of the country (Article I, Section 8). Furthermore, "No money shall be drawn from the Treasury, but in consequence of appropriations made by law" (Article I, Section 9). This provision is one of the legislature's most potent weapons in overseeing the executive branch.

Congress possesses potentially broad powers to promote the nation's economic well-being and political security. It has the power to regulate interstate and foreign commerce, and it has used this power to regulate not only trade but also transportation, communications, and such disparate subjects as labor practices, civil rights, and crime. This power is not unlimited and historically has been legally and politically contentious. Congress may also coin money, incur debts, establish post offices, build post roads, issue patents and copyrights, provide for a militia, and call forth the militia to repel invasions or suppress rebellions.

Although the three branches supposedly are coequal, the legislature takes the lead in formulating the structure and duties of the other two. The Constitution mentions executive departments and officers, but it does not specify their structure or duties, aside from those of the president. Thus the design of the executive branch, including cabinet departments and other agencies, is spelled out in laws passed by Congress and signed by the president. The judiciary, too, is largely a creation of statutes. It consists of a Supreme Court and "such inferior courts as the Congress may from time to time ordain and establish" (Article III, Section 1). Although the courts' jurisdiction is delineated, the Supreme Court's appellate jurisdiction is subject to "such exceptions" and "such regulations as the Congress shall make" (Article III, Section 2).

Congress's powers within the federal system were greatly enlarged by the Civil War amendments—the Thirteenth (1865), Fourteenth (1868), and Fifteenth (1870). The Radical Republicans, who had supported the war and controlled Congress in its aftermath, feared that former Confederate states would ignore the rights of blacks—the cause over which the war had been waged. Thus these amendments nationalized such citizens' rights as voting, due process, and equal protection of the laws. By implication, eventually recognized by court rulings, citizens were also protected against state actions that violated any of the Bill of Rights guarantees. To underscore such a basic change in the federal bargain, the three amendments' authors gave Congress the powers of enforcement by "appropriate legislation."

Congress is a full partner in foreign relations with its power to declare war, ratify treaties, raise and support armies, provide and maintain a navy, and make rules governing the military forces. Finally, Congress is vested with the power "to make all laws which shall be necessary and proper for carrying into execution the foregoing powers" (Article I, Section 8). This elastic clause, undoubtedly added to give Congress the means to implement its enumerated powers, has provoked far-reaching debates over the scope and reach of governmental activity.

Limits on Legislative Power

Congress's enumerated powers—those "herein granted"—are not boundless. The very act of listing the powers was intended to limit government, for by implication those powers not listed are prohibited. The Tenth Amendment reserves to the states or to the people all those powers neither explicitly delegated nor prohibited by the Constitution. This guarantee is a rallying point for those who take exception to particular federal policies or who wish broadly to curtail federal powers.

Eight specific limitations on Congress's powers are noted in Article I, Section 9. The most important bans are against bills of attainder, which pronounce a particular individual guilty of a crime without trial or conviction and impose a sentence, and ex post facto laws, which make an action a crime after it has been committed or otherwise alter the legal consequences of some past action. Bills of attainder and ex post facto laws are traditional tools of authoritarian regimes. Congress's enumerated powers are also limited in matters such as the slave trade, taxation, appropriations, and titles of nobility.

The original Constitution contained no bill of rights or list of guarantees for citizens or states. Pressed by opponents during the ratification debate, supporters of the Constitution promised early enactment of amendments to remedy this omission. The resulting ten amendments, drawn up by the First Congress and ratified December 15, 1791, are a basic charter of liberties that limits the reach of government. The First Amendment prohibits Congress from establishing a national religion, preventing the free exercise of religion, or abridging the freedoms of speech, press, peaceable assembly, and petition. Other amendments secure the rights of personal property and fair trial and prohibit arbitrary arrest, questioning, or punishment.

Rights not enumerated in the Bill of Rights are not necessarily denied (Amendment IX). In fact, subsequent amendments, legislative enactments, judicial rulings, and states' actions have enlarged citizens' rights to include the rights of citizenship, of voting, of privacy, and of "equal protection of the laws."

Separate Branches, Shared Powers

The Constitution not only delineates Congress's powers but also distinguishes them from those of the other two branches. Senators and representatives, while in office, are prohibited from serving in other federal posts; those who serve in such posts are in turn forbidden from serving in Congress (Article I, Section 6). This restriction forecloses any form of parliamentary government, in which leading members of the dominant parliamentary party or coalition form a cabinet to direct the ministries and other executive agencies.

Legislative Interdependence. Because the branches are separated, some people presume that the powers they exert should also be isolated. In practice, however, governmental powers are interwoven, even if the branches are separate. James Madison explained that the Constitution created not a system of separate institutions performing separate functions but separate institutions that share functions so that "these departments be so far connected and blended as to give each a constitutional control over the others." [12]

Congress cannot act alone, even in lawmaking. Although the Constitution vests Congress with "all legislative powers," these powers cannot be exercised without involvement by the president and by the courts. This same interdependency applies to executive and judicial powers. The president is a key figure in lawmaking. According to Article II, the president can convene one or both houses of Congress in special session. Although unable to introduce legislation directly, the president "shall from time to time give to the Congress information on the state of the Union, and recommend to their consideration such measures as he shall judge necessary and expedient." The president also has the power to veto congressional enactments. After a bill or resolution has passed both houses of Congress and been delivered to the White House, the president must sign it or return it within ten days (excluding Sundays). Overruling a presidential veto requires a two-thirds vote in each house.

Carrying out laws is the duty of the president, who is enjoined by the Constitution to take care that laws are faithfully executed. As head of the executive branch, the president has the power to appoint "officers of the United States," with the Senate's advice and consent. Although Congress sets up the executive departments and agencies, outlining their missions by statute, chief executives and their appointees manage the character and pace of executive activity.

In diplomacy and national defense, traditional domains of royal prerogative, the Constitution apportions powers between the executive and legislative branches. Following tradition, presidents are given wide discretion in such matters. They appoint ambassadors and other envoys, they negotiate treaties, and they command the country's armed forces. However, like other high-ranking presidential appointees, ambassadors and envoys must be approved by the Senate. Treaties do not become the law of the land until they are ratified by the Senate. Although the president may dispatch troops, only Congress has the power of formally declaring war. Reacting to the Vietnam War, Congress in 1973 passed the War Powers Resolution, intended to restrain presidents from making war without congressional involvement.

Historically, presidents and Congresses (and courts) have reached accommodations to exercise the powers they share. As Justice Joseph Story once wrote, the authors of the Constitution sought to "prove that rigid adherence to [separation of powers] in all cases would be subversive to the efficiency of government and result in the destruction of the public liberties." Justice Robert Jackson noted in 1952 that "while the Constitution diffuses power the better to secure liberty, it also contemplates that practice will integrate the dispersed powers into a workable government." [13]

Impeachment. Congress has the power to impeach and remove the president, the vice president, and other "civil officers of the United States" for serious breaches of the public trust: treason, bribery, or "other high crimes and misdemeanors." The House of Representatives has the sole authority to draw up and adopt (by majority vote) articles of impeachment, which are charges that the individual has engaged in one of the named forms of misconduct. The Senate is the final judge of whether to convict on any of the articles of impeachment. A two-thirds majority is required to remove the individual from office or to remove and also bar the individual from any future "offices of public trust."

Three attributes of impeachment fix it within the separation of powers framework. First, it is exclusively the domain of Congress. (Even though the chief justice presides over Senate trials of the president, his rulings may be overturned by majority vote.) The two chambers are free to devise their own procedures for reaching their decisions. The Supreme Court refused to review the Senate's procedures when a former federal judge, Walter L. Nixon Jr., objected that, although he had been convicted by the full Senate, the evidence in his case had been taken by a committee, not the full Senate. [14]

Second, impeachment is a legislative proceeding that is essentially political in character. The structure may appear judicial—the House a grand jury, the Senate a trial court—but lawmakers decide whether and how to proceed, which evidence to consider, and even what constitutes an impeachable offense. Treason is defined by the Constitution, and bribery by statute; but the words "high crimes and misdemeanors" are open to interpretation. They are usually defined (in Alexander Hamilton's words) as "abuse or violation of some public trust"—on-the-job offenses against the state, the political order, or the society at large.[15] This means they can be either more or less than garden-variety criminal offenses. Both presidential impeachment trials (Andrew Johnson, 1868; Bill Clinton, 1998–1999) were fiercely partisan affairs, in which combatants disputed not only the facts but also the appropriate grounds for impeachment.

Finally, impeachment is a clumsy instrument for punishing officials for the gravest of offenses. Congress has many lesser ways of reining in wayward officials. As for presidents and vice presidents, their terms are already limited. Although impeachments are often threatened, only fifteen Senate trials have taken place, and only seven individuals have been convicted. Significantly, all seven who were removed from office were judges—who, unlike executive officers, enjoy open-ended terms of office.[16]

Judicial Review

The third of the separated branches, the judiciary, has assumed a leading role in interpreting laws and determining their constitutionality. Whether the founders anticipated this function of judicial review is open to question. Probably they expected each branch to reach its own judgments on constitutional questions, especially those pertaining to its own powers. This reading of the founders' intent is called the doctrine of coordinate construction.

Whatever the original intent, Chief Justice John Marshall soon preempted the other two branches with his Court's unanimous assertion of judicial review in *Marbury v. Madison* (1803). Judicial review involves both interpretation and judgment. First, "it is emphatically the province and duty of the judicial department to say what the law is." Second, the Supreme Court has the duty of weighing laws against the Constitution, the "supreme law of the land," and invalidating those that are inconsistent—in the *Marbury* case a minor provision of the Judiciary Act of 1789.[17] Yet Congress, not the Court, remained the primary forum for weighty constitutional debates throughout the nineteenth century. Until the Civil War only one other law, the Missouri Compromise, had been declared unconstitutional by the Court (*Dred Scott v. Sandford*, 1857). Since the Civil War, however, the Court has been more aggressive in interpreting and judging congressional handiwork.

For the record, the Supreme Court has invalidated 152 congressional statutes, in whole or in part, in the 200 years since *Marbury*.[18] This count does not include lower court holdings that have not been reviewed by the Supreme

Court. Nor does it cover laws whose validity has been impaired because a similar law was struck down.

The justices' political leanings have historically worked either to expand or to contract the powers of Congress. Judges are said to exercise judicial restraint when using their power of judicial review sparingly, deferring to the judgments of the legislature (and executive) and intervening only in cases flagrantly at odds with the Constitution. Judicial activism involves more aggressive patrolling of the limits of the two elective branches' powers.

Judges are commonly labeled as practitioners of activism or restraint, but this is a false distinction. Ideology drives judges to activity on some subjects and passivity on others. Conservative courts from Reconstruction to the late 1930s, for example, fashioned the concept of "economic due process" to shield businesses from state and federal attempts at regulating the economy. At the same time, they generally deferred to legislative interpretations of civil rights and civil liberties, even when those actions fell far short of what seemed to be required by the Bill of Rights or the Civil War amendments. Court liberals of the 1950s and 1960s (Chief Justice Earl Warren's era) pushed far ahead of Congress to remedy long-standing violations of individual liberties and rights, but they rarely challenged congressional regulation of the economy.

Recently, conservative activists have seemingly been ascendant on the high court and a majority of federal appeals courts. The Supreme Court of Chief Justice William H. Rehnquist (1986–), though closely divided on many issues, has mustered a 5-to-4 majority to limit congressional powers in some thirty-odd cases since 1995. As one legal scholar put it,

> For nearly a decade, the court's five conservative justices have steadily usurped the power to govern by striking down or weakening federal and state laws regulating issues as varied as gun sales, the environment, and patents—as well as laws protecting women and . . . the disabled.[19]

Many court clashes with congressional powers turn on obscure or complex issues. One exception was a ruling (*Alabama v. Garrett*, 2001) that handicapped state employees cannot sue their own state government for discriminating against them in violation of the 1990 Americans with Disabilities Act (ADA).[20] Writing for the Court's majority, Rehnquist held that "states are not required . . . to make special accommodations for the disabled." The reason lay in an expanded notion of states' "sovereign immunity" from suits by private citizens, even if they can show they have been injured in violation of federal law—an interpretation dismissed by legal scholars as largely an invention of the Court's majority.[21]

Another dispute between the Court's majority and minority in *Alabama v. Garrett* involved opposing views of legislative and judicial powers. Rehnquist asserted what he called "the long-settled principle that it is the responsibility of this court, *not Congress*, to define the substance of constitutional guarantees"—

a claim far more grandiose than Chief Justice Marshall's duty "to say what the law is." [22] The ADA had been passed in 1990 by overwhelming margins and signed by President George Bush, who hailed it as a major advance in civil rights. Evidence of discrimination against disabled state employees had been amassed by congressional panels. Rehnquist dismissed this evidence as anecdotal.

Justice Stephen G. Breyer, writing for the minority, countered: "In fact, Congress compiled a vast legislative record documenting 'massive, society-wide discrimination' against persons with disabilities." He appended a thirty-nine-page list of findings from the ADA's legislative history. Breyer (a onetime Capitol Hill staff member) went on to remind his colleagues of the constitutional primacy of legislative judgments.

> Unlike courts, Congress can readily gather facts from across the nation, assess the magnitude of a problem, and more easily find an appropriate remedy. Unlike courts, Congress directly reflects public attitudes and beliefs, enabling Congress better to understand where, and to what extent, refusals to accommodate disability amount to behavior that is callous or unreasonable to the point of lacking constitutional justification. Unlike judges, members of Congress can directly obtain information from constituents who have first-hand experience with discrimination and related issues.

While the Court was narrowing the power of congressional laws regulating states, it tended to accept without question executive (and legislative) actions curtailing the rights of criminal defendants—for example, those accused (or merely suspected) of security breaches in the wake of the 2001 terrorist attacks. Such conflicts are rooted in political ideology: in this case, a conservative Supreme Court majority striking down ostensibly "liberal" socioeconomic laws and condoning restrictions on defendants' rights in the name of national security.

Yet another dimension of the conflict is the bifurcated career patterns of modern-day judges and elective officials. From Marshall's day through Earl Warren's, the Court typically included members steeped in legislative or executive experience. Today's sitting justices, in contrast, are drawn almost exclusively from lower federal or state courts. (Only one had ever held elective office: Sandra Day O'Connor, a onetime Arizona state senator.) The challenge of comprehending the legislative approach to policy questions has plagued the Court's treatment of other politically charged issues, such as racial gerrymandering and campaign finance.

None of this means, however, that the Supreme Court necessarily has the last word in "saying what the law is." Its interpretations of laws may be questioned and even reversed. If the congressional sponsors or supporters of a law disagree with the justices' readings of the text, they may clarify or modify the language in subsequent enactments. One study found that 121 of the Court's interpretive decisions had been overridden in the 1967–1990 period, an average of 10 per Congress. The author of the study concluded that "congressional committees in fact carefully monitor Supreme Court decisions" and that Congress was apt to override decisions of a closely divided Court, decisions that rely on the law's plain meaning, and decisions that clash with positions taken by federal, state, and local governments.[23]

Nor is the Court the sole arbiter of what is or is not constitutional. Courts routinely accept customs and practices developed by the other two branches. Likewise, they usually decline to decide sensitive political questions in the province of Congress and the executive. When courts strike down an enactment, Congress may turn around and pass laws that meet the courts' objections or achieve the same goal by different means.

Congress sometimes reacts to judicial holdings by trying to impede, modify, or reverse them or by simply ignoring them. The *Dred Scott* decision helped bring about the Civil War. Reconstruction laws and constitutional amendments after the war explicitly nullified the Court's holding. And despite *Immigration and Naturalization Service v. Chadha* (1983), Congress continues to enact legislative veto provisions, which were in large part outlawed but which administrators often feel obliged to honor out of political prudence.

The courts play a leading but not exclusive role in interpreting laws and the regulations emanating from them. When Congress passes a law, the policy-making process has just begun. Courts and administrative agencies then assume the task of refining the policy, but they do so under Congress's watchful eye. "What is 'final' at one stage of our political development," Louis Fisher observes, "may be reopened at some later date, leading to revisions, fresh interpretations, and reversals of Court doctrines. Through this never-ending dialogue, all three branches are able to expose weaknesses, hold excesses in check, and gradually forge a consensus on constitutional issues." [24]

Bicameralism

Although "the Congress" is discussed as if it were a single entity, Congress is divided internally into two very different, virtually autonomous chambers. Following the pattern initiated by Parliament and imitated by most of the states, the Constitution outlines a bicameral legislature. If tradition recommended the two-house formula, the politics of the early Republic commanded it. Large states preferred the "nationalist" principle of popularly based representation, but the smaller states insisted on a "federal" principle also ensuring representation by states.

The first branch—as the House was termed by Madison and Gouverneur Morris, among others—rests on the nationalist idea that the legislature should answer to the people instead of the states. As George Mason put it, the House "was to be the grand depository of the democratic principles of the government." [25] Many years later the Supreme Court ruled (in *Wesberry v. Sanders*, 1964) that these principles demanded that congressional districts within each state be essentially equal in population.

In contrast, the Senate embodied the federal idea. Each state would have two seats, the occupants to be chosen by the state legislatures and not by popular vote. The Senate would serve to curb the excesses of popular government. "The use of the Senate," explained Madison, "is to consist in its proceeding with more coolness, with more system, and with more wisdom, than the popular branch." [26]

Historical evolution overran the founders' intentions. In most cases, senators tended to voice dominant economic interests and shun the general public. British commentator Lord Bryce once remarked that the Senate seemed to care more for its "collective self-esteem" than it did for public opinion.[27] Yet state legislators often instructed their senators how to vote on vital issues. In some states legislative elections turned into statewide canvasses focusing on senatorial candidates. Such was the famous 1858 Illinois contest between Sen. Stephen A. Douglas and challenger Abraham Lincoln. The Democrats captured the legislature and sent Douglas back to Washington, but Lincoln's eloquent arguments against extending slavery to the territories west of the Mississippi River vaulted him into national prominence.

Direct election of senators came with the Seventeenth Amendment, ratified in 1913. A by-product of the Progressive movement, the new arrangement was designed to broaden citizens' participation and blunt the power of shadowy special interests, such as party bosses and business trusts. Thus the Senate became directly subject to popular will.

Bicameralism is the most obvious organizational feature of the U.S. Congress. Each chamber has a distinct process for handling legislation. According to the Constitution, each house sets its own rules, keeps a journal of its proceedings, and serves as final judge of its members' elections and qualifications. In addition, the Constitution assigns unique duties to each of the two chambers. The Senate ratifies treaties and approves presidential appointments. The House must originate all revenue measures; by tradition, it also originates appropriations bills. In impeachments, the House prepares and tries the case, and the Senate serves as the court.

The two houses jealously guard their prerogatives and resist intrusions by "the other body." Despite claims that one or the other chamber is more important—for instance, that the Senate has more prestige or that the House pays more attention to legislative details—the two houses staunchly defend their equal places. On Capitol Hill there is no "upper" or "lower" chamber.

Institutional Evolution

Written constitutions, even those as farsighted as the 1787 one, go only a short way in explaining how real-life governmental institutions work. On many questions such documents are inevitably silent or ambiguous. Issues that lie between the lines must be resolved in the course of later events.

In adapting to demands far removed from those of eighteenth-century America, Congress has evolved dramatically. Many of these changes can be subsumed under the term *institutionalization*—the process whereby structures and procedures take shape and become regularized. Instead of being unformed and unpredictable, the institution becomes structured and predictable, following settled traditions and widely held expectations about how it should perform. Institutionalization has shaped the two Congresses—Congress as deliberative body and Congress as individual representatives.

The Size of Congress

Looking at the government of 1789 through modern lenses, one is struck by the relatively small circles of people involved. The House of Representatives, that "impetuous council," was composed of sixty-five members—when all of them showed up. The aristocratic Senate boasted only twenty-six members, two from each of the thirteen original states.

As new states were added, the Senate grew. There were thirty-two senators in 1800, sixty-two in 1850, ninety by 1900, and one hundred today. (Since 1912 only the states of Alaska and Hawaii have been added.)

As for the House, the Constitution (Article I, Section 2) sets forth the method of apportioning its members—a decennial census. When the first census was taken in 1790, the nation's population count was fewer than four million—smaller than that of an average state today. "I take it for granted," Madison wrote in *The Federalist Papers* No. 55, "that the number of representatives will be augmented from time to time in the manner provided by the Constitution." [28] The House was raised to 104 members after the first census, and throughout the nineteenth century there were steady enlargements. The 1910 census, which counted ninety-two million people, led to a final expansion to 435 members. But following the 1920 census there was no size adjustment. And that is the way things stand to this day.

Enlarging the House is periodically urged—especially by states losing seats after a census. More seriously, some worry that congressional districts are too populous (only those in India are larger) to permit meaningful ties between citizens and their representatives. [29] The framers contemplated House districts of no more than thirty thousand people—huge by 1789 standards. Following that guideline would now require a House of some ninety-four hundred members. Modest enlargement would only marginally alleviate the problem. Most observers concur with Speaker Sam Rayburn, who served in Congress from 1913 to 1961, that the House is already at or above its optimum size for lawmaking.

Size profoundly affects an organization's work. Growth compelled the House to develop strong leaders, to rely heavily on its committees, to impose strict limits on floor debate, and to devise elaborate ways of channeling the flow of floor business. It is no accident that strong leaders emerged during the House's periods of rapid growth. After the initial growth spurt in the first two decades of the Republic, vigorous leadership appeared in the person of Henry Clay, whose speakerships (1811–1814, 1815–1820, and 1823–1825) demonstrated the potentialities of that office. Similarly, post–Civil War expansion was met with an era of forceful Speakers that lasted from the 1870s until 1910. Size is not the only impetus for strong leadership, but it also inevitably works to centralize procedural control.

In the smaller and more intimate Senate, vigorous leadership has been the exception rather than the rule. The relative informality of Senate procedures, not to mention the long-cherished right of unlimited debate, testifies to looser reins of leadership. Compared with the House's complex rules and voluminous precedents, the Senate's rules are brief and simple. Informal negotiations among senators interested in a given measure prevail, and debate typically is governed by unanimous consent agreements—agreed-upon ways of proceeding, brokered by the parties' floor leaders. Although too large for its members to draw their chairs around the fireplace on a chilly winter morning—as they did in the early years—the Senate today retains a clubby atmosphere that the House lacks.

The congressional establishment itself has changed in scale, with staffs added gradually. In 1891 a grand total of 142 clerks, 62 for the House and 80 for the Senate, were on hand to serve members of Congress. Many senators and all representatives handled their own correspondence. Keeping records and counting votes were the duties of committee clerks. After the turn of the twentieth century, House and Senate members, their clerks, and their committees moved into two ornate office buildings, one for each house. Today the legislative branch embraces some twenty-three thousand staff members. Housed in nearly a dozen Capitol Hill buildings, they include experts in virtually every area of government policy and constitute a distinct Washington subculture.

The Legislative Workload

During the Republic's early days, the government in Washington was "at a distance and out of sight." [30] Lawmaking was a part-time occupation. As President John F. Kennedy was fond of remarking, the Clays, Calhouns, and Websters of the nineteenth century could afford to devote a whole generation or more to debating and refining the few great controversies at hand. Rep. Joseph W. Martin, R-Mass., who entered the House in 1925 and went on to become Speaker (1947–1949, 1953–1955), described the leisurely atmosphere of earlier days and the workload changes during his service as follows:

> From one end of a session to another Congress would scarcely have three or four issues of consequence besides appropriations bills. And the issues themselves were fundamentally simpler than those that surge in upon us today in such a torrent that the individual member cannot analyze all of them adequately before he is compelled to vote. In my early years in Congress the main issues were few enough so that almost any conscientious member could with application make himself a quasi-expert at least. In the complexity and

volume of today's legislation, however, most members have to trust somebody else's word or the recommendation of a committee. Nowadays bills, which thirty years ago would have been thrashed out for hours or days, go through in ten minutes.[31]

The most pressing issue considered by the Foreign Affairs Committee during one session, Martin related, was a $20,000 authorization for an international poultry show in Tulsa, Oklahoma.

Congress's workload—once limited in scope, small in volume, and simple in content—has burgeoned since 1789. Some ten thousand bills and resolutions are introduced in the span of each two-year Congress; perhaps five hundred or so are enacted into law. By most measures—hours in session, committee meetings, floor votes—the congressional workload has about doubled over the past half century.

Legislative business has expanded in scope and complexity as well as in sheer volume. Today's Congress grapples with many issues that once were left to states or localities or were considered entirely outside the purview of governmental activity. Moreover, legislation tends to be more complex than it used to be. The average public bill of the late 1940s was two and a half pages long; by the late 1990s it ran to more than eighteen pages.[32]

For most of its history Congress was a part-time institution. Well into the twentieth century Congress remained in session for only nine of every twenty-four months, the members spending the rest of their time at home attending to private business. In recent decades legislative business has kept the House and Senate almost perpetually in session—punctuated by constituency work periods. During the average two-year Congress the Senate is in session nearly three hundred eight-hour days; the more efficient House gets by on somewhat less time.[33] The average senator or representative works an eleven-hour day when Congress is in session.[34]

Structures and Procedures

A mature institution exhibits not only the professionalism of its members but also the number and complexity of its structures and procedures. By that measure today's House and Senate are mature institutions indeed.

No trait illustrates Congress's institutional growth more dramatically than the division of labor through the committee system. Although fashioned gradually and seemingly inexorably, the committee system rests on precedents drawn from the British House of Commons, the colonial assemblies, and the Continental Congresses.[35] The first House standing committee (Elections) was created in 1789, but legislative business in both houses tended to be handled by temporary committees or on the floor. By the third decade of the nineteenth century, however, standing committees were firmly established.

The creation and, occasionally, abolition of committees parallel important historical events and shifting perceptions of public problems.[36] As novel policy problems arose, new committees were added. The House, for example, established Commerce and Manufactures in 1795, Public Lands in 1805, Freedmen's Affairs in 1866, Roads in 1913, Science and Astronautics in 1958, Standards of Official Conduct in 1967, Small Business in 1975, and Homeland Security in 2003. Numerous committees have existed at one time or another— as many as sixty-one in the House and seventy-four in the Senate.

Today the Senate has sixteen standing committees and the House has nineteen. These committees are only the tip of the iceberg, however. House committees now have nearly one hundred subcommittees; Senate committees, nearly seventy subcommittees. Four joint House–Senate committees have been retained. This adds up to some two hundred work groups, plus an abundance of task forces, party committees, voting blocs, informal caucuses, and the like.

The number of formal and informal leaders in Congress has grown as a function of proliferating work groups. Every committee and subcommittee has a chairman and a ranking minority member. The formal party leaders help organize the two chambers, assign members to committees, schedule business, and devise parliamentary strategy. Supplementing formal leadership posts in Congress are a host of informal leaders who represent factions, regions, economic interests, or issue positions. Thus formal leaders are now obliged to adopt what Barbara Sinclair calls a "strategy of inclusion"; that is, "drawing into the leadership's orbit and including in leadership efforts as many [partisans] as possible." [37] The result is ever more complex networks of give-and-take relationships in which less-informed members seek cues from better-informed colleagues, issue by issue. Today's Congress, in other words, abounds in leaders of every stripe.

In the early days, proceedings at the Capitol were disorderly, especially in the crowded, noisy, and badly ventilated chambers. "Debate has been rough and tumble, no holds barred, bruising, taunting, raucous, sometimes brutal," one historian related. "The floor of the House has been no place for the timid or the craven." [38] Before the Civil War, duels between quarreling legislators were not uncommon. One celebrated incident occurred in 1856, when Rep. Preston Brooks, a southern Democrat, stalked Sen. Charles Sumner, a Massachusetts Republican, and beat him senseless with a cane on the Senate floor for his views on slavery in the new territories.

As Congress matured, decorum by and large replaced chaos, and stricter rules of order came to govern the proceedings. Today there are formidable rules and precedents as well as numerous informal norms and traditions. Altering the rules is not a casual matter. (The House adopts its rules anew with each new Congress; as a continuing body the Senate has ongoing rules.) Most rules changes result from concerted effort by the leadership, party caucuses, or the respective rules committees. When major rules changes or committee realignments are considered, select committees may be established to make recommendations.

Despite institutional inertia the Senate and House repeatedly shift and adapt their ways of doing things—partly in response to changes in public and workload demands, partly in reaction to altered partisan or factional alignments, partly to accommodate shifts in membership. Just as physical anthropologists believe the earth's history is marked by periods of intense, even cataclysmic, change—punctuated equilibrium—so historians of Congress have identified several eras of extensive institutional change. "Reconstitutive change" is what Elaine K. Swift calls these instances of "rapid, marked, and enduring shift[s] in the fundamental dimensions of the institution." [39] During one such period (1809–1829), Swift argues, the Senate was transformed from an elitist, insulated "American House of Lords" into an active, powerful institution whose debates stirred the public and attracted the most talented politicians of the time. Another such period was the Progressive Era (roughly the first two decades of the twentieth century), when House leaders were toppled and the Senate became an elective body. The so-called reform era of the 1960s and 1970s qualifies as a third time of wide-ranging change, ushering in a period of heightened partisanship.

Not all institutional changes are so concentrated. Incremental changes of one kind or another are always unfolding. For example, the House in 1999 streamlined and codified its rules, and hardly anyone noticed. In a detailed examination of changes in committee jurisdictions, David C. King showed that periodic, large-scale jurisdictional "reform acts" were mainly compilations of gradually accumulated precedents created as novel bills were introduced.[40]

In short, Congress is no longer an informal institution. It bristles with norms and traditions, rules and procedures, committees and subcommittees. The modern Congress is highly institutionalized. How different from the First Congress, personified by fussy John Adams worrying about what forms of address to use. The institutional complexity of today's Congress enables it to cope with a staggering workload while for the most part containing personal conflict. Institutional complexity, however, carries its own costs—in rigidity and the cumbersome administrative apparatus needed to keep the system afloat.

Evolution of the Legislator's Job

What is it like to be a member of Congress? The legislator's job, like the institution of Congress, has evolved since 1789. During the early Congresses being a senator or representative was a part-time occupation. Few members regarded congressional service as a career, and from most accounts the rewards were slim. Since then the lawmakers' exposure to constituents' demands, their career expectations, and their factional loyalties have changed dramatically. Electoral units, too, have grown very large. After the 2000 census, which counted 282 million citizens, the average House constituency contained 650,000 people, the average state 5.6 million.

Constituency Demands

American legislators have been expected to remain close to their voters. From the very first, representatives reported to their constituents through circular letters, communications passed around throughout their districts.[41] In an era of limited government, however, there was little constituent errand running. "It was a pretty nice job that a member of Congress had in those days," recalled Rep. Robert Ramspeck, D-Ga., describing the Washington of 1911, when he came to take a staff job:

> At that time the government affected the people directly in only a minor way. . . . It was an entirely different job from the job we have to do today. It was primarily a legislative job, as the Constitution intended it to be.[42]

In those days a member's mail was confined mainly to awarding rural mail routes, arranging for Spanish War pensions, sending out free seed, and only occasionally explaining legislation. At most, a single clerk was required to handle correspondence. Members from one-party areas often did little personal constituency work. It was said that Democratic Speaker John Nance Garner, who entered the House in 1903 and ended his career as vice president (1933–1941), "for thirty years did not canvass his [south Texas] district and franked no speeches home." [43] His major constituency outreach consisted of barbecues given at his home in Uvalde, Texas.

This unhurried pace has long since vanished. Reflecting on his forty years on Capitol Hill, Representative Martin remarked on the dramatic upsurge of constituent awareness.

> Today the federal government is far more complex, as is every phase of national life. People have to turn to their Representative for aid. I used to think ten letters a day was a big batch; now I get several hundred a day. In earlier times, constituents didn't know their Congressman's views. With better communications, their knowledge has increased along with their expectations of what he must know.[44]

Even people of Martin's era (he left the House in 1967) would be astonished at the volume of constituency work now handled by House and Senate offices. Not only are constituents more numerous than ever before, but they are also better educated, served by faster communication and transportation, and mobilized by lobby organizations. Public opinion surveys show that voters expect legislators to dispense federal services and to communicate frequently with the home folks. Even though the crasser forms of pork barrel politics have come under attack, constituents' demands are unlikely to ebb in the future.

The Congressional Career

During its early years Congress was an institution composed of transients. The nation's capital was an unsightly place, its culture was provincial, and its summers were humid and mosquito-ridden. Members remained in Washington only a few months, spending their unpleasant sojourns in boardinghouses. "While there were a few for whom the Hill was more than a way station in the pursuit of a career," James Sterling Young observes, "affiliation with the congressional community tended to be brief." [45]

The early Congresses failed to command the loyalty needed to keep members in office. Congressional service was regarded more as odious duty than as rewarding work. "My dear friend," wrote a North Carolina representative to his constituents in 1796, "there is nothing in this service, exclusive of the confidence and gratitude of my constituents, worth the sacrifice. . . . Having secured this, I could freely give place to any fellow citizen, that others too might obtain the consolation due to faithful service." [46] Of the ninety-four senators who served between 1789 and 1801, thirty-three resigned before completing their terms, only six to take other federal posts. [47] In the House almost 6 percent of all early nineteenth-century members resigned during each Congress. Citizen legislators, not professional politicians, characterized that era.

Careerism mounted toward the end of the nineteenth century. As late as the 1870s more than half the House members at any given time were freshmen, and the mean length of service for members was barely two terms. By the end of the century, however, the proportion of newcomers had fallen to 30 percent, and average House tenure reached three terms, or six years. About the same time, senators' mean term of service topped six years, or one full term. [48] Today the average senator has served more than fifteen years (almost three terms); the average representative, more than eleven (nearly six terms). The data in Table 2-1 show changes since 1789 in the percentages of new and veteran members and the mean number of terms claimed by incumbents.

Rising careerism had a number of causes. The increase in one-party states and districts following the Civil War, and especially after the partisan realignment of 1896, made possible repeated reelection of a dominant party's candidates—Democrats in the core cities and the South, Republicans in the Midwest and the rural Northeast. Vigorous state and local party organizations dominated the recruitment process and tended to select party careerists to fill safe seats. [49] Around the turn of the twentieth century, however, electoral reforms—for example, direct primaries and the so-called Australian ballot (a uniform, secret, government-printed ballot)—blunted party control at the polling booth and encouraged candidates to appeal directly to their followers.

At the same time the power of the legislative branch, expressed in Woodrow Wilson's phrase "congressional government," made federal service ever more attractive and rewarding. [50] The government's subsequent growth enhanced the excitement and glamour of the national political scene, especially compared with state or local politics. Moreover, the physical environment of the nation's capital eventually improved. As Representative Martin related:

Table 2-1   Length of Service in House and Senate, 1789–2005

Chamber and terms	Congress			
	1st–56th (1789–1901)	57th–103d (1901–1995)	104th–107th (1995–2003)	108th (2003–2005)
House				
One (up to 2 years)	44.0%	23.3%	13.9%	12.4%
Two to six (3–12 years)	53.4	49.7	56.1	57.7
Seven or more (12+ years)	2.6	27.0	30.1	29.9
Mean number of terms[a]	2.1	4.8	5.2	5.7
Senate				
One (up to 6 years)	65.6%	45.6%	34.7%	30.0%
Two (7–12 years)	23.4	22.4	26.8	30.0
Three or more (12+ years)	11.0	32.0	38.5	40.0
Mean number of terms[a]	1.5	2.2	2.6	2.6

Source: Adapted from David C. Huckabee, *Length of Service for Representatives and Senators: 1st–103d Congresses,* Congressional Research Service Report No. 95–426GOV, March 27, 1995. Authors' calculations for the 104th through 108th Congresses.

[a] Figures are derived from the total number of terms claimed by members whether or not those terms were served out. For example, members in their initial year of service are counted as having one full term, and so on. Thus the figures cannot be equated precisely with years of service.

> The installation of air conditioning in the 1930s did more, I believe, than cool the Capitol: it prolonged the session. The members were no longer in such a hurry to flee Washington in July. The southerners especially had no place else to go that was half as comfortable.[51]

The rise of careerism, aided by turn-of-the-century political warfare between Progressives and the Old Guard (mainly within the dominant Republican Party), established the seniority rule to reward lengthy service. As long as senior members were scarce, they led their chambers and relied more on party loyalty than longevity in naming committees or chairmen. With careerists more numerous, greater respect had to be paid to seniority in distributing favored committee posts.

Seniority triumphed in both chambers at about the same time. In the Senate there was no decisive event. Seniority was largely unchallenged after 1877.[52] In the House strong post–Civil War Speakers, struggling to control the unruly chamber, sometimes bypassed seniority to appoint loyal lieutenants to major committees. But in 1910, when Speaker Joseph G. Cannon passed over senior members for assignments and behaved arbitrarily in other ways, the House revolted, divesting the Speaker of committee assignment power. With the Speaker's clout diminished, David W. Brady relates, "seniority came to be the most important criterion for committee assignments and chairmanships, and committees rather than parties became the major policy actors." [53]

Adherence to seniority fostered career patterns within the two houses. New members found themselves at the bottom of internal career ladders that they could ascend only through continued service. In recent decades seniority barriers have been lowered. After taking over the House in 1995, Republican leaders passed over several senior members in naming committee chairs. At the same time the GOP Conference limited chairs' terms to three years. The Committee on Committees holds interviews and selects chairs for committees and Appropriations subcommittees. Some of their choices depart from seniority, but all contenders are experienced members. Extended service, if not always seniority, remains a prerequisite for top party and committee posts.

Parties and Factions

Political parties had no place in the constitutional blueprint, which was deliberately fashioned to divide and dilute factional interests. However, when Treasury Secretary Alexander Hamilton unveiled his financial program in 1790, a genuine partisan spirit swept Capitol Hill. The Federalists, with Hamilton as their intellectual leader, espoused "energetic government" to deal forcefully with national problems. The rival Republicans, who looked to Thomas Jefferson and James Madison for leadership, rallied opponents of Federalist policies and championed local autonomy, weaker national government, and programs favoring lower-class or debtor interests.

When war broke out in Europe between revolutionary France and a coalition of old regimes, the Federalists sided with the dependable (and commercially profitable) British, while the Republicans tended to admire "French principles." By 1794 Sen. John Taylor of Virginia could write:

> The existence of two parties in Congress is apparent. The fact is disclosed almost upon every important question. Whether the subject be foreign or domestic—relative to war or peace—navigation or commerce—the magnetism of opposite views draws them wide as the poles asunder. [54]

U.S. House Speakers have always been political officers, and so they quickly came to reflect partisan divisions in wielding their powers. The other partisan institution in those early days was the congressional nominating caucus that selected a faction's presidential candidates. Not all members professed clear-cut partisan or factional affiliations, however. During the Era of Good Feelings (roughly 1815–1825), party voting was the exception rather than the rule. With the conspicuous exception of the nominating caucuses, no formal party apparatus existed. Between the quadrennial caucuses, Young explains, "the party had no officers, even of figurehead importance, for the guidance or management of legislative processes." [55] The nominating caucus collapsed after

1824, and the Jacksonians laid the foundation for something approaching a stable party system based on grassroots support.

Parties flourished in the years following the Civil War. Regional conflicts, along with economic upheavals produced by rapid industrialization, nurtured partisan differences. The Civil War and World War I mark the boundaries of the era of militant partisanship on Capitol Hill and in the country at large. At the grassroots level the parties were divided along class, occupational, and re-gional lines to a degree unimaginable today. Grassroots party organizations were massive and militant by American standards. Strong Speakers tamed the unruly House, and a coterie of statewide party bosses dominated the Senate. Even after the demise of the strong speakership (1910) and direct election of senators (1913), party caucuses or committees assumed responsibility for as-signing members to committees and sometimes even for formulating policy.

Today the parties' formal apparatus is extensive. There are policy com-mittees, campaign committees, research committees, elaborate whip systems, and numerous task forces. Some four hundred staff aides are employed by party leaders and perhaps an equal number by assorted party committees.[56] Party-oriented voting bloc groups (such as the conservative House Democrats' Blue Dogs or the Republicans' Mainstreet Coalition), class clubs (such as the Republican Freshman Class or the Democratic First Term Class), and social groups complement and reinforce partisan ties.

Partisanship and factionalism are very much alive on Capitol Hill. The first thing a visitor to the House or Senate chamber notices is that the seats or desks are divided along partisan lines—Democrats to the left facing the dais, Republicans to the right. Seating arrangements betoken the parties' role in or-ganizing the legislative branch. By means of party mechanisms, leaders are se-lected, committee assignments made, and floor debates scheduled. Parties also supply members with voting cues. Recent Congresses have seen modern-day peaks of party-line voting.

Partisanship has been underscored by recent events. Despite the Ameri-can public's professed antipathy toward partisanship (and toward the two major parties in particular), recent elections have had distinctly partisan ef-fects. Robust partisanship has led to congressional party platforms designed to attract voters and validate the party's bid for power. With gaping policy differ-ences and bitter personal battles, Capitol Hill political alignments are more rigid, and appeals to partisan loyalty more shrill, than at any time in nearly a century.

Conclusion

At its birth the U.S. Congress was an unstructured body. Although the founders understood the guiding principles of representative assemblies, they could not have foreseen what sort of institution they had created. They wrote into the Constitution legislative powers as they understood them and left the details to future generations. During its rich and eventful history, Congress has developed into a mature organization with highly articulated structures, procedures, routines, and traditions. In a word, it became institutionalized.

This fact must be taken into account by anyone who seeks to understand Congress. Capitol Hill newcomers—even those who vow to shake things up—confront not an unformed, pliable institution but an established, traditional one that must be approached largely on its own terms. This institutionalism has a number of important consequences, some good and some bad.

Institutionalization enables Congress to cope with its contemporary workload. Division of labor, primarily through standing committees, permits the two houses to process a wide variety of issues at the same time. In tandem with staff resources, this specialization allows Congress to compete with the executive branch in absorbing information and applying expertise to public issues. Division of labor also serves the personal and political diversity of Congress. At the same time, careerism encourages legislators to develop skills and expertise in specific areas. Procedures and traditions can contain and channel the political conflicts that converge upon the lawmaking process.

The danger of institutionalization is organizational rigidity. Institutions that are too brittle can frustrate policy making, especially in periods of rapid social or political change. Structures that are too complex can tie people in knots, producing inaction, delays, and confusion. Despite its size and complexity, however, today's Congress continues to adapt and change. Most recently, institutional changes following the Republican takeover in 1995 show vividly that Congress's evolution has by no means run its full course.

Generations Are Counting On You

Posters aimed at persuading Asian Americans to respond to the 2000 census canvass. All such posters featured variations of the message: "This is our future. Don't leave it blank." More minority candidates succeed in gaining election—as shown when sisters Linda and Loretta Sanchez, both California Democrats, raise their arms in victory on election night 2003.

3

Going for It:
Recruitment and Candidacy

In the Senate chamber, on the first day of the 108th Congress, a firefighter, a realtor, a college president, a newspaper reporter, two former cabinet secretaries, two founders of sizable firms, one Rockefeller, and twenty-two lawyers waited expectantly for their names to be called. They came from such places as Loveland, Colorado; Caribou, Maine; Seneca, South Carolina; Houston, Texas; and Brooklyn, New York. The sergeant at arms called them forward alphabetically in groups of four. Colleagues from their states escorted them to the front of the chamber, where the vice president, the Senate's constitutionally designated presiding officer, administered the oath of office. Newly elected or reelected, the senators were now officially members of "the world's greatest deliberative body," as the Senate likes to call itself. Over in the House chamber, 440 elected or reelected members were just sworn in as well.

How did these people get to Congress? The question has no simple answer. In the broadest sense all incumbent legislators are products of recruitment, the social and political process through which people achieve leadership posts. Social analysts agree that recruitment is a key to the effective functioning of all institutions, including legislatures. The first great book about politics, Plato's *Republic*, addressed the question of finding and enlisting the ablest individuals to lead their community. Conservatives, following Plato, believe that societies should be ruled by the most talented people—in John Adams's phrase, the "rich and the wise and the well-born." Marxists believe recruitment reflects a society's class structure, with the most privileged people landing in the ranks of leadership. Contemporary political scientists, whatever their ideology, eagerly chart the paths individuals travel to posts in Congress and other institutions of government.

Any recruitment process has both formal and informal elements. As for Congress, formal elements include the constitutional framework and state and federal laws governing nominations and elections. Equally important are informal, often unwritten, rules of the game. Some people are more ambitious than others for elective office; skills and attributes make some aspirants more eligible than others; and popular preferences persuade citizens to support certain aspirants and reject others. Taken together, such elements add up to a series of filters or screens. The recruitment process is a mix of rules, probabilities, and chance. Its biases, both overt and hidden, affect the day-to-day operation of the House and Senate, not to mention the quality of representation and decision making.

Formal Rules of the Game

The constitutional qualifications for holding congressional office are few and simple, though specific. The three are age (twenty-five years of age for the House, thirty for the Senate); citizenship (seven years for the House, nine years for the Senate); and residency in the state from which the officeholder is elected. Thus the constitutional gateways to congressional officeholding are fairly wide.

These qualifications cannot be augmented by the states (or by Congress, for that matter) without altering the Constitution itself, as the U.S. Supreme Court ruled in a 1995 case involving term limits.[1] By the early 1990s, twenty-three states had adopted restrictions on the number of terms their members of Congress could serve. The state of Arkansas, whose law the Court reviewed, argued that its scheme did not create an additional "qualification" for holding office (Article I, Sections 2 and 3) but had been written as a ballot-access measure within the state's power to regulate the "times, places, and manner of holding elections" (Article I, Section 4). Speaking for the Court, Justice John Paul Stevens spurned this subterfuge as "an indirect attempt to accomplish what the Constitution prohibits Arkansas from accomplishing directly." (State laws limiting the terms of state or local officials were unaffected by the ruling.)

As the term limits controversy showed, even the three simple requirements for holding congressional office can arouse controversy. The authors of the Constitution considered but eventually rejected several other proposed qualifications, such as property ownership and term limits. Trusting comments made by the framers (especially by the authors of *The Federalist Papers*), reelection of senators and representatives was left unrestricted because the framers did not wish to limit electors' choices; they regarded the reelection option as a powerful incentive for faithful service by officeholders; and they valued the expertise that experienced lawmakers could bring to legislative deliberations. Opposing term limits during the House's 1997 debate on the issue, Rep. Barney Frank, D-Mass., caustically remarked, "We must be the only profession in the world where an indication that your employers are satisfied with your work is taken as an indication that something is wrong."[2]

The residency requirement is traditionally stricter in practice than the Constitution prescribes. Voters tend to shun carpetbaggers and favor candidates with long-standing ties to their states or districts. The issue is sure to be raised when the candidate is an outsider. In New York's 2000 Senate contest, Republican representative Rick A. Lazio of Long Island leveled this charge at his opponent, first lady Hillary Rodham Clinton. Only by criss-crossing the state and learning about the issues affecting the Empire State was Clinton able to prove her qualifications. (A Long Islander, Lazio himself was something of an outsider to upstate voters.)

Americans' high geographical mobility has swollen the "carpetbagger caucus" on Capitol Hill. In the 108th Congress (2003–2005), about a third of the members of both chambers were born outside the states they represented. Especially in fast-growing areas, shrewd candidates can overcome objections to their outsider status. Barely a year after he settled in the state, Sen. John McCain, R-Ariz., a career navy officer, combat hero, and six-year prisoner of war in North Vietnam, beat three established politicians for a congressional nomination. He stifled carpetbagging charges by explaining that, as a navy officer and the son of one, he had never been able to put down roots: "The longest place I ever lived was Hanoi."

Senate Apportionment

The Senate was intended to add stability, wisdom, and forbearance to the actions of the popularly elected House. The founders stipulated that senators be chosen by the respective state legislatures, not by the voters themselves. This distinction between the two houses was eroded by the Seventeenth Amendment, which, in 1913, provided for the direct popular election of senators.

The states' equal representation in that body was the price for adoption of the Constitution and is virtually unamendable (Article V assures that no state can be deprived of its equal voice in the Senate without its own consent). Because states vary wildly in population, the Senate is the one legislative body in the nation where "one person, one vote" emphatically does not apply. By this measure "the Senate is the most malapportioned legislature in the world." [3]

The Senate's representative character has been further undermined by widening disparities in state populations. After the first census in 1790, the spread of House seats between the most populous state (Virginia) and the least populous one (Delaware) was nineteen to one. Today the spread between the most populous state (California) and each of the least populous states (Alaska, Delaware, Montana, North Dakota, South Dakota, Vermont, Wyoming) is fifty-three to one. Almost a third of U.S. citizens live in four megastates (California, Texas, New York, and Florida), represented by only eight senators. Such states complain that they are shortchanged in the federal bargain: Compared with lightly populated states, they contribute more revenue and receive fewer benefits. Thus in spite of constitutional barriers, Sen. Daniel Patrick Moynihan, D-N.Y. (1977–2001), warned that "sometime in the twenty-first century the United States is going to have to address the question of apportionment in the Senate." [4]

Although the Senate is malapportioned by design, it is not necessarily unrepresentative. When senators were chosen indirectly and states were less populous, the Senate tended to be a collection of promoters for dominant regional interests such as cotton, railroads, or tobacco. Today, however, a majority of states boast highly developed economies and reasonably competitive politics. Statewide electorates tend to display ethnic, racial, and social diversity; some are microcosms of the whole nation. Senators with large, diverse constituencies tend to approach their tasks with a generalist's or nationwide perspective. And Senate seats are more competitive than House seats—a state of affairs that would surely have confounded the framers.

House Apportionment

The 435 House seats are apportioned among the states by population. This apportionment process excludes the four delegates (American Samoa, the District of Columbia, Guam, and the Virgin Islands) and one resident commissioner (Puerto Rico). They speak for populations ranging from 70,000 (Samoa) to 3.8 million (Puerto Rico).

To allocate House seats among the states, a census of population—mandated by the Constitution—is taken every ten years by the Commerce Department's Bureau of the Census. Once the census figures are gathered, apportionment is derived by a mathematical formula called the method of equal proportions.[5] The idea is that proportional differences in the number of persons per representative for any pair of states should be kept to a minimum. The first fifty seats are taken because the Constitution allots to each state at least one representative. The question then becomes: Which state deserves the fifty-first seat, the fifty-second, and so forth? The mathematical formula yields a priority value for each seat, up to any desired number.

As the nation's population shifts, states gain or lose congressional seats. One state's gain means another's loss—because since 1910 the House's size has remained fixed. For some decades now, older industrial and farm states of the Northeast and Midwest have lost ground to fast-growing states of the South and West—the declining Rust Belt versus the booming Sun Belt. Within states, people have shifted from rural areas to cities and especially to suburbs.

The 2000 census showed what a difference ten years can make. Although all states added people, growth was slower in northeastern and midwestern states (only 5.5 percent in New York, for example). The South and West grew more rapidly. Nevada's growth rate, 66 percent, was the nation's highest, and its Second District (Las Vegas) was the nation's most populous (1.06 million). Arizona and six other western states all boasted gains of 20 percent or more. Figure 3-1 shows the 2000 allocation along with gains and losses since the 1990 census.

Census figures also govern how legislative seats are apportioned within the states. Moreover, the federal government uses population numbers and other census data to distribute funds—involving an estimated $185 billion—to states and other entities. Business firms, marketers, and researchers also rely upon these data.

Because population figures determine seats and affect power, controversy surrounds nearly every aspect of apportionment and districting. The Census Bureau's statisticians, who are civil servants, are conceded to be able and nonpartisan. But the bureau is part of the Commerce Department, a highly politi-

Figure 3-1   House Apportionment after the 2000 Census

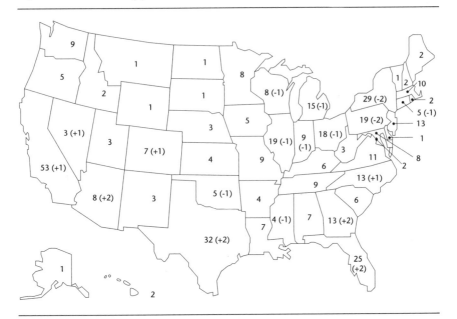

Source: Robert A. Rosenblatt and Nick Anderson, "State Picks Up House Seat as Sunbelt Grows," *Los Angeles Times,* Dec. 29, 2000, A1, A24.

Note: Numbers in parentheses show gains and losses from the 1990s apportionment.

cized entity whose political managers respond to White House pressures. And following the last two counts, diverse political forces—among them lawmakers, state and local officials, party strategists, minority groups, and courts—have waged battles over census numbers.

The decennial census is described as an "actual enumeration" (Article I, Section 2). But counting such a large and diverse population is logistically and methodologically daunting. Certain hard-to-contact groupings—transients, the homeless, renters, immigrants (legal or otherwise), children, and poorer people generally—elude census takers and are undercounted. (Some groups, such as college students living away from home, can be double-counted.)

After the 1990 count, representatives of areas where the hard-to-count were concentrated prevailed on the Census Bureau to undertake a recount. Using statistical projections to produce more accurate numbers, the bureau estimated that their original count had missed more than five million residents, or 2.1 percent of the total. Those missed were disproportionately minorities, mainly Latinos and African Americans. The undercount of non–Latino whites was neglible.[6] The Republican secretary of commerce chose the original figures amid cries from Democrats that both counts had been politically biased. The Supreme Court upheld his decision.

The issue of statistical sampling became the pivot for partisan and regional conflict over the 2000 census. The parties took predictable positions.

> Because Hispanics and African Americans—who in sheer numbers are the ones most undercounted—tend to be Democrats, Democrats almost universally see the wisdom in sampling and adjusting the totals, while Republicans, with very few exceptions[,] . . . do not.[7]

Census Bureau statisticians proposed to use statistical sampling and surveys to determine the rest. But Rep. Dave Weldon, R-Fla., chairman of the House Reform Committee's census panel, complained that any use of adjusted data "would be as flawed as the data itself."[8]

Although the 2000 count was more accurate than the prior one, the bureau analyzed a sample of households and projected that it had missed at least 6.4 million people and double-counted at least 3.1 million—a net undercount of some 3.3 million. As in 1990, blacks and Latinos tended to be undercounted; non–Hispanic whites were more apt to be overcounted. (Of the estimated half million Californians who were missed, three-fifths were Latinos.)[9] But the bureau was unsure that a statistical fix would be more accurate than the earlier numbers. As did his predecessor ten years earlier, the Republican commerce secretary embraced the original count.[10]

Because of population disparities between the states, reapportionment does not yield equal districts. (Congressional districts cannot cross state lines.) After the 2001 apportionment, Montana, with one representative for nearly a million people, was the nation's most populous district. The least populous was neighboring Wyoming, with fewer than half a million.

Districting in the House

Once congressional seats are apportioned, the states entitled to more than one seat must create districts. Each district is represented by a single member. A 1967 statute prohibits at-large or multimember elections in these states. Districts must be nearly equal in population within states—a standard rigorously enforced by the courts—and they must not dilute representation of racial minorities, an outgrowth of amendments to the Voting Rights Act of 1965.

Redistricting is a fiercely political process upon which hinges the fortunes of the Republican and Democratic parties, not to mention other intensely interested people—state legislators, governors, incumbent House members, lobbyists, and leaders of racial and ethnic causes. (Six states have turned the job over to nonpartisan overseers.) Even in California, where redistricting would seem a slam-dunk given that the state is safely in Democratic hands and a seat was added after 2000, the party and its consultants were buffeted by several clashing interests: state legislators, subject to term limits, who had their sights on Washington; nervous incumbents who seek safer reelection margins; minority groups insisting on more representation (especially Latinos, who account for a disproportionate share of the state's population growth); and national party leaders who counted on California to offset GOP districting gains elsewhere in the country and help Democrats retake control of the House.[11]

Both political parties poured money into statehouse elections in 2000 and into postcensus lobbying efforts. An Albany, New York, lobbyist hired to represent an upstate House member during the 2001 remapping put it bluntly: "No matter how successful [incumbents] are as lawmakers, nothing prepares them for the intensity and raw politics of the reapportionment process." [12]

In the redistricting wars no weapons are left untouched. Creating districts for elections from 2002 through 2010 thus hinged on how the contending parties utilized their array of national and state resources. Going into the redistricting cycle, the parties were well matched. Democrats controlled (that is, held the governorships and legislatures) in states with 135 seats; Republicans controlled states with 98 seats.[13]

Republicans are buoyed by the overall migratory patterns: away from the older industrial states and toward the South and West, and away from inner-core cities and toward suburbs. But GOP fortunes are clouded by other demographic trends. The ranks of Latino and African American voters (now virtually equal in numbers) are swelling; in the past they have tended to favor Democrats.[14] Moreover, the booming suburbs that once were GOP strongholds are becoming more diverse; many of them are hospitable to Democratic candidates. Older inner suburbs have become havens for racial and ethnic minorities anxious to escape the core cities. The more affluent outer suburbanites, while economically conservative, tend to hold more moderate views on social issues.

If a state's politicians become deadlocked on redistricting, or if they fail to observe legal guidelines, judges may step in to finish the job—sometimes awarding victory to parties that lost out earlier in the political fracas. Both parties engage in forum shopping, seeking the friendliest court to aid them in the remapping process. Republicans during both Bush administrations could rely on the Justice Department and a federal bench composed of a majority of GOP appointees. State courts can also become engaged in these battles. According to a Supreme Court ruling, they should be preferred over federal courts in drawing up redistricting plans.[15]

Because congressional seats are political prizes, districting is a tool for partisan, factional, or even personal advantage. Two historical anomalies of districting are malapportionment and gerrymandering.

Malapportionment

Before 1964 districts of grossly unequal populations often existed side by side. Within a single state, districts varied by as much as eight to one. Although metropolitan areas expanded in population and political clout, their representation lagged in Congress and even more in state legislatures. Sometimes malapportionment resulted from explicit actions. More often rurally dominated legislatures simply refused to redistrict, letting population movements and demographic trends do the job for them. This failure to act was called the silent gerrymander.

The courts were slow to venture into this political thicket. By the 1960s, however, the problem of unequal representation cried out for resolution. An activist Supreme Court, led by Chief Justice Earl Warren, ruled that state districting schemes that fell short of standards of equality violated the Fourteenth Amendment's equal protection clause (*Reynolds v. Sims,* 1964). State legislative seats, Warren held, must be apportioned "substantially on population"—even in bicameral arrangements.[16]

That same year, the Court applied the "one person, one vote" principle directly to the U.S. House of Representatives. An Atlantan who served in the Georgia senate, James P. Wesberry Jr. charged that the state's congressional districting violated equal protection of the laws, and the Supreme Court upheld his challenge (*Wesberry v. Sanders,* 1964). This decision was based on Article I, Section 2, of the Constitution, which directs that representatives be apportioned among the states according to their respective numbers and that they be chosen by the people of the several states. This language, argued Justice Hugo Black, means that "as nearly as is practicable, one person's vote in a congressional election is to be worth as much as another's."

How much equality of population is "practicable" within the states? The Supreme Court has adopted rigid mathematical equality as the underlying standard. In a 1983 case (*Karcher v. Daggett,*) a 5–4 majority voided a New Jersey plan in which districts varied by no more than one-seventh of 1 percent. "Adopting any standard other than population equality would subtly erode the Constitution's ideal of equal representation," wrote Justice William J. Brennan for the majority. The dissenting judges, speaking through Justice Byron R. White, contended that the majority opinion would ensure "extensive intrusion of the judiciary into legislative business." They also maintained it was an "unreasonable insistence on an unattainable perfection" that would encourage gerrymandering by making mathematics more important than geographic or political boundaries.

Population equality has been achieved at the expense of other goals. To attain strict parity in numbers of residents, district mapmakers must often violate political divisions, crossing city and county lines. It is not easy to follow economic, social, or geographic boundaries. The congressional district, therefore, tends to be an artificial creation, often bearing little relationship to real communities of interest—economic or geographic or political. "The main casualty of the tortuous redistricting process now under way," remarked journalist Alan Ehrenhalt, "is the erosion of geographical community—of place—as the basis of political representation."[17] The congressional district's isolation from other natural or political boundaries forces candidates to forge their own unique factions and alliances. It also aids candidates (incumbents especially) who have ways of reaching voters beyond relying on costly commercial media.

Traditional Gerrymandering

All districting is gerrymandering in the sense that single-member districts with a winner-take-all feature normally favor the majority party. The term *gerrymander* is usually reserved, however, for conscious line drawing to maximize seats for one's party or voting group. The gerrymander takes its name from Gov. Elbridge Gerry of Massachusetts, who in 1811 created a peculiar salamander-shaped district north of Boston to benefit his Democratic Party. Gerrymandering is used not only to gain partisan advantage but also to protect (and occasionally punish) incumbents, boost aspirants' political prospects, and help or hinder racial or ethnic groups.

From the mid-nineteenth to the early twentieth century, congressional statutes usually required that districts be equal in population and contiguous in territory. However, a 1911 law specifying "contiguous and compact territory" lapsed and has not been replaced, despite attempts to enact congressional districting standards. For most of its history, Congress has regarded gerrymandering as part of the spoils of partisan warfare.

Two gerrymandering techniques are cracking and packing. Cracking a district splits an area of partisan strength among two or more districts, thus diluting that party's voting leverage. Packing a district draws the lines to encompass as many of one party's voters as possible, thus rendering the district safe—either to make your own party's representatives more secure or to confine your opponents' seats. Whatever the motivation, packed districts waste votes because the party wins with far more votes than it needs.

Partisan Gerrymandering. The most common form of gerrymandering, partisan districting, occurs in states in which one political party clearly controls the process. In the 2001–2002 cycle, GOP-controlled Florida added three seats for the party—two new districts and defeat for one Democrat in a redrawn district. In Pennsylvania the controlling Republicans committed "a brilliant and legal manslaughter" that threw together three pairs of incumbents to yield a net gain of four seats." [18] Remapping in Democratic Maryland yielded two seats—both swing areas that were redrawn to favor Democrats.

Such clear partisan gains from districting are no sure thing. Remapping can serve party fortunes simply by padding the margins of incumbents in competitive districts. To capitalize on favorable districts, moreover, parties must field able candidates and exploit current voter concerns. Thus post–2000 Democratic schemes in Alabama and Georgia, for example, yielded only mixed results. Finally, the net effects of such districting tend to wash out in the nation as a whole and in later elections within the decade. "Partisan gerrymandering is, to say the least, an inexact science," Bruce E. Cain and David Butler caution. "[I]t is hard to predict whether a change in district composition will lead to a change in electoral outcome." [19]

On the issue of partisan gerrymandering the Supreme Court (like Congress) has chosen to look the other way. In a 1986 case involving Indiana state legislative districts, a Court majority held that gerrymandering was a justiciable issue (*Davis v. Bandemer*). [20] If the gerrymandering were substantial, long-standing, and truly harmful to the political minority, it could violate the Constitution's equal protection clause. At the same time, the Court's majority was not convinced the Indiana gerrymander met those tests. Although the Court invited legal challenges to partisan districting schemes, it has never confronted the problem of measuring inequities. And by 1999 the Court was ready explicitly to embrace a state's right to engage in "constitutional political gerrymandering"—whatever that might mean (*Hunt v. Cromartie*)." [21]

Pro-incumbent Gerrymandering. Bipartisan or sweetheart gerrymanders are those with lines drawn to protect incumbents. Any gains or losses in the number of seats are shared by the two parties. These gerrymanders are often by-products of divided party control—within the legislature or between the legislature and the governor. Such was the case in New York, which lost two seats after the 2000 count. In the end two pairs of incumbents (one from each party) were thrown together, resulting in two retirements. The remaining twenty-seven districts were drawn for incumbents (with Vice President Dick Cheney intervening to protect one rising GOP star).

The big story of the post–2000 redistricting was the large number of populous states—California, Illinois, Michigan, New York, Ohio, and Texas—that chose in the main to hoard their parties' existing assets. "Neither party [wanted] to lose its hard-won gains," election analyst Rhodes Cook explained. "With the partisan balance almost even, every seat counts."

> Incumbent protection [was] the path of least resistance for state legislatures redrawing the lines. Unlike in 1992, there were comparatively few retirements this time that would naturally create competitive, open-seat districts. And there were fewer districts that [were] competitive by virtue of their internal contradictions—for example, voting for one party's candidate for president and the other party's for Congress. In 2000, the number of such "split-ticket" districts was at its lowest level in nearly 50 years. [22]

No more than 10 percent of the 2002 races nationwide were competitive, hardly any of them in the large states. In California, home of 12 percent of all House seats, the dominant Democrats opted to play it safe and claim only the added seat awarded by the census. So the redrawn map eliminated one swing district (its Republican incumbent retired) to craft a new Latino district in Los Angeles County, created a new GOP seat in the Central Valley, and shored up several swing-district members. (The snake-shaped Twenty-fourth District, for example, spans some 250 miles of coastland to corral liberal votes for Democratic representative Lois Capps. See Figure 3-2.) The result: All of the state's fifty incumbents were reelected, only one of them garnering less than 60 percent of

Figure 3-2 Bipartisan Gerrymandering: California 2001

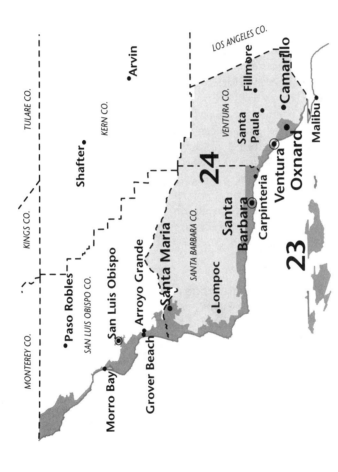

Source: Map adapted from Map Resources.

Note: In the 2001 redistricting, California Democrats opted for a bipartisan protection plan. Dividing central and south coast voters, the Twenty-third District stretched over some 250 miles of coast—from the San Luis Obispo county line to Oxnard in Ventura County—to enhance the fortunes of Democrat Lois Capps. The more conservative inland voters in two of the counties were grouped into Republican Elton Gallegly's Twenty-fourth District.

the vote (Representative Capps got 59.4 percent). The sole competitive race was in scandal-ridden Republican representative Gary Condit's rural Eighteenth District; after Condit lost his primary, his former aide won by some 10 percentage points.

Partisan advantage and incumbent advantage sometimes compete in districting. Safe districts, naturally preferred by incumbents, squander the majority party's votes by furnishing outsized victories. More competitive or marginal districts (those won by, say, less than 55 percent of the votes) are tougher for a party to capture and hold, but they hold the promise of yielding legislative seats with a modest number of voters (that is, a minimal winning coalition). In the case of California for the 2000s, the minimalist remapping dismayed national Democratic strategists and angered Latino leaders who had counted on gaining more House seats.

By yielding more safe districts than competitive districts, gerrymandering has been blamed for contributing to the rising success of incumbents since the late 1960s. But incumbents are reelected just as frequently in unredistricted areas as in redistricted ones. (As an example, Iowa's five districts were drawn by a nonpartisan panel to be competitive in 2002. The four incumbents who ran—thought to be vulnerable—were all returned to office.) Compared with other advantages of incumbency, districting seems to play a secondary role. Yet incumbents still seek and gain specific benefits from districting—for example, retention of familiar voters or exclusion of potential challengers.[23] Moreover, districting can affect the representation of political minorities, including racial and ethnic groupings.

Racial Gerrymandering

Another form of gerrymandering is intended to promote the election of racial minorities. The Voting Rights Act, enacted in 1965 to ensure the right of blacks to vote in elections, is credited with drastically curtailing voting discrimination. Coverage of language minorities was added in 1975. Amendments in 1982 barred election laws having the intent or effect of reducing minority voting power (Section 2). Sixteen states (mainly southern) that historically discriminated against minorities are required (under Section 5 of the act) to "pre-clear" changes in election rules with federal authorities to ensure that the changes do not have the purpose or effect of "denying or abridging the right to vote on account of race or color."

Under cover of the 1982 provisions, states not only were restrained from diluting (cracking) minority votes, but also were encouraged to pack districts to elect minority officeholders (majority-minority districts). Some commentators claimed that the act mandated or implied quotas for minority representation, even in the face of a proviso denying that the act "establishes a right to have members of a protected class elected in numbers equal to their proportion in the population." In a 1986 decision the Supreme Court enunciated tests for determining whether a minority's representation had been compromised. Is the group large enough and located in a compact enough area to elect a representative if grouped into a single district? Is the group politically cohesive? Is there evidence of racially polarized voting by the majority against candidates of that group?[24]

Faced with redistricting after the 1990 census, a number of states set about creating majority-minority black or Latino districts. States targeted as past offenders by the Voting Rights Act had additional prodding from the Bush administration's Justice Department. Its aggressive reading of Section 5 of the act dictated maximizing the number of majority-minority districts. (The Justice Department's maximization policy—requiring states to create majority-minority districts wherever possible—was found by the Supreme Court's conservative majority to have exceeded Congress's intent in the Voting Rights Act, forcing states to engage in "presumptively unconstitutional race-based districting.")

The 1990s thus saw the creation of fifteen new African American districts, thirteen of them in the South (for a total of thirty-two nationwide, seventeen of them in the South), and nine new Latino districts (totaling twenty). Many of these were artfully contrived to concentrate minority voters, making Governor Gerry's 1811 creation look innocent by comparison.

Racial redistricting contributed to the Democratic Party's southern meltdown in the 1990s. It was not lost on Republican Party strategists that confining minority (mostly Democratic) voters into safe (mainly urban) districts would strengthen the GOP in outlying suburban areas. Political scientist Charles S. Bullock noted that "all districts held by Democrats in 1991 in which redistricting reduced the black percentage by more than 10 points have now fallen to the Republicans."[25] The GOP captured and held four of these districts in 1992 and three more in subsequent elections. Bullock summarized the impact of racial gerrymandering in the South:

> After 1994, Republicans received handsome rewards while black Democrats were becoming an increasing numerical force within the minority party. The replacement of moderate white Democrats with conservative Republicans, even with the addition of a few African American legislative seats, bodes ill for the ability of African American legislators to find the allies they need to achieve their policy goals.[26]

Political scientist David Lublin termed the outcome a "paradox of representation." Majority-minority districts fostered more minority lawmakers but also led to a more conservative House and thus reduced minorities' leverage over legislative outcomes.[27]

Minority officeholders and groups supporting them view racially gerrymandered districts as "the political equivalent to the ethnically homogeneous neighborhood," in the words of law professor Lani Guinier. "They are a safe haven for members of that group, a bit of turf that one ethnic grouping controls, a place where their voice is pre-eminent." [28] But categorizing voters by race and ethnicity troubles critics. It creates majority-minority enclaves while further bleaching nonminority districts. "Racial districting is a vision of America deeply at odds with that upon which the civil rights revolution was built," warned Abigail M. Thernstrom, a leading opponent. "Race-based districting has been unprincipled, unnecessary—and (to top it off) a gross distortion of the law." [29] In Supreme Court Justice Sandra Day O'Connor's words, racial districting conveys "the belief . . . that individuals should be judged by the color of their skin." [30]

Others doubt that racial gerrymandering is the best way to advance minorities' interests. Concentrating minorities in their own districts wastes their votes by producing outsized electoral majorities for the winning candidates. In doing so, minority voters, along with whatever leverage they have, are drained from areas surrounding the new districts. Even if the number of minority officeholders rises, "the number of white legislators who have any political need to respond to minority concerns goes down as their minority constituents are peeled off to form the new black and Hispanic districts." [31]

A better strategy for maximizing the political influence of minorities might be to maintain substantial minorities, say 40 percent or so, in a larger number of districts (termed "influence districts") to keep officeholders responsive to minority needs. [32] So it was no surprise that it in the wake of the 2000 census Democratic strategists, concluding that racial gerrymandering had hurt their party, set about unpacking some of the minority districts—an effort that was in the main unsuccessful. [33]

The Court Enters the Quagmire

Since the 1960s the Supreme Court has repeatedly ruled against districts drawn deliberately to disadvantage a racial or ethnic group. In 1960 the Court declared unconstitutional the "obscene, 28-sided" boundaries of Tuskegee, Alabama, that disfranchised blacks by excluding them from the city (*Gomillion v. Lightfoot*). [34] Courts upheld the Voting Rights Act of 1965 and its later amendments, which forbid electoral arrangements, including district boundaries, that dilute the voting power of racial or language minorities. But would districting aimed at increasing minority officeholders pass constitutional muster?

Wading its way through the 1990s cases, the Supreme Court established a pair of guidelines for states to follow.

Race-Based Districting. First, race cannot be the predominant factor in drawing districts, unless the state can show a compelling reason for it. Moreover, states must not violate the Fourteenth Amendment's equal protection clause by drawing irregularly shaped districts based solely or primarily upon racial considerations.

In a 1993 case, *Shaw v. Reno*, the Court recoiled at two oddly shaped North Carolina congressional districts, the First and Twelfth. White citizens contended that such blatant gerrymandering violated their right to equal protection under the law by diluting their votes. By a narrow 5–4 majority, the Court agreed that nonminority citizens (whites, in this case) had standing to sue the state over racial gerrymandering. Although conceding that race-conscious districting might be permissible, the Court's majority expressed shock at the bizarre boundaries of the Twelfth District. Writing for the majority, Justice O'Connor questioned "districting so highly irregular that, on its face, it rationally cannot be understood as anything other than an effort to segregate voters . . . on the basis of race."[35]

In *Miller v. Johnson* (1995), the Supreme Court took a giant step along the path it began in *Shaw* by rejecting two Georgia districts drawn with race as the "predominant factor."[36] "To challenge a districting scheme as violating the equal protection clause," wrote Justice Anthony M. Kennedy for a 5–4 majority, a plaintiff must prove that "race was the predominant factor motivating the legislature's decision to place a significant number of voters within or without a particular district." To prove racial predominance, it must be shown that "the legislature subordinated to racial considerations traditional race-neutral districting principles, including but not limited to compactness, contiguity, and respect for political subdivisions of communities defined by actual shared interests."

In the next five years federal courts ruled on districting plans in several states—most notably, California, Florida, Georgia, Louisiana, North Carolina, Texas, and North Carolina (four times). By the decade's end several states had drawn new district maps in response to the Court's ruling in *Miller.* Affected majority-minority districts were in Texas (two of thirteen redrawn districts), Georgia (two), North Carolina (two), and Florida, Louisiana, and Virginia (one each). North Carolina's shoestring Twelfth District remained under a legal cloud after two remappings (see Figure 3-3).

Virtually all the minority members running in their new districts won subsequent elections, some with widened margins. Foes of racial gerrymandering seized on the results as vindication. "The idea that minorities have to have a super-majority of black voters to win in their districts, that's history now," declared the lawyer who had challenged the Georgia districts. Black officeholders credited their success to incumbency, which they argued was made possible by racial gerrymandering. They won reelection by combining overwhelming black support with 20 percent or more of the white vote.[37]

Taking Race into Account. A second Court-adopted principle softens this stance against racial districting: If race is only one of many factors considered in drawing a district, then the state need not meet the same constitutional barrier against race-based districting.

A decade of redistricting cases revealed that the Supreme Court, like outside commentators, was ideologically torn. The five conservative justices who comprised the majority in *Shaw* and *Miller* saw racial gerrymandering as a brand of political affirmative action repugnant to the Constitution—a departure from race-neutral standards that courts had a duty to review.

Figure 3-3   Racial Gerrymandering in the 1990s and 2000s:
North Carolina's First and Twelfth Congressional Districts

After the 1990 census (1992)

Two remaps later, after federal court decisions (1998)

After the 2000 census (2001)

Sources: Congressional Districts in the 1990s: A Portrait of America (Washington, D.C.: Congressional Quarterly, 1993), 548; *Congressional Staff Directory* (Washington, D.C.: CQ Press, 1999); *CQ s Politics in America 2004* (Washington, D.C.: CQ Press, 2003), 741.

Note: North Carolina's First and Twelfth Districts were drawn to give the state its first black representatives in ninety-three years. First elected in 1992, the two African-American representatives were subsequently reelected; after the First District representative retired in 2003, she was replaced by another African American.

The four Court liberals, in contrast, regarded race-based districting as just a new variant of a venerable political practice. The Court's minority in *Miller*, speaking through Justice Ruth Bader Ginsburg, noted that "legislative districting is a highly political business" and that "apportionment schemes, by their very nature, assemble people in groups." Historically, many ethnic groups sought and gained power through their own voting districts. "Until now, no constitutional infirmity has been seen in districting Irish or Italian voters together, for example." Why, she asked, shouldn't African Americans be accorded the same right? Courts should intervene only to protect the rights of minorities. In Ginsburg's words: "Special circumstances justify vigilant judicial inspection to protect minority voters—circumstances that do not apply to majority voters."

This argument offered a path for the Court to beat a strategic retreat from its hard-line stance on racial gerrymandering. The final decisions on 1990s' redistricting involved the much litigated North Carolina Twelfth District, whose black population had been whittled from 57 to 47 percent after two remappings. A group of the district's white voters had persuaded a lower court that the newly remapped district was still racially gerrymandered. The state, for its part, argued that it simply wanted to create a district of loyal Democrats, many of whom happened to be black. A unanimous Court sent the case back to the district court, which was instructed to take into account the state's point of view (*Hunt v. Cromartie*, 1999). Writing for the Court, the conservative Justice Clarence Thomas declared:

> A jurisdiction may engage in constitutional political gerrymandering, even if it so happens that the most loyal Democrats happen to be black Democrats and even if the state were conscious of that fact. Evidence that blacks constitute even a supermajority in one Congressional district while amounting to less than a plurality in a neighboring district will not, by itself, suffice to prove that a jurisdiction was motivated by race in drawing its district lines when the evidence also shows a high correlation between race and party preference.[38]

All nine judges agreed with the decision, but the four liberal dissenters from earlier cases declined to sign Justice Thomas's opinion. In a concurring opinion written by Justice Stevens, they held that the evidence of race-based districting in this instance was weak. At the very least, the guideposts erected in *Hunt* gave the states "very significant breathing room" in the post-2000 round of redistricting.

Two years later—just as states were beginning their next round of redistricting—the Court moved in the direction indicated by Justice Thomas (*Easley v. Cromartie*, 2001). Weighing the final challenge to North Carolina's redrawn Twelfth District, a three-judge district court had ruled that the districting was driven by race. By yet another 5–4 vote, the Court disagreed, describing as "clearly erroneous" the district court's findings. "The evidence taken together," wrote Justice Stephen G. Breyer, "does not show that racial considerations predominated in the drawing of District 12's boundaries. That is because race closely correlates with political behavior."[39] Justice Thomas, now writing for the minority, did not dispute the facts but simply held that the Court should have deferred to the lower court's factual findings.

More to Come. Race-conscious districting is likely to be contested well beyond the 2000 census. As a North Carolina state senator in charge of his chamber's redistricting efforts quipped to a reporter: "If the Lord God Almighty threw down lightening bolts and carved plans into the side of Mount Mitchell, and we adopted them, there would still be challenges to redistricting under every legal theory devised."[40] In 2003, the Court held in *Georgia v. Ashcroft* that it is permissible for states to consider a variety of factors to promote minority influence in the electoral process other than "packing" black voters in predominately minority districts. For instance, spreading black voters among more districts when legislative maps are redrawn could strengthen minority influence on a greater number of lawmakers. These cases raise complex issues of minority power and partisan balance.

On the one hand, courts can be expected to protect minority voting power from being unconstitutionally diluted—in Justice Kennedy's words, "eradicating invidious discrimination from the electoral process." But states have a good deal of leeway in making such political arrangements. Nonminority voters challenging such plans, Justice Breyer explained, must show how the state legislature "could have achieved its legitimate political objectives" in another way.

On the other hand, Justice Breyer noted, judges should be reluctant to second-guess state legislators on such intensely political matters. Majority-minority districts can be valid if they are properly drafted by the states to serve compelling state governmental interests and adhere to what the judges regard as traditional principles. For example, California's 1990s plan, while race conscious, was upheld by the Court as a fair, thoughtful application of desirable districting standards.[41]

The leading question is whether the Supreme Court means to back away from its activist stance of the early 1990s. After all, the Court has never defined what districting would be allowable. Apparently the justices have adopted a version of Justice Potter Stewart's test for identifying obscenity: You know it when you see it. And given the closeness of its past decisions—every major case on this question has turned on a 5–4 vote—the Court could again shift its direction in response to, say, a change in its membership.

Becoming a Candidate

Very few of those who are eligible for Congress vie for a seat. Candidates who meet the legal qualifications must weigh a variety of considerations—some practical and rational, others personal and emotional. Candidacy decisions are often the pivotal moments in the entire recruitment process, although students of politics have only recently given them the attention they deserve. "The decision to run obviously structures everything else that goes on in the primary process," writes Louis Sandy Maisel. "Who runs, who does not run, how many candidates run. These questions set the stage for the campaigns themselves." [42]

Called or Chosen?

In their heyday—roughly from the time of Andrew Jackson in the 1830s to the decline of big-city machines in the 1960s—local party organizations customarily enlisted and sponsored candidates. Then, as such organizations withered, the initiative passed to the candidates themselves: self-starters who pulled their own bandwagons. "The boys in the back room aren't going to decide who stays in this race," one representative remarked. "There are no boys anymore." [43] "The skills that work in American politics at this point in history," writes Alan Ehrenhalt, "are those of entrepreneurship. At all levels of the political system, from local boards and councils up to and including the presidency, it is unusual for parties to nominate people. People nominate themselves." [44]

Although typically launching their own careers, aspirants for Congress soon encounter national networks of party committees and allied interest groups. At the heart of these networks are the two major parties' House and Senate campaign committees, now active in nearly all phases of congressional elections. [45] They seek out and encourage promising candidates at the local level, sometimes even taking sides to help ensure their nomination. Once nominated, candidates receive help in nearly every phase of the campaign, from fund-raising to finding seasoned campaign managers to digging up dirt on opponents. Filing deadlines must be met, backers lined up, and financing sought. Candidates may be free to keep their national party at arm's length, but few nonincumbents can turn their backs on party sponsorship. Most would-be officeholders seek advancement within the two major parties, which boast not only the brand loyalties of a majority of voters but extensive financial and logistical resources as well.

During the recruiting season (beginning in early 2003 for the 2004 contests) the two major parties' leaders and campaign committee staffs "reach out across the country in search of political talent. Like college football coaching staffs in hot pursuit of high-school prospects, they are . . . putting together the lineups of the future." [46] Prospects can expect calls from the president, former presidents, governors, high-profile financial backers, and other notables.

Not all recruiting takes place on the road. Because open seats—newly created districts or those in which incumbents have died or retired—are less secure, party leaders strive also to discourage their incumbent colleagues from retiring.

The most celebrated party recruitment apparatus was GOPAC, founded in 1979 to "fund a 'farm team' of Republican candidates at the state level who would then be available to run for higher office." [47] When then Georgia representative Newt Gingrich took over GOPAC in the mid-1980s, he transformed it into a machine for building a Republican House majority. GOPAC's core was a research shop that developed and packaged conservative issue messages based on extensive surveys, focus groups, and workshops. "Republican state legislators across the country," a Gingrich ally related, "in drives back and forth across their states have been listening to Newt's tapes for nearly a decade. They have become whips, leaders, committee chairmen, and even speakers." [48] GOPAC's methods paid off when many of its farm-team recruits reached Capitol Hill in the 1990s. Its methods have been widely imitated—most recently by the Democratic Leadership Council (DLC) and the Green Party. [49]

In light of citizens' professed coolness toward the two major parties, independents and minor-party candidates not surprisingly are entering congressional contests. Some forty-seven party labels appeared on ballots in 2002. Two minor-party candidates that year captured about one of every five votes in their respective races. They offered voters a credible alternative, inasmuch as only one major party fielded a candidate in those races. Although few such candidates have been elected in recent decades, they occasionally draw enough votes to swing the election results. (Only two Independents now serve in Congress, both of them Vermonters: Sen. James M. Jeffords and Rep. Bernard Sanders.)

Nonparty groups also sponsor congressional candidates. The leading small-business lobby, the National Federation of Independent Business (NFIB), has been a major contributor to the GOP cause. After the party's 1994 victories, NFIB counted four senators and thirty-three representatives among its members. In the 1995–1996 cycle the NFIB began to pick potential candidates from its own membership, train them, and help them run for office. "We're trying to develop a farm team for down the road," explained the federation's national political director, "so we can work in more of a proactive instead of a reactive way," fielding, not just endorsing, candidates who support the small-business agenda. [50] Other organizations with strong grassroots networks now pursue the same course.

Amateurs and Pros

How do would-be candidates, whether self-starters or handpicked by party leaders, make up their minds to run? The answer depends on whether the individual is an amateur or a strategic politician.

Amateurs are by definition candidates without previous political experience. Despite their liabilities—inexperience and low name recognition (celebrities are an exception)—many amateurs run for Congress, and a few of them manage to win. Some amateurs are serious political strategists whose behavior resembles that of experienced politicians. Others run to bring a specific issue before the public; they are less interested in winning than in advancing a cause. But most are what David T. Canon calls "hopeless amateurs"—people with little or no chance of winning. [51] A long-shot bid is their only way of becoming a candidate. They run because "it was something they knew they were going to do sometime and for whatever reasons it appeared to be the right time." [52] "I think his chances have gone from absolutely out of the question to extremely remote," remarked the wife of one hopeless contender. "But he's learning a lot, and I think he has enjoyed it." [53]

Strategic politicians, unlike all but the savviest amateurs, painstakingly weigh the pros and cons of launching a campaign. They ask: Do the rewards exceed the drawbacks of the office, especially compared with what I am doing now? What are the chances of success, and what will it cost to succeed? If there is an incumbent, what are his or her weaknesses? What are my strengths and weaknesses in campaigning, voter appeal, and fund-raising? What local or national trends will boost, or lower, my chances?

The circle of people pondering these questions (the challenger pool) is large or small, depending on the office and the circumstances. [54] Any number of elected officials—especially state legislators (many facing retirement from state term limits), county officers, mayors, city council members, even governors—are weighing a race for Congress.

Of all the inducements to launch a candidacy, the odds of winning stand at the top. A seat that is clearly winnable seldom lacks for candidates eager to capture it. Open seats especially attract contenders. Given less-than-rigid party ties, races lacking an incumbent candidate are more likely to be competitive and to shift in party control than those with an incumbent. Party strategies thus pinpoint those races.

In most House and Senate contests, however, incumbents will be running, and most of them will be reelected. As Gary C. Jacobson writes, "Nearly everything pertaining to candidates and campaigns for Congress is profoundly influenced by whether the candidate is an incumbent, challenging an incumbent, or pursuing an open seat." [55] With somewhat less force, the same could be said of the Senate.

Anyone contemplating a congressional race would do well to study Table 3-1 with care. Since World War II, on average, 93 percent of all incumbent representatives and 80 percent of incumbent senators running for reelection have been returned to office. Historically, incumbents' reelection rates have always been robust, whereas voluntary turnover declined in the late nineteenth century and has remained low ever since. In 2002, winners included 96 percent of all House members who ran and almost as many senators (85 percent of those who ran). Eighty-one of those incumbents faced no major-party opponent in the general election.

Higher than normal casualty rates occur periodically: for example, the post–World War II generational shift (1946–1948), a midterm recession (1958), Barry Goldwater's failed candidacy (1964), the Watergate burglary fallout (1974), and a combination of generational shift and conservative realignment (1978–1980). During the early 1990s, political unrest, Capitol Hill scandals, an economic recession (in 1992), and voter anger at those in charge (the Democrats and President Bill Clinton in 1994) conspired to produce the largest turnover in two generations. But subsequent elections favored

Table 3-1 Reelection Rates in the House and Senate, 2002, and by Decades, 1950–2000

Decade	House					Senate				
	Sought reelection	Faced no opponent	Lost primary	Lost general election	Percent reelected	Sought reelection	Faced no opponent	Lost primary	Lost general election	Percent elected
1950s	402	85	6	25	93.2%	30	4	1	6	77.3%
1960s	404	52	8	26	91.5	32	1	2	4	80.8
1970s	289	57	2	23	92.3	27	1	2	6	67.7
1980s	403	67	13	15	95.7	29	1	0	3	88.0
1990s	385	36	8	18	93.6	26	0	0	3	87.4
Fifty-year average	376.6	59.4	7.4	21.4	93.3	28.9	1.4	1.0	4.4	80.2
2002	390	77	8	8	95.9	27 [a]	4	1	3	85.2

Source: Congressional Quarterly Weekly Report, April 5, 1980, 908; November 8, 1980, 3302, 3320–3321; July 31, 1982, 1870; November 6, 1982, 2781; November 10, 1984, 2897, 2901; November 12, 1988, 3264, 3270; November 10, 1990, 3796–3805; November 7, 1992, 3557–3564, 3570–3576; November 12, 1994, 329ff; February 15, 1997, 447–455; November 7, 1998, 3027–3035; November 11, 2000, 2694–2706; and December 14, 2002, 3289–3297.

Note: Statistics for each decade are election-year averages for the five elections conducted under that decade's reapportionment of House districts. For example, the 1950s include the five elections 1952 through 1960. Percent reelected includes both primary and general election defeats.

[a] Not counted as running in 2002 were Robert G. Toricelli, D-N.J., who withdrew from the race, and Paul Wellstone, D-Minn., who died in a plane crash less than two weeks before election day. The 2000 Senate class numbered 33, plus Jean Carnahan, D-Mo., who was appointed to the seat posthumously won by her husband, Missouri governor Mel Carnahan. She ran in 2002 to complete the unexpired term and lost.

incumbents. Decennial redistricting also produces a flurry of retirements and defeats.

Nowadays defeating a House incumbent is an uphill struggle, short of a major scandal or misstep. This is a relatively recent phenomenon. Although incumbents have been fattening their margins of victory for some time, through the 1970s they were just as vulnerable to defeat as they had been earlier. That is, incumbents were, on average, just as apt to lose any given election as before; but when they won, it was by higher margins.[56] By the 1980s, however, incumbents had erected imposing barriers against defeat by amassing campaign war chests and aggressively exploiting perquisites. Therefore, competition for their House seats dropped to exceedingly low levels. Incumbent advantage fell perceptibly in the early 1990s. The anti-incumbent atmosphere emboldened many strategically minded nonincumbents to try for House or Senate seats. Even so, turnover resulted less from electoral defeats than from retirements (some of them involuntary, to be sure). In those years of upheaval from 1990 to 1994, 194 members retired and 112 were defeated for reelection.[57]

Senate races tend to be closer, and so challengers—more often well known and generously financed—have a stronger chance of unseating incumbents than do those seeking House seats. In the past two decades Senate contests have become somewhat more competitive overall than have House races. This competitiveness is mainly a by-product of the South's dramatic shift from a Democratic to a Republican bastion—a statewide development that spread into House districts only in the 1990s. In nonsouthern states, however, Senate contests are less competitive than formerly. Four of five incumbents win the contests they enter. The proportion of marginal elections (candidates winning by less than 60 percent) has dropped. Winning candidates receive more than 60 percent of the vote in almost half of nonsouthern Senate elections.[58]

In Senate contests, the size of the state affects all elections, not just those in which an incumbent is running. Frances E. Lee and Bruce I. Oppenheimer find that "Senate elections in more populous states tend to be decided by much closer margins than Senate elections in less populous states"—mainly because larger states are more diverse and tend to be more competitive.[59] Yet small-state senators reap no real incumbency advantage. Although they are better known and tend to enjoy higher public approval than their big-state colleagues, their challengers, too, can more easily win visibility and support.

Why are incumbents so formidable? Political scientists have launched a veritable cottage industry to answer this question. It is no secret that incumbents have built-in methods of promoting support—through speeches, press coverage, newsletters, staff assistance, and constituent service. The average House member enjoys perquisites valued above $2 million over a two-year term; senators, with six-year terms, command between $12 million and more than $20 million in resources.

Everyone concedes the value of incumbents' perquisites, but scholars differ sharply on how they affect electoral success. One view is that incumbents exploit their resources to ensure reelection, seizing upon their ability to assist constituents in dealing with the bureaucracy to build electoral credit. Others counter that legislators simply are responding to constituents' demands, aided by technological advances in communications. Still others question whether incumbents' resources are directly translatable into votes. However these questions are resolved, incumbents and their staffs spend much of their time and effort forging links with their voters, and these links typically hold fast on election day.[60]

An incumbent's most effective electoral strategy is to scare off serious opposition. "If an incumbent can convince potentially formidable opponents and people who control campaign resources that he or she is invincible," Jacobson observes, "he or she is very likely to avoid a serious challenge and so will be invincible—as long as the impression lasts."[61] Any sign of weakness may invite opponents the next time around. That is why wise incumbents try to sustain wide electoral margins, show unbroken strength, keep up constituency ties, and build giant war chests of funds. If these tactics fail, there is always the option of retiring more or less gracefully.

Finding the Quality Challengers

The quality of challengers and the vigor of their campaigns are critical factors in many battles for congressional seats.[62] The parties' November triumphs hinge on their efforts during the recruitment season. Often races turn on bids that are not made.

Broadly speaking, quality challengers are people who are attractive to voters and skilled in presenting themselves as candidates. Attractiveness typically means having gained experience in public office, which implies visibility among, and credibility with, the voters. Alternatively, fame or notoriety may overcome lack of relevant background or experience. Attributes include physical appearance, personality, speaking ability, and a talent for organizing or motivating others.

Fund-raising ability or potential is an essential attribute of quality challengers. "I understand the significance of raising money," successful challenger Mike Ross, D-Ark., said in announcing his candidacy. "That's why the first person I've hired is not a press secretary or a campaign manager, but a finance director."[63] An opponent's war chest is also appraised—often as indicated in the Federal Election Commission (FEC) reports issued sixteen months before the election. When the incumbent in Virginia's Eleventh District reported less than $25,000 on hand in 1993, now House GOP campaign chair Rep. Thomas M. Davis III decided to take the plunge. "If she would have had $250,000, I would not have gotten into the race."[64]

All too often candidates of high caliber prefer to remain on the sidelines. The road to public office can be arduous and costly, and the odds are often long, especially against a dominant party or an entrenched incumbent. Therefore, quality challengers may not surface. Low-quality challengers raise less money and are less successful than the handful of blue-ribbon contenders. The dynamic works in Senate as well as House elections. "The quality of Senate challengers varies, and the higher the quality of a challenger the more votes he or she receives and the more likely the challenger is to defeat an incumbent."[65]

Most successful candidates are seasoned politicians long before they run for Congress. Grassroots organizations and movements are a breeding ground for a number of candidates—for example, environmental activists in the 1970s, religious conservatives and antiregulation businesspeople in the 1990s. More often, elective offices are the springboards: mayors, district attorneys, or state legislators for the House; and governors, lieutenant governors, and attorneys general—who have already faced a statewide electorate—for the Senate. House members, especially from smaller states, are also strategically positioned. For example, forty-six senators in the 108th Congress had moved over from the House.

Amateurs with highly visible nonpolitical careers may be nicely positioned to move into politics. Astronauts, war heroes, entertainers, and athletes are in big demand as candidates. Local or statewide television personalities also make attractive contenders. Only occasionally do other nonpolitical careers have such visibility. First elected to the Senate in 1988, Democrat Herb Kohl was familiar throughout Wisconsin from his family's food stores long before he wrote an $18.5 million check in 1985 to keep the Milwaukee Bucks basketball team from moving elsewhere—not a bad advertisement for a would-be senator. And in 2000 Republican Tom Osborne captured 80 percent of the vote in Nebraska's open Third District even though he wholly lacked political experience. But everyone in the state knew him as a twenty-five-year football coach of the University of Nebraska's Cornhuskers.[66]

A quick tour of recent recruitment drives reveals the complex interplay of individual decisions and political context. Take, for example, the Republicans' recruiting bonanza for the 1994 and 1996 contests. Given citizens' unrest and President Clinton's unpopularity, strategic politicians throughout the country realized that Democrats were vulnerable and that joining the GOP ticket offered them unusually good odds for advancement. Democrats, for their part, felt the foul political winds and decided to get out of the gale. Fourteen of the party's senators and fifty representatives declined to run, while scores of potential candidates did not enter the races. Two senators and five representatives even switched to the GOP. As a result, the Democratic Party fielded a relatively weak team of challengers in 1996. Only about a fifth of their candidates, for example, had previous experience in elective office.[67]

By the time of the 1996 balloting, citizens' anger had cooled, President Clinton's stock had rebounded, and it was the Republicans—blamed for shutting down the federal government in the winter of 1995–1996—who struggled to cut their losses. But the Democratic challengers were too weak to recapture the House. They netted only eight of the eighteen seats they needed for a majority. Although twelve of the experienced challengers bested GOP incumbents, too few of the amateurs were successful. The Democrats' failure to recapture the House can be attributed in part to their tepid recruitment season some months earlier. As for the Republicans, their majority status attracted strategically minded politicians and enabled them to recruit more experienced candidates than their opposition. In politics, nothing succeeds like success.

The playing field again shifted in 1998. Both parties recruited zealously. With Clinton's reelection and the party's gains in the House, Democrats were able to nail down quality candidates early—before the White House sex scandal broke. The party also showed a willingness to seek out contenders in swing districts who did not fit the party's profile—who were, for example, conservative or anti-abortion.[68] By November these candidates were well positioned to ride the wave of anti-impeachment sentiment, and the party gained five more House seats—still short of a majority.

The run-ups to 2000 and 2002 again featured fierce recruiting seasons, as both parties sought lineups that could win them House and Senate majorities. Then minority leader Richard A. Gephardt, D-Mo., led mostly successful recruiting efforts—encouraging quality challengers to enter the electoral arena and at the same time coaxing popular senior members to defer retirement. But with prosperity and few hot-button issues, 2000 turned out to be a very good year for incumbents of both parties; the Democrats gained only two seats. Recruitment for 2002 was complicated by redistricting, the midterm election phenomenon, and eventually the terrorist attacks. In the end the GOP, having more than held its own in redistricting, fielded slightly stronger candidates in close races and gained a net of seven seats.

The Personal Equation

Personal attributes also determine who is urged to run, and who decides to run, for Congress. Stamina, background, personal style, and physical appearance determine whether someone has "the right stuff" for campaigning. Ambition and a keen desire for public life and congressional perquisites lead people to become candidates and help them to succeed.[69]

Many potential candidates—no one knows how many—disqualify themselves because they are physically or emotionally unprepared for the rigors of campaigning. Not everyone has the capacity to hit the road nonstop, meet new people, attend meetings, sell themselves, ask for money, and endure verbal abuse—all the while appearing to enjoy it. "People who do not like to knock on strangers' doors or who find it tedious to repeat the same 30-second introduction thousands of times," explains Ehrenhalt, "are at a severe disadvantage in running for office."[70]

Raising the money needed to run an effective race is a major deterrent to would-be candidates. This stumbling block was cited twice as often as any other factor by the potential contenders in two hundred districts surveyed by L. Sandy Maisel and Walter J. Stone.[71] Other candidates reject campaigns because of the cost to their personal lives, incomes, and families. From the number of successful politicians who complain about such sacrifices, however, one can only conclude that many misjudge the costs before taking the plunge. Many simply indulge in self-delusion. Maisel, a political scientist who wrote candidly of his unsuccessful congressional primary campaign, described politicians' "incredible ability to delude themselves about their own chances. If I could honestly think that a young, liberal Jewish college professor from Buffalo could win a primary and then beat a popular incumbent in Downeast Maine, any level of delusion is possible."[72]

Nominating Politics

Nominating procedures, set forth in state laws and conditioned by party customs, help to shape the potential pool of candidates. Historically, they have spread to ever wider circles of participants—a development that has diminished party leaders' power and thrust more initiative upon the candidates themselves. In most states the direct primary is the formal mechanism for nominating congressional candidates.

Despite the prevalence of primaries, state and district party organizations are not without leverage in nominations. Party organizations play no active part in the primary process in the majority of states.[73] But in nine states, parties have conventions that influence candidates' access to the primary ballot—for example, by conferring preprimary endorsements. Elsewhere, party organizations informally influence the process, through endorsements or other actions that can boost favored candidates.

Who should be permitted to vote in a party's primary? The states have adopted varying answers. Party leaders naturally prefer strict rules that reward party loyalty, discourage outsider candidates, and maximize the leaders' influence upon the outcome. States with strong party traditions therefore tend to have closed primaries. This arrangement, found in twenty-six states, requires voters to declare party affiliation to vote on their parties' nominees. (Their affiliation is considered permanent until they take steps to change it.) In open primaries, conducted in twenty states, voters can vote in the primary of either party (but not in both) simply by requesting or selecting the party's ballot at the polling place.

Four states have experimented with a scheme that diminishes the parties' role even further. In blanket primaries (politicians call them jungle primaries), voters in three states (Alaska, California, and Washington) received a single ballot listing all candidates running for office, regardless of party affiliation. People voted for one candidate for each office, moving back and forth between parties if they wished. More people would come to the polls, California's lawyers told the Supreme Court, "because candidates will be more representative of the electorate and more broadly reflect the views of the voters."[74]

Louisiana employs a nonpartisan primary variant held on election day, when all candidates appear on one ballot. If a candidate receives a majority, he or she is elected; if no one gains a majority, the top two vote-getters, regardless of party, move to a runoff election.

The California scheme, a voter initiative, was adopted overwhelmingly in 1996. Four California parties (Democrats, Republicans, Libertarians, and Peace and Freedom) opposed the initiative and then challenged it in court as a violation of their First Amendment right to free association. The U.S. Supreme Court upheld their challenge by a 7–2 vote.[75] Calling the blanket primary a "stark repudiation of freedom of political association," Justice Antonin Scalia argued that it invited nonparty members to raid the primary and select a candidate who did not share the party's core beliefs. "In no area is the political association's right to exclude more important than in the process of selecting its candidates." In dissent, Justice Stevens observed that while a party's internal governance was a private matter, "an election, unlike a convention or a caucus, is a public affair." (Early civil rights cases established that parties could not arbitrarily exclude classes of persons from their nominating processes.)

The 2000 ruling served to invalidate primaries in the three blanket-primary states, though advocates of the device vowed to try and devise a Court-proof version. (The Court explicitly excluded nonpartisan primaries, such as Louisiana's, from its decision.) Some observers speculated that the Court's ruling cast constitutional doubt on all open primaries, though that seemed unlikely.

Not all primaries are competitive races. In the 1982–1996 period, nearly 70 percent of representatives and 60 percent of senators faced no challenge at all for renomination. Only twelve incumbents faced closely contested primaries; only 30 percent had any contests at all.[76]

Contests usually occur in both parties if the House or Senate seat is open and within the challenging party if the seat is deemed competitive. The level of competition depends on the party's prospects in the general election. "If a district party is without an incumbent, and has a fighting chance in November," Harvey L. Schantz writes, "there is a strong possibility of a public contest for the U.S. House nomination."[77] In one-party areas the dominant party's nomination is tantamount to election. Within that party, open seats are virtually certain to be contested, and in some states runoff primaries are held when no one receives a majority. Contests also are likely in two-party competitive areas.

National parties increasingly insert themselves into nominating contests. To gain a Republican Senate in 2002, Senate Republicans and the Bush White House targeted seats that were open or held by vulnerable Democrats: recruiting promising GOP candidates, elbowing other contenders aside to forestall divisive primaries, and channeling resources to the campaigns. Democrats were not far behind. As one observer reported,

Republicans "cleared the field" in Missouri, Minnesota, and South Dakota while Democrats did the same in Arkansas, New Hampshire, and Colorado. Even in open seat races—which normally draw throngs of candidates—political parties managed to load the dice. Republicans did this in Texas and South Carolina and Democrats did this in Tennessee and South Carolina.

Both parties persuaded '800-pound gorillas' to run in North Carolina, making the Senate primary virtually a foregone conclusion [between former Clinton chief of staff Erskine Bowles, D, and eventual winner and former cabinet member Elizabeth Dole, R].[78]

Some local politicians resented such intrusions, and not all nationally sponsored choices won nomination. But the parties' calculations usually panned out. Their favored candidates tended to win, while interlopers were less successful.[79]

The votes had hardly been tallied when party strategists turned their attention to 2004 races. "Who's' the president going to call?" was the question on the mind of a prominent Illinois Republican concerning his state's open Senate seat. Illinois Republican senator Peter G. Fitzgerald had just declined to run for reelection after only one term, citing family and campaign costs. But undoubtedly the real reasons were sagging poll numbers and lack of support from his party, financial and otherwise. (A maverick, Fitzgerald had irked the Bush White House and was feuding with the state's most important Republican, House Speaker J. Dennis Hastert.) Who would run in his place? The GOP activist spelled out the alternatives:

> The president convinces somebody like a Jim Edgar [former governor] or maybe a Judy Baar Topinka [state treasurer and GOP chairwoman], or somebody he thinks can win, or there's just a big, messy primary just like the Democrats are going to have.[80]

The direct primary was one of the reforms adopted early in the twentieth century to overcome corrupt, boss-dominated conventions. It has certainly permitted more participation in selecting candidates. Yet primaries normally attract a narrower segment of voters than do general elections (except in some one-party states, where primaries dictate the outcomes). In 2002 only 17 percent of eligible voters showed up to vote in the primaries—about the same number as in 2000 and less than half the number who voted in the midterm general elections.[81] Less publicized than general elections, primaries tend to attract voters who are somewhat older, wealthier, better educated, more politically aware, and more ideologically committed than the electorate as a whole.[82]

Primaries also have hampered the political parties by encouraging would-be officeholders to appeal directly to the public and construct support networks apart from the party machinery. Leaders still strive to influence who enters their primaries and who wins them. In recent years local and national Republican leaders pushed three controversial House freshmen into retirement, coaxed a former member to succeed one of them (with the promise of a committee chairmanship), and worked to quash primary challenges to several incumbents. GOP leaders, however, have sometimes been rebuffed when their moderate choices in swing districts suffer defeat in primaries to candidates with right-wing appeal—who usually lose in the general election.

Finally, primaries are a costly way of choosing candidates. Unless candidates begin with overwhelming advantages (such as incumbency), they must mount virtually the same kind of campaign in the primary that they must repeat later in the general election.

The Money Factor

"Money is the mother's milk of politics," declared California's legendary boss Jess Unruh. Money is not everything in politics, but many candidates falter for lack of it, and many others squander valuable time and energy struggling to get it. Money attracts backers (who in turn give more money), it can frighten away rivals, and it can augment or lessen the gap between incumbents and challengers. Every candidate, writes Paul S. Herrnson, wages not one but two campaigns—a campaign for resources that precedes, and underwrites, the more visible campaign for votes.[83]

Campaigns in the United States are very costly. In the 2001–2002 electoral cycle, congressional candidates raised more than a billion dollars and spent most of it. The average Senate race cost $3.6 million. House contests average $667,000.[84] Twenty-five years ago (when modern record keeping began) no House candidate spent that much.[85] Even controlling for inflation, expenditures for congressional campaigns have more than doubled over the last twenty-five years. And beyond what candidates spend, interest groups of all stripes throw untold millions of dollars into independent efforts aimed at changing election outcomes.

No mystery surrounds these skyrocketing costs. Inflation, population growth, and new campaign technologies—media ads, polling, and consultants of all kinds—account for much of the increase. Moreover, long-term changes in the campaign process itself have escalated costs. In old-style campaigns, candidates were chosen by party insiders in a caucus or convention. At the general election stage, candidates relied upon the party's legions of volunteers to mobilize loyal voters and to canvass precincts. Contrast that process with modern campaigns in which candidates are nominated by winning a primary election and then must face general election voters who can be reached most effectively through direct mail, phone banks, or electronic media. Campaign services once provided by well-oiled local parties must now be purchased on the open market. That is why today's costs of reaching voters are so high.

Campaign price tags also depend on the level of competition and other characteristics of the electoral unit. "Candidates for open seats tend to raise and spend the most money because when neither candidate enjoys the benefits of incumbency, both parties normally field strong candidates, and the election is usually close."[86] Costs in competitive races can be astronomical. In close House races (gaining less than 55 percent of the vote), the average winner in 2002 spent more than $1.5 million.

A district's demography also affects campaign costs. One study showed that suburban districts have the most expensive campaigns and urban districts the least expensive, with rural districts somewhere in between.[87] In the suburbs partisan loyalties are weaker and contests volatile. Lacking stable party organizations, candidates must advertise through paid media. In rural districts wide-open spaces keep costs high. Candidates must travel farther and advertise in many small media markets to get their messages across. In cities candidates shun media contests because of the huge cost and wasted effort of televising to adjoining districts. Here, too, party organizations are strongest.

The Haves and Have Nots

Although incumbents need less money than do challengers, they receive more—a double-barreled financial advantage (see Figure 3-4). Because they are better known and have government-subsidized ways of communicating with constituents, incumbents usually can communicate their message less expensively than challengers can. Incumbents tend to attract more money than challengers do because contributors see them as better investments. As Jacobson points out, "Incumbents can raise whatever they think they need. They are very likely to win, and even when they lose, it is almost always in a close contest."[88]

Many incumbents finish their campaigns with a surplus. After the 2001–2002 electoral cycle, the average returning House member had more than $300,000 on hand. This money can be hoarded for future races, dispensed to needier candidates, or used to buy constituency goodwill through outreach projects or charitable donations.

The incumbency advantage in fund-raising, especially in House contests, is bipartisan. Prior to 1994, the advantage worked to the benefit of Democrats, who had more incumbents than Republicans had. Since then the parties have achieved rough parity. As a party, the GOP has consistently been more effective at raising funds than have the Democrats. When in the majority, the Republicans harvest a bounty from lobby groups, eager as always to back winners to gain access to the policy-making process. As long as Democrats hover within striking distance of majority status, however, they will gather funds from groups eager to bet on their prospects.

Shaking the Money Tree

Raising money preoccupies all candidates. Incumbents need it to scare off opponents, challengers need it to gain visibility, and contenders for open seats need it to gain an edge. Fund-raising is time-consuming, odious, and demeaning. "I'd rather wrestle a gorilla than ask anybody for another fifty cents," grumbled John Glenn, D-Ohio, as he departed in 1998 after twenty-four years in the Senate.[89]

Figure 3-4   Average Campaign Expenditures for Incumbents, Challengers, and Open-Seat Candidates, House and Senate (1972–2002)

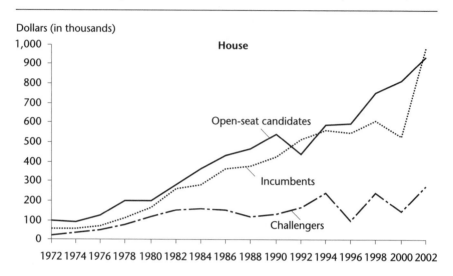

Sources: Congressional Research Service reports by Joseph E. Cantor, *Cost of Congressional Elections, 1972–1982: Statistics on Total Average Campaign Spending,* August 6, 1984; Joseph E. Cantor and David Huckabee, *House Campaign Expenditures, Receipts, and Sources of Funds: 1980–1992,* June 1993, 20; Joseph E. Cantor and David Huckabee, *Senate Campaign Expenditures, Receipts, and Sources of Funds: 1980–1992,* May 19, 1993, 20; Norman J. Ornstein, Thomas E. Mann, and Michael J. Malbin, *Vital Statistics on Congress, 1999–2000* (Washington, D.C.: American Enterprise Institute, 2000), 80–81, 86–89; Federal Election Commission, "1998 Congressional Activity Declines," news release, December 29, 1998; Federal Election Commission, "Congressional Financial Activity Sources for 2000," news release, January 9, 2001; and Federal Election Commission, "Election Overview: 2002 Cycle, Incumbent Advantage," opensecrets.org.

Funding sources include individuals (including the candidates and their families), party committees, and political action committees (PACs). Their motivations fall into two major categories. Consumers, usually individuals, want simply to show their support for a candidate or a cause, tending to respond to candidates most in need of funds. Investors—PACs, for example—give to gain personal or institutional benefits. Because they seek access or support from winning candidates, they tend to disregard the candidates' needs and support those (mainly incumbents) most likely to win.[90]

Individuals. Two-thirds of the money raised by Senate candidates, and more than half raised in House races, come from individuals. Individuals may lawfully contribute up to $2,000 per candidate for primaries and $2,000 per candidate in the general elections (the figure will be indexed in the future), totaling no more than $37,500 in any given year. Primary, runoff, and general contests are regarded as separate elections. Individuals may contribute up to $20,000 a year to a political party committee and $5,000 to any PAC, and they may spend an unlimited amount independently to promote parties, causes, or candidates. Expenditures greater than $250 must be reported, and the individual must declare that the money was not spent in collusion with the candidate. Many individual donations are solicited by interest groups, which seek to magnify their influence by collecting and then forwarding these personal checks to the designated candidates, a practice known as bundling.

Congressional candidates are not restricted in how much they may contribute to their own cause. (Donations and loans from family members also are unrestricted.) Especially in long-shot races, a candidate's ability to shoulder the financial burden may attract support from party or group leaders. In other cases heavy spending by the candidate may help pad a front-runner's margin of victory or boost an underdog's chances of winning. Sen. John D. Rockefeller IV, D-W.Va., spent about $10 million of his fortune to win his Senate seat in 1984—more than $27 for every vote he received.

Federal law requires strict accounting by candidates and political committees. All contributions of $50 or more must be recorded; donors of more than $100 must be identified. Accounting of funds must be made by a single committee for each candidate, and receipts and expenditures must be reported regularly.

Party Committees. National, congressional, and state party campaign committees may contribute $5,000 apiece to each House candidate at each stage of the electoral process—primary, runoff, and general election. The national and senatorial committees can give a combined total of $17,500 to each Senate candidate in an election cycle, whereas state committees can give $5,000. Inflation has shrunk the buying power of these sums. Party funds do not begin to cover the costs of campaigns today. Party contributions in 2002 amounted to an average of 6 percent of the total receipts in House and Senate races—mostly in the form of coordinated expenditures, not direct contributions.

Political parties are also permitted to make coordinated expenditures, funds a party pays for services (polling, producing ads, or buying media time) requested by a candidate who has a say in how they are spent. For Senate races, party committees may spend two cents (adjusted for inflation) for every person of voting age. In 2000 these figures ranged from $135,120 (in Delaware) to just under $3.3 million (in California). For House races, committees may spend no more than $33,780 in coordinated funds. (This amount is doubled for states with only one House seat.) Coordinated funds are used in general elections but not in primaries.

Since its rebuilding effort after the post–Watergate electoral disaster of 1974, the Republican Party has had spectacular success in raising money— much of it from modest contributions solicited through targeted mailings and phone banks. In the 2001–2002 cycle, Republican committees raised $692 million, compared with $513 million for their Democratic counterparts.[91] Especially in Senate contests, the parties can pump in huge sums of money by means of cooperative arrangements among state committees and the several national committees.

Political parties could also—before passage of the 2002 campaign reform law—raise soft money, over and above funds generated according to legally prescribed limit. These are individual, corporate, or union gifts to party entities to be used for grassroots party-building activities but not for individual campaigns (see Figure 3-5). The parties' soft-money spending—the bulk of which supports their national organizations—exceeds their contributions to congressional candidates. But activities fueled by such funds (for example, generic advertisements, voter registration, and get-out-the-vote drives) indirectly help all the party's candidates.

Funding patterns affect candidates' strategies and, on occasion, electoral outcomes. The Republican Party's fund-raising edge, some argue, has helped to swell victories in good years and to minimize losses in bad years.[92] In the decades before 1994, however, House Democrats relied on the funding advantages of their many incumbents to offset the GOP's national fund-raising superiority. But once in the majority, the Republicans' basic fund-raising superiority was augmented by the inevitable windfalls of incumbency. In the 2001–2002 cycle, Republican representatives raised an average of more than $1 million, compared with Democrats' $875,000.[93]

Interest Groups. Under existing law, corporations, federal contractors, and labor unions may not contribute funds directly to candidates. But such groups may indulge in independent spending for or against candidates but without the candidates' cooperation or consent. Corporations, labor unions, and membership organizations may recommend to their stockholders, personnel, or members the election or defeat of a candidate. Unions and corporations also may pay for nonpartisan voter registration or participation drives directed at their members, stockholders, or employees. Such group expendi-

Figure 3-5   National Party Fund-Raising, 1993–2002

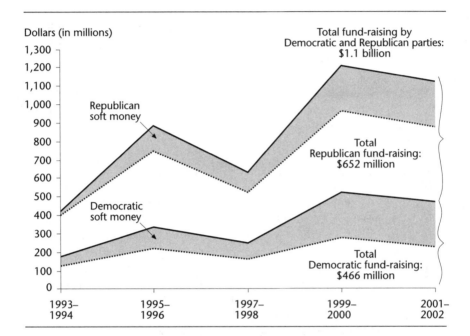

Source: Federal Election Commission, "Party Fundraising Escalates," news release, January 12, 2001; and opensecrets.org.parties (2001–2002 figures).

Note: Figures are overall party receipts through ten days following the election. Federal, or hard, money can be used to fund individual candidates' campaigns. Nonfederal, or soft, money may be used for a variety of partisan activities—staffing, voter registration, generic ads, including issue ads that are often indistinguishable from candidate ads.

tures are unlimited, although amounts over $2,000 must be reported to the Federal Election Commission.

Independent expenditures from all sources amounted to nearly $21 million in 2001–2002. Barely half the funds (55 percent) wound up favoring candidates; the rest went to negative campaigns. The most talked-about group activity in recent years has been organized labor's high-profile campaign of advertisements and voter mobilization on behalf of Democratic candidates in targeted districts. Business groups responded with similar ads. Whatever the outcome of that rivalry, Republicans benefited most from independent spending. Nearly three-quarters of the funds directed at GOP candidates were for positive efforts. Where Democratic candidates were concerned, seven of every eight independent dollars were aimed at defeating them.

PACs. Corporations, labor unions, and membership groups may also underwrite administrative or fund-raising costs of political action committees.

For some years PACs have been the preferred method of channeling corporate or union energies into campaign war chests. Corporate executives contribute to PACs with such names as the Good Government Fund. Most unions have PACs, the best known of which is the AFL-CIO's Committee on Political Education (COPE). Ostensibly, such groups are voluntary. However, it does not take a confirmed cynic to assume that subtle coercion and social pressure help draw money into the coffers.

Other kinds of groups are embraced by existing finance laws. Multicandidate committees may give no more than $5,000 per election to a candidate. These committees must have more than fifty members and must support five or more candidates. Such committees also may contribute up to $15,000 per year to a political party.

Political action committees are thriving, in part because the finance laws encourages them. At the end of 1974 there were 608 PACs; by 2002, more than 3,700. All types of PACs grew in numbers, but corporate PACs grew most of all—from 89 in 1974 to 1,523 in 2002. The growth of PACs has changed the way campaigns are run. Candidates are forced to make the rounds of PACs to beg for funds. Incumbents attract PAC support by finding a lucrative committee assignment and compiling a good voting report card. Nonincumbents gain support by knocking on doors, filling out forms, and being interviewed.[94]

PACs also have grown in financial clout. In 1972 they contributed $8.5 million to House and Senate candidates; in 2002 their contribution was $243 million. PAC donations are more significant in House races than in Senate races. In 1999–2000 PAC donations accounted for 30 percent of House campaign receipts but only 12 percent of Senate campaign receipts.

Because they are campaign investors, PACs favor incumbents and shun all but the most promising nonincumbents. Incumbents seeking reelection receive, on average, six times the PAC donations that their challengers receive. Increasingly, members are using their fund-raising prowess to start leadership PACs. These PACs trade on the name of their sponsor but are separate from the sponsor's own war chest. They are normally used to contribute to other candidates' campaigns as a way of gaining a party majority and earning their colleagues' gratitude. As a respected insider, J. Dennis Hastert, for example, collected a respectable $130,000 for his Keep Our Majority PAC during 1997–1998. After he was catapulted to the speakership, in the first six months of 1999 Hastert raised $1.25 million and $4 million more for his Republican colleagues.[95] In political vernacular this is called catching the late train. By that time Hastert was spending Mondays, Fridays, and weekends raising funds for candidates.

After the GOP takeover, PAC giving flowed to the victors. "The shift in PACs from the Democrats to the Republicans was dramatic and almost overnight," noted Larry Makinson of the Center for Responsive Politics, a nonprofit reform group. "When the Republicans took over all these chairmanships and subcommittees, they reaped a whirlwind of money."[96] Still, with control of the House in doubt, many PACs hedged their bets in post–1994 campaigns. Democrats still received the bulk of PAC money from labor and from groups such as the Association of Trial Lawyers of America (determined to stave off GOP efforts to restrict lawsuits against business).

Pressure comes from both directions. PAC officers complain that they are dogged by incumbents, many of whom do not need the contributions, and that members of Congress keep mental accounts of contributors. "I've had congressmen open up the door and look down a list to see if we have contributed," one of them said. "And I've had them say, 'Well, I like your organization but you haven't given me a contribution.' "[97]

Candidate Funding: A Regulated Industry?

Financial inequalities—between incumbents and nonincumbents and between wealthy donors and average citizens—inevitably lead to demands for legal ways of monitoring or even controlling campaign finance. Laws have been passed not only to clean up campaigns but also to shift political influence from those who rely on financial contributions to those who depend on other resources. Several techniques have been employed. The primary ones thus far have been disclosure of campaign contributions and expenditures, limits on campaign contributions and expenditures, and (in presidential races) public financing of campaigns.

Reacting to campaign scandals of the early 1970s, Congress decided to erect regulatory standards for financing federal election campaigns. On October 15, 1974, President Gerald R. Ford signed into law a broad-gauged campaign finance law, the Federal Election Campaign Act Amendments of 1974. Major features of the act included limits on individual contributions, limits on party and nonparty group contributions, and reporting requirements for all contributions.

The Supreme Court, ruling on a challenge to the law, held that Congress may limit contributions to congressional candidates but that it may not limit expenditures by candidates themselves, their campaign committees, or individuals or organizations independent of the candidate (*Buckley v. Valeo,* 1976). The reasoning was that, as a form of free expression protected by the First Amendment, spending to influence elections cannot be constrained. To end the confusion and meet the Court's constitutional objections, Congress quickly passed a revised act aimed at reconciling the Court's rulings with the original congressional intent.

The *Buckley* decision, experience has shown, undercut Congress's intentions and ultimately rendered the law unworkable. The Court's reasoning has been criticized as wrongheaded. First, it stretched the First Amendment to treat the spending of money in federal campaigns as pure, protected speech. More logically, such spending might be treated as, say, economic activity—which can be regulated. As dissenting Justice Stevens put it: "Money is property; it is not speech."[98] "In fact," writes lawyer-novelist Scott Turow, "given *Buckley's* rationale, I've never figured out why outright vote-buying isn't also protected by the First Amendment."[99] Second, with no enforceable restrictions on campaign spending, politicians and interested groups were free to exploit creative ways of maximizing their financial leverage, in the process stripping from the law the one fig leaf the Court sanctioned: contribution limits. The free-for-all system that resulted, critics charge, has replaced the principle of "one person–one vote" with a "regime of one dollar–one vote," which "distorts the fundamental principle of political equality underlying the First Amendment itself."[100]

The law is enforced by the bipartisan Federal Election Commission (FEC), appointed by the president and confirmed by the Senate. The commission may issue regulations and advisory opinions, conduct investigations, and prosecute violations of the law. Most important, the FEC compiles and disseminates campaign finance data from the reports it receives. Disclosure of the sources and uses of campaign money is the one aspect of current regulations that everyone agrees is a success.

Campaign financing laws have failed to limit the influence of big money in politics. Big money is alive and well in American elections, although now it flows through more issue and candidate groups than in the past. The best that can be said is that many of the best-funded PACs depend on large numbers of mail-solicited donations instead of on a few from fat cats. The 1976 act, moreover, failed utterly to reduce inequalities between incumbents and challengers. The changes may even have helped incumbents and made it harder for challengers to raise the money they need to win.[101] Finally, the reforms have blurred the distinction between interest groups and political parties. Labor unions, business and industry associations, consumer and environmental organizations, ideological movements, and a host of special issue groups have invaded the electoral arena as never before. By boosting and even recruiting candidates—and hindering others—they hope to win favorable treatment for their causes on Capitol Hill.

Campaign finance laws are so loosely drawn that money pours freely into congressional elections. Parties and PACs use tax-exempt foundations to take donations in excess of legal limits. Creative accounting and independent spending on behalf of candidates are used to skirt legal limits on what PACs can give directly to candidates. Bankers and other moneyed people can lend money or extend credit to candidates under permissive rules. And money is moving underground, thwarting federal enforcement and disclosure efforts. "You can do just about anything, as long as you take care," said one party official.[102]

In campaign financing debates, where you stand depends on where your money comes from. Change is resisted by those who thrive under existing rules. Republicans tend to shun monetary limits—for the very good reason that the party overall is very adept at fund-raising. Many conservatives would abolish all limits on contributions to candidates and parties, relying solely upon better reporting through electronic filing and Internet dissemination.

Some critics advocate public funding of Senate and House campaigns. As for presidential campaigns, the 1974 act included an optional public financing scheme that was intended to provide sufficient resources for candidates who agreed to use it—as most of them have done. But that has not stopped candidates and parties from raising money over and above the public funds, in violation of both the spirit and the letter of the law. In any event, Congress declined to extend public financing to its own elections. The public funding option, moreover, runs afoul of public antipathy toward spending more tax dollars on politicians.

Perhaps the most promising way to level the playing field, at least for incumbents and challengers, would be to provide the latter with subsidized mailings and free radio and TV time. This option, predictably, is fiercely opposed by broadcasters—a potent lobby because politicians crave the exposure their outlets provide. Even the innocuous provision that broadcasters offer time for political messages at the lowest prevailing rates has drawn opposition.

The Bipartisan Campaign Reform Act (BCRA), which became law in March 2002, was something of a political miracle, given the opposition to reform from across the political spectrum (see box on bipartisan campaign reform act). The drive to tighten up the 1974 law began in the mid-1980s and raged through four presidencies, multiple floor votes, a 1992 veto by President George Bush, and repeated parliamentary setbacks. In the mid-1990s the cause was taken up by Sens. John McCain, R-Ariz., and Russell D. Feingold, D-Wis., and in the House by Reps. Christopher Shays, R-Conn., and Martin T. Meehan, D-Mass. Scandals associated with the 1996 and 2000 elections—and the growth of unregulated soft-money spending—kept the issue alive. And a final scandal in 2002—involving Enron, the elusive energy firm whose political connections kept it alive despite its economic collapse—pushed the bill over the top. "What McCain said repeatedly was right," Senator Feingold remarked. "It would take a scandal—might take more than one scandal—but we would prevail." [103]

The future of BCRA remains in doubt. Court challenges quickly surfaced. The act's complexities bitterly divided a special three-judge panel whose four opinions, issued in May 2003, ran to more than sixteen hundred pages. By a 2–1 majority, the judges found that congressional reformers had made a convincing case for controlling soft-money sham-issue ads. But other soft-money uses were struck down, as were certain limits on corporate and labor union spending. Both sides were cheered by the results, but the act dictates that the Supreme Court must ultimately rule on it. Lacking a clear road map from the lower court, the justices will have to find their own way in reconsidering issues first raised in *Buckley* nearly thirty years earlier. [104]

Although reform commands public support, it does not seem to be a salient issue—a fact not lost on those who benefit from the current state of affairs. The Court's notion that spending money is protected speech is another

The Bipartisan Campaign Reform Act of 2002

Signed into law by President George W. Bush, the Bipartisan Campaign Reform Act of 2002 (BCRA) was the first major enactment since the advent of modern campaign finance regulations in 1974. More than ninety pages long, BCRA has a variety of provisions but was touted mainly for its ban on soft money and for regulating election-time issue advertising on radio and television by corporations, unions, and interest groups. Following are the major provisions of the law, known as McCain-Feingold for its principal Senate sponsors, John McCain, R-Ariz., and Russell D. Feingold, D-Wis.:

Hard-Money Contribution Limits. Individual contribution limits for House and Senate candidates are doubled to $2,000 per election, indexed to grow with inflation; aggregate contribution limits for individuals are $ 95,000—$37,500 to candidates and $ 57,500 to parties and political action committees (PACs). Contribution limits for PACs are unchanged: $5,000 per candidate per election, plus $15,000 to a national party committee and $5,000 combined to state and local party committees.

Soft Money. National party committees cannot accept or spend soft money—unregulated contributions from corporations, labor unions, and wealthy individuals ostensibly intended for party-building activities, such as voter registration, but often used for campaign-related purposes.

State and Local Parties. Non-national political parties cannot spend soft money on federal election activities. They may spend soft money for voter registration and mobilization under certain conditions.

Independent and Coordinated Expenditures. The Federal Election Commission (FEC) must issue new rules covering coordination between candidates or parties and outside groups. The rules cannot require formal evidence of coordination to treat spending by outside groups as a regulated contribution instead of an unregulated independent expenditure.

Tax-Exempt Organizations. National, state, and local parties may neither solicit money from nor contribute to any nonprofit that spends money on federal elections. They also may not contribute to or solicit money from so-called 527 organizations that intervene in campaigns but do not expressly advocate any candidate's election or directly subsidize federal campaigns.

Electioneering Communications. Broadcast, cable, or satellite communications that name candidates for federal office or show their likeness and are targeted at candidates' states or districts—known as electioneering communications—may not be issued within sixty days of a general election or thirty days of a primary.

Unions and Corporations. Labor unions and corporations are prohibited from directly funding electioneering communications and can pay for such advertising only through political action committees with regulated hard money.

Nonprofits and 527s. One contingent provision bars electioneering communications by nonprofit organizations except through PACs. If that provision were held unconstitutional, an alternative provision would allow nonprofits to pay for such ads only with individual contributions, not from corporations or unions.

Effective Date, Judicial Review. The law took effect November 6, 2002 (the day after the 2002 election), and provides for expedited judicial review. A panel of three U.S. district court judges would try the case in Washington, D.C., and the decision would go directly to the U.S. Supreme Court, bypassing the U.S. Court of Appeals.

Source: Revised and reprinted from *CQ Researcher*, November 22, 2002, 974 huge obstacle. That interpretation has its critics, but few public figures want to campaign publicly for a narrower reading of the First Amendment.

Although conceding that further controls are desirable, most political scientists are skeptical about the benefits of many of the proposed changes in campaign financing. Overall spending limits must be approached cautiously. Challengers need to be able to spend money to offset incumbents' advantages, and because they start from behind they get more value for every dollar they spend. As for PAC contributions, they are easily stigmatized, but they are nonetheless a lawful way for interested groups to give money—gifts that at least are recorded and scrutinized. Independent campaign activities of individuals or groups are forms of free expression that should be accorded wide elbowroom. Even the much-maligned soft money served in part to underwrite party activities. Abolishing it will surely force interest groups to shun the parties altogether and spend the money on their own.

Finally, there is what journalist Chuck Alston calls the "whack a mole" problem. In the arcade game "the mole pops up in one hole, and you whack him down. But then he pops up somewhere else. Similarly, campaign spending, whenever it is suppressed in one form, always pops up elsewhere." [105] That fate will surely confound any reform that is adopted.

Conclusion

The rules of the game that narrow the potential field of congressional contenders can be thought of as a series of gates, each narrower than the one before. First are the constitutional qualifications for holding office. Then there are complex rules of apportionment and districting. Beyond these are nominating procedures (usually, though not always, primaries) and financial requirements. These gates cut down sharply the number of persons who are likely to become real contenders.

Most important, individuals must make up their own minds about running for the House or Senate. Such choices embrace a range of considerations—many personal and emotional but all based on some estimate of the likely benefits and costs of their candidacy. This winnowing process presents voters with a limited choice on election day: two, rarely more, preselected candidates. From this restricted circle senators and representatives are chosen.

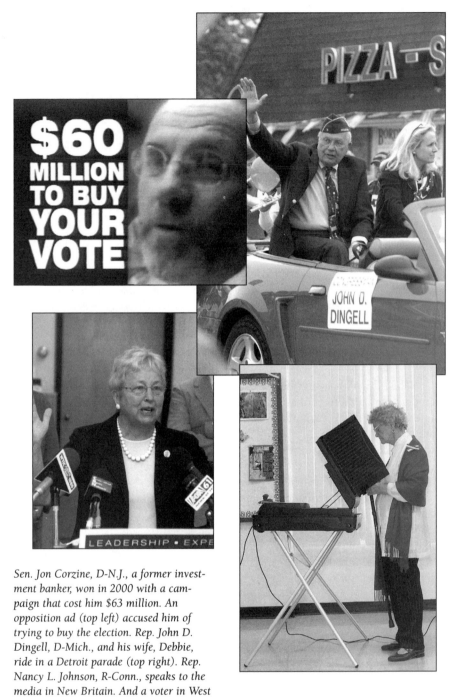

Sen. Jon Corzine, D-N.J., a former investment banker, won in 2000 with a campaign that cost him $63 million. An
opposition ad (top left) accused him of
trying to buy the election. Rep. John D.
Dingell, D-Mich., and his wife, Debbie,
ride in a Detroit parade (top right). Rep.
Nancy L. Johnson, R-Conn., speaks to the
media in New Britain. And a voter in West
Palm Beach (bottom right) uses a new voting machine in 2002
as Florida strives to erase the stigma of its election fiasco two
years earlier.

4

Making It: The Electoral Game

The New Jersey Senate race in 2000 was, hands down, the most expensive congressional election in U. S. history. The winner, Democrat Jon Corzine, was a wealthy Wall Street investment banker and twenty-five-year resident of Summit, New Jersey, who was virtually unknown to the state's voters when he launched his campaign. By the time he took the oath of office in January 2001 he had spent some $63 million, virtually all of it from his own fortune.[1]

Corzine's deep pockets made him a formidable candidate from the start. They fueled expensive media buys—the campaign's air war. Such appeals are especially costly and inefficient in New Jersey, which lies between two of the biggest media markets in the country (New York and Philadelphia). Corzine's funds also underwrote the campaign's ground war: aggressive efforts to woo the state's Democratic leaders and to get out the party's voters. To win endorsements from state and local party leaders, Corzine began dispensing contributions to Democratic state and county organizations and individual candidates in the 1999 state elections. His generosity extended to clubs, civic organizations, and charitable institutions—for example, black churches, which he attended and, as one cleric put it, "made tithes and general offerings." [2]

Corzine's willingness to spend whatever it took to win shaped the primary and general election candidate pool. Several potential Democratic candidates ran for cover or were pushed aside by party leaders, who "saw [Corzine] as a moneybags who could finance his own race and help win the state for the ticket." [3] Nervous party bosses also wanted him to save them from the one primary candidate who was not scared away: former governor James J. Florio, whose proposed tax hikes a decade earlier had disastrous results for the party and Florio himself. Several Republican would-be contenders—including Gov. Christine Todd Whitman (who had beaten Florio in 1993)—also backed out of the race. GOP funding sources were reluctant to invest money in what seemed a hopeless cause.

Corzine's primary opponent, ex-governor Florio, was crushed by an onslaught of media ads. The primary alone cost Corzine $35 million, or roughly $140 per vote. In the general election campaign, the underfinanced Republican candidate, former representative Robert D. Franks, fought gamely and hit Corzine for trying to buy the election. But Franks's message was drowned out by a $15 million television barrage over the campaign's last two months, telling voters that Corzine was "unbought and unbossed" and that "I won't owe anything to anyone but you." [4]

As election day approached, Corzine's funds underwrote legions of workers for the get-out-the-vote (GOTV) campaign. In the field were an estimated seven thousand precinct workers, given lunch, provided transportation, and rewarded with what party machines call walking-around money. Even so, money did not buy him a landslide victory. Corzine received 51 percent of the vote against 47 percent for Franks, whose $6.4 million bid was simply overwhelmed.

The New Jersey contest was singular but not unique. The New York Senate race next door, between Hillary Rodham Clinton and Rick A. Lazio, was nearly as costly. Fifty Senate candidates that year spent in excess of $1 million. These campaigns are waged in the new-fashioned way—through seasoned campaign specialists underwritten by truckloads of money. Jeff Pilletts of the *Bergen* (N.J.) *Record* summed up the lessons of the campaign: "Money supplies everything in politics—access, friends, even credibility. [Corzine] not only purchased commercials, he purchased the party machinery and the people who run it. That made all the difference." [5]

Campaign Strategies

Campaigns are volatile mixtures of personal contacts, fund-raising, speech making, advertising, and symbolic appeals. As acts of communication, campaigns are designed to convey messages to potential voters. The goal is to win over a plurality of those who cast ballots on election day.

Asking the Right Questions

Candidates, whether incumbents or challengers, strive to set the basic tone or thrust of their campaign. Their overall approach determines the allocation of money, time, and personnel. In mapping out a successful strategy, a candidate asks himself or herself: What sort of constituency do I have? Are my name, face, and career familiar to voters, or am I relatively unknown? What resources—money, group support, volunteers—can I attract? What leaders and groups are pivotal to a winning campaign? What issues or moods are uppermost in the minds of potential voters? What are the most efficient ways of reaching voters with my message? When should my campaign begin and how should it be paced? And what are my chances for victory? The answers to such questions define the campaign strategy.

The constituency shapes campaign plans—not only in its partisan balance, but in other ways as well. Senate candidates in larger states must typically appeal to diverse economic and social groups, scattered over wide areas and typically partitioned into multiple media markets. In fast-growing states, Senate incumbents must introduce themselves to hordes of new voters who have arrived in the intervening six years. Few Senate candidates can know their states as intimately as House candidates know their districts. Most House districts are narrower entities than states, often paralleling no natural geographic, community, media market, or political divisions. They have fewer automatic forums or media outlets for candidates, not to mention fewer ready-made partisan organizations.[6] Would-be representatives are on their own to piece together a network of supporters.

Because incumbents are usually tough to beat, the presence or absence of an incumbent colors the entire electoral undertaking. Also important is the partisan distribution within the electorate. Candidates whose party dominates a given area stress party loyalty, underscore long-standing partisan values (called valence issues), and sponsor GOTV drives—because high voter turnout usually aids their cause. Minority-party campaigns strive to highlight personalities, obscure partisan differences, and exploit factional splits within the majority party, perhaps by means of issues capable of prying voters away from their majority-party home (called wedge issues).

The perceptions and attitudes of voters, finally, must be reflected in campaign planning. Through sample surveys, focus groups, or informal pulse taking, strategists try to detect what is on voters' minds and what, if anything, they know or think about the candidate. Well-known candidates try to capitalize on their visibility; lesser-known ones run ads that repeat their names over and over again. Candidates with a reputation for openness and friendliness highlight those qualities in ads. Those who are less outgoing stress experience and competence, at the same time displaying photos or film clips reminding voters that they, too, are human. Candidates who have made tough, unpopular decisions are touted as persons of courage. And so it goes.

As popular moods change, so do the self-images candidates seek to project. Candidates' appearances, speeches, advertising, and appeals are designed to exploit such voter preferences. In the wake of scandals, honesty and openness are on display. Thus in the early 1990s, challengers sold themselves as outsiders (even when they were political veterans). Incumbents of both parties countered by portraying themselves as independent-minded apostles of change. By the decade's end political experience was back in fashion. The Capitol dome and its marble halls reappeared in campaign ads. And in crisis times, voters prefer experience, competence, and reassurance.

Choosing the Message

The average citizen is barraged with media messages of all kinds—an hour of television commercials per day, among other things. The candidate's overarching challenge is how to project an image through this morass of media appeals, including those from other candidates. "The only way to cut through this communication clutter," a political marketing executive points out, "is to adopt the strategy proven effective by successful businesses. Create a brand. And manage the message with discipline and impact."[7]

In other words, forge a message that will stand out from all the competing messages in the media marketplace. A candidate's message is usually distilled into a single theme or slogan that is repeated on radio, TV, and billboards and in campaign literature. "A good message . . . is a credible statement that can be summed up in a few sentences and frequently ends with a kicker slogan. . . . In most races, messages define campaigns."[8]

Strategists use these messages to *frame* the campaign—that is, to pose the election's core issue in such a way that voters respond favorably to their candidate or negatively to the opponent. "There's only three or four plots," explained Carter Eskew, a Democratic consultant. Plots for incumbents are Representative X is different from the rest; X can deliver; X stands with you. And the perennial plot for challengers is (fill in the blank) years are long enough; it is time for a change.[9]

Two basic plots framed the choice in the 1999 special election in Louisiana's conservative First District (New Orleans suburbs) following the dramatic withdrawal of Bob Livingston, Appropriations chair and presumptive heir to the House speakership. The hasty campaign to pick Livingston's successor featured a clash of themes between the two leading candidates, both Republicans. Former governor, House member, and "Mr. Republican," seventy-year-old David C. Treen was endorsed by virtually every Republican figure in the state as the party's insurance against a long-shot contender, ex–Ku Klux Klan leader David Duke. Treen's theme: "Send an experienced Congressman back to Washington." His main opponent was thirty-seven-year-old David Vitter, equally conservative but an independent and reform-minded state legislator who had alienated his state House colleagues. Vitter was, however, a resourceful GOP candidate with a solid voter base in his district. His theme—"The right way, not the old political way"—was backed up with brochures detailing his stands on policies. "When the politicians ran from the tough issues," read one flyer, "one person stood up for us and made a difference."[10] Vitter and Treen were the front-runners in the primary; in the runoff Vitter scored an upset in a close race, 50 to 49 percent, and has subsequently been reelected.

Incumbency can have its liabilities. An extensive public record gives enterprising opponents many potential openings to exploit. Votes or positions may be highlighted, and sometimes twisted, to discredit the officeholder. Incumbents may be shackled to unpopular issues, such as nuclear waste dumps or hikes in Medicare premiums, or to unpopular personalities on the national scene.

Incumbents, too, can become careless and take their home base for granted. One of only six candidates to topple an incumbent in 2000 was Republican Rob Simmons in Connecticut's Second District. His theme was "Rob Simmons is a perfect fit for the district. [Sam] Gejdenson [the ten-term Democratic incumbent] is out of touch with the district, and it is time for a change." One TV spot began with a picture of an iron gate and an announcer who began: "Living outside our district in a gated community, Sam Gejdenson no longer shares our values. Rob Simmons does."[11]

Simmons won narrowly, bucking a strong Democratic trend in the state. One campaign consultant summed up the lesson of such races: "You have to earn that support every two years. A lot of members of Congress forget how to run. . . . Voters will change members of Congress like they change shoes if they think it makes the outfit look better." [12]

Campaign Resources

Campaigns require resources to play out the strategy that has been devised. The cleverest strategy in the world is of no avail without the wherewithal to bring its message to voters. The type of state or district, incumbency status, candidate visibility, and party margin matter little if the candidate lacks two essential resources: money and campaign organization.

Allocating Resources

The importance of money in campaigns cannot be overemphasized. Virtually any kind of campaign can be mounted with enough money, as the Corzine case showed. Old-fashioned cut-rate alternatives, such as door-to-door canvassing or use of volunteer organizations, are still available, although they eat up time and resources that might be used to reach larger numbers of voters. Candidates facing tough contests in both primary and general elections and lacking Senator Corzine's reserves have an especially vexing dilemma. Should they ration their outflow of funds and risk losing the primary, or should they wage an expensive primary campaign and risk running out of money later on?

Especially useful is early money—funds on hand at the outset of the campaign, or even earlier. EMILY's List—Early Money Is Like Yeast ("It makes the 'dough' rise")—a group begun in 1985, was formed on this premise. EMILY's List collects (bundles) checks for Democratic women candidates who support abortion rights. In 2002 this meant 101,000 contributions totaling $9.7 million. The group claims to have helped some sixty-six women win seats in the House or Senate.[13] The Republican counterpart is Women in the Senate and House (WISH). Incumbents stockpile funds to scare off would-be challengers, whereas lackluster fund-raising emboldens them. Challengers and open-seat candidates raise money to gain visibility, win credibility, and get a head start over other contenders. (For one open-seat candidate's fund-raising efforts, see Table 4-1, page 86.) "Failure to raise enough money creates a vicious spiral," explains political analyst Thomas B. Edsall. "Some donors become reluctant to invest their cash, and then state and national parties are less likely to target their unlimited 'soft money' for party building and get out the vote drives in those races." [14]

Late blitz money also can turn the tide, although money alone rarely makes the difference. The final weeks of a campaign are tough because both sides are trying to reach undecided voters. "You've got to move that 10 or 15 percent, many of whom are not paying much attention," a Democratic consultant explained. "Unfortunately, the way to do that is with negative or comparative ads." [15] Late in the game, opponents frantically attack and—despite the scant time—counterattack.

Incumbents raise more money and also spend more on their campaigns than challengers do (see Figure 4-1). Because incumbents are better known than challengers, their spending often has strategic purposes. Preemptive spending involves constant fund-raising, which, along with surpluses from previous campaigns, can dissuade serious opponents. "If you look like a 900-pound gorilla, people won't want to take you on," remarked a GOP campaign aide.[16]

If a strong, well-financed challenger surfaces, incumbents can spend reactively to stave off defeat. The 1990s found incumbents spending more than ever to counter challengers (who were better financed than usual). In 2002 House incumbents spent more than $800,000 on average defending their seats—nearly five times what their challengers spent.[17]

New incumbents tend to invest heavily in preemptive and reactive spending because they are more likely than longtime veterans to face vigorous challenges. More senior members raise and spend less than junior members, especially in the early campaign stages (before July of an election year). Incumbents who are sure-fire vote-getters over the long haul—with five or more terms—may establish such commanding positions that they rarely have serious challenges.

Sometimes established incumbents deliberately overspend for reasons that lie beyond the race at hand. A decisive victory can establish a claim to higher office. Representatives may cast their eye on the Senate; senators may hope to be presidential contenders. Others strive to impress colleagues or interest groups with their electoral prowess. They may bid for freedom to concentrate on Capitol Hill business or other pursuits. Or they may distribute unused funds to needy colleagues in return for future support, perhaps in a leadership contest.

Incumbents' overspending is motivated, finally, by their sense of uncertainty and risk. "Because of uncertainty," Gary C. Jacobson explains, "members tend to exaggerate electoral threats and overreact to them. They are inspired by worst-case scenarios—what would they have to do to win if everything went wrong?—rather than objective probabilities."[18]

Challengers, for their part, spend all the money they can raise to make their names and faces known to voters. And, because normally they start far behind, their campaign dollars tend to be more cost-effective than those of incumbents. As Jacobson has demonstrated, the more a challenger spends, the more votes he or she is likely to attract.[19] The seven challengers who toppled incumbents in 2002 were all adequately financed, though none of them matched their opponents' resources.

Spending Campaign Funds

As exercises in communication, campaigns are driven, and their budgets shaped, by the need to reach the largest number of voters at the lowest cost. Spending patterns vary widely between the House and the Senate, among congressional districts and states, and between incumbents and challengers.

Figure 4-1 Average House Campaign Expenditures by Incumbency and Party, 1978–2002

Dollars (in thousands)

Source: Norman J. Ornstein, Thomas E. Mann, and Michael J. Malbin, *Vital Statistics on Congress, 2001–2002* (Washington, D.C.: American Enterprise Institute, 2002), 87–88; Federal Election Commission figures reported by the Center for Responsive Politics (Web site: opensecrets.org).

As a rule, statewide Senate races are mass media contests with messages conveyed mainly through radio and television. Costs are especially high in densely populated states with numerous metropolitan media markets. Senate candidates spend far more on media advertising and fund-raising than do their House counterparts, who spend correspondingly more on traditional means of voter contact. The most expensive House contests are in states where the population is small and spread out.[20]

Despite its astronomic costs, television advertising is popular because candidates find it cost-effective, and they believe it works. They are probably right. Political scientist Thomas Patterson estimated that as early as the 1980s it cost only about one-half cent to get to a single television viewer, compared with one and a half cents to reach a newspaper reader and twenty-five cents to reach a direct-mail recipient.[21]

Not all states feature such high-tech campaigns. Residents in smaller states usually expect personal appearances by the candidates at festivals, parades, or annual county fairs. Politicians are supposed to show up. "If you ain't seen at the county fair, you're preached about on Sunday," remarked a politician as he led his party's Senate candidate around the hog and sheep barns in Ada, Oklahoma.[22] In small states, first-name relationships are often valued. Of Vermont's voters, political scientist Garrison Nelson remarks, "They want to know you." Independent representative Bernard Sanders's bumper stickers there simply say, "Bernie."[23] In Bristol, on Rhode Island's coast, the Fourth of July parade—the oldest in the country—is "the first and perhaps biggest event of the campaign season."[24] Candidates are expected. By town decree, only public officials may march in the parade; nonofficeholders must work the crowd from the sidelines.

The character of candidates and their party organizations also affects the media mix and budgeting. Confident incumbents can channel their money into newspaper ads or phone banks that direct their messages to activists, partisans, and supporters. Lesser-known candidates must turn to broad-scale media, such as television or outdoor advertising, to promote name recognition.[25] Both House and Senate challengers spend more on media and less on traditional campaigning than do incumbents. And, although challengers presumably need more money to get their messages across, they spend less in fund-raising than incumbents do.

Incumbents also spend more on constituent gifts and entertainment and donations to others. Campaign funds have been barred from personal use since 1989, and in 1995 the Federal Election Commission (FEC) tightened its definition of permissible uses—though the issue remains a thorny one. The FEC still allows gifts of nominal value to constituents. Spending reports from members' campaigns and their related political action committees (PACs) disclose a surprising array of activities, such as buying flowers, leasing cars, organizing athletic teams, sponsoring contests and prizes, purchasing tickets to sporting events, and subsidizing travel and entertainment.[26]

Organizing the Campaign

Implementing the campaign strategy is the job of the candidates and their organizations. Waging a campaign is not for the fainthearted. Take the case of psychology professor Brian Baird, a Democrat who won Washington's Third District seat in 1998. Having lost to the incumbent by a mere 887 votes two years earlier, Baird vowed to run full tilt the second time, when the incumbent bowed out to run for the Senate. His campaign schedule is summarized in Table 4-1. Baird spent nearly all his waking hours on the campaign during the peak campaign months (July through October)—more than ten hours a day for 123 days. By far the largest block of time—more than one-third—was spent raising the $1.3 million he needed to win the open seat. Most of those hours he sat in a tiny room he called his bunker, wearing a headset and phoning potential contributors. Many of his meetings with individuals, groups, or other politicians were also related to fund-raising. Travel ate up many valuable hours in the average-size Third District (Olympia and southwest Washington). His days of hard campaigning are by no means over. Although he won reelec-

Table 4-1 See How He Ran: Candidate Brian Baird's Time Budget, July–October 1998

Activity	Hours and minutes spent[a]	Percentage of time
Fund-raising call time	397:30	32
Other fund-raising	36:00	3
Meeting with individuals, groups, politicians	146:00	12
Public events	96:00	8
Meeting with media	31:00	2
Voter contact	89:15	7
Meeting with staff	58:45	5
Travel	203:15	16
Personal time	201:30	16
Total hours	1,259:15	100[b]
Hours per day	10:12	

Source: Baird for Congress Campaign, 1998. Reported in James A. Thurber and Carolyn Long, "Brian Baird's 'Ring of Fire': The Quest for Funds and Votes in Washington's Third District," in *The Battle for Congress*, ed. James A. Thurber (Washington, D.C.: Brookings Institution, 2001), 188.

[a] Excludes the three days of campaigning in November: 33 hours, 15 minutes, mostly in voter contact.

[b] Percentages do not add to 100 because of rounding.

tion by widening margins in 2000 and 2002, his district will continue to be targeted by both parties.

In certain strong party areas, voter contact is the job of ward, precinct, and block captains. As in the Corzine case, candidates in strong party areas still dispense walking-around money to encourage precinct captains to get out the vote and provide small financial rewards for voting. Few neighborhoods today boast tight party organizations. In their place, national parties, partnered with their allied interest groups, can provide the fuel for grassroots campaigns— Republicans with small businesses and such groups as the National Rifle Association (NRA) and the Christian Coalition, Democrats with organized labor, environmental groups, and racial and ethnic associations.

As long as they can pay the price, candidates today can procure campaign services from political consulting firms. Some companies offer a wide array of services; others specialize in survey research, direct-mail appeals, phone banks, advertising, purchase of media time, coordination of volunteer efforts, fund-raising, or financial management and accounting. Despite the hype they often receive, consultants rarely turn a campaign around. At best they can make the most of a candidate's resources and help combat opponents' attacks.

They cannot compensate for an unskilled or lazy candidate or for a candidate's staff that does not follow through on details.

Reliance upon professional firms raises its own set of problems. Not all firms are scrupulous in adhering to professional or ethical standards. One example is opposition research, the purpose of which is "to get the skinny on the client's opponents and, if all goes well, expose them as hypocrites, liars, thieves, or just plain unsavory characters."[27] Most campaigns invest in opposition research. Some of them go too far, straying beyond the public record into private-eye snooping into personal matters. Another debatable form of campaigning is the push poll. This is a survey instrument that features questions intended to change the opinion of the contacted voters. It divulges negative information about the opponent with the hope of pushing the voter away from him or her and pulling the voter toward the candidate paying for the polling.

Campaign Techniques

Campaigns are designed to convey candidates' messages to people who will lend support and vote in the election. Campaigns are not necessarily directed at all voters. Often narrower groups are targeted, mainly those groups most likely to vote for the candidate—most notably, the political parties' core supporters. Campaign techniques are distinguished by the breadth and kind of audiences they seek to reach.

The Air War: Media and Other Mass Appeals

Candidates reach the largest numbers of voters by running advertisements and making televised appearances. Especially in statewide elections, media efforts may be the only way for candidates to get their messages to the mass of voters. Television is the broadest spectrum medium and often the most cost-effective. In the 2002 election cycle, $336 million was spent for political advertising on network television alone.[28]

Media efforts vary in the degree to which their preparation and distribution are controlled by the candidate. Paradoxically, some of the most effective appeals—news coverage and endorsements, for example—are determined by persons other than the candidate. Journalists' interviews can raise unwanted or hostile questions, so many politicians seek out the friendlier environments of talk shows hosted by nonjournalists. Even more congenial are appeals bought and paid for by the candidate—newsletters, media ads, and direct mail—but these are less credible because they are seen as promotional material.

Three-fourths of all citizens get their campaign news primarily from television—network, local, or cable. Less than a third rely mainly on newspaper, and smaller portions on radio, magazines, and the Internet.[29] Yet campaign coverage by the news media is sketchy, especially for House races.[30] Therefore, most candidates are left to their own devices in reaching voters. Herein lies a major difference between House and Senate races; the former are covered less than the latter by the news media. Although Senate contenders draw wider publicity, they have less control over its content than do House candidates.

Positive Advertising. Most campaign themes call for promotions that evoke positive responses from citizens. Little-known candidates must initially boost name familiarity. Their ads introduce the candidates to voters, underscore their personal and public qualities, and tell of their accomplishments. Running in California's Twenty-second District (Santa Barbara, San Luis Obispo) following her husband's sudden death, Lois Capps, D, introduced herself by stressing her local ties and associating herself with popular issues:

> CAPPS: For thirty-three years I've lived and raised my family here. My husband, Walter, had the honor of representing you, and now I'm running to finish his term. As a teacher and a mother, I'll make improving our schools a top priority. I'll use my experience as a nurse to fight for health care that protects seniors and the right to choose our own doctor, and I'll support tax reform and tax relief for working families.
>
> ANNOUNCER: The experience of a lifetime makes Lois Capps the qualified choice for Congress.[31]

Between January and November 1998, Capps ran and outpolled her opponents in four separate contests—the special election and subsequent runoff for the partial term and then the primary and general election for a full term. Ads like hers present candidates in warm, human terms to which citizens can relate. Democrat Dennis Moore, a 1998 challenger in Kansas's Third District (northeast; Kansas City suburbs) had a superb résumé, but it was his talent as an amateur singer and guitar player that enabled him to connect with voters on a personal level. Moore had to be coaxed into making a hokey TV spot entitled "Guitar Lessons." After mentioning a style of music (country, rock, blues), he would play a short tune and then apply it to an issue. Example: "Rock: We need to make Social Security solid as a rock."[32] Moore captured the seat, a feat he twice repeated.

If skillfully done, TV ads can be artful as well as effective in bringing home the candidates' themes. A case in point was the series of brilliant, funny—and inexpensive—television ads that helped a little-known Wisconsin state legislator, Russell D. Feingold, win the Democratic primary over better-known and better-financed rivals and then to defeat a two-term incumbent senator.[33] As his opponents battered each other with negative ads, Feingold ran clever, personal spots describing himself as the "underdog candidate." One showed Elvis, alive and endorsing Feingold. Another showed Feingold walking through his modest home, opening up a closet and saying, "No skeletons." In another he posted his three key pledges on his garage door. Although outspent in both the primary and the general election, Feingold became one of five successful challengers in the 1992 Senate races.

Some media appeals are coordinated with field operations. Trolling for the student vote in Madison, Wisconsin, Democratic candidate Tammy Baldwin ran what her staff called the "Bucky" ad (for the University of Wisconsin mascot "Bucky Badger"). It ran on MTV and youth-oriented shows. The ad said that "there is one candidate who understands our issues" and ended with a pitch to get out and vote, with phone number and Baldwin's Web site. Every time the ad ran, all the headquarters phone lines would light up.[34]

Negative Ads. Different from positive ads are those known as contrast ads, which separate the candidate from the opponent, and attack (truly negative) ads, which strike at the opponent's views or behavior. The line between contrast ads and negative ads is not always clear. Dennis Moore's gun control spot was a contrast ad. The message was delivered by a seedy looking gunman prowling outside a school playground, and the "this could happen here" theme was played off against the incumbent's votes and positions on gun control. The ad was a hit with women in focus groups, but the wary campaign managers decided to use it only at the end of the campaign and only during nonprime hours.[35] Ads slide into negativism when they mainly attack the opponent.

In many races, voters' opinions are tracked throughout the campaign, and damaging opposition tactics are countered at once. More than one politician has lost by hesitating to counter opponents' thrusts. Technology now enables reactive ads to be produced and distributed in a few hours. They can be sent by satellite to television stations on the campaign trail. Numerous attack and response ads may be produced in the course of a hard-fought campaign.

Attack ads are common in modern campaigning because politicians believe they work. Recent experiments by two noted communications researchers tend to confirm this intuition. Negative ads, the scholars found, do lift voters' information levels, even if the information conveyed is distorted or trivial. Neither positive nor negative ads have much effect on partisans. Ads tend to reinforce previously held views and only slightly raise (or lower) their predisposition to vote. But negative ads work powerfully on citizens who have little information to begin with and on those with little or no party allegiance—a growing proportion of the electorate.[36]

These provocative finds were challenged by other researchers. "We should not necessarily see negative ads as a harmful part of our electoral system," contends Kenneth Goldstein, head of the University of Wisconsin's political advertising project. "They are much more likely [than positive ads] to be about policy, to use supporting information, and to be reliable. Few negative ads are on personal issues." [37] One study of 189 different Senate campaigns found that "negative campaigning . . . generally *mobilizes*, rather than *demobilizes*, the electorate." [38] But people react differently: Political independents, for example, were turned off by all forms of negative advertising.

Distortions and Dirty Tricks. Like other forms of product promotion, political campaigns often stretch or distort the truth to make their point. Sometimes the disinformation is so blatant that the term *dirty tricks* applies. This includes not only misinformation but also using doctored photographs or faking news reports or news headlines. An especially sinister tactic is blaming an opponent for bad events over which the person had no control. For example, several candidates were slammed in 2002 for their "Enron values," when they had no ties to the failed energy company.

Candidates who are victims of smear tactics have some weapons of defense. The campaign can respond promptly, at least accusing the offender of mudslinging. Formal complaints can sometimes persuade local broadcasters to kill the offending ads. Media outlets find themselves in the unwanted role of arbitrating between contending candidates. (The legal situation is murky. Courts have held that candidates have a right to buy ads even if their content is challenged, but broadcasters are not legally required to air ads from party organizations or advocacy groups.)[39]

Some have proposed tighter controls on campaign advertising—for example, requiring candidates to appear in all ads that talk about their opponents or requiring them to state their approval of a broadcast ad. No jurisdictions, as far as we are aware, have been so bold as Minnesota, which passed a law that set criminal penalties for candidates who knowingly made demonstrably false claims in the course of their campaigns. An unsuccessful 1994 House contender was indicted for allegedly false accusations made against his opponent in a television spot. A state court dismissed the case, holding that Minnesota's law violated the First Amendment's guarantee of free speech. Two years later a Republican House member from Oregon was indicted (and later convicted) on charges that he had misrepresented his military service in state voter guides, which are official documents, after party leaders had already shoved him into retirement over this and other questions raised about his past record.[40]

Formal or legal remedies against campaign misrepresentations are very unlikely to work because they raise thorny constitutional questions, not to mention the specter of excessive regulation and litigation. Instead, citizens surely are better off trusting that "the give-and-take of campaign thrust-and-parry and the activity of a free and skeptical press create a balance" between contenders.[41]

Mass Media Shortcomings. Media campaigns increasingly display what political scientist Darrell West describes as a law of diminishing returns. "It becomes difficult to break through the clutter," he observes, "and at this point there is a lot of clutter out there."[42] There are far more media outlets: cable TV channels, specialized publications, and Web-based sources. And these media are crowded with ads, most of them nonpolitical. Some 1.5 million thirty-second spots were aired in the 2002 campaign season; that year, some twenty-one thousand commercials were run by the two candidates in lightly populated South Dakota's competitive Senate race.[43]

"We are moving into a new world," said former Democratic leader Rep. Richard A. Gephardt of Missouri, "and I think the traditional model we have gone on for 30 years, jamming millions of dollars into a television set and driving enough folks to the polls on Election Day, is a passing method."[44] In short, politicians were rediscovering the virtues of retail as opposed to whole-sale campaigning: personal appeals to voters.

The Ground War: Pressing the Flesh and Other Forms of Close Contact

Direct personal appeals remain the best way to gather votes. Although not as cost-effective as media campaigns in reaching masses of people, personal-ized techniques can be aimed at those most apt to go to the polling booth: loy-alists within the parties' core constituency groups. As political reporter David S. Broder put it: "More and more political strategists are coming to believe that the high-tech tools that have dominated campaigns for the past four decades —TV spots, mass mailings and professionally staffed phone banks—are far less effective [in motivating voters] than the old-fashioned way of turning out the vote." [45]

Direct appeals to voters through personal appearances by the candidate—at shopping centers, factory gates, or even door to door—are part of every campaign. In his first Senate campaign in 1948, Lyndon B. Johnson swooped out of the sky in a helicopter to visit small Texas towns, grandly pitching his Stetson from the chopper for a bold entrance. (An aide was assigned to retrieve the hat for use at the next stop.)[46] Other candidates, preferring to stay closer to the ground, stage walking tours or other events to attract attention. Few elected officials get by without doing a great deal of what is inelegantly called pressing the flesh. In his first campaign—for a House seat in 1978—Senate Democratic leader Tom Daschle of South Dakota recalls that forty thousand homes were contacted door to door. "In rural states you can still do a lot on a person-to-person basis," he explained. He won by 139 votes.[47]

One-on-one campaigning is physically and emotionally challenging, and the payoff is often elusive. "The hardest doorbell for a candidate to ring is the first one," campaign specialist Ron Faucheux recalls of his canvassing days. "Canvassing takes an enormous amount of time and a serious commitment." [48] At best, he cautions, canvassers reach only about 30 percent of an area's voters. Only about 60 percent of the people will be home, and the person who comes to the door may represent only half the household's eligible voters. To reach more voters per visit, candidates seek out shopping malls, organized groups, fairs, or rallies. Leafleting or targeted mailings reach even more voters.

Candidates or their surrogates need to make sure constituents are regis-tered, distribute campaign leaflets, produce crowds at rallies, trudge door to door, and muster voters on election day. All these tasks can be hired for a price, but they are most effective when carried out by someone who can connect with the potential voter. In a controlled experiment conducted by two Yale po-litical scientists, a preelection phone call to a randomly selected group of col-lege students from local young people boosted turnout an average of 8 percent over a similar group of students who received no such contact. "These young people just don't feel a connection to the campaign, and when someone like them calls, it turns 22-year-olds into 36-year-olds [whose community ties make them more frequent voters]."[49]

Some campaigns make a point of mobilizing cadres of volunteers.[50] Rep. Tammy Baldwin's winning run in 1998 for an open seat in Wisconsin's Second District (Madison) was boosted by some three thousand volunteers, seventeen hundred of them University of Wisconsin (UW) students. Most of these helpers did a literature drop or two, or they worked the phones for an evening. But some—thirty-five during the general election race—worked full time. Much of the volunteer effort targeted Madison's forty thousand UW students, notoriously indifferent voters who make up 10 percent of the district's potential electorate. Baldwin found their weekly field meetings rejuvenating:

> I would go to these meetings just to listen to the discussion and to get fired up. Joe [the field consultant] would be on the speaker phone in the middle of the room barking out questions. "OK, how many building and floor captains do we have in the dorms?" Someone would answer, "We have 87 of the 150 positions." "How many more can we get by next week?" he would ask. . . . Everyone was energized by these meetings. In many ways our campaign was an old-fashioned, person-to-person effort. It really came together in the last week of the campaign.[51]

The volunteer effort paid off. Baldwin topped 70 percent of the vote in the six wards with the highest concentration of UW students.

Other groups can similarly be goaded to the polls by personal appeals. Aided by labor unions and other groups, Democrats in 1998 and 2000 boosted their turnout by some 4 percent, thanks to vote-pulling operations in the campaigns' final days. In 2002 the Democratic National Committee together with labor unions spent nearly $35 million on such activities. "In most states union members will be contacted between fourteen and twenty-four times by other union members in some fashion," AFL-CIO's political director reported.[52]

Republicans struck back that year with their own "72-hour Plan" (masterminded by White House strategist Karl Rove and Georgia party chair Ralph Reed). They tested it in off-year elections and in 2002 rolled it out in thirty-one states. The party recruited more volunteers, made more phone calls, rang more doorbells, and pulled out more votes from Republican households than ever before. In Georgia, for example, the party's operating head

> hired a supervisor and nine field operatives and made turnout their mission. They recruited organizers and volunteers at Rotary Clubs and churches all over the state. Volunteers walked their target areas over the summer, identifying Republican voters and issues they cared about. Weeks later, voters started getting direct-mail advertisements and phone calls from local volunteers talking about those issues.[53]

In the final weeks volunteers at telephone banks—"neighbors calling neighbors"—spoke with thousands of people who had voted in GOP primaries. "And those were live phone calls, not recorded messages," explained victorious Sen. Saxby Chambliss's campaign manager. "In the last election cycle [the money] would've been spent on TV. This cycle, it went into manpower." [54] This revamped ground game was credited with the party's defeat of Georgia's Democratic governor, U.S. senator, and statehouse leaders.

The Parallel Campaigns

The big story about recent congressional campaigns is the soaring activity of groups not formally affiliated with the candidates or the parties. Campaigns no longer resemble boxing matches between two combatants. They are more like mud wrestling contests in which anyone can take part.

Groups interested in congressional election outcomes have every reason to mount their own campaigns. Direct contributions by individuals to candidates have little impact. The legal contribution limits are tiny drops in the bucket. But groups can indulge in unlimited independent spending for or against candidates, as long as it is reported to the Federal Election Commission (FEC) and not coordinated with the candidates' own fund-raising. Better yet is issue advocacy, messages aimed at influencing voters' choices without explicitly advocating the election or defeat of specific candidates. Although such efforts are clearly designed to affect federal elections—most are indistinguishable from candidate advertising—the courts have on First Amendment grounds rebuffed the FEC's attempts to limit them and are likely to do the same with limitations contained in the 2002 Bipartisan Campaign Finance Act (BCRA).

Today, interest group involvement in congressional elections resembles an arms race. Hundreds of organizations engage in congressional campaigning, most of them in league with one of four major power centers. [55] One conservative power center is the Business Industry Political Action Committee (BIPAC), a group that advises and coordinates election activities of businesses and industry associations. Another group, spearheaded by the U.S. Chamber of Commerce, embraces a wide spectrum of business groups such as the National Federation of Independent Business (NFIB), which has 600,000 members from small companies. Besides mobilizing these members, the NFIB in 2002 rolled out a GOTV drive aimed at some twenty House races and eight Senate-race states. [56] Another power cluster is the Wednesday Group, a loose-knit collection of staff representatives from ideologically conservative groups—those opposed to taxes, gun control, and abortion and those favoring term limits, prayer in schools, and home schooling.

On the left side of the spectrum, the AFL-CIO, the umbrella organization for seventy-seven labor unions, began with media campaigning but increasingly pours its money and personnel into GOTV efforts. "Magically, we have learned that when we talk to union members on the phone or face to face in the workplace and get them information, they vote—and they vote for the candidates and positions we have endorsed," explained the AFL-CIO's political chief.[57] The liberal equivalent of the Wednesday Group is the Progressive Network, described as "a progressive political coffee klatch where we exchange information, gossip, hearsay and innuendo."[58] An alliance of environmental, feminist, gay, and lesbian organizations, its influential members include the Sierra Club and the National Abortion and Reproductive Rights Action League (NARAL). Other influential environmental groups include the League of Conservation Voters and the Natural Resources Defense Council.

Right-wing groups such as the Christian Coalition, the National Rifle Association, and the small-business lobby helped propel the Republicans' takeover of Congress as a result of the 1994 elections. Democrats and their allies mobilized to retake Congress, and while they made gains over the next three elections they fell short of victory. Widely publicized work on their behalf by labor and environmental groups prodded pro–GOP organizations to dig deeper into their pockets for late ad blitzes. In 2002 the NRA spent some $10 million in the election; the Christian Coalition had an October convention to encourage members to get out the vote and distribute its voters' guides.[59]

Many of the new players in the electoral game are little known, even to seasoned political observers. One example is Triad Management Services, a for-profit consulting firm that advises conservative donors on which candidates and PACs to support. Triad also finds people willing to donate to nonprofit groups with names such as Citizens for Reform or Citizens for the Republic Education Fund, which then turn around and hire Triad to produce ads and buy media time. These entities have the appearance of paper organizations aimed at laundering money for campaign purposes. As a major broker, Triad "played the role of an orchestra leader," said Bill Hogan of the Center for Public Integrity, a nonprofit research group. "They had an ocean of money, and where it comes from and where it goes doesn't have to be disclosed. . . . It's secret money, and the level of it is worse today than during Watergate."[60] It is but one more manifestation of the "whack a mole" phenomenon described by journalist Chuck Alston. Campaigns parallel to, but formally independent of, the efforts of candidates and their parties are popping up everywhere.

Who Votes?

Although Congress is supposed to be the people's branch of government, less than half of voting-age citizens take part in House elections in presidential years, and less than 40 percent vote in off years. Nearly 79 million citizens cast ballots in the 2002 elections, 39.3 percent of the voting-age population, or VAP (all residents age eighteen and over).[61] As Figure 4-2 indicates, voting participation in national elections has declined since 1960.

Political analysts disagree over the reasons for the anemic voting levels in the United States, the lowest among all the Western democracies. Several explanations—not all of them compatible—have been suggested.[62]

Figure 4-2   Turnout in Presidential and House Elections, 1932–2002

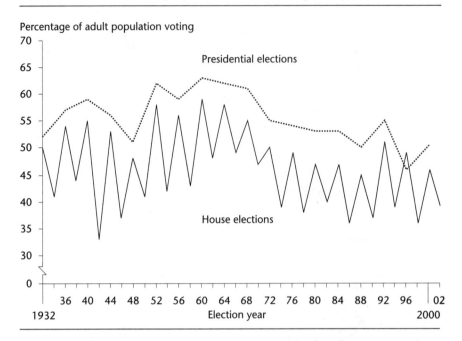

Percentage of adult population voting

Sources: U.S. Bureau of the Census, *Statistical Abstract of the United States 1982–1983*, 103d ed. (Washington, D.C.: U.S. Government Printing Office, 1982), Table 801; U.S. Bureau of the Census, *Statistical Abstract of the United States 1989*, 109th ed. (Washington, D.C.: U.S. Government Printing Office, 1989), Table 433; Norman J. Ornstein, Thomas E. Mann, and Michael J. Malbin, *Vital Statistics on Congress, 1999–2000* (Washington, D.C.: American Enterprise Institute, 2000), 48; "Overstated Turnout Woes," *Campaigns & Elections*, February 1999, 9; Dana Calvo, "Vote Turnout Is Low Despite Tight Race," *Los Angeles Times*, November 9, 2000, A44; and Edward Walsh, "Election Turnout Rose Slightly," *Washington Post*, November 8, 2002, A10.

One is demographic. Certain growing segments of the population—such as jailed felons and undocumented aliens—are formally excluded. And today's populace embraces expanding categories of people with traditionally low voting rates: for example, young voters, African Americans, and Latinos. Young people (ages eighteen through twenty-nine) are the least likely to vote of all age groups—in part because they have fewer of those life events (mortgages, taxes, school-age children, community ties) that propel older people toward activism. Yet other trends ought to raise turnout. For example, the single factor most closely linked with political engagement of virtually all kinds—education level—has been on the rise among the population.[63]

A second explanation stresses barriers to voting. Only about 70 percent of the VAP are registered to vote. Unlike their European counterparts, U.S. citizens must initiate the registration process. The National Voter Registration Act of 1993—the so-called motor voter law—linked voter registration to motor vehicle licensing. After five years, registration of eligible voters had risen about 3.8 percent nationwide, but that did not substantially raise voting levels, especially among the young and the poor, who were the targets of the measure.[64] "Motor Voter is a howling success as a registration tool," remarked Kentucky's chief election officer, "but turnout is still a dog."[65]

Other disincentives can be blamed on the electoral system itself. Citizens are asked to vote far more often than people in parliamentary regimes; and election days are not holidays. As uncovered in the 2000 Florida voting scandals (and Florida was by no means the sole offender), careless or biased election administration can turn away voters or miscount their ballots. Yet over the past generation many states have modernized their elections, lowering many barriers to registering and voting. Absentee balloting is common. Some states permit ballots to be submitted over a period of time. Oregon citizens may vote by telephone. And, prompted by the 2000 fiasco, the Bipartisan Campaign Reform Act of 2002 (P.L. 107-252) raised federal election standards and promised money to help states meet those standards.

A third explanation is citizen disaffection. Poor candidates and contentious or negative campaigning supposedly has kept people away from the polling booths. Apathy and cynicism are, to be sure, part of the picture. Surveys sponsored by Harvard University's *Vanishing Voters* project found that four out of ten nonvoters in 2000 claimed to care little about politics and public affairs. A quarter were dismayed or confused by the barrage of campaign messages. And another quarter were simply angry or cynical over politics.[66]

Fourth, citizens may be rationally abstaining from voting in favor of other forms of political participation, including membership in political groups and activism on issues. Even in 2000—whose razor-thin results underscored that "every vote counts"—few congressional races were truly competitive. With so many electoral outcomes a foregone conclusion, citizens may seek more meaningful participation elsewhere. Or they may simply prefer to spend their time doing something else. One study of the 1996 elections discovered that one in five people who registered but did not vote said they were too busy or could not take time off from work.[67]

Finally, even taking all these disincentives into account, it may be that the level of nonvoting has been vastly exaggerated. For one thing, the VAP measure has become so unreliable that, according to Samuel L. Popkin and Michael P. McDonald, "it significantly overstates the size of the eligible electorate and, therefore, artificially depresses the turnout rate." Recalculating the VAP for every national election since World War II, the two political scientists estimated turnout ranging from 52.7 to 60.6 percent—still nothing to be proud of, but "a lot less dismal than is generally believed."[68]

Voting is the broadest and most accessible form of political involvement, but it is still biased in favor of people at the higher rungs of the social and generational ladders—those who are more mature, more affluent, better educated, and more in touch with political events. Eight of ten people whose annual incomes exceed $50,000 vote in a typical election. This is twice the voting rate of the poor, defined as people with incomes of less than $15,000. Moreover, this gap has been widening over the past decade or so. In one recent election year poor people—who are nearly 20 percent of the voting-age population—accounted for only 7.7 percent of voters.[69]

Alternative forms of political participation are even more sharply biased. For example, giving money—which the Supreme Court equates with free speech—is mainly an elite activity. In the sample Sidney Verba and his colleagues examined, 35 percent of all political money flowed from the 4 percent of people making more than $125,000 a year. Poor people, who were 19 percent of the sample, made only 2 percent of political donations.[70]

Turnout varies according to whether the election is held in a presidential or a midterm year (even in presidential years the congressional vote typically lags behind the presidential vote by about 5 percent). Midterm races often lack the intense publicity and stimulus to vote provided by presidential contests. Since the 1930s, turnout in midterm congressional elections has averaged about 12 percent below that of the preceding presidential election. Midterm electorates include proportionately more people who are interested in politics and, incidentally, who are more affluent and better educated.[71] Turnout also varies by region. Less than 20 percent of the voters turn out in certain one-party areas; in competitive states turnout well above 50 percent is common.

How Voters Decide

What induces voters to cast their ballots for one candidate and not another? When American voters enter the polling booth, they typically do not carry much ideological or even issue-specific baggage. As a general rule, voters reach their decisions on the basis of three considerations: party loyalties, candidate assessments, and overall judgments about the state of the nation—the government, the economy, and what are perceived as the most pressing issues. The relative strength of these forces varies over time and among specific races.

Although American voters are often uninformed—or even indifferent—about political issues and candidates, they employ low-information rationality, or gut reasoning, to reach their voting-booth decisions. People "triangulate and validate their opinions in conversations with people they trust and according to the opinions of national figures whose judgments and positions they have come to know."[72] Thus voters work their way through imperfect information to make sensible choices, not very different from the sorts of choices they would have made with perfect information.

Party Loyalties

Political analysts over the years have found party identification the single most powerful factor in determining voters' choices. It remains the strongest single correlate of voting in congressional elections. In 2002, nine of every ten

Democrats and Republicans voted for their parties' candidates. Independents split their votes more evenly.[73]

The 2002 elections found the electorate divided roughly in thirds among Republicans (33 percent), Democrats (32 percent), and independents (31 percent).[74] These preferences, as measured by indexes of party identification, have remained relatively stable over the past several elections, despite short-term fluctuations.

According to surveys, however, most people who claim to be independents are in fact closet partisans who lean toward one party or the other. These independent leaners—about a quarter of the total electorate—hold attitudes similar to those of partisans: Not only do they favor one of the two parties, they also share many (though not necessarily all) of the party's values and say they will vote for the party's candidates—if they bestir themselves to vote.

Only 6 percent of all citizens are true independents, and they split in three ways—a third for each party and another third who do not know or who admit they will not vote. True independents are unpredictable and have very low turnout rates. "I would encourage candidates not to play to them," advises David Magleby of Brigham Young University, "because they tend to jump on bandwagons, to follow tides. You're better off [working] on getting your weak partisans and your leaners." [75]

Party Decline and Surge. The latter half of the twentieth century saw partisan loyalty decline among the American electorate. A variety of factors were at work. In their heyday the party organizations supplied voters with political information and cues, a range of personal services, and even entertainment—benefits now furnished elsewhere in society. During congressional campaigns of the past generation, fewer than one in five voting-age citizens reported having been contacted by a political party worker.[76] Candidates today are able to, and often are obliged to, bypass party organizations in taking their messages to voters. Elected officials have taxpayer-provided resources for reaching constituents. Finally, partisan voting cues in that era may simply have conveyed less meaning. As Jacobson put it, "The party label became less informative and thus less useful to voters as a shorthand cue for predicting what elected officials would do once in office. Information about individual candidates became more important." [77]

Weakened party ties led to an epidemic of split-ticket voting—in which voters supported a presidential candidate of one party and congressional candidates of another. A certain level of ticket splitting—by perhaps one in ten voters—can be expected in every election. In surveys between 1952 and 1988 the number of voters who reported that they split their ticket between presidential and House candidates increased from 12 percent to 25 percent. Those who split their ballots between different parties' House and Senate candidates grew from 9 percent to 27 percent.[78]

In the past three presidential elections, however, ticket splitting was back down to 9 percent—exactly the 1956 level. By the same token, the number of

House districts voting for one party's presidential candidate and the other party's candidate for the House of Representatives rose even more dramatically, only to fall back in recent elections. In 2000, eighty-six House members (forty-six Democrats and forty Republicans) were elected from districts carried by the opposite party's presidential candidate—the lowest figure in nearly half a century.[79] Democrats who bucked George W. Bush's tide tended to be in southern or border states; Republicans elected in Al Gore's best districts tended to come from the Northeast.

A look at the demographics of ticket splitting helps to identify voters whose traditional partisan loyalties were at odds with at least some of the choices they faced in the voting booth. In the 1980s many ticket splitters were so-called Reagan Democrats—voters who preferred the GOP's national tickets while backing Democrats in other races. Many of them were white southern conservatives who were making a slow but steady trek from their Democratic roots toward their new home with the Republicans. Responding to the call of the GOP's southern strategy, these voters were attracted to such candidates as Dwight D. Eisenhower in the 1950s, Barry Goldwater in 1964, and Ronald Reagan in the 1980s. For the time being, they continued to back Democrats in congressional and state races because the party put up conservative candidates and because it controlled legislative chambers and could deliver the most benefits to constituents. The same phenomenon occurred to a lesser degree in the Northeast, where the Democrats' national policies led voters to support their presidential candidates along with moderate to liberal Republican representatives or senators.[80] In short, the bulge in split-ticket voting seems to have been a by-product of gradual partisan realignment.

Recent party realignment, however, worked to bring party affiliation into sync with policy and ideological preferences. Although the process extended over many years, the long Republican courtship of southern conservatives was consummated in 1994. The Democratic Party's acceptance by GOP moderates and liberals, though less dramatic, is a parallel trend. Finding acceptable candidates up and down the ballot, these voters have less need to pick and choose—hence, revived partisanship and dwindling split tickets.

Divergent results in some recent elections reveal a lingering ticket splitting: the pull of candidate versus party appeal and local versus national forces. George Bush's 1988 presidential victory was accompanied by a two-seat loss of GOP House seats. Bill Clinton won a plurality of votes in 1992, while his party lost ten House seats. In 1996 he bested Bob Dole by nearly eight million votes, but his party gained only ten House seats. In 2000 George W. Bush and Al Gore battled each other to a virtual tie, whereas Democrats were gaining a net of five Senate seats and two House seats.

Politicians once talked about coattails—how House and Senate candidates could be helped into office on the coattails of a popular presidential candidate of the same party. Ronald Reagan, for example, boosted his party's congressional votes by 2 to 3 percent in 1980 and 4 to 5 percent in 1984. But the 1992, 1996, and 2000 elections saw little measurable pull from the presidential candidates.[81] Conversely, presidential candidates can gain from their party's local strength. In either case, spillovers from one contest to another are less frequent than they once were.

Midterm Elections. Historically, partisan forces have operated differently in presidential years and midterm years. Until about 1960, presidential-year races displayed a high correlation between votes cast for president and votes cast for House members on a district-by-district basis. After that the correlation declined as ticket splitting became more of an option for voters.

What happens when presidential candidates are not on the ballot? The midterm electorate is both smaller than and different from the presidential-year electorate. Normally, midterm elections result in losses for the party that captured the White House two years earlier (see Table 4-2). In midterm elections during recent decades the presidential party lost an average of twenty-eight House seats and almost four Senate seats. In 1994 the Democrats lost a net of fifty-two seats in the House and eight in the Senate, a result that was certainly related to President Clinton's unpopularity at the time. The 1998 and 2002 results were surprises, however. President Clinton's Democrats gained five seats in the House and held their own in the Senate in 1998, in the midst of an impeachment scandal. Four years later President Bush's GOP gained seven House and two Senate seats, despite a lagging economy. (The only other anomaly occurred in 1934, when President Franklin D. Roosevelt's popularity strengthened the Democrats' hold in both chambers.)

The surge and decline theory held that shrinkage of the electorate in midterm years explains the normal falloff in the presidential party's votes. That is, a presidential surge, swollen by less motivated voters attracted by presidential campaigns, is followed two years later by a decline as these voters drop out of the electorate. But other studies suggest that midterm voters are no more or less partisan than those in presidential years and share most of their demographic characteristics.[82]

Another theory argues that midterm elections serve in part as a referendum on the president's popularity and performance in office during the previous two years.[83] Voters may hold the president's party responsible for the nation's economic health or its political or moral climate. This provides plausible explanations for such outcomes as the Democrats' 1974 post–Watergate bonus of fifty-two representatives and four senators, their 1982 recession harvest of twenty-six House seats, and the Republicans' 1994 bonanza. Yet in other years the referendum aspect of midterm elections is harder to discern.

What explains the seemingly anomalous results of the last two midterm elections, in which the president's party defied historical precedents? In the 1998 case, off-year contests reflected a mostly satisfied public that expressed confidence in the high-flying U.S. economy and, by a margin of two to one,

Table 4-2 Midterm Fortunes of Presidential Parties, 1934–2002

Year	President	Seats gained or lost	
		House	Senate
1934	Franklin D. Roosevelt (D)	+9	+10
1938	Roosevelt (D)	–71	–6
1942	Roosevelt (D)	–55	–9
1946	Roosevelt and Harry S. Truman (D)	–45	–12
1950	Truman (D)	–29	–6
1954	Dwight D. Eisenhower (R)	–18	–1
1958	Eisenhower (R)	–48	–13
1962	John F. Kennedy (D)	–4	+3
1966	Lyndon B. Johnson (D)	–47	–4
1970	Richard M. Nixon (R)	–12	+2
1974	Nixon and Gerald R. Ford (R)	–48	–5
1978	Jimmy Carter (D)	–15	–3
1982	Ronald Reagan (R)	–26	+1
1986	Reagan (R)	–5	–8
1990	George Bush (R)	–8	–1
1994	Bill Clinton (D)	–52	–8
1998	Clinton (D)	+5	0
2002	George W. Bush (R)	+7	+2
Average seats lost (18 elections)		–25.7	–3.2

Source: Compiled by the authors.

rejected impeaching the president. The two parties thus turned to their core voters. To energize its loyalists, and anyone likely to be incensed over the president's behavior, the House GOP campaign committee launched Operation Breakout, a $10 million advertising assault on Clinton. The pretested ads were beamed at thirty House districts, and for only a few days before the election.[84] But the ad campaign was widely reported in the press, a fact that solidified people's perception of Republicans as "the impeachment party." As two commentators concluded, "The Republicans' drive to turn the election into a referendum on President Clinton ran head-on into an electorate less interested in the Monica S. Lewinsky scandal than in maintaining the status quo of a healthy economy." [85]

The 2002 midterm elections were equally intriguing. Most pundits predicted Democratic gains, based not only on the historical record (forgetting 1998, however) but also on surveys showing that the faltering economy was the No. 1 issue on the voters' minds. These factors were balanced, however, by positive feelings toward the president—his leadership since the 9/11 attacks and his calculated talk of waging war against Iraq. Thus, he was not blamed for the economic woes. The scales were certainly tipped in the Republicans' favor by their superior efforts in recruiting candidates, supporting them, and mustering core voters. President Bush's efforts were beamed laserlike to these voters. In races where he appeared in the final two weeks of the campaign, Republicans elected thirteen of eighteen senators and sixty of sixty-nine representatives.[86] Having framed the elections in terms of a likely Bush loss, media commentators now had to call the outcome a major victory.

"In any election," notes Curtis Gans, "the outcome is not determined by turnout, but by *who* turns out."[87] Recent off-year elections have been no exception. Traditional Democrats—in particular, organized labor and African American leaders—mounted aggressive ground wars in 1998 and 2000, and their efforts paid off. Polling data indicated that voters from union households made up 23 percent of the 1998 electorate, up from just 14 percent in the GOP-victory year of 1994. Black voters moved from 9 percent to 11 percent of the electorate.[88]

The Appeal of Candidates

"My theory on politics is ultimately that people vote for the person they like most," declares the revered former senator David Pryor, D-Ark. (1979–1997).[89] Apart from partisan loyalties, the appeal of given candidates is the strongest force in congressional voting. Not surprisingly, candidate appeal normally tilts toward incumbents. When voters abandon their party to vote for House or Senate candidates, they usually do so to vote for incumbents.

Over the past generation the incumbency factor has strengthened to the point that it rivals and sometimes eclipses partisanship. Scholars estimate the incumbency advantage in House and Senate races rose from about 2 percent of the vote totals during the 1954–1960 period to as much as 7 percent after 1960 (after controlling for national trends and district partisanship).[90] The proportion of marginal incumbents (those winning by less than 60 percent) fell by more than one-fourth. According to Jacobson, the proportion of marginal incumbents remained at this lower plateau (about 30 percent), dropping still further for a period in the late 1980s.[91] But wider reelection margins did not prevent incumbents from losing office at traditional rates—except for the late 1980s and late 1990s, bonanza periods for incumbents (see Table 3-1). However one measures incumbency effects, it remains true that incumbency confers powerful advantages upon officeholders who work to build and maintain support and who shrewdly exploit the resources available to them.

Although its effects are more pronounced in House elections, "incumbency now serves . . . as an important alternate voting cue to party" in Senate contests.[92] Statewide contests can be lively, especially in those southern states that have developed vigorous two-party competition over the past generation.

Yet in nonsouthern states competition for Senate seats has declined since 1958. Although Senate seats are more hotly contested than House seats, "a substantial proportion of Senate races are low-key affairs that attract scant notice: media coverage is limited, spending by the challenger is relatively low, and the outcome is often a foregone conclusion." [93]

Incumbents are better known than their opponents. Even if voters cannot recall officeholders' names in an interview, they can identify and express opinions about them when the names are presented to them—as in the voting booth. In the first National Election Study (NES) survey, nearly all respondents were able to recognize and rate Senate and House incumbents running for re-election (96 percent and 93 percent, respectively). Senate challengers were recognized and rated by 86 percent of the respondents, House challengers by only 44 percent. Open-seat candidates fell somewhere between incumbents and challengers in visibility. Thus most voters can recognize and express views about congressional candidates, except for House challengers. These opinions exert a powerful effect on voting decisions. In the eyes of some analysts they are the most potent influences on congressional voting. [94]

In evaluating candidates, voters normally favor incumbents over nonincumbents. Of voters' comments about incumbents in the NES survey, four out of five were favorable. In contrast, only 57 percent of the comments about challengers were positive. Most of the comments centered on the candidates' job performance or personal characteristics; relatively few dealt with issues. Voters evaluated House incumbents largely on the basis of personal characteristics and noncontroversial activities such as casework and constituent outreach. Even on the issues, references to incumbents were overwhelmingly positive. More than two-thirds of those voters claimed to have agreed with their legislator's votes, although only one in ten could cite how the representative had voted on a piece of legislation during the preceding two years.

Incumbents' popularity depends in large part upon their success in shaping information that constituents receive about them and their performance—through advertising, credit claiming, and position taking. [95] Not surprisingly, high levels of contact are reported with House and Senate incumbents. The more contact voters have with their legislators, the more positive their evaluations are likely to be. In the initial NES survey, only 10 percent of all voters said they had no exposure of any kind to their representative; only 6 percent reported no exposure to their senator. Many constituents receive mail from their representatives or read about them in newspapers. Almost a quarter have met the representative face to face. For senators, the major points of contact with voters are TV appearances or newspaper and magazine coverage.

The visibility gap between incumbents and challengers is wider in House races than in Senate races. Nine of every ten voters report some form of contact with their representative, but less than half that number have been exposed to challengers. Senate voters are more likely to be reached by both incumbent and challenger. Of those voters questioned in the initial NES survey,

82 percent reported contact with nonincumbent Senate candidates in their state, compared with 94 percent reporting contact with incumbent senators. In open seats the gap is narrower. Candidates for seats with no incumbent are able to reach nearly three-quarters of their potential House voters and 90 percent of potential Senate voters.

These findings explain why senators are more vulnerable at the polls than are their House counterparts. First, surveys indicate that representatives are viewed more favorably than senators—probably because they are judged primarily on noncontroversial acts, such as personal contact or constituent service, while senators are more closely linked to divisive national issues. Second, Senate challengers are far more visible than House challengers. Senate contests are more widely reported by the media, and challengers can gain almost as much exposure as incumbents. Media coverage of House races is more fragmentary than that of Senate races, throwing more weight to incumbents' techniques of contacting voters. Third, senators cannot manipulate voter contacts as much as representatives do. Voters largely get their information about Senate races through organized media, which senators do not control. Representatives gain exposure through focused means—personal appearances, mailings, and newsletters—which they fashion to their own advantage. "Somewhat ironically," observed Michael J. Robinson, "powerful senators are less able to control their images than 'invisible' House members." [96] Finally, senatorial elections are more competitive than House elections. There are proportionately fewer one-party states than one-party congressional districts.

Among senators, constituency size is a crucial variable in elections. Small-state senators in many respects resemble representatives. Compared with their large-state colleagues, they are more visible, more accessible, and more able to raise the campaign money they need. But they are not electorally safer—probably because their challengers, too, have an easier time mounting their campaigns and gaining visibility. [97]

Although incumbency offers many advantages, such as name recognition and media coverage, one must not exaggerate their causes or extent, as so often happens in journalistic or reformist accounts. Jacobson surely captured the normal state of affairs when he observed that "most incumbents face obscure, politically inexperienced opponents whose resources fall far short of what is necessary to mount a formidable campaign." [98]

Still, nonincumbents can and do win, with luck, timing, and attention to certain basic principles. Run for an open seat or against an incumbent whose support is slipping, or run in a year of voter restlessness. Be a credible, forceful candidate. Be prepared to spend money to erase the incumbent's visibility advantage. Blame the incumbent for the "mess in Washington." In some years (1992 and 1994, for example) this strategy works for many challengers. But even in years of political quiescence, as in the last three elections, a handful of challengers win by following these rules. That handful is usually enough to keep other incumbents on their guard. [99]

Issue Voting

According to conventional wisdom, issues and ideologies play a relatively minor role in voting, especially in congressional races. In their landmark 1962 study of House elections, Donald E. Stokes and Warren E. Miller found that voters knew next to nothing about the performance of either the parties or individual members of Congress.[100] Subsequent studies have done little to alter this judgment. Researchers have found that a large portion of those claiming to know House incumbents' stands on issues are wrong and that respondents resort mainly to guesswork when asked to place House or Senate candidates on a liberal–conservative scale.[101]

A slightly more optimistic picture emerged from later NES surveys. One-third of the respondents were able to name an issue they said was important to them in the House elections. Of those people, 40 percent preferred one of the candidates because of the issue they had cited. Yet 54 percent said the issue made no difference in their choice of candidates. Only 11 percent of the respondents, moreover, could remember how their representative had voted on any issue during the preceding two years; of those, 71 percent reported agreeing with the incumbent on that issue.[102]

As usual, a distinction must be made between House and Senate voting. House incumbents and challengers, on the one hand, can more easily sidestep divisive national issues and stress their personal qualities and district service. Senators, on the other hand, are more closely identified with issues. One study comparing incumbents' ratings by Americans for Democratic Action (ADA), a liberal group, with voters' self-classifications on a seven-point liberal–conservative scale found that ideology had "no discernible impact on evaluations of House candidates."[103] Contact was the prime influence on respondents' evaluations of House candidates; ideology and party identification were more important in evaluating Senate candidates. Another study, based on exit polls, found that "policy issues play an important role" in Senate elections, where "policy effects are substantial and systematic."[104]

Given the subordinate role of issues in influencing voters' decisions, how can recent efforts by parties and other groups to develop and market nation-wide platforms or themes for congressional campaigns be assessed? As early as the 1970s, House Democrats and Republicans were drafting platforms—lists of goals or talking points to supply ammunition to candidates in the field, especially nonincumbents.[105] The most daring use of this device occurred in September 1994, when more than three hundred GOP congressional candidates gathered on the steps of the U.S. Capitol's West Front to sign the Contract with America—a set of ten proposals that included a balanced-budget amendment, a presidential line-item veto, internal House reforms, term limits for members of Congress, and policy proposals on crime, welfare, business regulation, and tax cuts. The candidates pledged that, if a GOP majority were elected, they would put the measures to a House floor vote within the first hundred days of the new Congress. By signing what amounted to a national platform, the candidates seemingly defied the then-common assumption that issues did not win elections, as well as Speaker (1977–1987) Thomas P. "Tip" O'Neill Jr.'s dictum that "all politics are local."

Flush with victory that November, Republican leaders quickly claimed a popular mandate to enact the Contract with America. However, what we know about issues in elections—and about the contract in particular—entitles us to be skeptical of its specific impact on voting choice. First, candidates' use of the contract in their campaigns varied widely. Some used it to underscore themes they had already been employing. Others rarely mentioned it. "I didn't use the Contract that much," reported a typical GOP candidate. "I made very limited reference to it and the voters didn't know much about it. . . . I did talk about things that were in the Contract, but that's not the same as using the Contract per se." Second, most voters claimed not to have heard about the contract. At best, no more than three in ten voters were acquainted with it. "Almost all the GOP candidates admitted that few voters, aside from a few 'C-SPAN groupies,' could recognize what the Contract was by election day." [106]

Whatever one's verdict on the effect of congressional platforms, issues figure prominently in candidates' and parties' appeals. Although the vast majority of voters may make up their minds on other grounds, at least some of them are attentive to issues, even basing their choices on a specific issue or cluster of issues. Issues matter at the margins, and not a few elections turn on those margins.

Voters' responses to political issues show up in the different patterns of choice displayed by demographic groups. Many Americans sort themselves out politically according to their sex, their income or social class, their race or ethnicity, their age, their region, even their habits of religious devotion. True, these differences are typically reflected in people's long-term party loyalties, but issues can exert an independent force. Consider abortion. Although this issue cuts across party lines, the Democratic Party's generally pro-choice stance has cost it some support from its cadres of religious conservatives—for example, southern white Evangelicals, ethnic Catholics, and devout blacks and Latinos. The Republican Party's record (strongly anti-abortion) has hurt its standing among middle- and upper-class women who might otherwise prefer the party's candidates. Abortion is an example of what politicians call wedge issues—those that have the power to move voters away from their normal party loyalties. For certain voters in certain elections, such issues can overpower long-standing party loyalties and, if they persist over time, even displace those party loyalties.

A demographic snapshot of the two parties' voters would start at the much-discussed gender gap, which is the difference between the way men and women vote. This gap has amounted to as much as 10 percent in recent elections—women leaning toward Democratic candidates, men toward Republicans.[107] Gender gaps appear in virtually all recent contests. As pollster Celinda

Lake remarked, "You'll get [a gender gap] in a race for dogcatcher in Montana, if it's a Republican against a Democrat." [108] The presence of a female candidate affects but does not remove the phenomenon. The explanation for this phenomenon probably lies in men's and women's responses to political and social issues. Men are more attracted to issues such as military preparedness, tough anticrime laws, and restrictions on welfare recipients and immigrants. Women seem to respond more positively than men to social equality issues such as government-sponsored health benefits, job training, child care, and welfare aid. [109] A concerted effort by Republicans to talk about such issues as education and Medicare prescription drug support narrowed this gap in 2002 balloting.

A host of similar patterns are found among congressional voters. "There's a family gap, a generation gap, a gender gap," said GOP pollster Neil Newhouse of the fissures among the voting population. "They're all alive and well." [110] Many of the patterns are familiar. Republicans attract upper-income, conservative, well-educated voters who are not racial or ethnic minorities; Democrats draw in voters with opposite characteristics. Republicans draw upon married people, Protestants, and churchgoers; Democrats attract singles, Catholics, Jews, and occasional churchgoers. Such loyalties are built on issues and themes adopted by parties and candidates over the years.

Regardless of what nationwide surveys may show, therefore, legislators and their advisers are highly sensitive to voters' expected reactions to stands on issues. Much energy is devoted to framing positions, communicating them (sometimes in deliberately obscure words), and assessing their effect. Moreover, every professional politician can relate instances when issues tipped an election one way or another. Frequently cited is the electoral influence of single-interest groups. Some citizens vote according to a single issue they regard as paramount, such as gun control or abortion. Even if small in numbers, these groups can decide close contests. That is why legislators dislike taking positions on issues that evoke extreme responses, issues that prompt certain voters to oppose them regardless of their record on other matters.

No matter how issues sway voters directly, they exert powerful indirect effects upon election outcomes. For one thing, issues motivate the voters who are opinion leaders, who can lend or withhold support far beyond their single vote. Issues are carefully monitored by organized interests, including political action committees, that are in a position to channel funds, publicity, or volunteer workers to the candidate's cause. Legislators devote time and attention to promoting issues and explaining them to attentive publics because it pays them to do so.

Portrait of a Congressional Voter

What portrait can be constructed of voters in congressional elections? It is a complex picture in which three elements—party, candidates, and issues—play varying roles. A majority of voters seem to have reached a standing decision to vote for candidates according to party affiliation. Factors relating to individual candidates are, however, of substantial and enduring importance. Congressional candidates, especially incumbents, strive to fashion unique appeals based not simply on party loyalty but also on home style—a mixture of personal appeal, voter contacts, and constituent service.[111]

Because of their superior resources for cultivating attractive home styles, incumbents have an edge at the polls. Through media exposure, Senate challengers can more often overcome this advantage. Lacking such outlets for their message, fewer House challengers can do so. In periods of citizen unrest, however, incumbency can be effectively countered. Finally, issues and ideologies motivate a core of dedicated voters and tilt the outcomes of at least some elections.

Election Outcomes

The process by which representatives and senators reach Capitol Hill is an essential aspect of the two Congresses notion. House and Senate contests are waged one by one on local turf. Thomas E. Mann and Raymond E. Wolfinger expressed conventional wisdom when they declared that "in deciding how to cast their ballots, most voters are influenced primarily by the choice of local candidates."[112] At the same time, local contests are waged against a backdrop of national events, issues, and partisan alignments.

Top-down trends in 2002 included economic recession, uneasiness over terrorist threats, and a seemingly positive assessment of President Bush, especially his post 9/11 leadership. The increasing involvement of national party entities and their allied interest groups has imposed a large measure of national coordination upon congressional campaigns, especially those in marginal states and districts. The result is that a mix of local and national forces converge on congressional elections to shape their content and their results.

Party Balance

Despite the oft-claimed independence of candidates and voters, virtually all races are run with party labels, fought on playing fields sloped toward one party or the other, and aimed mainly at citizens who are likely to turn out for the parties' candidates.

In 2002 some forty-seven parties appeared on ballots somewhere in the United States, including the Reform, Green, Libertarian, Right to Life, Natural Law, and Socialist Workers parties. Only one independent won a seat that year.

In terms of governance, however, only two parties really count. The Democrats or the Republicans have controlled Congress since 1855. (Appendix A lists the partisan majorities in the House and Senate since 1901.) Between 1896 and 1920 the two parties had approximately equal numbers of partisans in the electorate, but lower participation rates in Democratic areas tended to favor the Republicans. The GOP's relative position improved after 1920, when women received the vote. The New Deal realignment of the 1930s shifted the balance to the Democrats. After that the Democrats became virtually a perennial majority and the Republicans a permanent minority on Capitol Hill. In all that time the Republicans controlled both chambers simultaneously for only four years (1947–1949, 1953–1955) and the Senate alone for only six years (1981–1987). Democratic sweeps in 1958, 1964, and 1974 padded Democratic majorities. Republicans eventually recovered from these setbacks, but Democratic dominance, especially in the House, was hard to overcome because incumbents learned how to exploit their reelection assets successfully.

In 1994, for the first time in forty years, the Republicans won control of both houses of Congress. Not one Republican incumbent was defeated that year, while thirty-four Democratic representatives and two senators lost their seats. In succeeding elections Republicans clung to their narrow majority in the House, with Democrats gaining ten (1996), then five (1998) and two (2000). The Senate had a Republican majority until 2000, when Democrats pulled even by gaining five seats. In 2002, however, the Republicans added to their majorities in both chambers.

Recent elections have confirmed historic shifts in the two parties' power bases. Historically, the Grand Old Party was dominant in the populous states of the Northeast and Midwest. "The Democracy," by contrast, owned the solid South from the Civil War era through the 1970s, as well as the large urban political machines. The tectonic plates of political alliances move slowly, but they sometimes produce results of earthquake proportions.

The 1994 earthquake underscored the Republican takeover of the South. For the first time in history, the GOP claimed a majority of the South's seats in the two chambers as nineteen House seats and four Senate seats moved into the party's fold. The party's grip on the region tightened in the ensuing decade. It now claims nearly two-thirds of the House seats in the eleven southern states, along with a majority of the senators. The GOP is the party of choice for conservative white southerners and is unquestionably their philosophic home. Breaking the Democrats' historic stranglehold in the southern states—with their rapidly growing population—was the step that gave the Republicans majorities on Capitol Hill.

Regionally, the South, along with the Mountain and Great Plains states (all of which went for Bush in 2000) form the backbone of the congressional GOP. The most solid GOP region is the Mountain West, where Democrats elect only 30 percent of the lawmakers. In the eight Great Plains states, Republicans account for nearly two-thirds of the senators and eight of every ten House members.

Democrats are strongest in the edges of the national map—the two coasts and parts of the Midwest. The eight states of the eastern Amtrak corridor, from Boston to Washington, D.C., are increasingly Democratic. In these states (all won by Gore in 2000) the party has an eighteen-seat House advantage and a ten-seat Senate margin. Similarly, the left-hand coast—the Pacific-rim states (excluding Alaska), again all won by Gore in 2000—have a Democratic margin of twenty House seats and six Senate seats.

Nationally the parties are evenly matched, even though Republicans represent the greater territory. That is simply because GOP districts in all regions tend to lie in rural areas, whereas Democrats overwhelmingly control the cities. Suburbs, traditionally GOP territory, are becoming more competitive.

Underlying this geographic distribution is a cultural divide between the two parties. Democrats tend to represent urban values, economic intervention by the government, environmental protection, and social tolerance. Republicans tend to be traditionalists—advocates of stricter values, along with cultural conservatism, generous support of the military, and limited use of the federal government in other sectors. Such long-standing divergencies give the lie to those citizens and commentators who claim that the two parties are largely the same.

Party Alignment and Realignment

Historically, political upheavals have shifted party control in the House or Senate with decisive results. Political scientists talk of "critical elections" or "critical periods," in which one party yields preeminence to another, or major voting groups alter the shape of the parties' coalitions, or both. Such watershed eras include the Civil War, the turbulent 1890s, the New Deal of the 1930s, and the unrest of the mid-1990s. Each of these upheavals brought to Capitol Hill new lawmakers, new voting patterns, and new legislative priorities.[113]

Recent trends clarify that post–New Deal realignment has occurred, at least from a congressional perspective. First, the Democratic Party's supremacy, established in the Roosevelt era of the 1930s, has been superceded by a competitive balance between the two major parties, though with an apparent Republican advantage. Second, the parties' infrastructures have shifted. The Democrats, long split by divisions between conservative southerners and liberal urban-dwellers, have consolidated their liberal base, in the process pushing away many white southerners but widening their reach to include blacks and other minorities. Republicans, for their part, have achieved more ideological consistency by co-opting southern and rural conservatives and by shedding most of their moderate wing—especially those from Northeastern, Mid-Atlantic, and Pacific states.

Meaningful changes can occur even without an underlying party realignment. The Wilson-era Democratic dominance (1913–1919), the Johnson-era Great Society Congresses (1965–1967), the post–Watergate Democratic landslide (1974), the Reagan juggernaut (1981–1982), and the Republican "revolution" of 1994–1995 involved changes in partisan strength on Capitol Hill that for one reason or another went far beyond any underlying shifts in attitudes or voting habits within the electorate as a whole. Elected officeholders, like most political activists, tend to be more committed to ideology or policy than are most voters, even those of the officeholder's own party. Congress turned leftward in the 1960s and 1970s and rightward in the 1990s as voters shifted their electoral choices but not necessarily their underlying attitudes.

Democratic dominance on Capitol Hill coexisted in the 1968–1992 period with Republican successes in capturing the White House. With their 1992 victory, Democrats had won twenty straight House elections, each time capturing from 53 to 68 percent of the seats. Their control of the Senate during this period was marred only by six years of Republican control (1981–1987). Meanwhile, Republicans had won six of the ten presidential contests, several by landslides. (Only once, in 1964, did a Democratic candidate win more than 50.1 percent of the popular vote.) Whether because of incumbents' strategies or voters' designs, GOP presidential successes had surprisingly little effect on party control of Congress. (Republican control of the Senate in the early 1980s was in part an exception to this rule, in part a product of unrelated factors.)

By the same token, when Democrats managed to capture the White House, they, too, had scant impact on electoral results on Capitol Hill. Jimmy Carter's election in 1976 had a negligible effect on his party's congressional fortunes (a net gain of one seat in the House, none in the Senate). Bill Clinton's victory in the three-way 1992 race (Clinton, Bush, and independent Ross Perot) was accompanied by no Democratic Senate gains and a loss of ten House seats.

The Democrats' and Republicans' separate conquests have often yielded long stretches of divided government, or split partisan control of the two policy-making branches. Some analysts argue that voters deliberately split their ballots to maintain ideological balance between the two branches or to make sure that the two branches check one another. This theory imputes great cunning to the average voter. Most voters are unlikely to engage in such a logical exercise to ensure divided partisan control. Indeed, many voters are unaware which party controls the government, especially when party control is divided.[114]

More plausible is the argument that voters, seeking different attributes in presidents and lawmakers, may find those attributes in candidates of different parties. Americans harbor inconsistent views about government, its benefits, and its burdens. Republican officeholders purvey a rhetoric of limited government ("no new taxes"), while Democrats in elective office traditionally promote government services that voters favor. Egged on by candidates' appeals, voters are encouraged to think they can have their cake and eat it, too.[115] This account of voters' behavior provides a commonsense explanation for recent periods of divided government.

Turnover and Representation

Reelection rates should not be confused with turnover rates. Even in years when few members are turned out of office by the voters, many leave Capitol Hill voluntarily—to retire, to run for another office, or to follow other pursuits. In 2002, a year of moderate turnover, eleven senators and sixty-one representatives did not return to office.

In other words, a natural process of membership change is continuous though fluctuating. When the 108th Congress convened in January 2003, a majority of senators and representatives had been elected in the previous five elections. The recent past, when most current House members came to Capitol Hill, began with a period of uncommonly low turnover (1984–1990) that brought only 162 newcomers to the House—an average of 9 percent per election, compared with a normal rate of 15 percent or more. In the early 1990s, however, high electoral turnover made the chamber significantly younger and more junior than it was when the decade began. These members have recently tended to remain in office, thus raising the chamber's average age and seniority. The Senate's membership has been altered to a lesser degree by recent elections. Despite respectable turnovers, however, the average age and seniority of senators have recently crept upward.

For Congress to be a responsive institution, a certain turnover of members is a given—whether by steady increments or by sudden, massive partisan realignments. Even when few lawmakers are turned out of office, all of them are keenly aware of the threat of defeat. Most take steps to prevent that eventuality by heightened attentiveness to constituents' needs through personal visits, speeches, newsletters, and polls. But are voters' views accurately reflected by the representatives they elect to Congress? This question is not easily answered. Popular control of policy makers is not the same thing as popular control of policies. Constituents' views are not precisely mirrored by legislators' voting behavior and the laws passed by the legislature.

Registering Voters' Views

What correlation exists between voters' attitudes and members' voting on issues? Miller and Stokes found that constituency attitudes correlated differently according to the kind of policy.[116] In foreign affairs a slight negative correlation existed between constituents' attitudes and legislators' votes; in social and economic welfare issues the correlation was moderate; in civil rights issues the correlation was very high. In other words, in at least one and possibly in two major policy areas the linkage was weak enough to cast some doubt on constituency control.

Political scientists explain the absence of strong linkages by noting how difficult it is to meet all the conditions needed for popular control of policies. Voters would have to identify the candidates' positions on issues, and they would have to vote by referring to those positions. Differences among candidates would have to be transparent, and winners would have to vote in accord with their preelection attitudes. These conditions are not routinely met. Candidates' stands are not always clear, and candidates do not invariably differentiate themselves on issues.

Political scientists John L. Sullivan and Robert E. O'Connor tried to test these conditions by submitting to all House candidates a questionnaire covering three issue areas—foreign affairs, civil rights, and domestic policies—and then following the successful candidates' voting records in the House.[117] Their findings suggest that elements of popular control are present. First, according to their inquiries, voters had meaningful choices among candidates. Second, winning candidates generally voted according to their preelection stands. Third, candidates were ideologically distinct, with Democrats invariably more liberal than Republicans. To these pieces of evidence we can add another: According to recent surveys, most congressional voters can rank their representative on a liberal–conservative scale, and most of these voters claim an affinity with their representative's ranking.[118] In other words, voters' attitudes and legislators' views are roughly parallel, even though they may diverge on numerous specific points.

After the Election Is Over

If ideological or attitudinal links between voters and their representatives are rough and variable, actual contacts between constituents and individual legislators are numerous and palpable. Individual legislators do not necessarily mirror their constituents, much less the nation as a whole, in terms of demographic characteristics. Yet much of their time and effort while in office is devoted to dealing with the folks back home. Constituency politics are ever present in the daily lives of senators and representatives.

The two worlds of a congressional leader. Senate Democrat Tom Daschle reads to school children in his home state of South Dakota (above). As his party's floor leader (below), he leads a press conference with fellow Democrats to show how many amendments were defeated by supporters of President George W. Bush's tax cuts.

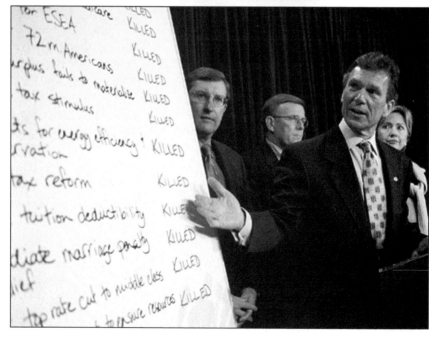

5

Being There:
Hill Styles and Home Styles

Touring his home state of South Dakota a few years ago, Democratic senator Thomas A. Daschle found himself stranded late one night after locking
himself out of his car:

> He telephoned the local locksmith. "What's your name?" asked the groggy-
> sounding voice on the other end of the line.
> "Tom Daschle," came the reply.
> The locksmith hung up, having concluded that the Senate Democratic
> Leader was a prank caller.[1]

The low-key Daschle tries to spend about seventy days a year in his home
state. For three weeks every August, he drives around the small towns and
rural communities of South Dakota, meeting and talking with constituents.
His tours are leisurely and unscheduled. Neither press nor staff accompany
him. He stops at coffee shops, health clinics, schools, civic clubs, and cattle
auctions.

Daschle relishes the time he spends talking with constituents. "It energizes
me," he says. "I really learn from them. I think it's awfully hard to get into a
debate on the floor of the Senate without having experiences like that."

The other side of Daschle's life in centered in the U.S. Senate, where he
has served since 1987. Eight years later he was chosen (by a one-vote margin)
as minority leader. In 2001 the word *minority* was dropped from his title. With
a fifty-fifty division, the two parties initially embarked on a precarious experiment in power sharing, which after four months was replaced by a narrow
Democratic majority (when Vermont Republican James M. Jeffords switched to
being an Independent and voted with the Democrats to organize the chamber). Republican gains in 2002 restored Daschle's earlier minority leader title.

Daschle's role as one of the two leading figures in the Democratic Party in
the 108th Congress (House leader Nancy Pelosi of California is the other)
might seem inconsistent with his representative role. South Dakota is a Republican state that went heavily for both George Bushes. But the linkages are
strong. Early in his presidency, George W. Bush sought to sell his budget plan
through a series of brief tours to states with Democratic senators whose constituents might be mobilized to support the administration. Before Bush arrived in Sioux Falls, Daschle alerted local newspapers that Bush's proposed tax

cuts might endanger the $273 million Lewis and Clark water project. Local officials were upset, and almost immediately Daschle's office received calls from the White House asking what the project was all about. During his Sioux Falls speech, President Bush made a point of expressing support for the Lewis and Clark project.

Local booster and Senate leader, Daschle personifies the two Congresses. All members of Congress live and work in these two worlds: one on Capitol Hill and the other back home in their states or districts.

Hill Styles

Members of Congress, as Richard F. Fenno Jr. says, spend their lives "moving between two contexts, Washington and home, and between two activities, governing and campaigning."[2] The two contexts and the two activities are interwoven. How members govern is deeply affected by their campaign experience, especially that of the most recent election. In turn, their Capitol Hill activities affect all their subsequent contacts with people back home.

Who Are the Legislators?

The Constitution names only three criteria for individuals serving in Congress: age, citizenship, and residency. However, entrance requirements are far more restrictive. Aristotle first observed that elections are essentially oligarchic affairs that involve few active participants. By almost any measure, senators and representatives constitute an economic and social elite. They are well educated. They come from a small number of prestigious occupations. The pay of senators and representatives ($150,000 in 2003) puts them in the top 1 percent of the nation's wage earners. Many possess or amass material wealth, but those who come from state or local posts boost their salaries when they arrive in Congress. And expenses are high, especially for members who maintain a residence in Washington as well as one back home. A federal pay commission reported more than a decade ago that "most members of Congress find it difficult to live on their current salaries."[3] Most of them have outside sources of income, although several such income sources have been shut down—including gifts, travel, and honoraria (fees provided by interest groups for speeches or other appearances).

Occupation. Historically, law and politics have been closely linked in this country. A humorist once quipped that the U.S. government "of laws and not men" is really "of lawyers and not men." When the 108th Congress convened in January 2003, 177 representatives and 59 senators were lawyers.[4]

Many lawyers view forays into electoral politics as a form of professional advancement. The legal profession stresses personal skills, such as verbalization, advocacy, and negotiation, that are useful in gaining and holding public office. Important, too, is lawyers' monopoly over offices that serve as stepping-stones to Congress—especially elected law enforcement and judicial posts.[5]

Unlike many other high-status professionals, lawyers can move in and out of their jobs without hurting their careers.

The historical dominance of lawyers on Capitol Hill has declined in recent decades. Lawyers are now outnumbered by members with other careers. Business is the next most prevalent occupation—especially on the rise since the Republican takeover in the mid-1990s. Members of the verbalizing professions—teaching, journalism, and public service—are also well represented. A hundred members of the 108th Congress spent part or all of their early careers in education; a couple dozen were in communications. As for prior public service, the 108th Congress included fourteen former governors, two former cabinet secretaries, a federal judge, two state supreme court judges, and 275 former state legislators. No less than 125 members had once served as congressional or White House staffers.

War heroes have often found their way to Capitol Hill. Following World War II, returning veterans surged into Congress. Among them were Reps. John F. Kennedy, Richard M. Nixon, Gerald R. Ford, and Bob Dole. By the 1970s more than seven of ten members were veterans. The number of veterans, especially those with combat experience, has since dwindled. Fewer than 30 percent of the 108th Congress's members had military service.

Today's media-centered campaigns have spawned a few celebrity legislators. Several astronauts, including Sen. Bill Nelson, D-Fla., have served. Former athletes and coaches in the 108th Congress included a member of the Baseball Hall of Fame: Sen. Jim Bunning, R-Ky., who once pitched a perfect game for the Philadelphia Phillies.

Many occupations are, and always have been, drastically underrepresented in Congress. Low-status occupations, including farm labor, service trades, manual and skilled labor, and domestic service, are rare on Capitol Hill. One blue-collar worker elected in recent years quit after one term in part because he was unhappy and self-conscious about his social status.

Education and Religion. By every measure, Congress is a highly educated body. All but a handful of members have college degrees. Three-quarters have graduate degrees, which are required in such heavily represented professions as law. Fifteen have medical degrees. Five Rhodes scholars serve in the House and three in the Senate.

Virtually every member of the 108th Congress professed a formal religious affiliation, compared with about seven of ten Americans in surveys.[6] More than one-quarter of all House and Senate members are Roman Catholics, the largest single contingent. That number is slightly above the nationwide proportion of Catholics. Most other legislators are Protestants, either from mainline denominations—Methodists, Episcopalians, Presbyterians, and Baptists—or from evangelical groups. Jews, who make up 2.6 percent of the total U.S. population, accounted for 7 percent of the 108th Congress. Catholics, evangelical Protestants, and Jews have enlarged their share of Congress's membership, while mainline Protestants have declined in numbers.

Sex and Sexual Orientation. Neither chamber accurately mirrors the nation in terms of sex or sexual identity. Congress historically has been a male bastion. Diversity has developed slowly.

Unable to vote until 1920, women have always been underrepresented in Congress. Beginning in 1916 with Jeannette Rankin, elected as a Republican from Montana, 199 women have been elected or appointed to Congress. In the 108th Congress a record number of women served—sixty-two representatives (sixteen of them in the California delegation) and fourteen senators. But that is only 14 percent of all members, compared with more than half of the nation's population.[7]

The presence of sizable numbers of women has changed Capitol Hill in several ways. Aside from obvious details (installing a Senate women's restroom, opening the gymnasiums to both sexes), the influx of women has brought adjustments in political agendas and ways of doing things. Policy concerns once labeled "women's issues" now receive respectful hearing. For the first time, workplace and women's health issues—gender discrimination and drive-by mastectomies, for example—had to be seriously addressed. Rep. Nita M. Lowey, D-N.Y., whose mother died of breast cancer, asked for increased funding for research on the disease. During debate over family leave policy, Sen. Patty Murray, D-Wash., talked about having to quit a secretarial job sixteen years earlier when she was pregnant with her first child. At a hearing on Social Security taxes for household help, Rep. Carrie P. Meek, D-Fla. (1993–2003), a granddaughter of slaves, brought her own vivid experiences to the proceedings. "I was once a domestic worker," she told her colleagues. "My mother was a domestic worker. All my sisters were domestic workers."[8] Referring to the women serving in the Senate, Senator Murray declared, "We've made it okay for men to talk about these [women's] issues, too."[9]

Gays and lesbians passed a milestone in 1998 when Tammy Baldwin, D-Wis., became the first lesbian representative whose sexual orientation was known before her initial election. The two gay men who also serve in the House (and several former representatives) revealed their sexuality or were outed after they had served for some time. Baldwin, who served six years in the state legislature, did not shy away from the issue. Her campaign slogan was "A different kind of candidate." Still, as Rep. Barney Frank, D-Mass., observed, the hardest part of running as a gay is "convincing voters that you will not disproportionately focus on that minority's issues."[10] That lesson applies to all candidates contending in districts where they are in the minority—for example, blacks running in majority-white areas.

Race. African Americans, who make up 12 percent of the nation's population, account for 7 percent of Congress's members. In 2003, thirty-nine African Americans (including two delegates) served in the House. In all U.S. history only 109 blacks have served in Congress, four of them in the Senate and the rest in the House. Nearly half of these served during the Reconstruction era after the Civil War. All were Republicans, loyal to the party of Abraham Lincoln.

No blacks served in Congress from 1900 to 1928, when Rep. Oscar De Priest, a Republican, was elected from a heavily black district on Chicago's South Side. In the next twenty-five years only three more blacks entered Congress, but after the 1960s African American representation rose steadily. All but four of the post–Reconstruction black legislators were Democrats.

Other minorities are represented in smaller numbers. Latinos make up 12 percent of the population but only 4.5 percent of the House membership (including one delegate); no Latinos serve in the Senate. Of the twenty-four Latino representatives, most are Mexican Americans, three are Cuban Americans, and three are of Puerto Rican descent. All but four are Democrats. Asians and Pacific Islanders claim five representatives and two senators—all Democrats. There are three Native Americans, a Senate Republican and one of each party in the House.

Most minority members of the House represent majority-minority districts, a number of them created since the 1990s. The goal of boosting minority representation through redistricting succeeded. All but one of these districts elected minority lawmakers. Only a handful of African Americans and Latinos are now elected from areas with less than 50 percent minority population. The ranks of such members must grow if minorities are to gain anything approaching proportionate representation.

Age and Tenure. When the 108th Congress convened, the average age of representatives was fifty-four; for senators, it was nearly sixty.[11] Tenure as well as age has risen since the early days. "Few die, and none retire," it was said as the twentieth century began. A century later, the average representative had served nearly eleven years, more than five and a half House terms. The average senator had served nearly sixteen years, or more than two and a half Senate terms.[12]

Even today, age and tenure levels fluctuate over time. Periods of relatively low turnover (the 1980s, for example) are punctuated by dramatic changing-of-the-guard periods, as in the 1970s and the 1990s, involving both senior and junior members of Congress.[13] Electoral defeats play some role, but the majority of members leave voluntarily. During the political upheavals of the early 1990s, older members wearied of the frantic pace and occasionally were dogged by scandal. Younger members wanted to earn more money and see more of their families.

A certain balance between new blood and stable membership is undoubtedly desirable for legislative bodies. The rapid turnover of the early 1990s heightened the generational conflict. Many newly elected members had indulged in Congress bashing in their campaigns and wanted to shake up the institution; not a few of them shunned the idea of making a career of public service. "They don't regard being defeated as the end of their life, just a change of jobs," then Speaker Newt Gingrich, R-Ga., remarked of his young colleagues. "That is very different than the sort of careerist view that had dominated for a long time."[14]

As the twenty-first century began, *incumbency* was no longer a dirty word, and turnover levels declined. Some of the firebrands who entered Congress promising to get out after six years had second thoughts. One of these was Rep. George Nethercutt, R-Wash., who in 1994 ousted Democratic Speaker Thomas S. Foley, a thirty-year veteran, with a promise that "six years is enough." By 2000 Nethercutt admitted that experience had shown him that issues were so complex that six years are "probably not enough."[15] He was not alone. Some two dozen members reconsidered their original pledges over the last three elections, and most of them (including Nethercutt) were reelected.[16]

Representation. Must Congress demographically mirror the populace to be a representative institution? The question is hotly debated. Hannah Finichel Pitkin distinguishes between two types of representation: *substantive* and *descriptive*.[17] To represent a category of people substantively, a legislator must consciously act for people and their interests, whether a member of that grouping or not. Legislators from farming districts can voice farmers' concerns even though they have never plowed a field; whites can champion equal opportunities for minorities. Few Asian Americans serve in Congress, but their proportion in a district affects a member's support of issues advocated by that group.[18] Conversely, white representatives from districts that lost black voters in gerrymandering after the 1990s became more conservative and less supportive of policies preferred by African Americans.[19]

By and large, Congress is a body of local political pros for whom speaking for constituents comes naturally. Most members keep in touch with the home folks without even thinking about it. A majority of representatives in one survey agreed with the statement: "I seldom have to sound out my constituents because I think so much like them that I know how to react to almost any proposal."[20]

Yet descriptive, or symbolic, representation can be as important as substantive representation. Symbolically, no real substitute exists for having a member of one's own grouping in a position of influence. "Even controlling for party membership," Katherine Tate found from surveying black constituents, "black legislators received significantly higher ratings on average than their white counterparts."[21] Moreover, tangible gains can be seen in the quality of representation. Studies indicate, for example, that women members of Congress are more likely than men to introduce, sponsor, and press for bills of special concern to women and children.[22]

Nor is representation restrained by state or district boundaries. When a member of an ethnic or racial minority goes to Congress, it is a badge of legitimacy for the entire grouping. Such legislators speak for people like them throughout the nation. Other, less obvious constituencies are likewise represented. One member who suffers from epilepsy defends job rights for other sufferers of the disease; another whose grandson was born prematurely champions funds for medical research into birth defects; a third, who fled the Nazis as a child in the 1940s, has sworn to perpetuate awareness of the Holocaust;

Table 5-1 House Members' Views on the Jobs Expected of Them

Volunteered responses	Percentage [a]
Legislator	87
Constituency servant	79
Mentor or communicator	43
Representative	26
Politico	11
Overseer	9
Institutional broker	7
Office manager	6
Jack-of-all-trades	6
All other roles	4

Source: House Commission on Administrative Review, *Final Report,* 2 vols., H. Doc. 95-272, 95th Cong., 1st sess., December 31, 1977, 2:874–875.

Note: N=146.

[a] Many members mentioned two or more jobs.

members who are openly gay speak out for the rights of homosexuals. Such causes are close to members' hearts, even though they often pay scant political dividends and are rarely noticed by the press and the public.

How Do Legislators Describe Their Jobs?

In the late 1970s the House Commission on Administrative Review asked 153 representatives to list "the major kinds of jobs, duties, or functions that you feel you are expected to perform as an individual member of Congress." This question elicited not so much the members' own priorities as their diverse perceptions of what colleagues, constituents, lobbyists, and others expect of them. The responses, summarized in Table 5-1, form a snapshot of members' views of their jobs. Although this survey has not been repeated, it remains a reasonably accurate representation of members' jobs as they see them.

Legislator. The rules, procedures, and traditions of the House and Senate impose many constraints on members' behavior. To be effective, new members must learn their way through the institutional maze. Legislators therefore stress the formal aspects of Capitol Hill duties and routines: legislative work, investigation, and committee specialization. Charles E. Schumer, D-N.Y., in elective office for more than half his life (he was elected to the state assembly at age twenty-three and served nine terms in the U.S. House), explained his commitment as a professional legislator during his successful 1998 Senate campaign:

I love to legislate. Taking an idea—often not original with me—shaping it, molding it. Building a coalition of people who might not completely agree with it. Passing it and making the country a little bit of a better place. I love doing that.[23]

Most legislators pursue information and expertise on issues, not only because it is the way to shape public policy but also because it sways others in the chamber.

The legislator's role dovetails with that of representing constituents. Most members seek committee assignments that will serve the needs of their states or districts. One House member related how his interest in flood control and water resource development impelled him to ask for a seat on the committee responsible for those issues. "The interests of my district dictated my field of specialization," he explained, "but the decision to specialize in some legislative field is automatic for the member who wants to exercise any influence."[24]

Members soon learn the norms, or folkways, that expedite legislative bargaining and maximize productivity. Examining the post–World War II Senate, Donald R. Matthews identified six folkways governing behavior that were enforced informally. Senators should (1) serve an apprenticeship (exercising restraint and deference to elders in the early years); (2) concentrate on Senate work instead of on gaining publicity; (3) specialize in issues within their committees or affecting their home states; (4) act courteously to colleagues; (5) extend reciprocity to colleagues—that is, provide willing assistance with the expectation that it will be repaid in kind one day; and (6) loyally defend the Senate, "the greatest legislative and deliberative body in the world."[25]

In recent years certain Senate folkways have faded in importance. New senators now actively take part in most aspects of the chamber's work, ignoring the apprenticeship norm. Many senators, especially those with an eye on higher office, work tirelessly to attract national publicity and personal attention. Committee specialization, although still common, is less rigid than it once was. Senators now have many overlapping committee assignments and are expected to express views on a wide range of issues. The norms of courtesy and reciprocity are still invoked, but institutional loyalty wears thin in an era of harsh partisanship and cynicism about government.

The House relies more on formal channels of power than on informal norms. From interviews, however, Herbert B. Asher uncovered seven norms: (1) friendly relationships are desirable; (2) the important work of the House is done in committee; (3) procedural rules of the House are essential; (4) members should not personally criticize a colleague on the House floor; (5) members should be prepared to trade votes; (6) members should be specialists; and (7) freshmen should serve apprenticeships.[26]

Even this loose network of norms has come unraveled. New members, impatient to make their mark, plunge into the work of the House even before they learn their way around. Leadership comes earlier to members than it used to. Specialization is still attractive—more so than in the Senate—but many members branch out into unrelated issues. No longer are committees the sole forums for influencing legislation. Looser norms of floor participation and voting have expanded members' chances for shaping bills outside their own committees' jurisdictions. Many ideologically driven new members, like those elected in 1994, dismissed norms such as specialization, reciprocity, and compromise. The conflict-ridden House (and Senate) reminded political scientist Eric M. Uslaner of "day care centers in which colicky babies [get] their way by screaming at the top of their lungs."[27]

Legislation-minded members reacted by reasserting the decaying norms and decrying the rancorous outbursts that have marked recent Congresses. Reassertions of the importance of civility and a spirit of reciprocity suggest that traditional institutional norms are not dead. Asked to compare the House with his earlier career (as an economics professor), retiring majority leader Dick Armey, R-Texas, remarked, "Here you're working with a more pleasant group of people. There isn't the petty meanness in Congress that you find in university politics."[28] So even in an era of high partisanship, reciprocity and compromise are acknowledged as necessary if members' disparate goals are to be reconciled into legislation that can be passed.

Constituency Servant. Nearly eight of ten respondents in the House survey mentioned the role of constituency servant. The constituency servant attempts to give voice to citizens' concerns and solve their problems. This role was cited by half the House members. Typically, the task is performed by legislators and their staffs as casework—individual cases triggered by constituent letters or visits. It is a chore that weighs heavily on members, even though most of them delegate it to staff aides. The philosophy of most legislators is expressed by one House member like this:

> Constituent work: that's something I feel very strongly about. The American people, with the growth of the bureaucracy, feel nobody cares. The only conduit a taxpayer has with the government is a congressional office.[29]

Sometimes members stress their constituency service to gain breathing room for legislative stands that stray from district norms.

Constituency servants typically make sure their states or districts get their fair share of federal money and assistance. "It's a big pie down in Washington," Michael "Ozzie" Myers, then a Democratic representative from Pennsylvania, told FBI agents posing as aides of an Arab sheik during the so-called Abscam probe of influence peddling in the late 1970s:

> Each member's sent there to bring a piece of that pie back home. And if you go down there and you don't—you come back without milkin' it after a few terms . . . you don't go . . . back.[30]

The words are inelegant and the context sleazy, but they characterize members' traditional view of constituency advocacy, even if they rail against pork barrel spending in other people's areas.

In recent years a number of candidates have publicly spurred this tradition of bringing home the bacon. Vocally committed to downsizing the federal establishment, they seek plaudits from constituents who oppose deficits, taxes, and federal bureaucrats. In times of tight budgets, fewer discretionary dollars may be available to distribute to localities. If members are unable to win earmarked funds for their constituents, however, they can nonetheless seek non-fiscal benefits—for example, favorable regulatory rules or trade concessions for local industries.[31]

There is no reason, however, to think that pork has vanished from the congressional diet. Even when budgets are lean, pork barrel advocacy will survive. Remaining government programs with highly visible local benefits—highway and mass transit grants, for example, or homeland security contracts—are smothered with attention. Particularized benefits normally trump collective benefits. An Arkansas lobbyist tells the story of going to visit one of his state's Republican members who was known for his anti-pork speeches. "I know you're anti-pork," the lobbyist began, "but I have to tell you about our needs and how to position yourself." "What do you mean?" the congressman retorted. "As far as I can tell, it's not pork if it's for Arkansas." [32]

Mentor-Communicator and Representative. The mentor-communicator role is linked both to legislating and to constituency errand running. Most members who stress this role view it in connection with issues that must be debated and voted on. Another aspect of the mentor-communicator role is the act of keeping in touch with constituents by mail, by personal appearances, and by print and electronic media. Republican Barber B. Conable Jr. conducted what he called a "dialogue of representation" by means of 254 newsletters to his Rochester, New York, constituents during his tenure in the House (1965–1985). "Conable never campaigned," a local professor explained, "he just conducted seminars every other year" (actually, a majority of his newsletters went out during nonelection years).[33]

Closely allied is the role of the issue emissary (representative), articulated by a quarter of the House members. Constituents expect their representatives to understand and express their views in Washington. This role is the essence of elective office, both in theory and in practice, and incumbents take it very seriously.

Other Roles. Some members pose as outsiders who adopt a maverick posture, but others act as Capitol Hill insiders. Some stress party leadership duties, others their social obligations, still others institutional brokerage—dealing with the executive branch, interest groups, and state and local governments. And, yes, a few members of Congress focus merely on campaigning and gaining reelection. One former member placed this goal in perspective: "All members of Congress have a primary interest in being reelected. Some members have no other interest." [34]

How Do Legislators Spend Their Time?

Time is the most precious commodity for senators and representatives. The lack of it is their most frequent complaint about their jobs.[35] Allocating time requires exceedingly tough personal and political choices.

According to a 1993 congressional survey, members' daily priorities are roughly as follows: (1) meeting on legislative issues with constituents, either at home or in Washington; (2) attending committee hearings, markups, and other committee meetings; (3) meeting with government officials and lobbyists on legislative issues; (4) studying pending legislation or discussing legislation with other members or staff; (5) working with informal caucus groups of colleagues; (6) attending floor debate or watching the debate on television; (7) doing nonlegislative work (casework) for constituents in Washington; (8) managing personal office operations and staffs; (9) raising funds for the next campaign, for others' campaigns, or for the political party; (10) working with party leaders to build legislative coalitions; (11) overseeing how agencies are carrying out laws or policies; and (12) making appearances on legislation outside the state or district (see Table 5-2).[36] Staff members usually prepare daily schedules for members of Congress to refer to as they whirl through a busy day on Capitol Hill.

Scheduling is complicated by the large number of formal work groups—mainly committees and subcommittees, but also joint, party, and ad hoc panels. Despite downsizing in recent Congresses, the average senator sits on three full committees and seven subcommittees; representatives average two committees and four subcommittees.

With so many assignments, lawmakers are hard-pressed to control their crowded schedules. Committee quorums are difficult to achieve, and members' attention is often focused elsewhere. All too often working sessions are composed of the chairman, the ranking minority member, perhaps one or two colleagues, and staff aides. Recent House rules tightening quorum requirements have only made scheduling problems worse.

Repeated floor votes, which lawmakers fear to miss, are another time-consuming duty. In a typical Congress more than one thousand recorded votes may be taken in the House chamber and perhaps six hundred in the Senate. "We're like automatons," one senator complained. "We spend our time walking in tunnels to go to the floor to vote."[37]

Lawmakers' daily schedules in Washington are "long, fragmented, and unpredictable," according to a study based on time logs kept by senators' appointment secretaries.[38] "In Congress you are a total juggler," recalls former representative Patricia Schroeder, D-Colo. (1973–1979), now a trade association executive. "You have always got seventeen things pulling on your sleeve."[39] Members' schedules are splintered into so many tiny bits and pieces that effective pursuit of lawmaking, oversight, and constituent service is hampered. According to a management study of several senators' offices, an event occurs every five minutes, on average, to which the senator or the chief aide must

Table 5-2   Activities of Members of Congress: Actual and Ideal
(in percentages)

Activity	Members actually spending time				Members preferring to spend more time
	Great deal	Moderate amount	A little	Almost none	
Representation					
Meet with citizens in state or district	68%	30%	1%	0%	17%
Meet in Washington with constituents	45	50	5	0	17
Manage office	6	45	39	10	13
Raise funds for next campaign, for others, for party	6	33	45	16	7
Lawmaking					
Attend committee hearings, markups, other meetings	48	46	6	0	43
Meet in Washington on legislative issues	37	56	6	0	31
Study, read, discuss pending legislation	25	56	17	2	78
Work with informal caucuses	8	43	36	13	25
Attend floor debate, follow it on television	7	37	44	12	59
Work with party leaders to build coalitions	6	33	43	18	42
Oversee how agencies are carrying out policies and programs	5	22	43	29	53
Give speeches about legislation outside state or district	5	23	49	23	16

Note: A total of 161 members of Congress (136 representatives, 25 senators) responded to this survey, conducted in early 1993 under the auspices of the Joint Committee on the Organization of Congress. This series of questions elicited responses from 152 to 155 members. U.S. Congress, Joint Committee on the Organization of Congress, *Organization of Congress, Final Report,* H. Rept. 103-413, 103d Congress, 1st sess., December 1993, 2:231–232, 275–287.

respond personally.[40] Often members have scant notice that their presence is required at a meeting or a hearing. Carefully developed schedules can be disrupted by changes in meeting hours, by unforeseen events, or by sessions that run longer than expected. (After the terrorist attacks of 9/11, members were issued BlackBerry pagers so they could keep track of developments.)

Political scientists may pretend that Congress runs in harmony with members' needs, but the members know otherwise. In a survey of 114 House and Senate members, "inefficiency" was the thing that most surprised them about Congress (45 percent gave this response).[41] "[Congress] is a good job for someone with no family, no life of their own, no desire to do anything but get up, go to work, and live and die by their own press releases," quipped former representative Fred Grandy, an Iowa Republican (and TV sitcom star) who left Congress in 1995. "It is a great job for deviant human beings."[42]

Nearly half the respondents in a 1987 survey agreed that they had "no personal time after work"; a third said they had "no time for family."[43] When they came to power in 1995, Republican leaders promised a "family friendly schedule," but the frantic pace of the next two years was anything but that. Subsequent Congresses took a more leisurely pace. House members and their families even held several weekend retreats to get to know one another better.

The dilemma legislators face in allocating their time is far more than a matter of scheduling. It is a case of conflicting role expectations. Look again at Table 5-2, where lawmakers' activities are arrayed to illustrate the tensions inherent in the two Congresses, from the representative Congress (at the top of the list) to the legislative Congress (at the bottom). More members want to devote extra time to legislative duties than would choose to spend more time on constituency and political chores. According to the 1993 survey, an average of 43 percent of the members would like to spend more time on the eight legislative tasks, whereas on average only 14 percent of them would give more time to the four representation items. Eight of ten members would study more thoroughly the legislation they vote on; six of ten would follow floor debate more closely.[44] The two Congresses pull members in different directions. As a retiring House committee chairman remarked:

> One problem is that you're damned if you do and damned if you don't. If you do your work here, you're accused of neglecting your district. And if you spend too much time in your district, you're accused of neglecting your work here.[45]

The Shape of the Washington Career

Once a short-term activity, congressional service has become a career. Accompanying this careerism, or longevity, is a distinctive pattern of Washington activity: The longer members remain in office, the more they sponsor bills, deliver floor speeches, and offer amendments. Despite the democratizing trends of the reform era (1960s and 1970s), senior lawmakers continue to lead in all these categories. "The *apprenticeship norm* may or may not be dead, but *apprenticeship* is stronger than it has been in decades," John R. Hibbing concluded from his painstaking study of four cohorts of members who entered the House between 1957 and 1971.[46]

Long tenure also pulls members toward greater legislative specialization. Members settle into their committee slots, cultivate expertise in a distinct policy field, and spend their time managing legislation and conducting oversight in that field. Seniority tends to boost legislative achievement. Veterans usually enjoy more success than do freshmen in getting their bills passed.

The correlation between members' service and effectiveness reflects the indispensable role careerists play in the legislative process. As Hibbing observed:

> Senior members are the heart and soul of the legislative side of congressional service. . . . Relatively junior members can be given a subcommittee chairmanship, but it is not nearly so easy to give them an active, focused legislative agenda and the political savvy to enact it. Some things take time and experience, and successful participation in the legislative process appears to be one of those things.[47]

The wisdom of this statement is repeatedly borne out. The newcomers elected in the 1990s brought with them zeal, energy, and fresh approaches. At the same time, many of them lacked patience, bargaining skills, institutional memory, and respect for the lawmaking process. Not a few of them demanded overnight reversals of long-standing policies and practices and vowed to retire voluntarily after a few terms.

Looking Homeward

Not all of a representative's or a senator's duties lie in Washington, D.C. Legislators not only fashion policy for the nation's welfare, but they also act as emissaries from their home states or districts.

What Is Representation?

Although found in virtually all political systems, representation is the hallmark of democratic regimes dedicated to sharing power among citizens. In small communities decisions can be reached by face-to-face discussion, but in populous societies this sort of personalized consultation is impossible. Thus, according to traditional democratic theory, citizens can exert control by choosing "fiduciary agents" to act on their behalf, deliberating on legislation just as their principals, the voters, would do if they could be on hand themselves.[48] Pitkin puts it this way:

> The representative must act in such a way that, although he is independent, and his constituents are capable of action and judgment, no conflict arises

between them. He must act in their interest, and this means he must not normally come into conflict with their wishes.[49]

The arrangement does not always work out precisely as democratic theory specifies. Unless it works fairly well most of the time, however, the system is defective.

Incumbent legislators give high priority to representation. Four of five House members interviewed in 1977 saw themselves as constituency servants. Many were mentor-communicators, others issue spokespersons. In an earlier survey of eighty-seven members, the role most often expressed was called the tribune: the discoverer, reflector, or advocate of popular needs and wants.[50]

Although legislators agree on the importance of representation, they interpret it differently. One point of departure is Edmund Burke's dictum that legislators should voice the "general reason of the whole," not speak merely for "local purposes" and "local prejudices."[51] This conception of the legislator as Burkean trustee has always had its admirers. Speaking to a group of newly elected House members, Rep. Henry J. Hyde, R-Ill., voiced the Burkean ideal:

> If you are here simply as a tote board registering the current state of opinion in your district, you are not going to serve either your constituents or the Congress well. . . . You must take, at times, a national view, even if you risk the displeasure of your neighbors and friends back home. . . . If you don't know the principle, or the policy, for which you are willing to lose your office, then you are going to do damage here.[52]

Representative Hyde followed his own precepts as chairman of the Judiciary Committee that in 1998 voted to impeach President Bill Clinton. Defying the weight of expert opinion, national opinion polls, and even some within his own party, he carried his committee's articles of impeachment to the full House, which adopted two of them, and then to the Senate, which rejected them.

Nearly every member can point to conscience votes cast on deeply felt issues. A few, such as Rep. Mike Synar, D-Okla. (1979–1995), compile a contrarian record, challenging voters to admire their independence if not their policies. Synar was an unabashed liberal Democrat from a state that now elects mostly conservative Republicans. "I want to be a U.S. congressman from Oklahoma, not an Oklahoman congressman," Synar declared when he arrived in the capital.[53] If turned out of office by hostile sentiment (as Synar later was), the Burkean can at least hope for history's vindication.

Electoral realities imperil the Burkean ideal. Burke himself was ousted from office for his candor. Modern electorates, motivated by self-interest and schooled in democratic norms, prefer instructed delegates—lawmakers who follow instructions rather than exercise independent judgments. In a recent survey 63 percent of those polled said they wanted members of Congress to "stick closely to American public opinion . . . including results of polls" when making legislative decisions. Only 34 percent thought members should "do what they think is best." [54]

In practice, legislators assume different representational styles according to the occasion. They ponder factors such as the nation's welfare, their personal convictions, and constituency opinions. "The weight assigned to each factor," writes Thomas E. Cavanagh, "varies according to the nature of the issue at hand, the availability of the information necessary for a decision, and the intensity of preference of the people concerned about the issue." [55]

Respondents in the 1977 House survey cited two categories of issues they reserved for personal conscience or discretion: grave national issues, such as foreign policy and national defense, and issues that tap deep-seated convictions, such as abortion, gun control, or constitutional questions. In contrast, members said they deferred to districts on bread-and-butter issues, such as public works, social needs, military projects, and farm programs. They give unqualified support to local needs because, as they see it, no other member is likely to do so.

Members of Congress are called upon to explain their choices to constituents—no matter how many or how few people truly care about the matter.[56] The anticipated need to explain oneself shapes a member's choices and in fact is part of the dilemma of choice. A cynical saying among lawmakers asserts that "a vote on anything [is] a wrong vote if you cannot explain it in a 30-second TV ad." [57] Votes to increase congressional pay and perquisites, for example, often fail simply because members fear having to defend their stand in front of skeptical constituents.

What Are Constituencies?

No senator or representative is elected by, interacts with, or responds to all the people in a given state or district. The constituencies fixed in lawmakers' minds as they campaign or vote may be quite different from the boundaries found on maps. Fenno describes a "nest" of constituencies, ranging from the widest (geographic constituency) to the narrowest (personal constituency), which is made up of supporters, loyalists, and intimates.[58]

Geographic and Demographic Constituencies. The average House district today numbers more than 650,000 people. As for senators, fourteen represent states with only one House district; the rest represent multidistrict states with as many as thirty-four million people.[59] Such constituencies differ sharply from one another. More than half the people in Manhattan's Upper East Side (New York's Fourteenth Congressional District) have college degrees, compared with only 5 percent in south Los Angeles (California's Thirty-fourth District). Average per capita income in these same two districts is, respectively, $41,000 and less than $7,000. You can buy an average home for $23,200 in Democratic representative Carolyn Cheeks Kilpatrick's central Detroit district (Michigan's Thirteenth); in Democratic representative Henry A. Waxman's Beverly Hills district (California's Thirtieth), you would pay well over $500,000.[60] Such disparities among districts animate their representatives' outlooks.

There is also the political equivalent of microclimates. Democrat Nita Lowey's Eighteenth District of New York snakes southward from the upscale suburbs of Westchester County through a working-class sliver of the Bronx, jumps across Long Island Sound to an immigrant corridor in Flushing, and continues toward the tidy homes of southern Queens. Republican Mary Bono's sprawling southern California Forty-fifth District embraces smog-ridden suburbs east of Riverside, irrigated farmland of the Coachella Valley, and wealthy desert oases of Palm Springs and Palm Desert, where retired Hollywood stars reside. Even these geographical distinctions grossly simplify the complex and subtle mixtures of ethnic, economic, and social categories that make up these communities.

Demographically, constituencies may be homogeneous or heterogeneous.[61] Some constituencies, even a few whole states, remain uniform and one-dimensional—mostly wheat farmers or urban ghetto dwellers or small-town citizens. Because of increasing size, economic complexity, and educational levels, however, virtually all constituencies, House as well as Senate, have become more heterogeneous than they used to be. The more heterogeneous a constituency, the more challenging is the representative's task.

Another attribute of constituencies is electoral balance, especially as manifested in the incumbent's reelection chances. Heterogeneous districts tend to be more competitive than uniform ones. Incumbents predictably prefer safe districts—those with a high proportion of groups sympathetic to their partisan or ideological stance. Not only do safe districts favor reelection, but they also imply that voters will be easier to please.[62]

Truly competitive districts are not the norm, especially in the House of Representatives. Four out of five House victors in 2002 boasted margins of 60 percent or more; nearly one in five faced no major-party foe. A mere 10 percent of the seats were truly competitive (won by 55 percent or less). As Table 5-3 shows, competitiveness varies over time. The mid-1990s elections, for example, were unusually competitive because short-term factors (retirements, scandals, and voter unrest) put more seats into play. Since then, competition has plummeted. Senate seats are more likely to be closely contested than House races, but many senators still win in a walk.

Whatever the numbers show, few incumbents regard themselves as truly safe. The threat of losing is very real. Most lawmakers have a close call at some time in their congressional careers, and a third of them eventually suffer defeat.[63] Incumbents worry not only about winning or losing but also about their margins of safety. Downturns in normal electoral support narrow the member's breathing space in the job, may invite challengers for future contests, and could block chances for advancement.[64]

Political and Personal Constituencies. As candidates or incumbents analyze their electoral base, three narrower constituencies can be discerned:

Table 5-3 House and Senate Margins of Victory, 1974–2002

Chamber and election year	Percentage of vote				
	Under 55	55–59.9	60 plus	Unopposed	(N)
House					
1974	24%	16%	46%	14%	(435)
1976	17	14	56	12	(435)
1978	17	14	53	16	(435)
1980	18	14	60	8	(435)
1982	16	16	63	6	(435)
1984	12	13	61	14	(435)
1986	9	10	64	17	(435)
1988	6	9	67	18	(435)
1990	11	16	58	15	(435)
1992	20	18	58	3	(435)
1994	22	17	52	9	(435)
1996	22	18	57	3	(435)
1998	10	17	63	10	(435)
2000	23	12	59	15	(435)
2002	10	10	80	18	(435)
Senate					
1974	41	18	35	6	(34)
1976	30	33	30	6	(33)
1978	24	33	36	6	(33)
1980	58	18	21	3	(34)
1982	30	27	43	—	(33)
1984	18	21	58	3	(33)
1986	38	15	47	—	(34)
1988	33	15	52	—	(33)
1990	26	11	49	14	(34)
1992	34	34	32	—	(35)
1994	32	34	34	—	(35)
1996	59	18	24	—	(34)
1998	29	9	62	—	(34)
2000	29	15	55	—	(34)
2002	38	18	44	4	(34)

Source: CQ Weekly and authors' calculations.

Note: Percentages may not add to 100 because of rounding. "Unopposed" includes districts or states where only one major-party candidate was on the ballot.

supporters (the reelection constituency), loyalists (the primary constituency), and intimates (the personal constituency).[65] Supporters are expected to vote for them on election day, but some do not. Candidates and their advisers repeatedly monitor these voters, reassessing precinct-level political demography—registration figures, survey data, and recent electoral trends. The more elections incumbents have survived, the more precisely they can identify supporters. Areas and groups with the biggest payoff are usually targeted.

Loyalists are the politician's staunchest supporters. They may be from preelectoral ventures—civil rights, environmental, or anti-abortion activism, for example. They may be concentrated in religious or ethnic groups, or political or civic clubs. They may be friends and neighbors. They are willing volunteers who can be counted on to lend a hand in reelection campaigns.

Candidates dare not ignore these loyalists. A favorite story of House Speaker Thomas P. "Tip" O'Neill Jr., D-Mass., came from his first, losing, campaign for city council. A neighbor supposedly told him, "Tom, I'm going to vote for you even though you didn't ask me." "Mrs. O'Brien," replied a surprised O'Neill, "I've lived across the street from you for 18 years. I shovel your walk in the winter. I cut your grass in the summer. I didn't think I had to ask you for your vote." To this the lady replied, "Tom, I want you to know something: people like to be asked." [66] Expressions of gratitude are equally important. The Bush family, for example, is noted for personal thank-you notes to supporters. George Bush reportedly "always carried a box of note cards with him on the campaign trail and penned a personal note immediately following each event to the volunteers and hosts." [67] Such catering to core supporters helped send both Bushes, father and son, to the White House.

Even entrenched officeholders worry about keeping their core supporters energized. Loyalists are also a politician's defenders in times of adversity. "There's a big difference between the people who are for you and the people who are excitedly for you," an Iowa politician told Fenno, "between those who will vote if they feel like it and those for whom the only election is [your] election. You need as many of that group as you can get." An inadequate base of core support, the informant explained, spelled the downfall of two one-term Democratic senators elected from Iowa in the 1970s. One had a base that was a mile wide and an inch deep; the other's support was an inch wide and a mile deep.[68]

Intimates are close friends who supply political advice and emotional support. Nearly every candidate or incumbent knows a few of them. They may be members of the candidate's family, trusted staff members, political mentors, or individuals who shared decisive experiences early in the candidate's career. The setting and the players differ from state to state and from district to district. Tip O'Neill's inner circle was the "boys" of Barry's Corner, a local clubhouse in Cambridge, Massachusetts, whose families O'Neill had known intimately over more than fifty years of political life. When Rep. David E. Price, D-N.C., first decided to run for Congress, he relied on what he called the

"Wednesday night group," which he described as "an inner circle without whom the effort would never have gotten off the ground."[69] Such intimates play an indispensable role. They provide unvarnished advice on political matters and serve as sounding boards for ideas and strategies.

Politicians confront the constant dilemma of deciding which advisers to trust. More than most, they pay a public price for those who let them down. The danger is that intimates may give faulty advice or inaccurately assess the larger constituencies. Long-term incumbents run a special risk if their intimates lose touch with constituency shifts.

Home Styles

Legislators evolve distinctive ways of presenting or projecting themselves and their records to their constituents—what Fenno calls their home styles. These styles are exhibited in members' personal appearances, mailings, newsletters, press releases, telephone conversations, radio or television spots, and home pages on the Internet. Little is known about how home styles arise, but they are linked to members' personalities, backgrounds, constituency features, and resources. The concept of home style shifts the focus of constituency linkage from representation to presentation. As Fenno states, "It is the style, not the issue content, that counts most in the reelection constituency."[70]

Presentation of Self. The core ingredient of a successful home style is trust—constituents' faith that legislators are what they claim to be and will do what they promise.[71] Winning voters' trust does not happen overnight; it takes time. Three major ingredients of trust are qualification, the belief that legislators are capable of handling the job, a critical threshold that nonincumbents especially must cross; identification, the impression that legislators resemble their constituents, that they are part of the state or region; and empathy, the sense that legislators understand constituents' problems and care about them.

Given variations among legislators and constituencies, countless available home styles can effectively build the trust relationship. The legendary Speaker "Mr. Sam" Rayburn represented his East Texas district for nearly fifty years (1913–1961) as a plain dirt farmer. Once back in his hometown of Bonham, his drawl thickened; his tailored suits were exchanged for khakis, an old shirt, and slouch hat; and he traveled not in the Speaker's limousine but in a well-dented pickup truck. A biographer relates:

> If Rayburn ever chewed tobacco in Washington, a long-time aide could not recall it, but in Bonham he always seemed to have a plug in his cheek. He made certain always to spit in the fireplace at his home when constituents were visiting, so that if nothing else, they would take away the idea that Mr. Sam was just a plain fellow.[72]

Today's legislators are no less inventive in fashioning home styles. Congressman A's direct style features face-to-face contacts with people in his primary constituency. He rarely mentions issues because most people in his district agree on them. Congressman B, a popular local athlete, uses the national defense issue to symbolize his oneness with a district supportive of the military. Congresswoman C, articulate and personable, comes across as "everybody's sister." Congressman D displays himself as an issue-oriented and verbal activist, an outsider ill at ease with conventional politicians. And so on. The repertoire of home styles is limitless.

Voters are likely to remember style long after they forget issue pronouncements or voting records. Even so, legislators know full well that they must explain their decisions to others.[73]

Explaining Washington Activity. Explaining is an integral part of decision making. In home district forums, constituents expect members to be able to describe, interpret, and justify their actions. If they do not agree with the member's conclusions, they may at least respect the decision-making style:

> They don't know much about my votes. Most of what they know is what I tell them. They know more of what kind of a guy I am. It comes through in my letters: "You care about the little guy."[74]

Although few incumbents fear that a single vote can defeat them, all realize that voters' disenchantment with their total record can be fatal. Members therefore stockpile reasons for virtually every position they take—often more than are needed. Facing especially thorny choices (for example, on abortion policy or Medicare reform), they may find an independent stance to be the best defense. Inconsistency is not only mentally costly, but it can be politically costly as well. Thus, while subject matter may vary, politicians give much the same account of themselves, no matter what group they are talking to (contrary to the popular belief that politicians talk out of both sides of their mouths).

Legislators' accounts of Congress to constituents rarely convey any of the chummy comfort they may enjoy as part of the institution. Often members defend their own voting record by belittling Congress—portraying themselves as knights-errant battling sinister forces and feckless colleagues.

Constituency Careers. Constituency ties evolve over the course of a senator's or representative's career. Constituency careers have at least two recognizable stages: expansionism and protectionism. In the first stage the member constructs a reelection constituency by solidifying the help of hardcore supporters and reaching out to attract added blocs of support. This aggressive expansionism—plus exploitation of the perquisites of incumbency, such as fund-raising and an election-year avalanche of communications to constituents—accounts for the "sophomore surge," in which newcomers typically boost their margin in their first reelection bid.[75] In the second stage the member ceases to expand the base of support, content with protecting already won support. Once established, a successful style is rarely altered.

Certain developments, however, can lead to a change in a member's constituency style. One is a contextual change in the constituency, as a population shift or redistricting forces a member to cope with unfamiliar voters or territory. A second cause is a strategic reaction, as a fresh challenger or a novel issue threatens established voting patterns. Because coalitions may shift over time, members and their advisers scrutinize the results of the past election (and, whenever available, survey findings).

Finally, home styles may change with new personal goals and ambitions. A member may seek higher office or may lose touch with voters and reject the reelection goal entirely. Growing responsibilities in Washington can divert attention from home state business, from family responsibilities, and, frankly, from amassing wealth. For Sen. William S. Cohen, R-Maine (1979–1997), the epiphany came with the death of his father and a heightened sense that "tomorrow is not promised to any of us."

> I really asked myself, is this what I want to do for the next six years? . . . Waiting to answer a senseless quorum call for no other reason than to have a quorum call? The endless back and forth and waste of time? The sense that rather than painting the broad landscape we're engaged in a pointillist approach—each little aspect of the dots?[76]

Cohen retired after eighteen years in the Senate. (Far from leaving public life, he became President Clinton's third secretary of defense.) His sentiments are echoed by many veteran legislators. Faced with new aspirations or shifting constituency demands, not a few members decide to retire. Others struggle ineffectively and are defeated. Still others rejuvenate their constituency base and survive.

Office of the Member Inc.

Home style is more than a philosophy for weighing constituents' claims. It affects the way a member answers day-to-day questions: How much attention should I devote to state or district needs? How much time should I spend in the state or district? How should I maintain contact with my constituents? How should I deploy my staff aides to deal with constituents' concerns? One of the most vexing problems is how to balance demands for being in Washington with the need to be back home with constituents.

Road Tripping

During the nineteenth century legislators spent much of their time at home, traveling to Washington only when Congress was in session. After World War II, however, congressional sessions lengthened until they spanned virtually the entire year. Legislators began to set up permanent residence in the nation's capital, a practice that in earlier times would have struck citizens as arrogant. By the 1970s both houses had adopted parallel schedules of sessions punctuated with brief district work periods (House) or nonlegislative periods (Senate).

At the same time, the two houses authorized members to make more paid trips to states or districts. In the early 1960s senators and representatives were allowed three government-paid trips home each year. Today they are allowed as many trips home as they want, subject to the limits of their official expense allowances.

Currently fashionable home styles entail frequent commutes. Although travel has increased for all members, the more time-consuming the trip home, the less often it is made. (Members from Alaska and Hawaii make about a dozen round trips a year—each requiring an elapsed twenty-four hours and spanning four or five time zones.)[77] When their families remain at home, members are more inclined to travel. They tend to avoid their districts during periods of congressional unpopularity, but they spend more time there during periods of adverse economic conditions. As election day approaches, representatives stay close to their districts.[78]

Seniority is also a factor. Senior members tend to make fewer trips to their districts than do junior members—perhaps reflecting junior members' greater attentiveness to their districts. Finally, members' decisions to retire voluntarily are usually accompanied by large drops in trips home. "There was no reason to go back," one member told Hibbing. "My engagement calendar used to be booked up for seven or eight months in advance; after I announced, no one seemed anxious to have me. I stayed in town and found out that Washington was not as bad as I had thought all those years."[79]

Constituency Casework

"All God's chillun got problems," exclaimed Rep. Billy Matthews, D-Fla. (1953–1967), as he pondered mail from his constituents.[80] In the early days lawmakers lacked staff aides and wrote personally to executive agencies for help in such matters as pension or land claims and appointments to military academies. The Legislative Reorganization Act of 1946 provided de facto authority for hiring caseworkers, first in Senate offices and later in the House.

What are these cases all about? As respondents in a nationwide survey reported, the most frequent reason for contacting a member's office (16 percent of all cases) is to express views or obtain information on legislative issues. Requests for help in finding government jobs form the next largest category, followed by cases dealing with government services such as Social Security, veterans benefits, or unemployment compensation. Military cases (for example, transfers, discharges, personal hardships) are numerous, as are tax, legal, and immigration problems. Constituents often ask for government publications: copies of legislative bills and reports, executive branch regulations, agricultural yearbooks, infant care booklets, and tourist information about the nation's capital. And there are requests for flags that have flown over the U.S. Capitol.

Most cases come to legislators' offices by letter, although phone calls, e-mails, faxes, or walk-ins at district or mobile offices are not uncommon.

Occasionally, members themselves pick up cases from talking to constituents. Many hold office hours in their districts for this purpose. When a constituent's request is received, it is usually acknowledged immediately by a letter that either fills the request or promises that an answer will be forthcoming.

If the request requires contacting a federal agency, caseworkers communicate by e-mail, phone, letter, or buckslip (a preprinted referral form).[81] Usually, the contact in the executive agency is a liaison officer, although some caseworkers prefer to deal directly with line officers or regional officials. Once the problem has been conveyed, it is a matter of time before a decision is reached and a reply forwarded to the congressional office. The reply is then sent along to the constituent, perhaps with a cover letter signed by the member. If the agency's reply is deemed faulty, the caseworker may challenge it and ask for reconsideration, and in some cases the member may intervene in person to lend weight to the appeal.

Although not all members are eager to handle casework personally, they all concede that prompt and effective casework pays off at election time. This principle applies to senators no less than to representatives. "Many freshmen view their role differently than twenty-five years ago, when a senator was only a legislator," Sen. Richard C. Shelby, R-Ala., observed as early as 1987. "Now a senator is also a grantsman, an ombudsman, and a caseworker, and cannot ignore those other roles. When we are asked by our constituents to help, we can't say we don't have time because we are focusing on national and international issues."[82]

Keeping up with incoming communications is a priority for all congressional offices. During fiscal 1998, representatives received some forty million pieces of mail; senators, thirty-five million. Low-cost phone calls, faxes, and e-mail messages, often prompted by concerted group efforts, have boosted constituents' communications to unprecedented (and uncounted) levels. All representatives and senators now have Internet e-mail addresses and home pages, some of them interactive.

The volume of Internet communications has, to all accounts, swamped congressional offices. House and Senate offices received an estimated eighty million messages in 2000, and the rate is rising by a million messages each month.[83] Representatives' offices may receive as many as eight thousand e-mails a month; for senators the figure is fifty-five thousand or more. The number of messages skyrocketed during the Clinton impeachment deliberations and then subsided, but at higher levels than before. The controversial nomination of former senator John Ashcroft, R-Mo. (1995–2001), as attorney general early in 2001 generated so much mail that the Senate's computer system was brought to a near standstill.

Casework loads vary from state to state and from district to district. In both chambers senior legislators apparently receive proportionately more casework requests than do junior members.[84] Perhaps senior legislators are considered more powerful and better equipped to resolve constituents' problems.

Legislators themselves certainly cultivate this image in seeking reelection. Demographic variations among electorates can affect casework volume. Some citizens simply are more likely than others to have contact with government agencies.

Comparing senators and representatives, casework loads depend mainly on constituency size. Frances E. Lee and Bruce I. Oppenheimer found that

> [s]enators as a group are not different from House members in the amount of contact they have with constituents. Instead, senators who represent constituencies that are similar in size to House districts have contact levels that mirror or exceed those of House members.[85]

Thus large-state senators would draw proportionately fewer requests than small-state senators. "As state population decreases . . . House members and senators look increasingly similar in accessibility and responsiveness."[86] As for clout, however, senators win hands down (they are 1 out of 100 instead of 1 out of 435). So constituents in small states are more than twice as likely to contact their senator than people in larger states, who tend to rely on their House member.

From all accounts, casework pays off in citizens' support for individual legislators. In one National Election Study (NES) survey, 17 percent of all adults reported that they or members of their families had requested help from their own representatives. Eighty-five percent of them said they were satisfied with the response they received; seven in ten felt the representative would be helpful if asked in the future.[87] "Casework is all profit," contends Morris P. Fiorina. If so, the profit statements may be written in disappearing ink. Only 16 percent of all citizens in the NES survey could remember anything specific the representative had done for the people of the district while in office.[88] A sensible middle-ground view holds that "service responsiveness has an electoral payoff for incumbents regardless of issue positions or other factors. Casework does not operate to supplant issue positions, however."[89]

Some criticize constituency casework as unfair or biased in practice. Citizens may not enjoy equal access to senators' or representatives' offices. Political supporters or cronies may get favored treatment at others' expense. But in the great bulk of cases, help is universally dispensed.

Personal Staff

Legislators head sizable office enterprises that reflect their two Congresses responsibilities within the institution and toward their constituents. In 2003 each House member was entitled to an annual staff allowance covering no more than eighteen full-time and four part-time employees. The average House member's full-time staff numbers about fourteen. Representatives also are entitled to an annual office allowance, used for travel, telecommunications, district office rental, office equipment, stationery, computer services, and mail.[90]

Senators' personal staffs range in size from thirteen to seventy-one; the average is about thirty-four full-time employees. Unlike the House, the Senate places no limits on the number of staff a senator may employ from their two personnel accounts: an administrative and clerical account (which varies according to a state's population) and an account for hiring legislative assistants. A senator's office expense account depends upon factors such as the state's population and its distance from Washington, D.C. Separate categories for mailing, stationery, local offices, and furniture can be shifted within the overall financial allotments.

Members' offices always seem crowded and overburdened, but the freezing of staff size has been partially offset by computerization, shifting to state and district offices, and use of volunteers. These offices depend heavily on unpaid help, mainly college-age interns. On average, each House and Senate office uses about nine interns every year (see Appendix B for information on internships).

Staff Organization. No two congressional offices are exactly alike. Each is shaped by the personality, interests, constituency, and politics of the individual legislator. State and district needs also influence staff composition. A senator from a farm state likely will employ at least one specialist in agricultural problems; an urban representative might hire a consumer affairs or housing expert. Traditions are important. If a legislator's predecessor had an enviable reputation for a certain kind of service, the new incumbent will dare not let it lapse.

The member's institutional position also affects staff organization. Committee and subcommittee chairmen have committee staff at their disposal. Members without such aides rely heavily on personal staff for committee work.

Staff Functions. Most personal aides in the House and Senate are young, well educated, and transient. Senate and House aides have served on average less than four years in their posts. Their salaries, although somewhat above the average for full-time workers in the United States, fall well below those for comparably educated workers.[91]

The mix of personal staff functions is decided by each member. Most hire administrative assistants, legislative assistants, caseworkers, and press aides as well as a few people from the home state or district. The administrative assistant supervises the office and imparts political and legislative advice. Often he or she functions as the legislator's alter ego, negotiating with colleagues, constituents, and lobbyists. Legislative assistants work with members in committees, draft bills, write speeches, suggest policy initiatives, analyze legislation, and prepare position papers. They also monitor committee sessions that the member is unable to attend.

To emphasize the personal touch, many members have moved casework staff to their home districts or states. Virtually all House and Senate members have home district offices in post offices or federal buildings. Some members have as many as five or six. With the decline of party workers to assist local citizens, members' district staffs fill this need and, simultaneously, enhance members' reelection prospects. Senators have an average of four home state offices and deploy a third of their staff there. Representatives have an average of 2.3 offices and deploy almost half of their aides in their districts.[92]

Other reasons are cited for decentralizing constituent functions. Congressional office buildings on Capitol Hill are crowded. Field offices have lower staff salaries and lower overhead. They also are more convenient for constituents, local and state officials, and regional federal officers. Computers and fax machines make it easy for Washington offices and district offices to communicate. This decentralizing trend, which is likely to persist, implies a heightened division between legislative functions based on Capitol Hill and constituency functions based in field offices. In other words, "Office of the Member Inc." is increasingly split into headquarters and branch divisions—with the Capitol Hill office dealing with legislative duties and the state or district office dealing with constituents.

Members and the Media

Office allowances in both chambers amply support lawmakers' unceasing struggle for media attention. A member's office bears some resemblance to the communications division of a medium-size business. Nearly every day, stacks of printed matter and electronic messages are released for wide distribution. In addition to turning out press releases, newsletters, and individual and mass mailings, members communicate through telephone calls, interviews, radio and TV programs, and videotapes. Most of the time, these publicity barrages are aimed not at the national media but at individual media outlets back in the home state or district.

Direct Mail

The traditional cornerstone of congressional publicity is the franking privilege—the right of members to send out mail at no cost to them with their signature (the frank) instead of a stamp. The practice, which in this country dates from the First Continental Congress in 1775, is intended to facilitate official communication between elected officials and the people they represent (a rationale accepted by federal courts in upholding the practice). In recent times members found that aggressive use of the frank could aid reelection. Rep. Bill Frenzel, R-Minn. (1971–1991), noted that both parties teach newcomers three rules for getting reelected: "Use the frank. Use the frank. Use the frank."[93]

Critics point out that franked mail is largely unsolicited and politically motivated. First, outgoing mail costs are much higher in election years than in nonelection years. Second, most items are mass mailings, not individual letters. These mass mailings are either general-purpose newsletters blanketing home states or districts, or special messages targeted to certain categories of voters. Recipients are urged to share their views or contact local offices for help. Sometimes the newsletter may feature an opinion poll asking for citizens' views on selected issues. Whatever the results, the underlying message is that the legislator cares what folks back home think.

The current franking law confers wide mailing privileges but forbids use of the frank for mail "unrelated to the official business, activities, and duties of members." It also bars the frank for a "matter which specifically solicits political support for the sender or any other person or any political party, or a vote or financial assistance for any candidate for any political office." In addition, chamber rules forbid mass mailings (five hundred or more pieces) sixty days (Senate) or ninety days (House) before a primary, runoff, or general election. In the two months before the beginning of each cutoff period, streams of Postal Service trucks are seen pulling away from loading docks of the congressional office buildings. During the period, moreover, many members skirt the requirement by sending out similar letters in batches of 499 or fewer.

Criticisms of such abuses led both houses to impose new franking restrictions in the 1990s. Most important, mailing costs have been integrated into members' office allowances, which forces trade-offs between mail and other expenditures, such as travel or staff. Caps have been placed on newsletters and on total outgoing mail—one piece for each address in the state for senators, three pieces for each address in the district for representatives. Rules governing newsletters curb their advertising features—for example, personal references or pictures of the member.

The recent reforms have reversed the upward spiral of congressional mail costs, from $113.4 million in fiscal 1988 to $30.8 million in fiscal 2002.[94] Members have turned toward discounted bulk mailings and away from mass newsletters and first-class letters. Although it can still be abused, the franking privilege is essential to sustain communications between lawmakers and their constituents. A former chairman of a House oversight commission posed the issue: "How do you write rules and regulations that distinguish between a thoughtful discussion of some important public issue and a self-promoting thing with the photograph of a member on every other page?"[95]

The advent of e-mail poses the problem of whether, or how, the much-debated franking restrictions should apply. The Senate has generally applied the franking rules to electronic mail. The House, however, has declined to adopt such strict rules. As Vernon J. Ehlers, R-Mich., says,

> It is not partisan, it is just simply an informational summary of these bills that were taken up, this is the result of the bills. My constituents are finding that useful, the e-mail list is growing. I think my constituents . . . will find it a bit strange to suddenly, three months before the election, they are not allowed to hear from me about what the Congress has done in a non-partisan way.[96]

Feeding the Local Press

News outlets in this country are highly decentralized and dispersed. About 1,500 daily newspapers and 6,500 weeklies are published in the United States. There are also more than 13,000 radio stations, 1,700 TV stations, and 11,800 cable systems throughout the country.[97] Virtually all these media outlets are locally based because of the vitality of local issues and local advertising.

Taken as a whole, local media outlets have inadequate resources for covering what their congressional delegations are doing in the nation's capital. Few of them have their own Washington reporters. Most rely on syndicated or chain services that rarely follow individual members consistently. "If they report national news it is usually because it involves local personalities, affects local outcomes, or relates directly to local concerns," stated a Senate report.[98]

Relations with the press receive careful attention from members. Most legislators have at least one staffer who serves as a press aide; some have two or three. Their job is to generate coverage highlighting the member's work. Executive agencies often help by letting incumbents announce federal grants or contracts awarded in the state or district. Even if the member had nothing to do with procuring the funds, the press statement proclaims, "Senator So-and-So announced today that a federal contract has been awarded to XYZ Company in Jonesville." Many offices also prepare weekly or biweekly columns that small-town newspapers can reprint under the lawmaker's byline.

The House, the Senate, and the four Capitol Hill parties have fully equipped studios and satellite links where audio or video programs or excerpted statements (called actualities) can be produced for a fraction of the commercial cost.[99] Some incumbents produce regular programs that are picked up by local radio or television outlets. More often, these outlets insert brief audio or TV clips on current issues into regular news broadcasts—to give the impression that their reporters have gone out and obtained the story. Members also create their own news reports and beam them directly to hometown stations, often without ever talking to a reporter. With direct satellite feeds to local stations, members regularly go "live at five" before local audiences.

Rep. Kenny Hulshof, R-Mo., typifies today's media-savvy lawmakers. Each week he holds a telephone conference with radio stations in his central Missouri district. Each month he hosts a half-hour television show in Columbia, his hometown and his district's largest city. Periodically he talks about the day's issues in links with local television outlets. A reporter described one such session:

> On the afternoon he appeared on satellite, from a GOP studio with red, white and blue drapes and a mural of the Capitol, Hulshof was questioned, in turn, by reporters from television stations in Quincy and Jefferson City about a bill to restructure the Internal Revenue Service (H.R. 2676) that Republicans had just passed.[100]

Aggressive media outreach was a logical strategy for Hulshof. In 1996 he ousted, by a 2 percent margin, a twenty-year Democratic incumbent who was widely perceived as being out of touch with his constituency. Hulshof's strategy seemed to have worked. He has won reelection handily ever since.

Some members invite controversy as a way of showing their accessibility. For example, Rep. Mark Souder, R-Ind., tapes five-minute reports every weekday for local airing and hosts an hour-long call-in show every Sunday—unofficially dubbed "Bark at Mark"—on a popular talk radio station in Fort Wayne.[101]

Like printed communications, radio and TV broadcasts pose ethical questions. House and Senate recording studios are supposed to be used only for communicating about legislation and other policy issues, but the distinction between legitimate constituent outreach and political advertising remains blurred. (Political party facilities, such as the one used by Representative Hulshof, have no such limits.) Some radio and television news editors have qualms about using members' programs. "It's just this side of self-serving," said one television editor of the biweekly "Alaska Delegation Report." [102] Others claim to see little difference between these electronic communications and old-fashioned press releases. Local editors and producers still have to decide whether to use the material, edit it, or toss it.

Local Press Boosterism?

In the eyes of home district media outlets, incumbents fare splendidly. Michael J. Robinson cited the case of "Congressman Press," a midlevel House member, untouched by scandal, who had an average press operation. One year Congressman Press issued 144 press releases, about three a week. That year the major paper in his district ran 120 stories featuring or mentioning him. More than half the stories drew heavily on the press releases. "On average, every other week, Congressman Press was featured in a story virtually written in his own office." [103]

Even when local stories are not drawn from press releases, they tend to be respectful if not downright laudatory. Hometown stories during one of the re-election campaigns of Rep. William Steiger, R-Wis. (1967–1978), were so fulsome in their praise, his press aide confessed, that no self-respecting press secretary would have dared put them out.[104] A detailed study of the local press corps in eighty-two contested races highlighted the journalists' tendency toward "safety and timidity." Incumbents were rendered respectful coverage based on their experience; in contested open seats, journalists tended to keep their distance.[105]

Electronic media are even more benign than print media. As one legislator said, "TV people need thirty seconds of sound and video at the airport when I arrive—that's all they want." [106] Most local reporters for radio and TV are on general assignment and do little preparation for interviews. Their primary goal is to get the newsmaker on tape. This is especially true of outlets in smaller markets, few of which have access to a Washington bureau. As a Jefferson City, Missouri, TV editor explained his station's handling of an appearance initiated by Representative Hulshof's office:

> He's trying to manage the information aspect of all of this [the Internal Revenue Service reform issue]. But we get the information we need, so we don't mind it too much. . . . We're in TV. We want to see him talk to us. We don't want phone calls.[107]

Local radio and television's weakness for congressionally initiated communications magnifies the advantages incumbents enjoy. ABC-TV correspondent Cokie Roberts concludes, "The emergence of local TV has made some members media stars in the home towns and, I would argue, done more to protect incumbency than any franking privilege or newsletter ever could, simply because television is a more pervasive medium than print."[108] Representative Hulshof states blandly: "I've been treated very fairly back home by the media, who have been content to just report the facts."[109]

Reports on Congress from the national press corps are far more critical than those from local news organizations. Following the canons of investigative journalism, many national reporters are on the lookout for scandals or evidence of wrongdoing. The national press reports primarily on the institution of Congress, whereas the local press is interested mostly in local senators and representatives. Individual members tend to be reported far more favorably than the institution. The content and quality of press coverage underscore the two Congresses. Congress as collective policy maker, covered mainly by the national press, appears in a different light from the politicians who make up the Congress covered mainly by local news outlets.

Conclusion

How members of Congress manage the two Congresses dilemma is reflected in their daily tasks on Capitol Hill and in their home states or districts. Election is a prerequisite to congressional service. Incumbent legislators allocate much of their time and energy, and even more of their staff and office resources, to the care and cultivation of voters. Their Hill styles and home styles are adopted with this end in mind. Yet senators and representatives do not live by reelection alone. Not a few turn their backs on reelection to pursue other careers or interests. For those who remain in office, reelection usually is not viewed as an end in itself but as a lever for pursuing other goals—policy making or career advancement, for example. Fenno challenged one of the representatives whose constituency career he had followed, remarking that "sometimes it must be hard to connect what you do here with what you do in Washington." "Oh no," the lawmaker replied, "I do what I do here so I can do what I want to do there."[110]

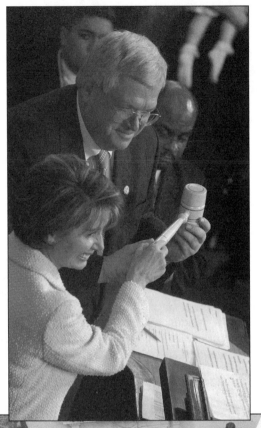

In an historic event, House minority leader Nancy Pelosi, D-Calif., the first woman ever nominated for the speakership, hands the gavel to J. Dennis Hastert, R-Ill., upon his election as Speaker on the opening day of the 108th Congress. President George W. Bush, meeting with Vice President Dick Cheney and the bipartisan congressional leadership on the war in Iraq, delivers remarks to the media. Seated to the president and vice president's left are Pelosi and Hastert, and to their right, Senate majority leader Bill Frist, R-Tenn., and Senate minority leader Tom Daschle, D-S.D. Frist, below left, and House majority leader Tom DeLay, R-Tex., wait for the president at a 2003 Congress of Tomorrow luncheon.

6

Leaders and Parties in Congress

Do congressional leaders matter? Reflecting on Newt Gingrich, R-Ga., who at the time was House Speaker and was widely credited with ending forty years of Democratic control of the House in the November 1994 elections, Rep. Sherwood Boehlert, R-N.Y., said: "Gingrich is the one responsible for leading the Republican Party out of the wilderness of the minority . . . to the promised land of the majority. He is singularly responsible for us being where we are now." [1] Four years after that electoral triumph Gingrich was out as Speaker and subsequently resigned as a member of Congress, the victim of personal scandals and his party's poor showing in the 1998 midterm elections.

Three days after the 1998 elections, Appropriations chairman Bob Livingston, R-La., announced his candidacy for the speakership and soon won the endorsement of House Republicans. However, on the same day in December 1998 that the House impeached President Bill Clinton, Livingston stunned his colleagues by declaring he would no longer seek to become Speaker and would resign from the House. Again, personal scandals were to blame. Most of his colleagues were willing to forgive his adultery, but about a dozen conservatives were miffed that he had not been candid on this matter and threatened to withhold their votes from him when the House elected the new Speaker.

House Republicans turned to J. Dennis Hastert of Illinois, the GOP's chief deputy whip since 1995. A popular and well-liked lawmaker, he so quickly locked up the support of his partisan colleagues that he headed off any potential challengers.[2] On January 6, 1999, the opening day of the 106th Congress, Hastert was elected Speaker. Dubbed the "accidental Speaker" by the press, "he's the right man at the right time," declared a House GOP leader. Or, as Rep. Ray LaHood, R-Ill., said, "He does not come into the job radioactive, controversial from the get go." [3]

Two years later Hastert was no longer viewed as a caretaker Speaker. Instead, his talent for unifying his party, devising effective legislative strategies, and forging compromises helped Republicans to stall a strong Democratic election challenge and hold onto the House majority in the November 2000 elections. Despite the razor-thin victory, the popular Hastert emerged a stronger Speaker as Republicans won control of the House for the fourth straight election, a feat not accomplished since 1924. However, it was also the third consecutive election in which Republicans lost House seats. That string of losses ended with the November 2002 midterm elections when Republicans defied history and picked up seats, as Hastert predicted would happen six weeks before the election.[4] Hastert's extensive travel schedule and fund-raising on behalf of GOP candidates (for instance, he spent twenty-six days during the August 2002 recess traveling coast to coast, raising an estimated $1.5 million), combined with the aggressive campaigning of President George W. Bush, broke the electoral pattern in place since 1934 that the party of the chief executive loses seats during the first midterm election.[5] The GOP made a net gain of six House seats.

These examples of the relationship between leaders and followers parallel the constant interaction between the two Congresses—between the lawmaking institution and the representative assembly. In their inside role, party leaders guide institutional activities and influence policy. Leaders also must find ways of persuading members who represent different constituencies, regions, ideologies, values, and interests to support legislation that addresses national concerns. "The only thing that counts is 218 votes, and nothing else is real," explained a House Democratic leader. "You have to be able [to attract a majority of the House] to pass a bill."[6]

Implicit in this party leader's statement is recognition that mobilizing winning coalitions is not easy. Party leaders encounter what scholars call a "collective action" dilemma.[7] How can leaders mobilize a majority to pass legislation (for the collective or public good) when it is often in the self-interest of many lawmakers to do little or nothing to secure the measure's enactment, even if they favor it, because the bill's advocates will invest whatever time and effort are required to achieve the collective result? Thus, many lawmakers may take a free ride on the efforts of their colleagues and then claim credit and receive benefits from the bill's enactment. Too many free riders and little lawmaking may be the result. Congressional leaders usually resolve the collective action problem in two main ways: devising sufficient incentives (political, policy, or procedural, for example) to attract majority support and coordinating the work of the bill's champions to win desired objectives. Leadership in legislatures, then, "can be seen as having been instituted to ameliorate the problems of collective action. . . . [P]arty leaders are seen as agents of the members who select them and charge them" with acting on their behalf to achieve a number of goals, including the production of collective goods.[8] This scholarly view of party leadership is sometimes called the principal-agent model. Party leaders (the agents) are selected by the partisan rank and file (the principals) to advance policy and electoral goals.

In their outside role, party leaders formulate and publicize issue agendas designed to galvanize the support of partisans and swing voters nationally. They help recruit candidates for Congress and assist in their campaigns. Leaders also must serve as the party's link to the president, the press, the public, and the partisan faithful.

The leaders' inside and outside roles interact constantly. For example, party leaders calculate how their actions on the House or Senate floor can give a boost to their party's candidates in the next election. Today, in a period of party parity, ideological polarization, and intense electoral competition, the line between campaigning and governing on the major issues that divide the two parties has all but disappeared. The permanent campaign approach to lawmaking aims to generate public support and momentum to force legislative action on party priorities. "The reality is, to get something done in this town you've got to deal with the policy and the politics," exclaimed Rep. Rob Portman, R-Ohio.[9] Congress is a partisan body. Stated differently, legislative organization is partisan organization. The majority party in the House or the Senate controls not only the top leadership posts and each chamber's agenda of activities but also the chairmanships and majorities on committees and subcommittees.

Leaders of the House

House rules permit a determined majority to achieve its policy objectives. During much of the nineteenth century, the struggle between majority rights and minority rights was paramount until the majoritarian principle became embedded in House procedures by the turn of the twentieth century. Stalling tactics by the minority during the pre– and post–Civil War House often prevented action. Finally, Republican Speaker Thomas "Czar" Reed of Maine broke the minority's capacity to frustrate House decision making. The House adopted new rules (the famous Reed Rules) to facilitate majority rule and action. "No dilatory motion shall be entertained by the Speaker" is an 1890 House rule that remains in effect today.

The Speaker

No other member of Congress possesses the visibility and authority of the Speaker of the House. The Constitution states that the House "shall chuse their Speaker." Although the Constitution does not require the Speaker to be a House member, all of them have been. Rep. John Conyers Jr., D-Mich., in the lead-up to the November 2002 elections, urged the dean of the House, John D. Dingell, D-Mich., to retire so as to avoid a divisive primary against another Democratic member. If Democrats won majority control, a grateful House, said Conyers, might "reward Dingell's sacrifice by making him the first non-Member to be elected Speaker of the House." [10] Dingell turned down the proposal, prevailed in the primary, and won reelection to his twenty-fifth term. Under the Presidential Succession Act of 1947, the Speaker is second in line behind the vice president to succeed to the presidency.

For a time House Speaker Gingrich was a virtual rival to the White House in setting the nation's course. In an unprecedented event mirroring what presidents often do, Gingrich made a prime-time, nationally televised address on April 17, 1995, highlighting the accomplishments of Congress and outlining the country's future direction. Not since the early 1800s when Speaker Henry Clay put forward an agenda (titled "The American System") for strengthening the nation's infrastructure has a Speaker so exploited the position's bully pulpit. Under Gingrich, the speakership became a platform for focusing public debate on crucial issues of national governance. Speaker Hastert, by contrast, maintains a lower public profile and shares with other Republicans the national spokesman's role. As Hastert said: "I don't think I have to be [at] the head of every news release or press conference . . . and didn't have to be on every Sunday talk show." [11] Hastert, noted one account, "is not known for the pithy sound bites that modern politics demands." [12]

The office of Speaker combines procedural and political prerogatives with policy and partisan leadership. Speakers preside over the House, rule on points of order, announce the results of votes, refer legislation to the committees, name lawmakers to serve on conference committees and select committees, and maintain order and decorum in the House chamber. In addition to these procedural prerogatives, they exercise important political powers. They set the House's agenda of activities, control the Rules Committee, chair their party's committee assignment panel, bestow or withhold various tangible and intangible rewards, coordinate policy making with Senate counterparts, and, in this age of videopolitics, present party and House positions to the public at large.

Before 1899 it was not uncommon for Speakers to have only a few years of service as representatives. Whig Henry Clay of Kentucky was elected to the speakership on November 4, 1811—his first day in the House. Speakers elected since 1899 have served, on average, more than twenty years before their election to the post. Hastert served a dozen years before becoming Speaker on January 6, 1999.

Once in position, Speakers traditionally have been reelected as long as their party controlled the House. Not since 1923 has there been a floor battle over the speakership because one party has always had a clear majority. Typically, members vote for the speakership along straight party lines. As chief parliamentary officer and leader of the majority party (see Figure 6-1), the Speaker enjoys unique powers in scheduling floor business and in recognizing members during sessions. Occasionally, Speakers will relinquish the gavel to join in floor debate. They usually vote only in case of a tie.

The Speaker is also in charge of administrative matters. When Speaker Gingrich took office, he revamped the administrative structure and management of the House. Administrative units and positions were abolished, management was streamlined and modernized, an outside independent audit of the accounting systems was undertaken, and a new chief administrative officer—elected by the House at the start of each Congress—was assigned overall responsibility for running the House's administrative operations in a professional manner.[13] Speaker Hastert retained this administrative structure.

Cannon and Rayburn. During the Republic's first 120 years, Speakers gradually accrued power. By 1910 Speaker Joseph G. Cannon, R-Ill., dominated the House. He assigned members to committees, appointed and

Figure 6-1 Organization of the House of Representatives, 108th Congress (2003–2005)

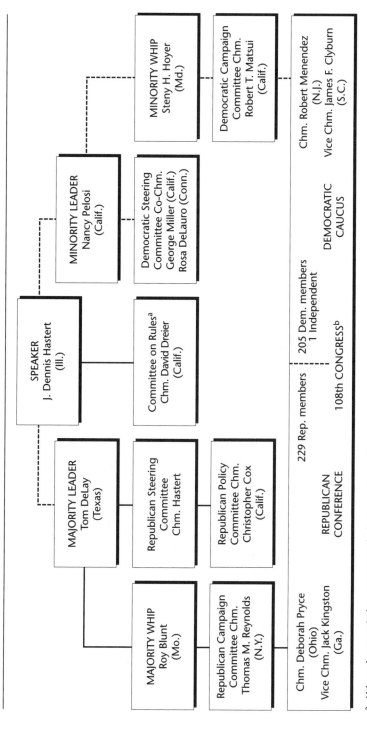

[a] Although not strictly a party panel, the Rules Committee in modern times functions largely as an arm of the majority leadership.
[b] As of February 2003.

removed committee chairmen, regulated the flow of bills to the House floor as chairman of the Rules Committee, referred bills to committee, and controlled floor debate. Taken individually, Cannon's powers were little different from those of his immediate predecessors, but taken together and exercised to their limits they bordered on the dictatorial. The result was a revolt against Cannon.

The House forced Cannon to step down from the Rules Committee in 1910. The next year, when Democrats took control of the House, the new Speaker (James B. "Champ" Clark of Missouri) was denied the authority to make committee assignments, and his power of recognition was curtailed. The speakership then went into long-term eclipse. Power flowed to the majority leader, to the committee chairmen, and for a while to party caucuses.

Speakers after Cannon exhibited various leadership styles that reflected their personalities, the historical context in which they operated, and the partisan divisions and level of conflict within the chamber. Democrat Sam Rayburn of Texas (Speaker, 1940–1947, 1949–1953, 1955–1961) was a formidable leader because of his personal prestige as well as his long political experience and immense parliamentary skills. As he explained, "The old day of pounding on the desk and giving people hell is gone. . . . A man's got to lead by persuasion and kindness and the best reason—that's the only way he can lead people." [14] Rayburn lent coherence to a House in which power was diffused among a relatively small number of powerful committee chairmen who were often called the "dukes" and "barons" of Capitol Hill.

The relationship between these two centers of institutional power—committee and party—provides a useful analytical framework for evaluating the extent of centralized (party dominance) versus decentralized (committee autonomy) authority in the legislature. The Cannon era was plainly a time of party power. Much of the twentieth century, with the seniority principle exercising primacy in the selection of House and Senate committee chairmen, was a period in which the balance of power tilted toward committee leaders. Today, it is not that committees are unimportant but that party leaders are more important in influencing action on the priority issues of the day. Both power centers, meanwhile, can be fettered by majority vote of the chamber's membership.

Revival of the Speakership. The distribution of internal power changed fundamentally after Rayburn. To curb the power of the committee barons, lawmakers elected during the Vietnam War and the Watergate era combined forces with longtime members disgruntled with the status quo. The majority Democrats changed their party rules to require that committee chairs be elected by secret ballot of the Democratic Caucus. Committee chairs were obligated to share power with subcommittee chairs. At the same time the reformers in the late 1960s and 1970s strengthened the hand of the party leadership. The Speaker, for example, gained the right to name all the majority party members of the Rules Committee, including the chair. House rules were further amended to permit the Speaker to refer measures to more than one committee.

Three Democratic Speakers—Thomas P. "Tip" O'Neill Jr. of Massachusetts (1977–1987), Jim Wright of Texas (1987–June 1989), and Thomas S. Foley of Washington (June 1989–1995)—were the beneficiaries of these changes, which strengthened their persuasive powers and ability to assemble winning coalitions. O'Neill held the speakership for ten consecutive years, the longest uninterrupted service of any Speaker. Using a strategy of inclusion to draw Democratic rank and file into the leadership orbit, he expanded the whip structure and encouraged junior Democrats to back partisan priorities by appointing them to leadership task forces.[15] During the first six years of the Reagan presidency, when the Senate was also in Republican hands, O'Neill became the Democratic Party's national spokesman. In the process he transformed the speakership into an office of high national visibility.

O'Neill's successor was Jim Wright, who pushed the prerogatives of office even further. In domestic and foreign policy, Wright took bold risks. Whereas O'Neill strived for consensus, Wright laid out an agenda and then worked diligently, by himself if necessary, to mobilize support. "The Congress," declared Wright, "should not simply react, passively, to recommendations from the president but should come forward with initiatives of its own."[16] His unyielding personal style and knack for making "minority status more painful," as one House GOP leader put it, embittered Republicans (and even some of his own party).[17]

"If Wright consolidates his power, he will be a very, very formidable man," warned Representative Gingrich. "We have to take him on early to prevent that."[18] Gingrich brought ethics charges against the Speaker, and they were investigated by the Committee on Standards of Official Conduct. That panel eventually charged Wright with violating House rules by accepting gifts from a close business associate and circumventing limits on members' outside income through bulk sales of his 1984 book *Reflections of a Public Man* to lobbyists and interest groups. Wright did not survive these ethical and political challenges and left the House in June 1989. Eight years later—as political payback—many House Democrats tried to force Gingrich from the speakership for ethical violations.

End of an Era: Foley (1989–1995). Next in line to succeed Wright as Speaker was Majority Leader Foley. Elected to the House in November 1964, Foley had risen through the ranks to become Speaker during an era of sharp partisan, political, and personal infighting. The new Speaker had a reputation for being a judicious, low-key, and consensus-oriented leader. His initial objectives as Speaker were to restore civility, integrity, and bipartisan cooperation to the House and to provide policy direction. Although Republicans found Foley easier to deal with than Wright, they soon lamented the Speaker's willingness to use procedural rules to frustrate GOP objectives. When Democrat Bill Clinton was elected president in 1992, Foley's instincts for conciliation became an asset as he worked to foster harmony among House Democrats and good ties with the Clinton White House. However, problems that afflicted the

Wright speakership—scandals (revelations in the early 1990s of check bouncing at the House bank by nearly three hundred members) and intraparty divisions—continued under Foley. In November 1994, after a thirty-year congressional career, Speaker Foley lost his reelection bid and Democrats lost the House.

Gingrich: A New Style of Speaker (1995–1999). There is little doubt that Newt Gingrich was a unique Speaker. His Democratic predecessors, he once said, were "essentially legislative leaders speaking to the press about legislative matters." He went on to say, "I, on the other hand, was essentially a political leader of a grassroots movement seeking to do nothing less than reshape the federal government along with the political culture of the nation." [19] Gingrich, summarized a commentator, was "first a leader of a national movement, then a Republican spokesman and, only third, Speaker of the House.[20]

As his party's unanimous choice for Speaker, Gingrich took the office to new heights. His ten-point party platform titled the Contract with America, which the House acted upon within the promised first hundred days of the 104th Congress, set the agenda for Congress and the nation during that period. Three factors help explain his influence: recognition on the part of most GOP lawmakers in the House that they owed their majority status to him; broad commitment on their part to the GOP's agenda, especially cutting spending and balancing the budget; and the new majority's need to succeed at governance after forty years in the minority.

A centralizing aspect of Gingrich's speakership was his influence over committees. Not only did Gingrich personally select certain Republicans to chair several standing committees, ignoring seniority in the process, but he also required the GOP members of the Appropriations Committee to sign a written pledge that they would heed the Republican leadership's recommendations for spending reductions. Furthermore, he often bypassed committees entirely by establishing leadership task forces to process legislation. Party power during this period dominated committee power.

Gingrich's speakership went through four main phases prior to his departure from the House. The first was characterized by the triumphalism of the first hundred days: Everything in the ten-point contract passed the House except term limits for lawmakers. As an aggressive and strong-willed Speaker, Gingrich for a time reversed the principal-agent leadership model. Instead of acting as the agent of the GOP rank and file, he dictated to them a common agenda that was in their best interest to pass. It was a different story in the Senate, where opponents stalled action on many contract items.

In the second phase, Gingrich's confrontational strategy with the White House produced political disaster for Republicans. In a face-off with President Clinton, Republicans were publicly blamed for twice shutting down the government in late 1995 and early 1996. Further, their revolutionary plans for downsizing government by eliminating cabinet departments and reducing spending for education, environment, and health programs were successfully characterized by Democrats as extreme. Gingrich's public popularity plummeted, and the Speaker became a campaign issue in many 1996 congressional races.

The lead-up to the November 1996 campaign ushered in the third phase of Gingrich's speakership. Worried that President Clinton would campaign against a do-nothing Congress, congressional Republicans and the White House cooperated and passed health, minimum wage, and welfare reform legislation. Each side wanted something positive to campaign on. The result was that Clinton won reelection to a second term, and the Republicans—although they lost nine House seats—held majority control of Congress.

A narrower majority was not Gingrich's only problem when the House convened in the 105th Congress (1997–1999). A few weeks earlier, on December 21, 1996, Gingrich admitted that he had provided inaccurate and incomplete information to the House ethics committee regarding his solicitation of tax-deductible contributions, which were used for partisan purposes contrary to federal law. Two weeks after Gingrich's reelection as Speaker, the House voted 395–28 to reprimand him for ethical misconduct and to fine him $300,000. He became the first Speaker formally disciplined by the House for ethical wrongdoing.

Weakened by the ethics charge, Gingrich no longer dominated the House as he once did. In the 105th Congress, the final phase of his leadership, he decided on a modest agenda (keeping the House in session the fewest number of days in two decades) and focused on hot-button issues (late-term or "partial-birth" abortion, education vouchers, tax cuts) designed to energize the GOP electorate for the 1998 midterm elections. Rank-and-file Republicans and his top leadership lieutenants became frustrated with Gingrich's impulsive leadership style. Rep. Peter T. King, R-N.Y., recommended that Gingrich step aside as Speaker because his low popular standing (below 30 percent job approval) made him unable to boost Republican priorities. "As roadkill on the highway of American politics," wrote King, "Newt Gingrich cannot sell the Republican agenda." [21] *Time* magazine's 1995 "Man of the Year" had fallen far. Top GOP leaders and a small band of ideologically hard-line junior conservatives complained that Gingrich compromised too much with the Democrats. As a result, a coup plot in the summer of 1997 was hatched by the hard-liners with the encouragement of some in the leadership. The plan to depose Gingrich was uncovered and averted, but it exposed the deep frustration with the Speaker within Republican ranks. [22]

On the eve of the November 3, 1998, elections, the Speaker took a high-risk political gamble. Despite polls showing the public was sick of hearing about President Clinton's sexual relationship with White House intern Monica S. Lewinsky, Gingrich gave the order to GOP campaign officials to blanket selected House districts with multimillion-dollar TV ads highlighting the scandal. When the House adjourned two weeks before the election, Clinton-preoccupied Republicans had no coherent agenda to promote. Furthermore, they had allowed the president to win large spending increases in an omnibus appropriations bill nearly four thousand pages in length, which no one had time to read and which was filled with pork. Many Republicans and conservative voters were angry with the Speaker about this end-of-session budget deal.

When the midterm results came in, Republicans were shell-shocked at their poor showing. Scores of Republicans blamed Gingrich for another election in which they lost seats despite the early predictions, including those of the Speaker, that their party would gain seats and coast to victory. The traditional principal-agent model had returned: A leader who fails to fulfill or jeopardizes the needs, expectations, and preferences of his partisan colleagues soon loses their support. Gingrich became an early casualty of the election. He abruptly departed the race for the speakership and resigned from the House. A skillful insurgent leader as a minority lawmaker, Gingrich had difficulty adjusting to the formidable job of governing the House.

The Coach as Speaker: Dennis Hastert (1999–). A former high school wrestling coach and Illinois state legislator, Hastert took office in the aftermath of the contentious House impeachment proceedings against President Clinton. The new Speaker promised to restore some semblance of bipartisanship between Democrats and Republicans and to unite his often fractious and divided party. Known as a patient, congenial, behind-the-scenes workhorse, Hastert excelled at counting votes as then chief deputy whip to Majority Whip Tom DeLay, R-Texas, and at crafting compromises and winning coalitions. Employing the coaching metaphor, Hastert explained his leadership role. "A good coach knows when to step back and let others shine in the spotlight," he said. "A coach worth his salt will instill in his team a sense of fair play, camaraderie, respect of the game and for the opposition. Without those, victory is hollow." [23] He added, "They call me speaker, but they probably ought to call me the listener because I just do a lot of it." [24]

A strong conservative, Hastert became Speaker without having served in an elective leadership post—something that had not occurred since the 1919–1925 period, when Frederick Gillett, R-Mass., was Speaker. For much of the 106th Congress, Hastert's speakership was a work in progress as he developed new relationships with the other GOP leaders, the committee chairs, and the factional groups in the House. Among Hastert's new departures was "ceding substantial authority to committee chairmen, delegating his role as party spokesman to a variety of Members, hiring seasoned staff who work well with the other leadership offices and playing a more active role in the day-to-day gruntwork of legislating." [25]

Subsequently, Hastert acted to consolidate power in a trio of leaders—himself (as Speaker), the majority leader, and the majority whip. This leadership team was not reluctant to inform rank-and-file members or committee chairmen that they needed to toe the line on issues or importance to Republicans. For example, during a GOP Conference meeting, the Veterans' Affairs chairman criticized the Republicans' budget resolution and the White House's

A Comparison of the Speakerships of Gingrich and Hastert

Newt Gingrich, R-Ga. (Speaker 1995–1999)	J. Dennis Hastert, R-Ill. (Speaker 1999–)
A visionary leader who often set aside traditional legislative procedures	A pragmatic leader who emphasized the regular order of lawmaking
Decreased power of committees	Restored committees' prerogatives but exercised leadership control on priority issues
Set aside seniority in naming several committee chairs	Employed interview process in naming committee chairs
Delegated floor management duties to the majority leader	Personally managed the floor schedule
Increased use of party task forces	Limited use of party task forces
Assumed large public spokesman role	Played relatively small role as public spokesman
Contributed to partisan rancor	Eased partisan tension in the House
Relished national spotlight	Operated behind the scenes
Exercised confrontational style of leadership	Exercised accommodating style of leadership
Bypassed committees on occasion to achieve his party's legislative ends	Relied on committee chairs

spending proposals. Speaker Hastert "got up and shut him down," said a witness to the tongue-lashing. "That was off the charts. I've never seen anything like that. . . . It was scathing." [26] A tight-knit team, the three have been able to move "top agenda items while wielding a historically small margin of control in a remarkably polarized House." [27] In brief, Hastert's style of leadership was different from Gingrich's because each operated in a different legislative context and with different personal skills. (See box for a summary comparison of some of the differences between Gingrich and Hastert.)

Hastert's leadership role also changed when Republican George W. Bush was inaugurated president on January 20, 2001. No longer did he need to develop agendas and strategies to counter the plans of a Democratic president. With his party in control of all three elective branches—only until June 2001 in the 107th Senate because of Vermont senator Jim Jeffords's party switch; unified control returned with the 108th Congress for effectively the first time since the 83d Congress (1953–1955)—Speaker Hastert worked with President

Bush to coordinate communications strategies and to move the administration's priorities through Congress. "It's my job to make sure that we can pass bills the president can sign," stated Hastert, "and if we [pass] bills the president can't support, then I'm derelict in my duty." [28]As part of his effort to promote effective legislative-executive relations, Hastert named Rep. Rob Portman of Ohio to be the chairman of the House GOP leadership team. Portman served in the first Bush administration and advised the Texas governor in his race for the White House. He also enjoys close ties with the Bush family. In his leadership capacity, said Speaker Hastert, Portman "will chair the leadership meetings, act as a liaison with the Bush administration and serve as an additional set of eyes and ears for the Republican leadership." [29]

The Speaker's Influence: Style and Context. Congressional analysts suggest a number of ways to study the primary determinants of the Speaker's influence. (See box for a brief review of the principal scholarly theories about congressional leadership.) Analysts generally emphasize context over personal style as the main factor affecting the Speaker's institutional clout. Personal style refers to the skills, abilities, and qualities of the Speaker, such as intelligence, talent for coalition building, or political acumen. Advocates of the individualist school of leadership stress that personally adroit and forceful Speakers can lead by molding circumstances and opportunities to their own objectives.[30] Here is how one analyst viewed Newt Gingrich's impact on the House: "If Newt Gingrich had been run over by a truck in 1993, it is almost certain that there would not be a Republican majority in the House. Few other congressional politicians have made such a difference in partisan history." [31] Speakers' personal capacities, in short, allow them to exercise that elusive quality called leadership—persuading others to follow their lead.

Consider the assertive styles of Speakers Wright and Gingrich. Both were willing to dictate to committee chairmen; advance party agendas; take procedural actions, as circumstances warranted, to hamstring the minority party; and challenge the White House. Wright and Gingrich had the advantage of serving with a president of the opposite party, reducing their need to carry out his programs. Their personal talents were augmented by formal and informal procedural changes that allowed them to accomplish more of their objectives than if they lacked these powers. For example, whether a Democrat or a Republican occupies the speakership today, he chairs his party's committee on committees (the assignment panel), a significant resource that the Speaker can employ strategically when appointing colleagues to coveted panels. On expected close floor votes, which the Speaker needs to win, he may remind wavering lawmakers of how they won their preferred committee position. Different personal styles, as in the "nice guy" Speakers who succeeded Wright (Foley) and Gingrich (Hastert) and who also had the same formal powers as their predecessors, can produce a leader less likely to exert intense pressure on colleagues to vote a certain way, to utilize the full range of his parliamentary prerogatives to achieve party objectives, or to advance political

Theories of Congressional Leadership

Political scientists have developed different theories to explain why congressional leaders appear to be stronger during some eras than others. The most prominent is called conditional party government.[a] A competing theory—the pivotal voter theory—suggests that the influence of party leaders is marginal with respect to their ability to shift policy outcomes away from what a majority of the chamber prefers toward the policy preferences of the majority party.[b]

Proponents of each theory view party leaders as agents of their principals—their rank-and-file partisans. Members want their party leaders to help them accomplish their fundamental goals: getting reelected, making good policy, and gaining—or maintaining—power in the House or Senate. A correspondence in leader-member views means that party leaders will work to advance the majority preferences of the rank and file. After all, party leaders hold their positions at the sufferance of their partisan colleagues and they usually want to be reelected to those leadership posts.

Conditional Party Government Theory. Under this model, the power of congressional leaders hinges on the degree of homogeneity within the majority party concerning policy and on the extent of interparty conflict between Democrats and Republicans. With both conditions in play, the theory goes, rank-and-file party members are supportive of changes that strengthen their party leaders, such as the Speaker. A cohesive majority party can pass legislation without any support from the minority party. Conversely, when parties' policy goals are fragmented, partisan lawmakers have little incentive to give their leaders more authority. They may use their power against the political and policy interests of many in the rank and file.

Pivotal Voter Theory. This theory challenges the conditional party government model by suggesting that policy outcomes on the floor rarely diverge from what is acceptable to the pivotal voter—the member who casts the 218th vote in the House. Rarely does everyone in the majority party support a particular policy. Why, then, should majority members change their policy views to back a party position with which they disagree? Instead, they will join with members of the other party to form the winning coalition. According to this theory, these pivotal voters determine chamber outcomes.

Moreover, if each party is internally united in its policy preferences, as the conditional party government theory states, there will be no difference between what the majority party wants and what the chamber membership will agree to. Simply observing party leaders engaged in frenetic activity—often seeking pivotal votes—does not mean they can skew legislative outcomes beyond what is acceptable to a majority of the entire membership.

[a] See, for example, John H. Aldrich and David W. Rohde, "The Transition to Republican Rule in the House: Implications for Theories of Congressional Politics," *Political Science Quarterly* (winter 1997–1998): 541–567.
[b] See Keith Krehbiel, *Pivotal Politics: A Theory of U.S. Lawmaking* (Chicago: University of Chicago Press, 1998).

and policy positions independent of any consensus within his party caucus or conference.

An important explanation that accounts for such variance among individual Speakers is context.[32] Context refers to the House's external and internal environment, both of which overlap and change over time. External elements include whether the Speaker's party controls the White House, the public's demand for legislation, the complexity of national problems, the popularity of the president, and the strength of partisan identification within the electorate. As the electoral constituencies of the two parties predominantly select either a liberal Democrat or a conservative Republican, a pattern of the last quarter century, the Speaker can set an agenda that enjoys wide support among partisans. Internal elements that condition the Speaker's influence are the configuration of forces within the House, such as the size and cohesiveness of the majority party, the diffusion of power among members, and the autonomy of committees.

A prominent scholarly theory that applies the principal-agent model, called conditional party government, suggests that when rank-and-file partisans share common policy views and confront an opposition party with sharply different substantive perspectives, then these dual conditions favor strong centralized leadership. Rank-and-file partisans empower their party leaders to advance an agenda that nearly all of them support and, conversely, oppose conflicting policies advocated by the other party. As the two leading proponents of the theory state:

> These two considerations—preference homogeneity [or policy agreement within parties] and preference conflict [or policy disagreement between parties]—together form the "condition" in the theory of conditional party government. As they increase, the theory predicts that party members will be progressively more willing to create strong powers for leaders and to support the exercise of those powers in specific instances. But when diversity grows within parties, or the differences between parties are reduced, members will be reluctant to grant greater powers to leaders. This is the central prediction of [conditional party government].[33]

A dynamic interaction exists between context and style that is often hard to untangle. Both factors shape to varying degrees the limits and possibilities of leadership.

Floor Leaders

The Speaker's principal deputy—the majority leader—is the party's floor leader. Elected every two years by secret ballot of the party caucus, the floor leader is not to be confused with a floor manager. The floor managers, usually two for each bill, are frequently the chairman and ranking minority member of the committee that reported the bill. They try to steer the bill to a final decision.

The House majority leader is usually an experienced legislator. When Tom DeLay took the post at the start of the 108th Congress (2003–2005), he had served in the House for eighteen consecutive years. He was elected majority whip when Republicans took control of the House following the November 1994 elections. As majority whip, DeLay established himself as perhaps the most effective party whip in the House's history and the chamber's most influential Republican, except for Gingrich. When Gingrich departed the House, DeLay mobilized his formidable whip organization to line up speakership support first for Livingston and then for Hastert—DeLay's chief deputy whip.

Nicknamed "The Hammer" by colleagues for his combative style—"I fight for what I believe in and I don't back off"—DeLay is proficient at what is known as multitasking.[34] He is an accomplished vote counter and enforcer, an aggressive campaign fund-raiser, a skillful coordinator of the party's connections to K Street (a street in the District of Columbia where numerous lobbying firms have their offices), and a shrewd campaign activist. During the November 2002 elections, for instance, DeLay formed the Strategic Taskforce to Organize and Mobilize People (STOMP), a highly successful get-out-the-vote initiative. STOMP raised millions of dollars to bus GOP "volunteers from safe congressional districts to ones where Republicans face a fight." [35]

A mark of his vote mobilization skills occurred after Majority Leader Dick Armey, R-Texas, announced on December 12, 2001, his retirement from the House at the end of the 107th Congress. Within thirty-six hours, DeLay had lined up the votes to succeed him. DeLay's backing also secured top leadership posts in the 108th House for two protégés: Roy Blunt, R-Mo., as majority whip, and Deborah Pryce, R-Ohio, as chair of the GOP Conference, the fourth ranking party position and the highest leadership post ever occupied by a woman in the majority party. As one conservative analyst exclaimed, "Everyone now in leadership basically was put there by [DeLay]." [36]

By modern custom, neither the Speaker nor the Democratic or Republican floor leader chairs committees. Sometimes there are exceptions. During the 107th Congress (2001–2003), Majority Leader Armey chaired the Select Committee on Homeland Security, which reported the bill signed into law by President Bush creating the Department of Homeland Security. The majority and minority leaders, as well as the Speaker, may serve on formal or informal task forces or panels. For example, the Speaker and minority leader are ex officio members of the Permanent Select Intelligence Committee.

House and party rules are largely silent about the majority leader's duties. By tradition, the primary duties are to be principal floor defender, negotiator, and spokesman for the party. "The role of the majority leader puts you in a spokesman role, but I won't be a show horse," declared Majority Leader DeLay.[37] The majority leader helps to plan the daily, weekly, and annual legislative agendas; consults with members to gauge sentiment on legislation; coordinates chamber action with the majority party floor manager and other party leaders; confers with the president about administrative proposals, particularly when the president is of the same party; urges colleagues to support or defeat measures; and, in general, works to advance the purposes and programs of the majority party. As one majority leader said: "The Majority Leader has prime responsibility for the day-to-day working of the House, the schedule, working with the committees to keep an eye out for what bills are coming, getting them scheduled, getting the work of the House done, making the place function correctly." He added: "[Y]ou are also compelled to try to articulate to the outside world what [your party stands] for, what [your party is] fighting for, what [your party is] doing." [38]

The minority leader is the floor leader of the loyal opposition. (Speakers assume that role for the majority.) Like the Speaker, these party leaders bring different styles to their roles. In general, the minority leader promotes unity among party colleagues, monitors the progress of bills through committees and subcommittees, and forges coalitions with like-minded members of the opposition party. Bertrand Snell, R-N.Y., minority leader from 1931 to 1939, thus described the duties:

> He is spokesman for his party and enunciates its policies. He is required to be alert and vigilant in defense of the minority's rights. It is his function and duty to criticize constructively the policies and program of the majority, and to this end employ parliamentary tactics and give close attention to all proposed legislation.[39]

Perhaps the most important task of the minority leader is to work to win back majority control of the House. For example, Minority Leader Richard A. Gephardt, D-Mo. (1995–2003) campaigned for scores of partisan colleagues, raised millions of dollars for Democrats, persuaded senior Democrats not to retire but to run again, stymied GOP initiatives in the House, and worked to inspire his partisan troops. He even "appeared before [the Democratic] caucus in the war paint and breastplate of the Scottish freedom fighter William Wallace, highlighted in the movie 'Braveheart.'"[40] His efforts fell short. Thus, at the end of the November 2002 elections, when Democrats lost seats, Gephardt chose not to seek reelection as minority leader and to focus on running for president in 2004. (He also chose not to sit on any House committees both to concentrate on his race for the presidency and to open up choice committee slots for other Democrats.)

In his place, Democrats promoted their minority whip, Nancy Pelosi of California, to be their party leader.[41] An eight-term veteran of the House, her election made congressional history. She became the highest-ranking female in either the House or Senate ever to lead a political party. An exceptional fundraiser, tireless campaigner, shrewd party strategist, and telegenic personality, Pelosi is well known as a San Francisco liberal. Some analysts suggested that her selection would allow Republicans to cast her in a negative light as a poster child for liberal orthodoxy (gun control, for example) among swing voters. She responded: "I don't think [my Democratic colleagues] chose me as an outspoken San Francisco liberal. I think they chose me as a person who can lead the caucus to victory, as a person who can build coalitions among various segments of our caucus and as a person who represents various points of view within the caucus." [42]

Pelosi, to be sure, reflects mainstream Democratic views. As the conditional party model suggests, a conservative Nancy Pelosi could no more be elected party leader by the liberal-oriented Democratic caucus than a liberal Republican could be chosen Speaker by the conservative-dominated GOP Conference. Her victory underscores that colleagues believe she can accomplish the principal functions of any minority leader: party spokesperson, fundraiser, coalition builder, and deviser of a party agenda to catapult Democrats into the majority. "I've communicated to my colleagues," she said, "that safety and soundness are our issues—the safety of the American people and the soundness of our economy." [43]

The Whips

Another top elective party post is the whip. As the term implies, the duties of a whip are to encourage party discipline, count votes, and, in general, mobilize winning coalitions on behalf of partisan priorities. These objectives are accomplished primarily through persuasion and hard work and with the assistance of an efficient whip organization.

In recent years both parties have expanded their whip systems to include a variety of deputy, regional, or assistant whips who meet regularly to discuss issues and strategy. Naming more members as whips involves them in leadership decision making and gives them additional incentives to back their top leaders. With about a sixty-person GOP whip organization in the 108th Congress, headed by Majority Whip Blunt, it is feasible "to reach everybody in the [Republican] conference and deliver their votes when it counts." [44] Having more whips also ensures leadership representation for important party groups and broadens the party's appeal to outside constituencies.

For example, Blunt named sophomore Eric Cantor, Va., as his chief deputy whip—a once obscure position that has become a stepping-stone to higher party office. Cantor is the only Jewish Republican in the 108th House, and he brings both geographical balance and credibility in reaching out to a constituency that generally votes against Republicans. "We have a great opportunity to reach out to Jewish voters, and Eric's been doing that already," remarked Blunt. [45] Blunt also names the assistant whips, such as freshman Katherine Harris, the former Florida secretary of state who was a central figure in the 2000 presidential election.

Majority Whip Blunt and his chief deputy whip meet weekly with their deputy and assistant whips to count votes, share intelligence, and ensure that everything is being done to marshal support for GOP proposals. Blunt's main mission is to "grow the vote," working with lobbyists, trade associations, the

White House, and others to plan strategy on how best to reinforce the support of colleagues on key votes and to persuade reluctant lawmakers to vote for legislation they may not support. An effective public spokesperson and vote counter, Blunt is among a handful of Republicans touted as a potential future GOP Speaker when Hastert leaves the post.[46] (In 2003, in a successful House rules change advocated by Blunt, the House deleted the provision setting an eight-year term limit on service as Speaker. The idea was put in place when Gingrich became Speaker in 1995.)

Minority Whip Steny H. Hoyer of Maryland—who had failed twice in his quest to be party whip, including a 2001 loss to Nancy Pelosi—heads a large whip organization composed of about one-third of the Democratic members of the House. They assist Hoyer in vote counting, preparing alternatives to GOP programs, monitoring the interests and needs of party members, tracking the views of informal party groups, and devising party strategy. A centrist member skilled in consensus building, Hoyer assists Minority Leader Pelosi in developing a Democratic message that resonates with the party's base supporters and swing voters. He asserts, too, that Democrats need to be more aggressive in challenging the agenda of the Bush White House.

In terms of gathering votes, Hoyer does not wait until a bill is being debated on the floor. Instead, he starts "talking to members much earlier, when the [priority] bill is introduced." [47] Hoyer understands that Democratic victories are hard to come by in a House noted for the sharp ideological divide between the two parties. "In many instances, as the minority whip, it's how much you lose by" that measures success, he said. "But there are opportunities to prevail. There are opportunities to reach across the aisle" and attract votes for Democratic issues.[48]

Each party's whip prepares weekly whip notices advising members of the upcoming floor agenda. Because scheduling changes can occur frequently, Blunt issues "The Whipping Post," a one-page daily bulletin. It identifies the time when the House is to convene and when the last vote is expected; it spells out what action is to take place that day on the floor, in the Senate, and in selective committees; and it forecasts the next day's schedule of floor business.

Leaders of the Senate

Today's Senate, more than the House, is an institution that tolerates and even promotes individualism. Candidate-centered elections, the decline of partisan affiliation in the electorate, the proliferation of policy-oriented interest groups, the large role of money in campaigns, and the huge influence of the press and media in political life are among the factors that have led to today's individualistic Senate. Senators cherish their independence, which exacerbates the challenges faced by those elected to lead them. Unlike House leaders, Senate leaders lack the buttress of rules designed to expedite business and so must rely heavily on personal skills and negotiation with their colleagues.

Presiding Officers

The House majority's highest elected leader, the Speaker, presides over the House. By contrast, the Senate majority leader, the majority party's highest leader, almost never presides in the Senate chamber.

The Senate has three kinds of presiding officers. First, the constitutional president of the Senate is the vice president of the United States (see Figure 6-2). Except for ceremonial occasions, the vice president seldom presides over Senate sessions, and he can vote only to break—not make—a tie. When votes on major issues are expected to be close, party leaders make sure that the vice president is presiding so that he can break tie votes. Vice presidents experienced in the ways of Congress, such as former senators Al Gore (Bill Clinton), Dan Quayle (George Bush), and Walter F. Mondale (Jimmy Carter), can help bridge the gap between Capitol Hill and the White House.

Vice President Dick Cheney's congressional role looms especially large for President George W. Bush's administration and in the closely divided Senate. A former House Republican whip, chief of staff to President Gerald R. Ford, and defense secretary, Cheney is widely respected among lawmakers. He meets regularly with House and Senate Republicans and exercises significant influence in shaping legislation and developing floor strategy to move Bush's priorities through Congress. The real possibility of tie votes in the Senate underscores Cheney's position as the "101st senator" and means close coordination between Senate Republicans and the GOP-controlled executive branch. In an unprecedented action, Speaker Hastert provided Cheney with office space near the House chamber—the first time a vice president "has ever had space on both sides of the Capitol." [49] Another sign of Cheney's elevated Capitol Hill role is his establishment of a legislative liaison team focused on the House and Senate that is separate from the White House's congressional affairs office. [50] Both liaison operations coordinate and consult with each other.

Second, the Constitution provides for a president pro tempore to preside in the vice president's absence. In modern practice this constitutional officer is the majority party senator with the longest continuous service. Sen. Ted Stevens of Alaska, for example, became president pro tempore of the Republican-controlled 108th Senate. If Democrats reclaim majority control, then Sen. Robert C. Byrd, W. Va., would become the president pro tempore. By passing a simple resolution, the Senate sometimes appoints a deputy president pro tempore. This majority party official, who presides over the Senate in the absence of the vice president and president pro tempore, is part of the leadership group that meets periodically at the White House with the president.

Third, a dozen or so senators of the majority party, typically junior members, serve approximately half-hour stints each day as the presiding officer. The opportunity to preside helps newcomers become familiar with Senate rules and procedures.

Figure 6-2 Organization of the Senate, 108th Congress (2003–2005)

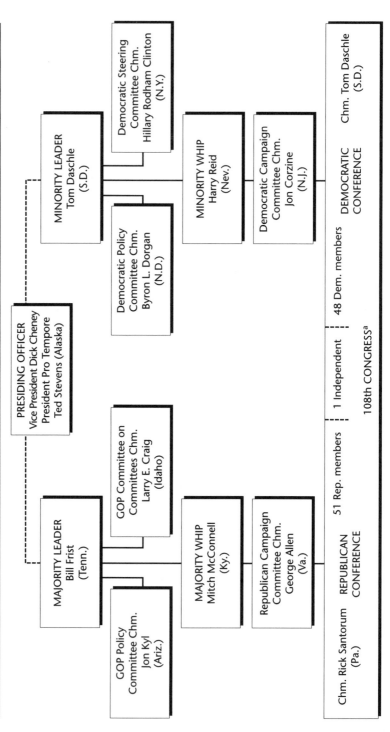

ᵃ As of February 2003.

Floor Leaders

The majority leader is the head of the majority party in the Senate, its leader on the floor, and the leader of the Senate. Similarly, the minority leader heads the Senate's minority party. (Nowadays, minority leaders prefer to be called "Republican leader" or "Democratic leader," as the case may be.) The majority and minority leaders are elected biennially by secret ballot of their party colleagues. Neither position is mentioned in the Constitution, and each is a relatively recent creation that dates from the early 1900s.

The Emergence of the Floor Leader. Historically, the Senate has always had leaders, but no single senator exercised central management of the legislative process in the fashion of today's floor leader. During the Senate's first century or so—especially in the 1790s and early 1800s, when there was no system of permanent standing committees or organized senatorial parties—leadership flowed from the personal talents and abilities of individual legislators. The small size of the early Senate and its tradition of viewing members as ambassadors from sovereign states promoted an informal and personal style of leadership.

Throughout the nineteenth century scores of prominent senators were called "leaders" by scholars and other observers. Some were sectional or factional leaders; others headed important committees (by the mid- to late 1840s committees and their chairmen had become centers of power); and still others (such as Henry Clay, John C. Calhoun, and Daniel Webster) exercised wide influence because of their special political, oratorical, or intellectual gifts. Even as late as 1885, however, Woodrow Wilson could write, "No one is *the Senator*. . . . No one exercises the special trust of acknowledged leadership." [51]

By the turn of the twentieth century the political landscape had changed. Party structures and leaders emerged as clearly identifiable forces in organizing and managing the Senate's proceedings. This important development occurred, according to a historian of the Senate, because of the influx of a "new breed" of senator who valued party unity and "the machinery of [party] organization," especially the party caucus. [52] Soon those senators who chaired their respective party caucuses acquired levers of authority over senatorial affairs. They chaired important party panels, shaped the Senate's agenda of business, and mobilized party majorities behind important issues. From the caucus chairmanship, scholars agree, the position of majority leader had informally emerged by 1913. [53]

Not until Lyndon B. Johnson (LBJ) became majority leader in 1955 was the post transformed into one of immense authority and prestige. [54] Considered by many analysts to be the most influential majority leader ever, the Texas Democrat had an extensive network of trusted aides and colleagues who made him better informed about more issues than any other senator. Opposition party control of the White House gave the aggressive Johnson the luxury of choosing which policies to support and which strategies to employ to get them enacted. And his pragmatic outlook, domineering style, and arm-twisting abilities made him the premier vote gatherer in the Senate. The majority leader's awesome display of face-to-face persuasion was called the Johnson Treatment.

> The Treatment could last ten minutes or four hours. It came, enveloping its target, at the LBJ Ranch swimming pool, in one of LBJ's offices, in the Senate cloakroom, on the floor of the Senate itself. . . . Its tone could be supplication, accusation, cajolery, exuberance, scorn, tears, complaint, the hint of threat. It was all of these together. It ran the gamut of human emotions. Its velocity was breathtaking, and it was all in one direction. Interjections from the target were rare. Johnson anticipated them before they could be spoken. He moved in close, his face a scant millimeter from his target, his eyes widening and narrowing, and his eyebrows rising and falling. From his pockets poured clippings, memos, statistics. Mimicry, humor, and the genius of analogy made The Treatment an almost hypnotic experience and rendered the target stunned and helpless.[55]

Buttressing Johnson was an inner club, a bipartisan group of senior senators, mainly southern Democrats such as Richard B. Russell, Ga., who was their leader. (A lawmaker of immense influence who endorsed Johnson as Democratic leader, the Russell Senate Office Building on Capitol Hill is named after the Georgia senator.) The club, observers said, wielded the real power in the Senate through its control of chairmanships and committee assignments.[56] Furthermore, unwritten rules of behavior (for example, junior members should be seen and not heard) encouraged new senators to defer to the establishment.

Every successor to Johnson as majority leader encounters a much different Senate from the one led by Johnson. Gone was the seniority-ruled, club-like, relatively closed Senate of old, ended largely by three key developments: (1) the influx of independent-minded and activist senators who wanted and expected to be major policy participants; (2) internal senatorial changes that promoted egalitarianism, such as the provision of staff resources to all members; and (3) external developments in the broader political environment (the twenty-four-hour news cycle, for instance).

Together, these developments led to an individualistic Senate where leaders are expected to serve members' personal needs and advance their individual agendas. As former majority leader Robert Byrd (1977–1981; 1987–1989) once remarked about the egalitarian, individualistic, assertive, independent, and C-SPAN-covered Senate, "Circumstances don't permit the Lyndon Johnson style. What I am saying is that times and things have changed. Younger Senators come into the Senate. They are more independent. The 'establishment' is a bad word. Each wants to do his 'own thing.' "[57] Unlike the demanding and aggressive Johnson, Byrd as majority leader referred to himself as "slave" to the needs of his senatorial colleagues.

Limits on Today's Leadership: Individualism and Partisanship. If individualism characterizes the post–Johnson Senate where activist members, under the Senate's permissive rules, can engage in extended debate, offer scores of amendments, and participate in any policy domain, another development added to the leader's difficulties in managing and processing the Senate's business: escalating partisanship. Why the uptick in partisanship? The bottom line: The conditional party government model discussed in the context of the House also marks the Senate. The two Senate parties have become, wrote journalist David Broder, "more cohesive internally and further apart from each other philosophically." [58] Or as Sen. Orrin G. Hatch, R-Utah, phrased it: "Today, most Democrats are far left; most Republicans are to the right; and there are very few in between." [59] The two Congresses theme is also in play as Democratic senators initiate and support policies backed by their core national constituencies (environmentalists, single women, gays, minorities, and union members, for instance) and Republican lawmakers do the same for their constituency base (the religious right, business owners, white males, rural Americans, gun owners, and pro-life advocates, for example).

Good indicators of heightened partisanship are the large number of party-line votes (a majority of Democrats facing off against a majority of Republicans) and the increase in party cohesion on those votes. For example, the percentage of party-line votes went from 39 percent in the 1970s to 58 percent in the 1990s. Even more striking is the growth in cohesion—call it discipline or philosophical agreement—within both party caucuses. In the 1970s, on partisan roll calls, the average member of Congress backed the party position 65 percent of the time. In the 1980s, the average degree of partisan loyalty rose to 73 percent; and in the 1990s to 81 percent. In 2001 and 2002, it has been 87 percent.[60] Other factors, too, contributed to more partisanship in the Senate, such as a decline in the number of centrists who acted as bridge-builders between the two parties.

What all this means for the majority leader is extraordinary difficulty in achieving consensus to enact legislation and approve nominations. Any senator has awesome parliamentary powers to stymie action, which puts a premium on the leader's skill in deal making, negotiating, and compromising. Absent formidable leadership tools to exert tight control over chamber proceedings, leaders rely heavily on patience, perseverance, personal ties, and, on occasion, procedural hardball to try and move legislation. Yet if one or more senators decide to filibuster (extended debate) a matter, the leader needs sixty votes to invoke a procedure called cloture (closure of debate) if he is to provide the Senate with an opportunity to vote on the measure or matter. As former majority leader Trent Lott, R-Miss. (1996–June 2001), stated:

> It's a tough job [being majority leader], and it has gotten tougher and tougher. Part of it is that now you don't need 50 votes—you've got to have 60 votes. The filibuster and cloture used to be used occasionally for big issues. [In more recent years], it has become an instrument used on almost

every bill. You can have 51 votes, you can have 55 votes, but if you don't get 60 votes, [the bill] can die. And it is very hard to dredge up 60 votes.[61]

Dredging up sixty votes is especially taxing given partisan parity within the Senate and in the country at large. With intense electoral competition the order of the day, each party carefully assesses how legislative actions—or inactions—may affect the next election and majority control of the chamber. One party, for instance, may block action on a bill to prevent the other from claiming a legislative victory. The tenuousness of party control in the 107th Congress (2001–2003) produced a number of unexpected developments, several of which affected the 108th Congress. Consider the number of times the majority leadership shifted back and forth between the two parties.

When the 107th Senate convened on January 3, 2001, it was equally divided between Democrats and Republicans. For its first seventeen days, Democrat Tom Daschle of South Dakota was the majority leader. With Vice President Al Gore still presiding and able to break tie votes until Republican Dick Cheney took the oath of office on January 20—the constitutional date set for the inauguration of the president and vice president—Daschle was in charge of running the Senate.

With Cheney as president of the Senate, Republican Lott became the majority leader. He and Daschle then negotiated an historic 50–50 power sharing agreement. Among other things, the agreement provided for an equal number of Democrats and Republicans on all Senate committees; an equal division of office space and staff; and a commitment by the two leaders to schedule measures of prime importance to each party.[62]

On May 24, 2001, moderate senator Jim Jeffords of Vermont announced that he was changing his party affiliation from Republican to Independent and caucusing with the Democrats for organizational purposes. Jeffords was unhappy with the conservative direction of GOP policy. Officially, Democrats became the majority party on June 5, 2001, with Daschle back as majority leader and Lott as minority leader. The shift in party control ended the 50–50 power sharing agreement, and another arrangement was negotiated between the two party leaders. Consented to on June 29, 2001, it stated, for example, that Democrats would have a one-seat majority on all Senate committees except Ethics, which is always divided equally between the parties. Majority Leader Daschle said of the Jeffords switch: "We have just witnessed something that has never happened before in all of Senate history—the change of power during a session of Congress." [63] An angry Lott blamed Jeffords for staging a "coup of one" to give Democrats control of the Senate.[64] However, now sensitized to the concerns of moderate Republicans, Lott created a new leadership post and appointed moderate senator Arlen Specter, R-Pa., to it.

Following the November 2002 elections in which Republicans won control of the Senate, Congress reconvened in a lame duck session. It began November 12 and ended November 20. Daschle remained majority leader because the newly elected senators would not be sworn in until January 3, 2003. Because Dean Barkley—named by Minnesota's governor to replace Democratic senator Paul Wellstone, who died in a plane crash days before the November election—chose not to affiliate with either party during the lame duck session, the party makeup of 49 Democrats, 49 Republicans, 1 Independent, and Barkley meant that Daschle stayed on as majority leader. If the lame duck session had lasted longer, the post of majority leader would have shifted on November 23 "when papers arrived from Missouri certifying Republican Jim Talent as the winner of a special election" to fill the unexpired Senate term of Democrat Mel Carnahan, who although deceased was still elected to the Senate in the November 2000 election by Missouri's voters. His widow, Jean Carnahan, had been appointed to the Senate by Missouri's governor, and she lost in the special election to Talent. As further icing on the cake for Senate Republicans, newly elected Alaska governor Frank H. Murkowski named his daughter, Lisa Murkowski, to fill his unexpired Senate term. She was sworn in on December 20, 2002. Never before had a senator been appointed by her father.

On November 13, 2002, Trent Lott was unanimously reelected by his GOP colleagues to be majority leader of the 108th Senate composed of 51 Republicans, 48 Democrats, and Independent Jeffords. Three weeks later, on December 5, 2002, Lott made racially charged comments at retiring GOP South Carolina senator Strom Thurmond's one hundredth birthday party. Lott praised Thurmond's 1948 run for the presidency on a segregationist Dixiecrat platform. A political firestorm developed as Lott's remarks were denounced by many in his party, including President Bush (who, many believe, quietly orchestrated Lott's eventual ouster). In a case of an agent (Lott) damaging the political expectations and legislative goals of the principals (rank-and-file Republicans), momentum built for Lott to step down as party leader even though he apologized five times for his comments. Lott had become a liability to his party. On December 20, 2002, Lott announced his resignation as majority leader. (To ease his fall from power, Republicans elected Lott to be chair of the Committee on Rules and Administration.)

Three days after Lott's resignation, Senate Republicans elected, by acclamation, Tennessee senator Bill Frist as the new majority leader. In another history-making event, Frist became the first majority leader to be elected via a telephone conference call. GOP senators were scattered across the country and unable to convene quickly in Washington. The Senate's only physician (a practicing heart surgeon), Frist enjoys close relations with the White House and received help from President Bush to succeed Lott. As chair of the GOP senatorial campaign committee, Frist worked closely with White House political strategist Karl Rove to devise the electoral game plan that led to the Republican senatorial victory in November 2002.

Majority Leader Frist's job in leading a closely divided Senate will not be easy. He is an untested party leader with limited procedural and senatorial experience, first winning election in 1994 and promising to serve only two terms in the Senate. Frist noted: "The frustration here of needing 60 votes" to get action on almost anything that becomes controversial "requires collaboration, reaching out, negotiation." [65] An observation made by Senator Daschle when he became majority leader of the 107th Senate applies equally well to Frist's leadership of the 108th Senate: "You still have the close division of philosophies, so I don't think anything becomes easier. The only thing that radically changes is who sets the agenda." [66]

Minority Leader. The Senate minority leader consults continually with the majority leader, because the Senate operates fundamentally by consensus. To get things done typically requires cooperation across party lines. If a member of the president's party, the minority leader has the traditional duties of trying to carry out the administration's program and answering partisan criticisms of the president. If a member of the opposite party, the minority leader has to calculate when to cooperate and when to confront the president.

As minority leader, Daschle meets regularly with Senate Democrats and with his House counterpart to develop and communicate a party agenda (assignments made harder without the bully pulpit of the White House), coordinate strategy, craft policy alternatives, devise tactics to block or modify Republican initiatives, and promote his party's political interests. The minority leader is always searching for ways to win back control of the Senate. Daschle was successful in this quest when he encouraged GOP senator Jeffords to leave the Republican Party, turning control over to the Democrats. He was unsuccessful, however, in holding the Senate for Democrats in the November 2002 elections despite expending enormous effort and enduring personal attacks in many GOP campaigns. "It's time for Congressional Republicans," wrote a GOP political consultant, "to personalize the individual that is standing directly in the way of economic security, energy security, and even national security. Remember what the Democrats did to Gingrich? We need to do exactly the same thing to Daschle." [67]

Party Whips. The Senate's whip system carries out functions that are similar to those of the House's system, such as counting noses before crucial votes and fostering party consensus. When Mitch McConnell, R-Ky., became majority whip at the start of the 108th Congress, he brought energy, organization, and coordination to the GOP's whip system of deputy and regional whips. A seasoned parliamentary tactician who for years almost single-handedly blocked Senate action on campaign finance reform, McConnell's focus is on day-to-day floor operations. "I'll be on the floor a lot," he said, "trying to make the trains run on time, which is always difficult in the Senate, as well as handling the traditional role of the whip, which is trying to win votes. And that means not only Republicans, but Democrats as well." [68]

Harry Reid of Nevada is the Democrats' second in command. He heads a whip structure that includes a chief deputy whip and four regionally appointed deputy minority whips. Reid's primary objectives are to ensure party unity, devise party strategy, defend the floor against GOP criticisms of the Democratic Party, and assist his party's leader. Daschle has delegated to Reid major responsibility for managing and coordinating day-to-day Democratic floor actions. Reid "will help line up speakers and coordinate with the GOP on the scheduling of debate and amendments. He also will fill in for the Democratic floor manager of a bill who has to leave the chamber." [69]

Selection of Leaders

Before the beginning of each new Congress, senators and representatives elect their top leaders by secret ballot in their party caucuses. Although the whole House votes for the Speaker, the election is a pro forma one. With straight party voting the unspoken rule on this and other organizational matters, the majority party has always elected the Speaker.

Since the 1980s candidates for party leadership positions have usually waged elaborate campaigns to win support from their partisan colleagues. Occasionally, last-minute entrants successfully bid for leadership positions. But whether short or long, campaigns for party leadership positions are intense. Members understand that a party leadership post can be a "career launching pad . . . either within the [Congress] or outside it." [70]

The two parties treat their hierarchies differently in the House: the Democrats as something like a ladder and the Republicans as a slippery slope. Democrats have a history of elevating their next-in-line officer—from whip to majority leader to Speaker—as vacancies occur. Republicans have a history of pushing people off the leadership track because of turmoil in their ranks. For example, in 1959 Charles A. Halleck of Illinois ousted Joseph W. Martin Jr. of Massachusetts as the GOP leader; in 1965 Gerald R. Ford of Michigan turned the tables on Halleck; in 1980 John J. Rhodes of Arizona was persuaded by his colleagues to step down as party leader; and in 1994 Robert H. Michel of Illinois retired in the face of Gingrich's stated intention to challenge him.

Seniority in Congress is only one of many criteria that influence the election of party leaders. Other considerations are ideological or geographical balance within the leadership; parliamentary expertise; competency in organizational matters; skill in forging winning coalitions; fund-raising prowess; communication skills; sensitivity to the mood of the membership; and personal attributes, such as intelligence, fairness, persuasiveness, political shrewdness, and media savvy.

Serving as a party leader in the House is typically a full-time position, although top party leaders sometimes serve ex officio or in some other capacity on committees. By contrast, every party leader in the Senate sits on several committees. The smaller size of the Senate allows leaders to participate in committee work while discharging their leadership duties. For example, in the 108th Senate, Frist, McConnell, Daschle, and Reid each served on several standing committees.

Leadership Activities

House and Senate leaders have basically the same job: to bring coherence, direction, and efficiency to a largely decentralized and individualistic legislative body. Leadership duties can be described in terms of institutional maintenance (ensuring that Congress and its members perform their lawmaking and oversight duties effectively and preserving Congress's reputation and integrity) and party maintenance (crafting winning coalitions among partisan colleagues and providing assistance to their members).[71] Both kinds of general functions point toward the parties' objectives of influencing policy making in conformity with their political leanings. Leaders, too, are expected to boost their partisan colleagues electorally through strategic and tactical actions designed to win them majority control of their chamber. As journalist David Broder said about Speaker Hastert: "[He] has gained stature among his colleagues because he has managed the agenda to their benefit and because he has been assiduous in campaigning for them in their districts." [72]

Institutional Tasks

From an institutional perspective, party leaders have a number of obligations associated with their positions. Most of these assignments devolved formally upon party leaders. They are provided with extra staff resources beyond those accorded individual lawmakers to assist in carrying out these diverse responsibilities.

Organizing the Chamber. Party leaders influence congressional organization and procedure. They select the chief administrative officers of the House or Senate, oversee committee jurisdictional revisions, and revise congressional rules. In 1995 Speaker Gingrich backed the abolition of three standing committees. In 1999 Speaker Hastert supported a major recodification of House rules, the first since 1880. Four years later he supported creation of a new Select Committee on Homeland Security to oversee the newest cabinet department. In the Senate, Daschle and Lott twice had to make crucial power-sharing decisions in the 107th Congress. The first agreement was reached when the Senate was evenly divided, and the second came after Senator Jeffords bolted the Republican Party and shifted majority control to the Democrats.

At the start of the 108th Congress, Frist and Daschle had to hammer out an accord over how to divide committee funds between Republicans and Democrats and how to allocate committee space between the parties. Republicans argued that a Senate precedent dating from the 1970s entitled them to two-thirds of committee funds, space, and staff with minority Democrats receiving one-third. Daschle insisted, however, that committee resources in the 108th Congress be split proportionately as they were in the 107th Senate. Lacking control of any elective branch, Democrats need the extra staff and financial resources to challenge the majority Republicans and the Bush White House. Democrats threatened to filibuster the Senate's organizing resolution (designating committee leaders and members) until their demands were met. Until the organizing resolution was agreed to, Frist was recognized by the presiding officers as the majority leader but Democrats continued to chair the committees and new members were without committee assignments. In the end, funding for the committees was apportioned on a 51–49 basis with GOP committee chairmen getting "an additional 10 percent for administrative expenses." [73]

Scheduling Floor Business. "The power of the Speaker of the House is the power of scheduling," Speaker O'Neill once declared. [74] Or, as Newt Gingrich put it, "When you are Speaker you get to set the agenda. . . . [Y]ou get to decide what legislation is up." [75] After consulting with committee leaders, interested members, the president, and others, House and Senate party leaders decide what, when, and in which order measures should come up for debate. Setting the chamber's agenda and schedule is perhaps the single most important prerogative of the Speaker and Senate majority leader.

Once a bill is scheduled for action, the leaders' job is to see that members vote—a task more difficult than merely herding bodies into the chamber. Party leaders may seek out certain members to speak on an issue because their endorsement can persuade other legislators to support it. Or they may delay action until the bill's sponsors are present. "The leadership must have the right members at the right place at the right time," said Byrd when he was the Senate majority whip. [76] In short, the leaders' scheduling prerogatives mold policy; arranging the time that bills reach the floor can seal their fate. A week's delay in scheduling a controversial White House initiative, for instance, gives the president, lobbying groups, and others additional time to mobilize votes for the proposal.

Legislative business is also scheduled with forthcoming elections in mind. Measures are postponed to avoid an electorally embarrassing defeat or, alternatively, they are brought to the floor to satisfy groups allied with each party. What better time to take up legislation revamping the Internal Revenue Service or a constitutional amendment affecting the internal revenue code than on or around April 15, the filing deadline for federal income taxes? The period close to July 4 is also popular for scheduling consideration of constitutional amendments banning the desecration of the American flag. Both parties commonly use the floor as an election platform to raise issues that appeal to their outside partisans. When it passes measures advocated by its electoral base, a party can say, "Look what we did for you." Conversely, a party that fails to pass a measure can say to its bedrock supporters, "Look what we tried to do."

Influencing Colleagues. Party leaders also have the task of persuading members to support their legislation. In the modern Congress arm-twisting means pleading and cajoling to coax votes. "If you have no sense of what other people's judgments, values or goals are," stated Representative Foley, who served as Speaker from 1989 to 1995, about the negotiating process, "you're in a very poor position to evaluate how you might accommodate them." [77] Although leaders generally seek to influence members of their own party and chamber, they also try to win cooperation from the other chamber and from the opposition party. Senate GOP leader Frist and Speaker Hastert, and their top aides, meet regularly to coordinate agendas, priorities, and strategies. Frequent meetings between Pelosi and Daschle, the two Democratic leaders, to coordinate political, policy, and public relations strategies are more important than ever because they lack the megaphone of a Democratic president.

Party leaders do not have to rely solely on their powers of persuasion, however. Informal political networks and access to strategic information give them an edge in influencing colleagues.

> Because of an improved whip system and because members will respond more candidly to leadership polls than to lobbyist or White House polls, [leaders] have perhaps the most important information in a legislative struggle—information on where the votes are and (sometimes) what it will take to win certain people over.[78]

Top leaders also can bestow or withhold a variety of tangible and intangible rewards, such as naming legislators to special or select committees, influencing assignments to standing committees, aiding reelection campaigns, and smoothing access to the White House or executive agencies.

Consulting the President. A traditional duty of party leaders is to meet with the president to discuss the administration's goals and to convey legislative sentiment about what the executive branch is doing or not doing. This consultative duty is performed mainly by leaders of the president's party. Presidents also consult with opposition leaders and the joint bipartisan leadership of the House and Senate. President Bush, for instance, periodically has the joint bipartisan leadership to the White House to discuss issues such as the global war on terrorism and his domestic economic policy plans.

Party Tasks

From a party perspective, congressional party leaders have a number of formal and informal responsibilities. Formally, the rules of each party specify certain roles and responsibilities for their leaders. Parliamentary precedents and chamber rules also assign certain duties to party leaders. Informally, party leaders have assumed a wide range of duties, such as devising and implementing strategic decisions.

Organizing the Party. Congressional leaders help to organize their party by selecting partisan colleagues for standing committees, revising party rules, choosing other party leaders, appointing party committees, and influencing policy formation. Two examples serve as illustrations. First, House minority leader Pelosi named fellow Californians Robert T. Matsui to chair the Democratic Congressional Campaign Committee and Jane Harman to be the ranking Democrat on the Permanent Select Intelligence Committee. Second, House majority leader DeLay was instrumental in winning the chairmanship of the House Resources Committee for Richard W. Pombo, Calif., who leap-frogged over several more senior Republicans on the panel to gain the post. "This is the guy DeLay wanted," said Rep. Joel Hefley, R-Colo.[79]

Promoting Party Unity. Another leadership assignment is to encourage party unity in Congress on priority legislation. Everett Dirksen (minority leader, 1959–1969) used social gatherings to accomplish this goal.

> Dirksen brought party members together in a series of social affairs. He held cocktail parties at a Washington country club, inviting all Republican senators and sometimes their wives too. These were calculated by Dirksen to improve party harmony and to build a friendly feeling for himself with the Republican senators.[80]

Party leaders' assistance to the rank and file goes far beyond extending them social invitations. Leaders schedule members' bills, provide them with timely political information, advise them on electoral issues, visit with their constituents, help them obtain good committee assignments, and work with them to forge policy agendas. "You really have to make people feel part of the process, and I guess it is a little bit like a shepherd," remarked Senator Daschle. "You really want to keep as much as you can the flock together, and that takes different approaches with different people." [81] Periodically, leaders organize partisan retreats where members discuss party and policy goals, consider specific legislative initiatives, air differences, and resolve disputes.

Publicizing Party Views. Leaders are expected to publicize their party's policies and achievements. They give speeches in various forums, appear on radio and television talk shows, write newspaper and journal articles, hold press conferences, organize town meetings around the country, and establish Web sites that highlight party issues and images. Leaders are also expected to develop public relations strategies that neutralize the opposition's arguments and proposals. The spokesperson's role has increased in importance in recent years in part because of the political effect of the mass media. "We've created a situation," noted a scholar, "where the real way you drive the legislative process is by influencing public opinion, rather than by trading for votes." [82]

The House Republican Conference, like the other party caucuses on Capitol Hill, provides its members with talking points for meetings with journalists or constituents. (The Bush White House also provides House and Senate Republicans with talking points and themes so party members are all sending a unified public message.) These party units often create communications teams that meet regularly to discuss message and delivery and to recommend their more telegenic members to present party positions on television. "We're focused on making sure we deliver the [party] message both here in Washington and out in the hinterlands," said Sen. Rick Santorum, Pa., chairman of the Senate Republican Conference.[83]

Providing Campaign Assistance. Leaders must be energetic campaigners and fund-raisers on behalf of their partisan colleagues. They assist party incumbents and challengers in raising campaign funds. They establish their own leadership PACs, such as DASHPAC after Senator Daschle, to raise money and donate it to candidates of their party. They help to raise large sums of money so issue ads can be run on television in the months leading up to the November elections. They travel to numerous House districts or states to campaign with either incumbents or challengers of their party. They encourage outside groups to raise money for the party. They also develop ways to boost the re-election chances of their partisan colleagues, such as creating working groups to provide members running for reelection with greater public exposure.[84]

Members anticipating a run for a leadership post distribute campaign funds as standard operating practice. As one account noted about a party leader's ability to raise money, "It seems that the job of fundraiser is becoming more important to senators' expectations of what a majority leader should do. The candidates [for this leadership position] thus are not trying to buy votes so much as to demonstrate how well they can fulfill that role." [85] The ability to raise funds for colleagues is an increasingly important criterion for judging prospective party leaders and another reminder that leaders stand at the conjunction of the two Congresses: the representative assembly, where money is needed to join, and the lawmaking body, where power calls the shots.

Party Caucuses, Committees, and Informal Groups

House and Senate leaders operate in different institutional contexts. In the larger, more impersonal House, majority party leaders sometimes ignore the wishes of the minority party. This seldom happens in the Senate, which emphasizes individualism, minority rights, reciprocity, and mutual accommodation. Despite these differences between parties in the House and Senate, they are organized into the same three components: caucuses, committees, and informal party groups.

Party Caucuses

The organization of all partisans in a chamber is called the conference or (in the case of House Democrats) the caucus. Party conferences or caucuses elect leaders, approve committee assignments, provide members with services, debate party and legislative policies, encourage party unity, appoint task forces or issue teams, develop themes to keep members on message, enable members to vent their frustrations, and discuss outreach programs that appeal to voters. In an explanation that applies equally well to how the caucus in both parties and chambers can serve to promote consensus on issues, a senior House Democrat said:

The caucus is the place where a great deal of freewheeling debate over an issue takes place and where sometimes a consensus develops. . . . Most of the discussions, although they have taken place at leadership meetings and at chairmen's meetings and in whips' meetings, have ended up in the broader forum of the caucus where every member of the Democratic party participates. You don't take a vote, but you try to develop a consensus and make concessions where they're necessary and develop the strongest possible position that can be supported by the maximum number of Democrats.[86]

In brief, party caucuses are useful forums where party members and leaders can assess and sway sentiment on substantive or procedural issues. On rare occasions, party caucuses vote to strip members of their committee seniority or to oust committee leaders. Committee leaders are removed from their posts when legal action is taken against them (for example, if they are indicted). Sometimes presidents attend their party's House or Senate caucus to rally the troops as President George W. Bush did soon after taking office before an unprecedented joint session of the House and Senate GOP Conferences. In another unprecedented action, Bush spoke at retreats of House and Senate Democrats to win backing for his agenda and to promote productive relationships.[87]

Party Committees

Each of the four congressional parties—Senate and House Democrats, Senate and House Republicans—establishes committees to serve partisan needs and objectives (see Table 6-1). Three of the four parties on Capitol Hill have policy committees, for example. House Democrats disbanded their policy committee at the direction of Minority Leader Pelosi. In its place, she established a revamped Steering Committee, which has a policy part (headed by George Miller of California) and a committee assignment component (chaired by Rosa DeLauro of Connecticut).[88] The committees do not make policy, but they provide advice on scheduling, encourage party unity, research substantive and political issues, distribute policy papers, track party votes on issues, and discuss and implement party policy. Their influence has varied over the years, assuming greater importance when the party does not control the White House and thus needs policy guidance. The two Senate and House GOP policy committees maintain Web sites that party members and staff can access at any time for pertinent information. Other important party panels are the campaign and committee assignment committees.

Informal Party Groups

In addition to party committees, a variety of informal groups operate on Capitol Hill. House and Senate leaders also employ party task forces to devise policy alternatives, formulate strategy, and coordinate floor action. In 2003 there were more than two hundred informal groups on Capitol Hill. They are

Table 6-1 Party Committees in the Senate and House

Committee	Approximate number of members	Function
Senate Democratic		
Policy	20	Considers party positions on specific measures and assists the party leader in scheduling bills
Steering and Coordination	18	Assigns Democrats to committees and works to coordinate policy, legislative, and message issues for the Democratic Conference
Campaign	14	Works to elect Democrats to the Senate
Technology and Communications	11	Promotes internal and external communications among Democrats
Senate Republican		
Policy	26	Provides summaries of GOP positions on specific issues; researches procedural and substantive issues; drafts policy alternatives
Committee on Committees	9	Assigns Republicans to committees
Campaign	6	Works to elect Republicans to the Senate
House Democratic		
Steering	36	Assists the leadership and Democratic Caucus in establishing, implementing, researching, and communicating party priorities; assigns Democrats to committees
Campaign	40	Aids in electing Democrats to the House
House Republican		
Policy	39	Considers policy alternatives to majority proposals and works for consensus among Republican members
Steering	29	Assigns Republicans to standing committees
Campaign	31	Seeks to elect Republicans to the House

Note: The official names of the parties' campaign committees are as follows: Democratic Senatorial Campaign Committee, National Republican Senatorial Committee, Democratic Congressional Campaign Committee, and National Republican Congressional Committee. The sizes of these panels vary over time.

partisan or bipartisan, unicameral or bicameral in composition, and have names such as the boating, steel, mining, soybean, rural health, electricity, automotive, children's, bicycle, or Internet caucus.

The close party division in the 108th Congress strengthens the ability of different party groups to sway voting outcomes. "I think we could be the deciding factor" in shaping policy outcomes in the 108th Congress, stated moderate senator John B. Breaux, La., a leader of the Senate's New Democrat Coalition.[89] Informal groups also influence public opinion. When President Bush in early 2003 renominated Charles Pickering Sr. of Mississippi to a federal appeals court judgeship—Pickering had been turned down for the position in March 2002 by the Democratically controlled Judiciary Committee—the Congressional Black Caucus announced its dismay with the White House nomination, particularly given the racially insensitive remarks of Mississippi senator Lott at Strom Thurmond's one hundredth birthday party a few weeks earlier. The House has many other party groups, such as the moderate Republican Tuesday Group, the conservative Republican Study Committee, the centrist New Democrat Coalition, and the Blue Dog coalition (fiscally conservative Democrats).

Party Continuity and Change

Several features of the contemporary party system on Capitol Hill stand out. Among these features are the vigor of the congressional parties, the persistence of the two-party system, and the advent of new coalition-building practices.

Vigorous Congressional Parties

By any test one can use, the four Capitol Hill parties are flourishing. The organizational elements are healthy and active, leaders are increasingly prominent, and party voting is at relatively high levels. The congressional parties are assisted by well-staffed and professional congressional campaign committees whose ultimate task is either to win or to keep majority control of the House or Senate.[90] These campaign panels recruit and train candidates, raise money, engage in research on the opposition party, target competitive districts, furnish polling advice and services, develop election strategies, and, in general, do everything they can to support congressional campaigns by their party's candidates.[91]

Demographic factors also contribute to the vigorous partisanship on Capitol Hill. Constituency changes in the South have led to the election of Democrats who are more ideologically compatible with their party colleagues from the rest of the country. The once prominent conservative coalition of Republicans and southern Democrats no longer is an important voting bloc in Congress. The South, as recent elections have shown, is now largely in the GOP camp. For the first time since Reconstruction, more lawmakers from the South are Republicans than Democrats. Meanwhile, the disappearance of liberal "Rockefeller Republicans" from GOP ranks has led to the dominance of conservative lawmakers in that party. (House redistricting also plays a role in heightened partisanship as many lawmakers represent constituencies filled predominately with Democratic or GOP voters.)

In addition, the electoral element triggers trench warfare between the two parties. Recent highly competitive elections have demonstrated that neither party has been able to solidify its hold on the House or Senate. Both legislative parties jockey to win public credit for their agenda and issue positions and to block the goals and aims of the opposition. As one congressional scholar put it:

> We can no longer try to understand congressional behavior simply as the pursuit of individual goals [such as reelection, gaining power, or making good policy]. Instead, we must also see how Republicans and Democrats seek the collective goal of majority status. In this sense, they resemble armies, which try to get their troops to subordinate their narrow self-interest to the good of the whole. [Thus, a key job of party leaders is] to rally the troops for electoral ground war.[92]

Further, as voting turnout has gone down, lawmakers from each party are more beholden to activists who vote in the primary and general elections. As a result, lawmakers may be reluctant to vote for bipartisan compromises that antagonize the vocal concerns of well-organized groups, such as the Christian Coalition, the National Rifle Association, or labor unions. As one analyst observed, moderate members of Congress in the Republican Party today,

> even popular incumbents who would win a general election by overwhelming margins, are hostage to the party's right wing. With few exceptions, they are vulnerable because of low turnouts in the primary elections, in which a relative handful of determined conservatives could oust the most popular incumbent while most voters are not paying attention.[93]

The heightened partisanship in Congress—fomented by the legislative and electoral prevalence of attack politics—motivates party leaders to demand, and often get, party loyalty on various votes. "Procedure is always a party vote," declared House GOP leader DeLay.[94] To reinforce that view, DeLay and Speaker Hastert have told GOP whips that "any lawmaker who votes against the leadership on a procedural matter will be booted from the whip team." [95]

By the 105th Congress (1997–1999) the rancorous partisan atmosphere had gotten so bad in the House (Speaker Gingrich and Minority Leader Gephardt, for instance, refused to speak to each other for a year) that a bipartisan group of lawmakers organized a weekend retreat in March 1997 for all members and their families. The so-called civility retreat was designed to allow members with different partisan viewpoints to get to know each other better. This result might then encourage them to work together on a bipartisan basis to resolve the nation's problems. Only marginal improvements flowed from this event. Three other civility retreats were held—in March 1999, March 2001, and March 2003—with similar limited improvements in comity among the members and between the parties, in part because of fundamental policy and ideological disagreements that often spark angry clashes and personal attacks. Episodes of sharp partisanship occur even in the usually sedate Senate. As Sen. Olympia J. Snowe, R-Maine, remarked, "The whole Congress has become far more polarized and partisan so it makes it difficult to reach bipartisan agreements. The more significant the issue, the more partisan it becomes." [96]

The call for bipartisanship is a common refrain among many lawmakers and pundits. An important issue, however, is who defines bipartisanship. There are at least two versions. First, there is the bipartisanship in which, as Senate majority whip McConnell stated, "some Democrats join Republicans to do things that Republicans would like to do." [97] Or as House majority leader DeLay phrased it: "We'll write conservative bills and ask the Democrats to participate" by providing votes. The other type requires the two parties to work together with the White House so that legislation reflects the views of both Democrats and Republicans. As conservative House Democrat Chris John, La., said: "We want to be involved on the front end, not just be counted on for votes after the legislation is written" by Republicans.[98]

There are virtues in sharp partisanship. For one, it enables voters to better comprehend the different views, values, and principles of the two parties. For another, party leaders sometimes prefer confrontation over bipartisan compromise as a way to minimize the need to make concessions to the other party and to underscore interparty differences. "Confrontation fits our strategy," stated Dick Cheney when he was in the House (1979–1989). "Polarization often has very beneficial results. If everything is handled through compromise and conciliation, if there are no real issues dividing us from Democrats, why should the country change and make us the majority?" [99] Partisanship, too, can either be policy- or process-oriented. Policy partisanship is when one of the two congressional parties advances substantive measures—so-called wedge issues or wedgislation (abortion rights or affirmative action, for instance)—to unite their own and to foment political divisions within the other party. Process partisanship involves efforts by party leaders to structure the procedural playing field to advance their own agenda and to stymie the other party's goals.[100] Process partisanship is easier to invoke in the majority-run House (assuming unity within the majority party) than in the Senate, where power is more evenly divided among all senators.

The Two-Party System

The Democratic and Republican parties have dominated American politics and Congress since the mid-nineteenth century. Scholars have posited various theories for the dualistic national politics of a country as diverse as the United States. Some trace the origins of the national two-party system to early conflicts between Federalists (advocates of a strong national government) and Antifederalists (advocates of limited national government). This dualism continued in subsequent splits: North versus South, East versus West, agricultural versus financial interests, and rural versus urban areas.[101] Constitutional, political, and legal arrangements are other bases of the two-party system. Plurality elections in single-member congressional districts encouraged the creation and maintenance of two major parties. Under the winner-take-all principle, the person who wins the most votes in a state or district is elected to the Senate or House. This principle discourages the formation of third parties. In addition, many states have laws that make it difficult to create new parties.

Whatever mix of causes produced the two-party system, one thing is clear: Few third-party or independent legislators have been elected to Congress during the last century. The high-water mark was the 63d Congress (1913–1915), which had one Progressive senator and nineteen representatives elected as Progressives, Progressive-Republicans, or independents. Since the post–World War II period, only a handful of lawmakers have been elected from minor parties or as independents.[102] Most legislators convert to one of the major parties or vote with them on procedural and substantive matters. The 108th Congress has two independents: Progressive representative Bernie Sanders, Vt., aligns with the Democrats and Senator Jeffords, I-Vt., caucuses with the Democrats. Third-party members have no institutional status. Their participation in Democratic or Republican matters is by invitation only.

Minor party candidates and independents can affect the outcome of congressional races and influence party control of the House or Senate. Ralph Nader, the 2000 Green Party presidential candidate, argues that the large Green Party turnout in the state of Washington enabled Democrat Maria Cantwell to defeat incumbent Republican senator Slade Gorton by twenty-three hundred votes. The "enormous Green spillover vote in Washington state," said Nader, "made a difference in her election over Sen. Slade Gorton and sent her as the 50th Democratic senator to the U.S. Senate, setting the stage for Sen. Jim Jeffords to hand the Senate over to the Democrats in June 2001." [103]

Advances in Coalition Building

To get the legislative results they desire, party leaders increasingly use media strategies, omnibus bills, and strategic planning. Procedural innovations also are important elements in the arsenal of the party leaders, such as multiple referrals, ad hoc task forces, creative rules from the House Rules Committee, and unanimous consent agreements in the Senate.

Media Strategies. Party leaders understand that media strategies (the use of the press, television, radio, polls, the Internet, speeches, and so on) are essential to move or block legislation. They form issue teams, message groups, or theme teams to orchestrate, organize, and coordinate political events and communications strategies that promote the party's message to the general public. No longer is the inside game—working behind the scenes to line up votes—sufficient to pass major, controversial measures. Also necessary is the outside game—influencing public opinion, coordinating with advocacy groups, and creating grassroots support for policy initiatives. Today, media and parliamentary strategies are complementary processes that both parties use to, among other things, raise issues, communicate with voters, define and frame priorities, or respond to partisan criticisms. For example, members of the House GOP theme team "remain close to the chamber during difficult votes, ready to stand up and either object or simply respond to Democratic charges" that Republicans are pushing costly or ineffective economic, or foreign policies.[104] Dueling news conferences may follow with each party blaming the other for irresponsible behavior.

Both congressional parties understand the importance of words as political weapons. GOP consultants found, for example, that characterizing the estate tax as the "death tax"—and having GOP officeholders repeat it again and again over several years—aroused public ire against the tax. This sentiment was instrumental in accomplishing the temporary repeal of the inheritance tax as part of President Bush's successful 2001 tax cut plan. Two years later, the president advocated the permanent demise of the "death tax." Playing off the title of the president's major educational enactment in the 107th Congress—the No Child Left Behind Act—Senator Daschle employed communications strategies as a way to undermine public support for the president's 2003 tax-cutting economic plan. He dubbed it the "Leave No Millionaire Behind Act." At a time when the nation is engaged in a war on terrorism, both parties employ "national security" as a way to advance their agenda. Congressional Republicans, for example, frame the debate over drilling for oil and gas in the Arctic National Wildlife Refuge (ANWR) as a way to reduce the nation's dependency on oil from the volatile Middle East and add that Bush's tax-cutting initiative is a way to strengthen "economic security." Democrats castigate Republicans for not spending more on homeland (recast as "home town") security, such as "border security," "port security," or "nuclear power plant security."

With President Bush having the megaphone of the White House to advance GOP initiatives, congressional Democrats understand that they lack a single messenger who can focus the nation's attention in the same manner as the president. As a result, they use the House and Senate floor and a wide variety of communications techniques to shape national debate. The two Democratic leaders—Pelosi and Daschle—hold press conferences, appear on diverse media outlets, organize town meetings, prepare talking points for the press (and their own members), develop party themes (bashing corporate corruption, for instance), write newspaper editorials, circulate data and statistics that skewer Republican proposals, organize policy forums, and engage in a variety of other actions to promote their legislative agenda to the public and to challenge GOP initiatives. As Senator Daschle said after Democrats returned to the minority after the November 2002 elections, "We are going to think a lot more [about] how we can more forcefully and more successfully get our message out." [105]

Omnibus Bills. A phenomenon of modern lawmaking is the rise of mega-bills—legislation that is hundreds or thousands of pages in length and which encompasses disparate policy topics. Many of Congress's most significant policy enactments are sometimes folded into four or five omnibus bills. There are many reasons that account for the use of these packages. For instance, some initiatives are incorporated into megabills to improve their chances of enactment. Bundling popular programs with painful spending cuts increases the chances of enacting megabills. This tactic limits the number of difficult votes lawmakers cast and provides them with political cover. Members can explain to angry constituents or groups that they had to support the indivisible whole because its discrete parts were not open to separate votes.

Joining several bills may increase the chances of garnering more support. (The reverse concern is that a megabill may attract a coalition of minorities with the votes needed to reject the measure.) Sweeteners can be added to woo supporters, or provisions that are unable to win majority support in stand-alone bills can be buried in megabills. Megabills can also strengthen Congress's leverage with the executive branch. Measures that presidents might veto if presented to them separately can be folded into megabills and be enacted in that fashion.

Party leaders command the resources and authority to exercise coordinative and substantive influence over the packaging process. "Omnibus bills place a huge amount of power in the hands of a few key leaders and their staffs," remarked one House member.[106] Rank-and-file members look to party leaders to formulate a package acceptable to at least a majority of members. However, these megabills sometimes arouse the ire of lawmakers. As one member said about their increasing prevalence, "These omnibus bills—often gauged more by weight than the number of pages—are abominations. No one member of Congress has a chance to read much of them, let alone under-stand7them, before they are voted on." [107]

Strategic Planning and Coordination. On major policy issues, strategic planning and coordination are crucial to the leadership's ability to forge successful coalitions. House and Senate leaders meet regularly with their partisan allies to craft their plans, to anticipate the legislative moves of the opposition, and to develop their countermoves. For example, party leaders employ defensive messages as a way to protect their members from political attack. The objective is to appropriate the other party's popular issues by blurring the distinctions between congressional Democrats and Republicans. For example, on an immigration reform issue, Democrats called their package the Latino and Immigrant Fairness Act; Republicans dubbed their initiative the Legal Immigration Family Equity Act.[108]

In the 108th Congress, congressional GOP leaders calculated that the House would take the lead on passing much of President Bush's legislative agenda. As Senate GOP Policy Committee chairman Jon Kyl, R-Ariz., stated: "The House has to initiate some things, like money bills, and because the Republican leadership in the House can control things better than the Republican leadership in the Senate, it will be the first to act on the president's agenda in some circumstances." [109] House Republican leaders call this strategy "willful triangulation." They plan to push some of Bush's policies beyond what he suggests—"compromising up," in the words of a GOP leadership aide—to ensure that legislation emerging from a House-Senate conference closely tracks the president's original recommendation. "We set the bar high to pass ambitious, bold legislation," the aide said, noting: "In the final analysis, we want to work down to the president's proposal and don't want [Bush's] plan to be watered down." [110]

Conclusion

Congressional parties have elaborate organizations, and their leaders fulfill a multiplicity of roles and duties. The Senate majority leader, explained Byrd when he held that post, "facilitates, he constructs, he programs, he schedules, he takes an active part in the development of legislation, he steps in at crucial moments on the floor, offers amendments, speaks on behalf of legislation and helps to shape the outcome of the legislation." [111] Party leaders can do many things, but they cannot command their colleagues. Their leadership rests chiefly on their skill in providing others with reasons to follow them.

The party principle organizes Congress. The committee principle, however, shapes the measures Congress acts upon. These two principles are often in conflict. The first emphasizes aggregation, the second fragmentation. Party leaders struggle to manage an institution that disperses policy-making authority to numerous work groups. In short, leaders provide the centripetal force to offset committees' centrifugal influence.

Three faces of committee work. Above, Secretary of State Colin Powell testifies at a hearing on the Iraq war. Sen. Olympia Snowe, R-Maine, consults with Sen. John Breaux, D-La., during a Finance Committee markup. Below, NASA Administrator Sean O'Keefe hands a document to his staff aides during a joint House-Senate hearing on the Columbia *space shuttle accident.*

7

Committees:
Workshops of Congress

Committees serve two broad purposes: individual and institutional. Individually, lawmakers look for ways from their committee perches to benefit their constituents. "As far as I can see, there is really only one basic reason to be on a public works committee," admitted a House member. "Intellectual stimulation" is not it. "Most of all, I want to be able to bring home projects to my district." [1] With scores of representatives seeking assignment to this panel, it has grown to be the largest (seventy-five members) in congressional history. Members of Congress understand the reelection connection between their committee assignments and their electoral opportunities.

Committees also enable legislators to utilize or develop expertise in areas that interest them. A former teacher, for instance, may seek assignment to the committee overseeing education policy. And some panels, such as the tax and appropriations power committees, enable members to wield personal influence among their colleagues. Members ask to be on the House Appropriations Committee, explained a GOP leader, because "instantaneously . . . they have a host of new friends, and we all know why"—that panel controls the distribution of discretionary federal money. [2]

Institutionally, committees are the centers of policy making, oversight of federal agencies, and public education (largely through the hearings they hold). By dividing their membership into a number of "little legislatures," the House and Senate are able to consider dozens of proposed laws simultaneously. [3] Without committees a legislative body of 100 senators and 440 House members could not handle roughly 10,000 bills and nearly 100,000 nominations biennially, a national budget over $2 trillion, and a limitless array of controversial issues. Although floor actions often refine legislation, committees are the means by which Congress sifts through an otherwise impossible jumble of bills, proposals, and issues.

Congressional committees serve another important institutional function in the political system. They act as safety valves, or outlets for national debates and controversies. Military and economic responsibilities, demographic shifts, trade agreements, global environmental concerns, the drug war, the social dislocations caused by technological advances, and the rising cost of health care place enormous strains on the political system. As forums for public debates, congressional committees help to vent, absorb, and resolve these strains. Moreover, the safety-valve function gives the citizenry a greater sense of participation in national decision making and helps educate members about public problems.

The individual and institutional purposes of the committee system can conflict. Because members tend to gravitate to committees for constituency or career reasons, they are not the most impartial judges of the policies they authorize. "It's one of the weaknesses of the system that those attracted to a committee like Agriculture are those whose constituents benefit from farm programs," acknowledged Sen. Charles E. Schumer, a Democrat from New York. "And so they're going to support those programs and they're not going to want to cut them, even the ones that are wasteful." [4]

The Purposes of Committees

Senator Schumer's comment highlights an ongoing debate about the development and fundamental purposes of the committee system. To explain the organization of legislatures, scholars have advanced the distributional, informational, and party hypotheses.

The distributional hypothesis suggests that legislatures create committees to give lawmakers policy influence in areas critical to their reelection. Members seek committee assignments to bring home the bacon (public goods and services) to their constituents. Because lawmakers self-select these kinds of committees, the committees become filled with what scholars call preference outliers—members whose homogeneous preferences for benefits to their constituents put them out of step with the heterogeneous views of the membership as a whole. Chamber majorities, in brief, may need to rein in overreaching committees by rejecting or amending their recommended actions. [5]

The informational hypothesis proposes that legislative bodies establish committees to provide lawmakers with the specialized expertise required to make informed judgments in a complex world. Furthermore, the division of labor under the committee system augments Congress's role in relation to the executive branch. Instead of being composed primarily of preference outliers, committees under this model will consist of a diverse membership with wide-ranging perspectives. The basic goal of committees, then, is to formulate policies that resolve national problems. [6]

The party hypothesis views committee members as agents of their party caucuses. According to this perspective, committee members are expected to support their party's programs.

The committee system in fact encompasses aspects of all three models. Lawmakers are concerned with local issues, but every district and state is also affected by broad national concerns—the condition of the economy and the environment, for example. Issues may lend themselves on occasion more to the distributional than to the informational or party theory of policy making. (See box for a review of comparable hypotheses.)

Three Views on the Role of Committees

Political scientist Forrest Maltzman has described three common views of committees: the committee-autonomy perspective, the chamber-dominated perspective, and the party-dominated perspective.

The committee-autonomy perspective portrays committees as "autonomous units that are able to control policy outcomes pertaining to their jurisdictions. Since members are allocated their committee seats in a fashion that is unresponsive to the chamber's policy preferences, and, after being assigned, . . . accept committee norms and receive biased information, [they may] . . . advance policies that are contrary to the preferences of the chamber as a whole." According to this view, the committee system is "a locus of institutionalized parochialism and logrolling."

The chamber-dominated perspective is based on the premise that members of the House want to belong to an effective institution and create good public policy. "In order to accomplish these goals, the institution needs information and expertise. Through the division of labor, the committee system provides such expertise," explains Maltzman. As a check on the committees' use of their position to benefit their own members, "the chamber retains the right to amend or reject committee recommendations and, if necessary, abolish or restructure its committees."

The party-dominated perspective is based upon two premises: All members of Congress seek electoral success for their party, and this success depends upon a party's capacity to form and enact a platform. According to this view, "the party caucuses organize the chamber so as to promote the party agenda. In order to prevent contingents from shirking their collective party responsibilities, the party appoints loyal members to committees and punishes those that ignore the needs of the party."

Sources: Forrest Maltzman, "Committee-Chamber-Party Relations in the Post-Reform House," paper presented at the annual meeting of the Midwest Political Science Association, Chicago, April 9–11, 1992, 2–3. See also Forrest Maltzman, *Competing Principals: Committees, Parties, and the Organization of Congress* (Ann Arbor: University of Michigan Press, 1997), chap. 2.

Because good public policy may be impeded by the parochial orientations of individual members, Congress has a small number of control, or centralizing, committees that promote institutional and policy integration over committee and programmatic particularism. For example, each house has a Budget Committee, which proposes limits on how much Congress can spend for designated functional areas.[7] However committees are characterized, they focus and concentrate the policy and oversight activities of individual lawmakers.

Evolution of the Committee System

Committees in the early Congresses generally were temporary panels created for specific tasks. Proposals were considered on the House or Senate floor and then were referred to specially created panels that worked out the details—the reverse order of today's system. The Senate, for example, would "debate a subject at length on the floor and, after the majority's desires had been crystallized, might appoint a committee to put those desires into bill form." [8] About 350 ad hoc committees were formed during the Third Congress (1793–1795) alone.[9] The parent chamber closely controlled these temporary committees. It assigned them clear-cut tasks, required them to report back favorably or unfavorably, and dissolved them when they had completed their work.

The Senate by about 1816—and the House a bit later—had developed a system of permanent, or standing, committees, some of which are still in existence. Standing committees, as historian DeAlva Stanwood Alexander explained, were better suited than ad hoc groups to cope with the larger membership and wider scope of congressional business. Another scholar, George H. Haynes, pointed out that the "needless inconvenience of the frequent choice of select committees" taxed congressional patience. Lawmakers recognized that debating bills one at a time before the whole chamber was an inefficient way of processing Congress's legislative business. Perhaps, too, legislators came to value standing committees as counterweights to presidential influence in setting the legislative agenda.[10] Permanent committees changed the way Congress made policy and allocated authority. The House and Senate now reviewed and voted upon recommendations made by specialized, experienced committees. Standing committees also encouraged oversight of the executive branch. Members have called them "the eye, the ear, the hand, and very often the brain" of Congress.[11]

As committees acquired expertise and authority, they became increasingly self-reliant and resistant to chamber and party control. After the House revolted against Speaker Joseph G. Cannon, R-Ill., in 1910, power flowed to the committee chairmen, who took on substantial powers. Along with a few strong party leaders, they held sway over House and Senate policy making during much of the twentieth century. In rare instances committee members rebelled and diminished the chairman's authority. But most members heeded the advice that Speaker John W. McCormack, D-Mass. (1962–1971), gave to freshmen: "Whenever you pass a committee chairman in the House, you bow from the waist. I do." [12]

The chairmen's authority was buttressed by the custom of seniority that flourished with the rise of congressional careerism. The majority party member with the most years of continuous service on a committee automatically became its chairman. There were no other qualifications, such as ability or party loyalty. As a result, committee chairmen owed little or nothing to party leaders, much less to presidents. This automatic selection process produced experienced, independent chairmen but concentrated authority in a few hands. The have-nots wanted a piece of the action and objected that seniority promoted the competent and incompetent alike. They objected, too, that the system promoted members from safe one-party areas—especially conservative southern Democrats and midwestern Republicans—who could ignore party policies or national sentiments.

The late 1960s and 1970s saw a rapid influx of new members, many from the cities and suburbs, who opposed the conservative status quo. Allying themselves with more senior members seeking a stronger voice in Congress, they pushed through changes that diffused power and shattered seniority as an absolute criterion for leadership posts. Today, House and Senate committee chairmen (and ranking minority members) must be elected by their party colleagues. No longer free to wield arbitrary authority, they must abide by committee and party rules and be sensitive to majority sentiment within their party's caucus or conference. For example, the House Republican Conference adopted party rules for the 108th Congress that state, "The Chairman on each committee has an obligation to ensure that each measure on which the Republican Conference has taken a position is managed in accordance with such position on the Floor of the House of Representatives."

Types of Committees

Congress today has a shopper's bazaar of committees—standing, select, joint, and conference—and within each of these general types there are variations. Standing committees, for example, can be characterized as authorizing or appropriating panels. Authorizing committees (such as Agriculture, Armed Services, and Judiciary) are the policy-making centers on Capitol Hill. As substantive committees, they propose solutions to public problems and advocate what they believe to be the necessary levels of spending for the programs under their jurisdictions. The House and Senate Appropriations Committees recommend how much money agencies and programs will receive. Continuing conflict not surprisingly exists between the two types of panels. Typically, authorizers press for full funding for their recommendations, while appropriators are in the habit of recommending lower spending levels.

Standing Committees

A standing committee is a permanent entity created by public law or House or Senate rules. Standing committees continue from Congress to Congress, except in those infrequent instances when they are eliminated or new ones are created. Table 7-1 compares the standing committees in the 108th Congress in terms of their sizes, party ratios, and number of subcommittees.

Standing committees process the bulk of Congress's daily and annual agenda of business. Seldom are measures considered on the House or Senate floor without first being referred to, and approved by, the appropriate committees. Put negatively, committees are the burial ground for most legislation. Stated positively, committees select from the thousands of measures introduced in each Congress those that merit floor debate. Of the hundreds of bills that clear committees, fewer still are enacted into law.

Table 7-1   Standing Committees of the House and Senate, 108th Congress (2003–2005)

Committee	Size and party ratio	Number of subcommittees
House		
Agriculture	51 (R 27/D 24)	5
Appropriations	65 (R 36/D 29)	13
Armed Services	61 (R 33/D 28)	6
Budget	43 (R 24/D 19)	—
Education and the Workforce	49 (R 27/D 22)	5
Energy and Commerce	57 (R 31/D 26)	6
Financial Services	70 (R 37/D 33)	5
Government Reform	44 (R 24/D 20)	7
House Administration	9 (R 6/D 3)	—
International Relations	49 (R 26/D 23)	6
Judiciary	37 (R 21/D 16)	5
Resources	52 (R 28/D 24)	5
Rules	13 (R 9/D 4)	2
Science	47 (R 25/D 22)	4
Small Business	36 (R 19/D 17)	4
Standards of Official Conduct	10 (R 5/D 5)	—
Transportation and Infrastructure	75 (R 41/D 34)	6
Veterans' Affairs	31 (R 17/D 14)	3
Ways and Means	41 (R 24/D 17)	6
Senate		
Agriculture, Nutrition, and Forestry	21 (R 11/D 10)	4
Appropriations	29 (R 15/D 14)	13
Armed Services	25 (R 13/D 12)	6
Banking, Housing, and Urban Affairs	21 (R 11/10 D)	5
Budget	23 (R 12/11 D)	—
Commerce, Science, and Transportation	23 (12 R/11 D)	7
Energy and Natural Resources •	23 (12 R/11 D)	4
Environment and Public Works	19 (10 R/9 D)	4
Finance	21 (11 R/10 D)	5
Foreign Relations	19 (10 R/9 D)	7
Governmental Affairs	17 (9 R/8 D)	3
Health, Education, Labor and Pensions	21 (11 R/10 D)	4
Judiciary	19 (10 R/9 D)	6
Rules and Administration	19 (10 R/9 D)	—
Small Business and Entrepreneurship	19 (10 R/9 D)	—
Veterans' Affairs	15 (8 R/7 D)	—

Source: CQ Weekly, "CQ Guide to the Committees," April 12, 2003, C3–C37.

Sizes and Ratios. Biennial election results frame the party negotiations that establish committee sizes and ratios. At the beginning of each new Congress, each chamber adopts two separate resolutions, one offered by the Democrats and the other by the Republicans, that elect members to the committees and thus set their sizes and ratios (the number of majority and minority members on a panel). In practice, committee sizes and ratios are set in the House by the majority leadership. Because the majority party has the votes, it can be the final arbiter if the minority protests its allotment of seats.

In the Senate, sizes and ratios are negotiated by the majority and minority leaders. Once it became clear after the November 2002 elections by what margin the Republicans had taken control of the 108th Congress, the two party leaders agreed that the GOP would have a one-seat majority on Senate committees. In the House, despite picking up six seats, Republicans kept the same ratio on committees in the 108th Congress that they had in the 107th. "What we have right now is working pretty well and there's no reason to change it," stated the spokesperson for Speaker J. Dennis Hastert, R-Ill.[13] Hastert's decision to maintain the status quo avoided partisan charges common at the start of a new Congress that the majority was stacking the deck and robbing the minority of their rightful number of committee seats. However, some committees, such as Budget and Rules, traditionally have disproportionate ratios to ensure firm majority party control.

Some panels may be enlarged by party leaders to accommodate lawmakers competing for membership on the same committees. They recognize that party harmony can be maintained by boosting the number of committee seats. Or members may be granted waivers from chamber or party rules limiting their service on standing committees. Waivers are sometimes granted to permit members to sit on an extra major committee that they deem important to their reelection prospects. This is another example of the two Congresses, the institution bending to suit individual preferences.

Subcommittees. Subcommittees perform much of the day-to-day lawmaking and oversight work of Congress. Like standing committees, these subunits of committees vary widely in rules and procedures, staff arrangements, modes of operations, and relationships with other subcommittees and the full committee. For example, the House Appropriations Committee uses full committee seniority to determine who will head its thirteen subcommittees; Senate Appropriations employs seniority on each subcommittee to determine who will head each of its thirteen subunits.

Subcommittees are created for various reasons, such as lawmakers' need to subdivide a committee's wide-ranging policy domain into manageable pieces, their desire to chair these panels and to have a platform to shape the legislative agenda, and their wish to respond to the policy claims of specialized constituencies. In a major subcommittee restructuring on the House Appropriations Committee, Chairman C. W. Bill Young, R-Fla., created in early 2003 a new Homeland Security Appropriations Subcommittee while keeping the total number of subcommittees at the panel's traditional thirteen. "Eight sub-committees have jurisdiction over facets of the new department under the current committee structure," said Chairman Young. "Creating one subcommittee will allow us to focus our attention and resources on the unique challenges confronting the new department." [14] The Senate Appropriations Committee also created an Appropriations subcommittee on homeland security.[15] During the 108th Congress the nineteen House standing committees together created eighty-eight subcommittees; the sixteen Senate standing committees collectively established sixty-eight subcommittees.

Under House rules adopted in 2003, Republicans limited most standing committees to no more than five subcommittees. Committees bound by the limit of five may create a sixth subcommittee if it is devoted to oversight. This requirement, championed by Speaker Hastert, was intended to encourage his GOP-run committees to emphasize programmatic oversight (evaluating agency and program performance). Committees permitted to have more than five subcommittees are Appropriations (thirteen), Government Reform (seven), and Armed Services, International Relations, and Transportation, all with six. Various reasons account for committees having more than five subcommittees, such as long-standing custom, the acquisition of additional jurisdiction, accommodation of a lawmaker, or bicameral considerations. For example, when Duncan Hunter, R-Calif., assumed the Armed Services chairmanship at the start of the 108th Congress, he reorganized the subcommittee structure.

> By [receiving House approval to add] a sixth panel . . . and realigning the [subcommittees] to focus on individual military services, not broad areas such as "procurement" or "research and development," he has created a structure for the House committee that closely follows the organization of the [GOP-controlled] Senate Armed Services Committee. That should clear the way for easier conferences when the two panels meet in future years to negotiate differences over the annual defense authorization bill.[16]

Another House rule limits members to no more than four subcommittees. These limits on the number of subcommittees for each standing committee and subcommittee assignment restrictions for each member are designed to make Congress "more deliberative, participatory, and manageable by reducing scheduling conflicts and jurisdictional overlap." [17] In contrast to the practice when Democrats ran the House, GOP committee chairmen manage their committees without having to contend with independent subcommittee chairmen. GOP party rules stipulate that the selection of subcommittee chairmen "shall be at the discretion of the full Committee Chairman." Some House GOP chairmen willingly cede more authority to their subcommittee leaders. Energy and Commerce chairman Billy Tauzin, La., for example, has assigned at least one significant issue to each of the six subcommittee chairmen and allowed each to hire his own staff director and develop his own bills. "We are moving away from an authoritarian structure," said Rep. James C. Greenwood, R-Pa., the subcommittee chairman of Energy's Oversight and Investigations Subcommittee. "We are going to emphasize teamwork." [18]

Although silent on the number of subcommittees that standing committees may establish, Senate rules set subcommittee assignment limits for senators and prohibit them from chairing more than one subcommittee on any one committee. The number of subcommittees not surprisingly often equals the number of majority party members on a committee. Typically, subcommittee chairmen and assignments are determined in one of two ways: by the full chair in consultation with the ranking member or by senators' order of seniority on the full committee.

Select, or Special, Committees

Select, or special, committees (the terms are interchangeable) are usually temporary panels that go out of business after the two-year life of the Congress in which they were created. But some select committees take on the attributes of permanent committees. The House, for example, has a Permanent Select Intelligence Committee. Select committees usually do not have legislative authority (the right to receive and report out measures); they can only study, investigate, and make recommendations.

Select panels are created for several reasons. First, they accommodate the concerns of individual members. The chairmen of these panels may attract publicity that enhances their political careers. For example, Democrat Harry S. Truman of Missouri came to the public's (and President Franklin D. Roosevelt's) attention as head of a special Senate committee investigating World War II military procurement practices. Second, special panels can be a point of access for interest groups, such as the elderly and owners of small businesses. Third, select committees supplement the standing committee system by overseeing and investigating issues that the permanent panels lack time for or prefer to ignore. Finally, select committees can be set up to coordinate consideration of issues that overlap the jurisdictions of several standing committees. A good example occurred at the start of the 108th Congress when the House created a Select Committee on Homeland Security with both legislative (the right to receive and report measures to the House) and oversight jurisdiction.

Scores of House standing committees have jurisdiction over various issues pertaining to homeland security. For example, among other homeland security topics, Agriculture has jurisdiction over animal and plant health; Energy and Commerce over public health; Financial Services over defense production; Judiciary over the Federal Bureau of Investigation (FBI); Science over computer security; Transportation and Infrastructure over transportation security; and Ways and Means over the Customs Service. To provide the new Department of Homeland Security, formed from the merger of twenty-two agencies with 170,000 employees, with a central point of contact in the House, Speaker

Hastert and other lawmakers "wanted a single point of oversight for the massive new department." [19] The select committee also has the responsibility to recommend to the Committee on Rules, by September 30, 2004, "possible changes in committee jurisdiction with respect to homeland security." [20] (The Senate has kept oversight authority for the new department in its Committee on Governmental Affairs.)

Joint Committees

Joint committees, which include members from both chambers, have been used since the First Congress for study, investigation, oversight, and routine activities. Unless their composition is prescribed in statute, House members of joint committees are appointed by the Speaker, and senators are appointed by that chamber's presiding officer. The chairmanship of joint committees rotates each Congress between House and Senate members. In 2003 there were four joint committees: Economic, Library, Printing, and Taxation. The Joint Library Committee and the Joint Printing Committee oversee, respectively, the Library of Congress and the Government Printing Office. The Joint Taxation Committee is essentially a holding company for staff who work closely with the tax-writing committees of each house. The Joint Economic Committee conducts studies and hearings on a wide range of domestic and international economic issues.

Conference Committees

Before legislation can be sent to the president to be signed, it must pass both the House and the Senate in identical form. Conference committees, sometimes called the third house of Congress, reconcile differences between similar measures passed by both chambers. They are composed of members from each house. A representative highlighted their importance:

> When I came to Congress I had no comprehension of the importance of the conference committees which actually write legislation. We all knew that important laws are drafted there, but I don't think one person in a million has any appreciation of their importance and the process by which they work. Part of the explanation, of course, is that there never is a printed record of what goes on in conference.[21]

Conference bargaining roughly can be classified in four ways: traditional, offer-counteroffer, subconference, and pro forma. Traditional conferences are those in which the participants meet face to face, haggle among themselves about the items in bicameral disagreement, and then reach an accord. The bulk of conferences are of this type. In offer-counteroffer conferences, often used by the tax-writing committees, one side suggests a compromise proposal; the other side recesses to discuss it in private and then returns to present a counteroffer. Conferences with numerous participants (on omnibus bills, for example) usually break into small units, or subconferences, to reconcile particular matters or to address special topics. Pro forma conferences are those in which issues are resolved informally—by preconference negotiations between conferee leaders or their staffs. The conference itself then ratifies the earlier decisions.[22]

Some scholars argue that congressional committees are influential because they possess unilateral authority at the conference stage to veto or negotiate alterations in legislation. Others dispute this contention and claim that the "ex post veto is not a significant institutional foundation of congressional committee power."[23] Another model suggests that conferees serve as agents of their respective chamber majorities and advocate their policy positions instead of committee viewpoints.[24] Increasingly, the top party leaders in each chamber are taking a more direct and active role in determining who should (or should not) be a conferee.

The Assignment Process

Every congressional election sets off a scramble for committee seats. Legislators understand the linkage between winning desirable assignments and winning elections. Newly elected representatives and senators quickly make their preferences known to party leaders, to members of the panels that make committee assignments, and to others. At the same time, incumbents may be trying to move to more prestigious panels.

The Pecking Order

The most powerful, and so most desirable, standing committees are House Ways and Means and Senate Finance, which pass on tax, trade, Social Security, and Medicare measures, and the House and Senate Appropriations Committees, which hold the federal purse strings. The Budget Committees, established in 1974, have become sought-after assignments because of their important role in economic and fiscal matters and their guardianship of the congressional budgeting process. The House and Senate Commerce Committees are also influential panels for two main reasons: their significant jurisdictional mandate and the campaign cash that committee members can raise from the many interest groups affected by the panel's decisions.

Among those that seldom have waiting lists are the Senate Ethics and House Standards of Official Conduct Committees. The House and Senate ethics panels are required to have an equal number of Democrats and Republicans. These committees in both chambers are unpopular because legislators are reluctant to sit in judgment of their colleagues. "Members have never competed for the privilege of serving on the ethics committee, and I am no exception," remarked Rep. Howard L. Berman, D-Calif., after the Democratic leader prevailed on him to join the ethics panel. Or as a GOP member said after serving as ethics chairman, "I've paid my debt to society. It's time for me to be paroled."[25]

The attractiveness of committees can change. For instance, the Senate Foreign Relations Committee, long an attractive panel (especially during the Vietnam War era), often has had trouble since the end of the cold war in filling vacancies. Senators often viewed it as largely a debating society without much influence either within or outside the Senate. Today, given heightened public concern about the global war on terrorism and a large array of other international issues, Foreign Relations chairman Richard G. Lugar, R-Ind., has worked successfully to make the panel a force to be reckoned with in influencing international decision making. A foreign policy expert underscored the renewed importance of the panel: "Yeah, they've got clout. You control money, you control nominations, you control treaties, and you control the microphone" to discuss an array of global issues. "That's a lot of power in Washington." [26]

Preferences and Politicking

In an analysis of six House committees, Richard F. Fenno Jr. found that three basic goals of lawmakers—reelection, influence within the House, and good public policy—affect the committee assignments that members seek. Reelection-oriented members were attracted to committees such as Resources (then called the Interior Committee). Appropriations and Ways and Means attracted influence-oriented members. Policy-oriented members sought membership on what are now called the Education and the Workforce Committee and the International Relations Committee. Members with similar goals find themselves on the same committees, Fenno concluded. This homogeneity of perspectives may result in harmonious but biased committees. [27]

Since Fenno's study, scholars have elaborated on the relationship between members' goals and committee assignments. They have divided House committees into reelection (or constituency), policy, and power panels and concur that some mix of the three goals motivates most activity on the committees. They agree, too, that members' goals "are less easily characterized in the Senate than in the House." [28] Almost every senator has the opportunity to serve on one of the top committees, such as Appropriations, Armed Services, Commerce, and Finance. Hence, the power associated with a particular committee assignment is less important for senators than for representatives (see Table 7-2).

In the weeks after an election, members campaign vigorously for the committees they prefer. When Rep. Robert B. Aderholt, R-Ala., was a freshman, he set out to win a coveted spot on the Appropriations Committee. He solicited the help of the majority leader and lobbied each member who sat on the GOP's committee assignment panel. "It was almost like this was another congressional campaign," Aderholt explained. "While a lot of [new] members were driving around house hunting and interviewing staff members, I was working" to win appointment to Appropriations. [29] Rep. Jennifer Dunn, R-Wash., provided all incoming GOP freshmen with a how-to booklet on securing com-

Table 7-2 House and Senate Committee Comparison

Category	House	Senate
Number of standing committees	19	16
Committee assignments per member	About 6	About 11
Power or prestige committees	Appropriations, Budget, Commerce, Rules, Ways and Means	Appropriations, Armed Services, Commerce, Finance, Foreign relations[a]
Treaties and nominations submitted by the president	No authority	Committees review
Floor debate	Representatives' activity is somewhat confined to the bills reported from the panels on which they serve	Senators can choose to influence any policy area regardless of their committee assignments
Committee consideration of legislation	More difficult to bypass	Easier to bypass[b]
Committee chairs	Subject to party and speakership influence that limits their discretionary authority over committee operations	Freer rein to manage committees
Committee staff	Often assertive in advocating ideas and proposals	More aggressive in shaping the legislative agenda
Subcommittee chairmanships	Representatives of the majority party usually must wait at least one term	Majority senators, regardless of their seniority, usually chair subcommitees

[a] Almost every senator is assigned to one of these committees.
[b] For example, by allowing riders—unrelated policy proposals—to measures pending on the floor.

mittee assignments. She suggested a three-part strategy emphasizing personal, political, and geographical factors. For example, Dunn suggested face-to-face meetings with members of the Steering Committee, letters and phone calls to committee chairmen, and personal contact with party leaders. "Do not be afraid to go to each Member of the Leadership to let them know of your political needs. Leadership has proven . . . open to placing freshmen Members on key committees," she advised the newcomers. Dunn also suggested that the freshmen seek help from key GOP members in their state or region.[30]

Although both parties try to accommodate assignment preferences, some members inevitably receive unwelcome assignments. A classic case involved Democratic representative Shirley Chisholm of Brooklyn (1969–1983), the first African American woman elected to Congress. She was assigned to the House Agriculture Committee her first year in the House. "I think it would be hard to imagine an assignment that is less relevant to my background or to the needs of the predominantly black and Puerto Rican people who elected me," she said. Chisholm's protests won her a seat on the Veterans' Affairs Committee. "There are a lot more veterans in my district than there are trees," she later observed.[31] Yet some urban lawmakers welcome service on the Agriculture Committee, where they can fuse metropolitan issues with rural issues through food stamp, consumer, and other legislation.

How Assignments Are Made

Each party in each house has its own panel to review members' committee requests and hand out assignments: the Steering Committee for House Republicans, the Steering Committee for House Democrats, the Republican Committee on Committees for Senate Republicans, and the Steering and Co-ordination Committee for Senate Democrats. The decisions of these panels are the first and most important acts in a three-step procedure. The second step involves approval of the assignment lists by each party's caucus. Finally, there is pro forma election by the full House or Senate.

Formal Criteria. Both formal and informal criteria guide the assignment panels in choosing committee members. Formal criteria are designed to ensure that each member is treated equitably in committee assignments. For example, the House Republican Conference divides committees into three classes: exclusive, nonexclusive, and exempt. A member assigned to an exclusive panel (Appropriations, Budget, Energy and Commerce, Rules, and Ways and Means) may not serve on any other standing committee unless the GOP Conference waives this party rule for certain members. Republicans may serve on only two nonexclusive panels: Agriculture, Armed Services, Budget, Education and the Workforce, Financial Services, Government Reform, International Relations, Judiciary, Resources, Science, Small Business, Transportation and Infrastructure, and Veterans' Affairs. The exempt committees are House Administration, Select Intelligence, and Standards of Official Conduct. House minority leader Nancy Pelosi, D-Calif., enforced Democratic Caucus rules that limit ranking members from serving on certain other committees without a waiver as a way to distribute more choice assignments to her party colleagues. For instance, Pelosi declined to grant a waiver "to allow Barney Frank, D-Mass., the new ranking minority member of the Financial Services Committee, to continue on the Judiciary Committee." [32]

Since 1953, when Senate Democratic leader Lyndon B. Johnson of Texas announced his "Johnson rule," all Senate Democrats are assigned one major committee before any party member receives a second major assignment. In 1965 Senate Republicans followed suit. Senate rules also classify committees into different categories, which are popularly called "A," "B," and "C." There is even a separate category in the A group informally called "Super A." Senators may serve on only one of the four Super A panels (Appropriations, Armed Services, Finance, and Foreign Relations) unless the rule is waived for them. Senate rules state that members must serve on no more than two committees in the A category, which includes the four Super A panels; one in the B grouping (Budget, Rules and Administration, and Small Business, for example); and any number of C committees (Ethics, Indian Affairs, Joint Library, Joint Printing, and Joint Taxation).

Informal Criteria. Many informal criteria affect committee assignments, including the members' own wishes. Lawmakers who represent districts or states with large military installations may seek assignment to the Armed Services Committee. Party leaders, mindful of the two Congresses, may assign vulnerable lawmakers to choice committees as a way to boost their reelection chances. Gender may affect assignments as well. With President Bill Clinton's impeachment hearings on the horizon in the fall of 1998, party leaders recruited Rep. Mary Bono, R-Calif., the widow of Rep. Sonny Bono, to serve on the Judiciary Committee as the panel's only female Republican. They hoped she might "soften the harsh image projected by some committee conservatives" and demonstrate the party's gender sensitivity at hearings where allegations of sexual exploitation could play a role.[33]

Worth underscoring is the reality of the two Congresses in assignment decisions. Each party seeks through the appointments process to give electoral advantage to lawmakers of their party. House GOP and Democratic leaders, for instance, commonly grant their electorally vulnerable freshmen an extra committee assignment to broaden their appeal as they head into the November elections. "All of these committees have constituents," said Democratic whip Steny H. Hoyer, Md. "And all of these [freshmen Democratic appointees] have people in their districts who are members of these constituencies." [34]

Seniority. Normally, the assignment panels observe seniority when preparing committee membership lists. The member of the majority party with the longest continuous committee service is usually listed first. Senate Republicans, unlike House Republicans and House and Senate Democrats, apply seniority rigidly when two or more GOP senators compete for either a committee vacancy or chairmanship. As a senator noted: "When I first came to the

Party Assignment Committees

House Republicans. Before the 104th Congress began in 1995, incoming Speaker Newt Gingrich, R-Ga., revamped his party's committee on committees, which he would chair. Gingrich renamed it the Steering Committee; transformed it into a twenty-nine-member, leadership-dominated panel; eliminated a weighted voting system wherein a GOP member of the assignment panel cast as many votes as there were Republicans in his or her state delegation; and granted the Speaker control over about one-fourth of the total votes on the panel with the Speaker personally casting the most votes (five). These reforms continued in the subsequent Congresses. The Speaker also appoints all GOP members of the Rules and House Administration Committees.

House Democrats. Democrats on the House Ways and Means Committee functioned as their party's committee on committees from 1911 until 1974, when the Democratic Caucus voted to transfer this duty to the Steering and Policy Committee. Renamed the Steering Committee at the beginning of the 104th Congress, the thirty-six-member assignment panel in the 108th Congress was chaired by Rosa DeLauro of Connecticut.

Senate Republicans. The chairman of the Republican Conference appoints the assignment panel of about eight members. In addition, the floor leader is an ex officio member. Idaho senator Larry Craig chaired the panel during the 108th Congress.

Senate Democrats. The Steering and Coordination Committee makes assignments for Democrats. Its size (about twenty-five members) is set by the party conference and may fluctuate from Congress to Congress. The party's floor leader appoints the members of this panel and its chairman (Sen. Hillary Rodham Clinton of New York, for the 108th Congress).

Senate, I was skeptical [of the seniority tradition]. But as I've become more senior, I've grown more fond of it." [35] By contrast, the two House parties do not observe seniority as strictly as Senate Republicans. House GOP Conference rules even state that the member designated as chair by the party's committee on committees (the Steering Committee) "need not be the Member with the longest consecutive service on the Committee." (See box on party assignment committees.)

When Newt Gingrich, R-Ga., was Speaker, he bypassed the seniority custom on several occasions to give chairmanships to Republicans who could move the party's agenda despite their having less committee longevity than some others on those panels. Further, in 1995 the House imposed a six-year term limit on committee and subcommittee chairmen, which triggered a round of musical chairmanships in 2001. Although several GOP chairs tried to repeal the rule or to obtain waivers so they could continue in their position beyond six years, they were all forced to give up their positions. With thirteen chairmanship vacancies, the GOP Steering Committee, headed by Speaker Hastert, had to settle a number of highly competitive contests among Republicans competing to chair the various committees.

Speaker Hastert decided upon an unprecedented interview procedure by which the Steering Committee would make its recommendations for chairman to the full Republican Conference, which votes to approve each nominee. In a letter to GOP members, Speaker Hastert explained several basic features of the interview process. "The candidates will be given an opportunity to discuss their legislative agenda, oversight agenda, how they intend to organize the committees, and their communication strategy," he wrote.[36] Fund-raising prowess was another consideration. "You can't tell me a Member who raises $1 million for the party and visits 50 districts is not going to have an advantage over someone who sits back and thinks he's entitled to a chairmanship. Those days are gone," said a top GOP leadership aide.[37] Only the chair of the Government Reform Committee was subject to a term limit at the start of the 108th Congress. Unsurprisingly, the GOP Steering Committee selected Thomas M. Davis III, Va., who raised millions of dollars as head of the Republican congressional campaign committee during the 2000 and 2002 election cycles, over two other competitors for the post.

In effect, many of the criteria employed to designate GOP chairmen are comparable to those that top party leaders must possess: coalition-building skills, fund-raising ability, and talent for media advocacy. (Party loyalty is another important criterion.) And like party leaders, GOP candidates for vacant chairmanships launch their own campaigns to influence, in this case, the Hastert-led Steering Committee. Some enlist the support of outside groups, others make PowerPoint presentations to the panel, several may develop memorandums or briefing books to highlight their plans as chairman, and still others hand out home-state products, such as peanuts or raisins, to the Steering members.

Senate Republicans followed the House's term-limit decision by adopting a party rule, effective in 1997, restricting committee chairmen (or ranking members) to six years of service. "The whole thrust behind this," said the Senate author of the term-limit change, "is to try to get greater participation, so new members of the Senate don't have to wait until they've been here 18 years to play a role." [38] However, in the lead-up to the November 2002 elections, Senate Republicans modified their party rule on term limits. With Senator Jeffords's midsession 2001 party switch, which put Democrats in charge of all Senate committees, concern arose about how to count the interrupted service of the GOP chairs. Some GOP senators wanted a strict six-year limit, counting service as both chair and ranking member, which would have produced large turnover in chairmanships after Republicans recaptured control of the 108th Senate. Other senators wanted to abolish the six-year limit entirely. In the end, Senate Republicans adopted a complex compromise that reaffirmed and clarified the six-year ban. Under the compromise,

> Republicans will be allowed to serve a total of six years as chairman and six as ranking Republican. But anyone who has served six years as chairman can no longer serve as ranking member. On the other hand, a senator who has

served six years as chairman can no longer serve as a ranking member but less than that as chairman could finish out a six-year tenure as chairman.[39]

Under the change, Republicans who served as chairmen in the 107th Senate until the Jeffords's switch still had two years left to chair their committee. For example, Sen. Ted Stevens, R-Alaska, who chaired the Appropriations Committee since 1997 until the June 2001 switch in party control of the Senate, was back for two more years as chair of Appropriations in the 108th Congress. "Once he hits that six-year total as chairman, he can no longer chair the [Appropriations] committee or serve as ranking member," but he was not prohibited from seeking the chairmanship of another committee.[40]

Biases. The decisions made by the assignment panels inevitably determine the geographical and ideological composition of the standing committees. Committees can easily become biased toward one position or another. Farm areas are overrepresented on the Agriculture Committees and small business interests on the Small Business Committees. No wonder committees are policy advocates. They propose laws that reflect the interests of their members and the outside groups and agencies that gravitate toward them.

Who gets on a panel or who is left off affects committee policy making. Committees that are carefully balanced between liberal and conservative interests can be tilted one way or the other by new members. A committee's political philosophy influences its success on the House or Senate floor. Committees ideologically out of step with the House or Senate as a whole are more likely than others to have legislation defeated or significantly revised by floor amendments.

Approval by Party Caucuses and the Chamber

For most of the twentieth century each chamber's party caucuses either ratified the assignment decisions of their committees on committees or took no action on them at all. Beginning in the 1970s, however, party caucuses became major participants in the assignment process. Chairmen and ranking minority members were subjected to election by secret ballot of their partisan colleagues. Clearly, committee leadership is no longer an automatic right.

Although seniority still encourages continuity on committees, the seniority system has now become more flexible and is under caucus control. House GOP rules for the 108th Congress stated that the "Conference shall vote by secret ballot on each recommendation of the . . . Steering Committee for the position of Chairman. If the Republican Conference fails to approve a recommendation . . . the matter shall be automatically recommitted without instruction to [the Steering] Committee." In the Senate the parties can exercise control over committees but nearly always defer to the seniority rankings of lawmakers in determining who heads a committee or subcommittee.

Each chamber's rules require that all members of standing committees, including chairmen, be elected by the entire House or Senate. The practice, however, is for each party's leaders to offer the caucus-approved assignment lists to the full chamber. Normally, these are approved quickly by voice vote.

Committee Leadership

Committee leaders are usually the chairmen and the ranking minority members. Committee chairmen call meetings and establish agendas, hire and fire committee staff, arrange hearings, recommend conferees, act as floor managers, allocate committee funds and rooms, develop legislative strategies, chair hearings and markups, and regulate the internal affairs and organization of the committee.

The procedural advantages of a chairman are hard for even the most forceful minority members to overcome. The chairman may be able to kill a bill simply by refusing to schedule it for a hearing. Or a chairman may convene meetings when proponents or opponents of the legislation are unavoidably absent. The chairman's authority derives from the support of a committee majority and a variety of formal and informal resources, such as substantive and parliamentary experience and control over the agenda, communications, and financial resources of the committee. When told by a committee colleague that he lacked the votes on an issue, then House Energy and Commerce chairman John D. Dingell, D-Mich., replied, "Yeah, but I've got the gavel." [41] Dingell banged his gavel, adjourned the meeting, and the majority had no chance to work its will before the legislative session ended.

The top minority party member on a committee is also an influential figure. Among his or her powers are nominating minority conferees, hiring and firing minority staff, sitting ex officio on all subcommittees, appointing minority members to subcommittees, assisting in setting the committee's agenda, managing legislation on the floor, and acting as committee spokesperson for his party.

Policy Making in Committee

Committees foster deliberate, collegial, fragmented decisions. They encourage bargaining and accommodation among members. To move bills through Congress's numerous decision points from subcommittee to committee, authors of bills and resolutions typically make compromises in response to important committee members. These gatekeepers may exact alterations in a bill's substance. The proliferation of committees also multiplies the points of access for outside interests.

Overlapping Jurisdictions

The formal responsibilities of a standing committee are defined by the rules of each house, various public laws, and precedents. Committees with overlapping jurisdictions sometimes formulate a written memorandum of understanding that informally outlines how policy topics are to be referred among them.[42] Committees do not have watertight jurisdictional compartments. Any broad subject overlaps numerous committees. The Senate has an Environment and Public Works Committee, but other panels also consider environmental legislation; the same is true in the House. These House bodies, along with a brief sketch of some of their environmental responsibilities, are as follows:

Agriculture: pesticides; soil conservation; some water programs

Appropriations: funding for environmental programs and agencies

Energy and Commerce: health effects of the environment; environmental regulations; solid waste disposal; clean air; safe drinking water

Financial Services: open space acquisition in urban areas

Government Reform: federal executive branch agencies for the environment

International Relations: international environmental cooperation

Resources: water resources; power resources; land management; wildlife conservation; national parks; nuclear waste; fisheries; endangered species

Science: environmental research and development

Small Business: effects of environmental regulations on business

Transportation and Infrastructure: water pollution; sludge management

Ways and Means: environmental tax expenditures

Jurisdictional overlaps can have positive results. They can enable members to develop expertise in several policy fields, prevent any one group from dominating a topic, and promote healthy competition among committees. However, healthy competition can quickly turn to intercommittee warfare.

In recent Congresses the House Energy and Commerce, Resources, and Science Committees have clashed over issues that do not fit neatly into any single panel's area of responsibility (energy and environmental issues, for instance). Committees' formal jurisdictional mandates have not kept pace with change—nor can they. Another trigger of turf battles is forum shopping by outside interests who want their carefully drafted bills referred to sympathetic committees. The expansionist tendency of some committees also can create intercommittee tussles. As ranking member on the Commerce Committee, Sen. Ernest F. Hollings, D-S.C., offered this opinion of the Senate Banking chairman, "He does everything in the world to come in on our jurisdiction." [43]

Multiple Referrals

When a bill is introduced in the House, it usually is referred to a single committee. Until 1975 House rules made no provision for multiple referrals, although informally occasions have arisen when more than one panel reviewed the same bill. In that year, however, the rules were changed to permit several types of multiple referrals. This change augmented the Speaker's authority and granted him additional flexibility in referring measures to various committees.

When Republicans assumed control of the House in 1995, they streamlined multiple referrals and placed them firmly under the Speaker's control. The Speaker must "designate a committee of primary jurisdiction upon the initial referral of a measure to a committee." The primary committee concept is designed to increase accountability for legislation while retaining for the Speaker flexibility in determining whether, when, and for how long other panels can receive the measure.

At the time of initial referral, the Speaker identifies the primary committee. It has predominant responsibility for shepherding the legislation to final passage. The Speaker may also send the measure to secondary panels. The House parliamentarian calls this practice an additional initial referral. In the following example of referral language, the Judiciary Committee is the primary committee and Resources is the additional initial panel:

> H.R. 2555. A bill to preserve the authority of the States over waters within their boundaries . . . to the Committee on the Judiciary, and in addition to the Committee on Resources, for a period to be subsequently determined by the Speaker, in each case for consideration of such provisions as fall within the jurisdiction of the committee concerned.

At the start of the 108th Congress, Republicans again modified the House rule on multiple referrals. Because of jurisdictional difficulties in determining which committee is primary in matters of health—Energy and Commerce or Ways and Means—Republicans authorized the use of joint referrals, a practice utilized by Democrats when they controlled the House. Rules chairman David Dreier, R-Calif., explained the intent of the new rule: "This change is meant only as a minor deviation from the normal requirement under the rules for the designation of one committee of primary jurisdiction and should be exercised only in extraordinary jurisdictionally deserving instances." [44]

Multiple referrals may promote integrated policy making, broader public discussion of issues, wide access to the legislative process, and consideration of alternative approaches. They also enhance the Speaker's scheduling prerogatives. The Speaker can use the referral power to intervene more directly in committee activities and even to set deadlines for committees to report multiply referred legislation. The reverse is also possible: The Speaker can delay action on measures by referring them to other committees. Thus, multiple referrals can be employed to slow down legislative decision making.

The Senate usually sends measures to a single committee—the committee with jurisdiction over the subject matter that predominates in the legislation. Although multiple referrals have long been permitted by unanimous consent, they are infrequently used, mainly because senators have many opportunities to influence policy making on the floor.

Where Bills Go

Many bills referred to committee are sent by the chairman to a subcommittee. Others are retained for review by the full committee. In the end, committees and subcommittees select the measures they want to consider and ignore the rest. Committee consideration usually consists of three standard steps: public hearings, markups, and reports.

Hearings. When committees or subcommittees conduct hearings on a bill, they listen to a wide variety of witnesses. These include the bill's sponsors, federal officials, pressure group representatives, public officials, and private citizens—sometimes even celebrities. Movie-star witnesses can help give a bill national visibility. When Elizabeth Taylor appeared before a Senate panel to testify on acquired immune deficiency syndrome (AIDS), the chairman said of the press coverage, "I haven't seen anything like this in the 30 days we have had hearings." [45] Or as Sen. Arlen Specter, R-Pa., put it, "Quite candidly, when Hollywood speaks, the world listens. Sometimes when Washington speaks, the world snoozes." [46]

Equally important are witnesses who can add drama to hearings because of their first-hand experience with an issue or problem. The Senate Finance Committee, for example, attracted national headlines with its hearings on alleged wrongdoings by the Internal Revenue Service (IRS). Taxpayers recounted their horrendous experiences, and IRS agents donned black hoods to tell about the organization's mistreatment of taxpayers.[47] Testimony by employees who lost their retirement savings because of corporate scandals (Enron Corp. and WorldCom Inc., for example) helped to galvanize congressional enactment of corporate accounting and accountability laws. Hearings, in brief, are often orchestrated as a form of political theater where witnesses who put a human face on a public problem tell a story that may generate public momentum for legislation.

Hearings provide opportunities for committee members to be heard on the issues. Frequently, lawmakers present their views on legislation in their opening statements and in the guise of asking questions of witnesses. Most hearings follow a traditional format. Each witness reads a prepared statement. Then each committee member has a limited time (often five minutes) to ask questions before the next witness is called. To save time and promote give-and-take, committees occasionally use a panel format in which witnesses sit together and briefly summarize their statements.

After 1997 new House rules were adopted to promote opportunities for longer exchanges between lawmakers and witnesses. The majority and minority on a committee now can designate one of their panel members or committee staff aides to question a witness for a total of one hour.

Gradually, committees are beginning to harness contemporary technology to conduct Capitol Hill hearings. Several House and Senate panels have used interactive video, teleconferencing, and other technology to collect testimony from witnesses who may be located in other parts of the nation or world. The Internet has been used to transmit testimony, and cable television viewers have e-mailed or faxed questions to witnesses.[48] The House Agriculture Committee in September 1998 became "the first congressional panel to broadcast its proceedings in live audio format over the internet." [49]

Among the overlapping purposes served by hearings are

- to explore the need for legislation;
- to build a public record in support of legislation;
- to publicize the role of committee chairmen;
- to review executive implementation of public laws;
- to provide a forum for citizens' grievances and frustrations;
- to educate lawmakers and the attentive public on complex issues; and
- to raise the visibility of an issue.

When Democrats lost control of the Senate following the November 2002 elections, they also lost the ability to schedule hearings, issue subpoenas, or initiate investigations of the Republican administration. As a result, they sometimes schedule informal partisan hearings (policy forums with outside experts, for instance) to air their criticisms of the Bush administration and to highlight their own alternatives.[50] Sometimes committees conduct field hearings around the country to generate and assess public support for measures or hold joint hearings with other House or Senate panels. For example, the House and Senate Intelligence Committees conducted joint hearings in the aftermath of the September 11, 2001, terrorist attacks to assess why the intelligence agencies failed to detect and prevent the assault on the United States.

Hearings are shaped mainly by the chairman and staff, with varying degrees of input from party leaders, the ranking minority member, and others. By revealing patterns of support or opposition and by airing substantive problems, hearings indicate to members whether a bill is worth taking to the full chamber. Chairmen who favor bills can expedite the hearings process; conversely, they can kill with kindness legislation they oppose by holding endless hearings. When a bill is not sent to the full chamber, the printed hearings are the end product of the committee's work. Committee chairmen can also use hearings to try and win reelection by addressing issues that appeal to various voting groups in their state or district.

Markups. After hearings have been held, committee members decide the bill's actual language; that is, the bill is marked up or amended (see box on committee decision making). The chair may circulate his or her mark to committee colleagues via the Internet and solicit their comments and suggestions. Just as committees and the hearings process differ one from the other, so, too, do markups vary among committees. Some panels adhere closely to parliamentary rules during this committee amending phase, others operate by consensus with few or no votes taken on the issues, and still others have concep-

Committee Decision Making: A Formal Model

Political scientists are using a variety of sophisticated techniques to better understand legislative decision making. Employing concepts from economics such as rational choice—the notion that individuals (or lawmakers) have preferences or desires and that they will act in their self-interest to achieve their goals—these scholars utilize a number of analytical tools to consider how lawmakers devise strategies to accomplish their policy objectives. One such analytical approach is called spatial theory. The term *spatial* refers to a mathematical idea that theorists rely on called a policy space. An easy-to-understand example is that certain policy preferences can all be arrayed along a straight line, or unidimensional continuum. So, for example, one end of the line might be labeled "more spending" and the other "less spending." Different spending preferences could be placed at different points, or spaces, along the line.

In employing spatial theory to model legislative decision making, scholars make a number of assumptions. Two are especially important: (1) lawmakers hold consistent preferences and (2) members have an ideal policy outcome that they prefer. Put differently, lawmakers will vote for policy alternatives that bring them closer to their policy ideal and oppose those that do the reverse. The work of these scholars highlights the importance of institutional rules and procedures in determining which of several policy alternatives will prevail. Analysts have also found that the median voter—the midpoint lawmaker with an equal number of other members to his or her left or right—is the ultimate determiner of outcomes in unidimensional cases. Another way to view the median voter is the 218th vote in the House, the Supreme Court justice who casts the fifth vote in a 5 to 4 decision, or the member who casts the sixth vote in a committee of eleven members.

To depict this graphically, assume that a House Appropriations subcommittee has sent to the floor a spending bill that reflects its committee median (CM). The subcommittee also must take into account a floor median (FM) if it wants its majority position to carry the day on the floor. The current policy status quo (Q) means that, if the bill does not pass, last year's funding level remains in force. If the subcommittee's bill is brought to the floor under a no-amendment rule, then the House membership can either accept or reject the panel's position. If the House rejects the subcommittee's policy recommendation, it has agreed to retain the status quo. Whether the subcommittee's position prevails on the floor can be depicted using these two examples.

These simple examples illustrate that if the subcommittee's position is to win on the House floor, it must devise a strategy that takes account of the majority preferences

---

tual markups. Sen. Rick Santorum, R-Pa., explained that Finance Committee markups "are not about legislative language. There are concept documents that are then put into legislative language and brought to the floor." [51] Concepts may include, for instance, whether going to school counts as work for welfare recipients or what kind of tax plan best fosters economic growth.

Proponents try to craft a bill that will muster the backing of their colleagues, the other chamber, lobbyists, and the White House. This process can be arduous because members often face the two Congresses dilemma: whether

Example 1

More   Less
Spending ──────────────────────────────── Spending
                FM   CM   Q

In Example 1, the preferences of a majority of the House clearly are closer to the committee's position than the status quo. Hence, the committee's position prevails.

Example 2

More   Less
Spending ──────────────────────────────── Spending
                FM   Q   CM

In Example 2, a majority of the House clearly favors the policy status quo instead of the committee's position, which loses in an up-or-down floor vote.

of the membership. This condition also means that the subcommittee must have some way to acquire information about the policy options likely to be accepted by at least a majority of the House. These types of considerations are commonplace in the real world of Capitol Hill policy making.

Most bills concern not a single dimension, such as more or less spending, but a multitude of dimensions. For example, a bill might be close to a member's ideal point on the spending dimension but be far away on another dimension, such as which governmental level (federal or state) should handle the issue. The introduction of additional dimensions (multidimensionality) produces greater difficulty in analyzing legislative decision making. By employing spatial theory and other analytical approaches, political scientists strive to better understand and explain congressional politics and decision making.[a]

[a] See, for example, Kenneth Shepsle and Mark Boncheck, *Analyzing Politics* (New York: W. W. Norton, 1977); Charles Stewart, *Analyzing Congress* (New York: W. W. Norton, 2001); and Gerald Strom, *The Logic of Lawmaking: A Spatial Theory Approach* (Baltimore: Johns Hopkins University Press, 1990).

to support a bill that might be good for the nation or oppose it because of the opposition of their constituents. Not surprisingly, the bill that emerges from markup is usually the one that can attract the support of the most members. As Rep. Dan Rostenkowski, D-Ill., said when he chaired the House Ways and Means Committee, "We have not written perfect law; perhaps a faculty of scholars could do a better job. A group of ideologues could have produced greater consistency. But politics is an imperfect process." [52]

Outside pressures are often intense during markup deliberations. Under House and Senate sunshine rules, markups must be conducted in public, except on national security or related issues. Compromises can be difficult to achieve in markup rooms filled with lobbyists watching how each member will vote. Hence, committees sometimes conduct pre-markups in private to work out their positions on various issues.

After conducting hearings and markups, a subcommittee sends its recommendations to the full committee. The full committee may conduct hearings and markups on its own, ratify the subcommittee's decision, take no action, or return the matter to the subcommittee for further study.

Reports. If the full committee votes to send the bill to the House or Senate, the staff prepares a report, subject to committee approval, describing the purposes and provisions of the legislation. Reports emphasize arguments favorable to the bill, summarizing selectively the results of staff research and hearings. Reports are noteworthy documents. The bill itself may be long, highly technical, and confusing to most readers. "A good report, therefore, does more than explain—it also persuades," commented a congressional staff aide.[53] Furthermore, reports may guide executive agencies and federal courts in interpreting ambiguous or complex legislative language.

The Policy Environment

Executive agencies, pressure groups, party leaders and caucuses, and the entire House or Senate form the backdrop against which a committee makes policy. These environments may be consensual or conflictual. Some policy questions are settled fairly easily, while others are bitterly controversial. Environments also may be monolithic or pluralistic. Some committees have a single dominant source of outside influence, while others face numerous competing groups or agencies.

Environmental factors influence committees in at least four ways. First, they shape the content of public policies and thus the likelihood that these policies will be accepted by the full House or Senate. The Judiciary Committees are buffeted by diverse and competing pressure groups that feel passionately on volatile issues such as abortion, school prayer, and gun control. The committees' chances for achieving agreement among their members or on the floor depend to a large extent on their ability to deflect such issues altogether or to accommodate diverse groups through artful legislative drafting.

Second, policy environments foster mutual alliances among committees, federal departments, and pressure groups—the iron triangles. The House and Senate Veterans' Affairs Committees, for example, regularly advocate legislation to benefit veterans groups, the second point in the triangle. This effort is backed by the Department of Veterans Affairs. At the very least, issue networks emerge. These are fluid and amorphous groups of policy experts who try to influence any committee that deals with their subject area.[54]

Third, policy environments establish decision-making objectives and guidelines for committees. Clientele-oriented committees, such as the House and Senate Small Business Committees, try to promote the policy views of their clientele groups, such as small-business enterprises. Alliances between committees and federal departments also shape decisions.

Finally, environmental factors influence the level of partisanship on committees. Some committees are relatively free of party infighting, but other committees consider contentious social issues such as poverty and welfare that often divide the two parties. The House Judiciary Committee is filled with conservative Republican and liberal Democratic firebrands. Their sharp ideological clashes got wide publicity during the panel's nationally televised impeachment proceedings against President Bill Clinton.[55]

Committee Staff

Throughout the three principal stages of committee policy making—hearings, markup, and report—staff aides play an active part. Representatives and senators (to a greater degree because there are fewer of them) cannot handle the large workload on their own and so must rely heavily on the unelected lawmakers. Part of the Democratic motivation for nearly equal committee budgets and staff aides in the closely divided 108th Senate is their need to counter the expertise lodged in the Bush-controlled executive branch. In the House, committee resources are generally divided between the majority and minority parties on a two-thirds to one-third basis. Informally, congressional Democrats rely on a network of outside experts, such as former Clinton administration officials, to help them scrutinize and evaluate proposals from the GOP administration.

The discretionary agenda of Congress and its committees is powerfully shaped by the congressional staff. Their influence can be direct or indirect, substantive or procedural, visible or invisible. In the judgment of one former senator, "most of the work and most of the ideas come from the staffers. They are predominantly young men and women, fresh out of college and professional schools. They are ambitious, idealistic, and abounding with ideas."[56] Staff turnover on Capitol Hill is fairly high. In 2002, the average tenure for House personal staff members was 3.3 years, a slight increase from two years earlier. However, staff tenure is still low. According to a study by the Congressional Management Foundation, "Over 60% of House staff have less than two years of experience in their current position, including 40% of Chiefs of Staff, 58% of Legislative Directors, and 72% of Press Secretaries."[57] The average tenure for Senate aides is 5.3 years. Yet 70 percent of all Washington-based Senate staff and nearly two-thirds of state-based senatorial staff have less than two years of experience.[58] Many committee, personal, and leadership aides use their experience as a stepping-stone to other jobs, such as lobbying.

Policy proposals emanate from many sources—the White House, administrative agencies, interest groups, state and local officials, scholars, and citizens—but staff aides are strategically positioned to advance or hinder these proposals. As one Senate committee staff director recounted, "Usually, you draw up proposals for the year's agenda, lay out the alternatives. You can put in some stuff you like and leave out some you don't. I recommend ideas that the [chairman's] interested in and also that I'm interested in." [59] Many committee staff are active in outside communications and issue networks (health or environment, for example) that enhance lawmakers' ability to make informed decisions.[60]

Staff aides negotiate with legislators, lobbyists, and executive officials on issues, legislative language, and political strategy. Sometimes they travel to foreign countries to conduct investigations. Congress's investigative power undergirds its ability to make informed judgments on policy matters. And staff members are the ones who do the essential spadework that can lead to changes in policy or new laws. Staff aides sometimes make policy decisions. Consider their crucial role on a defense appropriations bill:

> The dollar figures in the huge piece of legislation [were] so immense that House-Senate conferees, negotiating their differences . . . , relegated almost every item less than $100 million to staff aides on grounds that the members themselves did not have time to deal with such items, which Sen. Ted Stevens (R-Alaska) called "small potatoes." [61]

During hearings, aides recruit witnesses, on their own or at the specific direction of the chairman, and plan when and in what order they appear. In addition, staff aides commonly accompany committee members to the floor to give advice, draft amendments, and negotiate compromises. The number of aides who can be present on the floor is limited, however, by House and Senate regulations.

For information, analyses, policy options, and research projects, committee staff can turn to the three legislative support agencies: the Congressional Research Service, established in 1914; the General Accounting Office, established in 1921; and the Congressional Budget Office, established in 1974. The Office of Technology Assessment, a support agency created in 1972 to assist lawmakers in making scientific and technological policy, was abolished by the Republican-controlled Congress in 1995. One factor in the office's demise was the perception that its research duplicated that performed by other public and private organizations.[62] Unlike committee or personal aides, the Congressional Research Service, the General Accounting Office, and the Congressional Budget Office operate under strict rules of nonpartisanship and objectivity. Staffed with experts, they provide Congress with analytical talent matching that in executive agencies, universities, or specialized groups.

Staffing reflects members' dual roles in the two Congresses: individual policy maker and constituency representative. It can be a controversial process. A New Jersey senator, for example, was criticized by African American clergy in his state for "failing to appoint blacks to important positions on his personal staff" as he had promised during his mid-1990s senatorial campaign. The senator responded that he had hired professional black staffers and "defended his efforts to hire members of racial minorities." [63]

Committee Reform and Change

Since passage of the Legislative Reorganization Act of 1946, Congress has made numerous attempts to reform the committee system but has only rarely succeeded. In 1973 and 1974 the Select Committee on Committees, headed by Rep. Richard Bolling, D-Mo. (1949–1983), tried to eliminate several standing committees and make extensive changes in the jurisdiction of other committees. Instead, because of strong opposition from members who stood to surrender subcommittee chairmanships or favored jurisdictions, the House adopted a watered-down version of the committee proposal. In 1977 a Senate select committee, chaired by Adlai E. Stevenson, D-Ill. (1970–1981), tried committee reform with somewhat greater success.

Since then, given the mixed results of these earlier efforts, Congress has moved gingerly to restructure committees. A House select committee proposal in 1979 to create a standing committee on energy failed, and a Senate select panel, created in 1984 to address committee reform and assignment limitations, had few of its recommendations acted upon by the full Senate.

Many witnesses who appeared before the 1993 Joint Committee on the Organization of Congress urged a major overhaul of the House and Senate committee systems. Others argued for modest changes: reducing committee sizes, eliminating subcommittees, or restricting the use of multiple referrals. Neither the House nor the Senate acted during the 103d Congress on the reform recommendations of the joint committee.[64] Then came the electoral earthquake of November 1994, and Republicans took control of the Congress. Significantly, three standing committees with Democratic constituencies—District of Columbia, Merchant Marine and Fisheries, and Post Office and Civil Service—were abolished and their functions assigned to other standing committees. In addition, there were a number of other formal (amendments to House rules) changes—six-year term limits for committee and subcommittee chairs, for instance—and informal (the Speaker selects committee chairs, ignoring seniority) developments.

Committees, however, are remarkably durable, resilient, and stable institutions despite the periodic forces for change (public criticism of Congress, reformist sentiment among institutionally minded lawmakers, and so on) that buffet them. Major committee restructuring plans, as the several committee reform efforts since the post–World War II period attest, almost always fail or they produce marginal adjustments in committees' jurisdictional mandates, policy-making influence, or method of operation. Scholars and lawmakers posit various theories to explain why it is difficult to accomplish major jurisdictional realignment. For example, given that the control of jurisdictional turf is viewed as power, Speaker Thomas P. "Tip" O'Neill Jr., D-Mass., explained the House's rejection of a major 1973–1974 committee realignment plan in this succinct manner: "The name of the game is power, and the boys don't want to give it up." [65] A political scientist offered an electoral explanation, which embodies the two Congresses concept, for the demise of committee reshuffling plans.

> [A] primary and constant force hindering committee restructuring move-ments has been the electoral objectives of members of Congress. Under pres-sure to bolster their reelection prospects in order to achieve long-term leg-islative and personal goals, rational politicians with the ability to shape legislative structures utilize the arrangement of rules and procedures to se-cure targeted government benefits for needy constituents and voting blocs. Any widespread change in the established order of policy deliberation—par-ticularly its centerpiece—the committee system—would create far too much uncertainty in members' electoral strategies and therefore would be broadly opposed from the start.[66]

Whatever variety of other factors (interest group, party leadership, or committee staff opposition, for instance) impedes major committee overhaul, these workshops of Congress evolve in response to new events and circum-stances. Several recent developments merit mention because they highlight the dynamic quality of the committee system. These include ebbs and flows in the authority of committee chairs, the employment of proxy voting, the use of task forces, and the circumvention of the committee process.

Constricting the Authority of Committee Chairmen

When Republicans took control of the Congress in the mid-1990s, many GOP committee chairmen had to take more direction from their top leaders, especially in the House. Committee chairmen "have been at the mercy of top House and Senate Republicans leaders," wrote two congressional analysts, "who—given the high level of partisanship and the small size of their majori-ties—have resorted to dictating legislation from the top down in order to maintain some semblance of control." [67] Centralized control over committees was particularly pronounced during the speakership of Gingrich (1995–1999), who sometimes circumvented committee consideration of legislation, dictated legislative changes to committees, used the Rules Committee to re-draft committee-reported measures, and engaged in other actions that under-mined the committee system, such as creating partisan task forces. Speaker Hastert, by contrast, has encouraged committees to reclaim their prerogatives. "You are now beginning to see the committees re-establish themselves," said Ways and Means chairman Bill Thomas, R-Calif.[68] The enhancement of the chairmen's authority comports with Speaker Hastert's general leadership style of involving and delegating responsibility to chairmen and others for imple-menting the GOP agenda hammered out in discussions among the members, in leadership circles, and with the George W. Bush administration.

However, Speaker Hastert and the GOP leadership are not reluctant to rein in committee chairs. At the start of the 108th Congress, Hastert and Majority Leader Tom DeLay, R-Texas, were instrumental in winning passage of a party rules change that gave themselves and their allies on the Steering Committee (the GOP's committee on committees) the authority to name all thirteen subcommittee chairs of the Appropriations Committee. Collectively, the subcommittee chairs—equivalent in stature to full committee chairs—are informally called the college of cardinals because of their large influence over spending measures. These subcommittee leaders had been previously designated solely by the Appropriations chairman without review by the majority leadership. This change was triggered by a variety of factors: insufficient deference by the subcommittee chairs to the majority leadership, complaints by conservatives that the appropriators spend too freely, and the chairs' lack of accountability to the Republican Conference. As one Appropriations subcommittee chair put it, "Now the leadership gets to have the Cardinals come in and grovel before them." [69] The upshot was that the subcommittee chairs were reappointed but not before they gave assurances that they would support and advance the party's programs.

Occasions also arise when Senate committee chairs are subject to party leadership direction. For example, toward the late 1990s when political momentum began to build for a patients' bill of rights bill, the majority leader took the issue away from the chairman of the Health, Education, Labor, and Pension Committee and "created a [party] task force headed by [then] Majority Whip Don Nickles of Oklahoma to write the GOP version of the bill." [70] When Sen. Tom Daschle, D-S.D., was majority leader, he gave the Finance Committee a deadline to report a priority bill or else he would call up the proposal that he favored. "I told the Finance Committee they have a window, and I'd love to have them pass out a bill and give it to us and then we'll take it up," said Daschle. "If that fails, we'll have to go to the floor with another vehicle." [71] The point is that, on measures of utmost party importance, congressional leaders will override the prerogatives of committee chairs to take control of crucial agenda items. (Term limits for today's Republican House and Senate chairs inhibit their ability to accumulate powers akin to those held by committee leaders during the heyday of a rigid seniority system.)

Proxy Voting in Committee

When the Republicans took control in 1995, they passed a House rule banning proxy (absentee) voting in committee and subcommittee. The Republicans remembered too many occasions when their members were present at committee sessions only to be outvoted by the Democratic chair who cast the proxy votes of absent partisan members. (The Senate permits proxy voting in committee subject to certain restrictions specified in their rulebook.) Republicans prohibited proxy voting to promote greater participation in committees so that the product would reflect the work of all members, instead of a few. This ban, however, is not popular with everyone. Given the frenetic pace and heavy workload, and the narrow GOP majority on most committees, the ban on proxy voting has made life difficult for committees and their members. Many lawmakers must sprint to cast votes in committees that are conducting business simultaneously. Or they must run back and forth from committee to the House floor to cast their votes. On a few occasions, GOP chairs even lost votes because their partisan committee colleagues were absent. Top Republican leaders and some committee chairmen tried to institute a limited form of proxy voting in the 107th Congress (2001–2003), but the recommendation was rejected by vote of the GOP Conference.

However, Republicans in the 108th Congress amended House rules and handled the issue successfully in an artful manner. "Committees can now adopt a rule that allows committee and subcommittee chairmen to postpone votes almost indefinitely when a record of votes has been ordered, to avoid embarrassing losses and to reschedule when they can be sure they have the votes." [72] As Representative Dingell said of the new House rule: "[B]y permitting votes to be postponed to a time certain, Members will no longer have to attend committee markups while important amendments are being debated. Instead, they will merely have to show up at a specified time to vote. It sounds an awful lot like proxy voting to me." [73]

Task Forces

Speaker Gingrich created numerous party task forces in part because he could determine their mandate and timetable, appoint the chair and members, and assign a deadline for drafting a product. Many of these task forces did little, but some wrote legislation. Task forces, in sum, can forge consensus, draft legislation, coordinate strategy, promote intraparty communication, and involve noncommittee members and junior members in issue areas.

Gingrich's use of task forces provides a practical look at the three theories of legislative organization: the distributional hypothesis, the informational hypothesis, and the party hypothesis. The Speaker's Task Force on California was established in large measure to ensure that the politically important state of California received its fair share of federal funds from the GOP-controlled House. This panel's formation buttressed the committee autonomy or distributive politics view of congressional organization: Committees are designed to accommodate important constituencies. The Task Force on Immigration highlights the chamber-dominated, or informational, perspective. Its work enhanced the expertise of all members by providing them with specialized information on the complexities of immigration policy. Finally, the Task Force on the Environment was formed in part to promote the GOP's deregulatory agenda. A partisan perspective shaped much of its work.

Speaker Hastert has deemphasized the use of party task forces, but they are still occasionally employed to address issues of importance to the party. Hastert, for instance, created task forces to deal with health and terrorism issues. Minority Leader Nancy Pelosi also employs task forces to mobilize support behind party priorities.

The Senate Republican leader also forms party task forces. For instance, to showcase GOP senators up for reelection and to promote Republican priorities, the GOP leader established a number of task forces to focus on such issues as Medicare, education, defense, and Social Security. Democratic leader Daschle also employs task forces selectively. He named New York senator Schumer, for example, to head a Homeland Security Task Force to monitor the government's antiterrorism efforts, including the activities of the Department of Homeland Security. Furthermore, sometimes leaders establish bipartisan task forces or working groups.

Bypassing Committees

Sen. Robert C. Byrd, D-W.Va., and other senators were upset with then Budget chairman Pete V. Domenici, R-N.M., when he decided to forgo committee markup of the concurrent budget resolution for fiscal 2002, which largely tracked the budget recommendations of President Bush. With the likelihood of deadlock on the Budget Committee given its 10 to 10 membership, Domenici decided to avoid a contentious markup and call up the resolution in the Senate. "[C]ircumventing a committee markup of the budget resolution is unprecedented and has never been done in the history of the Senate Budget Committee," declaimed Senator Byrd.[74] In the judgment of Sen. Don Nickles, R-Okla., a tendency exists today to circumvent the committee process. "This Senate is becoming more and more willing to bypass committees" and take "bills directly to the floor without ever going through committee, not giving committee Members the opportunity to have amendments, to have discussion, to have vetting, offer alternatives, or come up with bipartisan approaches." [75]

Circumventing committees is not unique to the Senate. On the same day that Senator Byrd was urging that a markup go forward, a House member was upset that a bill had been called up on the floor that had not been the subject of consideration by the House committee of jurisdiction. "I was flabbergasted," he said, "when I found out . . . that [this bill] was coming to the floor of the House without hearings, without committee deliberation, without the ability to offer amendments." [76]

These examples highlight the tendency of party leaders or individual members to bypass some or all of the stages of committee consideration of legislation. Various techniques are employed to accomplish this purpose, such as establishing task forces. In general, the circumvention of committees reflects the dominance of party power over committee power. Other specific reasons are also noteworthy. For instance, heightened partisanship in certain committees encourages party leaders to take charge of priority measures to avoid negative media coverage of committee markups. Or factional disputes within committees may prevent committees from reaching agreement on measures deemed important to party leaders. Party leaders, too, may believe insufficient time exists for committees to hold hearings and markups on major bills that they want to consider within a specific time period. Allies of Senator Daschle when he was majority leader argued that "there are few consequences if [committees are bypassed] because nobody outside Congress cares whether a bill went through committee or not." [77] Today, committee review of major legislation can sometimes be problematic.

Conclusion

Several generalizations can be made about congressional committees today. First, they shape the House and Senate agendas. Not only do they have negative power—pigeonholing legislation referred to them—but they have positive power as well. The bills they report largely determine what each chamber will debate and in what form. As one House chairman stated in his testimony before the Joint Committee on the Organization of Congress,

> [Committees] provide Congress with the expertise, skill, and organizational structure necessary to cope with the increasingly complex and technical questions in both the domestic and international arenas. They also ensure a forum for the broadest possible participation of diverse interests and constituencies in the formative stages of the legislative process. They are, in short, the window through which much of the democratic participation in lawmaking is made possible.[78]

Second, committees differ in their policy-making environments, mix of members, decision-making objectives, and ability to fulfill individual members' goals. Recruitment methods reinforce the committees' autonomy. Committees frequently are imbalanced ideologically or geographically. They are likely to advocate policies espoused by agencies and outside groups interested in their work.

Third, committees often develop an esprit de corps that flows across party lines. Committee members usually will defend their panels against criticisms, jurisdictional trespassing, or any attempt to bypass them.

Fourth, committees typically operate independently of one another. This longtime custom fosters an attitude of mutual noninterference in the work of other committees. However, multiple referrals of bills spawn broader interrelationships among committees.

Fifth, the committee system contributes fundamentally to policy fragmentation, although a few committees—Rules and Budget, for example—act as policy coordinators for Congress. "This is one of the anomalies here," remarked a House member. "In order to attain legislative efficiency, we say that we have to break down into committees with specialized jurisdictions. When you do that, you lose your ability to grapple with the big problems." [79] Party leaders, as a result, are more involved than ever in coordinating policy making and forging winning coalitions in committees and on the floor.

Finally, committee autonomy is increasingly under pressure from assertive party leaders who strive to move the party's agenda forward and enforce party discipline—with or without the committee leaders' cooperation. In theoretical terms, it may be seen as a shift in committee roles from distributional purposes to partisan-programmatic goals.

A view from the back of the House chamber spotlights the Speaker's rostrum, gallery, and lawmakers' seats. Unlike the Senate, House members do not have assigned seats.

8

Congressional Rules and Procedures

Congress needs written rules to do its work. Compiling the Senate's first parliamentary manual, Thomas Jefferson stressed the importance of a known system of rules:

> It is much more material that there should be a rule to go by, than what the rule is; that there may be uniformity of proceeding in business not subject to the caprice of the Speaker or captiousness of the members. It is very material that order, decency, and regularity be preserved in a dignified public body.[1]

Jefferson understood that how Congress operates affects what it does. Thus Congress's rules protect majority and minority rights, divide the workload, help contain conflict, ensure fair play, and distribute power among members. Because formal rules cannot cover every contingency, precedents—accumulated decisions of House Speakers and Senate presiding officers—fill in the gaps. These precedents are codified by House and Senate parliamentarians, printed, and distributed. There are also informal, unwritten codes of conduct such as courtesy to other members. These folkways are transmitted from incumbent members to newcomers.[2]

Before bills become laws, they typically pass successfully through several stages of life or death in each house (see Figure 8-1). Bills that fail to attract majority support at any critical juncture may never be passed. Congress, in short, is a procedural obstacle course that favors opponents of legislation and hinders proponents. This defensive advantage promotes bargaining and compromise at each decision point.

Congressional rules are not independent of the policy and power struggles that lie behind them. There is very little that the House and Senate cannot do under the rules so long as the action is backed by votes and inclination. Yet votes and inclination are not easily obtained, and the rules persistently challenge the proponents of legislation to demonstrate that they have both resources at their command. Little prevents obstruction at every turn except the tacit understanding that the business of the House and Senate must go on. Members recognize that the rules can be redefined and prerogatives taken away or modified. Rules can also be employed against those who use them abusively. In brief, rules can be employed to block or advance actions in either

Figure 8-1 How a Bill Becomes Law

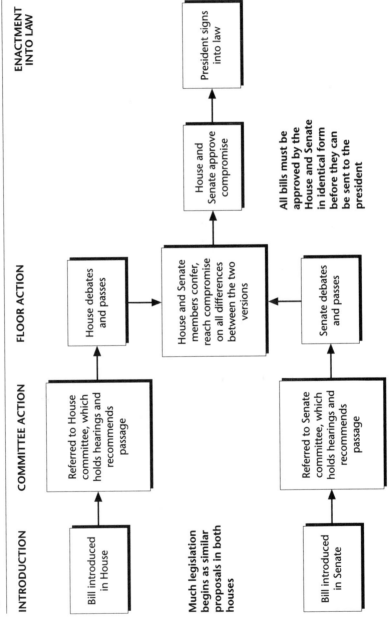

INTRODUCTION **COMMITTEE ACTION** **FLOOR ACTION** **ENACTMENT INTO LAW**

Bill introduced in House

Referred to House committee, which holds hearings and recommends passage

House debates and passes

House and Senate members confer, reach compromise on all differences between the two versions

House and Senate approve compromise

President signs into law

Much legislation begins as similar proposals in both houses

Bill introduced in Senate

Referred to Senate committee, which holds hearings and recommends passage

Senate debates and passes

All bills must be approved by the House and Senate in identical form before they can be sent to the president

chamber and proponents or opponents of measures or matters do not look on them as neutral devices.

Introduction of Bills

Only members of Congress can introduce legislation. The reasons that they introduce the bills they do are fascinating and numerous.

> Lawmakers are led to their choice of legislation by many factors: parochial interest, party preference, and crass calculation connected to campaign fund raising. But there is a motivator that is rarely discussed that can be just as potent: a personal brush with adversity. Congress is an intensely human place where personal experience sometimes has powerful repercussions.[3]

As Sen. Gordon H. Smith, R-Ore., stated: "Each of us, as United States senators, comes to . . . this public place with the sum of our beliefs, our personal experience and our values, and none of us checks them at the door."[4] For example, Sen. Pete V. Domenici, R-N.M., whose daughter suffers from mental illness, is Congress's acknowledged champion for the mentally ill. "In the field of mental health," said a Democratic House member, "I think it's possible that nothing at all would have been done by Congress if it weren't for legislators like Domenici who were galvanized by personal experience."[5] Personal experience, however, is not the only source of legislative proposals. Often members get ideas for bills from the executive branch, interest groups, scholars, state and local officials, constituents, the press and media, and their own staff.

A member who introduces a bill becomes its sponsor. This member may seek cosponsors to demonstrate wide support for the legislation. Outside groups also may urge members to cosponsor measures. "We were not assured of a hearing," said a lobbyist of a bill that his group was pushing. "There was more hostility to the idea, so it was very important to line up a lot of cosponsors to show the over-all concern."[6] As important as the number of cosponsors is their leadership status and ideological stance. Cosponsors are not always like-minded politically. Massachusetts senator Edward M. Kennedy, a liberal Democrat, once said of conservative South Carolina senator Strom Thurmond, "Whenever Strom and I introduce a bill together, it is either an idea whose time has come, or one of us has not read the bill."[7]

Although identifying a bill's sponsors is easy, pinpointing its real initiators may be difficult. Legislation is "an aggregate, not a simple production," wrote Woodrow Wilson. "It is impossible to tell how many persons, opinions, and influences have entered into its composition."[8] President John F. Kennedy, for example, usually is given credit for initiating the Peace Corps. But Theodore Sorensen, Kennedy's special counsel, recalled that the Peace Corps was

> based on the Mormon and other voluntary religious service efforts, on an editorial Kennedy had read years earlier, on a speech by General [James] Gavin,

on a luncheon I had with Philadelphia businessmen, on the suggestions of [Kennedy's] academic advisers, on legislation previously introduced and on the written response to a spontaneous late-night challenge he issued to Michigan students.[9]

In short, the ideas behind many bills have tangled histories.

Required legislation, particularly funding measures, makes up much of Congress's annual agenda. Bills that authorize programs and specify how much money can be spent on them (authorization bills) and bills that provide the money (appropriation bills) appear on Congress's schedule at about the same time each year. Other matters recur at less frequent intervals, every five years perhaps. Emergency issues require Congress's immediate attention. Activist legislators also push proposals onto Congress's program. Bills not acted upon die automatically at the end of each two-year Congress. "Anybody can drop a bill into the hopper [a mahogany box near the Speaker's podium where members place their proposed bills]," said a House GOP leader. "The question is, Can you make something happen with it?" [10]

Drafting

"As a sculptor works in stone or clay, the legislator works in words," observed one member.[11] Words are the building blocks of policy, and legislators frequently battle over adding, deleting, or modifying terms and phrases. Members increasingly give their bills eye-catching titles. The Republicans' celebrated Contract with America bristled with items such as the American Dream Restoration Act (tax code reform), the Common Sense Legal Reforms Act (tort and product liability changes), and the Taking Back Our Streets Act (crime control). Lawmakers sometimes use the names of famous sports figures to gain publicity and support for their ideas, such as the Muhammad Ali Boxing Reform Act, or they affix popular phrases to legislation, such as the patients' bill of rights. As Sen. Trent Lott, R-Miss., pointed out: "If you ask [voters], 'Are you for the Bill of Rights?' Yeah, they're for the Bill of Rights. 'Bill of Rights' is a great term. It's the new term. It may even be supplanting reform." [12] Instead of proposals to reduce estate taxes, they are called bills to end death taxes. "Whoever controls the language controls the debate," asserted one commentator.[13]

Although bills are introduced only by members, anyone may draft them.[14] Expert drafters in the House and Senate offices of legislative counsel assist members and committees in writing legislation. Executive agencies and lobby groups often prepare measures for introduction by friendly legislators. Many home-state industries, for instance, draft narrowly tailored tariff or regulatory measures that enhance their business prospects. These proposals are then introduced by the local lawmakers—another instance of the two Congresses linkage. As a senatorial aide said, the senator "just introduces it as a courtesy to his constituents." [15] (See box outlining the four basic types of legislation: bills, joint resolutions, concurrent resolutions, and simple resolutions.)

Types of Legislation

Bill. Most legislative proposals before Congress are in a bill form. Bills are designated H.R. (House of Representatives) or S. (Senate) according to where they originate, followed by a number assigned in the order in which they were introduced, from the beginning of each two-year congressional term. *Public bills* deal with general questions and become public laws if approved by Congress and signed by the president. *Private bills* deal with individual matters, such as claims against the government, immigration and naturalization cases, and land titles. They become private laws if approved and signed.

Joint Resolution. A joint resolution, designated H. J. Res. or S. J. Res., requires the approval of both houses and the president's signature, just as a bill does, and has the force of law. No significant difference exists between a bill and a joint resolution. The latter generally deals with limited matters, such as a single appropriation for a specific purpose. Joint resolutions also are used to propose constitutional amendments, which do not require presidential signatures but become a part of the Constitution when three-fourths of the states have ratified them.

Concurrent Resolution. A concurrent resolution, designated H. Con. Res. or S. Con. Res., must be passed by both houses but does not require the president's signature and does not have the force of law. Concurrent resolutions generally are used to make or amend rules applicable to both houses or to express their joint sentiment. A concurrent resolution, for example, is used to fix the time for adjournment of a Congress and to express Congress's annual budgeting plan. It might also be used to convey the congratulations of Congress to another country on the anniversary of its independence.

Resolution. A simple resolution, designated H. Res. or S. Res., deals with matters entirely within the prerogatives of one house. It requires neither passage by the other chamber nor approval by the president and does not have the force of law. Most resolutions deal with the rules of one house. They also are used to express the sentiments of a single house, to extend condolences to the family of a deceased member, or to give advice on foreign policy or other executive business.

Nowadays, Congress frequently acts on comprehensive or omnibus bills or resolutions (called packages or megabills by the press). Packages contain an array of issues that once were handled as separate pieces of legislation. Their increasing use stems in part from members' reluctance to make hard political decisions without a package arrangement. A House Budget Committee chairman once explained their attractiveness:

> You can use large bills as a way to hide legislation that otherwise might be more controversial, as a way to be able to slam-dunk issues that otherwise might be torn apart, as a way to avoid hard votes that Members would have to account for at election time, as a way to avoid angering special-interest groups that use votes [to decide] contributions to campaigns and as a way to guarantee that the President will have to accept it.[16]

Sometimes Congress has little choice but to use the omnibus approach. Months overdue in passing eleven regular appropriations bills, Congress in early 2003 packaged the unfinished measures into one huge bill. In this way, procedural action on the outstanding measures was expedited by GOP congressional leaders, who minimized opportunities for further delay if each bill had been taken up separately.

Timing

"Everything in politics is timing," Speaker Thomas P. "Tip" O'Neill Jr., D-Mass., used to say. A bill's success or failure often hinges on when it is introduced or brought to the floor. A bill that might succeed early in a session could fail as adjournment nears. However, controversial legislation sometimes could be rushed through during the last hectic days of a Congress.

Elections greatly influence the timing of legislation. Policy issues can be taken off or kept on Congress's agenda because of electoral circumstances—a good illustration of how the two Congresses are inextricably connected. For example, coming off a major success in the 2002 midterm elections, congressional Republicans moved to capitalize on their momentum by acting quickly early in 2003 on a number of their priority bills. Among the measures were late-term abortion, a ban on human cloning, and welfare reform. In February, for example, House GOP leaders brought welfare reform legislation directly to the floor, bypassing committee review.

Referral of Bills

After bills are introduced, they are referred formally to appropriate standing committees by the Senate presiding officer or the House Speaker. (In practice, the reference of measures is done by the Senate or House parliamentarian, who is the official procedural adviser to each chamber's presiding officer.) A bill's phraseology can affect its referral and hence its chances of passage. This political fact of life means that members use words artfully when drafting legislation. The objective is to encourage the referral of their measures to sympathetic, not hostile, committees. If a bill mentions taxes, for example, it invariably is referred to the tax panels. To sidestep these committees, Senator Domenici avoided the word *tax* in a bill proposing a charge on waterborne freight.

> If the waterway fee were considered a tax—which it was, basically, because it would raise revenues for the federal treasury—the rules would place it under the dominion of the Senate's tax-writing arm, the Finance Committee. But Finance was chaired by Russell B. Long, of Louisiana, whose state included two of the world's biggest barge ports and who was, accordingly, an implacable foe of waterway charges in any form. Domenici knew that Long could find several years' worth of bills to consider before he would voluntarily schedule a hearing on S. 790 [the Domenici bill]. For this reason, [Domenici staff

Referral Strategy

Sometimes, the Senate's rules can be so arcane that it takes major strategy sessions to get even the most routine bills through the bureaucracy.

That was the case when Sen. Bob Graham, D-Fla., drafted a bill [targeted only at Florida] to permit the Forest Service to sell eighteen tracts of land and use the proceeds to buy up patches of private lands within the Apalachicola National Forest. To ensure that such a low-profile bill moved, Graham wanted it to go through the Energy and Natural Resources Committee, on which he sat.

Instead, Parliamentarian Alan S. Frumin told Graham's aides that the bill, which was soon to be dropped, would be referred to the Agriculture, Nutrition, and Forestry Committee. Because Graham was not a member, such a move could have guaranteed the bill a quiet death.

Why the Agriculture Committee? For at least three decades, the jurisdiction over land bills was split between the two committees. Bills affecting land east of the 100th Meridian—which runs through North and South Dakota and the middle of Texas—are assigned to Agriculture, while bills that affect lands west of it go to Energy.

Graham's bill dealt with the wrong side of the country. To change Frumin's mind, Graham's aides needed to turn the rules to their advantage.

They found their opportunity by uncovering the roots behind the 100th Meridian rule. The idea was to divide jurisdiction between public lands and privately owned lands. Because most land on the East Coast is privately owned, that side of the country went to Agriculture, which had jurisdiction over private lands. Everything in the West fell to Energy, which had jurisdiction over public lands.

Graham's aides, however, found out that a majority of tracts in Florida were always public lands. That persuaded Frumin that the bill belonged to the Energy panel.

Source: Adapted from David Nather, "Graham Turns Rules to His Advantage," *CQ Weekly,* June 8, 2002, 1494.

---

aides] had been careful to avoid the word *tax* in writing the bill, employing such terms as *charge* and *fee* instead.[17]

Domenici's drafting strategy worked. His bill was jointly referred to the Commerce and Environment Committees on which he served. Because committees' jurisdictional mandates are ambiguous or overlap, it is not unusual for legislation to be referred to two or more Senate or House committees—the concept of "one bill, many committees." (See the box illustrating that parliamentary convention also affects the reference of legislation.)

Of the thousands of bills introduced annually, Congress takes up relatively few. During the 107th Congress, 7,439 public bills and joint resolutions were introduced; of these only 377 became public laws (see Table 8-1). Many reasons can be cited for the general decline in the enactment of laws, such as

Table 8-1　Bills Introduced and Legislation Enacted, 80th–107th
Congresses (1947–2003)

Congress and years		Bills and joint resolutions introduced			Laws enacted	
		Total	House	Senate	Public	Private
80th	(1947–1949)	10,797	7,611	3,186	906	458
81st	(1949–1951)	14,988	10,502	4,486	921	1,103
82d	(1951–1953)	12,730	9,065	3,665	594	1,023
83d	(1953–1955)	14,952	10,875	4,077	781	1,002
84th	(1955–1957)	17,687	13,169	4,518	1,028	893
85th	(1957–1959)	19,112	14,580	4,532	936	784
86th	(1959–1961)	18,261	14,112	4,149	800	492
87th	(1961–1963)	18,376	14,328	4,048	885	685
88th	(1963–1965)	17,479	14,022	3,457	666	360
89th	(1965–1967)	24,003	19,874	4,129	810	473
90th	(1967–1969)	26,460	22,060	4,400	640	362
91st	(1969–1971)	26,303	21,436	4,867	695	246
92d	(1971–1973)	22,969	18,561	4,408	607	161
93d	(1973–1975)	23,396	18,872	4,524	649	123
94th	(1975–1977)	21,096	16,982	4,114	588	141
95th	(1977–1979)	19,387	15,587	3,800	634	170
96th	(1979–1981)	12,583	9,103	3,480	613	123
97th	(1981–1983)	11,490	8,094	3,396	473	56
98th	(1983–1985)	10,559	7,105	3,454	623	52
99th	(1985–1987)	9,885	6,499	3,386	664	24
100th	(1987–1989)	9,588	6,263	3,325	713	48
101st	(1989–1991)	10,352	6,683	3,669	650	16
102d	(1991–1993)	10,513	6,775	3,738	590	20
103d	(1993–1995)	8,544	5,739	2,805	465	8
104th	(1995–1997)	6,808	4,542	2,266	333	4
105th	(1997–1999)	7,732	5,014	2,718	394	10
106th	(1999–2001)	9,158	5,815	3,343	580	24
107th	(2001–2003)	7,439	5,115	2,284	377	5

Source: Rozanne M. Barry, *Bills Introduced and Laws Enacted: Selected Legislative Statistics, 1947–1992,* Congressional Research Service Report, January 15, 1993, 2. See also U.S. Congress, *Congressional Record,* daily ed., 106th Cong., 1st sess., January 19, 1997, D29; U.S. Congress, *Congressional Record,* daily edition, 107th Cong., 1st sess., January 30, 2001, D45; and 107th Cong., 2nd sess., December 16, 2002, D1193.

legislative interest in limiting the size of the national government, an emphasis on community and private action for resolving problems, the complexity of issues, the intensity of partisanship, legislative-executive conflicts, the narrow party divisions in Congress, and significant sentiment in both chambers that more laws may not be the answer to the nation's problems.

Lawmaking, too, is an arduous and intricate process. As a Senate GOP leader noted, "That's the way Congress works. You work for two years and finally you get to the end and either it all collapses in a puddle or you get a breakthrough." [18] Or as John D. Dingell, D-Mich., the most senior House member, phrased it: "Legislation is hard, pick-and-shovel work," and it often "takes a long time to do it." [19] For example, in 2003, Rep. Charlie Norwood, R-Ga., began his seventh year trying to get Congress to enact a patients' bill of rights measure.

Once committees complete action on the bills referred to them, House and Senate rules require a majority of the full committee to be physically present to report out any measure. If this rule is violated and neither waived nor ignored, a point of order can be made against the proposal on the floor. (A point of order is a parliamentary objection that halts the proceedings until the chamber's presiding officer decides whether the contention is valid.)

Bills reported from committee have passed a critical stage in the lawmaking process. The next major step is to reach the House or Senate floor for debate and amendment. We begin with the House because tax and appropriation bills originate there—the former under the Constitution, the latter by custom.

Scheduling in the House

All bills reported from committee are listed in chronological order on one of several calendars—lists that enable the House to put measures into convenient categories. Bills that raise or spend money are assigned to the Union Calendar. The House Calendar contains all other major public measures. Private bills, such as immigration requests or claims against the government, are assigned to the Private Calendar, and generally noncontroversial bills are placed on the Corrections Calendar. There is no guarantee that the House will debate legislation placed on any of these calendars. The Speaker, in consultation with other party leaders, largely determines if, when, how, and in what order bills come up. The power to set the House's agenda constitutes the essence of the Speaker's institutional authority.

Shortcuts for Minor Bills

Whether a bill is major or minor, controversial or noncontroversial, influences the procedure employed to bring it before the House. Most bills are relatively minor and are taken up and passed through various shortcut procedures.

One shortcut is the designation of special days for considering minor bills. Measures on the Corrections Calendar, for example, are in order for floor consideration on the second and fourth Tuesdays of the month. The Corrections Calendar is an innovation of Speaker Newt Gingrich, R-Ga. (1995–1999). He wanted an expeditious way to repeal what he considered the silliest rules, regulations, and laws on the books. The House adopted the calendar on June 20, 1995, by amending its rules. The Speaker has sole authority to determine whether a bill, which must have been favorably reported from a committee, is to be on the Corrections Calendar. A three-fifths vote (261 votes if all 435 members are present) is required to pass corrections legislation.

Another shortcut is the suspension-of-the-rules procedure (informally referred to as the suspension calendar), which is controlled by the Speaker through his power of recognizing who may speak. Most public laws enacted by the House are accomplished through this procedure. A study by Donald Wolfensberger, former staff director of the House Rules Committee, determined that in the 107th Congress (2001–2003) nearly three-quarters of bills enacted into public law came to the floor via this procedure, compared with around 33 percent two decades ago. Members may use this timesaving device every Monday and Tuesday (and on Wednesdays until mid-April 2003 under a House rules change adopted at the start of the 108th Congress) to pass relatively noncontroversial measures. Measures considered under suspension of the rules do not have to be reported from committee before the full House takes them up. The procedure permits only forty minutes of debate, allows no amendments, and requires a two-thirds vote for passage. The procedure is often favored by bill managers who want to avoid unfriendly amendments and points of order against their legislation.

The heightened partisanship in the closely divided House raises the question, Why is the suspension procedure, which requires bipartisanship to attract the two-thirds vote, increasingly employed in such a polarized institution? The answer seems to involve a trade-off. "As members are increasingly being denied opportunities in special rules to offer amendments to more substantive bills on the floor," declaimed Wolfensberger, "the leadership is providing alternative mechanisms to satisfy members' policy influence and re-election needs through the relatively non-controversial and bipartisan suspension process." [20] Thus, greater use of suspensions serves two prime purposes: providing an outlet for members to achieve their policy and political goals and keeping the lid on members' frustration with limited or closed amendment procedures.

The current rules of the House Republican Conference establish some guidelines for the Speaker in using the suspension procedure. For example, the Speaker cannot schedule any bill or resolution under suspension of the rules that "fails to include a cost estimate, has not been cleared by the minority, was opposed by more than one-third of the committee members [who] reported the bill, and exceeds $100,000,000 in authorized, appropriated, or direct or indirect loan commitments or guarantees."

Still another expedited procedure is unanimous consent. However, the Speaker will recognize a lawmaker to call up bills or resolutions by unanimous consent "only when assured that the majority and minority floor leadership and committee and subcommittee chairmen and ranking minority members have no objection." [21] Absent these clearances, unanimous consent is not a viable avenue to the floor.

Major measures reach the floor by different procedures. Budget, appropriation, and certain other measures are considered privileged and may be called up from the appropriate calendar for debate at almost any time. Most major bills, however, do not have an automatic green light to the floor. Before they reach the floor they are assigned a rule by the Rules Committee.

The Strategic Role of the Rules Committee

A House Rules Committee has existed since the First Congress. During its early years the committee prepared or ratified a biennial set of House rules and then dissolved. As House procedures became more complex with increases in membership and workload, the committee became more important. In 1858 the Speaker became a member of the committee and the next year its chairman. In 1880 Rules became a permanent standing committee. Three years later the committee launched a procedural revolution. It began to issue rules (sometimes called special rules), which are privileged resolutions that grant priority for floor consideration to virtually all major bills.

Arm of the Majority Leadership. In 1910 the House rebelled against the arbitrary decisions of Speaker Joseph G. Cannon, R-Ill., and removed him from the Rules Committee. During the subsequent decades, as the committee became an independent power, it extracted substantive concessions in bills in exchange for rules, blocked measures it opposed, and advanced those it favored, often reflecting the wishes of the House's conservative coalition of Republicans and southern Democrats.

The chairman of the Rules Committee from 1955 to 1967, Howard W. "Judge" Smith, D-Va., was a diehard conservative and a master at devising delaying tactics. He might abruptly adjourn meetings for lack of a quorum, allow requests for rules to languish, or refuse to schedule meetings. House consideration of the 1957 civil rights bill was temporarily delayed because Smith absented himself from the Capitol. His committee could not meet without him. Smith claimed he was seeing about a barn that had burned on his Virginia farm. Retorted Speaker Sam Rayburn, D-Texas, "I knew Howard Smith would do most anything to block a civil rights bill, but I never knew he would resort to arson." [22]

Liberals' frustration with the coalition of conservatives who dominated the committee boiled over. After John F. Kennedy was elected president in 1960, Speaker Rayburn realized he needed greater control over the Rules Committee if the House was to advance the president's activist New Frontier program. Rayburn proposed enlarging the committee from twelve members to fifteen. This proposal led to a titanic struggle between Rayburn and the archconservative Rules chairman.

> Superficially, the Representatives seemed to be quarreling about next to nothing: the membership of the committee. In reality, however, the question raised had grave import for the House and for the United States. The House's answer to it affected the tenuous balance of power between the great conser-

vative and liberal blocs within the House. And, doing so, the House's answer seriously affected the response of Congress to the sweeping legislative proposals of the newly elected President, John Kennedy.[23]

In a dramatic vote the House agreed to expand the Rules Committee. Two new Democrats and one Republican were added, which loosened the conservative coalition's grip on the panel.

During the 1970s the Rules Committee came under even greater majority party control. In 1975 the Democratic Caucus authorized the Speaker to appoint, subject to party ratification, all Democratic members of the committee. (Thirteen years later Republicans authorized their leader to name the GOP members of the Rules Committee.) The majority party maintains a disproportionate ratio on the panel (nine Republicans and four Democrats in the 108th Congress). The Rules Committee, in short, has become the Speaker's committee. As GOP Rules vice chairman Porter J. Goss of Florida said about the panel's relationship with the Speaker, "How much is the Rules Committee the handmaiden of the Speaker? The answer is, totally." [24] Rep. David Dreier, R-Calif., chairs the panel in the 108th Congress.

The Speaker's influence over the Rules Committee ensures that he can both bring measures to the floor and shape their procedural consideration. Because House rules require bills to be taken up in the chronological order listed on the calendars, many substantial bills would never reach the floor before Congress adjourned. The Rules Committee can put major bills first in line. Equally important, a rule from the committee sets the conditions for debate and amendment.

A request for a rule usually is made by the chairman of the committee reporting the bill. The Rules Committee conducts hearings on the request in the same way that other committees consider legislation, except that only members testify. The House parliamentarian usually drafts the rule after consulting with committee leaders and staff. The rule is considered on the House floor and is voted on in the same manner as regular bills (see box on example of a rule from the Rules Committee).

Types of Rules. Traditionally, the Rules Committee has granted open, closed, or modified rules as well as waivers. An open rule means that any germane amendments can be proposed. A closed rule prohibits the offering of amendments. A modified rule comes in two forms: modified open and modified closed. The distinction hinges on the number of amendments made in order by the Rules Committee—few under modified closed, more under modified open. Waivers of points of order set aside technical violations of House rules to allow bills to reach the floor. Waivers are commonly included in the different types of rules.

Whether Democrats or Republicans control the House, their majority on the Rules Committee displays procedural creativity and imagination.

Example of a Rule from the Rules Committee

The following modified open rule (H. Res. 472), which required members to preprint their amendments in the Congressional Record *at least one day before the bill was considered, set the terms for debating and amending the Arming Pilots against Terrorism Act of 2002.*

Resolved, That at any time after the adoption of this resolution the Speaker may, pursuant to clause 2(b) of the rule XVIII, declare the House resolved into the Committee of the Whole House on the state of the Union for consideration of the bill (H.R. 4635) to amend title 49, United States Code, to establish a program for Federal flight deck officers, and for other purposes. The first reading of the bill shall be dispensed with. All points of order against consideration of the bill are waived. General debate shall be confined to the bill and shall not exceed one hour equally divided and controlled by the chairman and ranking minority member of the Committee on Transportation and Infrastructure. After general debate on the bill shall be considered for amendment under the five-minute rule. It shall be in order to consider as an original bill for the purpose of amendment under the five-minute rule the amendment in the nature of a substitute recommended by the Committee on Transportation and Infrastructure now printed in the bill. The committee amendment in the nature of a substitute shall be considered as read. All points of order against the committee amendment in the nature of a substitute are waived. No amendment to the committee amendment in the nature of a substitute shall be in order except those printed in the portion of the Congressional Record designated for that purpose in clause 8 of rule XVIII and except pro forma amendments for the purpose of debate. Each amendment so printed may be offered only the Member who caused it to be printed or his designee and shall be considered as read. At the conclusion of consideration of the bill for amendment the Committee shall rise and report the bill to the House with such amendments as may have been adopted. Any Member may demand a separate vote in the House on any amendment adopted in the Committee of the Whole to the bill or to the committee amendment in the nature of a substitute. The previous question shall be considered as ordered on the bill and amendments thereto to final passage without intervening motion except one motion to recommit with or without instructions.

Source: U.S. Congress, *Congressional Record,* daily ed., 107th Cong., 2d sess., July 10, 2002, H4435.

Instead of choosing from among a few patterns the Rules Committee has demonstrated a willingness to create unique designs by recombining an increasingly wide array of elements, or by creating new ones as the need arises, to help leaders, committees, and members manage the heightened uncertainties of decision making on the House floor.[25]

The trend toward creative use of complex rules reflected several developments: the desire of majority party leaders to exert greater control over floor procedures, members' restlessness with dilatory floor challenges to committee-reported bills, the rise of megabills hundreds of pages in length, and efforts by committee leaders either to limit the number of amendments or to keep unfriendly amendments off the floor. The sharp rise in partisanship also triggered an increase in restrictive rules.

When Republicans took control of the House, they remembered their bitter experience with rules that restricted their right to offer amendments. They promised more openness and greater opportunities for all lawmakers to offer floor amendments to pending legislation. Republicans did work to provide more open amendment procedures when they first took control of the House in 1995, although Democrats contended that the Republicans fell short of meeting their claims that about 70 percent of special rules would be open. (Republicans exceeded the 70 percent target by taking up 16 of 22 Contract with America measures under open or modified open rules.) However, as Republican majorities dropped from 235 in the 104th Congress [1995–1997] to 222 in the 107th [2001–2003], the Rules Committee moved away from open rules. Open and modified open rules declined from 57 percent in the 104th Congress to only 37 percent in the 107th Congress (see Table 8-2).

This downturn underscores that open rules sometimes clash with a fundamental objective of any majority party: passage of priority legislation even at the cost of restricting members' amending opportunities. Under an open rule, minority Democrats could offer scores of dilatory amendments to stall action on the GOP's agenda. Such actions prompted a Rules chairman to say, "It looks like we're going to have to increasingly restrict rules if the Democrats won't cooperate." [26]

The Republicans not only have used most of the known creative rules (see box on examples of creative rules), but they also have devised new rules of their own. When they were in the minority, Republicans opposed the so-called king-of-the-hill rules crafted by the Democrats. These rules made in order a limited number of major amendments but stipulated that only the last alternative voted on is the one that counts for purposes of accepting or rejecting national policy. The yeas and nays on the other amendments were free votes; that is, they provided political cover to lawmakers who could explain them however they wished. Republicans argued that these rules "violated the democratic principle that the position with the strongest support should prevail." [27] The GOP-controlled Rules Committee now issues queen-of-the-hill rules, by which the major amendment that wins the most votes among all the amendments voted upon in the Committee of the Whole is forwarded to the full House for a vote on final passage.

Another GOP innovation, the time-structured rule, allows lawmakers to offer their amendments but only within specified time limits set by the Rules Committee. A ten-hour cap for debating and voting on amendments is an example of such a rule. Democrats criticize this type of rule as not being genuinely open. They argue, for instance, that a ten-hour cap may leave only seven hours for amendments because the time for voting is counted against the

Table 8-2 Open and Restrictive Rules, 95th–107th Congresses
(1977–2003)

Congress and years	Total rules granted	Open rules		Restrictive rules	
		Number	Percent	Number	Percent
95th (1977–1979)	211	179	85	32	15
96th (1979–1981)	214	161	75	53	25
97th (1981–1983)	120	90	75	30	25
98th (1983–1985)	155	105	68	50	32
99th (1985–1987)	115	65	57	50	43
100th (1987–1989)	123	66	54	57	46
101st (1989–1991)	104	47	45	57	55
102d (1991–1993)	109	37	34	72	66
103d (1993–1995)	104	31	30	73	70
104th (1995–1997)	151	86	57	65	43
105th (1997–1999)	142	72	51	70	49
106th (1999–2001)	184	93	51	91	49
107th (2001–2003)	112	71	37	71	63

Sources: U.S. Congress, *Congressional Record,* daily ed., 103d Cong., 2d sess., October 7, 1994, H11278. For the 104th see December 10, 1996, press release, House Rules Committee. For the 105th Congress, the Rules Committee issued a total of 207 rules, but many did not directly involve bills and resolutions. As a result, the authors selected 142 as the number of rules granted for bills and resolutions. Minority Democrats have made their own calculation of the kinds of rules granted by the committee. They identify a total of 163 rules of which 38 are open (23 percent) and 115 (77 percent) are restrictive. See *Survey of Activities of the House Committee on Rules,* 105th Cong. 2d sess. (Washington, D.C.: U.S. Government Printing Office, 1999). For the 106th Congress, the Rules Committee issued 267 rules with 184 directly affecting the amending process on the floor. Hence, the authors employ the 184 figure instead of 267, which included rules, for example, that permitted the House to go to conference with the Senate. See *Survey of Activities of the House Committee on Rules,* 106th Cong., 2d sess. (Washington, D.C.: U.S. Government Printing Office, 2001). for the 107th Congress, the panel issued 191 rules with 112 directly related to the amendment process for the consideration of bills and resolutions. See *Survey of Activities of the House Committee on Rules,* 107th Cong., 2d sess. (Washington, D.C.: U.S. Government Printing Office, 2003).

overall time restriction. Republicans reply that it is up to the Democratic leadership to decide which amendments have priority over others. These and other kinds of creative rules enable the majority party to advance its policy and political agenda and to cope effectively with today's substantive and procedural complexities.

In summary, rules establish the conditions under which most major bills are debated and amended. They determine the length of general debate, permit or prohibit amendments, and may waive points of order. Writing the rules is the majority party's way of ensuring that measures reach the floor under

Examples of Creative Rules

Queen-of-the-Hill Rule. Under this special rule, a number of major alternative amendments—each the functional equivalent of a bill—are made in order to the underlying legislation, with the proviso that the substitute that receives the most votes is the winner. If two or more alternatives receive an identical number of votes, the last one voted upon is considered as finally adopted by the membership.

Self-Executing Rule. This special rule provides that when the House adopts a rule it has also agreed simultaneously to pass another measure or matter. Adoption of a self-executing rule means that the House has passed one or more other proposals at the same time it agrees to the rule. Whether this rule is controversial or not usually depends on the nature of the policy being agreed to in the two-for-one vote.

Restrictive Rule. The essential feature of the restrictive rule is that it limits the freedom of members to offer germane amendments to the bills made in order by those rules. The number of restrictive rules has increased since the 1980s. Rank-and-file members often rail against these rules because they restrict their opportunities to amend committee-reported measures or majority party initiatives.

Multiple-Step Rule. This type of rule facilitates an orderly amendment process. One variation is for the Rules Committee to report a rule that regulates the debating and amending process for specific portions of a bill and then report another follow-on rule to govern the remainder of the measure and amendments to it. Another variation is for the Rules Committee to state publicly that, if a measure encounters difficulties on the floor, the panel will report a subsequent rule that limits time for further debate or further amendments.

Anticipatory Rule. To expedite decision making on the floor, the Rules Committee may grant a rule even before the measure or matter to which it would apply has been reported by a House committee or conference committee.

---

terms favorable to the party's preferred outcomes on bills and amendments. Put differently, the majority party limits and structures the votes to get the results they intend. They are often as important to a bill's fate as a favorable vote out of committee.

Dislodging a Bill from Committee

Committees do not necessarily reflect the point of view of the full chamber. What happens when a standing committee refuses to report a bill or when the Rules Committee does not grant a rule? To circumvent committees, members have three options, but they are extraordinary actions and are seldom successful: the discharge petition, the Calendar Wednesday rule, and the ability of the Rules Committee to extract a bill from committee.

The discharge petition permits the House to relieve a committee from jurisdiction over a stalled measure. This procedure also provides a way for the rank and file to force a bill to the floor even if the majority leadership, the committee chairman, and the Rules Committee oppose it. If a committee does not report a bill within thirty legislative days after the bill was referred to it, any member may file a discharge motion (petition) requiring the signature of 218 members, a majority of the House. Once the signatures are obtained, the discharge motion is placed on the Discharge Calendar for seven days. It can then be called up on the second and fourth Mondays of the month by any member who signed the petition. If the discharge motion is agreed to, the bill is taken up right away. Since 1910, when the discharge rule was adopted, only two discharged measures ever have become law. Its threatened or actual use, particularly as the number of signatures close in on 218, may stimulate a committee to act on a bill and the majority leadership to schedule it for floor action.

The minority party also uses discharge petitions to spotlight the two Congresses. For example, Democrats identify their high-priority issues and circulate discharge petitions "in an attempt to force House votes—and provide a contrast with Republicans in an election year." [28] Outside groups also may run ads in selected lawmakers' districts to discourage them from signing discharge petitions on legislation they oppose.

The discharge rule also applies to the Rules Committee. A motion to discharge a rule is in order after seven legislative days, instead of thirty days, as long as the bill made in order by the rule has been in committee for thirty days. Any member may enter a discharge motion, but majority members seldom break ranks with their party leaders to sign the petition. When Rep. Christopher Shays, R-Conn., signed a successful discharge petition to force House action on a major campaign finance reform bill (the Bipartisan Campaign Reform Act of 2002) opposed by the GOP leadership, there were charges of treason against Shays and rumblings that he might face a GOP challenger in the Republican primary. Signing discharge petitions, "along with other kinds of procedural betrayals, are being considered and discussed by members" of the GOP's committee on committees, remarked the GOP Conference chair.[29] Shays was subsequently passed over as chair of the Government Reform Committee, even though he had more seniority than the two other Republicans in contention.

Adopted in 1909, the Calendar Wednesday rule provides that on Wednesdays committees may bring up from the House Calendar or Union Calendar their measures that have not received a rule from the Rules Committee. Calendar Wednesday is cumbersome to employ, seldom used, and generally dispensed with by unanimous consent. Since 1943 fewer than fifteen measures have been enacted into law under this procedure.[30]

Finally, the Rules Committee has the power of extraction. The committee can propose rules that make bills in order for House debate even if the bills have been neither introduced nor reported by standing committees. Based on an 1895 precedent, this procedure is akin to discharging committees without the required 218 signatures. It stirs bitter controversy among members who think it usurps the rights of the other committees and is seldom used.

House Floor Procedures

The House meets Monday through Friday, usually convening at noon. In practice, it conducts the bulk of its committee and floor business during the middle of the week (the so-called Tuesday to Thursday Club). This scheduling pattern helps representatives juggle legislative business with weekend trips to their districts—weekly testimony to the two Congresses.

At the beginning of each day's session, bells ring throughout the Capitol and the House office buildings, summoning representatives to the floor. The bells also notify members of votes, quorum calls, recesses, and adjournments. Typically, the opening activities include a daily prayer; recitation of the Pledge of Allegiance; approval of the *Journal* (a constitutionally required record of the previous day's proceedings); receipt of messages from the president (such as a veto message) or the Senate; announcements, if any, by the Speaker; and one-minute speeches by members on any topic. There is also a period of morning hour debate, on Mondays and Tuesdays, which occurs after the opening preliminaries but before the start of formal legislative business.

After these preliminaries, the House generally begins considering legislation. For a major bill, a set pattern is observed: adopting the rule, convening in Committee of the Whole, allotting time for general debate, amending, voting, and moving the bill to final passage.

Adoption of the Rule

The Speaker, after consulting the majority leader and affected committee chairmen, generally decides when the House will debate a bill and under what kind of rule. When the scheduled day arrives, the Speaker recognizes a majority member of the Rules Committee for one hour to explain the rule's contents. By custom, the majority member yields half the time for debate to a minority member of the Rules Committee. At the end of the debate, which usually takes less than the allotted hour, the House votes on the rule.

Opponents of a bill can try to defeat the rule and avert House action on the bill itself. But rules seldom are defeated because the Rules Committee is sensitive to the wishes of the House. Since 1999, when J. Dennis Hastert, R-Ill., became Speaker, the House has rejected only three rules offered by the Rules Committee. Splits within the majority party account for the defeats. Once the rule is adopted, the House is governed by its provisions. Most rules state that "at any time after the adoption of [the rule] the Speaker may declare the House resolved into the Committee of the Whole."

Committee of the Whole

The Committee of the Whole House on the State of the Union is a parliamentary artifice designed to expedite consideration of legislation. It is simply the House in another form with different rules. For example, a quorum in the Committee of the Whole is only 100 members, compared with 218 for the full

House. The Speaker appoints a majority party colleague to preside over the committee, which then begins general debate of a bill.

General Debate

A rule from the Rules Committee specifies the amount of time, usually one to two hours, for a general discussion of the bill under consideration. Controversial bills will require more time, perhaps four to ten hours. Control of the time is divided equally between the majority and minority floor managers—usually the chairman and ranking minority member of the committee that reported the legislation. (When bills are referred to more than one committee, a more complex division of debate time is allotted among the committees that had jurisdiction over the legislation.) The majority floor manager's job is to guide the bill to final passage; the minority floor manager may seek to amend or kill the bill.

After the floor managers have made their opening statements, they parcel out several minutes to colleagues on their side of the aisle who wish to speak. General debate rarely lives up to its name. Most legislators read prepared speeches. Give-and-take exchange occurs infrequently at this stage of the proceedings.

The Amending Phase

The amending process is the heart of decision making on the floor of the House. Amendments determine the final shape of bills and often dominate public discussion. Illinois Republican Henry J. Hyde, for example, repeatedly and successfully has proposed amendments barring the use of federal funds for abortions.

An amendment in the Committee of the Whole is considered under the five-minute rule, which gives the sponsor five minutes to defend it and an opponent five minutes to speak against it. The amendment then may be brought to a vote. Amendments are routinely debated for more than ten minutes, however. Legislators gain the floor by saying, "I move to strike the last word" or "I move to strike the requisite number of words." These pro forma amendments, which make no alteration in the pending matter, simply serve to give members five minutes of debate time.

If there is an open rule, opponents may try to load a bill with so many objectionable amendments that it will sink of its own weight. The reverse strategy is to propose sweetener amendments that attract support from other members. Offering many amendments is an effective dilatory tactic because each amendment must be read in full, debated for at least five to ten minutes, and then voted on.

In this amending phase the interconnection of the two Congresses is evident: Amendments can have electoral as well as legislative consequences. Floor amendments enable lawmakers to take positions that enhance their reputations with the folks back home, put opponents on record, and shape national policy. For example, "put them on the spot amendments," as one representative dubbed them, can be artfully fashioned by minority lawmakers to force the majority Republicans to vote on issues (such as Social Security or veterans' benefits) that can be used against them in the next campaign.[31]

The minority party's policy preferences often are expressed through amendments. "Since the . . . leadership more often than not refuses to schedule hearings on our bills," wrote a House member, "we counter by offering our legislation in the form of amendments to other bills scheduled for consideration by the House."[32]

The minority also guards the floor to demand explanations or votes on amendments brought up by the majority. When Republicans were in the minority, one of their floor guardians wrote, "So long as a floor watchdog exists all members of the House are afforded some additional protection from precipitous actions."[33] With Democrats in the minority since the mid-1990s, Rep. Barney Frank, D-Mass., and others assumed this role for their party.

Voting

Before the 1970 Legislative Reorganization Act was passed, the Committee of the Whole adopted or rejected amendments by voice votes or other votes with no public record of who voted and how. Today, any legislator supported by twenty-five colleagues can obtain a recorded vote. (The member who requested a recorded vote is counted as one of the twenty-five who rise to be counted by the chair.)

Since the installation of an electronic voting system in 1973, members can insert their personalized cards (about the size of a credit card) into one of more than forty voting stations on the floor and press the Yea, Nay, or Present button. A large electronic display board behind the press gallery provides a running tally of the total votes for or against a motion. The voting tally, said a representative, is watched carefully by many members.

> I find that a lot of times, people walk in, and the first thing they do is look at the board, and they have key people they check out, and if those people have voted "aye," they go to the machine and vote "aye" and walk off the floor.
>
> But I will look at the board and see how [members of the state delegation] vote, because they are in districts right next to me, and they have constituencies just like mine. I will vote the way I am going to vote except that if they are both different, I will go up and say "Why did you vote that way? Let me know if there is something I am missing."[34]

After all pending amendments have been voted on, the Committee of the Whole rises. The chairman hands the gavel back to the Speaker, and a quorum once again becomes 218 members.

Final Passage

As specified in the rule, the full House must review the actions of its agent, the Committee of the Whole. The Speaker announces that under the rule the previous question has been ordered. This parliamentary term means that no further debate is permitted on the bill or its amendments. The Speaker then asks whether any representative wants a separate vote on any amendment. If not, all the amendments agreed to in the committee will be approved.

The next important step is the recommittal motion, which provides a way for the House to return, or recommit, the bill to the committee that reported it. By precedent, the request is always made by a minority party member who opposes the legislation. Recommittal motions rarely succeed, but they do serve to protect the rights of the minority. When Republicans won majority control, they amended House rules to guarantee the minority leader or his designee the right to offer a recommittal motion with instructions (the instructions embody the minority's policy alternative).

After the recommittal motion is defeated, the Speaker then declares, "The question is on passage of the bill." Final passage is usually by recorded vote. Passage of the bill, by the House in this case, marks about the halfway point in the lawmaking process. The Senate must also approve the bill, and its procedures are strikingly different from those of the House.

Scheduling in the Senate

Compared with the larger and more clamorous House, which needs and follows well-defined rules and precedents, the Senate operates more informally. And, unlike the House, where the rules permit a determined majority to make decisions, the Senate's rules emphasize individual prerogatives (unlimited freedom to debate and to offer amendments, including nonrelevant amendments) and minority rights (those of the minority party, a faction, or even a single senator). "The Senate," said one member, "is run for the convenience of one Senator to the inconvenience of 99." [35] No wonder some commentators say the Senate has only two rules (unanimous consent and exhaustion) and three speeds (slow, slower, and slowest). As Sen. Byron L. Dorgan, D-N.D., said, "The only thing it's easy to do in the Senate is slow things down. The Senate is 100 human brake pads." [36]

The scheduling system for the Senate is relatively simple. The Calendar of Business is used for all public and private bills and the Executive Calendar for treaties and nominations. The Senate has nothing comparable to the scheduling duties of the House Rules Committee, and the majority and minority leadership actively cooperate in scheduling. The Senate majority leader is responsible for setting the agenda and is aided in controlling the scheduling by the priority given him when he seeks recognition on the floor. Despite the Senate's smaller size, establishing a firm agenda of business is harder in the Senate than in the House. As a former majority leader once said:

The ability of any Senator to speak without limitations makes it impossible to establish total certainty with respect to scheduling. When there is added to that the difficulty and very demanding schedules of 100 Senators, it is very difficult to organize business in a way that meets the convenience of everybody.[37]

Legislation typically reaches the Senate floor in two ways: by unanimous consent or by motion. Senators, too, can offer nonrelevant amendments to pending business and force Senate consideration of their proposals. Unanimous consent, however, is of utmost importance, and its use is regulated by the majority leader in consultation with the minority leader.

Unanimous Consent Agreements

The Senate frequently dispenses with its formal rules and instead follows negotiated agreements submitted to the Senate for its unanimous approval (see box on unanimous consent agreement). The objective is to expedite work in an institution known for extended debate, to impose some measure of predictability on floor action, and to minimize dilatory activities. As Democratic leader Tom Daschle of South Dakota observed:

We aren't bringing [measures] to the floor unless we have [a unanimous consent] agreement. We could bring child-care legislation to the floor right now, but that would mean two months of fighting. We want to maximize productive time by trying to work out as much as we can in advance [of floor action].[38]

It is not uncommon for party leaders to negotiate piecemeal unanimous consent agreements—limiting debate on a specific amendment, for example—and to hammer them out in public on the Senate floor.

Unanimous consent agreements (also called time-limitation agreements) limit debate on the bill, any amendments, and various motions. In effect, these accords are a form of voluntary cloture. Occasionally, they specify the time for the vote on final passage and typically impose constraints on the amendment process. For example, to facilitate enactment of an omnibus crime package that contained provisions with widespread Senate support, senators agreed to a unanimous consent request barring floor amendments on controversial issues such as gun control or the death penalty.[39]

The Senate's unanimous consent agreements are functional equivalents of special rules from the House Rules Committee. They waive the rules of their respective chambers, and each must be approved by the members—in one case by majority vote and in the other by unanimous consent. These accords are binding contracts and can only be terminated or modified by another unanimous consent agreement. Senators and aides often negotiate and draft unanimous consent agreements privately, whereas the Rules Committee hears requests for special orders in public session.

Example of a Unanimous Consent Agreement

S. 27

2.—*Ordered,* That on either Monday, March 19, 2001, or Monday, March 26, 2001, at a time to be determined by the Majority Leader, after consultation with the Democratic Leader, the Rules and Administration Committee be immediately discharged from consideration of S. 27, a bill to amend the Federal Election Campaign Act of 1971 to provide bipartisan campaign reform, as introduced, and that the Senate proceed to its immediate consideration.

Ordered further, That following the reporting of S. 27 by the Clerk, the bill become the pending business to the exclusion of all other business, except for a motion to temporarily postpone consideration of the pending legislation made by the Republican Leader, following approval of the Democratic Leader; and that no call for the regular order serve to displace this item, except one made by the Republican Leader, after approval of the Democratic Leader.

Ordered further, That when a first degree amendment is offered, there be up to 3 hours for debate only, with the time to be evenly divided in the usual form, after which a motion to table may be made; that if a motion to table fails, the amendment then be fully debatable and amendable; that if a motion to table is not made at the expiration of the 3 hours, a vote occur on the amendment, without any intervening action, motion, or debate, provided that no points of order be considered as having been waived by this agreement.

S.J. RES. 4

3.—*Ordered,* That during or immediately following disposition of the McCain-Feingold bill, S. 27, the Senate proceed to the consideration of S.J. Res. 4, proposing an amendment to the Constitution of the United States relating to contributions and expenditures intending to affect elections, that it become the pending business, and that no amendments be in order to S.J. Res. 4.

Ordered further, That there be 5 hours debate thereon, with 2 hours under the control of the Senator from South Carolina (Mr. Hollings); 2 hours under the control of the Senator from Utah (Mr. Hatch), or his designee; and 1 hour, to be equally divided, between the Republican and Democratic Leaders or their designees.

Ordered further, That upon the use or yielding back of time, the Senate, without intervening action, motion or debate, proceed to vote on passage of S.J. Res. 4.

Source: U.S. Senate, Calendar of Business, 107th Cong., 1st sess., March 14, 2001, 4.

Ways to Extract Bills from Committee

If a bill is blocked in committee, the Senate can do one of several things to obtain floor action. It can add the bill as a nonrelevant floor amendment to another bill, bypass the committee stage by placing the bill directly on the calendar, suspend the rules, or discharge the bill from committee. Only the first two procedures are effective; the other two are somewhat difficult to employ and seldom succeed.[40]

Because the Senate has no general germaneness (or relevancy) rule, senators can take an agriculture bill that is stuck in committee and add it as a nonrelevant floor amendment to a pending health bill. "Amendments may be made," Thomas Jefferson noted long ago, "so as to totally alter the nature of the proposition." It is not uncommon, however, for unanimous consent agreements to limit or prohibit nonrelevant amendments.

Bypassing committees also occurs when senators invoke one of its formal rules (Rule XIV). Typically, when senators introduce bills or joint resolutions (or when bills or joint resolutions are passed by the House and sent to the Senate), they are referred to the appropriate committee of jurisdiction. Rule XIV specifies that those measures are to be read twice by title on different legislative days before they are referred. If a senator interposes an objection after the first reading and again after the second reading, the bill or joint resolution is automatically placed on the Senate's calendar of business. Although not used for the vast majority of measures, Rule XIV is often invoked on party issues of high priority. The majority leader, for example, may employ it to circumvent committees because no time is available for lengthy committee review, or he wants an issue ready to be called up at his discretion.

Senate Floor Procedures

The Senate, like the House, regularly convenes at noon, sometimes earlier, to keep pace with the workload. Typically, it opens with a prayer. This is followed by the Pledge of Allegiance and then leader's time (usually ten minutes each to the majority leader and the minority leader to discuss various issues). If neither leader wants any time, the Senate typically either permits members who have requested time to make five-minute statements or resumes consideration of old or new business under terms of a unanimous consent agreement. The Senate, too, must keep and approve the *Journal* of the previous day's activities. Commonly, the *Journal* is "deemed approved to date" by unanimous consent when the Senate adjourns or recesses at the end of each day.

Normal Routine

For most bills the Senate follows four steps:

1. The majority leader secures the unanimous consent of the Senate to an arrangement that specifies when a bill will be brought to the floor and the conditions for debating it.
2. The presiding officer recognizes the majority and minority floor managers for opening statements.
3. Amendments are then in order, with debate regulated by the terms of the unanimous consent agreement.
4. A roll call vote takes place on final passage.

As in the House, amendments in the Senate serve various purposes. For example, floor managers might accept "as many amendments as they can without undermining the purposes of the bill, in order to build the broadest possible consensus behind it." [41] Some amendments highlight the two Congresses and bestow benefits to the electorate or embarrass members who must vote against them. "My amendment can be characterized as a 'November amendment,' " remarked a Republican senator, "because the vote . . . will provide an opportunity for Senators to go home and say, 'I voted to reduce Federal taxes' and 'I voted to cut Federal spending.' " [42] As another example, Senate Democrats make "vigorous use of amendments to strike a contrast with Republican policies." [43] Unless constrained by some previous unanimous consent agreement, senators generally have the right to offer an unlimited number of floor amendments.

A bill is brought to a final vote whenever senators stop talking. This can be a long process, particularly in the absence of a unanimous consent agreement. On some bills unanimous consent agreements are foreclosed because of deliberate obstructive tactics, particularly the filibuster. In these instances bills cannot be voted upon until the filibuster has ended.

Holds, Filibusters, and Cloture

The old-style filibuster has long been associated with the 1939 movie *Mr. Smith Goes to Washington*, which featured Jimmy Stewart conducting a dramatic solo talkathon to inform the public about political wrongdoing. In its new incarnation the filibuster is usually threatened more than invoked to gain bargaining power and negotiating leverage.

Filibusters involve many blocking tactics besides extended debate in which senators hold the floor for hours of endless speeches. Many contemporary filibusters are waged by those who skillfully use Senate rules. For example, senators might offer scores of amendments, raise points of order, or demand numerous and consecutive roll-call votes. Holds also function as a form of silent filibuster.

Holds. A hold permits one or more senators to block floor action on measures or matters by asking their party leaders not to schedule them. A hold, explained Sen. Charles E. Grassley, R-Iowa, is "a notice by a Senator to his or her party leader of an intention to object to bringing a bill or nomination to the floor for consideration." [44] Neither Senate rules nor precedents make provision for holds; they are an informal custom. The majority leader decides whether, or for how long, he will honor a colleague's hold. The power of holds is grounded in the implicit threat of senators to conduct filibusters or to object to unanimous consent agreements.

Holds have come under criticism because they often lead to delays or even the death (choke holds) of measures or nominations. Originally intended as a way for senators to get information about when the majority leader planned action on a measure, holds have become devices to kill measures by delaying them indefinitely or to gain bargaining leverage by, for instance, stalling action on presidential nominations. On one occasion, so many holds on nominations were pending before the Senate that Democratic leader Daschle felt left out. As he explained: "I'm going to have to pick out a nominee to get to know him or her a lot better because it works that way. I mean, it's 'Hello, I'm your holder . . . come dance with me.' " [45] Periodically, proposals are made to reform the practice, such as ending secret holds, but such initiatives have been neither easy to accomplish nor easy to enforce. [46]

Filibusters and Cloture. The right of extended debate is unique to the Senate. Any senator or group of senators can talk continuously in the hope of delaying, modifying, or defeating legislation. In 1957 South Carolina senator Strom Thurmond, then a Democrat, set the record for the Senate's longest solo performance—twenty-four hours and eighteen minutes—trying to kill a civil rights bill.

The success of a filibuster depends not only on how long it takes but also on when it is waged. A filibuster can be most effective late in a session because there is insufficient time to break it. [47] Even the threat of a filibuster can encourage accommodations or compromises between proponents and opponents of legislation.

Defenders of the filibuster say it protects minority rights, permits thorough consideration of bills, and dramatizes issues. "In many ways," noted Sen. Robert C. Byrd, D-W.Va., "the filibuster is the single most important device ever employed to ensure that the Senate remains truly the unique protector of the rights of our people." [48] Critics contend that talkathons enable minorities to extort unwanted concessions. During most of its history, the Senate had no way to terminate debate except by unanimous consent, exhaustion, or compromise. In 1917 the Senate adopted Rule XXII, its first cloture (debate ending) rule. After several revisions, Rule XXII now permits three-fifths of the Senate (sixty members) to shut off debate on substantive issues or procedural motions. (A two-thirds vote is required to invoke cloture on a proposal to change the rules of the Senate.) Once cloture is invoked, thirty hours of debate time remain before the final vote.

Senators complain about the frequent use of filibusters and cloture attempts. In the past, filibusters generally occurred on issues of great national importance; today they occur on a wide range of less momentous topics. As one majority leader pointed out:

> Not long ago the filibuster or threat of a filibuster was rarely undertaken in the Senate, being reserved for matters of grave national importance. That is no longer the case. . . . The threat of a filibuster is now a regular event in the Senate, weekly at least, sometimes daily. It is invoked by minorities of as few as one or two Senators and for reasons as trivial as a Senator's travel schedule. [49]

Unsurprisingly, many commentators call it the "sixty-vote Senate."

Attempts to invoke cloture also have increased. For example, in the decade from 1961 to 1971, there were 5.2 cloture votes per Congress; during the 107th Congress (2001–2003), there were 61 cloture votes.[50] Moreover, the norm of one cloture vote per measure has changed. The modern Senate reached a record of eight cloture votes (all unsuccessful) on a controversial campaign financing measure during the 100th Congress (1987–1989).

This upward trend reflects the willingness of senators today to employ their procedural prerogatives to gain concessions, delay the consideration of legislation, or accomplish other objectives through greater use of filibusters and threatened filibusters (as well as holds, the use of cloture, and nongermane amendments). Two examples illustrate the point. First, the majority leader usually requests and receives unanimous consent to bring legislation to the Senate floor. If senators object to that request, perhaps signaling that blocking actions will be taken on the measure, the majority leader may then offer a debatable motion to take up the legislation. Recent Congresses have witnessed an increase in the number of cloture petitions filed on the leader's motion to take up measures. From only two cloture motions filed during the 96th Congress (1979–1981), the 1990s regularly saw cloture motions in the double digits on the leader's motion to bring legislation to the floor. The high-water mark was thirty-five cloture petitions filed during the 102d Congress (1991–1993) on the leader's motion to take up legislation.

Second, cloture is also employed for purposes unrelated to ending a filibuster. The purposes are usually twofold: to expedite the Senate's business by limiting debate and to impose a germaneness, or relevancy, requirement on all amendments. (If invoked Rule XXII requires all amendments to be germane to the clotured measure.) When he was majority leader, Senator Lott sometimes filed cloture on the first day the Senate took up a measure. His objective in trying to invoke cloture was to prevent Democrats from offering their agenda priorities as nonrelevant amendments to the pending legislation and thus protect electorally vulnerable Republicans from casting votes on difficult issues. "I fear my colleagues on the Democratic side are trying to change the subject," stated Senator Lott. "Let's have relevant amendments" to this bill, added Lott.[51] Senator Daschle railed against the practice of filing cloture on a bill as soon as it is taken up. "How do you end debate that you haven't even started?" he exclaimed.[52]

These actions reflect the Senate's shift away from its norms of collegiality and accommodation. The various explanations for this development include the election to the Senate of House members who have brought with them the aggressive partisanship common to the lower house and heightened demands placed on senators by constituents and lobbyists and the escalating costs of campaigns. "Daily priorities [are] shaped more by personal agendas—campaign needs, interest-group demands, personal staff, obligations to meet constituents, and off-the-Hill speeches—and less by the expectations of colleagues and the needs of Senate colleagues," wrote Steven Smith. "Pressed by constituencies and lobbyists and more strongly motivated to grab a headline, senators now more routinely and more fully exploit their procedural prerogatives than at any other time in the Senate's history." [53] The upshot of these developments is a more individualistic and partisan Senate, which means that compromises and accommodations are harder to achieve on significant substantive issues.

Resolving House–Senate Differences

Before bills can be sent to the president, they must be passed by the House and the Senate in identical form. One way this occurs is if one chamber simply accepts the other body's bill. Another approach is to ping-pong House and Senate amendments between the chambers until each chamber is satisfied with the product. If neither chamber will accept the other's changes, a House-Senate conference committee is usually appointed to reconcile the differences. Under each chamber's rules and precedents, conference committees meet to resolve the matters in bicameral dispute; they are not to reconsider provisions already agreed to, nor are they to write new law by inserting matter that neither house may have considered. However, parliamentary rules are not self-enforcing, and either chamber can waive or ignore them. It is not unusual for conference reports to contain new matter that neither chamber debated nor amended in committee or on the floor. No wonder conference committees are called the third house of Congress. As Sen. Arlen Specter, R-Pa., stated,

> [Conference committees] are when the work is concluded. Everything else which is done is really of much less significance than the conferences, where the final touches are put on legislation which constitutes the laws of the country.[54]

Most public laws are approved without conferences (roughly 70 percent). Either they pass each chamber without any changes or the House and Senate amends a bill in turn until both chambers agree on the wording (about 20 percent of laws follow this shuttle route). Only about 10 percent of the measures passed by Congress—usually the most important and controversial—are subject to bicameral reconciliation by conference committees.

Selection of Conferees

Conferees usually are named from the committee or committees that reported the legislation. Congressional rules state that the Speaker and the Senate presiding officer select conferees. In fact, that decision typically is made by the relevant committee chairmen and the ranking minority members. House and Senate party leaders commonly get involved in naming conferees on major legislation. For example, when Gingrich was Speaker, he took a strong role in the selection of House conferees. In precedent-setting events for the modern House, Gingrich several times even named conservative minority Democrats (in part to woo them to convert to the Republican Party) to serve as conferees on the House Republican conference delegation. Speaker Hastert, too, has not been reluctant to do the selecting of GOP conferees on legislative priorities of the Republican Party.

Knowing that the GOP leadership opposed many provisions in a campaign finance reform bill passed by the Senate early in the 107th Congress and long championed by Sen. John McCain, R-Ariz., Senate Democratic leader Daschle offered to appoint McCain as a conferee on the bill if Republicans refused to do so.[55] (The so-called McCain-Feingold bill, named for McCain and Sen. Russell D. Feingold, D-Wis., would ban soft money. In 2002 it was signed into law as the Bipartisan Campaign Reform Act.) Daschle made the same offer to moderate GOP senator Lincoln Chafee, R.I., on a bill of which he was a prime sponsor. GOP leader Lott made it clear that Chafee was unlikely to be chosen a conferee. (Both McCain and Chafee were viewed by Democrats as possible party switchers, as in the James M. Jeffords of Vermont case.)

Each chamber may name as many conferees as it wants, and in recent years some conference delegations have grown large. The 1981 omnibus reconciliation conference set the record, with more than 250 House and Senate conferees working in fifty-eight subconferences to resolve more than three hundred matters in bicameral disagreement.

Today's conference committees represent a sharp departure in size and composition from the pre-1980 era, when conference delegations generally ranged from five to twelve conferees from each house. And before the mid-1970s conferees nearly always were the most senior lawmakers from the committees that reported the legislation. Although seniority frequently determines who the conferees will be, it is not unusual for junior and even first-term members to be conferees. Further, conferees today commonly are chosen from many standing committees and sometimes reflect intricate selection arrangements. For example, House conferees may be named to negotiate only certain items in disagreement instead of the entire bill. Multiple referrals and megabills are the driving forces behind these two developments.

In conference each chamber has a single vote determined by a majority of its conferees, who are expected generally to support the legislation as it passed their house. But, a senator confessed, as conference committees drag on, the "individual attitudes of the various members begin to show." [56] House conferees on some occasions have a "knowledge advantage" over Senate conferees. Because representatives serve on fewer committees than do senators, they have greater opportunities to specialize in various policy areas. This means that representatives on conference committees often find that they are "arguing with Senate staff. For a House member, that's a frustrating experience." [57]

The ratio of Republicans to Democrats on a conference committee generally reflects the proportion of the two parties in the House or Senate. When the Senate was evenly divided from January to early June 2001, GOP leader Lott and Democratic leader Daschle disagreed over the conference ratio ques-

---

Appropriations, Live

For true legislative junkies, there was nothing like the coverage by the Cable Satellite Public Affairs Network (C-SPAN) of the exhaustive House-Senate conference committee negotiations May 11–13, 1999, over the midyear supplemental spending package. C-SPAN televised a rare glimpse of the good, the bad, and the ugly in the normally closed world of congressional appropriations.

The show got better ratings than *ER* in the Capitol, alerting Speaker J. Dennis Hastert, R-Ill., to a surprise development and inspiring other members to rush to the floor and demand special votes to affect the talks.

Reviews from those in the camera's gaze were mixed, raising the question of whether the appropriators would invite C-SPAN back. "The answer is, I don't know," said Senate Appropriations chairman Ted Stevens, R-Alaska, who was visibly angry at several points. What galled Stevens was that, while one lawmaker would be speaking, C-SPAN cameras panned the room showing others chatting, reading, or just relaxing. Sometimes microphones picked up the sounds of lawmakers laughing and joking. All that is normal in any lengthy meeting, but, Stevens said in an interview, "When you're having a private conversation or chewing out a staffer, we don't want that picked up."

Stevens, whose language is not always G-rated, added: "My wife told me I had to stop swearing."

C-SPAN officials said they have covered high-profile appropriations conferences in the past. What was different in this case was that the appropriators did not boot out the press and public, as they are wont to do.

Source: Adapted from Carroll J. Doherty, "Appropriations, Live," *CQ Weekly,* May 22, 1999, 1185.

---

tion. Lott wanted at least a one-vote GOP majority on Senate conference delegations; Daschle insisted on an equal number of Democratic and Republican conferees. For months the Senate was at an impasse over the composition of its conference delegation. The stalemate ended when Democrats assumed majority control following Senator Jeffords' switch in party status.

Openness

Secret conference meetings were the norm for most of Congress's history. In 1975 both houses adopted rules requiring open meetings unless the conferees from each chamber voted in public to close the sessions. Two years later the House went further, requiring open conference meetings unless the full House agreed to secret sessions. Sometimes the Cable Satellite Public Affairs Network (C-SPAN) will televise conference proceedings (see box on appropriations, live).

The open conference is yet another instance of individual-institutional cleavage. Under the watchful eye of lobbyists, conferees fight harder for provisions they might have dropped quietly in the interest of bicameral agreement. Private bargaining sessions still permeate conference negotiations. As one senator noted:

> When we started the openness thing we found it more and more difficult to get something agreed to in the conferences; it seemed to take forever. So what did we do? We would break up into smaller groups and then we would ask our [conference] chairman . . . to see if he could find his opposite number on the House side and discuss this matter and come back and tell us what the chances would be of working out various and sundry possibilities.[58]

Senators and representatives expect certain bills to go to conference and plan their strategy accordingly. For example, whether to have a recorded vote on amendments can influence conference bargaining. In the absence of a recorded vote, amendments may be easier to drop in conference.

The Conference Report

A conference ends when its report (the compromise bill) is signed by a majority of the conferees from each chamber. House and Senate staff then prepare the conference report and the accompanying joint explanatory statement, which summarizes the conferees' recommendations. The House and Senate then vote on the conference report without further amendment. If either chamber rejects the conference report—an infrequent occurrence—a new conference may be called or another bill introduced. Once passed, the compromise bill is sent to the president for approval or disapproval.

Conclusion

The philosophical bias of House and Senate rules reflects the character of each institution. Individual rights are stressed in the Senate, majority rule in the House. In both chambers, however, members who know the rules and precedents have an advantage over procedural novices in affecting policy outcomes. Senator Byrd is an acknowledged procedural expert in the Senate. Byrd understands that passing measures often involves unorthodox processes and procedures (for example, forgoing committee hearings or markups or even floor debate).[59]

In addition to congressional rules, persistence, strategy, timing, compromise, and pure chance are also important elements in the lawmaking process. To make public policy requires building majority coalitions at successive stages where pressure groups and other parties can advance their claims. Political, procedural, personal, and policy considerations shape the final outcome. Passing laws, as one former representative said, is like the "weaving of a web, bringing a lot of strands together in a pattern of support which won't have the kind of weak spots which could cause the whole fabric to fall apart." [60]

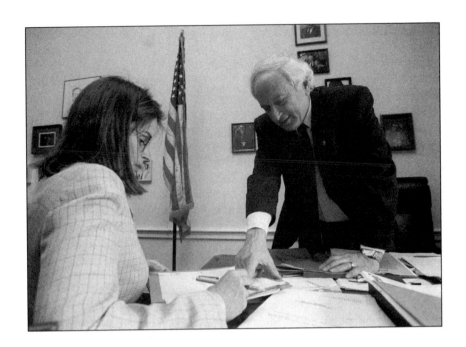

Members face daily decisions about allocating time and casting votes. Above, Rep. Sander M. Levin, D-Mich., consults with his chief of staff, Hilarie Chambers. To record members' votes (below), the House employs an electronic system. Members insert plastic cards in voting boxes throughout the chamber and vote "yea," "nay," or "present." Votes are scrutinized and rated by hundreds of interest groups, including (bottom inset) state PIRGs (public interest research groups).

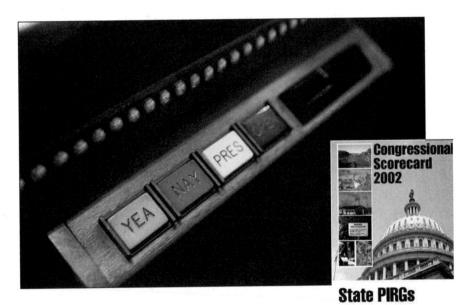

9

Decision Making in Congress

The House of Representatives took formal action in October 1998 to deal with the scandal involving President Bill Clinton and White House intern Monica S. Lewinsky. Since it had been revealed nine months earlier, the scandal had fascinated the public and commandeered nonstop media coverage. Independent counsel Kenneth W. Starr's controversial report, with supporting documents, was sent in August to the House, which referred it to the Judiciary Committee. The committee released Starr's report to the public and the Internet on October 11. By the end of the following day, twenty-five million people had viewed the report online; the conventional media brought it to millions more.

On October 18 the issue reached the House floor in the form of H. Res. 581, a Republican-drafted resolution directing the Judiciary Committee to conduct an open-ended impeachment investigation of the president. Now individual lawmakers had to take a stand on the matter. One of them was Gerald D. Kleczka, a seven-term Democrat from Milwaukee, Wisconsin's south side.

> Kleczka stood transfixed in the center of the House, voting card in hand and eyes on the tote board above him. Should he support the third presidential impeachment inquiry in the nation's history?

> Kleczka . . . hesitated for several minutes and talked to a couple of Judiciary Committee members. Finally, he punched in his card.[1]

The vote that Kleczka cast was "no." All but thirty-one Democrats voted against impeachment, as Kleczka did. But the Republican resolution was approved, 258–176. Earlier, a Democratic alternative that would have limited the scope of the investigation and finished it by the end of the year was voted down, 198–236.

The vote on H. Res. 581 was probably the most fateful and symbolic action taken by the ideologically divided 105th Congress. It set Congress and the nation on a five-month course that led to the president's impeachment by the House and acquittal by the Senate. It ensured that the whole process would be marked by boisterous partisanship. The vote itself was accompanied by catcalls and angry exchanges. Even without the Democratic defectors, the unanimous Republican majority commanded the votes to conduct the impeachment process on their own terms. But with only thirty-one Democrats supporting them at the outset, it was going to be a bitter, partisan affair to the very end.

The votes on the impeachment inquiry are a reminder that members of Congress are free agents obliged, according to the Constitution, to make public commitments that they alone can answer for, regardless of the appeals of party leaders, lobbyists, or even the president of the United States. These votes also show that lawmakers today tend to follow their party's direction. "Can I trust the Republicans to conduct this in a fair and expeditious manner?" Kleczka asked himself. His answer: "They are content to draw this out as far into next year as possible."[2]

The Power to Choose

Although not all votes command as much attention as the impeachment of a president, every decision has the capacity to shape government. In both chambers every legislator has the right, indeed the obligation, to vote. Legislators cast their own votes; no colleague or staff aide may do it for them. To exchange their votes for money or for any other thing of value would be to accept a bribe, which is a federal crime.

Nor are there any legal grounds for attacking legislators for performing their duties, at least in legislative deliberations and votes. Anxious to prevent reprisals against legislators in the conduct of office, the Constitution's authors specified in Article I, Section 6, that "for any speech or debate in either House, they shall not be questioned in any other place."

Recorded votes on the House or Senate floor or in committee, though the most visible decisions made by legislators, are imperfect measures of their stewardship. From his study of members' committee activity, Richard L. Hall distinguishes between formal and informal modes of participation.[3]

Much of Congress's decision making is a matter of public record: voting as well as taking part in formal meetings, markups, debates, and amending activities. But equally important are the complex informal negotiations that surround nearly every enactment—away from the prying eyes of reporters and lobbyists and often conducted by staff aides.

For a full accounting of lawmakers' performance, one must inquire not only how members participate in floor or committee deliberations but also how much effort they expend overall. How much attention do they pay to issues, how do they gain expertise on them, and how do they discharge party or caucus affairs? How do they allocate time between legislative and constituent duties? How do they hire and deploy and supervise their staff? Countless such decisions—some reached with the solemnity of a vote to commit troops abroad, others made hastily or inadvertently—define what it means to be a member of Congress.

Capitol Hill norms strongly underscore lawmakers' individual responsibility for their decisions. Although party leaders may plead, coax, or warn, using roughhouse tactics against members can backfire. Exhibit A would be Sen. James M. Jeffords of Vermont—a liberal Republican from a liberal state— who endured a series of petty snubs by Senate leaders and the White House after he balked at President George W. Bush's tax and education initiatives. In mid-2001, Jeffords resigned from the party, becoming an independent and voting with the Democrats on organizational matters, thus shifting Senate control from Republican to Democratic hands. "The party establishment . . . has to understand it is nonproductive for them to threaten retaliation on people who don't vote their way," declared John McCain of Arizona, another Republican senator who had risked the wrath of his party's leaders.[4]

"It's déjà vu all over again," quipped Norman J. Ornstein. He recalled that the Clinton administration had employed hardball tactics against Alabama senator Richard C. Shelby, a conservative Democrat who opposed the Clinton-Gore economic package. With each White House confrontation, Shelby's popularity soared in his home state, and nobody was surprised when he switched to the GOP.[5]

The issues of members' independence came up again in 2002 as the closely divided Senate considered President Bush's dividend tax-cut plan. Again the White House tried a full-court press on several wavering senators, including lobby group ads and presidential speeches in the members' home states. The administration won narrowly with votes of George V. Voinovich, R-Ohio, and Ben Nelson, D-Neb., both of whom claimed they had won key concessions in exchange. But three other GOP targets—Lincoln Chaffee, R.I.; John McCain, Ariz.; and Olympia Snowe, Maine—were unmoved by the president's efforts.[6]

Types of Decisions

One of the most basic decisions made by legislators is how much time to spend in the nation's capital. Members within air-commuting range often remain at their home bases, commuting to Washington for midweek sessions. Many of these Tuesday to Thursday Club members rarely if ever spend a weekend in Washington. Others, with varying degrees of enthusiasm, plunge into the capital's social and political activities. Such individuals rarely "go back to Pocatello," as the saying goes. Between these two extremes are many variations.

A more subtle question for lawmakers is how to spend their time and energy while in the nation's capital. Some labor to digest the mountains of studies and reports that cross their desks; in the parlance of Capitol Hill, they "do their homework." Others, by contrast, seem to know or care little about legislative matters. They prefer other aspects of the job (correspondence, outreach, and visits with constituents or lobby groups, for example). Such members rarely contribute to committee or floor deliberations. Their votes are usually prompted by cues from party colleagues, staff aides, the White House, or interest groups. They are found in the ranks of the Obscure Caucus, a list of unnoticed members compiled periodically by *Roll Call,* a Capitol Hill newspaper. "These members kept their noses down for the most part, made the welfare of their district their number one priority, and largely avoided joining any contentious national debates." [7]

Either of these strategies can be successfully pursued, and distressingly few voters can tell the difference. Still, most legislators claim to prefer legislative tasks. They strive to make time for their legislative duties, regardless of distractions.

Specializing

Within the legislative realm, members may dig deeply in a particular area or range widely across issues and policies. Senators are more apt to be generalists, while representatives are inclined to cultivate a few specialties. Rep. Jim DeMint, R-S.C., head of the GOP class of '98 caucus, explains why members should specialize:

> If you've got 20 things you want to do, see where everything is. You'll find that maybe 10 of those are already being worked on by people, and that while you may be supportive in that role, you don't need to carry the ball. But you can find those two or three things that are important to you that no one seems to be taking the lead on. But if you try to play the lead on everything, you'll be wasting your time and recreating work that's already going on.[8]

In both houses key policy-making roles are played by those whom Rep. David E. Price, D-N.C., a political scientist, calls policy entrepreneurs—those recognized for "stimulating more than . . . responding" to outside political forces in a given field.[9]

Often nearly invisible to the mass of citizens, these legislators are known to specialized publics for their contributions to specific policies—for example, Rep. Charlie Norwood, R-Ga., on health care; Sen. Mitch McConnell, R-Ky., on campaign finance; Rep. Tom DeLay, R-Texas, on regulatory reform; and Sen. Tom Harkin, D-Iowa, on policies toward the disabled.

Legislative specialties are often dictated by constituency concerns. Alaska lawmakers focus on the policies toward government-controlled Alaska lands, while the delegation from Washington state (home of thousands of Boeing and Microsoft employees) must be attuned to needs of the aerospace and software industries. A pair of Senate liberals, Christopher J. Dodd, D-Conn., and Charles E. Schumer, D-N.Y., have honed their reputations as effective voices for, respectively, the insurance industry (Hartford, Connecticut, is the nation's insurance capital) and the banking industry (New York City is the world's financial center).

Committee assignments themselves may shape members' interests. Chairman Richard G. Lugar, R-Ind., and his colleagues Joseph R. Biden Jr., D-Del., and Chuck Hagel, R-Neb., use their seats on the Foreign Relations Committee to express thoughtful, independent views on foreign affairs. Such specialties may not excite home-state voters, but their assignments challenge them to undertake serious legislative work.

Specializations may also reflect personal interests nurtured by background or experience. As former senator Warren B. Rudman, R-N.H. (1980–1993), explained:

> Who are we when we're elected to the Senate? . . . We are men and women. We are not bland, neutral, blank-slate people who never suffered, and never were happy. You tend to be influenced by the sum total of life's experiences.[10]

Past experiences impel members to specialize in particular issues. Sens. Pete V. Domenici, R-N.M., and Paul Wellstone, D-Minn. (1991–2002), both of whom had family members suffering from mental illness, led a 1996 fight to require health plans to offer the same coverage for severe mental disorders as for physical disorders. They agreed on so little else that they were dubbed the "odd couple of health care." Wellstone and House Speaker J. Dennis Hastert, R-Ill., both former school wrestlers, formed another unexpected team. They came together to support provisions of higher education bills that bolster the place of "non-revenue-producing sports" such as wrestling, gymnastics, tennis, and track.[11]

Before the reforms of the 1960s and 1970s, lawmakers faced formidable obstacles if they wanted to affect policies not handled by their committees. Today, however, members have avenues of influence besides committee assignments—speeches, floor amendments, caucuses, and task forces, to name a few. When only in his second term, and not a member of the Armed Services Committee, Rep. Dick Armey, R-Texas (1985–2003), devised an ingenious scheme (involving an outside commission) for closing unneeded military bases. His proposal smoothed political sensitivities and won bipartisan support for passage in 1988. Such feats are not everyday occurrences, but the fluidity of today's procedures makes even the most junior member a potential policy entrepreneur.

Whatever a member's specialty, the ability to influence the decision-making process is what counts, as Sen. Edmund S. Muskie, D-Maine (1959–1980), explained:

> People have all sorts of conspiratorial theories on what constitutes power in the Senate. It has little to do with the size of the state you come from. Or the source of your money. Or committee chairmanships, although that certainly gives you a kind of power. But real power up there comes from doing your work and knowing what you're talking about. Power is the ability to change someone's mind. . . . The most important thing in the Senate is credibility. Credibility! That is power.[12]

Staking Out Positions

Lawmakers do more than specialize in a particular policy field. They are constantly forced to adopt positions or take stands—which may be governed by what Richard F. Fenno Jr. has called the "politics of timing." [13]

From his examination of a 1981 vote on selling AWACS (airborne warning and control system) reconnaissance planes to Saudi Arabia, Fenno identified three types of decision makers: early deciders, active players, and late deciders. Early deciders are fervent supporters who want to get out front in the debate. "I'd rather come out early and be part of the fight," said Rep. Peter T. King, R-N.Y., of his ready support for fast-track trade authority.[14] These members are often bypassed by lobbyists, because their fixed positions are known at the outset from declarations, bill sponsorship, or prior voting records.

Active players, in contrast, delay their commitment, inviting bids from various sides of the issue at hand and often giving them leverage over the final language of legislation.

Late deciders delay their decision (or reconsider an earlier commitment) until the very last moment. They forfeit influence over the basic framework of the measure. Chiding colleagues who resisted supporting President George W. Bush's tax cut, then GOP Whip Don Nickles of Oklahoma warned, "People that don't support [the budget] won't have very much impact on how it's put together." [15] But late deciders are eagerly courted by all sides and may gain specific concessions. "I love a 50–50 tie," confides Sen. John B. Breaux, D-La., a frequent end-game bargainer. "This is the kind of thing you dream about being involved in. It's a mandate for getting things done." [16] Such members are concerned not only about political payoffs and their need for political cover but also about their reputation for independence.

Individual senators and representatives differ widely in the rate at which they introduce and sponsor bills. Some lawmakers are inveterate initiators of bills and resolutions; others shy away from sponsoring measures. A Senate study by Wendy Schiller found that bills are most likely to be introduced by senior senators, those who are chairs or ranking members of high-volume committees (such as Commerce), and those who represent large, diverse states.[17]

Senate and House rules do not limit the number of members who can cosponsor bills or resolutions. Thus cosponsorship has become common. One survey found that a majority of bills introduced in both chambers were cosponsored; the average such bill had 7.2 cosponsors in the Senate and 22.2 cosponsors in the House.[18] Authors of measures often circulate a "Dear Colleague" letter detailing the virtues of the bill and soliciting cosponsors to demonstrate broad support and force committee action. According to another study, House members circulated no fewer than fifty-four hundred "Dear Colleague" letters over a year's time—an average of more than twelve letters per member.[19]

Cosponsorship, no less than sponsorship, is politically motivated, as freshman senator Dan Quayle, R-Ind. (1981–1989), understood when he asked the Senate's preeminent liberal, Edward M. Kennedy, D-Mass., to cosponsor his first major bill, the 1982 Job Training Partnership Act. Soliciting Kennedy's cooperation was a daring move for a young conservative embarking on his first subcommittee chairmanship. "The decision to travel the bipartisan route ... was his earliest strategic decision," wrote Fenno of Quayle's eventual legislative success. "It caused him a lot of trouble, but he never looked back." [20] Despite right-wing opposition and stonewalling from President Ronald Reagan's administration, Quayle's decision helped win passage of the job training act. It was his greatest Senate achievement (and a notable entry in his résumé when he was tapped for the vice presidency by George Bush).

Occasionally, however, cosponsors are shunned. Introducing his waterway users' fee bill, Senator Domenici decided against seeking cosponsors for several reasons.[21] First, as ranking Republican on the subcommittee, he could arrange for hearings without the support of cosponsors. Second, single sponsorship would be easier. ("If you've got cosponsors you have to clear every little change with them.") Third, if by chance he found no cosponsors, his effort might suffer a devastating initial setback. And, finally, if the bill became law, he would get full, undiluted credit. Thus, for a time, Domenici fought alone for his bill. In the end it was signed into law by President Jimmy Carter at a Democratic rally crowded with politicians who initially had opposed it. Domenici's role was barely mentioned. Such are the ironies of politics.

Do legislators favor the bills and resolutions they introduce? Normally they do, but as Sportin' Life, the *Porgy and Bess* character, said, "It ain't necessarily so." Members may introduce a measure to stake out jurisdiction for their committee or to pave the way for hearings and deliberations that will air a public problem. Or they may introduce measures they do not personally favor to oblige an executive agency or to placate a given interest.

Taking Part

As in any organization, some members of Congress take a passionate interest in what goes on; others pay selective attention to issues; a few seem just to be going through the motions. In his detailed study of three House committees, Richard L. Hall uncovered varying levels of participation among members, among committees and subcommittees, and among types of involvement.

Although members' attendance at committee and subcommittee sessions was respectable (about three-quarters of the members showed up for at least part of each session), active participation—taking part in markup debate, offering amendments, and the like—was far less common. Perhaps half a subcommittee's members could be considered players, by a generous counting. The rest are nonplayers. As a subcommittee staffer remarked, "On a good day half of [the members] know what's going on. Most of the time it's only five or six who actually mark a bill up." [22]

Constituency interests, as might be predicted, strongly propel members to participate in committee business. This is true even when the negotiations are informal and out of the public's sight. In formal subcommittee markup sessions, "the public forum has the benefit of allowing members to at once promote—through their votes, arguments, amendments, obstructionism—constituency interests and be seen doing so." [23]

Constituency-driven activity was most pronounced in the House Agriculture Committee, a panel historically driven by regional and commodity pressures. That committee also witnessed the most biased participation in that active members were unrepresentative of the full committee (much less the full House). Decisions on programs for dairy farmers and peanut growers, for example, were strongly tilted toward producers in those agricultural areas. Not even full committee or floor deliberations muted the enthusiastic advocacy of the dozen or so lawmakers from districts where those commodities were concentrated. In debates over job training legislation in another committee, participating members tended to represent areas with higher unemployment rates than those of nonparticipants. In the three additional cases, where concentrated district benefits were not at stake, Hall found no participatory biases.

Casting Votes

Lawmakers' most visible choices are embodied in the votes they cast. Voting is a central ritual in any legislative body. Members place great stock in their voting records, under the assumption (sometimes borne out) that constituents will judge them at reelection time. Outside groups are keen-eyed followers of the votes on specific measures. Scholars, too, have a long-standing love affair with legislative voting, no doubt because votes provide concrete, quantifiable indicators that lend themselves to statistical analysis.

Senators and representatives strive to be recorded on as many floor and committee votes as they can. The average member participates in about 95 percent of recorded votes on the floor. Members seek to cultivate a record of diligence to buttress their home styles and to forestall charges of absenteeism by opponents. House and Senate leaders make it easier for members to compile such records by avoiding votes on Mondays and Fridays, stacking votes back to back in midweek, and promising no votes several evenings each week.[24]

If members cannot vote in person, they can still be recorded on an issue. They may announce their views in floor statements or in press releases. Or they may pair themselves with someone on the opposite side of an issue. Pairing is a voluntary arrangement that allows members to go on record without voting or affecting the final tabulation.

The practice of allowing absent members to vote by proxy—entrusting their votes to an ally who is present at the session—has never been permissible in floor deliberations, and in 1995 it was suspended in House committees. During their forty years in the minority, House Republicans resented the fact that their members in attendance invariably were outvoted by chairmen voting the proxies they had collected beforehand from busy Democrats (though the tactic was used by both parties). By abolishing proxies, the new majority hoped to encourage members to attend their committee meetings, even though it made life more hectic for everyone.

Offering Amendments

A chief strategy for shaping legislation during committee or floor deliberations is to offer amendments. Sometimes amendments are intended to provide a test of strength. In 1993, during debate on reauthorizing the National Aeronautics and Space Administration, Rep. Tim Roemer, D-Ind. (1991–2003)—then a junior committee member—introduced an amendment to cancel the costly space station program. Instead of losing by a comfortable margin (as had happened in previous years), the amendment failed by a single vote, signaling plunging support for the space station and other "big science" projects such as the superconducting super collider.[25]

In the House, majority party leaders can shape outcomes by determining which, if any, members' floor amendments will be in order. The outcome of the 1997 debate over funding for the National Endowment for the Arts (NEA) hinged on the single floor amendment permitted by the leadership. Conservatives urged GOP leaders to honor their commitment to ax the NEA and uphold the Appropriations Committee's bill, which in essence ended the agency's funding. But fearing defeat by a bipartisan pro-arts coalition, Republican leaders seized upon an amendment proposed by Rep. Vernon J. Ehlers, R-Mich., and incorporated it into the Rules Committee's rule for the debate. This amendment would have eliminated the agency and sent the funds ($80 million) directly to the states for arts and education grants. The amendment satisfied neither of the warring camps, which pleaded for an up-or-down vote on NEA. By twisting arms, the leaders eked out a victory for the rule by one vote, 217–216. But the next day the Ehlers amendment itself went down to defeat, 155–271. And the bill went to the Senate with no NEA funding at all.[26]

In the Senate, which cherishes individual senators' prerogatives, amendments are more freely offered and form a central part of floor debate. With elections looming in 1996, Senator Kennedy won passage of two popular measures by vowing to introduce them as amendments for a variety of floor bills. These were a hike in the minimum wage and a provision that insurance companies could neither drop coverage when people switch jobs nor deny coverage for preexisting medical conditions. GOP leaders strongly opposed both measures but allowed floor votes to avoid having to face repeated embarrassments in an election year.

Amendments can also derail legislation. President Clinton's 1993 economic stimulus package came unglued in the Senate under a barrage of hostile amendments. While the bill's Democratic managers labored to keep the measure intact, Republicans put forward amendments to drop what they claimed were pork projects. When Democrats shut off amendments by a parliamentary maneuver, the Republicans' opposition hardened, and cloture could not be invoked.

Some amendments are designed to force members to declare themselves on symbolic issues that command public attention. Amendments on abortion funding or balanced budgets are prime examples. Others are killer amendments, or poison pills, intended to make a bill so unpalatable that it will fail. Senate and House sponsors of campaign finance reform faced opponents who offered nonseverability amendments. Advocates and opponents alike realized that any one of the bill's provisions—the soft-money ban, issue ad restrictions, or hard-money limits—could be struck down by the courts. The amendments provided that the entire act would fall if courts ruled against any portion of the measure. Authors of the Senate bill, McCain and Russell D. Feingold, D-Wis., beat back those amendments in close votes. Although killer amendments upset the sponsors and managers of bills, such roadblocks rarely alter a measure's ultimate fate. Examining seventy-six such amendments considered in the mid-1990s, John D. Wilkerson concluded that such amendments "rarely, if ever, cause bills to fail. . . . Most were easily defeated." Nor did these proposals tempt lawmakers to vote not on the amendment's policy substance but on its effect on future floor voting choices (so-called strategic voting).[27]

What Do Votes Mean?

Like other elements in the legislative process, voting is open to manifold interpretations. A vote may or may not be what it seems to be. Therefore, one must be cautious in analyzing legislative votes.

House and Senate floor votes are imperfect channels for registering members' views. Votes are frequently taken on procedural matters that evoke responses independent of the issue at hand. Or members may favor a measure but feel constrained to vote against the version presented on the floor. Conversely, as with the 2001 education bill (the so-called No Child Left Behind Act), members may go along because on the whole they deem it a step forward, even though they dislike specific portions. Or they may vote for a questionable proposal to prevent enactment of something worse. Or they may support a harmful amendment expecting that the other chamber or the conference committee will kill it. Finally, they may accede to party leaders' wishes on measures so long as their actions do not adversely affect their constituencies.

In some cases recorded votes are wholly misleading. A favorable vote may be negative, or vice versa. A Senate vote to attach a school prayer amendment sponsored by Sen. Jesse Helms, R-N.C. (1973–2003), to a 1979 measure dealing with Supreme Court jurisdiction was really a vote to kill the amendment; it was expected that the House would scuttle the bill. Later that year a vote against automobile air bags was only a token vote; it was tied to an authorizing bill that would have expired before the National Highway Traffic Safety Administration's air-bag regulations were to take effect. In such cases legislators' votes must be decoded to reveal their real meaning.

Sometimes voting conceals a legislator's true position. Given the multiplicity of votes—procedural as well as substantive—on many measures, lawmakers can come out on more than one side of an issue, or at least appear to do so. For instance, members may vote for authorizing a program but against funding it. Or they may vote against final passage of a bill but for a substitute version. This tactic assures the bill's backers that a lawmaker favors the concept, while pleasing voters who oppose the bill. Such voting patterns may reflect either a deliberate attempt to obscure one's position or a thoughtful response to complex questions. As in so many aspects of human behavior, lawmakers' motivations can be judged fully only in light of specific cases.

Lawmakers' voting rationales are sometimes hard to explain to outsiders. In some cases members face a dilemma: Either vote their convictions and face the consequences or swallow their reservations and vote for the sake of appearance. Rep. Mark Sanford, R-S.C. (1995–2001), chose the former course in 1998, when he joined fourteen other Republicans in voting against a popular bill authorizing U.S. sanctions against nations that persecute religious minorities—an appealing idea but fraught with problems. "This was an awfully awkward vote, and I know I'll hear from the folks back home," he explained. "But the devil was in the details." [28]

More often lawmakers decide to go with the crowd. Regarding a highly appealing constitutional amendment requiring a balanced budget, Sen. Ernest F. Hollings, D-S.C., admitted that he planned to vote for it because he got "tired of explaining" its deficiencies. It was easier "just to say put it in." [29] Such was the case in the Homeland Security Act of 2002—a massive, flawed bill that transferred some 170,000 federal workers to a new department. Members went along because they feared being labeled as against homeland security.

This point is important for students to understand because scholars often treat votes as if they were unambiguous indicators of legislators' views. It is important for citizens to discern because lobbyists and reporters frequently assess incumbents on the basis of floor votes. Many groups construct voting indexes to label "friendly" or "unfriendly" legislators. Citizens are advised to examine such indexes closely. How many votes does the index comprise, and are they a fair sample of the group's concerns? Does the index embody a partisan or ideological agenda, hidden or otherwise? The bottom line is: Beware of an interest group's voting scorecards, even if you agree with its policy leanings.

Determinants of Voting

Votes, particularly on single issues, should be examined, interpreted, and labeled with caution. Several factors shape congressional voting: party affiliation, ideological leanings, constituents' views, and presidential leadership.

Party and Voting

One way for members to reach voting decisions is to consult the views of their political party colleagues. Party affiliation is the strongest single correlate of members' voting decisions, and in recent years it has reached surprisingly

Figure 9-1   Party Unity Votes in Congress, 1970–2002

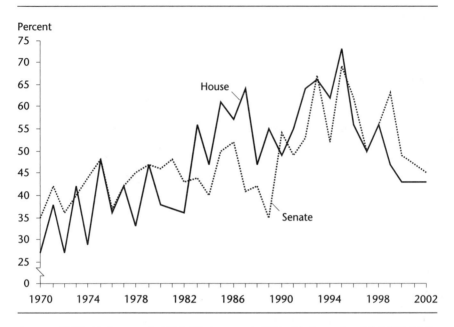

Source: CQ Weekly, January 9, 1999, 79; January 6, 2001, 56; December 14, 2002, 3240.

Note: Party unity votes are defined as the percentage of all House and Senate votes in which a majority of Democrats opposed a majority of Republicans.

high levels. Of all the floor votes cast by House and Senate members on articles of impeachment against President Clinton in 1998–1999, for example, 92 percent followed partisan battle lines—Republicans favoring impeachment, Democrats resisting it.

In a typical year from half to two-thirds of all floor votes could be called party unity votes, defined by *Congressional Quarterly* as votes in which a majority of voting Republicans oppose a majority of voting Democrats. Figure 9-1 depicts such House and Senate party votes from 1970 through 2002. An upward trend since the early 1980s can be discerned, although the frequency of such votes dipped in the 107th Congress (2001–2003). Today's revival of party voting recalls the militant parties era of a century ago. At that time at least two-thirds of all roll calls were party unity votes.[30]

Unlike parliamentary systems, however, the U.S. Congress rarely votes along absolutely strict party lines and almost never brings down the government in power (Richard M. Nixon's resignation in 1974 being the one exception). In the 107th Congress, Republicans won three-fourths of all party unity votes (63 percent in the Senate, 81 percent in the more disciplined House). Re-

Figure 9-2   Levels of Party Voting in Congress, 1970–2002

Sources: Derived from voting studies in *Congressional Quarterly Weekly Report,* December 22, 1990, 4212; December 19, 1992, 3849, 3905; December 18, 1993, 3432; January 27, 1996, 245; December 21, 1996, 3432; January 9, 1999, 80; January 6, 2001, 67; December 14, 2002, 3281.

Note: The graph shows the percentage of times the average Democrat or Republican in Congress voted with his or her party majority in partisan votes for the years listed. These composite party unity scores are based on votes that split the parties in the House and Senate—a majority of voting Democrats opposing a majority of voting Republicans. We have recomputed the scores to correct for absences.

publicans stood together unanimously in about one in ten votes; Democrats voted unanimously somewhat less frequently.

Party unity scores can be calculated for individual members—the percentage of party unity votes in which each member voted in agreement with the majority of his or her party colleagues. According to these scores, the average legislator now sticks with the party line on nearly nine out of ten votes. Aggregate party unity scores for Democrats and Republicans from 1970 through 2002 are displayed in Figure 9-2. Partisan voting blocs are evident also in many committees. From their painstaking study of voting in eight House committees as early as the mid-1970s, Glenn R. Parker and Suzanne L. Parker concluded that partisanship was a major factor in all of the panels except for Foreign Affairs (now International Relations), which has a bipartisan tradition.[31]

Party voting levels in both houses have risen by about 20 percent since the 1970s. Sharpened partisanship now dominates congressional politics, to the point that "partisan gridlock" has become a buzzword in recent campaigns.[32]

Partisan strength in voting is rooted in several factors. Some students argue that party loyalty is mainly a shorthand term for constituency differences. That is, partisans vote together because they reflect the same kinds of political and demographic areas—for example, rural areas and outer suburbs for Republicans, inner cities and minority clusters for Democrats. In the House, these demographic divisions are sharpened by partisan and bipartisan redistricting schemes.

According to this reasoning, legislators stray from party ranks when they feel their constituents will not benefit from the party's policies. Today's Democratic mavericks tend to be from nonminority southern districts, whose voters typically are to the right of the party's mainstream. Thirteen of them (ten representatives and three senators) decamped to the GOP during the last two decades. Republican mavericks are mostly from New England and the Northeast corridor, where voters fall to the left of the party's center. To win in these areas, elected officials must lean away from their parties' main thrust. (However, only two such members left the GOP.)

Partisan realignment—in which constituencies sorted themselves out according to ideological and policy preferences—helps explain the recent upsurge in lawmakers' party loyalty. Among Democratic representatives, increasing numbers of their southern flank are African Americans. The dwindling number of Democrats representing conservative districts (including the self-named Blue Dog Democrats) try to put distance between themselves and their leaders. By the same token, the Republican congressional party is more uniformly conservative than it used to be. In the South, the most conservative areas now tend to elect Republicans, not Democrats. Elsewhere many areas once represented by GOP liberals have been captured by Democrats. The decline of archconservative Democrats and liberal Republicans, especially in the House, underlies much of the ideological cohesion within, and chasm between, today's Capitol Hill parties.[33]

Party cohesion also flows from shared policy goals shaped early in a politician's career. Those who entered politics through the civil rights, environmental, or antiwar movements gravitated toward the Democratic Party and displayed their shared values in voting. By contrast, individuals who became active to cut taxes, downsize the federal government, or promote traditional values tended to gather under the GOP banner, intensifying that party's historical approach to such issues. Nowadays, candidates, and would-be candidates, receive an array of incentives and services from their parties' campaign committees, long before they take the oath of office.

Constituency and recruitment are not, however, the sole sources of Capitol Hill partisanship. Another source is institutional: the congressional parties and their activities to promote partisanship. New-member socialization is dominated by party organizations. Incoming members attend party-sponsored orientations, rely on party bodies for their committee assignments, and often organize into partisan class clubs. When seeking out cues for voting, moreover, legislators tend to choose party colleagues as guides for their own behavior.[34]

Party leaders repeatedly contact members to solicit views and urge them to support the party. The more visible an issue, the harder leaders must compete against other pressures for members' votes. Rep. Mark Souder, R-Ind., described the exhortations of House Speaker Newt Gingrich, R-Ga. (1995–1999), and his lieutenants during the GOP's first year in power:

> They pull us into a room before almost every vote and yell at us. . . . They say, "This is a test of our ability to govern," or "This is a gut check," or "I got you here and you hired me as your coach to get you through, but if you want to change coaches, go ahead." [35]

Leaders are more likely to muster votes if the issue is defined in procedural terms than if the issue is presented substantively. Whatever the legislator's personal leanings, the institutional push toward partisan voting cannot be ignored.

Finally, party leaders exploit each chamber's rules and procedures to encourage favorable outcomes. David W. Rohde calls this "process partisanship," which means "the degree to which each institution is structured or operates in a partisan fashion." [36] House procedures sharpen partisanship, inasmuch as a cohesive majority party can usually work its will. Through their control of key committees, their scheduling powers, and the use of special rules to structure floor debate and voting, majority party leaders can arrange votes they are likely to win and avoid those they are apt to lose. Senate leaders have fewer opportunities to engineer victories because that chamber's rules and procedures distribute power more evenly between the parties and among individual members than does the House. Yet Senate floor leaders can regulate the timing of debates to their advantage and (through their right to be recognized first to speak or offer amendments on the floor) influence the order and content of floor deliberations.

"Conditional party government" is how political scientists describe today's legislative parties. But considering the range of partisan influence, perhaps the word *conditional* could be dropped.

Ideology and Voting

Just as lawmakers are committed partisans, they also tend to harbor ideological views. From roll-call votes and interviews, Jerrold E. Schneider concluded that much congressional voting is ideological, that voting coalitions form because members carry with them well-developed ideological positions. Since then Keith T. Poole and Howard Rosenthal have derived from roll-call votes ideological scores for all members of Congress from 1789 to the present.[37] They find stable cleavages along two dimensions: race and government intervention in the economy.

When political scientists began to do serious voting analysis in the 1950s, party and ideology were distinct ingredients, despite measurable differences between the parties. The reason was deep ideological splits within the two parties. In the late 1930s a conservative coalition of Republicans and southern Democrats emerged in a reaction against the New Deal.[38] Historically, this coalition was stronger in the Senate than in the House, but its success rate in both chambers was formidable during the 1938–1964 period—no matter which party controlled the White House or Capitol Hill. In 1981 the coalition reappeared as President Ronald Reagan captured votes of conservative Democrats on budget, tax, and social issues, while pulling mainstream Democrats toward conservative positions on the other issues.[39]

Today the conservative coalition surfaces so rarely that the respected *CQ Weekly* has stopped scoring it.[40] Bipartisan conservatism fell victim to the hardening ideological consistency of both political parties. The Republicans are more uniformly conservative, and the Democrats more liberal, than they were in the period between the late 1930s and the mid-1980s. "Democrats are perched on the left, Republicans on the right, in both the House and the Senate as the ideological centers of the two parties have moved markedly apart," writes Sarah A. Binder.[41] In other words, the two parties are more cohesive internally and further apart externally than they were in the recent past.

The ideological center on Capitol Hill is thus a victim of partisan repositioning aided in the House by partisan gerrymandering. The proportion of political moderates—conservative Democrats or liberal Republicans—hovered at about 30 percent in the 1960s and 1970s. (Binder's definition of centrists is those members who are closer to the ideological midpoint between the two parties than to the ideological center of their own party.) Fewer than one in ten of today's lawmakers fall into this centrist category.[42] Conservative Democrats, the larger of the two centrist groupings, once represented a third of their party's members; a mere handful remain today. In the 107th Congress (2001–2003), they represented no more than 9 percent of their party in the House and 15 percent in the Senate. Most of these represented southern or border states. Even rarer were moderate to liberal Republicans, who accounted for no more than 2 percent of all House GOP members and 8 percent of senators.[43]

Polarization on Capitol Hill—in which partisanship and ideology are closely intertwined—can be shown spatially on a left-right (liberal to conservative) continuum. See Figure 9-3. If one asks the American public to locate themselves at points along a left-right scale, the result roughly follows a normal bell-shaped curve; that is, citizens tend to cluster toward the middle, their numbers declining toward the extreme ends of the scale (Panel A). Political elites—delegates to national political conventions, for example—are more opinionated than the public as a whole, and they cluster to the left and right of the median, nonetheless overlapping one another at the center. Data

Figure 9-3 Ideological Divisions in Congress and the Public

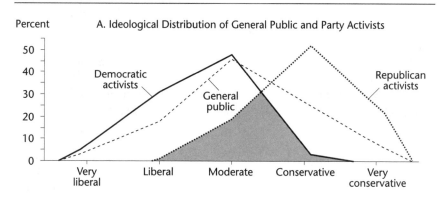

A. Ideological Distribution of General Public and Party Activists

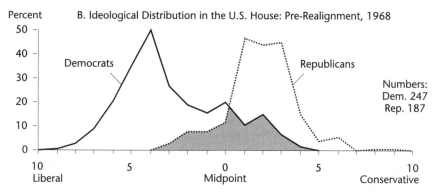

B. Ideological Distribution in the U.S. House: Pre-Realignment, 1968

Numbers:
Dem. 247
Rep. 187

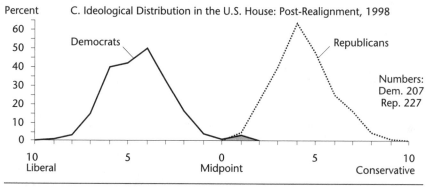

C. Ideological Distribution in the U.S. House: Post-Realignment, 1998

Numbers:
Dem. 207
Rep. 227

Sources: Panel A: *Washington Post*/ABC News surveys, *Washington Post,* August 11, 1996, M8; August 25, 1996, M4. Panels B and C: Adapted from Sean M. Theriault, "The Case of the Vanishing Moderates: Party Polarization in the Modern Congress," paper presented at the Western Political Science Association, Denver, Colo., March 2003, Figure 1. Data derived from Keith T. Poole and Howard Rosenthal's DW-NOMINATE ideology scores. See Keith T. Poole and Howard Rosenthal, *Congress: A Political–Economic History of Roll-Call Voting* (New York: Oxford University Press, 1997).

compiled by Sean M. Theriault allow ideological divisions in the House of Representatives to be viewed at two historical points: before and after the recent partisan realignment (1968 and 1998). Ideology in the pre-realignment House (Panel B) looks very similar to that of the party elites. Democrats appeared in almost every ideological niche, from far left to far right, whereas Republicans were more tightly clustered on the right, with a number spilling over to the liberal side of the scale (Panel B).[44] The contemporary Congress (1998, represented by Panel C) is almost completely polarized. Only a handful of members fall at the midpoint; not a single Republican falls on the liberal side of the scale, and only a handful of Democrats stray into the weakest conservative category.

Although the diagrams in Panels B and C are based on ideological categories drawn from members' voting records (following the Poole-Rosenthal scale), they now virtually mirror partisan labels. (The figures are for the House; patterns in the Senate are similar though somewhat less dramatic.) This polarization, and the resulting collapse of the middle, is an outgrowth of realignment that has produced legislative battle lines of a clarity not seen in nearly a century.

Constituency and Voting

To consider the potency of constituency, take how House members voted on an uncommonly partisan agenda: the Republicans' ten-point Contract with America in 1995. Fealty to the contract hinged mainly on partisanship and ideology, according to James G. Gimpel's multivariate analysis of the voting. Southern Democrats, for example, were more supportive than were non-southerners. Also significant were district characteristics: racial composition, median income, percentage of rural inhabitants, and percentage who voted for independent presidential candidate Ross Perot in 1992. Gimpel summarizes his findings:

> The plurality of legislators who found themselves on the losing side of these votes [on the contract] were from northern and western urban districts with significant minority and low-income populations. In this sense, the Contract with America was a legislative program supported most consistently by members from predominantly white, middle- and upper-income suburban and rural districts.[45]

Constituencies control lawmakers' choices in two ways. First, people can elect representatives whose views so mirror their own that floor votes automatically reflect the will of the constituents. In other words, representatives vote their constituency because they are simply transplanted locals. Certain constituency issues invariably override party or ideology—for example, farm subsidies, public lands management, and immigration.

Second, lawmakers are faced with the ever-present threat of electoral defeat. Only rarely do politicians' careers hang on a single vote, but it happens.

Pennsylvania Democrat Marjorie Margolies-Mezvinsky lost her swing district in 1994 because of her deciding vote that passed President Clinton's budget. Her constituents regarded her vote as a broken promise to oppose tax and spending increases. Naturally skittish in calculating voters' reactions, politicians usually play it safe. The choices they make, taken cumulatively, offer opportunities to expand or contract their electoral base of support. To explain how politicians calculate the electoral effect of their decisions, R. Douglas Arnold draws upon the distinction between attentive and inattentive publics first described by V. O. Key Jr.[46]

Attentive publics are those citizens who are aware of issues facing Congress and harbor decided opinions about what Congress should do. Such people usually, though not always, belong to interest groups that reinforce, mobilize, and voice their preferences. Politicians have little trouble discerning who is paying attention to a given issue and even grasping what the electoral consequences may be. Yielding to a group's strongly voiced preferences is a politician's natural instinct—unless the issue in question has mobilized two equally vociferous but opposing interests. Especially feared are single-interest groups that threaten to withhold electoral support if their preferences are not followed. Abortion and gun control are recent issues that have evoked such threats. Happily for lawmakers, most citizens, even highly motivated ones, are interested in a range of issues. Thus politicians can cultivate support over the long haul and encourage voters to gloss over wrong votes on particular issues.

Inattentive publics are people who lack extensive knowledge and firm preferences about a specific issue. This describes most people most of the time. People pay attention to only a small fraction of the issues being decided by Congress. Yet a reelection-minded legislator cannot afford to ignore those who seem indifferent to an issue. "Latent or unfocused opinions," Arnold cautions, "can quickly be transformed into intense and very real opinions with enormous political repercussions. Inattentiveness and lack of information today should not be confused with indifference tomorrow." [47]

Previously invisible issues—personal ethical lapses, the House bank overdrafts of the early 1990s, and the corporate scandals of the early 2000s, for example—may leap to the public spotlight, especially when prompted by aggressive media coverage or interest group activity. Legislators are well advised to approach even the most minor choices with this question in mind: Will my decision be defensible if somehow it appears on the front pages of major newspapers in my state or district?

Calculating the electoral consequences of a lawmaker's multitude of daily decisions is no easy task. Arnold summarizes the components of such calculations:

> To reach a decision, then, a legislator needs to (1) identify all the attentive and inattentive publics who might care about a policy issue, (2) estimate the direction and intensity of their preferences and potential preferences, (3) estimate the probability that the potential preferences will be transformed into

Figure 9-4   Presidential Success History, 1953–2002

Percent

Source: CQ Weekly, December 14, 2002, 3237, 3275.

Note: Presidential success is defined as the percentage of the times the president won his way on roll-call votes on which he had taken a clear position.

real preferences, (4) weight all these preferences according to the size of the various attentive and inattentive publics, and (5) give special weight to the preferences of the legislator's consistent supporters.[48]

Fortunately, lawmakers do not have to repeat these calculations every time they face a choice. Most issues have been around for some time. The preferences of attentive and even inattentive publics are fairly well known. Moreover, Congress is well structured to amass and assess information about individual and group preferences. And prominent officials—party leaders and acknowledged policy experts, for example—can often legitimize members' choices and give them cover in explaining those choices to voters.

The Presidency and Voting

Although Congress often pursues an independent course and members differ in their feelings toward the occupant of the White House, presidents do influence voting. Not only do presidents shape the legislative agenda, but they also can persuade members to lend support. Figure 9-4 depicts the percentage of times presidents from Dwight D. Eisenhower to George W. Bush have prevailed in congressional roll-call votes on which the president announced a position.

President Bush won 87 percent of the roll-call votes on which he took a position during the 107th Congress (2001–2003). This was the best presidential success record since 1965, when President Lyndon B. Johnson was at the summit of his influence. Bush's record owed much to his strategy of focusing on a few core initiatives. Although his administration changed profoundly after the September 11, 2001, terrorist attacks, his legislative success level was high in both of his first two years.

Presidential support votes—those on which presidents have taken an unambiguous stance—include a range of issues, from the momentous (tax cuts and the Iraqi war, in Bush's case) to large numbers of routine and noncontroversial matters (most Senate confirmations of executive nominations, for example). Still, the index roughly gauges presidents' standing on Capitol Hill and suggests several patterns.

First, modern presidents see their position prevail in two-thirds or more of House and Senate votes, though support levels can vary wildly from year to year. Many of their successes spring not so much from popularity or skill as from the routine nature of many of their initiatives. Yet some presidents—such as Eisenhower, John F. Kennedy, Lyndon B. Johnson, Reagan in his first year, and Clinton and George W. Bush in their first two years—enjoy extraordinary success in steering their proposals through Congress.

Second, presidents do better with their own partisans than with those of the opposition party. Members of the president's party feel obliged to lend their support whenever they can. The party ratio that presidents confront in Congress is the single most important determinant of success or failure. "We don't live in a parliamentary system," observed Senator Jeffords as he departed the Republican Party, "but it is only natural to expect that people such as myself, who have been honored with positions of leadership, will largely support the president's agenda." [49] In 2002 the average House Republican supported President Bush 82 percent of the time; the average Senate Republican 89 percent of the time. For Democrats, the figures were 32 percent for House members and 71 percent for senators.[50]

Third, partisan swings affect presidential success rates. As long as their party controls Congress, presidents win at least three of every four votes on which they have taken positions; when the government is divided, presidents fall well below that level. In his first two years in office, with Democrats controlling both chambers, President Clinton prevailed on 86.4 percent of all roll calls—comparable to President Bush's later numbers. Success smiled even upon Jimmy Carter, whose reputation on Capitol Hill was clouded by his stance as an outsider and the initial ineptness of his legislative liaison staff. With heavy partisan majorities in both chambers, Carter had a strong legislative record.[51]

When partisan control of the White House and Congress is divided, presidents' success levels are far less reliable. President Clinton's success rates on Capitol Hill plummeted to modern-day lows in 1995 and 1999. His overall success rates those years were 36 percent and 37.8 percent, respectively.[52] President Eisenhower's success rate fell 24 percent after the Democrats' big victories in the 1958 congressional elections. Building on the 1964 Democratic landslide, President Johnson achieved a modern high of 93 percent success. (Johnson's success rate was boosted by his habit of sending up messages supporting measures he already knew would pass.)

Fourth, presidents tend to lose congressional support as their administrations age. Reagan's experience dramatically confirmed this finding. His support score fell thirteen points after his first year and dropped still further after the 1982 midterm elections boosted the Democrats' majority in the House. After the Democrats recaptured the Senate in the 1986 election and his administration was damaged by the Iran-contra revelations, Reagan's success rate sagged to 43.5 percent.

Finally, presidents have taken clear-cut stands on fewer issues over time.[53] In 2002 President Bush took a position on only ninety-eight House or Senate votes—about half the number of such votes in the 1980s. The White House weighed in on 13 percent of all votes; at a comparable stage in his administration Eisenhower was taking positions on about three of five congressional votes.

Legislative Bargaining

Legislators decide on a bewildering variety of matters, in relatively short periods of time, often with inadequate information. First, each legislator has unique and sometimes conflicting goals and information. Second, whatever their goals or information levels, every legislator wields a single vote with which to affect the outcome.[54]

Such a state of affairs—disparate goals and widely scattered influence—is hazardous. Conflict may flare out of control if the contending policy objectives are not adequately met. However, stalemate is a constant threat. "Collective action problem" is how political scientists refer to the challenge of merging individual goals into group achievements. To overcome this predicament, members have to resort to politicking; that is, they must trade off goals and resources to get results. No wonder, then, that Congress is "an influence system in which bargain and exchange predominate." [55]

Implicit and Explicit Bargaining

Bargaining is a generic term that refers to several related types of behavior. In each case an exchange takes place. Goals or resources pass from a bargainer's hands in return for other goals or resources that he or she values. Bargains may be implicit or explicit.

Implicit Bargaining. Implicit bargaining occurs when legislators take actions designed to elicit certain reactions from others, even though no negotiation may have taken place. For example, legislators may introduce a bill or sponsor hearings not because they think the bill will pass but because they hope the action will prod someone else—an executive branch official, perhaps, or a committee chairman with broader jurisdiction on the question—into taking action on the problem. Or a bill's managers may accept a controversial amendment knowing full well that the objectionable provision will be dropped in the other chamber or in conference. These are examples of the so-called law of anticipated reactions.[56]

Another type of implicit bargaining occurs when legislators seek out or accept the judgments of colleagues with expertise on a given matter, expecting that the situation will be reversed in the future. Exchanges of voting cues are endemic in both chambers. What is being traded is information. The exchange not only saves the recipient the time and trouble of mastering the subject matter, but it may also provide a credible cover in defending the vote. A number of moderate House Republicans take cues from Sherwood Boehlert of New York on environmental issues. "I pay attention to how Sherry votes, and think other people do as well," said Christopher Shays, R-Conn. "He would not be in the mainstream of the Republican Party, but I think he's in the mainstream of American politics when it comes to the environment." [57]

Another instance of cue-giving came in Vermont senator Jeffords' musings upon the 1999 death of his friend John H. Chafee of Rhode Island—the Senate's most liberal Republican. Said Jeffords:

> I remember that if I ever had a question on how to vote or if I came in at the last minute and did not know what the issue was—I hate to admit that—I would first look to see how John voted. I knew, if nothing else, that if I voted as he did, I would probably not get in trouble.[58]

Chafee was soon succeeded by his son, leaving Jeffords as the senior dissenter within the Senate GOP caucus, before he left the party.

Exchanging cues is a key element in John W. Kingdon's model of representatives' decisions, derived from interviews with members immediately after their votes on specific issues.[59] Legislators have little difficulty making up their minds when they have strong personal convictions or when party leaders and interest groups agree and point them in the same direction. If all the actors in their field of vision concur, members operate in a consensus mode of decision making. Fellow members emerge as the most influential cue givers, with constituencies ranking second. As one lawmaker observed:

> I think that the other members are very influential, and we recognize it. And why are they influential? I think because they have exercised good judgment, have expertise in the area, and know what they are talking about.[60]

When members deviate from the consensus stance indicated by their cue givers, it is usually to follow their own consciences. Adding up these short-term forces, Kingdon in his model successfully predicted about 90 percent of the decisions.

Explicit Bargaining. Explicit bargains also take several forms. In making compromises legislators agree to split their differences. Compromises are straightforward in measures containing quantitative elements that can easily be adjusted upward or downward—for example, funding levels or eligibility criteria. Compromise on substance is also possible. For example, members who favor a major new program and members who oppose any program at all may agree to a two-year pilot project to test the idea.

"You cannot legislate without the ability to compromise," declared Sen. Alan K. Simpson, R-Wyo. (1979–1997), who often found fault with militant junior members of his own party. He recounted the following tale from the 104th Congress:

> On a recent bill, I went to [conservative House members] and said: "Here's what I'm doing. I've got six senators who will vote this far, and then the next time if you go any further, they will not be there." So [Sen.] Larry Craig [R-Idaho] and I delivered on this singular bill, and they said, "We want you to get more." And we said, "There is no more to get." Next vote on this bill, we lost six votes. Then they came in and said, "We are going to probably kill the whole thing." . . . [A]nd they got nothing.[61]

The lesson is that compromise is inevitable in crafting laws; those who are unwilling to give ground are bound to be disappointed.

Logrolling

Logrolling is bargaining in which the parties trade off support so that each may gain its goal. The term originated in the nineteenth century when neighbors helped each other roll logs into a pile for burning. In its most visible form, trading is embodied in a something-for-everyone enactment—known as pork barrel—on subjects such as public works, omnibus taxation, or tariffs and trade. Describing the classic logroll, former representative Edward J. Derwinski, R-Ill. (1959–1983), explained how the country's two million farmers put together a majority coalition every five years to pass the omnibus farm bill's basket of price supports, acreage allowances, and marketing agreements:

> What [the farmers] do is very interesting. The agriculture people from North Carolina, where agriculture means tobacco, discuss their problems with the man representing the rice growers in Arkansas or California. The sugar beet growers in Minnesota and sugar cane interests in Louisiana and Hawaii and the wheat and corn and soybean and other producers just gather together in one great big happy family to be sure there is a subsidy for every commod-

ity. They put those numbers together again so that they have at least 218 supporters in the House and 51 in the Senate. A supporter of the tobacco subsidy automatically becomes a supporter of the wheat subsidy, or the sugar quota, or the soybean subsidy, or whatever else follows.[62]

"This is for rural America," declared House Agriculture chairman Larry Combest, R-Texas, of the 2002 farm package (the Farm Security and Rural Investment Act).[63] Like its predecessors, the $180 billion bill aided U.S. farmers by sharply raising subsidies and price guarantees for a variety of crops—thus encouraging overproduction. As a result, the program's cost is borne not only by taxpayers here, but also by farmers in less developed countries, whose poverty is deepened when subsidized U.S. products reach the world market.

One of the most successful logrolling achievements in farm policy has been the food stamp program. It brought together farm lobbies that wanted to boost the agricultural market and urban welfare interests that wanted to feed low-income people. Environmentally minded lawmakers were lured to the farm bill because of subsidies linked to prudent land use. This logroll has proved inclusive and durable. In 1998, for example, a House-Senate agriculture conference report included a crop insurance provision for farmers and a provision restoring food stamps to a quarter-million immigrants who had lost them in the 1996 welfare overhaul. House Republican leaders decided to strip the food stamp provision from the agreement—a move calculated to please conservatives. The rule for debate was soundly defeated by an urban-rural coalition of 98 Republicans and 190 Democrats. "It was wrong to try to use procedure to amend a conference report that had such overwhelming bipartisan support," said Rep. Lincoln Diaz-Balart, R-Fla. "After today's vote, there is no doubt about food stamps." [64]

Logrolling draws individual lawmakers, at a personal level, into the finished legislative product by embracing (or anticipating) their special interests, proposals, or amendments. Henry M. "Scoop" Jackson, D-Wash. (House, 1941–1953; Senate, 1953–1983), when asked how he had assembled a majority for a new proposal, responded something like this: "Maggie said he talked to Russell, and Tom promised this if I would back him on Ed's amendment, and Mike owes me one for last year's help on Pete's bill." [65] Such reciprocity especially pervades the Senate, dominated as it is by individuals. Sponsors of a Senate bill often must placate most or all of the interested legislators to gain clearance to bring a bill to the floor.

Lawmakers who enter into, and stand to profit from, a logroll are expected to support the final package, regardless of what that package looks like. A broad-based logroll is hard to stop. "It's not a system of punishment. It's a system of rewards," explained Rep. Bill Frenzel, R-Minn. (1971–1991), about the House tax-writing process.[66] The 1998 transportation bill (the Transportation Equity Act for the Twenty-first Century), crafted mainly by House Transportation chairman Bud Shuster, R-Pa. (1973–2001), embraced so many highway and mass transit projects in so many congressional districts that it was impossible to stop—despite the fact that it bent earlier budget figures out of shape.

Fiscal constraints in recent years, however, have shifted the goal of logrolling. In a hostile fiscal environment, logrolling is often aimed at equalizing sacrifices instead of distributing rewards. Broad-spectrum bills—authorizations, omnibus tax measures, continuing resolutions, and budget resolutions—may include numerous less than optimal provisions, many of which would fail if voted on separately. Such a negative logroll enables lawmakers to support the measure as "the best deal we can get." In other words, members find it easier to accept hits to their favorite programs as long as they are sure that everyone else is taking their lumps through cutbacks or across-the-board formulas. Mark O. Hatfield, R-Ore., who served as chairman of the Senate Appropriations Committee (1981–1987; 1995–1997), explained that he would "hold my nose and do certain things here for the purpose of getting the job done, but certainly not with enthusiasm or anything other than recognizing that we are doing things under emergency." [67]

In times of fiscal stringency, legislators have fewer opportunities to claim credit for sponsoring new programs or obtaining added funding. Avoiding blame can displace claiming credit as a legislative objective, and these omnibus reverse logrolls are a result.[68] Aside from its political value, logrolling can have policy virtues. As R. Douglas Arnold notes,

> It can draw under a single umbrella coalition a whole series of programs, each of which targets funds according to need. Districts then receive substantial benefits where their needs are greatest and nothing where they are marginal.[69]

Logrolling, however, can turn narrowly targeted programs into broad-scale ones. In negotiating for passage of two high-priority measures—crime reduction and a national service corps—the Clinton administration had to scatter benefits so broadly that their effectiveness was severely impaired. The 1994 crime bill provided for 100,000 more police officers on the nation's streets, but it was diluted by spreading the funds throughout the entire country, not just in high-crime, inner-urban areas. Similarly, funds in the Americorps program were spread too thinly among too many sites to be successful.[70]

In a time logroll, members agree to support one measure in exchange for later support for another measure. Sometimes the logroll specifies an exchange; at other times it is open-ended until the donor decides to call in the chips. That is why President Clinton failed to gain passage of fast-track trade negotiation authority late in 1997. Four years earlier, Clinton had won a narrow victory for the North American Free Trade Agreement (NAFTA) by promising wavering Democrats programs that would help workers and industries hurt by freer trade. In 1997 members complained that the bargains had not been carried out. Explained Rep. Xavier Becerra, D-Calif., "I was one of those opposed to NAFTA, and I gave the president the benefit of the doubt." Clinton had pledged to negotiate side agreements protecting labor and the environment. "There was an utter failure to implement those proposals." [71]

In a logroll with side payments, support is exchanged for benefits on an unrelated issue—for example, a federal project for the state or district, a better committee assignment, inclusion in an important conference, or access to the White House. White House officials are adept at such maneuvering. In the aforementioned 1997 debate on fast-track authority, the following exchange took place on the House floor between Robert L. Livingston, R-La., then Appropriations chair, and his ranking minority member, Rep. David R. Obey, D-Wis.:

> Mr. OBEY: Does the gentleman know how many bridges the president has promised today for fast-track votes?
>
> Mr. LIVINGSTON: The gentleman does not have enough fingers for that.[72]

Although the side benefits of bargains often seem trivial or parochial, in many cases such payoffs help the member to achieve other valued goals.

Bargaining Strategy

For bargaining to take place, participants must be reasonably certain of each other's intentions and likely future actions. Rep. John P. Murtha, D-Pa., a master deal maker, cites two elements of power on Capitol Hill: "Develop expertise on an issue that makes you vital to colleagues, and keep your word." [73] Building on expertise in defense issues, Murtha often deals quietly in the back corner of the Democratic side of the House. His orbit includes the ultraconservative majority leader, Tom DeLay of Texas, whom he regards as an honest broker. When DeLay needs something, Murtha told a reporter, "He comes over to the corner and we work it out." On the Senate side of the Capitol, Majority Leader Bill Frist, R-Tenn., has not hesitated to do business with liberal icon senator Edward Kennedy. "He has always dealt straight with me," Frist said. "You know exactly where he's coming from." [74]

For bargaining to succeed, the participants must agree on the desirability of a legislative product. That is, the benefits of reaching a decision must exceed the costs of failing to do so. In the vast majority of cases—where there is sharp disagreement or concerted opposition—a negative political cost-benefit ratio results in no action at all. In other cases politicians may prefer a course of strategic disagreement, which John B. Gilmour describes as "efforts of politicians to avoid reaching an agreement when compromise might alienate supporters, damage their prospects in an upcoming election, or preclude getting a better deal in the future." [75] Such strategies are encouraged by today's competitive, polarized party system. As Rep. Barney Frank, D-Mass., observed,

Right now, the differences between the two parties are so great, it doesn't make sense for us to compromise. We'll show where we stand, and let the people decide." [76]

The result is often legislative inaction—which can be interpreted as stalemate or gridlock.

Are there inherent limits to negotiation? According to bargaining theory, a measure's sponsors will yield only what they absolutely must to gain a majority of supporters. Under this size principle, a minimum winning coalition occurs in ideal legislative bargaining situations—that is, when the bargainers act rationally and with perfect information.[77] Recounting Senate majority leader Lyndon B. Johnson's meticulous vote counting before a floor fight, political scientist John G. Stewart concluded, "And once a sufficient majority had been counted, Johnson would seldom attempt to enlarge it: Why expend limited bargaining resources which might be needed to win future battles?"[78]

Most legislative strategists, however, lack Johnson's extraordinary skills. Uncertainty about outcomes leads them to line up more than a simple majority of supporters. Moreover, at many points in the legislative process supermajorities are required—for example, in voting under suspension of the rules, in overriding vetoes, or in ending Senate filibusters. Not surprisingly, therefore, minimum winning coalitions are not typical of Congress, even in the majoritarian House of Representatives.[79]

Yet coalition size is the crux of legislative strategy. Bargainers repeatedly face the dilemma of how broadly or how narrowly to frame their issues and how many concessions to yield in an effort to secure passage.

Conclusion

The enterprise of lawmaking rests, nonetheless, on the premise that—at least where urgent matters are concerned—bargainers will normally prefer some sort of new outcome to none at all. As the legendary Senate Republican leader (1959–1969) Everett M. Dirksen, R-Ill., once remarked: "I am a man of fixed and unbending principle, and one of my principles is flexibility." [80] Especially is this the case with actions facing deadlines or imperiling government functions if not approved—reauthorizations, appropriations, debt ceiling adjustments, and the like.

The ultimate consequence of nonaction is government shutdown. Since 1981, budget confrontations between executive and legislative branches controlled by different political parties have left the government temporarily without funds to operate on sixteen separate occasions. Such funding gaps typically have lasted only a few hours or days, but in the winter of 1995–1996 the stalemate between the Clinton White House and GOP congressional majorities caused major disruptions. When the parties realized the escalating costs of inaction, the bargaining resumed.

Bargaining is reflected not only in the substance of legislation but also in many attributes of the legislative process—delay, obfuscation, compromise, and norms such as specialization and reciprocity. It is no exaggeration to say that bargaining is endemic to the legislative way of life. Legislative bargaining shapes the character of bills, resolutions, and other forms of congressional policy making. It is yet another point of contact and conflict between the two Congresses—the Congress of individual wills and the Congress of collective decisions.

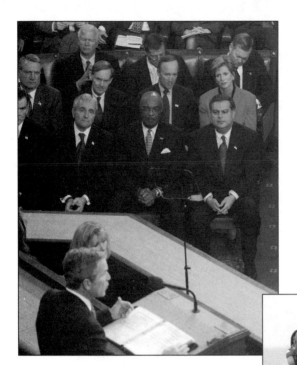

The different roles of the president. Above, President George W. Bush delivers the State of the Union address before a joint session of Congress. Center, as commander in chief, the president salutes as he lands on the aircraft carrier USS Abraham Lincoln *before announcing that the war with Iraq had ended. Below, he plays golf and conducts business informally with GOP House members Dan Burton of Indiana, Tom DeLay of Texas, and Michael Oxley of Ohio.*

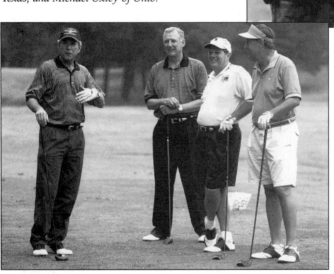

10

Congress and the President

Frustrated by President George W. Bush's inadequate consultation with Congress about the design of important domestic policies, several key lawmakers began to question why the administration advanced proposals without their input and without providing sufficient details. Senate Finance chairman Charles E. Grassley, R-Iowa, exclaimed that the White House had "botched" the development of a Medicare reform initiative. Added Sen. John B. Breaux, D-La., about the president's handling of the issue: "You don't just throw it up in the air and hope that people will decide it's wonderful." [1]

Tensions between the executive and legislative branches are inevitable. These two branches are organized differently; they have divergent responsibilities; they have different constituencies and terms of office; and they are jealous of their prerogatives. Executive officials see Congress as inefficient and meddlesome. Legislators perceive the executive branch as arrogant and arbitrary. At times these differences lead to conflicts that the media dramatize as "battles on the Potomac."

Yet day in and day out, Congress and the president work together. Even when their relationship is guarded or hostile, bills get passed and signed into law. Presidential appointments are approved by the Senate. Budgets are eventually enacted and the government is kept afloat. This necessary cooperation goes on even when control of the White House and the Capitol is divided between the two major parties. Conversely, as President Jimmy Carter sadly learned—and President Bill Clinton learned during his first two years in office—unified partisan control of both branches is no guarantee of harmony. In his third year in office, President George W. Bush also confronted complaints from the GOP-controlled Congress that he was offering some unpopular proposals that could never pass. Speaker J. Dennis Hastert, R-Ill., stated, for example, that he believed a Bush health proposal was "politically" unfeasible and not "practical." [2]

The President as Legislator

Presidents are sometimes called the chief legislators because they are closely involved in the decisions Congress makes. Article II, Section 3, of the Constitution directs the president from time to time to "give to the Congress Information of the State of the Union and recommend to their Consideration such Measures as he shall judge necessary and expedient." (Today, this means annually and during prime-time television.) Soon after delivering the annual

State of the Union address, the president sends to Congress draft administration bills for introduction on his behalf. By enlarging the list of messages required from the president—the annual budget and economic reports, for example—Congress has further involved the chief executive in designing legislation. Congress often delegates authority to the president, because it appreciates the strengths of the White House, such as its capacity for coordination, and recognizes its own shortcomings, such as its decentralized committee structure, which inhibits swift and comprehensive policy making. Crises, partisan considerations, and public expectations all make the president an important participant in congressional decision making. And the president's constitutional veto power ensures that White House views will be listened to, if not always heeded, on Capitol Hill.

The concept of the legislative presidency did not become widespread until after World War II. Only then could it be said that the role was institutionalized, performed not because of some unique combination of personality and circumstance but because everyone—including Congress, the press, and the public—expected it.[3] This expectation could change, but there is no indication of it happening any time soon.

To understand the chief executive's relations with Congress is no easy assignment. This appraisal is traceable in part to the founding fathers, who did not clearly define legislative-executive relationships. From the country's earliest days, the relationship has always been a work in progress. Presidents bring their own style to the relationship, which Charles O. Jones characterizes as the "partnership model" or the "independent model." The partnership model means that presidents consult regularly with lawmakers and involve them directly in the policy and political affairs of the White House. The independent model states that presidents minimize their involvement with Congress and strive to accomplish their top priorities on their own.[4] To be sure, Congress and the broad domestic and international context in which presidents operate are always evolving, and these factors affect legislative-executive relations.

Scholars and others have long analyzed America's complex system of separate institutions sharing and competing for power. Different theories or models, such as Jones's, have been formulated to suggest what constitutes effective presidential leadership. Scholars have produced such an array of studies in recent decades that they have been "marked by a bewildering succession of new models of the presidency, each the product of an admixture of empirical and normative assessments."[5] Some studies focus on the person in the White House; others on the institutional functions and structures of the presidency—arguably the fourth branch of government; and still others analyze discrete aspects of the relationship between Congress and the president, such as presidential spending power versus the legislative branch's power of the purse.[6] Here we employ five prominent presidential theories—persuasion, rhetoric, administrative, political time, and the "two presidencies"—as a way to illuminate important aspects of the chief executive's relations with Congress. To varying degrees, these analytical perspectives overlap one another and affect the activities of all presidents.

The Power to Persuade

Harvard professor Richard Neustadt (a former staff aide in the Truman White House and adviser to President-elect John F. Kennedy) wrote a classic study in 1960, read by President Kennedy and other presidents, that stated simply: "Presidential *power* is the power to persuade." [7] Power, according to Neustadt, meant more than the executive's ability to persuade Congress to enact a specific bill. "Strategically, the question is not how he masters Congress in a peculiar instance, but what he does to boost his chances for mastery in any instance." [8] To be successful, presidents must employ all their varied powers (constitutional, political, bureaucratic, personal, and more) to persuade Congress and others to do what they want. Setting Congress's agenda—determining the policies that the legislature pays attention to by taking them up in committee and on the floor—epitomizes the president's power to persuade. (The Office of Management and Budget has prime responsibility for central clearance—coordinating and sifting through departmental requests to Congress to ensure that they conform with the president's agenda.)

From the beginning, presidents have shaped Congress's agenda in varying degrees. The First Congress of "its own volition immediately turned to the executive branch for guidance and discovered in [Treasury secretary Alexander] Hamilton a personality to whom such leadership was congenial." [9] Two decades later (from 1811 to 1825) the "initiative in public affairs remained with [Speaker Henry] Clay and his associates in the House of Representatives" and not with the president.[10] Thus, dominance in national policy making may pass from one branch to the other. Strong presidents sometimes provoke efforts by Congress to reassert its own authority and to restrict that of the executive. Periods of presidential ascendancy often are followed by eras of congressional assertiveness. Still, Congress usually looks to the White House to outline its legislative program in the annual State of the Union message and in other formal and informal presidential messages.

Presidents follow different patterns in setting agendas. Two recent presidents—Reagan (1981–1989) and Carter (1977–1981)—were mirror opposites in their ability to persuade Congress to enact their policy priorities. Agenda control was the hallmark of Reagan's leadership during his first year in office. By limiting the number of legislative priorities, the president focused Congress's and the public's attention on one priority issue at a time. Most were encapsulated as Reaganomics—tax and spending cuts. He exploited the usual honeymoon period for new presidents by moving his agenda quickly and during a time of widespread anticipation of a new era of GOP national political dominance.

Reagan also dealt skillfully with Congress: meeting, negotiating, and socializing with lawmakers, including a private dinner for Democratic Speaker

Thomas P. "Tip" O'Neill Jr. of Massachusetts and his wife. After the March 30, 1981, assassination attempt hospitalized the president, Reagan returned a month later and made a dramatic appeal for his economic program. "The White House shrewdly tied Reagan's return to action to the budget and tax debate, scheduling an April 28 comeback speech before a joint session of Congress. It was a triumph, and people began to call him the 'Great Communicator.' " [11] After only eight months in office, Reagan scored some of the biggest victories of his entire eight years in office. Later, when his control over the agenda slackened, Congress was still confined to a playing field largely demarcated by the president. It was forced to respond to, although not always accept, the positions the president had staked out on taxes, spending, defense, and social issues.

By contrast, Reagan's predecessor in the White House, Jimmy Carter, quickly overloaded Congress's agenda and never made clear what his priorities were. Three major consequences resulted:

> First . . . there was little clarity in the communication of priorities to the American public. Instead of galvanizing support for two or three major national needs, the Carter administration proceeded on a number of fronts. . . . Second, and perhaps more important, the lack of priorities meant unnecessary waste of the President's own time and energy. . . . Third, the lack of priorities needlessly compounded Carter's congressional problems. . . . Carter's limited political capital was squandered on a variety of agenda requests when it might have been concentrated on the top of the list.[12]

As for personal lobbying, Carter lacked the temperament for it. He met in formal sessions with a large number of members but shunned informal and personal contacts. He did not view informal discussions or negotiating meetings with members as a productive use of his time.

Most presidents recognize the importance of maintaining informal contacts with Congress, because they understand that it is not easy to persuade Congress to act in a certain way. As President Lyndon Johnson once declared: "Merely placing a program before Congress is not enough. Without constant attention from the administration, most legislation moves through the congressional process at the speed of a glacier." [13] Johnson regularly (and sometimes crudely) admonished his aides and departmental officers to work closely with Congress. "[Get off] your ass and see how fast you can respond to a congressional request," he told his staff. "Challenge yourself to see how quickly you can get back to him or her with an answer, any kind of an answer, but goddamn it, an answer." [14] And at least since Harry S. Truman, presidents have maintained a formal White House legislative liaison office to promote the administration's program in Congress; to lobby outside groups, state officials, and others to do the same; to target members who could be coaxed for votes on certain issues; and, more generally, to foster a cooperative legislative-executive atmosphere.

In addition, to persuade members to support their programs, presidents commonly grant or withhold their patronage resources. Broadly conceived, patronage involves not only federal and judicial positions but also federal construction projects, location of government installations, campaign support, availability of strategic information, plane rides on *Air Force One,* White House access for important constituents, and countless other favors, large and small. Some presidents even keep records of the political favors they grant to lawmakers: IOUs that they can cash in later for needed support in Congress. Limits, however, do exist to the persuasive power of patronage. As one head of the White House congressional relations office said: "The problem with Congressional relations is that with every good intention, at the end of the day you can't accommodate all the requests that you get." [15] More significantly, many factors influence how members vote on issues important to the White House. Although the persuasive skills of presidents are significant, other considerations—lawmakers' constituency interests, policy preferences, and ideological dispositions, as well as public opinion and the number of partisan seats in each chamber—usually are more important in shaping congressional outcomes.

Going Public: The Rhetorical President

"With public sentiment, nothing can fail; without it nothing can succeed," Abraham Lincoln once observed.[16] Lincoln's idea is the essence of the rhetorical presidency—how and when a chief executive strategically employs contemporary campaign techniques and the technology of the mass media to promote "himself and his policies in Washington by appealing to the American public." [17] The rhetorical president's ultimate objective is to produce an outpouring of public support that encourages lawmakers to push his ideas through the congressional obstacle course. Going public on an issue, however, is not without its risks. The president can raise expectations that cannot be met, make inept presentations, lose control over issues, infuriate legislators whose support he needs, or further stiffen the opposition. Furthermore, many legislators are more popular than the president in their districts or states. The president goes public to gather support, because "if he had the votes he would pass the measure first and go to the public only for the bill-signing ceremonies." [18]

President Reagan was an acknowledged master at using the electronic media to orchestrate public support. The Hollywood actor turned president was at home in front of cameras and microphones, and he had a keen sense of public ritual and symbolism as means of rallying support. Reagan's adroitness with the media, primarily during his first year in office, is where his legacy will loom large for future presidents and Congresses. He showed that "one man using the White House's immense powers of communication can lift the mood of the nation and alter the way it does business." [19]

President George Bush's public relations techniques "abandoned the elaborate, tightly controlled machinery developed in recent years to project, manipulate and polish a presidential image" in the television age.[20] Instead, Bush used traditional methods—meeting with small groups of reporters, inviting journalists to lunch, or traveling outside Washington—to build public support through communications.

President Clinton, by contrast, was innovative in using media technologies to reach voters and in employing campaign-style practices to generate public support for his programs. The April 1995 Oklahoma City bombing—and Clinton's empathetic response—reminded the public of the human face of the federal government, the very entity Republican "revolutionaries" were warring against. When Republicans added provisions to a flood relief bill that Clinton opposed, the president used the bully pulpit to paint the GOP position as "extreme" and generated a flurry of favorable publicity for his position. As one account noted:

> News accounts portrayed Republicans as, well, crazy extremists bent on playing games with flood victims. Rank-and-file Republicans writhed in political agony. Michigan Republican Fred Upton's mother watched the news accounts with alarm and warned her son, "You're getting killed." "When your mom tells you that, you know you're in trouble," said Upton.[21]

The White House also used "nightly tracking polls and weekly focus groups to help determine its daily message and the approach President Clinton should take to important national issues." [22]

George W. Bush was initially dubbed "the reticent president" by some analysts for several reasons: his preference not to seize the public spotlight and address every major event or issue that might arise; his determination to stay "on message" by sticking to prepared talking points; his predilection for carefully staged and scripted appearances; and his capacity to make verbal gaffes. Nonetheless, Bush works diligently to win the battle for popular opinion and to mobilize public and political support for his policy and political objectives.[23] For example, he and his cabinet officers, in coordination with House and Senate GOP leaders, traveled across the country to promote broad public support for administration priorities. Bush also became the first president to deliver his weekly radio address in Spanish—political recognition of the electoral potential of the growing Hispanic population.

Bush came into his own as both communicator in chief and commander in chief in the aftermath of the terrorist attacks on the World Trade Center in New York City and the Pentagon. Several times he gave powerful and eloquent speeches in a variety of forums, such as before Congress and at the United Nations (UN), on the need to go after terrorists who threaten the United States and to disarm and end Saddam Hussein's regime in Iraq. His direct and confident manner of speaking resonated with most Americans and boosted domestic and congressional support for his military and international campaign against terrorists and regimes deemed to be associated with them.

In addition, the Bush White House has gone to great lengths to use television to promote the president, employing many former network television aides who are expert at lighting, camera angles, and backdrops. For example, in a speech in Indianapolis urging public backing of his tax cut, White House aides "went so far as to ask people in the crowd behind Mr. Bush to take off their ties . . . so they would seem more like the ordinary folk the president said would benefit from his tax cut." [24] Perhaps the most elaborate—and also criticized—event was Bush's flight to and speech on the aircraft carrier *Abraham Lincoln* announcing the end of military combat in Iraq. White House aides "choreographed every aspect of the event, even down to the members of the Lincoln crew arrayed in coordinated shirt colors over Mr. Bush's right shoulder and the 'Mission Accomplished' banner placed to perfectly capture the president and the celebratory two words in a single shot." [25]

The Administrative President

Presidents understand that getting Congress to pass legislation is an arduous process and, even when laws are enacted, bureaucratic indifference may hamper implementation of presidential initiatives. Thus, the core idea of the administrative strategy for presidents is to win policy goals by statute when that is feasible and, if not, to accomplish those aims through organizational or managerial techniques. A variety of methods are employed by administrative presidents, such as naming loyal political appointees to supervise and monitor agency activities, reorganizing executive departments to better accomplish presidential goals, using the budget process to reduce unwanted programs or increase favorite activities, and employing executive orders to implement policies blocked by Congress. [26]

Stymied by the GOP-controlled Congress on issues such as antismoking legislation, a patients' bill of rights, and subsidies for school construction, President Clinton expanded the use of executive authority. Issuing executive orders—a form of administrative lawmaking to carry out authority delegated by the legislative branch—was a favorite technique of the president to bypass the Republican Congress. Presidents have long employed executive orders. [27] President Truman, for example, issued an executive order to integrate the armed services. But Clinton used them extensively. "His formula includes pressing the limits of his regulatory authority, signing executive orders and using other unilateral means to obtain his policy priorities when Congress fails to embrace them." [28] To dramatize the importance of trigger locks on guns, a proposal that stalled in Congress, Clinton issued an executive order requiring trigger safety locks on new guns purchased for federal law enforcement officers. [29] Congressional Republicans railed against Clinton's "go it alone" governing.

George W. Bush also exploited the techniques of the administrative president. First, not only did the president fill cabinet positions with seasoned Washington hands, such as Secretary of State Colin L. Powell (chairman of the Joint Chiefs of Staff during the George Bush administration) and Defense secretary Donald H. Rumsfeld (a former House member, White House chief of staff, and defense secretary during the Ford administration), he also named numerous conservatives to his White House staff and to high administration positions, burnishing his reputation with conservative activists. The most prominent example was the appointment of former Missouri senator John Ashcroft, a pro-life conservative, to be attorney general. Many conservatives said that the president surpassed "even Ronald Reagan in the ideological commitment of his appointments." [30] These appointees work to ensure that bureaucratic intransigence does not hinder enforcement of Bush's policies.

Second, Bush quickly exercised executive authority to roll back, suspend, or challenge many Clinton-era regulations viewed as unnecessary, overly burdensome, or too costly. The president, too, moved with dispatch after September 11 to establish by executive order a White House Office of Homeland Security. Bush also is not reluctant to implement by executive fiat administration programs stalled in Congress. For example, when the Senate blocked action on Bush's faith-based initiative (assisting religious groups in winning government grants for charitable and social service work), the president ordered his administration to implement the program.

> Bit by bit, through executive orders and changes in agency regulations, the administration has been carrying out the initiative anyway. Its goal is to allow religious groups to compete more easily for federal funds to address underserved social needs, such as helping the homeless and the drug-addicted. Seven government departments now have faith-based offices, which steer religious groups toward billions of dollars in grant money. . . . The most controversial proposal to date has come out of the Department of Housing and Urban Development [HUD]: HUD has proposed a change in its rules to allow taxpayer money to be used for the construction, acquisition, or rehabilitation of houses of worship [so long as part of the building is used to provide social services].[31]

The president has employed executive authority on other matters blocked by Congress, such as permitting more logging in national forests and allowing industries more flexibility in meeting federal clean air regulations.[32] Senate Democratic leader Tom Daschle of South Dakota even set up a party watchdog panel to monitor and publicize the promulgation of regulations by the Bush administration that appear to benefit GOP-affiliated interest groups.[33]

The President and Political Time

Political scientist Stephen Skowronek spotlights the importance of political time—the evolving array of social, economic, and partisan forces in play during diverse presidential eras or "regimes," using Skowronek's word—in assessing how chief executives interact with the broader political system of which they are a part. Painting in broad historical strokes, for example, there are eras when Republicans dominate national politics; at other times, Democrats are in charge; and in still other periods, both parties coexist in rough parity until one breaks out to establish itself as the nation's majority party.

Karl Rove, President George W. Bush's top political adviser, likes to suggest that Bush's impending 2004 election may be equivalent politically and electorally to the 1896 presidential election of Republican William McKinley. During the two decades prior to McKinley's election, the two national parties were evenly balanced. McKinley's election, however, saw a large voter swing toward Republicans, who dominated nationally until the 1932 election of President Franklin D. Roosevelt. FDR's victory began nearly four decades of national Democratic dominance.[34] Skipping over a few decades when Republicans generally won the White House and Democrats held onto one or both chambers of Congress until the 2000 elections produced unified GOP control of the national elective branches, today's political era can be characterized as one of parity politics with a heavy dose of partisan polarization. Both parties are closely divided in the House and Senate, and they eye each other carefully to prevent one from gaining a political, policy, or electoral advantage over the other.

Skowronek's point is that presidential leadership is shaped by whether a White House occupant begins his service at the start (waxing) or end (waning), or someplace in-between, of a specific political era or regime. Thus, presidents can be compared not only by whether they are affiliated with the dominate national coalition of the period (if there is one), but also by how they perform within that historical context. "In the modern Democratic period," Skowronek states, "regime outsiders like Republicans Dwight D. Eisenhower and Richard Nixon faced different political problems from those confronted by regime insiders like John F. Kennedy and Lyndon B. Johnson." [35]

Leadership situations might also be differentiated according to political time; that is, when in a regime sequence the president engages the political-institutional order. Presidents Franklin Roosevelt, John Kennedy, and Jimmy Carter—all Democrats who enjoyed Democratic majorities in Congress—may be said to have faced different problems in leading the nation as they were arrayed along a sequence of political change that encompassed the generation and degeneration of the New Deal order.[36] More time needs to pass before informed judgment can be made about where Clinton or Bush fit in Skowronek's theory. For example, was Clinton a deviant president during a Republican regime, or was he (like Carter) at the tail end of a fading Democratic regime? Is George W. Bush a regime-creator at the start of a new national era of GOP dominance or a regime consolidator, completing the Reagan revolution?

A brief look at the context in which Clinton operated may provide analysts with clues as to where he fits in Skowronek's theory about the political life cycles of presidential regimes. Based on the increase in party-line legislative votes and the rise in incivility on Capitol Hill, Clinton served during a time of resurgent congressional partisanship, especially evident after Republicans won control of the House in November 1994. (Clinton won the White

House in 1992 after twelve years of GOP control. He won again in 1996 and became the first Democrat since FDR to win reelection. For their part, Republicans also won in 1996 and retained consecutive control of Congress for the first time since the 1927–1931 period. See Appendix A.)

The intense partisan era in which Clinton served largely shaped legislative-executive relations. Two vivid examples make the point. First, most House Republicans interpreted the November 1994 election as a mandate to implement an agenda (the Contract with America) whose main focus was shrinking the size and scope of the national government. As a result, they pushed budget plans fiercely opposed by the Democratic administration and they threatened to shut down the government if Clinton did not sign their legislation. "You have to realize we're serious," then House majority whip Tom DeLay, R-Texas, told Vice President Al Gore. "We'll shut down the government if we have to to balance the budget." [37] Clinton made it plain that he would not sign their bills. Twice, in late 1995 and early 1996, partisan warfare between the GOP Congress and the Democratic president forced the federal government into the longest ever temporary and partial shutdowns. To the fury of Republicans and their outside supporters, the public blamed Republicans for the shutdowns, in large measure because many were vociferous in saying, "Shut down the government. No one will notice."

Second, the partisan era led to Clinton's impeachment. Frustrated by Clinton's ability to reach out to the public and his general political adroitness, Republicans launched scores of investigations to uncover wrongdoing on the part of the president and his administration. Rep. Henry A. Waxman, D-Calif., declared that Republicans spent millions of dollars investigating the White House in a "concerted effort to undermine the authority of the President." [38] On the one hand, Clinton's popular support remained fairly robust even after it became known that he lied to a grand jury about having sexual relations with White House intern Monica S. Lewinsky and House Republicans launched a move to impeach the president. On the other hand, the public's appraisal of Clinton's personal character and integrity dropped dramatically.

Despite numerous polls showing the public opposed impeachment and conviction, Clinton became the first elected president to be impeached by the House, although he was acquitted by the Senate. The partisan voting on impeachment—98 percent of House Republicans voted to impeach Clinton, while 98 percent of House Democrats voted against—reflected a similar polarization between Democratic and Republican voters. "In poll after poll, a solid majority of self-identified Republicans favored Clinton's impeachment and removal, while more than 80 percent of self-identified Democrats remained opposed," wrote political scientist Gary Jacobson. Thus, added Jacobson, congressional Republicans "voted the way the majority of Republican voters wanted them to." [39] Whether one agrees or not with the charges (perjury and obstruction of justice) leveled against Clinton, it seems evident that the contemporary era of aggressive and angry partisanship provided the context that motivated Republicans to try and remove the president from office. The only time Clinton exceeded a 70 percent public approval rating was after his December 1998 impeachment, in large measure because of "a perception on the part of many voters that the Republican-led impeachment process was a partisan attack that went too far." [40]

The 'Two Presidencies'

"The United States has one president, but it has two presidencies; one presidency is for domestic affairs, and the other is concerned with defense and foreign policy." [41] This formulation by political scientist Aaron Wildavsky stated that presidential proposals are likely to achieve more success in the international than the domestic arena, in part because Congress asserts itself more in domestic policy making than the foreign policy field. Wildavsky's thesis has sparked considerable controversy, such as how to measure success rates in the two arenas and whether the concept is relevant in today's world where the international and domestic overlap constantly. [42] Whatever the strengths or weaknesses of the two presidencies idea as laid out by Wildavsky, the concept has some relevancy to the presidency of George W. Bush, considered before and after the September 11, 2001, terrorist attacks.

The Pre–9/11 Phase. Despite Bush's loss to Democratic candidate Vice President Al Gore in the popular vote tally, the absence of a clear mandate from the voters, public concern about the legitimacy of Bush's victory (which was determined on December 12, 2000, by the U.S. Supreme Court decision in *Bush v. Gore*), and the lack of any presidential coattails (the GOP lost seats in both chambers but held onto their majority in each), President Bush quickly advanced an ambitious agenda as if he had won a huge victory. He surprised many pundits who predicted that Bush would move slowly to implement his "compassionate conservative" campaign promises. "[T]his is the farthest thing from a caretaker administration you could get," declared a Brookings Institution analyst. "It's the farthest thing from a president saying I lost the popular vote, I'm here because of a 5 to 4 vote on the Supreme Court. I'd better [advance] some centrist positions." [43] That Bush could get off to a fast start was due in part to the public's favorable view of the new chief executive, especially in comparison to his predecessor, as an honest and trustworthy straight-shooter from Texas. And with a master's degree in business administration, Bush imposed a corporate model of governance at the White House, acting as chief executive officer who sets broad goals and policies and delegates responsibility for implementation to others. (See box for a comparison of Bush and Clinton.)

Strategically, Bush employed partisan and bipartisan models of governance to advance his agenda. He scored a major policy success early in his administration largely by staking out an assertive and partisan approach. When the government estimated in 2000 that it would run a projected surplus of $5.6 trillion over the next decade, the president soon after taking office sent a

Differences Between the Bush and Clinton Presidencies

George W. Bush	Bill Clinton
Disciplined White House	Less disciplined White House
Scripted presidency	Unscripted presidency
Strict focus on few key priorities	Wide-ranging policy focus
More reliance on vice president	Less reliance on vice president
Punctuality required for meetings with clear starting and ending times	Meetings start late and seldom end on time
Little use of the bully pulpit	More use of the bully pulpit
Direct public communicator	Skillful public communicator
Frequent reliance on experts to provide policy overviews	Well informed on policy issues
Somewhat more attentive to Congress and its members	Less attentive to Congress and its members
Large responsibilities delegated to aides	Close supervisory role maintained over all top aides
Preference for executive summaries	Enamored of thick briefing books
Regular working days observed insofar as practicable	A "24/7" president

ten-year $1.6 trillion tax cut plan to Congress. As Bush said, "We recognize loud and clear the surplus is not the government's money—the surplus is the people's money, and we ought to trust them with their own money," he stated.[44] (Later, when the economy dipped downward, Bush added another argument for his tax cut: the need to stimulate a slowing economy by putting refund checks in the hands of consumers.) Despite Democratic complaints that the tax cut was too large and doubts that the huge projected surplus would ever materialize, Bush's determination to win combined with GOP control of Congress and lawmakers' hesitancy to vote against any tax reduction that benefits their constituents produced the largest across-the-board tax cut since the presidency of Ronald Reagan.

Bush's tax cut plan first passed the House in several separate bills (repeal of the estate tax and income tax rate reductions, for instance)—all on a party-line vote. Bush's plan, however, faced a real challenge in the 50–50 Senate where moderates in both parties wanted to downsize the package. To generate support for his plan, Bush flew to several states that he carried, such as Montana, where ranking Finance Committee member Max Baucus was up for re-election in 2002, to pressure Democrats to back his proposal. Bush, too, refused to heed Democratic leadership calls to compromise, prompting then majority whip Harry Reid of Nevada to exclaim: "No one has talked more about bipartisanship and done less." [45] Bush's hardball approach carried the day. On June 7, 2001, the president signed a compromise $1.35 trillion tax cut into law, proclaiming victory for the centerpiece of his economic agenda. His victory came with political costs, "generating antagonism from Democrats and from some Republican moderates, including Sen. James Jeffords (Vt.), who quit the GOP and shifted leadership of the chamber to the Democrats." [46]

Bush chose a bipartisan approach to advance another major priority: the No Child Left Behind education bill. As Norman J. Ornstein explained:

> From the get-go, he aimed at negotiating an education package with liberal Democrats like Sen. Edward Kennedy (Mass.) and Rep. George Miller (Calif.). He dropped references to vouchers, to keep the most divisive issue off the table. He named Sandy Kress, a moderate Texas Democrat and close friend of the president, to head his negotiating team, underscoring his commitment to a bipartisan approach right down the middle of the ideological fairway. It took a bit longer, but the education bill also got enacted.[47]

The president's success in selectively using either a partisan or bipartisan approach to lawmaking kept both his electoral base happy and "the opposition party inside the tent." [48]

The Jeffords switch produced a different legislative dynamic, however. Democratic control of the Senate produced significant problems for the Bush administration. Now the Democrats could initiate and force votes on their priorities, hold hearings to spotlight their agenda and critique Bush's, modify or block administration bills coming from the GOP House, disapprove the president's nominations, and require the White House to develop "a defensive strategy for responding to Democratic ideas." [49] The result was that Bush set bipartisanship aside and opted to emphasize the partisan model of governance. Given the choice "between making concessions that create a broader bipartisan majority and narrowly passing a bill that more closely tracks his preferences, Bush will choose the latter," say top White House aides.[50]

The president soon encountered serious opposition to many of his ideas in Congress and among the electorate. Furthermore, polls indicated public concern about the direction of the country. Economically, the expected surplus was falling behind earlier projections because of the weak economy and the tax cuts. On energy and environmental policy, polls suggested that the public preferred Democratic approaches to the GOP's. In June 2001, Bush's public standing had fallen "to a tepid 50% approval rating, the lowest presidential approval rating in more than five years." [51]

Thus, as Congress returned to Washington in early September 2001 after its traditional August recess, Democrats were blaming Bush for the sagging economy, squandering the declining surplus on tax cuts for the rich, and raiding the Social Security trust fund to pay for government expenses. On the day before the terrorist assault, a Gallup poll indicated a 51 percent approval rating for the president. A thicket of political and policy problems seemed to lie ahead for the president.

The Post–9/11 Phase. The Bush presidency was transformed by the terrorist attacks. After the uncertainty of the first day, Bush became a confident, resolute, decisive, and strong commander in chief. Images of the president consoling firemen and others at the site of the World Trade Center, his calm and confident demeanor, and his eloquent statements to the public, including the September 20, 2001, national address before a joint session of Congress, rallied the nation to fight a global war against terrorists and those states that provide them safe haven. He called this global struggle "the first war of the 21st century," a war that could go on for years or decades as did the cold war.

Bush's public approval ratings soared to a record level 91 percent, breaking his father's previous record of 89 percent established during the 1991 Persian Gulf War.[52] The levels of bipartisanship on Capitol Hill were also remarkable in the initial weeks after the terrorist assaults. Congress moved quickly in bipartisan fashion to enact a number of significant measures to strengthen homeland security and to combat terrorism.

The president, for instance, won congressional support to federalize security at airports, to grant larger law enforcement authority to the Justice Department (U.S.A. Patriot Act), and to assist in recovery efforts at the World Trade Center and the Pentagon. He was also authorized by Congress to employ "all necessary and appropriate force" against those groups or nations involved in the terrorist attacks. Subsequently, the president directed the military to oust the Taliban regime in Afghanistan, which had provided safe haven for Osama bin Laden, the al-Qaeda leader who organized the September 11 attacks. Later, in his January 29, 2002, State of the Union address, the president declared that three nations—Iraq, Iran, and North Korea—were part of an "axis of evil" that threatened the world. The president focused on the Saddam Hussein–led Iraq regime and persuaded Congress in October 2002 to enact a joint resolution granting him unilateral authority to launch a preemptive military strike against Iraq and remove Hussein from power, which successfully occurred early in 2003 after a three-week military campaign.

Bipartisanship generally characterized action on antiterrorist and defense issues, but in many areas of domestic policy, Bush faced strong opposition from Congress. A good portion of legislative dismay with the president was his insistence that lawmakers do what he says. This administration "has the most executive-oriented view of government of any recent president," stated Thomas Mann of the Brookings Institution. "It believes that the president leads and Congress follows—that Republican members of Congress are there at his beck and call. That's not the way the constitutional system was designed."[53] Bush's assertive and partisan approach toward Congress sharpened legislative-executive tensions.

As for the minority Democrats, they are upset with Bush's penchant for either ignoring or attacking them. Cutting deals with Bush is something that many Democrats are not eager to do. They remember Bush's aggressiveness on the 2002 campaign trail even against Democrats who voted with him on issues such as the 2001 tax cuts or homeland security. A prime example Democrats cited was the defeat of incumbent senator Max Cleland, D-Ga., on the ground that he was "soft" on homeland security. "This is something that gnaws at us," said Sen. Richard J. Durbin, D-Ill. "A decorated and disabled Vietnam veteran [who lost three limbs in the war] would be discredited because of his stand in the homeland security debate." [54] Cleland favored civil service protections, opposed by Bush, for employees of the new Department of Homeland Security.

The distinction between the international and domestic realms inheres in the two presidencies theory. Each is surely to be a consequential force in shaping the 2004 election campaigns of President Bush and congressional Democrats. At issue is whether voters will give more weight to Bush's leadership in the global war on terrorism or the sluggish condition of the national economy, if it persists or worsens. "One thing we know is that presidential elections are performance-based and the economy is a very, very big factor in that," explained a public opinion analyst. "Whether it is going to be different after September 11 is the real question." [55]

The Veto Power

Article I, Section 7, of the Constitution requires the president to approve or disapprove of bills passed by Congress. In the case of disapproval, the measure dies unless it "shall be repassed by two thirds of the Senate and House of Representatives." Because vetoes are so difficult to override, the veto power makes the president, in Woodrow Wilson's words, a "third branch of the legislature." [56] Presidents usually can attract one-third plus one of their supporters in Congress to sustain a veto, and so presidential vetoes are not often overridden.

The decision to veto is a collective administration judgment. Presidents seek advice from numerous sources, such as agency officials, the Office of Management and Budget, and White House aides. Five reasons commonly are given for vetoing a bill: (1) the bill is unconstitutional, (2) it encroaches on the president's independence, (3) it is unwise public policy, (4) it cannot be administered, and (5) it costs too much. Political considerations may permeate any or all of these reasons. The cost rationale is a favorite of recent presidents.

The veto is more than a negative power, however. Presidents also use it to advance their policy objectives. Veto threats, for example, often encourage legislators to accommodate executive preferences and objections. Presidents also practice the politics of differentiation in using their vetoes. A veto fight with Congress may be just fine with presidents who want to underscore for voters how their views differ from the other party's. For its part, Congress can discourage vetoes by adding its desired items to must-pass legislation or to measures strongly favored by the president.

An Unsigned Bill Becomes Law

In November 1995 President Bill Clinton opposed legislation (S. 1322) that would relocate the U.S. embassy in Israel from Tel Aviv to Jerusalem. Clinton did not object in principle to moving the embassy to Jerusalem, which Israel has regarded as its capital since 1950. But he warned that ordering the shift would risk derailing the Middle East peace process because Arab nations strongly objected to the idea.

Both chambers of Congress approved S. 1322 by wide margins. Clinton decided not to veto the measure and face an almost certain override. Instead, he announced that he would allow the bill to become law without his signature and would make use of a provision added in the Senate after closed-door negotiations that would enable him to delay the move indefinitely for national security reasons.

Clinton's decision to distance himself from the embassy bill without actually vetoing it was by no means unprecedented, although it is an option rarely used by chief executives. S. 1322 was only the sixth bill to become law in this way since 1973.

Source: Adapted from Amy D. Burke, "An Unsigned Bill to Become Law Today," CQ's *Congressional Monitor,* November 7, 1995, 3.

Veto Options. Once the president receives a bill from Congress, he has ten days (excluding Sundays) in which to exercise one of four options.

1. He can sign the bill. Most public and private bills presented to the president are signed into law. Presidents sometimes issue signing statements that express their interpretation of a new law's provisions.[57]

2. He can return the bill with his veto message to the originating house of Congress.

3. He can take no action, and the bill will become law without his signature. This option, seldom employed, is reserved for bills the president dislikes but not enough to veto (see box on how an unsigned bill becomes law).

4. He can pocket veto the bill. Under the Constitution, if a congressional adjournment prevents the return of a bill, the bill cannot become law without the president's signature.

During the 1970s and 1980s Congress and the president sharply disagreed over the meaning of the word *prevents* in the fourth option. A federal appeals court ruled that President Reagan acted unconstitutionally when he pocket vetoed a measure during the holiday season between the first and second sessions of the 98th Congress. Congressional attorneys argued that during legislative recesses both chambers designate officials to receive executive communications, including veto messages. Pending action by the Supreme Court, the appeals court ruling makes clear that pocket vetoes are constitutional only when Congress adjourns *sine die* (that is, adjourns finally) at the end of its second session. President George Bush tried to expand the pocket veto to include midsession recesses and adjournments between the first and second sessions of a Congress, but congressional leaders disputed such actions.

Veto Strategies. George Bush was among the most successful chief executives in employing the veto against an opposition Congress. He used it to block unwanted legislation and as a potent bargaining weapon to get concessions from the Democratic-controlled Congress. Not until his term was nearly over (on October 5, 1992), and after thirty-five consecutive veto victories, did Congress manage to override a Bush veto of a popular bill—a measure to reregulate the cable television industry. Part of the explanation for Bush's veto successes was that he announced his intentions early and stuck by them unless the compromises he wanted were agreed to. Furthermore, he convinced congressional Republicans that their strength depended on sustaining the president's vetoes. (Of forty-six vetoes, Bush had only the cable bill overridden by Congress.) Frustrated by their inability to override presidential vetoes, congressional Democrats devised their own strategy: win by losing. To sharpen the policy differences between the two parties before the November 1992 election, they sent the president bills that he was certain to veto.

By contrast, President Clinton did not veto a single measure during his first two years in office—something that had not happened since the days of Millard Fillmore in the 1850s. Part of the explanation is that Congress was then controlled by Democrats. Clinton used his veto pen for the first time on June 7, 1995, rejecting an appropriations bill. Subsequently, the president either exercised or threatened to use the veto against numerous Republican-sponsored bills.

President George W. Bush stated that he would not hesitate to use his veto power to enforce his budgetary goals if Congress passed legislation he considered excessive. The threat of a veto, in short, often serves as a bargaining device that encourages lawmakers to accommodate the president's policy preferences. Like Clinton, however, Bush did not exercise his veto during his first two years in office, and counting, even though prominent Republicans such as Speaker Hastert have urged the president to wield his veto pen.

Bush sometimes choreographs bill-signing ceremonies to reward supporters and send messages. For example, "Bush signed [a bill dealing with corporate corruption] on a table adorned with a sign saying 'Corporate Responsibility,' a technique used by the White House image-makers to associate the president's picture with the gist of his message." [58] Occasions do arise when bills are signed in virtual secrecy, such as the 2003 measure raising the federal debt ceiling by nearly $1 trillion. On the day he quietly signed that bill into law, Bush held a public bill-signing ceremony for his $350 billion tax-cut measure.

Post-Veto Action. Just as the president may feel strong pressure to veto or sign a bill, Congress may feel intense political heat after it receives a veto message. A week after President Nixon's 1970 televised veto of a bill funding welfare programs, House members received more than fifty-five thousand telegrams, most of them urging support for the veto. Congress upheld the veto, in part because of Nixon's televised appeal. However, despite a massive telephone campaign to congressional offices (as many as eighty thousand calls an hour) urging support for President Reagan's veto of a 1988 civil rights bill, the House and Senate easily overrode the veto.[59]

Congress need not act at all upon a vetoed bill. If party leaders believe they lack the votes to override, the chamber that receives a vetoed measure may refer it to committee or table it. Even if one house musters the votes to override, the other body may do nothing. No amendments can be made to a vetoed bill—it is all or nothing at this stage—and the Constitution requires votes on vetoed bills to be recorded.

The Line-Item Veto. Congress's habit of combining numerous items into a single measure puts the president in the position of having to accept or reject the entire package. Presidents and supporters of executive power have long touted the advantages of allowing the president to veto items selectively. The legislative line-item veto was a mid-1990s priority in the GOP's Contract with America. Proponents argued that it would give the president an effective way to eliminate wasteful spending and reduce the federal deficit. Opponents countered that the item veto is about interbranch power and not fiscal restraint. Granting the item veto to the president, they said, would undermine Congress's power of the purse and give chief executives added bargaining leverage over lawmakers. "The president could say, 'I'm going to zap your dam, but I've got another piece of legislation coming around, and I won't be so inclined to do that [if you support me],' " said Rep. Jack Kingston, R-Ga.[60] After much debate, the 104th Congress expanded the president's rescission (cancellation of spending) authority. It eventually passed the line-item veto despite some concern among congressional Republicans that President Clinton might use it against GOP-passed riders (extraneous policy provisos) in appropriations bills.

The Line-Item Veto Act of 1996 gave the president a fifth veto option. After a president signed a bill into law, he could exercise the line-item veto prerogative to cancel dollar amounts specified in any appropriations law or even in the accompanying House or Senate committee reports; strike new entitlement programs or expansions of existing programs; and delete tax breaks limited to one hundred or fewer beneficiaries. After using the line-item veto, the president was required to send a special message to Congress identifying what he had rescinded. To overturn his decisions, Congress would have to pass another bill that the president could then veto, requiring Congress to override it by a two-thirds vote of each chamber. Under the law the president could block something if he had the support of only one-third plus one of the members of each chamber. The act became effective January 1, 1997, and was to expire at the end of 2004.

Right after the bill took effect, a bipartisan group of lawmakers filed a lawsuit challenging the law's constitutionality. The group argued that the law allowed the president to repeal statutory provisions unilaterally and that it eroded Congress's constitutional power of the purse.[61] Without addressing the law's constitutionality, the Supreme Court ruled that members of Congress lacked legal standing to bring the suit. They had suffered no specific personal injury—a requirement if the Court is to decide cases or controversies—because Clinton had never exercised the line-item act's cancellation authority. The Court's decision cleared the way for the president to exercise the line-item veto option, and he did so for the first time in August 1997.[62]

Contrary to expectations, President Clinton exercised caution in his use of the line-item veto. Apparently, the president chose not to anger lawmakers whose support he might need later to enact administration priorities. As one account noted, the president "has deferred to Congress on the overwhelming majority of projects that members added to budget bills, even when the Administration could find no compelling public interest to justify them." [63]

Several lawmakers subsequently brought another suit challenging the president's use of the line-item veto. On June 25, 1998, in the case of *Clinton v. New York City*, the Supreme Court by a 6–3 vote declared the Line-Item Veto Act unconstitutional because it gave the president "unilateral authority to change the text of duly enacted statutes," wrote Justice John Paul Stevens for the majority.[64] The administration soon announced that it would release funding for projects that had been subject to the line-item veto. Subsequently, several lawmakers introduced line-item veto alternatives, including a constitutional amendment. As a chairman of the House Ways and Means Committee said, "I am deeply concerned that our commitment to fiscal discipline will be eaten away" unless Congress enacts a constitutional line-item veto amendment.[65] Little momentum presently exists for further legislative action on the line-item veto, although President George W. Bush recommended in his fiscal year 2004 budget submission that Congress revive the proposal. Specifically, he asked Congress to adopt a constitutional line-item veto so presidents could reject spending or tax benefits viewed as "not essential" to government priorities.[66]

Sources of Legislative-Executive Cooperation

Unlike national assemblies where executive authority is lodged in the leader of parliament—called the prime minister or premier—Congress truly is separate from the executive branch. Yet the executive and legislative branches are mutually dependent in policy making. The 115 volumes of the *United States Statutes at Large* underscore the cooperative impulses of the two branches. Each volume contains the joint product of Congresses and presidents over the years, from the 108 public laws enacted by the First Congress (1789–1791) to the 377 enacted by the 107th Congress (2001–2003). These accomplishments are the result of party loyalties and public expectations, bargaining and compromise, and informal links between the president and lawmakers.

Party Loyalties and Public Expectations

Presidents and congressional leaders have met informally to discuss issues ever since the First Congress, when George Washington frequently sought the advice of Virginia representative James Madison. But meetings between the chief executive and House and Senate leaders did not become common until Theodore Roosevelt's administration. Today, congressional party leaders are two-way conduits who communicate legislative views to the president and inform members of executive preferences and intentions.

Presidents and members of their party are linked psychologically and ideologically. This means that "bargaining 'within the family' has a rather different quality than bargaining with members of the rival clan." [67] After winning unified control of the national government for the first time in almost fifty years, congressional Republicans wanted President George W. Bush to succeed in moving his agenda even though they did not always share his priorities. "I think everyone on our side realizes that if the president does well, we do well," declaimed GOP representative Tom Latham of Iowa.[68]

It is not uncommon for presidents and their partisan colleagues on Capitol Hill to have divergent goals, especially when the president's party is in the minority. The need for legislative results impels presidents to deal with whichever is the majority party. As one Clinton adviser explained about the administration's dealings with the GOP-controlled Congress, the "president must present himself as a national leader, as opposed to a Democratic leader, to an electorate increasingly dominated by voters who feel no allegiance to either party." [69] After tangling with the Clinton administration for eight years, some congressional Republicans took a while to adjust to Bush in the White House. "This is not a war anymore, folks," said a GOP House member. "Those bad guys are now our good guys." [70]

Bargaining and Compromise

The interdependence of the two branches provides each with the incentive to bargain. Legislators and presidents have in common at least three interests: shaping public policy, winning elections, and attaining influence within the legislature. In achieving these goals, members may be helped or hindered by executive officials. Agency personnel, for example, can heed legislators' advice in formulating policies, help them gain favorable publicity back home, and give them advance notice of executive actions. Executive officials, meanwhile, rely on legislators for help in pushing administrative proposals through the legislative process.

A classic illustration of effective presidential bargaining with Congress occurred on May 7, 1981, when the Democratic-controlled House adopted President Reagan's controversial budget package, intended to cut federal spending for social programs and to raise military spending. The plan easily passed the House because of Reagan's popularity and skill in dealing with representatives. The "greatest selling job I've ever seen," said Speaker O'Neill. Reagan, for instance, persuaded several governors to meet with members from their states who were opposing the program. He met or phoned conservative Democrats whose support was needed. Top executive officials were sent into targeted Democratic districts to drum up public support. Thus, on the key House vote all 191 GOP members and 63 Democrats backed the president's budget scheme.

Informal Links

Some presidents are able to deal with Congress more adeptly than others. Lyndon Johnson assiduously courted members. He summoned legislators to the White House for private meetings, danced with their wives at parties, telephoned greetings on their birthdays, and hosted them at his Texas ranch. He also knew how to twist arms to win support for his programs. Johnson's understanding of what moved members and energized Congress was awesome. "There is only one way for a President to deal with the Congress," he said, "and that is continuously, incessantly, and without interruption." [71]

After September 11, 2001, President Bush instituted a weekly breakfast with the bicameral leadership: the Speaker, House minority leader, Senate majority leader, and Senate minority leader. At the start of the 108th Congress, the White House added House majority leader DeLay "to the core group, giving him a voice in Washington's top-level Wednesday meeting." [72] Ultimately, however, presidential style and skills affect legislative success only "at the margins." [73] Far more important are contextual factors: the mood of the country, the state of the economy, the popularity of the president, the president's partisan strength in Congress, and so on.

Sources of Legislative-Executive Conflict

Legislative-executive conflicts were evident in 1789; they are present today; and they can be expected in the future for at least three reasons. First, the Constitution specifies neither the precise policy-making roles of Congress and the president nor the manner in which they are to deal with one another. Second, presidents and Congresses serve different constituencies. Third, important variations exist in the timetables under which the two branches operate.

Constitutional Ambiguities

Article I invests Congress with "all legislative powers," but it also authorizes the president to recommend and to veto legislation. In several specific areas the Constitution splits authority between the president and Congress. The Senate, for example, is the president's partner in treaty making and nominations under "advice and consent" clauses. And, before treaties can take effect, they require the concurrence of two-thirds of the Senate. The

Constitution is silent, however, on how or when the Senate is to render its advice to the president.[74]

In 1919 and 1920 a historic confrontation occurred when the Senate vehemently opposed the Treaty of Versailles negotiated by President Wilson. The treaty contained an agreement binding the United States to the proposed League of Nations. Many senators had warned the president against including the league provision in the treaty, and during floor deliberations the Senate added several reservations that were strongly opposed by the president. Spurning compromise, Wilson launched a nationwide speaking tour to mobilize popular support for the treaty. Not to be outdone, senators opposed to the pact organized a "truth squad" that trailed the president and rebutted his arguments. During his tour Wilson suffered a stroke from which he never fully recovered. In the end the treaty was rejected. The Constitution, in short, intermingles presidential and congressional authority but also assigns each branch special duties.

Different Constituencies

Presidents and their vice presidents are the only public officials elected nationally. To win, they must create vastly broader electoral coalitions than is necessary for legislators, who represent either states or districts. Only presidents, then, can claim to speak for the nation at large. It is important to note, however, that

> there is no structural or institutional or theoretical reason why the representation of a "single" broader constituency by the President is necessarily better or worse than the representation of many "separate" constituencies by several hundred legislators. Some distortion is inevitable in either arrangement, and the question of the good or evil of either form of distortion simply leads one back to varying value judgments.[75]

Presidents and legislators tend to view policies and problems from different perspectives. Members often subscribe to the view that "what's good for Portland is good for the nation." Presidents are apt to say that "what's good for the nation is good for Portland." In other words, public officials may view common issues differently when they represent diverging interests.

For example, a president might wish to reduce international trade barriers. A representative from a district where a manufacturer is threatened by imported Japanese products is likely to oppose the president's policy, while importers and retailers of Italian shoes are likely to support the president. The challenge to national policy making is to forge consensus within an electorate that simultaneously holds membership in two or more competing constituencies.

Disparities in constituencies are underscored by differences in the ways voters judge presidents and members of Congress. Studies of presidential popularity ratings suggest that presidents are judged on the basis of general factors—economic boom or bust, the presence or absence of wars or other crises, the impact of policies on given groups.[76] Legislators, by contrast, tend to be assessed on the basis of their personalities, their communication with constituents, and their service in material ways to the state or district. Not only do presidents and legislators serve different constituencies, but they also labor under divergent incentives.

Different Time Perspectives

Finally, Congress and the president operate on different timetables. Presidents have four years, at most eight, to win adoption of their programs. They are usually in a hurry to achieve all they can before they leave office. In practice, they have even less time—in view of the typical fall-off of presidential support after the initial honeymoon. In reality, presidents and their advisers have a year, perhaps less, to sell their basic program to Congress and the public.

Lawmakers' attitudes toward the president are likewise influenced by election cycles. For instance, the George W. Bush administration announced a national energy strategy in May 2001 designed to ameliorate the country's energy problems over the next several years. Congressional Republicans, worried about rising gasoline prices, escalating natural gas prices, and rolling electricity blackouts in California, wanted immediate actions to address those problems. They were concerned about voter backlash against Republicans in the November 2002 midterm elections. Rep. Thomas M. Davis III of Virginia, chairman of the National Republican Congressional Committee, communicated these concerns to the White House. "Do they get the message?" a journalist asked Davis. "No," he said. "They think in four-year terms; we think in two."[77]

On major, long-standing issues, however, Congress typically moves slowly. Seldom does it pass presidential initiatives quickly. Moreover, many legislators are careerists. Once elected, House members are likely to be reelected, and senators serve six-year terms. Most members hold office a good deal longer than the presidents they deal with. Skeptical legislators, reluctant to follow the president, realize that if they resist long enough someone else will occupy the White House.

The Balance of Power

"The relationship between the Congress and the presidency," wrote Arthur M. Schlesinger Jr., "has been one of the abiding mysteries of the American system of government."[78] Part of the mystery inheres in the Constitution, which enumerates many powers for Congress as well as those "necessary and proper" to carry them out, while leaving the president's powers largely ambiguous. Where does the balance of power lie? There is no easy answer, but at certain times the scale has tipped toward Congress and at other times toward the president. Scholars have even identified periods of "congressional government" or "presidential government."[79]

Four points need to be remembered about the ups and downs of Congress and the presidency. First, the power balance is in constant flux. The stature of either branch can be influenced by issues, events, partisan circumstances, personalities, or public opinion. Even during periods when one branch appears to dominate, actual relationships in specific policy areas may be far more complex.

The mid-1960s and early 1970s, for example, are cited as a time of "imperial presidents" and compliant Congresses.[80] But Congress was by no means passive during this period. While it enacted much of President Johnson's Great Society program, it also initiated scores of laws, including consumer, environmental, health, and civil rights legislation. Nor did executive actions go unchallenged. Nationally televised hearings conducted in 1966 by the Senate Foreign Relations Committee helped to mobilize congressional and public opposition to Johnson's Vietnam War policies.

Second, shifts of power occur within each branch. In Congress aggressive leaders may be followed by less assertive leaders. In the executive branch the forces for White House leadership regularly battle the forces for agency decentralization. These internal power fluctuations clearly affect policy making. As recently as the Eisenhower presidency in the 1950s, powerful committee and party leaders could normally deliver blocs of votes to pass legislation. Today, even with the resurgence of partisanship on Capitol Hill, the president can never be sure which of the 535 members will form a winning coalition.

Third, legislative-executive relationships are not zero-sum games. If one branch gains power, the other does not necessarily lose it. If one branch is up, the other need not be down. The expansion of the federal government since World War II has augmented the authority of both branches. Their growth rates were different, but each expanded its ability to address complex issues, initiate legislation, and frustrate proposals of the other. Conventional wisdom states that wars, crises, nuclear weapons, military expansion, and public demands fostered the imperial presidency. Such factors certainly enlarge the likelihood of executive dominance, but, for example, in the wars of 1812 and 1898, military action was encouraged in part by aggressive Congresses. Economic panics and depressions under Presidents James Monroe, James Buchanan, and Ulysses S. Grant did not lead to losses of congressional power.

Political scientist David Mayhew has asserted that it "does not seem to make all that much difference whether party control of the American government happens to be unified or divided" in influencing the productivity of laws and investigations.[81] Mayhew examined the period from 1946 to 1990, when the mobilization of cross-party majorities on Capitol Hill was commonplace. President Ronald Reagan, for instance, enjoyed large successes in 1981 on his policy priorities (tax cuts, defense hikes, and program reductions) when he won the support of conservative "Reagan Democrats" in the Democratically controlled House. Today, in an era of strong, evenly divided, and ideologically distinct congressional parties—reflecting the conditional party government model—presidents may confront heightened potential for partisan impasses, especially in the Senate, regardless of whether the government is unified or divided.

Conflict between Congress and the president is embedded in the system of separation of powers and checks and balances. But the founders also expected their governmental arrangement to promote accommodation between the branches. Historical patterns have veered between these two extremes. The two branches worked together in the early days of Woodrow Wilson's progressive New Freedom (1913–1916), during the New Deal (1933–1937) and World War II (1941–1945), in the brief Great Society years (1964–1966) following John F. Kennedy's assassination (1963), for the even briefer "Reaganomics" juggernaut during Ronald Reagan's first year in office (1981), and for some of George W. Bush's first two years in office (2001–2002). At other times they fought fiercely—during Wilson's second term (1919–1921); after 1937 during the Franklin D. Roosevelt (FDR) administration; after 1966 during the Lyndon B. Johnson administration; and for much of Richard M. Nixon's, Reagan's, George Bush's, and Clinton's tenures.[82]

More generally, President Bush and Vice President Cheney share the view that the White House needs to reclaim power that they perceive it lost to Congress, especially during the Clinton presidency. "I've seen a constant, steady erosion of the power and the ability of the president to do his job," declared Cheney, "and time after time after time, administrations have traded away the authority of the president to do his job. We're not going to do that in this administration." [83] The Bush administration, for example, did not hesitate to minimize the public's access to information; to challenge the right of Congress's investigative arm, the General Accounting Office, to gain access to records of a Cheney-led energy task force; or to refuse to cooperate with "even the most routine and basic congressional requests for information." [84] On many occasions, the Bush administration preferred acting unilaterally rather than collaboratively with Congress. While fierce interbranch conflicts in recent administrations (Reagan, George Bush, Clinton) had thwarted many executive initiatives, the president continued to exercise broad and even growing authority in nonlegislative areas—for example, through executive orders, administrative rulemaking, and aggressive use of the war powers.

Finally, a wide gap often separates what presidents want from what they can get. Congress can influence what, when, how, or even whether executive recommendations are sent to Capitol Hill. White House agendas frequently are shaped by expectations of what will pass Congress. This indirect priority-setting power of the House and Senate can affect whether the president even transmits certain proposals to Congress. It also works in the other direction. Recommendations may be forwarded or endorsed because the White House knows they have broad legislative support. "The president proposes, Congress disposes" is an oversimplified adage.

Congress and the president are institutions shaped by diverging imperatives. Executive officials want flexibility, discretion, and long-range commitments from Congress. They prefer few controls and consultations with a limited number of legislators. The executive tends to be hierarchical in decision making, whereas Congress is collegial. One of the legislative branch's strengths, however, is to give voice and visibility to diverse viewpoints that the executive branch may have overlooked or ignored. The dispersion of power can slow down decision making, but it can also promote public acceptance of the nation's policies. Hence, what are often viewed as Congress's vices have genuine virtue.

Conclusion

Legislative-executive relations are characterized by accommodation, conflict, and flux. Of these, accommodation is the most important. Neither branch is monolithic. Presidents find supporters in Congress even when they are opposed by a majority of either house. Both branches seek support for their policy preferences from each other and from outside allies.

Furthermore, confrontation is a recurring element in dealings between Capitol Hill and the White House. The framers of the Constitution consciously distributed and mixed power among the three branches. They left it unclear how Congress or the president was to assert control over the bureaucracy and over policy making. No wonder these two branches tend to be adversaries even when they are controlled by the same party.

Lastly, legislative-executive relations are constantly evolving. Either branch may be active on an issue at one time and passive on the same or different issues at another time. So many circumstances affect how, when, what, or why changes are brought about in their relationship that it is impossible to predict the outlook.

However, over the past generation Congress clearly has equipped itself with a formidable arsenal of resources. As a result, it can play a more active role, initiating policies of its own and overseeing executive branch actions. This development need not be a formula for stalemate. "Our proper objective," counseled Sen. J. William Fulbright, D-Ark., "is neither a dominant presidency nor an aggressive Congress but, within the strict limits of what the Constitution mandates, a shifting of the emphasis according to the needs of the time and the requirements of public policy." [85]

The newest cabinet department: Homeland Security. Above, Rep. Jane Harman, D-Calif., holds up the government's "Where's Waldo" chart to show the proliferation of federal agencies responsible for homeland security, underscoring the need for consolidation of homeland security issues in a new department. Center, in the aftermath of September 11, security tightens in Logan Airport in Boston. Below, Tom Ridge, center, the head of the Department of Homeland Security, greets Sen. Susan Collins, R-Maine, as Joe Lieberman, D-Conn., and Carl Levin, D-Mich., look on.

11

Congress and the Bureaucracy

In his 1981 inaugural address, President Ronald Reagan declared that "government is not the solution to our problem, government is the problem." Fifteen years later, in his State of the Union address, President Bill Clinton exclaimed, "The era of big government is over." On the 2000 campaign trail, George W. Bush said of his opponent, Vice President Al Gore, "He trusts Washington; I trust the people." Yet four months into his administration, President Bush asked Congress to fund the construction of nineteen hundred new oil refineries and power plants to deal with the nation's looming energy crisis. One analyst concluded that "if there is something that can be built—a missile defense system [a Bush priority] or 1,900 new power plants," the president is not a small-government conservative, but a "Big Engineering Project" Republican.[1] And, after 9/11, in the largest governmental reorganization since the creation of the Department of Defense in 1947, a new cabinet-level Department of Homeland Security (DHS), with about 180,000 employees, officially opened for business on January 24, 2003, with most of the twenty-two agencies composing the department transferred to it formally on March 1, 2003.[2] Other laws and federal funds bolstered the government's expanding role in all matters relating to security, law enforcement, and national defense. Exclaimed journalist David S. Broder,

> Bush is presiding over the biggest, most expensive federal government in history. He has created a mammoth Cabinet department, increased federal spending, imposed new federal rules on local and state governments, and injected federal requirements into every public school in America. Meanwhile, the U.S. military is expanding, too, [to track down terrorists, end Saddam Hussein's Iraqi regime, and foster the security conditions essential for democratic nation building].[3]

Why is it often so difficult for presidents or Congress to shrink the size, role, or reach of the federal government? Setting aside war, one basic reason is the ambivalence of the citizenry. Although professing to want to get government off their backs, Americans of virtually all ideological persuasions turn to government to fulfill their goals and to provide assistance during times of need. As William S. Cohen, former GOP senator from Maine and defense secretary during the Clinton administration, put it: "The government is the enemy until one needs a friend."[4] The paradox, then, is that citizens understandably oppose the general idea of big government (after all, most people do not like to pay taxes), but they support the government's specific roles—and may even welcome their selective expansion—in ensuring clean air and water, a strong national defense, quality health care, the safety of prescription drugs, crime prevention, and safety from terrorist attacks. Understandably, lawmakers typically defend governmental programs supported by their constituents.

Even when the GOP enjoyed unified control of Congress from the mid-1990s to mid-2001 and again starting in 2003 and vowed to devolve power to the states and localities, authority was still consolidated in Washington "when it proved the best way to implement [the Republican] agenda." [5] In state capitals across the nation, many people have noted "how limited the transfer of power to the states has been so far, at least compared with the scale of the promises once held out for the idea." [6] As a GOP senator said, "It's much easier to devolve when someone else is in power. When you've got the ball, the temptation is to replace those bad, old regulations with your good, new regulations, instead of sending it back to the states." [7]

The national government is not reluctant to preempt state authority to regulate electricity, define what constitutes drunk driving, or combat child abductions. Moreover, nationwide corporations often lobby for federal regulation so they do not have to contend with the different rules of the fifty states. In short, in today's complex and interdependent world, individuals and entities often look to the national government for such things as security, services, justice, or protection. As Sen. Ernest F. Hollings, D-S.C., said: "We have armies who protect us from enemies from without and the FBI protects us from enemies within. We have Social Security to protect us from the ravages of old age. We have Medicare to protect us from ill health. We have clean air and clean water [laws] to protect our environment. We have [laws that mandate] safe working places and safe machinery. Our fundamental duties here are to protect." [8]

Congress Organizes the Executive Branch

Both the president and Congress are responsible for the fourth branch of government—the bureaucracy. The Constitution requires the president to implement the laws, and by implication it empowers him to give managerial direction to the executive branch. But just as the president is a key player in the lawmaking process, so Congress "has at least as much to do with executive administration as does an incumbent of the White House." [9] Congress is constitutionally authorized to organize and fund the executive branch. But the framers could not have foreseen that their sparse references to "executive departments" would nurture the huge modern bureaucracy. George Washington supervised only three departments (State, War, and Treasury); George W. Bush heads fifteen. Congress establishes the departments and creates the independent agencies, government corporations, and intergovernmental commissions (see Figure 11-1).

The complex federal structure periodically undergoes four basic forms of reorganization. First, the president can recommend administrative changes,

Figure 11-1   The Government of the United States

The Constitution

Legislative Branch

Congress

Senate   House

Architect of the Capitol
U.S. Botanic Garden
General Accounting Office
Government Printing Office
Library of Congress
Congressional Budget Office

Executive Branch

The President

The Vice President

Executive Office of the President

White House Office
Office of the Vice President
Council of Economic Advisers
Council on Environmental Quality
National Security Council
Office of Administration

Office of Management and Budget
Office of National Drug Control Policy
Office of Policy Development
Office of Science and Technology Policy
Office of the U.S. Trade Representative

Judicial Branch

The Supreme Court
of the United States

U.S. Courts of Appeals
U.S. District Courts
Territorial Courts
U.S. Court of International Trade
U.S. Court of Federal Claims
U.S. Court of Appeals for the
   Armed Forces
U.S. Tax Court
U.S. Court of Veterans Appeals
Administrative Office of the
   U.S. Courts
Federal Judicial Center
U.S. Sentencing Commission

Agriculture Department

Commerce Department

Defense Department

Education Department

Energy Department

Health and Human Services Department

Homeland Security Department

Housing and Urban Development Department

Interior Department

Justice Department

Labor Department

State Department

Transportation Department

Treasury Department

Veterans Affairs Department

Independent Establishments and Government Corporations

African Development Foundation
Central Intelligence Agency
Commodity Futures Trading Commission
Consumer Product Safety Commission
Corporation for National and
   Community Service
Defense Nuclear Facilities Safety Board
Environmental Protection Agency
Equal Employment Opportunity
   Commission
Export-Import Bank of the U.S.
Farm Credit Administration
Federal Communications Commission
Federal Deposit Insurance Corporation
Federal Election Commission
Federal Emergency Management Agency
Federal Housing Finance Board
Federal Labor Relations Authority
Federal Maritime Commission
Federal Mediation and Conciliation Service
Federal Mine Safety and Health
   Review Commission

Federal Reserve System
Federal Retirement Thrift Investment Board
Federal Trade Commission
General Services Administration
Inter-American Foundation
Merit Systems Protection Board
National Aeronautics and Space Administration
National Archives and Records Administration
National Capital Planning Commission
National Credit Union Administration
National Foundation on the Arts and
   the Humanities
National Labor Relations Board
National Mediation Board
National Railroad Passenger Corporation
   (Amtrak)
National Science Foundation
National Transportation Safety Board
Nuclear Regulatory Commission
Occupational Safety and Health Review
   Commission
Office of Government Ethics

Office of Personnel Management
Office of Special Counsel
Panama Canal Commission
Peace Corps
Pension Benefit Guaranty Corporation
Postal Rate Commission
Railroad Retirement Board
Securities and Exchange Commission
Selective Service System
Small Business Administration
Social Security Administration
Tennessee Valley Authority
Trade and Development Agency
U.S. Arms Control and Disarmament Agency
U.S. Commission on Civil Rights
U.S. Information Agency
U.S. International Development
   Cooperation Agency
U.S. International Trade Commission
U.S. Postal Service

Source: The United States Government Manual, 2002/2003 (Washington, D.C.: U.S. Government Printing Office, 2002), 21.

Table 11-1   Growth of the Cabinet

Department	Year created
State	1789
Treasury	1789
War (reorganized and renamed Defense in 1947)	1789
Interior	1849
Justice (position of attorney general created in 1789)	1870
Agriculture	1889
Commerce (created as Commerce and Labor)	1903
Labor (split from Commerce and Labor)	1913
Health, Education, and Welfare (reorganized and renamed Health and Human Services in 1979)	1953
Housing and Urban Development	1965
Transportation	1966
Energy	1977
Education	1980
Veterans Affairs	1989
Homeland Security	2002

Source: CQ Daily Monitor, January 10, 2003, 3.

such as new strategies for management improvements. Second, Congress can authorize departments and agencies to reorganize themselves. Sometimes Congress establishes an outside commission to recommend how departments or agencies might be merged or abolished. Third, Congress can authorize the president to reorganize on his own initiative or to propose reorganization plans subject to some form of congressional review. Fourth, executive agencies and departments are created or abolished by law. The Department of Homeland Security is the newest cabinet creation (see Table 11-1).

Department of Homeland Security

Nine days after September 11, 2001, President Bush announced to a joint session of Congress that by executive order he was establishing an Office of Homeland Security within the White House. He named former Pennsylvania governor Tom Ridge to head the new office and also to be the assistant to the president for homeland security. Under Bush's executive order (E.O. 13228), "[t]he mission of the Office shall be to develop and coordinate the implementation of a comprehensive national strategy to secure the United States from terrorist threats or attacks" and "to coordinate the executive branch's" homeland security efforts.

In establishing the Homeland Office as an entity within the Executive Office of the President, Bush was following the administrative presidency strategy. Under this governing model, Bush not only could act quickly and unilaterally, but he also avoided the legislative hurdles and hassles of dealing with a House and Senate controlled by different parties. The president, however, soon encountered congressional criticism and resistance to his administrative approach, as both Democrats and Republicans contended that Ridge lacked adequate authority and resources under the executive order to coordinate the government's many agencies involved in antiterrorist activities. Ridge responded that his close access and ties to Bush provided him with all the authority he needed to carry out his mission.

Lawmakers were not convinced, however. Members such as Sen. Joseph I. Lieberman, D-Conn., and Rep. William M. "Mac" Thornberry, R-Texas, introduced legislation to establish a new homeland security department. They argued that Ridge could not accomplish his coordinative role out of an office in the White House. He needed the budgetary, legal, and human resources provided by a cabinet department. A related legislative-executive dispute soon enveloped the administration. Under orders from Bush, Ridge refused to testify before House and Senate committees.[10] Members of both parties responded to the challenge from the president. For instance, when Ridge refused to testify before GOP Oklahoma representative Ernest Istook's Appropriations subcommittee, Istook threatened to reduce funding for the Executive Office of the President. The result was that Ridge began to meet informally with House and Senate committees and members, a practice that did not satisfy everyone on Capitol Hill.[11]

The controversy over testifying, revelations about failures in executive agencies to analyze or share information that might have prevented September 11, and Ridge's inability to persuade cabinet members to cede some of their turf finally persuaded the president to support creation of the new department. In April 2002, four administration members—Ridge, Office of Management and Budget (OMB) director Mitchell E. Daniels Jr., White House chief of staff Andrew H. Card Jr., and White House counsel Alberto Gonzales—began to meet in secret to draft legislation to establish the new department.[12] On June 6, 2002, the president went on nationwide television to recommend creation of a new cabinet department on homeland security, something that he had opposed for months. The president sent a draft of his reorganization plan to Congress on June 18, 2002, and it was formally introduced (H.R. 5005) on June 24.[13]

Bush's proposal had no trouble passing the GOP-controlled House, which acted on July 22, 2002, by a 295 to 132 vote. The Senate, controlled by Democrats, was another matter. Initially, many senators hoped that the new department would be created by the September 11 anniversary, but, when that date came and went with no action, many lawmakers became "increasingly doubtful that [it] will get done before the November elections."[14] The stumbling block involved civil service and collective bargaining rights for the tens of thousands of federal employees from twenty-two federal agencies who would be transferred to the new department. President Bush wanted to exempt these employees from civil service protections so he would have the flexibility to hire, fire, or transfer these workers as circumstances dictated. Senate Democrats, backed by their union supporters, vigorously opposed the president on this issue. When it became clear that the Democrats had the fifty-one votes to pass legislation containing civil service protections, Republicans launched a filibuster. Democrats tried five times unsuccessfully to invoke cloture (or closure of debate), which requires sixty votes. In the end, the Senate recessed on October 17, 2002, for the November 5 midterm elections without passing its bill but agreeing to return with the House for a postelection, or lame duck, session in mid-November.

Both parties understood the politics of not having acted on homeland security. President Bush was already on the campaign trail lambasting Democrats for being more concerned about special interests than the nation's security. He repeated this message over and over as he criss-crossed the country on behalf of GOP candidates. Congressional Democrats were unable to neutralize the blame-game politics of the White House by castigating Republicans for their unwillingness to compromise and for preventing Senate action by filibustering the bill creating the new department. The midterm elections produced a victory for Republicans, who won back control of the Senate and increased the size of their majority in the House. Capitalizing on the electoral victory, Bush used that momentum to push his version of the DHS bill through the lame duck Senate. It passed on November 19 by a 90 to 9 vote. The House agreed to the amended version of the DHS bill (H.R. 5005), which the president signed into law on November 25, 2002.

Senate Confirmation of Presidential Appointees

High-level federal appointments—executive, diplomatic, and judicial—are subject to the Senate's "advice and consent" under Article II, Section 2, of the Constitution. After the president has decided whom to nominate, the Senate decides whether to confirm (see Figure 11-2). Senate committees usually elicit the following promise from departmental and agency nominees they have confirmed: "The nomination was approved subject to the nominee's commitment to respond to any requests to appear and testify before any duly constituted committee of the Senate." [15] The confirmation process also reflects the two Congresses principle. As a top Senate official once remarked, "It looks very, very good in California or some place to put out a press release that says, 'Today, I questioned the new Secretary of Transportation about the problems of our area.' " [16]

Presidents sometimes circumvent the Senate's role by making recess appointments during breaks in the Senate's session. (Recess appointees serve until the end of the next Senate session; for example, a person named in 2003 might serve until late 2004.) The Senate resents presidential use of this con-

Figure 11-2 The Appointments Process

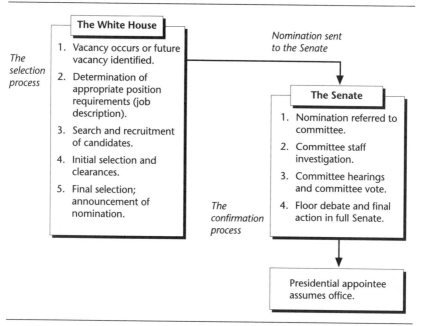

Source: G. Calvin Mackenzie, *The Politics of Presidential Appointments.* Copyright © 1981 by The Free Press. Reprinted with permission of The Free Press, a Division of Simon & Schuster, Inc.

stitutional option (see Article II, Section 2), and its opposition to some recess appointees has caused some of them to give up their posts. Another way for the administration to circumvent the confirmation process is to appoint officials on an acting basis. In 1998, 20 percent of the cabinet-level jobs requiring Senate confirmation were held by acting officials.[17] Anger at this practice precipitated enactment of the Vacancies Act of 1998. This law identifies individuals subject to the advice and consent of the Senate who can be named on an acting basis and sets limits on the length of their tenure.

Nominations to high executive posts today are subject to standards of judgment and evaluation that go beyond questions of competence or conflict of interest. Nominees' personal lives and morality are scrutinized as well. As one commentator explained:

> These days, if you want to run for office or accept a position of public trust, everything is relevant. Your moral, medical, legal and financial background, even your college records, become the subject of public scrutiny. In the old days, the scrutiny was done in private, and certain transgressions could be considered irrelevant.[18]

This shift in standards stems in part from a shift in attitudes by the press and public. The press now reports more aggressively than in years past the private activities of public officials.[19]

Today, there is substantial frustration with the confirmation process. "The nomination system is a national disgrace," wrote a scholar of the presidential appointment process.[20] The problems are many according to analysts and afflict both Democratic and Republican administrations—even when the same party controls the White House and the Senate. Although most nominees are eventually confirmed by the Senate, three concerns with the process merit mention.

First, it takes longer and longer to fill the full-time cabinet and agency positions requiring Senate confirmation. While President John F. Kennedy had his administrative appointees in place by April 1961, only 2.4 months after his inauguration, "the first Bush administration was not fully confirmed until early October [1991], and the Clinton administration not until mid-October [1993], more than eight months after the start of their respective presidencies.[21] Four months into the administration of President George W. Bush, "only 11 percent of its most senior government positions" had been filled.[22] On average, it has taken the Bush administration almost nine months to fill appointed positions that require Senate confirmation compared with the five-month average of the Reagan administration.

Second, bureaucratic developments contribute to the slowness of the confirmation process. Congress and the president have created more executive positions requiring Senate confirmation. For example, President Kennedy nominated fifteen undersecretaries in 1961; President George W. Bush will appoint almost fifty. "Kennedy nominated 87 assistant secretaries; Mr. Bush will appoint more than 220." [23] Further, nominees are required to complete complex and burdensome disclosure forms and undergo lengthy background checks by the Federal Bureau of Investigation (FBI). One result of the onerous review process, according to a study done by the Brookings Institution (a Washington-based think tank), is a drop-off in "the number of talented Americans willing to accept the call to presidential service. Presidential recruiters report that it takes more calls to find candidates willing to subject themselves to the process and more work to keep the candidates from bolting once the process begins." [24]

Third, the Senate's confirmation process can be mean and nasty, especially in this period of polarized politics. "With law so hard to make and so hard to change, influencing the choice of the implementers and adjudicators of the law becomes an essential strategic option." [25] Many nominees are subject to rough treatment. Ideological groups, for instance, may organize attack campaigns to defeat nominees who appear unsupportive of their agenda. Sometimes the purpose of Senate confirmation hearings "seems less to ensure that nominees are fit than to cripple the chief executive's political leadership. A defeated nomination can embarrass a president, demoralize his supporters, and reduce public confidence in his judgment." [26] Others argue that the confirmation process may be tough, but so are the positions for which nominees seek assignment. "If you can't fight your way through the process," stated former

Senate Holds on Presidential Nominees

Sen. Jeff Bingaman, D-N.M., frustrated by a Bush administration about-face, put a hold October 10, 2002, on the White House nominee to run the Food and Drug Administration (FDA).

Bingaman was seeking to gain leverage to pass a bill (S 724) that would expand the State Children's Health Insurance Program (S-CHIP) to cover pregnant women. The administration had backed off its previous support for the measure.

"Sen. Bingaman is as eager as anyone to fill the FDA position, but sometimes you have to do things to capture people's attention," a spokeswoman said.

The FDA nominee, White House health care policy adviser Mark B. Mc-Clellan, staked out the Senate chamber for hours to lobby Bingaman to allow a vote before lawmakers were scheduled to leave town the next week. But the standoff continued as the day neared an end.

At issue was a bill that would allow states to use S-CHIP to cover pre- and post-natal care for low-income women not eligible for Medicaid and a Bush administration regulation issued September 27, 2002, that would allow states to extend S-CHIP coverage to "unborn children" but would not fully cover pregnant women before, during, or after delivery.

Anti-abortion groups hailed the regulation, but women's rights groups said it denied needed care to pregnant women for conditions that might not affect their fetuses directly.

Source: Adapted from "Democrats Block FDA Nominee to Seek Action on Health Bill," *CQ Daily Monitor,* October 11, 2002.

Central Intelligence Agency (CIA) director Robert Gates, "you might not just do a hot job as director." [27]

Individual senators, too, are not reluctant to threaten filibusters or to place holds on nominations. For example, several Republican senators placed holds on two Defense Department nominees "to protest what the senators consider Secretary of Defense Donald H. Rumsfeld's lack of communication with Congressional leaders." [28] (See box on holds placed on nominations.) The Senate may also refuse to consider a nominee if members invoke senatorial courtesy. This tradition, dating from President Washington's administration, generally means that the Senate will delay or not act upon nominations for offices in a state if a senator of the president's party from that state opposes them.

The Personnel System

Congress wields wide authority—constitutionally, legally, informally—over the federal personnel system. The assassination of President James A. Garfield in 1881 by a disgruntled job seeker prompted Congress to curb the abuses of the spoils system, the practice of handing out federal jobs to

Table 11-2 Political Appointee Positions in the Executive Branch

Type of appointee	Full time	Part time	Total
Presidential appointee requiring			
Senate confirmation	966[a]	395	1,361
Presidential appointee not requiring			
Senate confirmation	123	139	262
Non-career Senior Executive Service	639	0	639
Schedule C[b]	1,421	3	1,424
Total	3,149	537	3,686

Source: Figures provided by Henry Hogue, Congressional Research Service, Library of Congress, who is an expert on the presidential appointee process. See also *fedscope.opm.gov.*

[a] Does not include Foreign Service and diplomatic positions in the Department of State; officer corps positions in the civilian uniformed services of the National Oceanic and Atmospheric Administration in the Department of Commerce; posts in the Public Health Service of the Department of Health and Human Services; the officer corps in the military services; and five positions in the legislative branch (architect of the Capitol, comptroller general, deputy comptroller general, librarian of Congress, and the public printer).
[b] Employees in policy-determining positions or those who are required to have a close, confidential working relationship with the head of an agency or other key appointed officials.

supporters of the party that had won the presidency. In 1883 Congress passed the first civil service law that substituted merit for patronage. But the early patronage practices have a modern equivalent: the political-appointee system. Currently, there are more than three thousand political appointments (see Table 11-2).

Political Appointees. In the 1970s, writes Paul C. Light, "Congress discovered executive structure . . . and began to mine it." [29] Since then Congress and the president have made numerous changes in the top four layers of officials in cabinet departments (secretary, deputy secretary, undersecretary, and assistant secretary). More new job titles in the top echelons of government have been created than ever before. Additional bureaucratic layers result—in some federal agencies there are as many as fifty layers between the president and front-line executive employees—which produce "a bureaucratic fog in which Congress and the president are hopelessly isolated from the people they most need to guide." [30] Among the numerous new titles are deputy to the deputy secretary, principal assistant deputy undersecretary, principal senior deputy assistant secretary, and associate principal deputy assistant secretary.[31] As a result of "title creep," it is becoming "impossible for the bottom to hear the top when messages go through dozens of interpretations on their journey down." [32]

The number of political appointees is small compared with the total number of federal employees (about 2.7 million civilian employees and 1.4 million uniformed personnel).[33] Yet concern has arisen about the politicization of high-level jobs in the civil service. "We entrust the administration of the largest 'company' in the country . . . to a cast of well-meaning political loyalists with little or no management experience," wrote a career civil servant with thirty-four years of federal service. "We accept the rather mindless notion that any bright and public-spirited dilettante can run a government agency, bureau, or office." [34]

Sens. Russell D. Feingold, D-Wis., and John McCain, R-Ariz., proposed that the number of political appointees be capped at two thousand.[35] In their judgment there are too many for the president to manage effectively. Far from enhancing responsiveness, said GOP senator Trent Lott of Mississippi, the large number of political appointees undermines "presidential control of the executive branch." [36] Not everyone agrees. Some contend that more political appointees are needed "to monitor the permanent government" and "to develop aggressively new policies." [37] Still others argue that the elimination of managerial layers would force many talented civil servants to leave the government. New layers "have been created for civil service workers so their agencies can offer them more competitive salaries and keep them from going into often better-paying private sector jobs." [38]

Pay and Other Legal Standards. By law, Congress has wide control over federal employees. It can establish special requirements for holding office; employee performance standards; wages, benefits, and cost-of-living adjustments (COLAs); personnel ceilings; and protections from reprisals for whistleblowers (employees who expose waste and corruption). The 1939 Hatch Act, named for Sen. Carl Hatch, D-N.M., restricts federal employees' partisan activity. The act was passed during the New Deal after reports that civil servants were being coerced to back President Franklin D. Roosevelt in his reelection efforts. Congress tried unsuccessfully several times to revamp the law and give federal employees wider opportunities to participate in the political process. Finally, in 1993, President Clinton signed into law the Hatch Act reform amendments. They encourage civil servants to participate in political activity in accordance with regulations prescribed by the Office of Personnel Management.

Under the Constitution, Congress determines its own pay. It legislates pay raises or accepts pay hikes recommended by the statutorily created Citizens' Commission on Public Service and Compensation. Members of Congress may also receive automatic cost-of-living adjustments by statute. These were intended to remove politics from the pay hike issue. However, periodic battles are still waged in Congress—often in election years—over the COLAs, and lawmakers have several times been successful in passing legislation to deny the increase. Public criticism of pay hikes is a real concern, as is the threat that potential opponents will seize upon the issue in the next election.[39] (Lawmakers are prohibited from accepting speaking fees, or honorariums, from special interests and other groups.)

In 1992 the Twenty-seventh Amendment to the Constitution (first proposed by James Madison in 1789) was finally ratified: "No law varying the compensation for the services of the Senators and Representatives shall take effect, until an election of Representatives shall have intervened." This amendment permits voters an opportunity to render their verdict on the pay hike before lawmakers receive it.[40]

After leaving public office, members, legislative staffers, and executive officers often pass through the revolving door to jobs with private firms that deal with the government. Responding to procurement abuses at the Pentagon, Congress restricted federal officials who leave public service from immediately joining a private company to work on projects or contracts they managed while in government service. Former federal employees who were "personally and substantially" involved in trade or treaty negotiations with a foreign government cannot lobby on behalf of foreign governments for a year after they leave office. When Congress passed the Lobby Disclosure Act of 1995, it prohibited the U.S. trade representative and his or her deputies from ever lobbying on behalf of foreign interests. The 1995 act also repealed the Ramspeck Act (named after Rep. Robert C. Ramspeck, D-Ga., 1929–1945), which allowed congressional employees who lost their jobs on Capitol Hill to enter the civil service without meeting the competitive requirements for government positions.

Size of Government. Americans have debated the size and scope of the federal government since the nation's founding. At issue is what functions (law enforcement, welfare, education, and so on) each level of government (local, state, or national) should be responsible for. In addition, people disagree about whether the federal government is bigger or smaller today than it was a few decades ago. Much of the disagreement centers on how governmental size is measured, such as federal expenditures as a share of the gross domestic product, the magnitude of the federal budget, or the number of federal employees. As to the first standard, "federal spending has shrunk relative to the size of the American economy," from 21.8 percent of gross domestic product in 1990 to 18.4 percent in 2000 but with a projected hike of 19.7 percent in 2004.[41] The federal budget keeps growing ($2.2 trillion in 2004), but so, too, have the nation's population and its economy.

Contrary to what many people believe, the federal workforce has remained relatively constant in size. How can the government continue to perform services while keeping its size down? One answer is that much of what the federal government does is to transfer money to eligible recipients, such as the elderly who receive Social Security. This function does not require large numbers of federal workers. Another answer is that federal work is being outsourced, or privatized, to contract employees. The Pentagon, for instance, reached a milestone of sorts at the start of the twenty-first century when the number of its private sector employees (734,000) exceeded its civilian workforce of 700,000. These contract employees "perform service jobs from mowing lawns to testing weapons systems." [42] Or consider the Department of Energy, which relies on contractors for "almost everything it does. More than 90 percent of its budget is paid to 100,000 outside workers." [43] A goal of President Bush is to make as many as 850,000 federal jobs subject to private competition.[44] As one analyst explained: "Everybody wants the federal government to look smaller than it really is. By contracting out jobs rather than having civilian workers in those jobs, you can say, 'Look, the government's smaller.' " [45]

When everyone who works directly or indirectly for the federal government is counted, it is much bigger than twenty years or thirty years ago. A scholar puts its "true size" at about 17 million employees: the 4.1 million civilian, military, and postal workers plus the 12.7 million "shadow" workers who are "off the books" because they "work under federal contracts and grants or mandates imposed on state and local governments." [46] An academic dean at Harvard University, however, disagrees. He argues that whom and how many people the federal government employs are "poor surrogates" for the size and scope of government. The conclusion he reaches is that the "federal government—measured by direct and indirect employment, by the dollars it spends and how it spends them—is doing less today than a generation ago." [47]

However this debate about governmental size is reconciled, privatizing the work of the federal government has advantages and disadvantages. Because companies under contract to the government are not directly responsible to Congress, the so-called third-party or shadow government presents serious problems of accountability.[48] Some believe certain functions are inherently governmental and ought not to be turned over to outside organizations. Yet third parties are sometimes faster, more flexible, and cheaper than the governmental machine.

Under an e-government initiative, the national government is working to deliver more of its services online. President Bush signed the E-Government Act into law on December 17, 2002. The law establishes an Office of Electronic Government within the Office of Management and Budget to be responsible for promoting easier online access to the public by, for instance, improving the federal government's Internet site (Firstgov.gov). E-government has implications for the size and work of government because federal employees "are accustomed to working regular business hours, [but] e-government services would operate around the clock." [49]

The Rulemaking Process

Although Congress creates executive agencies and lays down their mandates by law, it rarely can specify the details needed to implement policies. The landmark Telecommunications Act of 1996, for example, made it illegal to make "indecent" material available to minors. What material is indecent? That question rests with government regulators (the Federal Communications

Commission already bars "seven dirty words" from broadcasts) and ultimately the federal courts. In such cases, specifications must be written, details filled in, and procedures set forth. Thus agencies are empowered to make rules for carrying out the mandates contained in laws.[50]

In the Administrative Procedures Act of 1946 and later changes to it, Congress established standards for rulemaking by government agencies. Interested parties can take part in the process by testifying in public about the merits or demerits of proposed regulations. Regulations have all the force and effect of law. All regulations, explained Sen. Charles E. Grassley, R-Iowa,

> are based ultimately on authority granted by this Congress. When an agency promulgates a rule, it is engaging in a legislative task—in effect, filling in the gaps on the implementation of policies that we in Congress have established through statute. Accordingly, all regulations must be accountable to this Congress.[51]

In other words, rulemaking is a legislative process authorized by Congress but located in the executive branch or in independent regulatory bodies. Federal regulations may be overturned or even declared unconstitutional, as occurred with air quality standards promulgated by the Environmental Protection Agency (EPA). A federal appeals court in May 1999 ruled that Congress had delegated "too much legislative-like authority" to the EPA.[52] However, on February 27, 2001, the U.S. Supreme Court unanimously rejected that claim and upheld EPA's clean air rules as an appropriate exercise of the regulatory authority delegated to it by Congress.[53]

Congress and the White House frequently skirmish over rulemaking. During the Clinton administration, Republicans put the rollback of federal regulations high on their agenda. "Regulatory agencies have run amok and need to be reformed," House GOP leader Tom DeLay, R-Texas, declared.[54] This sentiment was triggered in large measure by business's animus toward regulatory growth (see Table 11-3). In general, about six hundred major rules and regulations are issued each year by executive agencies that require review by the White House regulatory czar, currently former Harvard professor John Graham. The regulatory czar heads the Office of Information and Regulatory Affairs within OMB, which analyzes the costs and benefits of significant regulations (those that "would cost industry more than $100 million to implement") and either rejects, requires their revision, or approves them as comporting with the president's priorities.[55]

Republican ire against Clinton's regulatory actions heightened when his administration "produced more than 26,000 pages of new regulations between November 2000 and January 2001"—dubbed "midnight regulations" by detractors or Clinton's "night deposit" by Bush officials.[56] Upon taking office, George W. Bush found himself in the position of other newly elected presidents. He had to review the many executive and regulatory actions of his pre-

Table 11-3 *Code of Federal Regulations* Page Count by Selected Presidencies

President	Average annual number of pages in the *Code of Federal Regulations*
Gerald R. Ford	71,982
Jimmy Carter	94,777
Ronald Reagan	109,599
George Bush	125,664
Bill Clinton	134,173

Source: Cornelius M. Kerwin, *Rulemaking: How Government Agencies Write Law and Make Policy,* 2d ed. (Washington, D.C.: CQ Press, 1999), 21.

decessor. On the day Bush was inaugurated, his chief of staff, Andrew Card, issued the "Card memo," which imposed a sixty-day moratorium for all new rules that had not officially taken effect. While Bush can overturn Clinton's executive orders with the stroke of his pen, that is not the case with regulations. "It is not easy for a President to stop a final rule that has been published in the *Federal Register* short of putting the whole process [as prescribed in the Administrative Procedures Act of 1946] in reverse and beginning a process of rule-making anew—with public notices, comment periods and agency reviews that could take years." [57]

Still, the Bush administration made it clear that proposed rules and regulations would be subject to stricter cost-benefit review. Critics of this approach note that it is often easier to quantify costs than benefits because the latter are often intangible and long term, such as future improvements in public health. In an unusual use of cost-benefit analysis triggered by the September 11 terrorist attacks, Graham wants this analytical tool employed to calculate the trade-offs between the benefits of greater security versus the costs of losing privacy or civil liberties. He requested that experts around the country come up with ways to assess the indirect costs of tighter security regulations, such as lost customers for airlines or fewer foreign students enrolled in American universities. Graham's initiative is backed, on the one hand, by an array of libertarians who worry that the government, in combating terrorism, is gaining too much power to spy on or arrest individuals and, on the other hand, by liberals who have long championed the rights of privacy and civil liberty. As one account noted:

> The domestic security push has in many ways turned the battles of cost-benefit analysis on their head. In the 1980s, consumer advocates like [Ralph] Nader often denounced cost-benefit analysis as a tool conservatives used to

swat down environmental and safety regulations. But just as business groups once viewed cost-benefit analysis as a way to curb restrictions on their activity, Mr. Nader and civil rights groups see it as a way to curb restrictions on government authorities.[58]

President Bush has another way to undo regulations he opposes: encourage Congress to use laws on the books to overturn unwanted regulations. For example, the Congressional Review Act of 1996 requires regulators to submit all proposed major rules and regulations to the House and Senate. Lawmakers then have sixty legislative days from the time a regulation is published to reject it under expedited procedures by enacting a joint resolution of disapproval. The law was never employed during the Clinton administration. Congress recognized that any disapproval measure would be vetoed by the president, and neither chamber had the two-thirds vote to override. The GOP-controlled House and Senate used the review act shortly after the 107th Congress (2001–2003) convened to repeal a controversial workplace safety rule designed to reduce repetitive stress injuries.[59] Bush signed the repeal measure into law (see box on overturning federal rules).

How valuable are regulations? Lawmakers, like their constituents, are of two minds. Some, such as Sen. Barbara Boxer, D-Calif., emphasize their positive achievements.

> The purpose of the Federal regulatory process is to improve and protect the high quality of life that we enjoy in our country. Every day, the people of our Nation enjoy the benefits of almost a century of progress in Federal laws and regulations that reduce the threat of illness, injury, and death from consumer products, workplace hazards, and environmental toxins.[60]

Others call for "more rational regulations," with "better analysis of costs, benefits, and risks, so that regulators will issue smarter, more cost-effective regulations." [61] A difficult challenge is to distinguish between inflexible, pointless, or overly burdensome and costly regulations and beneficial regulations that are necessary to promote and protect the public's health and safety. Events, too, shape public attitudes toward regulation. Businesses, for example, often complain about excessive government regulation hampering their initiative and creativity. In the wake of corporate scandals, such as Enron, many individuals and entities recognize the need for federal rules and regulations to protect investors and employee pensions and promote corporate responsibility.

The Electoral Connection

Some observers suggest that Congress enlarged the executive establishment by passing vague laws that bureaucrats had to embellish with rules and regulations. Many regulatory laws, for example, call for a "reasonable rate," without defining "reasonable." Frustrated by government rules, people turn to their senators and representatives for help. Lawmakers thus "take credit com-

Overturning Federal Rules

At the urging of business lobbyists, Republican leaders in 2001 dusted off an untested five-year-old statute to use to strike down some of the new regulations issued in the waning days of the Clinton administration.

Lobbyists saw the 1996 Congressional Review Act (P.L. 104-121) as a tool to nullify some of the new rules hustled into the *Federal Register* in President Bill Clinton's final months in office. The law allows Congress to erase regulations by passing a resolution of disapproval by a simple majority vote of both houses. The law was never used during the Clinton presidency because Clinton would have vetoed any disapproval resolution.

Topping the business community's hit list was the hotly debated set of ergonomics rules issued in December 2002 by the Occupational Safety and Health Administration. The rule, many years in the making, was designed to reduce repetitive-motion injuries on the job. The National Association of Manufacturers (NAM) and other trade group argued that it was too costly and unnecessary.

The review act offers a unique advantage: A resolution of disapproval is not subject to filibuster in the Senate, so its sponsors need only fifty-one votes there.

If Congress wants to disapprove a major regulation—one that costs the economy $100 million or more per year—it has to do so within sixty House "legislative days" after it is entered in the *Federal Register.* In the Senate, the time limit is sixty "session days."

According to GOP aides, the House parliamentarian concluded that that means Congress could review any regulation published on or after July 13, 2000. Because the sixty-day clock starts with the beginning of a new Congress, aides said, all those rules would be fair game until sometime around mid-spring 2001.

Source: Adapted from Peter Kaplan, *CQ Daily Monitor,* January 26, 2001, 7.

---

ing and going"—they claim credit for getting programs enacted and then for untangling the bureaucratic snarls they create.[62]

This electoral explanation of overall bureaucratic growth is unproved. There is little support for the argument that "congressmen's incessant quest for local benefits has somehow contributed to growth in government spending." In fact, the most costly federal programs, such as Medicare and Social Security, "deliver benefits as a matter of right, not privilege, and congressmen have fewer opportunities to claim responsibility for them." [63]

Many considerations affect how federal benefits are distributed. An agency may process the requests of the president's congressional backers quickly, while other members' proposals are encased in red tape. Or influential members of the committees with jurisdiction over certain agencies may receive the lion's share of federal benefits. Lawmakers eagerly earmark money in appropriations bills for projects in their states or districts. Presidential pork is also commonplace as chief executives promise jobs and projects in states crucial to their reelection.

Not all federal projects are worth attracting. Members compute the political risks of backing a missile base, hazardous waste dump, nuclear power plant, or other controversial project strongly resisted by their constituents. Some lawmakers oppose spending for projects even if they are in their own district. They have formed the Porkbusters Coalition to oppose what they view as wasteful federal expenditures on unjustified constituency projects. Senator McCain is especially vigilant in targeting what he considers to be wasteful spending. McCain's Internet Web site contains his floor statements against legislation containing what he considers pork. Still other members want to challenge unnecessary tax and spending subsidies for businesses and industries (corporate welfare).[64]

Whatever their view of federal projects, legislators must act as intermediaries between constituents and federal agencies. Constituents' problems are handled by personal staff aides called caseworkers. In addition to courting the electoral payoff of effective casework—evidence of the two Congresses once again—some members appreciate its value in oversight. "The very knowledge by executive officials that some Congressman is sure to look into a matter affecting his constituents acts as a healthy check against bureaucratic indifference or arrogance," wrote a former senator.[65]

Congressional Control of the Bureaucracy

"Congressional power, like chastity," explained a scholar, "is never lost, rarely taken by force, and almost always given away."[66] Congress allows executive officials considerable discretion in interpreting and implementing the laws it passes. This delegation of authority occurs because legislators lack the knowledge and expertise to address the complexities of contemporary society (licensing interstate communications, for example), and no law can be sufficiently detailed to cover every conceivable circumstance.

Congress is often criticized for drafting vague or sloppy legislation that gives executive officials and judges too much leeway in interpretation and administration. "Administration of a statute is, properly speaking, an extension of the legislative process," and therefore Congress must watch over its programs lest they undergo unintended change.[67] Given the size and reach of the executive establishment, Congress's oversight role is more important today than when Woodrow Wilson wrote that "[q]uite as important as lawmaking is vigilant oversight of administration."[68]

The Constitution does not refer explicitly to the oversight role; it is implicit in Congress's right to, among other things, make laws, raise and appropriate money, give advice and consent to executive nominations, and impeach federal officials. Congress, however, has formalized its oversight duties. The Legislative Reorganization Act of 1946 directed all House and Senate committees to exercise "continuous watchfulness" over the programs and agencies under their jurisdiction. Subsequent statutes and House and Senate rules extended Congress's authority and resources for oversight.

Members understand their review responsibilities. "Congress's duty didn't end in passing this law," remarked a senator. "We have to make sure the law works." Or as Senator Lott said: "I have always felt that one-third of the role of Congress should be in oversight." [69] House Speaker J. Dennis Hastert, R-Ill., has made it clear that he wants committees to focus more of their attention on oversight. The Speaker's "not so much interested in scandal as he is in how departments are being run, what programs work and which don't," said the Speaker's spokesperson.[70]

To ensure that laws are working, Congress utilizes an impressive array of formal and informal processes and techniques. Many of its oversight activities are indirect, ad hoc, and not subject to easy measurement or even recognition. "Oversight isn't necessarily a hearing," said John D. Dingell, D-Mich., a noted House overseer. "Sometimes it's a letter. We find our letters have a special effect on a lot of people." [71]

Hearings and Investigations

Many of Congress's most dramatic moments have occurred in legislative probes into administrative or business misconduct or man-made or natural disasters. Examples include the Teapot Dome inquiry (1923), the Senate Watergate hearings (1973–1974), the Iran-contra investigation (1987), the investigations undertaken in 1997–1998 into alleged illegal and improper campaign fund-raising practices during the 1996 election cycle, the 2000 Firestone and Ford hearings into whether vehicle crashes were caused by defective tires, and the 2003 joint hearings into the disintegration of the space shuttle *Columbia* as it was returning to Earth. But Congress's investigative authority is not without limits. Earl Warren, when he was chief justice, wrote in *Watkins v. United States* (1957):

> There is no general authority to expose private affairs of individuals without justification in terms of the functions of Congress. . . . Nor is the Congress a law enforcement or trial agency. These are functions of the executive and judicial departments of government. No inquiry is an end in itself; it must be related to, and in furtherance of, a legitimate task of the Congress.[72]

By collecting and analyzing information, House and Senate inquiries can clarify whether specific legislation is needed to address public problems. They also sharpen Congress's ability to scrutinize executive branch activities, such as the expenditure of funds, the implementation of laws, and the discharge of duties by administrative officials. (The executive branch has a number of ways of not cooperating with congressional investigations, such as inundating Capitol Hill with irrelevant materials or stalling in providing needed information.) And they inform the public by disseminating and revealing information.

"Congress provides a forum for disclosing the hidden aspects of governmental conduct," wrote two Senate members of the Iran-contra investigating committee. It allows a "free people to drag realities out into the sunlight and demand a full accounting from those who are permitted to hold and exercise power." [73] Hearings and investigations, in short, are valuable devices for making government accountable to the people. They can spawn new laws or their functional equivalent: unwritten laws that change bureaucratic operations.

Congressional Vetoes

With unelected executive officials necessarily involved in the complexities of modern decision making, Congress has little choice but to delegate sweeping authority to administrative agencies. There are strings attached, however. One of the most popular strings is the legislative veto (or congressional veto), a statutory enactment that permits presidents or agencies to take certain actions subject to later approval or disapproval by one or both houses of Congress (or in some cases by committees of one or both houses). Legislative vetoes are arrangements of convenience for both branches. Executives gain decision-making authority they might not have otherwise, and Congress retains a second chance to examine the decisions.

In 1983, in *Immigration and Naturalization Service v. Chadha,* the Supreme Court declared many forms of the legislative veto unconstitutional. The Court majority held that the device violated the separation of powers, the principle of bicameralism, and the presentation clause of the Constitution (legislation passed by both chambers must be presented to the president for his signature or veto). The decision, wrote Justice Byron R. White in a vigorous dissent, "strikes down in one fell swoop provisions in more laws enacted by Congress than the court has cumulatively invalidated in its entire history." [74]

Congress repealed some legislative vetoes, amended others, and employed its wide range of oversight techniques to monitor executive actions. Yet, despite the *Chadha* decision, legislative vetoes continue to be enacted into law. Public law scholar Louis Fisher sums up the status of legislative vetoes:

> Are they constitutional? Not by the Court's definition. Will that fact change the behavior between committees and agencies? Probably not. An agency might advise the committee: "As you know, the requirement in this statute for committee prior-approval is unconstitutional under the Court's test." Perhaps agency and committee staff will nod their heads in agreement. After which the agency will seek prior approval of the committee. [75]

Self-interest requires that agencies pay close attention to the wishes of members of Congress, especially those who sit on their authorizing or appropriating panels.

Mandatory Reports

Congress requires the president, federal agencies, and departments to assess programs and report their findings.[76] Reports can act "as a mechanism to check that laws are having the intended effect." They can "drive a reluctant bureaucracy to comply with laws it would otherwise ignore." [77] The House Permanent Select Intelligence Committee, for instance, threatened to reduce the funds to run the Central Intelligence Agency director's office if the intelligence agency did not "file dozens of overdue reports required by law" within a reasonable period of time.[78] Periodically, Congress passes legislation to eliminate obsolete or unnecessary reports. But, as Senator McCain noted, "Congress assigns about 300 new reports to the agencies each year." [79] By one estimate, executive agencies prepare more than five thousand reports for submission to Congress annually. Occasions also do arise, though, when lawmakers object to the discontinuation of reports that they believe provide useful information to policy makers and the public.

Nonstatutory Controls

Congressional committees also use informal means to review and influence administrative decisions. These range from telephone calls, letters, personal contacts, and informal understandings to statements in committee and conference reports, hearings, and floor debates.[80] Committee reports frequently contain phrases such as "the committee clearly intends that the matter be reconsidered" or "the committee clearly intends for the Secretary to promote" or "the committee clearly expects."

On occasion, OMB directors tell federal agencies to ignore appropriations report language because it is not legally binding. Lawmakers of both parties and chambers (and even executive officials) mobilize to thwart such directives, however. Sometimes they threaten to make all report language legally binding on agencies, thus limiting the agencies' flexibility and discretion in resolving issues.[81] Although there is no measure of their usage, nonstatutory controls may be the most common form of congressional oversight.

Inspectors General

In 1978 Congress created a dozen independent offices for inspectors general (IGs). Since then Congress has established inspector general offices in nearly every federal department and agency. Inspectors general submit directly to Congress reports on their efforts to root out waste, fraud, and abuse. For instance, the IG at the Education Department informed both Secretary Rod Paige and Congress that she had uncovered at least $100 million of recent fraud in the department's grant and loan programs.[82] "It is the IG's job," said a high executive official, "to offer independent analysis to Congress and the public on how the agency and the agency head are doing." Some IGs meet regularly with legislative officials. The State Department's IG, for instance, "meets with congressional staffers at least every other week to discuss his work and, as a result, is often asked by congressional committees to conduct specific audits and investigations." [83]

The Appropriations Process

Congress probably exercises its most effective oversight of agencies and programs through the appropriations process. By cutting off or reducing funds (or threatening to do so), Congress can abolish agencies, curtail programs, or obtain requested information. In 2000, for example, an agricultural appropriations bill stripped an undersecretary of the Agriculture Department of his supervisory authority over the U.S. Forest Service and the Natural Resources Conservation Service because of sharp and continuing clashes between GOP appropriators and the Clinton appointee.[84] By the same token, Congress can build up program areas by increasing their appropriations—sometimes beyond what the administration has requested.

The appropriations power is exercised mainly through the Appropriations Committees in the House and Senate (and especially through each panel's thirteen standing subcommittees). These panels annually recommend funding levels for federal agencies and departments, so they have the money to carry out their program responsibilities. The budgetary recommendations of the Appropriations subcommittees are generally accepted by their parent committee and by the House or Senate.

The Appropriations Committees and their subcommittees, or members from the House or Senate floor, may offer amendments that limit the purposes for which money may be spent or that impose other expenditure restrictions on federal agencies. The spending bills also may contain various policy directives to federal agencies—for example, imposing airline smoking bans or prohibiting agencies from using funds to promulgate or issue certain regulations. Such policy directives are often in the form of floor amendments called riders. "These amendments," wrote two GOP senators, "are an important way for Congress to save taxpayers from wasteful agency spending, and they enjoy a long-standing precedent because of their use by Republican and Democratic Congresses alike to rein in the excesses of Republican and Democratic administrations." [85]

Impeachment

Article II, Section 4, of the Constitution states:

> The President, Vice President, and all Civil Officers of the United States, shall be removed from office on Impeachment for, and Conviction of, Treason, Bribery, or other high Crimes and misdemeanors.

The ultimate governmental check is this removal power, and it is vested exclusively in Congress.[86] The House has the authority to impeach an official by majority vote. It then tries the case before the Senate, where a two-thirds vote is required for conviction.

Only in seventeen cases has the House voted to impeach; the Senate convicted seven persons, all of them federal judges.[87] The House impeached President Andrew Johnson in 1868, after Radical Republicans in the House charged that he had violated the Tenure of Office Act by dismissing the secretary of war. The Senate acquitted Johnson by a single vote. President Richard M. Nixon resigned in 1974, after the House Judiciary Committee voted articles of impeachment; he faced probable impeachment and conviction. In December 1998 President Clinton became the first elected president to be impeached by the House. (Johnson was not elected; he became president when Abraham Lincoln was assassinated.) The charges against Clinton were perjury and obstruction of justice. Two months later the Senate voted acquittal on both these articles of impeachment.[88]

Oversight: An Evaluation

Congress's greater willingness in recent years to conduct oversight stems from several factors: the public's dissatisfaction with government, revelations of executive agency abuses, the influx of new legislators skeptical of government's ability to perform effectively, the availability of congressional staff, and recognition by Congress that it must make every dollar count.[89]

Electoral and political incentives also encourage members to oversee the bureaucracy. One of these is the opportunity to receive favorable publicity back home (the two Congresses connection). Another is prodding by interest groups and the media. Committee and subcommittee chairmen "seek a high pay off—in attention from both the press and other agencies—when selecting federal programs to be their oversight targets." [90]

Divided government—the president of one party, the Congress of another—fosters vigorous congressional oversight. Opposition lawmakers, for example, may monitor and supervise agency activities and at the same time be on the lookout for ways to bash the administration's politics. President Clinton's press secretary complained that House Republicans requested information "not so they can evaluate the effectiveness of the government's performance but so that they can . . . [gum] up the works in order to intimidate and thwart those who might be carrying out the laws as they've been properly passed by Congress." In response, the press secretary to the House majority leader said, "They've gotten nothing from Democratic oversight chairmen [when that party was in charge] but postcards from Hawaii saying, 'Wish you were here.' Now they have to deal with the same type of oversight the Democrats had during the Reagan-Bush years." [91] When Dan Burton, R-Ind., chaired the House Government Reform Committee (1995–2003), he issued nearly one thousand subpoenas investigating the Clinton administration.[92] With George W. Bush in the White House, the GOP-controlled Congress is less likely to conduct oversight as a way to embarrass the administration. Nonetheless, House Judiciary chairman F. James Sensenbrenner Jr., R-Wis., informed Attorney General John Ashcroft and the FBI director that "just because I'm the chairman and the administration is of my party, they don't get a free pass on oversight." [93]

Congressional Republicans highlighted the oversight potential inherent in a little-known law passed by the Democratic-controlled 103d Congress: the Government Performance and Results Act (GPRA) of 1993. Under the law, federal agencies are required to submit strategic plans to Congress specifying how they intend to measure the achievement of their goals. (The administration also bases funding decisions on how well agencies perform in accomplishing program goals.) Republicans recognize that GPRA gives them "a powerful framework for establishing agency priorities and analyzing how [the agencies] perform." [94] They have urged their committee chairmen to eliminate wasteful and duplicative programs. To make this point a House GOP leader held up a pizza box: "If this were a cheese pizza, it would be inspected by the [Food and Drug Administration]. If it were a pepperoni pizza, it would be inspected by the [U.S. Department of Agriculture]. . . . . We definitely have a great deal of duplication here." [95]

On occasion, congressional oversight may not be as tough as some members would wish. Sweetheart alliances can develop among the committees that authorize programs, the agencies that administer them, and the interest groups that benefit from the services. Many committees are biased toward the programs or agencies they oversee. They want to protect and nurture their progeny and make program administration look good. Without concrete allegations of fraud or mismanagement, committees may lack the incentive to scrutinize and reevaluate their programs. This kind of cooperative oversight can dissuade committees from conducting hard-hitting inquiries.

A standard rationale for oversight is that it ensures that laws are carried out according to congressional intent. Because many laws are vague and imprecise, however, they are difficult to assess. Moreover, evidence that programs are working as intended can take years to emerge. Congressional patience may wane as critics conclude that there are no demonstrable payoffs for the taxpayer. Alternatively, oversight may identify program flaws but may not reveal what will work or even whether there is any ready solution.

Each oversight technique has limitations. Hearings, for example, tend to be episodic with minimal follow-up. The appropriations process is usually hemmed in by programmatic needs for financial stability. And statutes are often blunt instruments of control. Other obstacles to effective oversight include inadequate coordination among committees that share jurisdiction over a program; unsystematic review by committees of departmental activities; and frequent turnover among committee staff aides, a situation that limits their understanding of programs passed by Congress.

Critics who fault Congress's oversight may be erecting unattainable standards. Many analysts are looking for what scholars have come to call "police patrol" oversight—active, direct, systematic, regular, and planned surveillance of executive activities. Instead, Congress often waits until "fire alarms" go off from interest groups, the press, staff aides, and others about administrative violations before it begins to review in detail agencies' activities.[96]

Micromanagement

Because oversight tends to be specific instead of general, committees are open to complaints about micromanagement—legislative intrusion into administrative details. Perhaps to the chagrin of executive officials, Congress's focus on administrative details is as old as the institution itself. The structural fragmentation of the House and Senate encourages examination of manageable chunks of executive actions. Members understand that power inheres in details, such as prescribing personnel ceilings for agencies. Presidents who oppose certain programs can starve them to death by shifting employees to favored activities. Thus Congress may specify personnel ceilings for some agencies. "It is one of the anomalies of constitutional law and separated powers," writes Louis Fisher, "that executive involvement in legislative affairs is considered acceptable (indeed highly desirable) while legislative involvement in executive affairs screams of encroachment and usurpation."[97]

Conclusion

Because of continual shifts in the balance of legislative and executive prerogatives, the age-old issue of executive independence versus congressional scrutiny cannot be settled conclusively. Yet the recent interest in oversight has had little discernible effect on the size and scale of the executive branch or on the main roles and responsibilities of the legislative branch. After all, committees are not disinterested overseers but guardians of the agencies and programs under their jurisdictions. Together with their satellite interest groups, committees and agencies form subgovernments or issue networks that dominate many policy-making areas.

The Senate addresses issues concerning the judiciary—what Alexander Hamilton called the federal government's "least dangerous branch." Above, Senate Judiciary Committee chair Orrin Hatch, R-Utah, and ranking Democrat Patrick Leahy, Vt., discuss the judicial confirmation process. Center, Chairman Hatch lends his strong support to controversial circuit court nominee Miguel A. Estrada. Below, Chief Justice William Rehnquist holds a report urging pay hikes for federal judges at a news conference in Washington, D.C.

12

Congress and the Courts

[S] carcely any political question arises in the United States that is not re-solved, sooner or later, into a judicial one," wrote the famous French chronicler Alexis de Tocqueville in *Democracy in America,* his classic 1835 study of early American life.[1] From the beginnings of the republic, when federal courts handed down decisions that strengthened the national government, to many of today's most hotly debated issues—affirmative action, the war powers, racial redistricting, and abortion—federal judges have been at the storm center of numerous controversies. Bolstered by its prerogative of judicial review that the U.S. Supreme Court asserted in the landmark case of *Marbury v. Madison* (1803)—and the public's perception that the highest court is the primary, but not exclusive, interpreter of the Constitution—federal jurists regularly pass judgment on the compelling issues that confront the nation.[2] Meanwhile, Congress and the White House also interpret the Constitution. As the Supreme Court stated in *United States v. Nixon* (1974): "In the performance of assigned constitutional duties each branch of the Government must initially interpret the Constitution, and the interpretation of its powers by any branch is due great respect from the others."

The American constitutional system of separate institutions sharing power inevitably produces tension between Congress and the courts. While the framers outlined the structure and authority of Congress in some detail in Article I, little by comparison is in Article III dealing with the courts. Thus, the beginnings of the court owe less to constitutional mandates and more to legislation establishing its structure and to the rulings of the early justices, such as Chief Justice John Marshall (1801–1835). As a noted legal scholar explained:

> Congress was created nearly full blown by the Constitution itself. The vast possibilities of the presidency were relatively easy to perceive and soon, inevitably materialized. But the institution of the judiciary needed to be summoned up out of the constitutional vapors, shaped and maintained. And the Great Chief Justice, John Marshall—not single-handed, but first and foremost—was there to do it and did.[3]

These early jurists rebuffed challenges to judicial power and conclusively established the court's right to determine the constitutionality of acts of Congress.

Conflicts between Congress and federal courts are common when the elective branches are called to account by decisions of the nonelective judicial branch, composed of judges with lifetime tenure. A famous instance occurred during the New Deal when the Supreme Court, acting as a super-legislature, invalidated thirteen acts of Congress in one term (1935–1936). So frustrated was President Franklin D. Roosevelt that he tried to have Congress pass legislation expanding the size of the Court so he could nominate judges more sympathetic to his program. Widespread legislative opposition to the court-packing plan led to a huge defeat for Roosevelt. Nonetheless, sensitive to the changes under way in the country, the Court soon began to shift its attitude in constitutional interpretation. For example, the Court handed down a decision in 1937 upholding a minimum wage law that only a few months earlier it had ruled unconstitutional.[4] This turnabout by the Court, ending its penchant for limiting congressional power, was, as a wit of the period put it, "the switch in time that saved nine."

Constitutional Review

Whether it is enacting minimum wage, health, or other laws, Congress derives its policymaking authority from two key parts of the Constitution: Article I and the Fourteenth Amendment. Article I, Section 8, grants Congress the right to legislate in a number of specific areas, such as laying and collecting taxes, coining money, and raising and supporting armies. In addition, an elastic clause gives Congress the authority to "make all laws which shall be necessary and proper" to carry out its enumerated powers.

Under the post–Civil War Fourteenth Amendment, no state shall deny any person of life, liberty, or property without due process of law or the equal protection of the laws. The amendment provides that Congress "shall have the power to enforce [these provisions], by appropriate legislation." Congress, as the courts have noted, also has "implied" or "inherent" powers not specifically mentioned in the Constitution, such as its right to conduct investigations as an adjunct to its lawmaking function. Federal courts, however, can impose constraints on the exercise of these constitutional pillars of legislative authority.

As for the courts, Article III of the Constitution states: "[T]he judicial power of the United States shall be vested in one Supreme Court, and in such inferior courts as the Congress may from time to time ordain and establish." Left to Congress was the establishment of the elaborate judicial structure of district and circuit courts of appeals that exist today, not to mention the legislature's authority to create a number of specialized courts, such as bankruptcy courts, where judges serve fixed terms. The Constitution also specifies the "cases and controversies" over which the court has original jurisdiction, such as issues involving the Constitution, federal law, and treaties. In addition, the Supreme Court has appellate jurisdiction (the authority to review cases on appeal) under the Constitution but with such exceptions as Congress may determine. The composition of federal courts is subject to the "advice and consent" of the Senate. Basically, these provisions constitute the core of the federal judiciary.

The judiciary's policymaking role is carried out in three main ways. First, its interpretive decisions can uphold or broaden the legislative powers of Congress. "Congress acted within its authority," said Supreme Court justice Ruth Bader Ginsburg, the Court upheld a 1998 law further extending copyright privileges for authors, artists, and inventors, such as commercial artist Walt Disney, who created the world-famous animated cartoon character Mickey Mouse.[5] Second, it can check overreaching by the Congress through its implied power of judicial review. Third, and equally significant, the Supreme Court can act as a policymaking catalyst, especially when the House or Senate is stymied in making decisions. The landmark civil rights case of *Brown v. Board of Education* (1954) is a classic example. The decision struck down the separate but equal doctrine upholding state laws that permitted racially segregated public schools. Until this decision, majorities in the Senate could not enact civil rights bills because of filibusters conducted by southern senators. The *Brown* case galvanized Congress to enact the Civil Rights Act of 1957, the first civil rights law since 1875. "The genius of a system of divided powers," wrote a law professor, "is that when one branch is closed to the desires of the populace or the demands of justice, another may open up." [6] The *Brown* decision had little impact until Congress began to pass landmark legislation, such as the Civil Rights Act of 1964 prohibiting racial discrimination in public accommodations.

Each national branch of government has the constitutional wherewithal to influence the others. The Supreme Court affects Congress "whenever justices interpret the meaning of the Constitution, treaties, federal statutes, administrative [rules and regulations], and the decisions of [lower] federal and state courts." [7] In turn, Congress has the authority to affect the size, funding, and decisions of federal courts with the Senate directed under the Constitution to approve or reject court nominees chosen by the chief executive. And enforcement of judicial decisions falls to the president. President Andrew Jackson reportedly responded to an 1832 case handed down by the Supreme Court by saying: "Well, John Marshall has made his decision, now let him enforce it." [8] Alexander Hamilton, in distinguishing judicial power from legislative or executive power, wrote in the *Federalist Papers* No. 78: The judiciary "has no influence over either the sword [the president] or the purse [Congress] . . . and can take no active resolution whatever. It may truly be said to have neither Force nor Will, but merely judgment."

The Court as Referee and Umpire

The Supreme Court serves as both referee between the two nationally elective branches and as the umpire of federal-state relations. Ever since the Court claimed the power of judicial review in 1803 and struck down an act of Congress, it has considered a large number of separation of power issues, most notably during the New Deal and in the past few decades. Super-legislature, or legislating from the court (the charge of judicial activism), is an oft-repeated epithet used for the Court when it makes decisions that others believe should be settled by the elective branches of government. Someone's view of activism, however, often depends on whether he or she supports the direction of the court. Decisions that expand Congress's authority to legislate may be opposed by those who prefer matters to be handled by the states. Conversely, decisions that restrict the reach of the legislative branch are likely to be opposed by those who favor a national approach to problems. Criticism has been lodged against conservative judicial activism by the Rehnquist Court, which has struck down "nearly thirty federal enactments since 1995—"a record of activism against the national legislative branch." [9]

For example, in *United States v. Lopez* (1995), the Supreme Court overturned a federal law banning guns near school grounds. For the "first time since the New Deal . . . the Court found Congress to have exceeded the bounds of its constitutional authority to regulate interstate commerce"—in this case the movement of guns across state lines that could end up on school playgrounds.[10] Quickly, Congress moved to pass legislation that made clear its authority under the commerce clause to restrict guns from school zones. In 1996 it enacted a measure, which the president signed, that said, "It shall be unlawful for any individual knowingly to possess a firearm that has moved in or that otherwise affects interstate or foreign commerce at a place that the individual knows, or has reasonable cause to believe, is a school zone." [11]

Lawmakers are mindful of the court's umpire role and seek to employ it for their own goals. Increasingly, members turn to the court to accomplish ends they were unable to achieve in Congress. Often, they ask the court to defend congressional prerogatives against usurpation by the president. War making is the principal example. Not since World War II has Congress declared war, although it may enact legislation that is its functional equivalent. Recent presidents of both parties have committed American troops to combat on their own initiative. As scholar Louis Fisher pointed out with respect to war power suits brought by members:

> From the Vietnam War to the present day, members of Congress have gone to court to contest presidential wars and defend legislative prerogatives. In most of these cases, the courts held that the lawmakers lacked standing to bring the case. Even when legislators were granted standing, the courts refused relief on numerous grounds. Judges pointed out that the legislators represented only a fraction of the congressional membership and that often another group of legislators had filed a brief defending the president's action. Courts regularly note that Congress as a whole has failed to invoke its institutional powers to confront the president.[12]

Usually, courts dismiss these suits and offer two rationales: (1) the lawsuits raise political questions best left to the elective branches to resolve, and (2) they represent conflicts between groups of lawmakers pitted against each other, not constitutional clashes between Congress and the president.

As the federalism umpire, the Supreme Court has lately taken a more limited view of federal authority in relation to state prerogatives. Or as one law professor noted: "The revival of a doctrine of federalism that constrains the power of Congress has been a signature feature of the Rehnquist court." [13] The Court revived federalism through use of the Tenth Amendment (powers not delegated to the national government or prohibited to the states are reserved to the states or to the people) and the Eleventh Amendment (states are protected from being sued in federal court). "Over the past few terms," noted an analyst, Supreme Court "majorities have gradually chipped away at federal power and worked to strengthen the role of the states." [14] For example, in *Alabama v. Garrett* (2001) the Supreme Court held that states are immune from suits brought by state employees under the 1990 Americans with Disabilities Act. The Court asserts its review of legislative powers even as it affirms a congressional enactment—as when . . . . it upheld the right of state workers to sue their employers for violating the Family and Medical Leave Act of 1993, which permits women and men to take up to twelve weeks of unpaid leave a year to care for their sick children or relatives (*Nevada Department of Human Resources v. Hibbs, 2003*).[15] However, analysts suggest that the case did not represent a retreat from the Court's defense of state interests.

> The deeper message of Chief Justice William H. Rehnquist's opinion was that Congress was free to exercise the discretion the court chose to give it, and no more. The difference between the . . . disability discrimination statutes on the one hand and the family leave act on the other was that the court had, for the last several decades, identified sex discrimination as a problem for which, as with race discrimination, Congress simply had more freedom to devise remedies.[16]

Today, as the nation confronts an ongoing terrorist threat against the homeland, it is uncertain whether the Supreme Court's recent deference to state sovereignty will continue in that direction. "Whenever you see a national emergency, federalism disappears," stated a law professor. "In a national emergency, you give the national government the power to get done what needs to get done." [17] It is the president who gains power during wartime, when the balance between liberty and security tilts toward the latter and not the former.

A condition of perpetual war against terrorists raises a number of important issues: whether and to what extent federal courts will sanction infringements of individual privacy, allow terrorist suspects to be imprisoned without legal protections, permit greater governmental secrecy, and authorize searches of public library records without a criminal warrant (see box on book borrowing). After September 11, 2001, federal district judge Gladys Kessler said, "[T]he court fully understands and appreciates that the first priority of the executive branch in time of crisis is to ensure the physical security of its citizens." By the same token, she added, "the first priority of the judicial branch must be

Bill Would Close Book on Book Borrowing

After the U.S.A. Patriot Act was enacted, library patrons' borrowing records became an open book for FBI agents. But Rep. Bernard Sanders, I-Vt., in 2003 introduced a bill that would close them again. The bill (H.R. 1157) would exempt libraries and book sellers from a section of the act (P.L. 107-56) that expanded the FBI's ability to get information on terrorism suspects—including what books they purchased and borrowed.

"One of the cornerstones of our democracy is . . . to read printed material without government intrusion," Sanders said.

The FBI used to have to prove probable cause before compiling information about someone's reading habits. Now, it must only show that they would be "relevant" to an investigation.

Librarians and bookstores are concerned that people will quit reading. Others believe the section violates the Constitution.

The bill also would force the Justice Department to tell Congress just how much that section has been used and to what effect—information Attorney General John Ashcroft has so far refused to provide, citing national security. Some September 11, 2001, hijackers were suspected of having used library computers.

Source: Adapted from Kathryn A. Wolfe, *CQ Weekly,* March 8, 2003, 538.

to ensure that our government always operates within the statutory and constitutional constraints which distinguish a democracy from a dictatorship." [18] Congress also must address how to protect the homeland against terrorism without trampling on constituents' civil liberties. The challenge it faces is that partisan polarization in Congress "is so great that the institution as a whole doesn't seem to be able to reach conclusion on [many] critical things." [19]

Polarization on the Supreme Court is not unusual, as highlighted by its recent spate of 5–4 decisions on states' rights. These and other rulings have raised again the issue of how assertive courts should be in overturning decisions of the popularly elected Congress. Lawmakers are accountable to their constituents every time they face reelection. Although judges are not immune to the tides of public opinion, they do not face accountability through elections. The tension between policymaking by lawmakers versus judge-made decisions is perennial. However, it is useful to explore two traditional features of the Congress-court connection: statutory interpretation and legislative checks on the judiciary.

Statutory Interpretation

Communications between Congress and the federal courts are less than perfect. Neither branch understands the workings of the other very well.[20] Judges are generally aware that ambiguity, imprecision, or inconsistency may be the price for winning enactment of legislative measures. The more members try to define the language of a bill, the more they may divide or dissipate congressional support for it. Abner J. Mikva, a four-term House Democrat from Chicago who went on to become a federal judge and later counsel to President Bill Clinton, recounted an example from his Capitol Hill days. The issue involved a controversial strip-mining bill being managed by Arizona Democrat Morris K. Udall, then chairman of the House Interior (now called Resources) Committee:

> They'd put together a very delicate coalition of support. One problem was whether the states or the feds would run the program. One member got up and asked, "Isn't it a fact that under this bill the states would continue to exercise sovereignty over strip mining?" And Mo replied, "You're absolutely right." A little later someone else got up and asked, "Now is it clear that the Federal Government will have the final say on strip mining?" And Mo replied, "You're absolutely right." Later, in the cloakroom, I said, "Mo, they can't both be right." And Mo said, "You're absolutely right." [21]

Called upon to interpret statutes, judges may not appreciate the efforts required to get legislation passed on Capitol Hill or understand how to divine legislative history, as manifested in hearings, floor debate, and reports. The courts are debating what is the proper way to approach statutory interpretation. Should judges focus only on the plain meaning of the statutory language or should legislative history be consulted to help judges ascertain what Congress intended when it employed certain statutory phrases?

A group of federal judges, led by Supreme Court justice Antonin Scalia, argues that legislative history is open to manipulation by individual members of Congress, executive officials, congressional staffers, and lobbyists and therefore is unreliable as an indicator of statutory intent. (Decisions by executive and judicial officials are also influenced by the ideas, legal briefs, or written reports submitted to them by lobbyists, law clerks, and others.) Scalia contends that justices should follow a textualist approach and look at the words of laws or constitutional clauses and interpret them according to what they meant at the time of enactment.[22] Other federal judges, including Supreme Court justice Stephen G. Breyer, defend the value of legislative history, finding it useful in statutory interpretation. "It is dangerous," Breyer asserted, "to rely exclusively upon the literal meaning of a statute's words." [23]

The dispute over legislative history is well illustrated by Congress's passage of the Civil Rights Act of 1991. The law overturned, in whole or in part, seven civil rights cases decided by a conservative-leaning Supreme Court.[24] Yet the 1991 legislation was filled with ambiguities, and so lawmakers created their own legislative history during floor debate. A memorandum was even put in the *Congressional Record* stating that the written statement was the exclusive legislative history for certain contested provisions. During debate on the legislation, a Republican senator pointed out the pitfalls of relying on legislative history. His position essentially endorsed Justice Scalia's view that Congress should state clearly what it means or wants in the law instead of in floor debate or other explanatory statements.[25]

Supreme Court justice John Paul Stevens expressed a contrary opinion, saying that a "stubborn insistence on 'clear statements' [in the law] burdens the Congress with unnecessary reenactment of provisions that were already plain enough." Rep. Barney Frank, D-Mass.—who once stopped committee members from putting explanatory language in a committee report by saying "Justice Scalia"—added that, if Scalia's view on legislative history became dominant, Congress would be required to develop a new category of legislation: "the 'No, we really meant it' statute." [26] The disagreement between Congress and federal judges over the utility of legislative history was summed up by the chief counsel of the Senate Judiciary Committee: "The textual interpretation encourages us to write clearer legislation. But unclear bills are still written. If they were not, we would not have this fight over [the confirmation of] judges." [27] Judges who favor the plain meaning principle of statutory construction may still search legislative history to confirm their understanding of the legal language.

Legislative Checks on the Judiciary

Decisions of the Supreme Court can have profound effects on Congress and its members. Cases involving the redistricting of House seats, the line-item veto, and term limits for lawmakers are recent examples. If the court arouses the ire of Congress when it rules on statutory questions, the legislative branch can enact new legislation. Scores of interest groups also monitor court decisions, and, if they disagree with them, these groups are not reluctant to lobby Congress to seek their statutory reversal. Generally, if the court bases its decisions on constitutional grounds, then Congress can only change them by constitutional amendment.[28] Congress has other ways by which it can influence the Supreme Court and lower federal courts. In addition to the Senate's constitutional advice and consent role with respect to judicial nominations, there are three that merit some mention.

Withdrawal of Jurisdiction. Under its constitutional authority to determine the court's appellate jurisdiction, Congress may threaten to withdraw the Supreme Court's authority to review certain categories of cases, such as school prayer, abortion, or school busing. Senate Judiciary chairman Orrin G. Hatch, R-Utah, for instance, recommended that a single federal judge no longer have the authority to issue "an order halting the implementation of a state referendum." [29] Despite such legislative threats to constrict or withdraw jurisdiction, on only one occasion in U.S. history did Congress prevent the Supreme Court from deciding a case by removing its appellate jurisdiction.

This extraordinary action was taken by a Congress dominated by Radical Republicans who wanted to prohibit the Supreme Court from reviewing the constitutionality of the Reconstructions Acts of 1867. The acts substituted military rule for civilian government in the ten southern states that initially refused to rejoin the Union and established procedures for those states to follow to gain readmittance and representation in the federal government.[30]

Congress simply passed legislation repealing the Supreme Court's right to hear appeals involving these matters and prevented "a possibly hostile Court from using the power of judicial review to invalidate a piece of legislation that was of vital concern to those who controlled the legislative body." [31]

Furthermore, Congress may simultaneously urge the attorney general of the United States to appeal lower federal court decisions to the Supreme Court and threaten to limit the judiciary's jurisdiction. During 2002–2003, both chambers expressed strong opposition to a Ninth Circuit Court of Appeals decision that a 1954 federal law adding the phrase "one Nation under God" to the Pledge of Allegiance was unconstitutional on First Amendment grounds. As explained by the House Judiciary Committee in its response to the Ninth Circuit's ruling:

> The purpose of H. Res. 132 . . . is to express the sense of the House of Representatives that the phrase "one Nation under God," should remain in the Pledge of Allegiance; that the Ninth Circuit Court of Appeals ruling in *Newdow v. U.S. Congress* is inconsistent with the Supreme Court's interpretation of the First Amendment; that the Attorney General of the United States should appeal the Ninth Circuit's ruling; and the President should nominate, and the Senate confirm, Federal circuit court judges who will interpret the Constitution consistent with the Constitution's text.[32]

On March 20, 2003, the House adopted H. Res. 132 by a vote of 400 to 17. House majority leader Tom DeLay, R-Texas, reminded the court that Congress could do more than just adopt a sense of the House resolution. "I think that [legislation to limit the court's jurisdiction] would be a very good idea to send a message to the judiciary [that] they ought to keep their hands off the Pledge of Allegiance." [33]

Impeachment of Judges. Federal judges, like other national civil officers, are subject to impeachment under Article II of the Constitution. They are appointed for life "during good behavior." Only one Supreme Court justice, Samuel Chase, was impeached by the House. This occurred in 1804, during bitter partisan battles between Federalists and Jeffersonian Republicans. The judiciary was the last bastion of Federalist influence after Thomas Jefferson won the presidency in the 1800 election. Intemperate and arrogant behavior on Chase's part, including campaigning for John Adams's reelection in 1800, aroused the ire of the president and his Republican allies in Congress. On March 12, 1804, the House voted 73–32 along party lines to impeach Chase. The Senate, however, failed to convict Chase. The importance of Chase's acquittal by the Senate was underscored by today's chief justice, William Rehnquist.

The acquittal of Samuel Chase by the Senate had a profound effect on the American judiciary. First, it assured the independence of federal judges from congressional oversight of the decisions they made in the cases that come before them. Second, by assuring that impeachment would not be used in the future as a method to remove members of the Supreme Court for their judicial opinions, it helped to safeguard the independence of that body.[34]

Other Supreme Court justices have either been threatened with impeachment or been the subject of impeachment investigations (for example, William O. Douglas in 1953 and in 1970).

Fewer than a dozen federal judges have been impeached and even a smaller number have been convicted and removed from office. "The three most recent impeachment efforts led to the removal of Judges Harry E. Claiborne (1986), Walter Nixon (1989), and Alcee L. Hastings (1989)." [35] Claiborne was removed for tax evasion, Nixon for perjury, and Hastings for bribery. None of the three, however, was barred from holding further federal office by a separate Senate vote following their conviction. In 1992 Hastings was elected to the House of Representatives as a Democrat from Florida, where he has served continuously since his first election.

Size, Procedure, and Pay. Historically, on a half-dozen occasions the size of the Supreme Court has varied anywhere from six to ten members. "Generally, laws decreasing the number of justices have been motivated by a desire to punish the president; increases have been aimed at influencing the philosophical balance of the Court itself," such as Roosevelt's court-packing plan.[36] Not since 1869 has Congress changed the Supreme Court's size from its current nine justices.

Procedurally, lawmakers have sometimes proposed that court decisions overturning federal laws must be accomplished by a supermajority vote of the justices. Some of the "more extreme proposals have urged that such decisions be unanimous." [37] None of these initiatives has been agreed to by Congress. They are a form of message sending to highlight lawmakers' dissatisfaction with certain court decisions.

Recently, concern has arisen about fewer aspirants seeking federal judgeships. Part of the reason for this is pay. "Salaries are far lower [for federal judges] than what fresh-faced law-school grads can make at big corporate firms." [38] Chief Justice Rehnquist said judicial pay is "the most pressing issue facing the federal judiciary today," in part because many qualified candidates cannot afford to serve on the bench.[39] Lawmakers recognize this problem but have been reluctant to boost judicial salaries above their own (currently $154,700). The Senate Judiciary Committee did report a bill giving all judges a 16.5 percent pay hike, but it was combined with a proposal that most federal judges have opposed: opening courtrooms to television (see box on judiciary panel). Justices on the Supreme Court oppose the televising of their proceedings, in part because the cameras might alter decision making and intrude on the privacy of the justices, making them public celebrities.

Judiciary Panel Endorses Higher Judges' Pay and Cameras in the Courtroom

Federal judges would get a one-time, across-the-board pay increase of 16.5 percent under legislation approved by the Senate Judiciary Committee in 2003.

But the package comes with strings attached. The bill (S. 1023), as amended by the panel and approved 14–2, would give appeals and district court judges the option of allowing television cameras and other devices to record proceedings in their courtrooms.

The U.S. Judicial Conference for years has implored Congress to boost judges' salaries. At the same time, it has long opposed the use of cameras or other devices to record proceedings. All but two states allow cameras in their courtrooms, but the federal judiciary bans them.

Some senators—including Judiciary chairman Orrin G. Hatch, R-Utah—side with the Judicial Conference and oppose allowing cameras in federal courtrooms. A stand-alone bill (S. 554) that would give federal judges the option of allowing recordings was first approved 14–4 by the panel despite Hatch's opposition.

But Hatch and other Judiciary members then went along with a plan to combine the cameras bill with the legislation that would boost federal judges' salaries, effective January 1, 2004. The pay raise and cameras bills were combined by an amendment offered by Sen. Charles E. Schumer, D-N.Y., and adopted 13–5.

Charles E. Grassley, R-Iowa, who sponsored the cameras bill but opposed Hatch's pay raise measure, said the combination of the two will propel the legislation through the Senate.

"If we've got to pay judges more, I want to give them more work to do," Grassley said after the markup. "And the one more piece of work would be just to decide if there should be cameras in the courtroom."

Grassley's cameras measure would give appeals and district court judges the option of allowing television cameras and other devices to record court proceedings. Judges would be able to bar the recording of witnesses who ask that their identities be protected, unless the witnesses are named parties in the case before the court.

The pay raise bill, sponsored by Hatch, would boost the salaries of appeals court judges from $164,000 to $191,000. District court judges, who now earn the same salary as members of Congress—$154,700—would get roughly $188,200 under the measure. Supreme Court justices also would get the one-time 16.5 percent raise.

Source: Adapted from Jennifer Dlouhy, *CQ Today,* May 23, 2003, 15.

Constitutional Amendments. On four occasions, Congress successfully used the arduous process of amending the Constitution to overturn decisions of the Supreme Court. In *Chisholm v. Georgia* (1793), the Court held that citizens of one state could sue another state in federal court. To prevent a rash of citizen suits against the states, the Eleventh Amendment reversed this decision. It guarantees the states immunity from suits by citizens outside its borders. The *Dred Scott v. Sandford* (1857) decision that denied African Americans citizenship under the Constitution was nullified by the Thirteenth (abolishing slavery) and

Fourteenth (granting African Americans citizenship) Amendments. The Sixteenth Amendment overturned *Pollock v. Farmer's Loan and Trust Co.* (1895), which struck down a federal income tax. The Twenty-sixth Amendment invalidated *Oregon v. Mitchell* (1970), which said that Congress had exceeded its authority by lowering the minimum voting age to eighteen for state elections.[40]

Generally, lawmakers are reluctant to amend the Constitution. Rep. Melvin Watt, D-N.C., reflects the view of many members: "I just think the Constitution has served us very well over a long, long period of time and one needs to make a compelling case before we start amending the Constitution to do anything." [41] However, certain constitutional amendments appear regularly on the legislative agenda. Since 1995, for instance, the House has voted five times to approve a constitutional amendment banning desecration of the American flag. The proposed amendment—which is an especial favorite of many Republicans both inside and outside Congress who view flag burning as highly objectionable behavior—is a response to a 1989 Supreme Court ruling (*Texas v. Johnson*) that state laws banning flag burning violate the First Amendment right of free speech. Justice William Brennan, who wrote the majority opinion, stated: "We do not consecrate the flag by punishing its desecration, for in doing so we dilute the freedom that this cherished emblem represents." House votes on this proposed constitutional amendment are regularly scheduled near Flag Day (mid-June) or July 4. The Senate has never approved the measure.

Advice and Consent for Judicial Nominees

Article II, Section 2, of the Constitution states that the president "shall nominate, and by and with the advice and consent of the Senate, shall appoint." The founders opposed lodging the power to appoint solely in the executive. They also opposed giving it exclusively to Congress as a whole or to the Senate in particular. The framers compromised and provided that judicial selections required joint action by the president and the Senate. The president has the sole prerogative to nominate, but the power to confirm (or not) is the Senate's. Alexander Hamilton, in the *Federalist Papers* No. 66, viewed this division of responsibility in stark terms. "There will, of course, be no exertion of CHOICE on the part of the Senate. They may defeat one choice of the Executive and oblige him to make another; but they cannot themselves CHOOSE— they can only ratify or reject the choice he may have made."

Hamilton's perspective requires modification, however. Giving two elective institutions a voice in the appointments process necessarily meant that nominees would be subject to a political process. Individual senators, House members, interest groups, the American Bar Association (which, since 1952, has rated judicial candidates), the press and media, and even sitting judges all may play a role in influencing both the choice of judicial nominees and Senate action, if any, on those nominees.

Norms and Practices. Extraconstitutional norms and practices also shape the confirmation process. President George Washington quickly learned the importance of the norm of senatorial courtesy—an informal practice in which presidents consult home-state senators before submitting nominees for federal positions in their state. When Washington "failed to seek the advice from the Georgia senate delegation regarding a nomination for a federal position in Savannah, Washington was forced to withdraw the nomination in favor of the person recommended by the senators." [42]

Related to senatorial courtesy is the blue-slip policy of the Judiciary Committee, which applies only to district and circuit court nominees. It refers to "blue approval papers that senators are asked to submit on nominees for federal judgeships in their states. For the past few years, both home-state senators had to submit a positive blue slip for a nominee to be considered by the Judiciary Committee." [43] Although exceptions have been made to this policy, it does encourage the president to seek the advice of senators before he submits judicial nominees to the Senate. An array of other Senate practices influence whether any action occurs on judicial nominations, such as holds, the committee chair's prerogative of determining whether hearings will be held, and the majority leader's willingness to schedule floor consideration of the nominations.

An unresolved issue is the balance between advice and consent. Presidents often favor consent over advice. The Senate tilts in the other direction. "The [George W. Bush] administration seems to think that 'advice and consent' means 'advise and rubber stamp,' " declared Sen. Patrick J. Leahy of Vermont, ranking Democrat on the Judiciary Committee.[44] Adding to the controversy is the lack of agreement on what qualifications are appropriate for service as a federal jurist. The Constitution makes no reference to what presidents or senators should consider when exercising their respective roles. Setting aside the standard qualifications that everyone expects in prospective judges—legal experience, ethical behavior, recognized competence, and so on—an age-old question is whether people should be subject to litmus tests to be either nominated or confirmed for a judicial position. What place should a person's legal philosophy or ideology have in the appointments process? Here, for example, is the approach of the George W. Bush administration.

> The people counseling Bush on judicial appointments are convinced that his father erred in appointing some judges, notably David Souter, who has become a reliable vote for the Supreme Court's moderate wing and cast a pivotal vote for reaffirming *Roe v. Wade* [upholding a woman's right of abortion during the first trimester]. Consequently, Bush's counselors conduct extensive interviews with prospective nominees about their judicial philosophies. Many of the nominees have been active members of the Federalist Society, established in the early 1980s to organize, cultivate and sharpen conservative thinking about the Constitution. Activity within the Federalist Society con-

stitutes an important—and sometimes the only—evidence of a young conservative's ideological commitment.[45]

Each party, sensitive to electoral demands from supporters who want judges appointed who share their values and views, confronts a quandary somewhat akin to the one faced by Goldilocks as she sampled the bowls of porridge: Are the judicial nominees too liberal, too conservative, or just right?

Nomination Battles. Over the past two centuries, the Senate has "rejected about 20 percent of all Supreme Court nominees."[46] Most of the rejections occurred in the nineteenth century, with President John Tyler holding the record: Five of his six nominees were rejected by the Senate (see Table 12-1). After the Senate turned down John Parker in 1930, no Supreme Court nominee was rejected until the presidency of Lyndon B. Johnson. In June 1968 Chief Justice Earl Warren informed Johnson of his intention to retire. "Concern that Richard Nixon might win the presidency later that year and get to choose his successor dictated Warren's timing."[47] Johnson nominated his close friend on the court, Associate Justice Abe Fortas, to be the next chief justice. However, when Fortas's ethical violations (accepting private money) came to light, it triggered the first filibuster in the Senate's history on a Supreme Court nomination, which doomed Fortas. Cloture could not be invoked to end the filibuster and Johnson withdrew his nomination for the chief judgeship. The next year, enmeshed in further ethical controversies, Fortas resigned from the Court under threat of impeachment by the House.

Also in 1969 the Senate rejected President Nixon's nominee to fill the Fortas vacancy, Clement Haynsworth, on the grounds of insensitivity to civil rights issues. A year later another Nixon nominee, Harold Carswell, was rejected because of his mediocre record as a lower court judge. However, President Ronald Reagan's nomination of conservative Robert Bork to the Supreme Court in 1987 sparked the bitter confirmation battles that still continue today. During nationally televised hearings, members of the Democratically controlled Judiciary Committee probed Bork's extensive written record to evaluate his constitutional and philosophical beliefs. Because Bork's nomination came at a time of large public concern about the Supreme Court's ideological balance, and because Bork's views were perceived as too conservative and controversial by many senators and interest groups, the Senate rejected the nominee by a 58 to 42 margin. (Bork's nomination fight gave rise to a made-up verb—"to bork"—which means to attack nominees by launching a politically based campaign against them.)

Even more controversial was President George Bush's 1991 nomination of Clarence Thomas, who was narrowly approved by the Senate on a 52 to 48 vote. Law professor Anita Hill, who previously worked for Thomas, charged that he had sexually harassed her on the job. The charges and countercharges played out on national television during the Judiciary Committee's hearings. Many in the public were glued to their television sets to witness the dramatic

Table 12-1 Supreme Court Nominations Not Confirmed by the Senate

Nominee	President	Date of nomination	Senate action	Date of Senate action
William Paterson	George Washington	February 27, 1793	Withdrawn[a]	
John Rutledge[b]	Washington	July 1, 1795	Rejected (10–14)	December 15, 1795
Alexander Wolcott	James Madison	February 4, 1811	Rejected (9–24)	February 13, 1811
John J. Crittenden	John Quincy Adams	December 17, 1828	Postponed	February 12, 1829
Roger Brooke Taney	Andrew Jackson	January 15, 1835	Postponed (24–21)[c]	March 3, 1835
John C. Spencer	John Tyler	January 9, 1844	Rejected (21–26)	January 31, 1844
Reuben H. Walworth	Tyler	March 13, 1844	Withdrawn	
Edward King	Tyler	June 5, 1844	Postponed	June 15, 1844
Edward King	Tyler	December 4, 1844	Withdrawn	
John M. Read	Tyler	February 7, 1845	Not acted upon	
George W. Woodward	James K. Polk	December 23, 1845	Rejected (20–29)	January 22, 1846
Edward A. Bradford	Millard Fillmore	August 16, 1852	Not acted upon	
George E. Badger	Fillmore	January 10, 1853	Postponed	February 11, 1853
William C. Micou	Fillmore	February 24, 1853	Not acted upon	
Jeremiah S. Black	James Buchanan	February 5, 1861	Rejected (25–26)	February 21, 1861
Henry Stanbery	Andrew Johnson	April 16, 1866	Not acted upon	
Ebenezer R. Hoar	Ulysses S. Grant	December 15, 1869	Rejected (24–33)	February 3,1870
George H. Williams[b]	Grant	December 1, 1873	Withdrawn	
Cable Cushing[b]	Grant	January 9, 1874	Withdrawn	
Stanley Matthews	Rutherford B. Hayes	January 26, 1881	Not acted upon[a]	

Continued

Table 12-1 Continued

Nominee	President	Date of nomination	Senate action	Date of Senate action
William B. Hornblower	Grover Cleveland	September 19, 1893	Rejected (24–30)	January 15, 1894
Wheeler H. Peckham	Cleveland	January 22, 1894	Rejected (32–41)	February 16, 1894
John J. Parker	Herbert Hoover	March 21, 1930	Rejected (39–41)	May 7, 1930
Abe Fortas[b]	Lyndon B. Johnson	June 26, 1968	Withdrawn	
Homer Thornberry	Johnson	June 26, 1968	Not acted upon	
Clement F. Haynsworth Jr.	Richard M. Nixon	August 18, 1969	Rejected (45–55)	November 21, 1969
G. Harrold Carswell	Nixon	January 19, 1970	Rejected (45–51)	April 8, 1970
Robert H. Bork	Ronald Reagan	July 1, 1987	Rejected (42–58)	October 23, 1987

Source: Joan Biskupic and Elder Witt, *Guide to the U.S. Supreme Court*, 3d ed., vol. 2 (Washington, D.C.: Congressional Quarterly, 1997), 707.

[a] Later nominated and confirmed.
[b] Nominated for chief justice.
[c] Later nominated for chief justice and confirmed.

testimony of Hill and Thomas. Conservative groups were outraged at the way Bork and Thomas were treated by the Democratically controlled Senate. They bided their time until it was their turn to wreck havoc on Democratic nominees for the federal bench.

In 1995 Republicans took control of the Senate and Democrat Bill Clinton was in the White House. Many of Clinton's nominees never received hearings or waited years before any action took place on their nomination. For example, Richard Paez waited four years from his original nomination before he was confirmed to sit on the Ninth Circuit Court of Appeals. During the brief period from June 2001 to November 2002 when Democrats held the Senate because of Vermont senator Jim Jeffords's party switch, they blocked many of President Bush's judicial nominees through holds, blue slips, and other dilatory actions. In 2003, with Democrats again in the minority, it was their turn to block many of Bush's controversial nominees. Every time power shifted in Washington, an escalation of conflict over judicial nominees was launched by senators who viewed them as too controversial for one reason or another. It is "payback on top of payback on top of payback," exclaimed Sen. Mark Pryor, D-Ark.[48] Or, as one commentator put it, what distinguishes the judicial battles of the Clinton and Bush presidencies from those of earlier eras is that they have come "to resemble political blood feuds, in which each side seeks to avenge the earlier assaults by the other side." [49]

Consent and Dissent. The struggle over who should be a federal judge has intensified in recent years, especially during the Clinton and George W. Bush administrations. Traditionally, little controversy was associated with scrutinizing judges named to serve on the dozen regional courts of appeals and the ninety district (or trial) courts. Nominees to the Supreme Court often were the focus of sometimes bitter and lengthy confirmation battles between the White House and Senate.

Today, fierce political, strategic, and tactical conflicts between the parties and branches overlay the confirmation process for many judicial nominees, especially for the circuit courts. "The politicization of the judiciary has recently been the most focused, and most virulent, at the appellate, or circuit level," stated federal judge James Robertson.[50] Four main factors explain this development. First, both parties understand that although the Supreme Court is viewed as the "court of last resort," it only decides about 80 cases each year (a decade ago the number was 107). Circuit courts are "playing a more important role in setting law for vast areas of the country. A decision by the 9th Circuit, for example, is binding on nine states, where 19 percent of the nation's population lives." [51]

Second, circuit courts, especially the District of Columbia Circuit Court of Appeals, are often recruiting grounds for Supreme Court nominees. For example, three of the nine members of today's Supreme Court—Antonin Scalia, Ruth Bader Ginsburg, and Clarence Thomas—served previously on the D.C. circuit court. (Democrats are mindful that President George W. Bush has said that his favorite models as Supreme Court justices are Scalia and Thomas.)

Third, the contests over circuit court nominees are perceived by many as a warm-up for the impending battles involving Supreme Court vacancies. As Sheldon Goldman, an expert on judicial nominations, observed: "It's very transparent that we're in a high-stakes game, and this is all preparing for fights over the Supreme Court." [52] Conservative and liberal groups already have launched fund-raising, research, and advertising campaigns to be prepared for the expected nomination battles and to influence public opinion. In June 2003, for instance, the Naral Pro-Choice America Foundation was "making a pre-emptive strike with a television campaign . . . that highlights the importance of the court to abortion. The commercial shows a woman gasping as she reads the newspaper headline—'Abortion Outlawed—Court Overturns Right to Choose.' " [53]

Finally, the confirmation battles represent a clash between President Bush and Senate Democrats over who will control the ideological balance of power on the courts. President Bush "has been more consistent and insistent than, say, [Gerald R.] Ford or Reagan" in nominating conservatives to the bench, said a law professor.[54] "If Democrats just rolled over on Bush's nominations," said an analyst, "they would be guilty of oppositional malpractice." [55]

The bitter partisan battles and recriminations over judges play out in both the Judiciary Committee and on the Senate floor. The Judiciary Committee is "polarized to a degree that I've never seen," exclaimed Sen. Jeff Sessions, R-Ala., who sits on the panel.[56] Sen. John Cornyn, R-Texas, expressed a comparable view. "I'm very concerned not only about the broken judicial confirmation process, but also how badly it seems to have poisoned relations in the Senate . . . and hurt our ability to do other things as well." [57] Democratic senator Edward M. Kennedy of Massachusetts, who serves on the Judiciary panel, has a different take on why there are problems with the confirmation process. "What's broken is not the Senate confirmation process, it's the White House nominations process. The process isn't working now because President Bush is trying to stack the courts with right-wing extremists." [58]

Republicans heatedly deny that they are trying to pack the court with conservative activists. They contend that their nominees are highly qualified professionals who represent the mainstream of judicial thinking. These diverse perspectives are difficult to resolve because, unlike the lawmaking process, opportunities for compromise on controversial nominations are limited. It is typically a zero-sum game: President Bush either wins the confirmation battle and Senate Democrats lose, or the reverse scenario plays out.

Several other significant points are important to note about the contemporary confirmations process. Most judicial nominations are approved by the Senate, roughly an 85 percent approval rate for the period extending from the late 1970s to the late 1990s.[59] Both senatorial parties, however, present dueling and divergent statistics on how each processed a large number of nominations when it was in charge compared with the poor record of the other party when it held the majority.[60]

Recent judicial nominations confront longer confirmation delays. Sheldon Goldman devised an index of obstruction (no action on a nominee) and delay (it takes more than 180 days from the date of nomination to a Senate floor vote) for district and appeals court nominees from 1977 through 2002, accounting for periods of divided or unified government. He found an increasing pattern of delay and obstruction, especially for circuit court nominees. For example, the "average number of days from the date the nomination was reported [by the Judiciary Committee] to the date of confirmation [by the Senate] ranged from a low of 1.8 days for the 97th Congress [1981–1983] for district court appointees and 1.9 days for appeals court nominees to 38.3 days for district court nominees for the 105th Congress [1997–1999] and 68.5 days for appeals court nominees for the 106th [1999–2001]." [61]

A number of reasons account for the delays, especially for the relatively small number of nominees who wait many months or several years for confirmation. Scholars confirm, for instance, that an approaching presidential election, not to mention divided government, usually produces two outcomes: longer delays and more rejections of presidential election-year nominees.[62] A large number of other factors influence whether a nominee is confirmed quickly or subject to lengthy delays or outright rejection, such as a candidate's race or gender; the position to which a candidate is nominated, especially if it tips the balance of power on the court; the extent of bipartisan support for a nominee; the use of dilatory tactics by senators; the philosophic outlook of candidates; the extent of presidential consultation with senators; the likelihood that a candidate might be nominated to the Supreme Court; and more. President Bush has even offered his own plan to speed Senate action on judicial confirmations.[63]

The frustration and anger level has risen exceptionally high in the Senate, largely over filibusters against two Bush nominations. In spring 2003, as one account noted, the "number of Bush circuit court nominees the Senate has confirmed: 22. The number of Bush nominees confirmed to the district courts: 101. The number of Bush judicial nominees currently being filibustered: 2." [64] However, the two nominees for the circuit court—Miguel Estrada and Priscilla Owens—have sparked unusual partisan acrimony. Hearings have been held on the constitutionality of the filibuster; a day (March 11, 2003) was set aside for the Senate to debate the state of the nominations process, with Vice President Dick Cheney presiding to underscore the administration's concern; senators have threatened to file suit in court challenging the filibuster; the majority leader, Bill Frist, R-Tenn., has sponsored a resolution setting forth a procedure that prevents filibusters on judicial nominations; and Republicans are discussing a parliamentary nuclear option: one version would have Cheney invoke the Constitution, declare that a majority can change the chamber's formal rules, and state that Senate Rule 22, which requires sixty votes to stop a filibuster, does not apply to judicial nominations.

Senate Republicans charge that Estrada, who came to the United States from Honduras, is being subjected to a "piñata confirmation process," in which the nominee is chastised by critics "until they unearth some damning information" about his record.[65] Senate Democrats say that the procedural quagmire in which the Senate finds itself over the Estrada nomination can be resolved quickly if the Bush administration will "supply the memos from the Solicitor's Office [of the Department of Justice] while he worked there and that he wrote and allow more questioning of Estrada" at another round of Judiciary Committee hearings.[66] The administration refuses to release the memoranda written by Estrada, and the Senate remains gridlocked over this nomination.

How such controversial nominations as Estrada play out in the Senate is uncertain, but they reflect larger political and electoral factors. One is that each party employs these battles to bolster and energize their electoral base of supporters. Republicans, for instance, want to solicit votes from the expanding number of Hispanic voters, so they keep forcing cloture votes on Estrada to highlight that Democrats are holding back his elevation to the bench. They aim to portray Democrats as anti-Hispanic in battleground states, such as Florida. A second consideration is the extensive involvement of interest groups on the nominations process. Advocacy groups affiliated with each party ran pro- and con-Estrada television ads in the states of targeted senators. Women's groups refer to female conservative nominations such as Owens as "Scalia in a skirt." [67]A further factor is recognition by the parties that court battles are another manifestation of their fundamental policy differences. The composition of the federal bench can significantly shape Congress's work.

Conclusion

Federal courts, like Congress and the president, are important forums for resolving the political, social, and economic conflicts that characterize American society. All three branches of government constantly interact to shape and influence the laws Americans live under. Sometimes, as presidents say, "the buck stops here." In Congress the buck may stop nowhere, and either elective branch may pass the buck to the courts when it is unable to resolve certain issues. "Through this process of interaction among the branches," wrote scholar Louis Fisher, "all three institutions are able to expose weaknesses, hold excesses in check, and gradually forge a consensus on constitutional values." [68]

The influence of lobbying on the law. Above, AARP members lobby at the Capitol to add prescription drug care coverage to Medicare. Center, John Walsh, host of the television show America's Most Wanted, gives the "thumbs-up" to members and staff during a House-Senate conference committee on the Child Abduction Prevention Act. The three members seated at the conference table are Reps. Phil Gingrey, R-Ga., Peter Hoekstra, R-Mich., and Melissa Hart, R-Pa. Below, Sen. Debbie Stabenow, D-Mich., addresses environmentalists who oppose oil and gas drilling in Alaska's Arctic National Wildlife Refuge.

13

Congress and Organized Interests

A House subcommittee markup attracted scores of lobbyists representing Wall Street and other interests. Early each morning before a scheduled session, people formed long lines outside the meeting room for the limited number of seats. "Places on the line [were] being held for [the $500-an-hour] lobbyists by some people being paid almost $20 an hour.[1] As one line-stander said, "The lobbyists pay us, and then the interest groups and corporations seeking tax breaks pay the lobbyists." [2]

Capitol Hill lobbyists regularly fill committee hearings and markups, jam into conference committee rooms, and pack House and Senate galleries. These emissaries of organized interests do more than observe congressional events. They wield their vast resources—money, personnel, information, and organization—to win passage of legislation they favor and to reward the politicians who help them. Practically every major corporation, trade association, and professional group has Washington lobbyists. They even have their own associations: the American Society of Association Executives and the American League of Lobbyists. Like many other groups, both are based in Washington, D.C., which is home to more national associations than any other city.

Looking in the Washington telephone directory under "associations" reveals as much about what moves Congress as the Constitution does. More than eighty thousand employees work for various associations. Numerous law firms have moved to the District of Columbia, and growing cadres of consultants and lawyers represent diverse clients, including foreign governments. The lobbying community probably constitutes the third largest industry employer in the nation's capital behind government and tourism. In 2001 companies and special interests spent $130 million a month lobbying members of Congress, with the health care industry expending the most during the year ($234,724,579) and public employee unions and associations the least ($3,105,000). (Average spending for the first six months of 2002 was $143 million.)[3] Of the five top money-earning lobbying firms in 2001, the first-place group earned $30 million and the fifth-place firm earned nearly $16.3 million.[4]

A Nation of Joiners

Americans' zest for joining groups was observed long ago by the French chronicler Alexis de Tocqueville. Americans of all "conditions, minds, and ages daily acquire a general taste for association and grow accustomed to the use of it," he wrote in 1825.[5] During the 1990s about 65 percent of the population belonged to at least one organization.[6] All told, the United States is home to more than 138,000 national, regional, and local organizations.[7]

The First Amendment protects the people's right to "petition the Government for a redress of grievances." Throughout American history, groups speaking for different subsets of "the people" have swayed public policies and politics. The nineteenth-century abolitionists fought to end slavery. The Anti-Saloon League crusaded for Prohibition in the 1900s. Movements of the 1960s and 1970s protested the Vietnam War, racial discrimination, and abuse of the environment. Interest groups galvanized support for women's rights and anti-abortion efforts in the 1980s, term limits for lawmakers and balanced-budget amendments in the 1990s, tax cuts in 2001, and affirmative action and anti– or pro–Iraqi war in 2003.

A free society nurtures politically active groups. "Liberty is to faction what air is to fire," wrote James Madison in *The Federalist Papers,* No. 10. In recent years interest groups have grown in number and diversity. In particular, there are more narrow-based groups that focus on single issues such as abortion, gun control, or animal rights. Many factors account for proliferation of interest groups of all kinds: social and economic complexity; the surge in scientific and technological developments; the government's regulatory role; the competition for scarce federal dollars; and the diffusion of power in Congress and throughout the government, which enhances access for outside interests (see box on theories of interest group formation).

For decades the American Medical Association dominated health lobbying. Today hundreds of health advocacy groups woo lawmakers and orchestrate grassroots efforts. In 1975 there were about 90 health groups; today there are nearly 750. "You name a disease, there's probably a Washington lobby for it," said an official of the American Heart Association.[8] Lobbyists for specific diseases use an innovative technique: placement spots on television shows watched nationwide. For example, they might lobby Hollywood producers to use a story line on television that dramatizes certain afflictions, such as acquired immune deficiency syndrome (AIDS) or Hodgkin's disease. A mention on a hit show encourages viewers to donate money to the relevant health advocacy group.[9]

Some scholars contend, however, that people's civic engagement has declined. Harvard University's Robert Putnam argues that citizen participation in associations is on the wane, and he employs a good example to highlight his contention. More people are bowling but they are bowling alone, resulting in a drop in the number of bowling leagues.[10] "People would rather be alone in front of a television set than out with a group," added Putnam.[11]

Putnam's views about the lack of civic engagement and community involvement have been challenged by other scholars. "Civic America is in fact being renewed and extended, not diminished," stated Professor Everett Carll Ladd. Putnam rightly notes, says Ladd, that membership in longtime organi-

Some Theories of Interest Group Formation

Scholars have suggested a number of theories to explain the development of interest groups. Special interests have long been a source of fascination, in part because of their ability to influence policy making even though they may not reflect majority sentiment within the country. The case of intense minorities prevailing over apathetic or disengaged majorities often rivets scholarly attention. Among the various theories of group formation are the following.

The proliferation hypothesis suggests that, as society becomes more complex and interdependent, groups naturally form to reflect the country's intricate array of issues and entities. As new conditions, issues, or forces emerge, new groups are formed to reflect or respond to these developments. "The reasoning behind the proliferation hypothesis is straightforward: groups need a clientele from which to draw members." [a]

The disturbance hypothesis posits the notion of an unstable equilibrium among groups. If something disturbs the equilibrium, such as war, technological innovations, the emergence of new concerns (AIDS, homeland security, and so on), and the like, then new groups will emerge. As two scholars wrote, "Groups organize politically when the existing order is disturbed and certain interests are, in turn, helped or hurt." As an example, they noted: "Mobilization of business interests since the 1960s often has resulted from threats posed by consumer advocates and environmentalists, as well as requirements imposed by the steadily growing role of the federal government." [b]

The exchange hypothesis states that groups form because of the efforts of "entrepreneurs." The "argument asserts that group organizers invest in a set of benefits which they offer to potential members at a price—joining the group. Benefits may be material [private gains], solidarity [camaraderie], or expressive [the reward of belonging to a group with shared values and causes]." [c] The implication is that organized interests are "deemed more powerful than unorganized interests." [d]

[a] Scott H. Ainsworth, *Analyzing Interest Groups* (New York: W. W. Norton and Co., 2002), 40.
[b] Alan J. Cigler and Burdett A. Loomis, eds., *Interest Group Politics*, 6th ed. (Washington, D.C.: CQ Press, 2002), 8. See also David S. Truman, *The Governmental Process*, 2d ed. (New York: Knopf, 1971).
[c] Robert Salisbury, "An Exchange Theory of Interest Groups," *Midwest Journal of Political Science* (February 1969): 1. Mancur Olson, in *The Logic of Collective Action* (Cambridge: Harvard University Press, 1965), suggests that many individuals are unlikely to join organizations that may benefit them personally because they will still receive the gains without the costs (fees, attending meetings, and so on) of participating in the group. This is called the free-rider problem. "For Olson, a key to group formation—and especially group survival—was 'selective' benefits. These rewards—for example, travel discounts, informative publications, and cheap insurance—go only to members." See Cigler and Loomis, *Interest Group Politics*, 9.
[d] Ainsworth, *Analyzing Interest Groups*, 39.

zations, such as the Lions Club, Elks, or Masons, is down. By contrast, membership is on the rise in newer organizations, such as environmental or youth soccer groups. Many individuals also are using the Internet to form social or political communities. Furthermore, other important indicators of civic engagement—especially volunteering and charitable giving—register increases in participation.[12]

A clear difference, however, is evident in the activity levels of the advantaged and the disadvantaged. A bias in political participation advantages the well-off and the well-educated in U.S. society compared with those who are not so fortunate. Lawmakers hear disproportionately from the former. Each group is interested in different things. The advantaged talk about taxes, government spending, and social issues, while the disadvantaged are primarily concerned about "basic human needs . . . poverty, jobs, housing, and health." [13] Elected officials are inundated with messages from groups that represent the politically active (the elderly, veterans, small-business owners, for example). Lawmakers receive comparatively little information about the policy preferences of the needy, who often are only marginally engaged in civic life.

Pressure Group Methods

Groups have influenced congressional decisions from the beginning. During the nation's early technological and industrial expansion, railroad interests lobbied for federal funds and land grants to build their routes. Some of the lobbyists' methods—offering bribes, for example—helped foster the traditional public suspicion of pressure tactics. In 1874 Sen. Simon Cameron, R-Pa., described an honest politician as one who "when he is bought, stays bought" (or stays "rented" with a long lease).[14] Samuel Ward, the "king of the lobby" for fifteen years after the Civil War, once wrote to his friend Henry Wadsworth Longfellow:

> When I see you again I will tell you how a client, eager to prevent the arrival at a committee of a certain member before it should adjourn, offered me $5,000 to accomplish this purpose, which I did, by having [the member's] boots mislaid while I smoked a cigar and condoled with him until they could be found at 11:45. I had the satisfaction of a good laugh [and] a good fee in my pocket.[15]

Lobbying methods during the twentieth century became more varied, urbane, and subtle. But the move from limited government to big government deepened the mutual dependence of legislators and lobbyists.

> Groups turn to Congress as an institution where they can be heard, establish their positions, and achieve their policy goals. Members of Congress in turn rely on groups to provide valuable constituency, technical, or political information, to give reelection support, and to assist strategically in passing or blocking legislation that the members support or oppose. Groups need Congress, and Congress needs groups.[16]

Modern-day methods vary according to the nature and visibility of the issue and the groups' resources. Among the most important practices are direct and social lobbying, group alliances, grassroots support, and electronic advocacy.

These diverse techniques typically overlap. For example, a small group of business lobbyists regularly meet privately with House GOP leader Tom DeLay of Texas to formulate strategy on the party's issues and goals. The lobbyists then mobilize grassroots support for these initiatives through petition drives, rallies, radio and television advertising blitzes, national door-to-door campaigns, and other techniques.[17] Emulating the success of DeLay, top Senate Democratic staffers meet every Monday with "liberal interest groups and lobbyists to seek advice on how to counter the White House bully pulpit." [18]

This is the first time the Democratic leadership has held regularly scheduled, formal meetings with outside groups, which has long been the regular practice of the GOP. Senate Republican Conference chairman Rick Santorum of Pennsylvania regularly meets with K Street brokers, and the GOP leadership on both sides of the Capitol constantly participate in strategy sessions with lobbyists.[19]

Top leadership aides to House minority leader Nancy Pelosi, D-Calif., also participate in the meetings convened by Senate Democratic aides with various liberal interest groups.

Direct Lobbying

In the traditional method of direct lobbying, lobbyists present their clients' cases directly to members and congressional staff. If a group hired a prominent lawyer or lobbyist, such as Ken Duberstein, Anne Wexler, or Tom Korologos, the direct approach would involve personal discussions with senators or representatives. An aide to Speaker Thomas P. "Tip" O'Neill Jr., D-Mass. (1977–1987), explained the importance of the personal touch.

> [Lobbyists] know members of Congress are here three nights a week, alone, without their families. So they . . . [s]chmooze with them. Make friends. And they don't lean on it all the time. Every once in a while, they call up—maybe once or twice a year—ask a few questions. . . . Anne Wexler [a former official in the Carter White House, now a lobbyist] will call up and spend half an hour talking about . . . politics, and suddenly she'll pop a question, pick up something. They want that little bit of access. That's what does it. You can hear it. It clicks home. They'll call their chief executive officer, and they've delivered. That's how it works. It's not illegal. They work on a personal basis.[20]

Particularly effective at direct lobbying are Hollywood movie stars, the children and spouses of powerful members, former staff aides and government luminaries, famous sports figures, prominent business executives (such as Microsoft's Bill Gates), and some former members of Congress.[21] "Since I will continue to be active in the Congressional Prayer Breakfast Group, in the House gym, the members' Dining Room and on the House Floor, I will maintain contact with my good friends who affect legislation," a just-retired representative of twenty years wrote to prospective clients. He promised to "unravel red tape, open doors, make appointments, work with the Administration or government agencies, influence legislation, and assist in any other service required." [22]

Member-to-member lobbying can be uniquely effective. No outsider has the same access to lawmakers (or to certain areas of Congress) that former colleagues have. For example, ex–GOP senators who may be lobbyists are invited to attend the regularly scheduled Tuesday Republican Policy Committee lunch "where legislative tactics are plotted on issues ranging from tax cuts to foreign policy," information "that gives them a decided edge over other lobbyists." [23] But some are offended by the entree that former legislators who are lobbyists have to the floor and to other Capitol Hill locations not generally open to the public.[24] Since 1991 former lawmakers have been prohibited for one year from lobbying members of Congress directly, although they may plan strategy and advise others who do so.

Direct lobbying takes many forms. Lobbyists monitor committees and testify (or have their clients function as witnesses) at hearings, interpret Hill decisions to clients and clients' interests to legislators, perform services such as writing speeches for members, and give campaign assistance. The House offers more occasions for contacting members directly than does the Senate, where lobbyists are more likely to target the staff who surround each member. "Essentially, we operate as an extension of congressmen's staff," explained one lobbyist. "Occasionally we come up with the legislation, or speeches—and questions [for lawmakers to ask at hearings] all the time. We look at it as providing staff work for allies." [25] Or, as one of Washington's premier lobbyists, Thomas Hale Boggs Jr. (son of former House majority leader Thomas Hale Boggs Sr., D-La., and former representative Lindy Boggs, D-La.), explained, "Congressional staffs are overworked and underpaid. Lobbyists help fill the information vacuum." [26]

The direct approach is limited, however, by rapid turnover in Congress. Nonetheless, lobbyists are major players in congressional policy making. "Lobbyists contribute a lot to democracy," stated Rep. James P. Moran, D-Va. "They provide continuity and institutional memory. Most of them have been around longer than members." [27] Or as a GOP senator put it: "I would have to say the best information I get in the legislative process comes from people directly involved in the industry that is going to be affected—and from people who represent them: the 'nefarious' lobbyists." [28] Generally, the tendency of lobbyists is to work with lawmakers who share their policy views by providing them with appropriate information, data, and political intelligence.

Social Lobbying

Although the Washington social circuit is vastly overrated, some lobbyists gain access to members at dinner parties or receptions. "When you want to make an end run, meet someone at a party," explained an experienced power dealer.[29] Because of the public's clamor and members' concern about gifts and free meals and trips from lobbyists, the House and Senate in 1995 imposed tighter restrictions on gift giving. "By themselves, gifts and meals are not sufficient to corrupt the whole system," remarked Sen. Russell D. Feingold, D-Wis. "But they create a psychological feeling that you are obliged. Somebody might not be aware of it, but I think it does have that effect." [30]

Under the amended 1995 House rules, virtually all gifts—free meals, free trips, and presents—were banned. Representatives then complained about the complexities associated with the strict ban on free meals and gifts. (For example, is a gift of a pie or a can of popcorn unacceptable?) This confusion led the House four years later to again amend its gift rules to bring them into alignment with those of the Senate. The Senate's rules include a number of exceptions for meals and gifts. For example, senators may accept gifts, including meals, if the gift has a value of less than $50. Senators may not accept a gift, however, from any one source that exceeds $100 annually. Items of little monetary value, such as baseball caps or T-shirts, are exempt from the gift limitation. Neither chamber bans gifts to political organizations or to members' campaigns. Gifts of liquor flow freely to lawmakers' fund-raising events.[31]

In 2003 Republicans amended the House rulebook to relax the ban on gifts from lobbyists. One change permits lobbying firms to provide fancier catered food to House offices (dubbed the "pizza rule" by an aide to Speaker J. Dennis Hastert, R-Ill.). However, criticism of the revision led the Committee on Standards of Official Conduct to issue guidelines on when lawmakers can accept food from interest groups. The committee stated that food "must be refused entirely if the person offering it has a direct interest in the particular legislation or other official business on which the staff is working at the time." [32]

The other change allows charitable groups to pay for lawmakers' travel and lodging expenses for up to two nights if they attend a fund-raising charity function, such as participating in a celebrity golf tournament. Critics have expressed concern that corporations or other entities might underwrite a charity event and then send "its top executives and lobbyists to the event for a weekend of schmoozing with lawmakers." As the chairman of the House ethics committee stated, "I don't want sham charities out there so congressmen can have a nice vacation." [33]

A variation on social lobbying is offering legislators speaking fees (honorariums). Although members now are banned by law from pocketing honorariums, they still may accept speaking fees if they donate them to charities or other tax-exempt groups. Some critics suggest that this arrangement enables members to "obtain political benefits by directing contributions to favored organizations, and some tax-exempt groups are affiliated with politicians." [34]

House and Senate gift rules do permit lawmakers and staff aides to travel on fact-finding missions, attend educational seminars, and make speeches if they are connected with their official duties and the trips are disclosed within thirty days of their completion. Special interests and foundations sponsor many trips to locations throughout the United States and abroad. For example, the American Association of Airport Executives spent about $90,000 to send three House members and six staff aides to a January conference in Hawaii. "The sessions were substantive and timely, and sure, it was in a warm place," remarked a House member who sent an aide on the trip. "If they held it in Newark, a lot fewer people would go." [35]

Members are becoming wary of overseas travel, however. "If you travel a lot, your opponent will put a map of the world on the screen and have you, like a ping-pong ball, zigging and zagging all over the world," remarked Rep. Ileana Ros-Lehtinen, R-Fla. No matter who pays for it—special interests or taxpayers—travel can be a political liability, she noted.[36]

Campaign fund-raising events are another important aspect of social lobbying. "With politicians wanting money and lobbyists wanting access, lobbyists are paying big sums to spend time in fancy places with lawmakers." These getaways are legal "because the money comes as a campaign contribution and not as a gift." [37] One lawmaker invited lobbyists to attend a four-day "winter conference" in Vail, Colorado. Here is a chance, the lawmaker said in his invitation, for "members of the PAC [political action committee] community to make a $3,000 . . . contribution to my . . . Leadership PAC." [38] To raise money for their reelection, lawmakers sometimes invite lobbyists to hang out with them informally—on a Super Bowl weekend, a summer trip to Nantucket, or a spring baseball training excursion in Florida, for example.

Coalition Lobbying

"We have no permanent friends or permanent enemies—only permanent interests." This oft-repeated truism helps to explain why "coalitions, like politics, make strange bed fellows." [39] Rival lobbying interests sometimes forge temporary coalitions to promote or defend shared goals. For instance, an unusual coalition of groups was formed in 2001 to fight against campaign finance reform legislation sponsored by Sens. John McCain, R-Ariz., and Russell Feingold. The combination of groups, which included the American Civil Liberties Union, the Christian Coalition, and the National Rifle Association, opposed the bill because they believed it would unconstitutionally limit their right of free speech during political campaigns.[40] Alliances often form on either side of an issue to battle against each other. On President George W. Bush's signature $1.35 trillion tax cut bill that he pushed through Congress soon after taking office, liberal groups—unions, the Sierra Club, and the National Association for the Advancement of Colored People—joined to oppose it while a group of businesses created the Tax Relief Coalition to promote its enactment.[41]

Coalitions bring advantages—more resources, contacts, and money— to lobbying efforts, but one advantage is especially significant. With the diffusion of power on Capitol Hill, coalitions are better able than a single group to touch all the legislative bases. A drawback is that coalitions are marriages of convenience. It is difficult to keep them working in harness for very long. To coordinate their activities and keep all participants informed, some coalitions post Web sites on the Internet.[42]

Grassroots Lobbying

Instead of contacting members directly, many organizations mobilize citizens to pressure their senators and representatives—perhaps the most effective lobbying technique. Masters of grassroots lobbying know how to be specific. Here is what one lobbyist said when he called a sportsman about a proposal to make hunting a nondeductible business expense: "Hello, Johnny Bob? This is J. D. in Washington. Got a pencil handy? Now, this is who your congressman is. This is how you write him."[43]

Interest groups often send mass mailings to targeted congressional districts with enclosed letters or postcards for constituents to sign and mail to their legislators. Legislators understand that lobby groups orchestrate this outpouring of mail, but they do not wholly disregard it.

> Members have to care about this mail, even if it's mail that is almost identically worded. Labor unions do this sort of thing a lot. The congressman has to care that somebody out there in his district has enough power to get hundreds of people to sit down and write a postcard or a letter—because if the guy can get them to do that, he might be able to influence them in other ways. So, a member has no choice but to pay attention. It's suicide if he doesn't.[44]

Lawmakers sometimes have to distinguish between genuine grassroots and astroturf. Many so-called grassroots groups function as front organizations for their financial backers. For example, a group called the Citizens for Sensible Control of Acid Rain was funded by the coal and electric industry to lobby against the Clean Air Act.[45] When the House debated a major telecommunications bill in the mid-1990s, lawmakers were flooded with bogus constituent mail from children, dead people, and constituents who said they had not sent any mailgrams. The uproar from members led to an investigation of the incident by the Capitol police.[46]

Mass mobilizations have become so common that some firms specialize in "grass tops" lobbying. Whereas the goal of grassroots lobbying is to mobilize the masses, the goal of grass tops lobbying "is to figure out to whom a member of Congress cannot say no: his chief donor, his campaign manager, a political mentor. The lobbyist then tries to persuade that person to take his client's side" during talks with the lawmaker.[47] Big corporations may also hire stealth lobbyists—public relations specialists who work quietly to "influence the news media, sponsor grassroots activities and generate favorable scientific reports."[48]

Electronic Lobbying

"Through their computers, [lobbying] groups get to more of my voters, more often, and with more information than any elected official can do," complained one House member. "I'm competing to represent my district against the lobbyists and the special interests."[49] Many lobbyists today orchestrate support at the local level by means of sophisticated electronic technology. As one account noted:

> The mobile telephone allows a lobbyist sitting in a congressional hearing to alert a lobbying group's head office. The fax machine can be used to send out a "broadcast fax" to hundreds of sympathizers with one push of a button. . . . A laptop and printer can be set up at a protest meeting, so that people can type their name, address and a personal message into a standard letter which can then be printed and signed on the spot.[50]

Talk-radio hosts, such as Rush Limbaugh (who is heard weekly on 660 stations by about twenty million listeners), can trigger an outpouring of letters, telegrams, e-mails, and faxes to lawmakers. The potent combination of technology and politics makes "it easier to organize and send a political message across the country at warp speed."[51] Electronic outreach is now incorporated into the advocacy efforts of numerous special interests.

Many groups use computers to identify supporters, target specific constituencies, recruit people, or generate personalized mass mailings. Cyber-lobbying through the Internet is fast becoming an important form of grassroots activism. For example, opponents of a ban on indecent material online rallied Internet users and "orchestrated 20,000 phone, fax or e-mail messages to House and Senate offices in a single day."[52] With the emergence of interactive Web sites, lobbyists can communicate directly with prospective supporters, recruit volunteers, assign tasks, and get immediate feedback on any issue.[53]

With various software programs, computer users—students and homemakers as well as business professionals and interest groups—can send targeted letters to scores of lawmakers or organize a "billion byte march" on Capitol Hill.[54] In early 2003, for instance, a coalition of peace groups titled Win Without War organized a "Virtual March on Washington" in which individuals flooded "every Senate office with phone calls, e-mails, and faxes."[55]

Rep. Jesse L. Jackson Jr., D-Ill., may be the only member to use his Web site (jessejacksonjr.org) to create an electronic network of outside political activists and organizations to lobby Congress on behalf of his policies they support. His e-mail network of external allies can quickly be mobilized to launch lobbying blitzes. Members will be "getting ready to do something against my bill, and I'll go straight to the computer and I'll say, 'All right, folks, we're having a problem over here,'" explained Representative Jackson. "And then, whoomp!"[56] Scores of e-mails, faxes, letters, personal visits, and telephone calls will inundate lawmakers' offices.

Groups and the Electoral Connection

In the fall of 1995 an unusual event occurred. A group of congressional candidates descended on Capitol Hill to learn how to win elections. What made

Union Workers Trained As Lobbyists

The AFL-CIO brings a group of legislative interns to the capital four times a year. It pays them what they make in their normal jobs plus expense allowances, lodges them in hotels, and gives them desks in the Steel Workers' Offices near DuPont Circle. The visitors are technically on sabbaticals authorized by the union's collective bargaining agreements.

The program combines schooling and work. Interns often are sent to Capitol Hill to track down lawmakers or congressional aides to make the union's case on legislative issues. During a typical week, they also study congressional procedures and history, attend hearings, and observe union policy meetings. The purpose is to give rank-and-file workers a deeper knowledge of Congress and to inspire activism at the local level. The union hopes its interns will go home more politically savvy and better prepared to rally co-workers on union issues and at election time.

The steel union's program is unusual in intensity, length, and agenda. The union wants to bolster its grassroots efforts and deepen its pool of potential candidates for elected offices. Gary Hubbard, spokesman for the Steel Workers, said the union hopes the two-year-old program will "get more plumbers and steamfitters and electricians into public office."

Source: Matthew Tully, "Union Program Fields Blue-Collar Washington Lobbyists," *CQ Daily Monitor,* March 29, 1999, 7.

the group unusual was its members. They were not Democratic or Republican recruits but members of the National Federation of Independent Business, an organization that had handpicked them to run for Congress. "It's the final stage of sophistication when [interest groups] train their members to actually run for office," declared a business PAC official.[57] Labor unions, as well as business groups, are making the electoral connection (see box on union workers trained as lobbyists).

Congressional party leaders and their allied interest groups also connect electorally when they work together to promote the party's message and thereby encourage voters to back preferred candidates in the next election. For instance, the National Association of Manufacturers coordinated with House GOP leaders to generate public support for President Bush's 2001 tax cut. As commonly occurs on Capitol Hill, they assembled a group of average Americans to communicate the point, in this case, that the tax cuts benefited all taxpayers and not just the well-to-do as the Democrats and their interest group supporters argued in their message offensive.[58]

Interest groups help reelect members to Congress in three other ways. They raise funds and make financial contributions through political action committees, they conduct their own independent campaigns for or against issues and candidates, and they rate the voting record of legislators.

Groups and Campaign Fund-raising

Legislators who dislike raising money—seemingly a majority of them—turn to lobbyists or professional fund-raisers to sponsor parties, luncheons, dinners, or other social events where admission is charged. Lobbyists buy tickets or supply lists of people who should be invited.

Fund-raising events have consumed more and more of legislators' limited time and created new scheduling conflicts—further evidence of the imperatives of the two Congresses, the representative assembly and the lawmaking institution. Members cannot chase money and vote on bills at the same time. To minimize these conflicts between members' electoral and lawmaking responsibilities, windows are opened in the Senate schedule.

> A window is a period of time in which it is understood that there will be no roll-call votes. Senators are assured that they won't be embarrassed by being absent for a recorded vote. Windows usually occur between six and eight in the evening, which is the normal time for holding fundraising cocktail parties.[59]

Sen. Ernest F. Hollings, D-S.C., added that windows now occur Wednesday and Thursday during the lunch period. In his judgment, members devote "at least 20 to 25 percent" of their time to fund-raising.[60]

Veteran senator Robert C. Byrd, D-W.Va., complained that members must spend more time raising money than legislating.[61] A former senator said that he "had to become an expert [at fund-raising] to survive in California politics." He described three principles of raising money based on his experiences. First, "people who give once are likely to give again." If you stop asking, they will stop giving or give to someone else. Second, "it's a compliment . . . to ask someone for a large sum." Third, "people who have given to other causes may give to yours." For this reason, "keep track of all who give what to whom." [62] Congressional critics, and even legislators and lobbyists, question the propriety of fund-raising practices. Members are concerned about implied obligations when they accept help or money from groups. For their part, lobbyists resent pressure from members to give repeatedly to congressional campaigns.

Groups and Advocacy Campaigns

To win, congressional candidates must broaden their sights beyond their partisan opponents to well-funded issue advocacy media campaigns. "We don't just run against our opponent anymore," explained the political adviser to Sen. Tom Daschle, D-S.D. "We run against anybody who wants to come in and run ads." [63] Lobbyists also organize congressional staff focus groups to determine what arguments will most appeal to lawmakers.[64] The president of a telephone trade association described the importance of keeping congressional staffers informed. He even organized a retreat for congressional aides, in part to glean political intelligence about how best to frame his association's issues on Capitol Hill.[65]

Something like reverse lobbying also occurs. Lawmakers try to pass legislation designed to appeal to the outside groups aligned with their partisan and policy objectives. To ensure that a minimum wage bill (backed by organized labor) would be made palatable to corporate and small-business interests (traditional GOP supporters), Newt Gingrich, R-Ga., then House Speaker, met with officials of the National Federation of Independent Business: "So you guys need to tell us items on your agenda" that will make this bill acceptable. "Just give us the list." [66] In short, lawmakers now lobby the lobbyists. They aggressively solicit from their interest group allies legislative input as well as campaign funds.

GOP congressional leaders closely monitor the hiring practices of Washington-based special interests. Called the "K Street Project," GOP leaders pressure lobbying firms to hire Republicans over Democrats for plum positions. The pressure on corporations and associations to hire more Republicans for their top lobbying posts began in the mid-1990s as a way to minimize the influence of Democrats in the lobbying community after their party lost the House after four consecutive decades of majority control. The hiring pressure is especially intense now that the GOP controls the House, Senate, and the White House. "My perspective is, we want to have people at . . . associations who will be receptive to our message and be fair to our proposals," exclaimed Senate GOP Conference chairman Rick Santorum.[67]

Groups and the Policy Payoff

Today there are about four thousand political action committees, and they play a significant role in financing the election of lawmakers, especially incumbents. Journalists and campaign reform groups often posit a direct linear correlation between a member's vote and the amount he or she has received from a PAC. The Center for Responsive Politics, a nonprofit research group, analyzed fourteen heavily lobbied votes and found that "corporations that poured money into Congress typically got the votes they wanted." [68] The nonpartisan and nonprofit Center for Public Integrity also reported that "lawmakers devote themselves to protecting the industries that do them favors and pay for their campaigns." [69]

Other researchers have had a hard time proving such a cause-and-effect relationship. For one thing, groups tend to give money to members who are already favorably disposed to their objectives. Contributions cement a relationship more often than they create one. Moreover, the influence of money must be weighed against other considerations that influence how members vote. These include constituency pressures, party ties, friendship with fellow legislators or lobbyists, conscience, and personal idiosyncrasies and prejudices.[70] As Rep. Barney Frank, D-Mass., put it:

> Votes will beat money any day. Any politician forced to choose between his campaign contributions and strong public sentiment is going to vote public sentiment. Campaign contributions are fungible, you can get new ones. You can't get new voters.[71]

Access is another matter. "There is no question—if you give a lot of money, you will get a lot of access. All you have to do is send in the check," explained one corporate executive.[72] Or as one senator explained:

> If someone came in and said, "I contributed $1,000, or am about to contribute $1,000, to your campaign and I expect you to vote No," I think most Members would, if not kick 'em out of the office, at least make an outraged statement. But, a contributor calls you on a busy day when your inclination is not to take any calls, and if that person says, "I must speak to you urgently," the chances are you will take that call when you wouldn't have taken any other calls. So to that extent I think money does have impact.[73]

Rating Legislators

About a hundred groups keep pressure on legislators by issuing report cards on their voting records. Groups select major issues and then publicize the members' scores (on a scale of zero to one hundred) based on their right or wrong votes on those issues. Members are often warned by colleagues that certain votes will be scored. "You'll hear this as you walk into the chamber: 'This is going to be a scored vote. The environmentalists are going to score this vote, or the AFL-CIO is going to score this vote,' " stated Rep. Joel Hefley, R-Colo.[74] Congressional aides also telephone lobbying groups to determine if certain votes will be scored.

Scorecards not only attract the attention of lawmakers, but they also are used by interest groups to influence members' decisions on selected issues. The liberal Americans for Democratic Action and the conservative American Conservative Union issue score-based ratings that are well known and widely used. One must beware of the ratings game, however. It is always simplistic. The selected issues often are biased, self-serving, and in any case inadequate to judge a member's record. Group strategists, however, defend ratings as "a shorthand way for voters to tell something about their congressman."[75] Many groups that target members for electoral assistance or defeat assign them attention-catching names based on their scorecards: "heroes and zeroes" (from consumer advocates) or the "dirty dozen" (environmental polluters).

Groups use legislative scorecards to determine which candidates will win endorsements and which will receive campaign contributions. Incumbents who hold closely contested seats are usually careful when casting their votes. As a lawmaker who represents a marginal district once said, "If I cast a vote, I might have to answer for it. It may be an issue in the next campaign. Over and over I have to have a response to the question: Why did you do that?" [76] Some of the groups that rate lawmakers maintain Web sites where visitors can register "how they would have voted on the scorecard issues and then compare their own voting record to that of their senators or representatives." [77]

Groups and Legislative Politics

The lobbyist's job is time-consuming because power in Congress is diffused. "Instead of selling his idea to a few senior members," observed one lobbyist, "he must work all members of a committee, on both sides of the aisle, and repeat that work when legislation reaches the floor." [78] Reflecting on the changing styles of modern lobbying, a lawyer-lobbyist said:

> Because of the increasing sophistication of staff, you have to be armed with facts, precedents and legal points. Sure it's a political environment, but it's much more substantive. The old-style, pat-'em-on-the-back lobbyist is gone, or at least going.[79]

An annual survey conducted by the American League of Lobbyists underscored this observation. Lobbyists rated "good information/analysis" given directly to the member as the most effective way to influence a lawmaker.[80]

An open, decentralized institution, Congress affords lobbyists multiple opportunities to shape the fate of legislation. Groups affect, directly or indirectly, virtually every feature of the congressional environment, such as committee activities, legislative agendas, and floor decision making.

Lobbyists and Committees

Many congressional committees reflect the concerns of specific groups, such as farmers, teachers, or veterans. As long as an outside group wields political clout, Congress is unlikely to eliminate the committee it supports. Members, too, seek assignments to prestigious panels, because they provide a good perch from which to raise money from political action committees. For example, when Rep. Billy Tauzin, R-La., became chairman in 2001 of the Energy and Commerce Committee, he had raised over $385,000 during the previous two years from telecommunications, financial, energy, and other industry political action committees whose interests are tied to the panel's jurisdiction.[81] In campaigning for choice committee assignments, legislators sometimes enlist the support of outside organizations. Lobbyists also encourage friendly legislators to bid for committees and subcommittees that handle issues important to their group's interests.

At committee hearings lobbyists employ the usual techniques to win support for their issues. They enlist the assistance of their allies on committees and encourage favorite witnesses to testify. Finding a celebrity witness ensures members' attendance and media attention. An official of a health advocacy group made this observation:

Let me tell you, at hearings where Elizabeth Taylor has testified about AIDS, there wasn't a seat in the house. There were members there not even on the committee. The minute she left, they left.[82]

Committees often form alliances with the bureaucrats and lobbyists who regularly testify before them and with whom members and staff aides periodically meet. Scholars and journalists use the term *subgovernment* for the three-way, policy-making alliances of committees, executive agencies, and interest groups.

These triangular relationships dominate policy arenas less today than in the past. Other contending forces (citizens groups, aggressive journalists, assertive presidents) have ended their policy monopoly. Fluid issue networks, in which diverse participants and groups influence decision making, better characterize the relationships within and among policy domains. When Democrats ruled Capitol Hill, favored clusters of interest groups embraced such issues as welfare programs, environmental protection, and civil rights. With the GOP in charge, the insiders tend to represent such interests as small business, the family lobby, and the military. But many lobbying clusters—for example, big business and veterans—seem equally at home with both political parties. A few committees even have a formal staff position, such as "director of coalitions," that works with "various coalitions that back legislation" advocated by the committee.[83]

Lobbyists and Legislation

Lobbyists are active during all phases of the legislative process. During the committee phase, they draft bills and amendments for members and testify at hearings. They often "help the policy-making process by pointing out how different industries and regions might be affected by various provisions, perhaps in ways unintended by those who drafted them." [84] Sometimes groups blanket Capitol Hill with materials or devices to make a point. The Sierra Club, for instance, sent Hill offices a letter with a condom attached. "I'm sending you this condom," wrote the club's president, "to reinforce our message that international family planning programs, free speech, and environmental protection deserve extra protection." [85]

When measures reach the House and Senate floor, groups focus on influencing votes. They prepare arguments for and against expected floor amendments, work to round up their supporters for key votes, draft floor statements and amendments, and plan strategy with friendly lawmakers. For example, when the Senate passed a patients' bill of rights measure in summer 2001, lobbying coalitions on opposite sides of the issue planned grassroots efforts and legislative strategies with their supporters on and off Capitol Hill. "Our approach is a political campaign-approach," stated one lobbyist, including the use of nightly tracking polls to assess how public opinion was influencing lawmakers' views.[86]

Lobbyists and lawmakers also understand that the wording of legislation can be all-important. The deletion of one word—*nonprofit*—from an obscure passage of a four hundred-page welfare bill produced an immediate scramble for federal dollars. For-profit orphanages competed with nonprofit foster homes "for the billions of dollars that the Government spends each year to support poor children who are taken away from homes judged unfit." [87] Regularly, on behalf of the interests they represent, lobbyists supply lawmakers with the exact legislative language they want enacted into law. For their part, members sponsor bills and amendments that win them group support—again, the two Congresses at work.

On the one hand, groups help to frame Congress's policy and oversight agenda by pushing the House and Senate to address their concerns. Many legislative preoccupations of the past several decades—civil rights, abortion, environmental and consumer protection, deregulation, and child care among them—reflect vigorous lobbying. On the other hand, a lobbyist's job is often to stop things from happening. "Most of the stuff that we do in this business is protection—negative stuff," stated Tom Korologos, one of Washington's premier lobbyists. "For the most part, it's stop this regulation, stop that tax, stop this crazy scheme," including using the courts to challenge or bolster executive or legislative actions.[88] Often, lobbyists exercise more influence on obscure issues compared with topics that receive substantial public and press attention.

Informal Groups of Members

Congress always has had informal groups, caucuses, coalitions, clubs, alliances, blocs, and cliques. What makes today's informal congressional groups different from earlier ones is their greater number (over two hundred in the early 2000s), diversity, and capacity to monitor developments that affect their interests.[89]

Some state delegations, often including House and Senate members, meet frequently on either a partisan or bipartisan basis. At a weekly breakfast or lunch they discuss state and national issues and internal congressional politics, plan strategies to capture their share of federal funds and projects, champion colleagues for coveted committee assignments, or back candidates for party leadership positions.

Types of Groups

Many informal congressional groups have ties with outside interests. For example, the Steel Caucus maintains links with the steel industry and the Textile Caucus with textile manufacturers. Interest groups can be instrumental in forming these informal legislative entities. The idea for the Mushroom Caucus (to protect mushroom producers from foreign imports) originated at a May 1977 luncheon for House members, which was sponsored by the American Mushroom Institute.[90] The Black, Hispanic, Asian, and Women's Caucuses were established to give their national constituencies—and the members themselves—more recognition and clout in Congress.

Other groups have a regional purpose. Members of the Northeast-Midwest Congressional Coalition want to retain their share of energy supplies, encourage federal aid to cities, and promote manufacturing in the Frost Belt states. The Sunbelt Caucus, a southern representative explained, was established in 1979 "in large part to counter lobbying and information-disseminating activities of the Northeast-Midwest Coalition." [91] Each move to protect a region's interests is likely to prompt a countermove from another region.

Caucuses also are formed to focus on issues that overlap several committees' jurisdictions or that fail to receive sufficient committee attention. Sometimes caucuses can buttress their members' strength back home. The House Coal Caucus offered its initiator, Rep. Nick J. Rahall II, D-W.Va., significant political benefits in his coal-producing district, revealing another aspect of the two Congresses.

Legislative Effect of Caucuses

The effect of informal groups on policy making is not clear. Some legislators believe they undermine party unity and lead to the balkanization of the institution. Nonetheless, informal groups can shape Congress's policy agenda and influence policy making. For example, members of Congress who are on the Internet Caucus—many from rural areas—have been instrumental in shaping telecommunications legislation. The rural members of this caucus want to ensure that their constituencies are not left behind technologically. "There is a common theme with the belief that telecommunications can be a bridge for rural areas into the American economic mainstream," remarked Rep. Rick Boucher, D-Va., cochairman of the Internet Caucus. [92] To be sure, caucus members want to attract high-tech industries to their states or districts.

Informal groups serve as contact points for liaison officers in the executive branch. They provide executive and White House officials with information and can play an essential role in coordinating a legislative strategy and building coalitions. Caucuses permit members to discuss common strategies and join with other groups to pass or defeat legislation. Finally, caucuses enable lawmakers to align themselves publicly with a cause or interest. For many, these memberships are simply another way of taking a position. Paradoxically, informal groups foster both decentralizing and integrative tendencies in Congress. [93]

Regulation of Lobbying

For more than one hundred years Congress intermittently considered ways to regulate lobbying—a right protected by the First Amendment: "the right of the people . . . to petition the Government for a redress of grievances." Not until 1946, however, did Congress enact its first comprehensive lobbying law, the Federal Regulation of Lobbying Act (Title III of the Legislative Reorganization Act of that year). This law's ineffectiveness finally led to passage of the Lobby Disclosure Act of 1995. (A "Guide to the Lobbying Disclosure Act" can be found on the Web site of the clerk of the U.S. House of Representatives: http://clerk.house.gov.)

The 1946 Lobbying Law

The main objective of the 1946 act was to disclose lobbying activities to the public. Persons trying to influence Congress were required to register with the clerk of the House or the secretary of the Senate and to report quarterly on the amount of money received and spent for lobbying. The law's authors, although loath to propose direct control of lobbying, believed that "professionally inspired efforts to put pressure upon Congress cannot be conducive to well-considered legislation." Hence the law stressed registration and reporting:

> The availability of information regarding organized groups and full knowledge of their expenditures for influencing legislation, their membership and the source of contributions to them of large amounts of money, would prove helpful to Congress in evaluating their representations without impairing the rights of any individual or group freely to express its opinion to the Congress.[94]

The lobby law soon proved ineffective. In 1954 the Supreme Court upheld its constitutionality, but the decision (*United States v. Harriss*) significantly weakened the law. First, the Court said that only lobbyists paid to represent someone else must register, exempting lobbyists who spent their own money. Second, the Court held that registration applied only to persons whose "principal purpose" was to influence legislation. As a result, many trade associations, labor unions, professional organizations, consumer groups, and Washington lawyers avoided registering because lobbying was not their principal activity. Some lobbyists claimed immunity from the law on the pretext that their job was to inform, not influence, legislators. Finally, the Court held that the act applied only to lobbyists who contacted members directly. This interpretation excluded indirect lobbying activities that, for example, generated grassroots pressure on Congress.

Lawmakers tried repeatedly to plug the loopholes of the 1946 law. These attempts foundered largely because it was difficult to regulate lobbying without trespassing on citizens' rights to contact their elected representatives. Finally, after repeated efforts to "change the way Washington does business"—a campaign theme advocated by many members—the two parties came together to enact the first major overhaul of the 1946 act.

The Lobby Disclosure Act of 1995

Under the Lobby Disclosure Act of 1995, which became effective on January 1, 1996, new rules apply to individuals and firms who lobby Congress

Lobbying Reforms

The Lobby Disclosure Act of 1995 tightened the rules for lobbyists. An outline of the major changes follows:

- A lobbyist is defined as anyone who spends 20 percent or more of his or her time in paid lobbying.
- Lobbying activities include preparation and research intended to influence policy as well as direct contacts with policy makers and their staff.
- Lobbyists are required to register with Congress. They must disclose the names of their clients and the issues they are lobbying on and state approximately how much clients are paying for their services.[a]
- Lobbyists must file disclosure reports every six months. Those who fail to comply are subject to civil fines up to $50,000.
- Nonprofit groups under IRS Section 501(C)4 that lobby cannot receive direct federal grants.
- Former U.S. trade representatives and deputies are banned for life from lobbying for foreign interests.

Source: Washington Times, November 30, 1995, A14.

[a] There are some exemptions; for example, lobbyists paid $5,000 or less in six months are not required to register.

and senior executive branch officials (see box on lobbying reforms). The law broadened the definition of people who must register as lobbyists (all those who spend one-fifth of their time trying to influence lawmakers, congressional aides, or high executive officials). Registrations of lobbyists quickly soared. A study by the General Accounting Office determined that when the law took effect "only 6,078 individuals and organizations had registered" under the outdated 1946 act. "After the new law took effect, a total of 14,912 lobbyists registered" with 10,612 being first-time registrants.[95] The law is administered by the public records offices of the House and Senate.

Lobbyists are required to "provide semiannual disclosures showing who their clients are, what policies they are trying to influence and roughly how much money they are spending for lobbying."[96] Civil fines of up to $50,000 can be imposed on those who fail to comply. Grassroots lobbying is exempt from the law, as are lobbyists paid $5,000 or less semiannually and organizations that use their own employees to lobby. The 1995 lobby disclosure law was amended three years later to make several technical corrections, such as clarifying the definition of "lobbying contact."

Although the 1995 lobby law is better than the old one, it is minimally enforced, according to some analysts. Not a single firm or lobbyist has yet to receive an official notice for failure to file the required reports. Some firms and organizations even underreport their lobbying expenditures. "Companies, trade associations, and lobby firms often misreport—intentionally or inadvertently—how much money they shell out or take in." Administrators of the law contend, however, that there have been no serious cases of noncompliance or evasion.[97]

Foreign Lobbying

The 1995 law also amended the Foreign Agents Registration Act of 1938, which required those who lobby on behalf of foreign governments or political parties to register with the Justice Department. The 1995 law broadened the definition of foreign lobbyists to include individuals who lobby on behalf of foreign-owned commercial enterprises. It required them to register with the clerk of the House and the secretary of the Senate. About five hundred lobbyists have registered with the Justice Department as agents representing foreign governments or parties (see usdoj.gov/criminal/fara).

Given the role of the United States in the global economy and in military security, combined with the information technology era, many foreign nationals and Americans who work for foreign clients spend considerable time and money lobbying Capitol Hill and promoting their interests nationwide. After Turkey in 2003 turned down the United States' request to use its air bases from which to attack Iraq to oust Saddam Hussein, that nation boosted its "public relations work on Capitol Hill," having signed a $600,000 annual contract with a Washington-based lobbying firm. By way of comparison, Saudi Arabia paid Washington lobbyists $11.3 million in 2002.[98] Covert campaign contributions by foreign governments and foreign nationals to American elections are a problem that congressional committees have investigated.

The American Israel Public Affairs Committee (AIPAC) is not a registered foreign lobby because it is independent of foreign sponsorship and composed of American citizens who have a keen interest in the mother country. (Ethnic lobbying by citizens of Irish, Greek, or Polish lineage, for instance, is an effective form of advocacy, and it seems sure to grow in this period of increased immigrant flow to the United States.) Yet AIPAC is one of the most influential lobbying groups in the United States. For instance, AIPAC "sponsors tours of Israel for legislators and keeps in touch with all departments of the United States Government with the slightest involvement in Israel. It has student affiliates at more than 200 campuses."[99] Many other nations and international interests also have covered the costs of lawmakers and congressional aides who visit their countries on fact-finding missions.

The globalization of American lobbying efforts is also occurring. Worried that international restrictions and regulations might adversely affect the gun trade and the ability of Americans to acquire firearms, the National Rifle Association formed a transnational organization of gun groups and firearms manufacturers from eleven other countries (the World Forum).[100] The organization's objectives are to fend off international pressure for tighter gun controls in the United States and to defend the right to bear arms worldwide. As another example, multinational cigarette makers, such as Philip Morris and British American Tobacco, "have embarked on a global lobbying campaign to undermine a proposed international treaty that could place tight restrictions on cigarette advertising and smuggling." [101] Many U.S.-based corporations also hire lobbyists who can operate globally to protect their interests in Europe or other parts of the world when disputes arise about trade, agriculture, antitrust laws, the environment, and other issues.[102]

Globalization of the world's economy also influences congressional lobbying. In the late 1990s U.S. antitrust officials approved the Boeing aircraft company's merger with rival McDonnell Douglas in part because the global marketplace seems to require firms to be larger and more efficient to survive. This global imperative enhanced Boeing's political clout on Capitol Hill by broadening its ties beyond lawmakers in its home base in the state of Washington to include "congressional delegations from California, Missouri, Texas, Alabama, and Pennsylvania. . . . Through subcontractors and their employees, they can bring direct influence to bear on virtually every other delegation in Congress." [103] For example, Boeing executives enlisted machine and tool subcontractors in El Monte, California, to lobby their representatives to support the renewal of China's favorable trade status with the United States. Boeing executives said the suppliers readily agreed to lobby Congress because "their firms depend as much as Boeing does on business generated by aircraft sales to China." [104]

Conclusion

From the nation's beginning, lobbying and lawmaking have been twin phenomena. Lobbying "has been so deeply woven into the American political fabric that one could, with considerable justice, assert that the history of lobbying comes close to being the history of American legislation." [105]

Recent years have witnessed an explosion in the number and types of groups organized to pursue their ends on Capitol Hill. Compared with a decade ago, more industry associations, public affairs lobbies (such as Common Cause), single-issue groups, political action committees, and foreign agents are engaged in lobbying. Some of these groups employ new grassroots and technological lobbying techniques. Many victories today are won in Washington because of sophisticated lobbying campaigns back in home states or districts.

No one questions that groups and lobbyists have a rightful public role, but some aspects of lobbying warrant concern. Groups push Congress to pass laws that benefit the few and not the many. They exaggerate their members' views and hinder compromise. They frequently misrepresent the voting records of legislators in their rating schemes and pour money into campaigns of their allies (mainly incumbents). Lawmakers who defy single-issue groups find at election time that these organizations pull out all the stops to defeat them.

Built-in checks constrain group pressures, however. Legislators can play one competing group off against another, and knowledgeable staff aides can provide members with reports and studies to counter the lobbyists' arguments. Lawmakers' own expertise is another informal check on lobbyists. Finally, there are self-imposed constraints. Lobbyists who misrepresent issues or mislead members soon find their access permanently closed off.

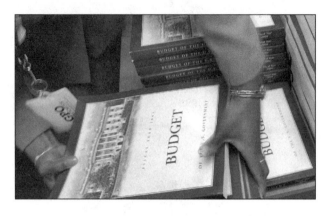

Policy making and budgeting are inextricably linked on Capitol Hill. Left, hot off the printing presses at the Government Printing Office, copies of President Bush's over $2.2 trillion budget for fiscal year 2004 are distributed to reporters. Right, House Appropriations chair C.W. Bill Young, R-Fla., left, and Senate Appropriations chair Ted Stevens, R-Alaska, put the finishing touches on a spending bill during a House-Senate conference meeting. Below, Speaker J. Dennis Hastert, R-Ill., shares a laugh with fellow GOP leaders Tom DeLay, R-Texas, Ways and Means chair Bill Thomas, R-Calif., and Richard Armey, R-Texas, during a telephone call to President Bush after the House passed his $1.35 trillion tax cut. Rep. J.C. Watts, R-Okla., is seated behind the Speaker.

14

Congress, Budgets, and Domestic Policy Making

The 2003 military victory ending Saddam Hussein's regime in Iraq turned congressional and presidential attention to a number of important and interconnected domestic and fiscal issues. One involved the costs associated with winning the peace, such as providing reconstruction and humanitarian assistance to Iraq. Another concerned the financial competition between "guns and butter"; that is, how to pay for military and homeland security needs and still address domestic requirements or party commitments, such as providing a prescription drug benefit for the elderly. Finally, many lawmakers believed that the country could not afford another round of tax cuts—President George W. Bush was the first chief executive to recommend cutting taxes in a wartime environment—when deficits were escalating and spending was increasing for security and other programs. Understandably worried about the outcome of his tax-cut plan (he initially requested $726 billion over ten years) in Congress, President Bush used his wartime popularity and launched "a nationwide campaign to pressure reluctant lawmakers to vote for his tax cut," which the administration retitled "the president's job and growth package." [1]

Federal budgeting involves setting priorities, but difficult fiscal decisions do not always come easily to either Congress or the president. On the one hand, Congress "does not make hard decisions," exclaimed Sen. George V. Voinovich, R-Ohio. In his judgment, "This place continues to say yes [to tax cuts and spending hikes] without any consideration of the next generation." [2] On the other hand, presidents confront a comparable circumstance. For instance, President Bush expressed a popular sentiment when he said: "Whatever it costs to defend our country, we will pay it." Yet he refused to ask citizens to pay for it. "On the contrary, in the face of massive new spending, he proposed *additional* tax cuts." [3] A rationale for the proposed tax cuts is that they will stimulate economic growth and produce the revenue to eliminate any deficit. Conflicts about policies and the money to pay for them inhere in the lawmaking process.

Definitions of Policy

Because policies ultimately are what government is about, definitions of policy and policy making—not surprisingly—are diverse and influenced by the beholder's eye. David Easton's celebrated definition of public policy as society's "authoritative allocations" of values or resources is one approach to the question. To put it another way, policies can be regarded as reflecting "who gets what, when, and how" in a society. A more serviceable definition of policy is offered by Randall B. Ripley and Grace A. Franklin: Policy is what the government says and does about perceived problems.[4]

How can one recognize policies? The answer is not as simple as it may seem. Many policies are explicitly labeled and recognized as authoritative statements of what the government is doing, or intends to do, about a particular matter. The measures may be far-reaching (financing the Social Security system, for example); they may be trivial (naming federal buildings after deceased public officials). Nonetheless, they are obvious statements of policy. They are usually written down, often in precise legal language. They boast documented legislative histories in committee hearings, reports, or floor deliberations that indicate what lawmakers had in mind as they hammered out the policy's final provisions.

Not all policies, however, are formal enough to be considered the law of the land. Some are articulated by officials but, for one reason or another, are never set down in laws or rules. The Monroe Doctrine, which declared U.S. resistance to European intervention in the Western Hemisphere, was inserted into the president's 1823 State of the Union report written by Secretary of State John Quincy Adams. It has been adhered to ever since by successive generations of policy makers. Other policies, especially of a symbolic or exhortatory nature, gain currency in the eyes of elites or the public without formal or legal elaboration.

Some policies stress substance—programs designed to build the nation's defense, for example. Others stress procedure, such as those imposing personnel ceilings on federal agencies, mandating program management standards, or requiring contractors' insurance for military weapons. Still others are amalgams of substance and procedure, such as fast-track provisions (renamed "trade promotion authority" by the George W. Bush administration) written into trade laws and other laws that expedite committee and floor action in each house. Ways of putting legislation on a fast track include time limits on committee consideration of a bill and on floor debate of the measure, prohibitions on the offering of floor amendments, and requirements obligating each chamber to pass identical legislation, thus obviating the need for a conference committee to iron out bicameral differences.

Finally, some policies are made by negation. Doing nothing about a problem often has results that are as profound as passing a law about it. The United States had no general immigration law before 1924 and no overall medical care program before 1965, but its policies on those matters—mainly favoring unregulated private activity—were unmistakable.

The process of arriving at these policies is policy making. The process may be simple or complex, highly publicized or nearly invisible, concentrated or diffuse. The policy may happen suddenly, such as air strikes ordered by the president. Or it may require years or even decades to formulate, as in the case of civil rights or Medicare for the elderly.[5]

Stages of Policy Making

Whatever the time frame, policy making normally has four distinct stages: setting the agenda, formulating policy, adopting policy, and implementing policy.

Setting the Agenda

At the initial stage, public problems are spotted and moved onto the national agenda, which can be defined as "the list of subjects to which government officials and those around them are paying serious attention."[6] In a large, pluralistic country such as the United States, the national agenda at any given moment is extensive and vigorously debated.

How do problems get placed on the agenda? Some are heralded by a crisis or some other prominent event—the bombing of a building by terrorists, a schoolyard shooting, a national disaster, or a campaign-funding scandal. Others are occasioned by the gradual accumulation of knowledge; for example, increasing awareness of an environmental hazard such as acid rain or ozone depletion. Still other agenda items represent the accumulation of past problems that no longer can be avoided or ignored. Finally, agendas may be set in motion by political processes—election results, turnover in Congress, or shifts in public opinion.[7] The 1994 election results gave the GOP control of Congress and a chance to pursue its "revolution" in downsizing government. The next four elections conveyed a different message—generally a recognition of government's key role in ensuring the nation's security and encouraging economic growth—to the GOP Congress and to presidents of both parties.

Agenda items are pushed by policy entrepreneurs, people willing to invest time and energy to promote a particular issue. Numerous Washington, D.C., think tanks and interest groups, especially at the beginning of a new president's term, issue reports that seek to influence the economic, social, or foreign policy agenda of the nation. Welfare and Social Security reforms, for instance, have long been advocated by various think tanks. Usually, however, elected officials and their staffs or appointees are more likely to shape agendas than are career bureaucrats or nongovernmental actors.[8] Notable policy entrepreneurs on Capitol Hill are party and committee leaders who push their party's policy initiatives.

Lawmakers frequently are policy entrepreneurs because they are expected to voice the concerns of constituents and organized groups and to seek legislative solutions. Politicians generally gravitate toward issues that are visible, salient, and solvable. Tough, arcane, or conflictual problems may be shunned because they offer few payoffs and little hope of success.

Sometimes only a crisis, such as the gasoline and natural gas price increases in the early 2000s, can force lawmakers to address difficult questions.

Paradoxically, despite the energy-saving innovations introduced in the aftermath of the oil shortages (triggered by an oil boycott led by OPEC—the Organization of Petroleum Exporting Countries) and long gasoline lines of the 1970s, Americans today are as dependent on imported oil as they were three decades ago and use more energy to power bigger homes and larger trucks and automobiles, such as sports utility vehicles (SUVs). Forecasters predict more short- and long-term energy woes unless steps are taken to develop alternative fuels, change habits of consumption, encourage conservation, and reduce the spiraling demand for oil, especially from the volatile Middle East. This kind of creeping crisis is often difficult for members of Congress to grapple with, in part because of the two Congresses dilemma. As conscientious lawmakers, members might want to forge long-term solutions. But as representatives of their constituents, they must respond to their immediate concerns about rising energy prices.

Formulating Policy

In the second stage of policy making, items on the political agenda are discussed and potential solutions are explored. Members of Congress and their staffs play crucial roles by conducting hearings and writing committee reports. They are aided by policy experts in executive agencies, interest groups, and the private sector.

Another term for this stage is *policy incubation,* which entails "keeping a proposal alive while it picks up support, or waits for a better climate, or while a consensus begins to form that the problem to which it is addressed exists." [9] Sometimes this process takes only a few months; more often it requires years. During Dwight D. Eisenhower's administration, for example, congressional Democrats explored and refined domestic policy options that, while not immediately accepted, were ripe for adoption by the time their party's nominee, John F. Kennedy, was elected president in 1960.[10]

The incubation process not only brings policies to maturity but also refines solutions to the problems. The process may break down if workable solutions are not available. The seeming intractability of many modern issues complicates problem solving. Thomas S. Foley, D-Wash. (Speaker, 1989–1995), held that issues had become far more perplexing since he came to Congress in 1965. At that time "the civil rights issue facing the legislators was whether the right to vote should be federally guaranteed for blacks and Hispanics. Now members are called on to deal with more ambiguous policies like affirmative action and racial quotas." [11] Add to these such complex contemporary topics as physician-assisted suicide, human cloning, and genetic discrimination.

Solutions to problems normally involve "some fairly simple routines emphasizing the tried and true (or at least not discredited)." [12] A repertoire of proposals—for example, blue-ribbon commissions, trust funds, or pilot projects—can be applied to a variety of unsolved problems. Problem solvers also must guard against recommending solutions that will be viewed as worse than the problem.

Adopting Policy

Laws are ideas whose time has come. The right time for a policy is what scholar John W. Kingdon calls the *policy window:* the opportunity presented by circumstances and attitudes to enact a policy into law. Policy entrepreneurs must seize the opportunity before the policy window closes and the idea's time has passed.

Once policies are ripe for adoption, they must gain popular acceptance. This is the function of legitimation, the process through which policies come to be viewed by the public as right or proper. Inasmuch as citizens are expected to comply with laws or regulations—pay taxes, observe rules, or make sacrifices of one sort or another—the policies themselves must appear to have been properly considered and enacted. A nation whose policies lack legitimacy is in deep trouble.

Symbolic acts, such as members voting on the House or Senate floor or the president signing a bill, signal to everyone that policies have been duly adopted according to traditional forms. Hearings and debates, moreover, serve not only to fine-tune policies but also to cultivate support from affected interests. Responding to critics of Congress's slowness in adopting energy legislation, Sen. Ted Stevens, R-Alaska, asked these questions:

> Would you want an energy bill to flow through the Senate and not have anyone consider the impacts on housing or on the automotive industry or on the energy industries that provide our light and power? Should we ignore the problems of the miner or the producer or the distributor? Our legislative process must reflect all of the problems if the public is to have confidence in the government.[13]

Legitimating, in other words, usually demands a measured pace and attention to procedural details. Another strategy is to move quickly in response to a public outcry—before opposition forces can mobilize—to enact bold changes, knowing that the details will have to be refined and adjusted later.

Implementing Policy

In the final stage, policies shaped by the legislature and at the highest executive levels are put into effect, usually by a federal agency. Policies are not self-executing; they must be promulgated and enforced. A law or executive order rarely spells out exactly how a particular policy should be implemented. Congress and the president usually delegate most decisions about implementation to the responsible agencies under broad but stated guidelines. Implementation determines the ultimate effect of policies. Officials of the executive branch can thwart a policy by foot dragging or sheer inefficiency. By the same token, overzealous administrators can push a policy far beyond its creators' intent.

Congress therefore must exercise its oversight role. It may require executive agencies to report or consult with congressional committees or to follow certain formal procedures. Members of Congress get feedback on the operation of federal programs through a variety of channels: media coverage, interest group protests, and even casework for constituents. With such information Congress can and often does pass judgment by adjusting funding, introducing amendments, or recasting the basic legislation governing a particular policy.

Types of Domestic Policies

One way to understand public policies is to analyze the nature of the policies themselves. Scholars have classified policies in many different ways.[14] Our typology identifies three types of domestic policies: distributive, regulatory, and redistributive.

Distributive Policies

Distributive policies or programs are government actions that convey tangible benefits to private individuals, groups, or firms. Invariably, they bestow subsidies, tax breaks, or advantageous regulatory provisions upon favored individuals or groups. The benefits are often called pork (usually special interest spending for projects in members' states or districts), although that appellation is sometimes difficult to define. After all, "one person's pork is another person's steak." The projects come in several varieties.

> Dams, roads and bridges, known as "green pork," are old hat. These days, there is also "academic pork" in the form of research grants to colleges, "defense pork" in the form of geographically specific military expenditures and lately "high-tech pork," for example the intense fight to authorize research into super computers and high-definition television (HDTV).[15]

The presence of distributive politics—which makes many interests better off and few, if any, visibly worse off—is natural in Congress, which as a non-hierarchical institution must build coalitions to function. A textbook example was the $1 billion-plus National Parks and Recreation Act of 1978. Dubbed the "Park Barrel" bill, it created so many parks, historical sites, seashores, wilderness areas, wild and scenic rivers, and national trails that it sailed through the Interior (now Resources) Committee and passed the House by a 341–61 vote. "Notice how quiet we are. We all got something in there," said one House member, after the Rules Committee cleared the bill in five minutes flat. Another member quipped, "If it had a blade of grass and a squirrel, it got in the bill."[16] Distributive politics of this kind throws into sharp relief the two Congresses notion: national policy as a mosaic of local interests.

The politics of distribution works best when tax revenues are expanding, fueled by high productivity and economic growth. When productivity declines or tax cuts squeeze revenues, it often becomes difficult to add new benefits or expand old ones. Yet distributive impulses remain strong even in these circumstances as lawmakers in both parties work to ensure that money is spent for particular purposes in their districts or states. For example, in 2003, amidst concern about rising deficits, the uncertainty of costs associated with reconstructing Iraq, and hikes in the price tag for homeland security, scores of House members asked the Transportation and Infrastructure Committee to funnel money for highway and transit projects to their districts. According to one account, the panel has received fifty-three hundred requests from Republicans and Democrats alike "worth more than $500 billion." [17] Congressional leaders also use the promise of projects in bills to secure the votes they need for passage of legislation.

Sen. Trent Lott, R-Miss., highlighted the two Congresses theme and the prevailing appeal of distributive policy making to members of Congress when he remarked: "Mississippi is getting tired of dirt roads; we want some asphalt. I also want some more asphalt for my buddies in Florida, Texas, and Alabama." [18] Or, as Lott's colleague Rick Santorum, R-Pa., said: "Republicans feel very strongly about infrastructure. It's an area where we feel real comfortable spending money." [19]

Regulatory Policies

Regulatory policies are designed to protect the public against harm or abuse that might result from unbridled private activity. For example, the Food and Drug Administration monitors standards for foodstuffs and tests drugs for purity, safety, and effectiveness, and the Federal Trade Commission guards against illegal business practices, such as deceptive advertising.

Federal regulation against certain abuses dates from the late nineteenth century, when the Interstate Commerce Act and the Sherman Antitrust Act were enacted to protect against transport and monopoly abuses. As the twentieth century dawned, scandalous practices in slaughterhouses and food processing plants led to meatpacking, food, and drug regulations. The stock market collapse in 1929 and the Great Depression paved the way for the New Deal legislation that would regulate the banking and securities industries and labor-management relations. Consumer rights and environmental protection came of age in the 1960s and 1970s.

Regulation is not popular with the recent GOP-controlled Congresses. Republicans wanted to cut back the government's role by repealing or modifying many federal regulations that they viewed as overly costly and burdensome, especially to businesses. Much of the clean-air debate, for instance, involves the basic issue of costs versus benefits: Do the public health benefits of cleaner air outweigh the financial costs?[20] Environmentalists and health advocates argue that tougher standards for regulating air pollution would prevent suffering and save the lives of thousands who are afflicted with asthma and other lung diseases. Industries and conservative groups attack these claims and contend that the "regulations are unnecessary, would be too costly and would yield only marginal health benefits." [21]

Redistributive Policies

Redistribution, which visibly shifts resources from one group to another, is the most difficult of all political feats. Because they are controversial, redistributive policies engage a broad spectrum of political actors—not only in the House and Senate chambers but also in the executive branch and among interest groups and the public at large. Redistributive issues tend to be ideological. They often separate liberals and conservatives because they upset relationships between social and economic classes. Theodore R. Marmor described the fight over medical care for the aged as "cast in terms of class conflict":

> The leading adversaries . . . brought into the opposing camps a large number of groups whose interests were not directly affected by the Medicare outcome. . . . Ideological charges and countercharges dominated public discussion, and each side seemed to regard compromise as unacceptable.[22]

Most of the divisive socioeconomic issues of the past generation—civil rights, affirmative action, school busing, welfare, homelessness, abortion, tax reform—were redistributive problems. A redistributive issue for the twenty-first century concerns the increasing share of the federal budget that goes to the elderly compared with everyone else in society. Tax dollars spent on entitlement programs such as Social Security and Medicare absorb an ever-increasing proportion of federal dollars, which then are unavailable for other important social, domestic, or security needs.

Federal budgeting is marked not only by conflict but also by techniques to disguise the redistributions or make them more palatable. Omnibus budget packages permit legislators to approve cuts en bloc instead of one by one, and across-the-board formulas (such as freezes) give the appearance of spreading the misery equally to affected groups. In all such vehicles, distributive elements are added to placate the more vocal opponents of change.

Characteristics of Congressional Policy Making

As a policy-making body, Congress displays the traits and biases of its membership and structure and of the larger political system. Congress is bicameral with divergent electoral and procedural traditions. It is representative, especially where geographic interests are concerned. It is decentralized, having few mechanisms for integrating or coordinating its policy decisions. It sometimes is inclined toward enacting symbolic measures rather than substantive ones. And it is generally reactive, mirroring conventional perceptions of problems.

Bicameralism

Several differences between the House and Senate—their terms of office, the character of their constituencies, and the size of their legislative bodies— powerfully influence the policies they make. Six-year terms, it is argued, allow senators to play the statesman for at least part of each term before they are forced by oncoming elections to concentrate on fence mending. This distinction may be more apparent than real, but empirical studies of senators' voting habits lend some support to it.

The various constituencies unquestionably pull in divergent directions. The more homogeneous House districts often promote clear and unambiguous positions on a narrower range of questions than those considered by senators, who must weigh the claims of many competing interests on a broad range of matters. The sizes of the two chambers, moreover, dictate procedural characteristics. House rules are designed to allow majorities to have their way. In contrast, Senate rules give individual senators great latitude to influence action. As a GOP senator once said: "The Senate has the strongest minority of any minority on Earth, and the weakest majority of any on Earth." [23]

The two chambers, in short, differ in outlook, constituency, and strategy. Bicameralism is less important in promoting or discouraging particular kinds of policies, writes Benjamin I. Page, than in "the furtherance of deliberation, the production of evidence, and the revealing of error." [24]

Localism

Congressional policies respond to constituents' needs, particularly those that can be mapped geographically. Sometimes these needs are pinpointed with startling directness. For example, an aviation noise control bill required construction of a control tower "at latitude 40 degrees, 43 minutes, 45 seconds north and at longitude 73 degrees, 24 minutes, 50 seconds west"—the exact location of a Farmingdale, New York, airport in the district of the Democratic representative who requested the provision.[25]

Usually, however, programs are directed toward states, municipalities, counties, or geographic regions. Funds are often transferred directly to local government agencies, which in turn deliver the aid or services to citizens. Lawmakers often require states and localities to fund some national programs. These unfunded mandates strain state budgets and arouse the ire of state and local officials. In 1995 President Bill Clinton signed into law the Unfunded Mandates Reform Act, which governs any proposed mandate that the Congressional Budget Office (CBO) estimates will cost state and local governments $50 million or more. Congress must either "make provision to pay for the mandate . . . or take a separate recorded vote to waive the requirement, thus holding members of Congress accountable for their decision." [26] Lawmakers must now consider the costs of any federal requirements they impose on state and local governments. However, the promise or intent of the law is not always met. The 2001 No Child Left Behind education law, for instance, imposes on today's cash-strapped states mandatory testing in all public schools. The fiscal 2004 estimate by the Bush administration to fund this requirement is $30 billion. "But the budget for it is only $21 billion. The states must make up the $9 billion difference." [27]

National and local policies are necessarily intertwined. National policies can be advanced by state and local governments, or states and localities can develop innovations that can spur national action. The threat of terrorist attacks in the United States means that any such calamity will be confronted by first responders—police officers, fire fighters, public health officials, and others on the state and local level. On other issues as well, the states are the testing grounds, or laboratories, for social, economic, and political experiments.

Many policy debates revolve around not only which governmental level can most effectively carry out a responsibility but also which level best promotes particular values. Liberals, for example, seek a significant role for the national government in the enforcement of civil rights and environmental protection. Conservatives support an activist national government on defense and security matters. Although empowerment and decentralization are popular concepts among today's conservatives, in previous decades they were powerful slogans for liberals who supported equal rights for women and local Head Start programs for children. When it suits their purposes, both liberals and conservatives are capable of advocating either national actions or local preferences, depending on which level of government would best serve their objective.

Piecemeal Policy Making

Policies all too often mirror Congress's scattered and decentralized structure. Typically, they are considered piecemeal, reflecting the patchwork of committee and subcommittee jurisdictions. Congress's segmented decision making is typified by authorizing and appropriating processes in which separate committees consider the same programs often without consulting each other.

The structure of a policy frequently depends on which committees have reported it. Working from varying jurisdictions, committees can take different approaches to the same problem. A program from the taxing committees will feature tax provisions, from the Appropriations Committees a fiscal approach, from the commerce panels a regulatory perspective, and so forth. The approach may be well or ill suited to the policy objective. It all depends on which committee was best positioned to promote the bill.

Symbolic Policy Making

At heart, congressional policy making often concerns appearances more than substance. Symbolic actions are important to all politicians. Often bills are passed to give the impression that action is being taken when the impact or efficacy of the measure is wholly unknown. Groups outside Congress continually demand, "Don't just stand there, do something." Doing something is often the only politically feasible choice, even when no one really knows what to do or whether inaction might be just as effective.[28]

Reactive Policy Making

Elected officials are seldom far ahead of or far behind the collective views of the citizenry. Hence it would be misguided to expect the national legislature routinely to express radical solutions to problems. Members know that radical views are unlikely to attract widespread public support. Congress is essentially a reactive institution. As one House member explained:

> When decision rests on the consent of the governed, it comes slowly, only after consensus has built or crisis has focused public opinion in some unusual way, the representatives in the meantime hanging back until the signs are unmistakable. Government decision, then, is not generally the cutting edge of change but a belated reaction to change.[29]

The reactive character of Congress's policy making is evident in its budget process. Under pressures to reform, Congress reacted in 1974, 1985, and again in the 1990s with changes in the way it makes budget decisions. The current budget process, dating from the mid-1970s, was intended to bring coherence to the way standing committees handle the president's budget. It has decisively shaped both Congress's internal decision making and its relations with the executive.

Congressional Budgeting

Congressional budgeting is a complex process that involves virtually all House and Senate members and committees, the president and executive branch officials, and scores of other participants. That congressional budgeting is usually contentious and conflict-laden should come as no surprise considering the high political and policy stakes associated with fiscal decision making. (See box for some of the terminology used in budgeting.)

Authorizations and Appropriations

Congress has a two-step financial procedure: authorizations and appropriations. Generally, Congress first passes authorization laws that establish or continue (reauthorizations) federal agencies and programs, recommends funding them at certain levels, and authorizes the enactment of appropriations to fund those agencies and programs. Congress then enacts annually appropriation laws that grant agencies legal authority to spend no more than the amount appropriated to it. An authorization is like an IOU that must be validated by an appropriation.

A Budget Glossary

Appropriations. The process by which Congress provides budget authority, usually through the enactment of thirteen separate appropriations bills.

Budget authority. The authority for federal agencies to spend or otherwise obligate money, accomplished through enactment into law of appropriations bills.

Budget outlays. Money that is actually spent in a given fiscal year, as opposed to money that is appropriated for that year. One year's budget authority can result in outlays over several years, and the outlays in any given year result from a mix of budget authority from that year and prior years. Budget authority is similar to putting money into a checking account; outlays occur when checks are written and cashed.

Discretionary spending. Programs that Congress can finance as it chooses through appropriations. With the exception of paying entitlement benefits to individuals (see mandatory spending below), almost everything the government does is financed by discretionary spending. Examples include all federal agencies, Congress, the White House, the courts, the military, and programs supporting space exploration and child nutrition. About a third of all federal spending falls into this category.

Fiscal year. The federal government's budget year. For example, Fiscal year 2004 runs from October 1, 2003 through September 30, 2004.

Mandatory spending. Made up mostly of entitlements, which are programs whose eligibility requirements are written into law. Anyone who meets those requirements is entitled to the money until Congress changes the law.

Examples are Social Security, Medicare, Medicaid, unemployment benefits, food stamps, and federal pensions. Another major category of mandatory spending is the interest paid to holders of federal government bonds. Social Security and interest payments are permanently appropriated. And although budget authority for some entitlements is provided through the appropriations process, appropriators have little or no control over the money. Mandatory spending accounts for about two-thirds of all federal spending.

Pay-as-you-go (PAYGO) rule. This rule requires that all tax cuts, new entitlement programs, and expansions of existing entitlement programs be budget-neutral—offset either by additional taxes or by cuts in existing entitlement programs.

Reconciliation. The process by which tax laws and spending programs are changed, or reconciled, to reach outlay and revenue targets set in the congressional budget resolution. Established by the 1974 Congressional Budget Act (P.L. 93-344), it was first used in 1980.

Rescission. The cancellation of previously appropriated budget authority. This is a common way to save money that already has been appropriated. A rescissions bill must be passed by Congress and signed by the president (or enacted over his veto), just as an appropriations bill is.

Revenues. Taxes, customs duties, some user fees, and most other receipts paid to the federal government.

Sequester. The cancellation of spending authority as a disciplinary measure to cut off spending above preset limits. Appropriations that exceed annual spending caps can trigger a sequester that will cut all appropriations by the amount of the excess. Similarly, tax cuts and new or expanded entitlement spending programs that are not offset under pay-as-you-go rules will trigger a sequester of nonexempt entitlement programs.

Source: Adapted from *CQ Weekly,* February. 6, 1999.

The authorization-appropriation sequence is an invention of Congress. It is required not by the Constitution, but by House and Senate rules. The dual procedure dates from the nineteenth century and stems from inordinate delays caused by adding riders—extraneous policy amendments—to appropriation bills. "By 1835," wrote a legislator, "delays caused by injecting legislation [policy] into these [appropriation] bills had become serious and John Quincy Adams suggested that they be stripped of everything save appropriations." [30] Two years later the House required authorizations to precede appropriations. The Senate followed suit.

Authorizations and appropriations can be annual, multiyear, or permanent. Through the end of World War II most federal agencies and programs were permanently authorized. They were reviewed annually by the House and Senate Appropriations Committees but not by the authorizing panels (such as Agriculture or Commerce). Since the 1970s the trend has been toward short-term authorizations, giving the authorizing committees more chances to control agency operations.[31] Agencies and programs are not terminated if their authorization law expires because Congress typically continues to appropriate money for them. In recent years, for example, "the total amount of unauthorized programs has ranged between about $90 billion and $120 billion annually." [32] Authorization (or reauthorization) measures sometimes cannot be passed for various reasons, such as conflicts over policy between the chambers or among the elective branches. Generally, authorizing committees strive to enact their bills, otherwise they cede their power to the appropriating panels. To generate public backing for the reenactment in 2003 of the Transportation Equity Act for the 21st Century, House Transportation chairman Don Young, R-Alaska, and ranking Democrat James L. Oberstar, Minn., even led a "reauthorization tour" to major media markets "across the country to drum up grass roots support." [33]

The Two Stages. Suppose, for example, that the authorizing committee recommends $20 million for a new Energy Department solar research and development program. Under the authorization-appropriation procedure, before the Energy Department has the authorization to establish the solar program, both houses must pass and the president must sign legislation providing for it.

The House Appropriations Committee (usually one of its thirteen subcommittees) must propose how much money the solar program should receive. The proposed amount is the budget authority (BA). It is equivalent to depositing money in a checking account. The budget outlay (BO) is the check written by the Treasury to meet a financial commitment. The Appropriations Committee can provide the whole $20 million (but not more), propose cuts, or refuse to fund the program at all. Assume that the House goes along with the Appropriations Committee and votes to approve $15 million. The Senate Appropriations Committee, acting somewhat like a court of appeals, then hears agency officials asking the Senate to approve the full $20 million. If the Senate accedes, a House-Senate compromise is worked out.

In practice, it is hard to keep the two stages distinct. Authorization bills sometimes carry appropriations, and appropriation bills sometimes contain legislation (or policy provisions). Chamber rules that forbid these practices can be waived. In the House limitation riders make policy under the guise of restricting agency use of funds. Phrased negatively ("None of the funds . . ."), limitations bolster congressional control of bureaucracy. The Senate, too, is not reluctant to add extraneous policy proposals to appropriations bills. Often controversial, policy riders can trigger disputes with the other body and veto threats from the president.

Committee Roles and Continuing Resolutions. Among the authorizing committees, House Ways and Means and Senate Finance have especially powerful roles in the budget process. Both House and Senate tax panels have access to the staff experts of the Joint Taxation Committee. Because the House initiates revenue measures, it usually determines whether Congress will act on measures to raise, lower, or redistribute taxes. (By custom, the House also initiates appropriations bills.) Occasionally, however, the Senate takes the lead. The Senate technically can comply with the Constitution by taking a minor House-passed revenue bill and adding to it a major tax measure. In 1981 the Republican-controlled Senate employed this tactic to act on President Ronald Reagan's sweeping tax-cut plan; it used the same ploy the next year on the president's tax-increase package. Usually the House jealously guards its constitutional authority to originate tax measures and may return to the Senate any bills that violate the origination clause.

Whenever Congress cannot complete action on one or more of the thirteen regular appropriations bills (one for each subcommittee) by the beginning of the fiscal year (October 1), it provides temporary, stopgap funding for the affected federal agencies through a joint resolution known as a continuing resolution. In the past, continuing resolutions were usually employed to keep a few government agencies in operation for short periods (usually one to three months). Some years Congress has packaged all thirteen regular appropriations bills into one massive continuing resolution. (A record twenty-one continuing resolutions were needed in 2000 before the GOP Congress and President Clinton compromised their differences on several appropriations bills that had not been enacted by the start of the fiscal year.) Congress also passes supplemental appropriations to meet unexpected contingencies, such as the $78.5 billion supplemental in spring 2003 to pay for the war in Iraq.

Backdoor Spending Techniques

To sidestep the appropriations ax, authorizing committees have evolved backdoor funding provisions that bypass the front door of the two-step authorization-appropriation sequence. Backdoors are authorization laws that mandate, not simply recommend, the expenditure of federal funds. This type of spending legislation, which is reported solely by the authorizing committees, is called direct spending as contrasted with the discretionary spending under the jurisdiction of the House and Senate Appropriations Committees. There are three types of backdoor or direct spending legislation. Contract authority permits agencies to enter into contracts that subsequently must be covered by appropriations. Borrowing authority allows agencies to spend money they have borrowed from the public or the Treasury. And mandatory entitlements grant eligible individuals and governments the right to receive payments from the national government.

The fastest growing of these three techniques is entitlements, which establish legally enforceable rights without reference to dollar amounts. Spending for entitlement programs (Medicare and Social Security, for example) is determined by the number of citizens who qualify and the benefit levels established by law; no fixed dollar amount is established for these programs.

Entitlements are the real force behind the escalation of federal spending (see Figure 14-1). More than half of all federal spending consists of entitlements that avoid the annual appropriations process review. The ratio today of discretionary (determined through yearly appropriations) to mandatory spending represents a dramatic reversal of what it was like four decades ago. Interest on the federal debt is another uncontrollable expenditure. Unlike defense or domestic discretionary programs—for which the Appropriations Committees recommend annual amounts and on which all lawmakers may vote—entitlement spending occurs automatically under the terms outlined in the statute. Moreover, around four-fifths of these programs "are not 'means tested,' or linked to the incomes of recipients." [34]

Congress has done a good job of containing discretionary spending. It is trying to rein in expenditures for costly entitlements, a much more difficult task. In 1996 Congress did pass legislation ending a decades-old national welfare entitlement program—Aid to Families with Dependent Children.[35] However, benefits to the elderly make up the largest share of entitlement spending, and senior citizens are protective of their entitlement programs and they vote. Given an aging society and a longer lived population (thanks to advances in often expensive medical technology), spending for Social Security and Medicare is sure to increase until steps are taken to revise these open-ended spending programs. Reform proposals are sure to be controversial, such as permitting recipients to use some of their benefits to establish private retirement accounts, reducing the rate of spending for the program by raising the retirement age, or means testing the program to require affluent retirees to pay taxes on their benefits.

Some analysts contend that the real entitlement budget buster of the future is not Social Security but Medicare. For instance, if prescription drug coverage is added to Medicare, an oft-repeated proposal on Capitol Hill, the Congressional Budget Office estimates that the program's beneficiaries "will consume $1.5 trillion worth of medications over the next decade." [36] Even more frightening from a budget perspective is the prospect of providing long-term nursing home or other care for the elderly. Long-term care, said Rep. Earl

Figure 14-1 Federal Spending by Major Category, Fiscal Years 1965 and 2004 (in billions)

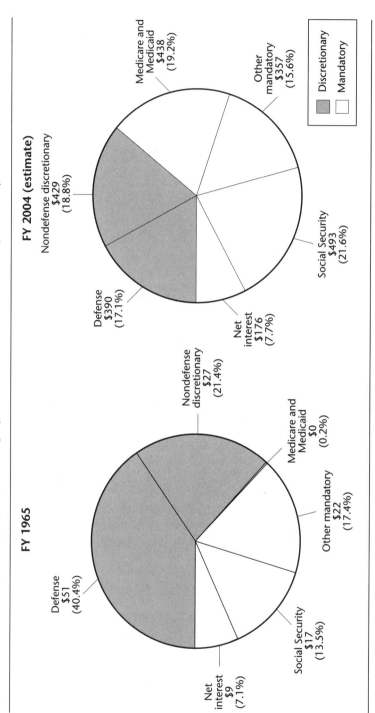

FY 1965

Defense
$51
(40.4%)

Net interest
$9
(7.1%)

Social Security
$17
(13.5%)

Other mandatory
$22
(17.4%)

Medicare and Medicaid
$0
(0.2%)

Nondefense discretionary
$27
(21.4%)

FY 2004 (estimate)

Nondefense discretionary
$429
(18.8%)

Medicare and Medicaid
$438
(19.2%)

Other mandatory
$357
(15.6%)

Social Security
$493
(21.6%)

Net interest
$176
(7.7%)

Defense
$390
(17.1%)

Discretionary

Mandatory

Source: Office of Management and Budget, *Budget of the United States Government: Fiscal Year 2004, Historical Tables* (Washington, D.C.: Government Printing Office, 2003), 123, 127, and 132. Charts prepared by Robert Keith, Government Division, Congressional Research Service.

Pomeroy, D-N.D., is "the elephant in the living room that no one's talking about." [37]

In short, an "entitlement revolution" is under way as the government today transfers more than half of federal monies to eligible families and individuals. "Call it government by A.T.M.," remarked an analyst, "you walk up, hit the buttons and the cash to which you're entitled pops out." [38] This transformation in the federal budget away from discretionary to direct (or mandatory) spending raises the question of the appropriateness of this funding ratio. Congress and the president face at least a dual fiscal challenge: the battle for scarce resources between entitlements versus discretionary spending and the struggle within the discretionary category between domestic versus defense spending. Added to this mix is another $800 billion in indirect spending called "tax expenditures"—revenue that is foregone through various tax credits, subsidies, or deductions, such as home mortgage deductions. Tax expenditures receive relatively little public attention compared with direct or discretionary spending.[39]

The 1974 Budget Act

Loose control of Congress's purse strings in the 1970s gave rise to charges of financial irresponsibility. President Richard M. Nixon blamed Congress for annual deficits, consumer price hikes, high joblessness, and inflation. He also refused to spend—impounded—monies duly appropriated by Congress. Although his administration lost every court challenge to the impoundments, Nixon won the political high ground. These diverse pressures prompted Congress to restructure its budget procedures.

The Budget and Impoundment Control Act of 1974 created the House Budget Committee, the Senate Budget Committee, and the Congressional Budget Office. The nonpartisan CBO prepares economic forecasts for Congress, scores the costs of proposed legislation, and issues fiscal, monetary, and policy reports. The 1974 act also limited presidential use of impoundments and established a timetable for action on authorization, appropriation, and tax measures. The timetable has been changed periodically, and Congress commonly misses some of the target dates (see box for the timetable).

Among many complex features of the 1974 act, two are central components of Congress's budget process: the concurrent budget resolution and reconciliation. These two features warrant discussion because they orient much of the time-consuming work of each annual legislative session, attract the attention of many interests and participants clamoring for fiscal resources, and influence policy decisions and outcomes.

Concurrent Budget Resolution

The core of Congress's annual budget process centers on adoption of a concurrent budget resolution. This measure is formulated by the House and Senate Budget Committees, which consider the views and estimates of nu-

The Congressional Budget Timetable

Deadline	Action to be Completed
First Monday in February	President submits budget to Congress
February 15	Congressional Budget Office submits economic and budget outlook report to Budget Committees
Six weeks after president submits budget	Committees submit views and estimates to Budget Committees
April 1	Senate Budget Committee reports budget resolution
April 15	Congress completes action on budget resolution
May 15	Annual appropriations bills may be considered in the House, even if action on budget resolution has not been completed
June 10	House Appropriations Committee reports last annual appropriations bill
June 15	House completes action on reconciliation legislation (if required by budget resolution)
June 30	House completes action on annual appropriations bills
July 15	President submits mid-session review of his budget to Congress
October 1	Fiscal year begins

Source: Bill Heniff Jr., "The Congressional Budget Process Timetable," 98-472 GOV, Congressional Research Service, December 9, 2002.

merous witnesses. The resolution consists of two basic parts. The first part deals with fiscal aggregates: total federal spending, total federal revenues, and the public debt or surplus for the upcoming fiscal year (October 1 to September 30). The budget resolution also sets multiyear targets for these fiscal aggregates. The second part subdivides the budget aggregates among twenty functional categories, such as national defense, agriculture, and energy, and it establishes spending levels for each. In effect, the budget resolution sets the overall level of discretionary spending for each fiscal year.

Under a House rule reinstated at the start of the 108th Congress (January 7, 2003)—it was dropped from the rulebook of the 107th House—"after successful adoption of the budget [resolution] the House would automatically be 'deemed' to have passed a bill to increase the debt ceiling"; that is, the total amount of outstanding public debt (savings bonds, Treasury securities, and other government obligations) permitted by law.[40] Votes to raise the federal debt ceiling are often controversial, in part because campaign challengers can charge lawmakers who support the hike as big spenders. The House's "deeming" procedure avoids this problem. The Senate has no comparable procedure and must vote separately on legislation to raise the debt ceiling, which was slated to be raised another trillion (to $7.4 trillion) in 2003.

The budget resolution is Congress's fiscal blueprint. It establishes the context of congressional budgeting; guides the budgetary actions of the authorizing, appropriating, and taxing committees; and reflects Congress's spending priorities. In a period of polarized politics, partisan considerations dominate debates on these resolutions as Democrats and Republicans battle over spending levels for their competing priorities. "I've always said the budget vote is the toughest vote because we have to carry that budget by ourselves," exclaimed House Speaker J. Dennis Hastert, R-Ill. "We don't get any help from across the aisle." [41] Sen. Bob Graham, D-Fla., explained the purposes of the budget resolution:

> [The budget] resolution would be analogous to an architect's set of plans for constructing a building. It gives the general direction, framework, and prioritization of Federal fiscal policy each year. Those priorities then drive the individual appropriations and tax measures which will support that architectural plan.[42]

The House and Senate each consider a budget resolution. In the House, budget resolutions are typically considered under special rules from the Rules Committee, which limit debate and impose restrictions on the number and types of amendments. In the Senate, unless members accept a unanimous consent agreement imposing time restrictions, the 1974 budget act sets a fifty-hour limitation for consideration of the budget resolution. However, amendments can be taken up and voted upon after the fifty hours, but without debate. This circumstance often leads to so-called vote-a-ramas, during which senators over several days may "cast back-to-back votes on a dizzying array of dozens of amendments," often with the two Congresses in mind—the votes will "serve as valuable campaign fodder" in the next election.[43]

When each chamber passes budget resolutions that contain different aggregate and functional levels, which is normal practice, the two chambers usually meet in conference to resolve their disagreements. The conference report is then submitted to the House and Senate for final action. Congress's budget resolution is not submitted to the president and thus has no legal effect. Instead, it outlines a fiscal framework that enables Congress, through its budget committees, CBO, and other devices, to monitor all budget-related actions that the House and Senate take during the course of a year.

Reconciliation

The 1974 budget act established a special procedure called reconciliation, which is an optional process authorized when Congress adopts the budget resolution. Its basic purpose is to bring revenue and direct spending (entitlement) legislation into conformity (or reconciliation) with the fiscal targets established in the concurrent budget resolution. As Sen. Robert C. Byrd, D-W.Va., declaimed: "[A] budget reconciliation process was established as an optional procedure to enhance Congress's ability to change current law in order to bring revenue and spending levels into conformity with the targets of the budget resolution." [44]

First used in 1980, reconciliation is a controversial and frequently employed process that "forces committees that might not want to reduce spending for entitlements under their jurisdiction to act and report legislation." [45] In practice, reconciliation has been used to reduce spending, primarily through entitlement savings, and either to increase revenues or cut taxes.

Reconciliation is a two-step process. In the first step, Congress adopts a budget resolution containing a provision that instructs committees to report legislation that changes existing law. The instructions embody three features. They designate, by name, the committees required to report legislation; they give each designated committee a dollar figure for mandated savings; and they establish a deadline for reporting legislation to achieve the savings. In the second step, the House and Senate budget committees compile into an omnibus reconciliation bill the legislative changes in revenue or direct spending programs recommended by each named committee.

The year 2003 witnessed an unprecedented agreement between the GOP-controlled House and Senate: two different tax reconciliation instructions for each chamber. "No budget resolution has even been approved with different tax numbers for the House and Senate"—$550 billion for the House (reflecting President Bush's new bottom line for the $726 billion tax cut he first recommended) and $350 billion for the Senate. [46] Two key moderate Senate Republicans—Olympia J. Snowe of Maine and George V. Voinovich—refused to accept a tax cut greater than $350 billion because of concerns over rising deficits. The incorporation of two different tax numbers in the reconciliation instructions—along with the promise by Finance chairman Charles E. Grassley, R-Iowa, that any conference report on the budget resolution would not exceed $350 billion—won the support of the two senators. As a result, the GOP Senate was able to pass the budget resolution by a 51–50 vote with Vice President Dick Cheney casting the tie-breaking vote, averting large embarrassment for Senate Republicans. The year before GOP senators had heaped criticism on Democrats, who controlled the chamber, for their inability to have the Senate adopt a budget resolution.

However, Grassley's commitment to hold the tax cut to $350 billion, which Senate majority leader Bill Frist, R-Tenn., agreed to, surprised House GOP leaders, who expected that a higher tax figure would be negotiated and reported by the conference committee on the budget resolution. The result was an angry outburst by House GOP leaders against Frist. To mend their differences so a new tax-cut strategy could be devised, numerous House-Senate GOP meetings took place, including a session with President Bush attended by Speaker Hastert and Senate majority leader Frist. "I have apologized" [to the Speaker], said Frist. "The big mistake, lesson learned, is 'no surprises,' " he said.[47]

Reconciliation bills are treated in the Senate differently from other bills or amendments. Reconciliation bills cannot be filibustered (there is a statutory time limit of twenty hours for debate); passage requires a simple majority instead of the supermajority (sixty votes) needed to stop a talkathon; and amendments must be germane (the Senate has no general germaneness rule). Little surprise that measures likely to arouse controversy in the Senate, such as tax-cut legislation, are attached to filibuster-proof reconciliation measures that could pass with fifty votes, if the vice president casts the tie-breaking vote. To prevent the Senate from putting issues (abortion, for instance) that are extraneous to deficit reduction into reconciliation bills, senators adopted the so-called Byrd Rule (named after Senator Byrd). Under this rule, "measures cannot be included in the Senate reconciliation package [including conference reports] if they do not have revenue or entitlement components or if such components are 'merely incidental' to a broader policy question. It takes 60 votes in the Senate to waive the Byrd Rule." [48]

The two Congresses also overlays reconciliation. For example, in 2003 the House Budget Committee instructed fourteen House committees to cut spending levels for programs under their jurisdiction by 1 percent over ten years. This directive posed potential electoral problems for Chairman Tom Davis of the Government Reform Committee. Davis represents scores of federal employees who reside in his suburban Virginia district next to the District of Columbia. His panel was instructed to produce savings of $1.1 billion in federal health and pension benefits programs. Threatening to mobilize votes against the budget resolution, Chairman Davis brokered a deal with GOP leaders, including Budget chairman Jim Nussle, R-Iowa, which avoided any need to make drastic cuts in the federal employee programs. Instead, the Government Reform Committee won approval to "generate [the required] savings by reforming procurement rules and reorganizing agencies. Even though the savings would come from programs under the jurisdiction of other committees, the Government Reform Committee would get the credit." [49]

Reconciliation, in sum, is a powerful procedure for fiscal retrenchment. President Reagan and GOP congressional leaders in 1981 used it for the first time on a grand scale. A reconciliation bill dictated deep, multiyear reductions (about $130 billion over three years) in domestic spending. Not long afterward, Congress also agreed to Reagan's tax legislation, which sharply cut tax rates for individuals and businesses. The revenue losses caused by the tax cut, combined with increased defense and entitlement expenditures and insufficient spending reductions in other areas, soon pushed annual budget deficits from double to triple digits. For nearly a quarter century, Congress has grappled statutorily and in other ways with deficits, with only a brief interlude of surpluses.

The Gramm-Rudman-Hollings Plan

The escalating growth of budgetary deficits after 1981 became the prime congressional issue as lawmakers and presidents adapted to a new world: the politics of deficit reduction. As the national debt (the accumulation of annual deficits) mounted, numerous proposals were put forth to deal with the problem. One notable example in the mid-1980s was the Gramm-Rudman-Hollings plan (named after Sens. Phil Gramm, R-Texas, Warren B. Rudman, R-N.H., and Ernest F. Hollings, D-S.C.).

Its core feature was the establishment in law of annual deficit reduction targets. If Congress did not meet the targets, the president would have to sequester funds; that is, impose automatic across-the-board spending cuts evenly divided between defense and domestic programs. This dire prospect was supposed to create an incentive for Congress and the president to decide how best to achieve deficit reduction. The plan did not work and deficits continued to climb. Congress exempted 70 percent of the budget from the threat of sequestration. Moreover, the yearly targets were met through budgetary gimmicks. Dissatisfaction with this law triggered enactment of another major budgetary reform: the Budget Enforcement Act (BEA) of 1990 (the product of a budget summit between President George Bush and congressional leaders). The law was subsequently amended several times and extended through 2002.

The Budget Enforcement Act

The Budget Enforcement Act once again changed the fiscal procedures of Congress. Three basic features undergird the law. First, it shifted Congress's attention from deficit reduction to spending control. Thus, the law removed the threat of automatic across-the-board reductions if conditions beyond Congress's control (inflation, a worsening economy, or emergency funding for crises or disasters) pushed the deficit upward.

Second, the BEA established caps, or limits, for discretionary spending. The spending caps can be changed, but Congress and the president would have to agree to the modification. If Congress exceeds the spending limits, the law provides for across-the-board reductions to bring spending in line with the caps. However, a loophole in the law enables Congress and the president to escape tight spending caps and avoid a zero-sum dilemma: paying for spending hikes in some discretionary programs by making cuts in other programs. If Congress and the president designate expenditures above the cap as emergency spending, they are exempt from the limits imposed by the BEA.

Third, the BEA subjected tax and entitlement programs to a new pay-as-you-go (PAYGO) procedure, which requires that any tax reductions or any increases in direct spending (that is, entitlement) programs must be offset by tax hikes or reductions in other direct spending programs. The enforcement mechanism is the threat of across-the-board cuts in direct spending programs not exempt under BEA. As the chief counsel of the Senate Budget Committee explained: "The 'pay-as-you-go' label implies that Congress and the President may cut taxes or create [new direct spending] programs—that is 'go'—if they also agree to provide offsetting increased revenues or spending reductions—that is 'pay.' " [50]

Throughout much of the 1990s, the GOP-controlled Congress and President Clinton waged fierce battles over deficit reduction. As part of their political game plan, Republicans sent Clinton appropriations bills making deep cuts in federal programs. The president vetoed the measures, forcing two partial shutdowns of the government. The public blamed Republicans for the shutdowns, the longest in congressional history, with the result that GOP congressional leaders changed their combative approach and reopened the government. The bitter fights reflected profound policy differences between the two parties and between Clinton and Congress. Still, the two sides made a fiscal and policy breakthrough when they announced on May 2, 1997, a joint plan to produce a balanced budget by 2002.

Surpluses Arrive Unexpectedly

To the surprise of many lawmakers and pundits, who talked regularly about the pain and sacrifice (tax hikes and spending cuts) that balancing the budget would require, a balanced budget became reality sooner than anyone expected. By the end of September 1998, the national budget was $70 billion in the black, something that last occurred in 1969. David A. Stockman, President Reagan's director of the Office of Management and Budget, once predicted deficits as far as the eye could see. Now economic forecasters were predicting surpluses as far as the eye could see.

Why the surge of black ink? Several factors contributed to the fiscal turnaround. First, the end of the cold war led to reductions in defense expenditures. Second, despite some soft spots, the America economy was strong and healthy. This factor, combined with a booming stock market, flooded the federal Treasury with tax and capital gains dollars provided mainly by the richest 1 percent of the populace. Third, the Federal Reserve kept inflation and interest rates under control through an effective monetary policy that promoted economic expansion. Fourth, presidential and congressional budgetary decisions, such as passage of the BEA of 1990 during the George Bush administration and President Clinton's 1993 economic package, encouraged fiscal restraint and led to budgetary savings. Finally, luck and timing contributed to the fiscal mix. "Just about everything broke right that could have broken right" is how Robert Reischauer, a former CBO director, explained the deficit-free picture.[51]

Not everyone believed that the politics of plenty had arrived or, if so, that it would last indefinitely. Some lawmakers suggested to their colleagues that budget surpluses stood for "b.s." Another economic recession could be around the corner. Economic forecasts are often unreliable or just plain wrong. A downturn in the domestic economy or an international economic crisis could undermine the optimistic fiscal projections. A military conflict could send defense expenditures skyrocketing and erode any budgetary surplus. Some analysts and lawmakers flatly denied that a surplus existed. "The truth is there is no surplus," contended Senator Hollings, citing a national debt at the time of $5.7 trillion.[52]

On January 30, 2001, CBO revised upward its surplus projections over the next decade to $5.6 trillion. This surplus figure was composed of two parts. The first surplus is generated from the payroll taxes of workers and employers, which is earmarked for deposit in the Social Security trust fund. Currently, more payroll taxes are going into the fund than are needed to pay benefits to elderly retirees. Today's excess in Social Security revenues is called the off-budget surplus. This favorable condition is projected to change around 2015 when the seventy-six million baby boomers (those born between 1946 and 1964) retire in droves and begin to draw down Social Security's extra revenues.

The second surplus is on the on-budget surplus. This is the amount of money generated from income taxes and other sources, excluding Social Security. These funds are used to finance federal agencies and programs. Of the estimated $5.6 trillion budget surplus, $2.5 trillion is in Social Security, and $3.1 trillion would accumulate from general revenue sources.

Both parties pledged not to touch the off-budget surplus. In 1998 President Clinton promised to "save Social Security first." No longer would Social Security be raided to pay for the general operations of the government. (For decades, both parties had masked the true size of the deficit by using the extra Social Security funds to help pay for general governmental programs.) Not to be outdone, Republicans embraced the lockbox concept. They promised to lock up 100 percent of the Social Security surplus.

The Return of Deficits

Given the projected $5.6 trillion surplus, President George W. Bush and congressional Democrats soon began to argue over what to do with the on-budget surplus of $3.1 trillion. Although many lawmakers and pundits recognized that the ten-year projection might be grossly wrong and never materialize because of a slowing economy, international crises, or other reasons, politicians in both parties had their own ideas on how the surplus should be spent. Here was a case of fiscal projections driving policy making, even though the money was not yet in the bank.

President Bush's top priority when he took office was a $1.6 trillion tax cut. And on June 7, 2001, the president signed into law the largest tax cut ($1.35 trillion) since Reagan's. A little more than three months later terrorists attacked the United States and new demands and challenges confronted the country. From a budget perspective, at least three significant developments merit some discussion. First, the rather brief era (1998–2002) of surpluses came to an early end after Congress and the White House spent nearly three decades making deficit reduction one of their primary goals. As Rep. David E. Price, D-N.C., pointed out:

> We had, at the start of the [Bush] administration, a projected $5.6 trillion surplus over ten years. That surplus now is not only gone . . . [but] we are looking at no surplus and, in fact, at a $2.1 trillion deficit for the same 10-year period. That is a fiscal reversal of almost $8 trillion, unprecedented in our country's history. The deficit for 2003 is projected to be over $300 billion and for 2004 around $307 billion.[53]

What happened to the surplus? It disappeared because the factors that produced it reversed themselves to trigger the return of deficits. Instead of defense cutbacks, the nation confronted a global war on terrorism, military conflicts in Afghanistan and Iraq and the reconstruction of those countries, and large expenditures for homeland security. A record ten years of uninterrupted economic growth ended, the economy turned sluggish, and the stock market performed poorly—factors that led to a decline in federal revenues. Another contributor to revenue shortfalls was the large tax cuts pushed by the Bush administration. The Bush White House had indicated that it will push a new tax cut every year as a way to further shrink the size of government and to keep the GOP base united.[54] Finally, Congress's budgetary controls—spending caps and PAYGO—expired on September 30, 2002. With the return of deficits, Congress now must decide whether to return to these forms of fiscal discipline, devise new processes, or rely on existing legislative procedures for budgetary control.

Some analysts, such as former CBO director Daniel Crippen, even state that the current congressional budget process is dead. Discretionary spending caps have sometimes been evaded by designating spending, even for the conduct of the decennial census, as emergency. Partisan conflicts frequently delay action on appropriations bills. Budget resolutions may be ignored or cannot be adopted. (In 2002, for the first time ever, the Senate failed to adopt a budget resolution. Four years earlier Congress was unable to agree to a budget resolution.) The lockbox is broken as surpluses in Social Security are once more being used to mask the size of the deficit. In the judgment of Crippen,

> The budget process as we know it is on its way out. That means, inherently, the executive branch will accrete more power on the budget, and the veto will be the primary impediment to spending—and the president will become more powerful in the process. So this has been a 25-year experiment to see whether the Congress could bring back [to itself] more budgetary power.[55]

Second, the two parties have switched fiscal positions. Democrats now spotlight the dangers of the deficit and use it on the campaign trail to criticize President Bush's handling of the economy. Many Republicans, contrary to the views of President Reagan, now contend that deficits may be a good thing. "Anything that will help us stop spending money, I'm in favor of," exclaimed conservative representative Sue Myrick, R-N.C. "This place is set up to spend money. . . . And if there's a deficit that may help us."[56] Cutting taxes, then, is an important way for Republicans to shrink the size and reach of the national government by starving it of funds, even if that means higher deficits. "If we had a little teeny government and a big deficit, I wouldn't care," said conservative GOP strategist Grover Norquist. "It's the size of the government we're focused on. It's also the size of the government the left is focused on."[57] Many Democrats want to curb the deficit so there is money to spend on scores of favored domestic programs, such as health, education, and environmental protection. Neither party is willing "to sacrifice their priorities for the sake of deficit reduction."[58]

Finally, if deficits continue to escalate in the years ahead, the federal government confronts a serious dilemma in funding competing priorities. Will the government, for instance, have the resources to pay the retirement and health benefits of the baby boomers? "This is a demographic time bomb that we are facing as a society," stated Sen. Kent Conrad, D-N.D. "It is unlike anything we have ever faced before because always in our history the succeeding generation has been much larger than the generation retiring" and thus provide sufficient payroll taxes to fund the retirement needs of the elderly.[59] A political consensus currently does not exist on how to address the impending explosion in the costs of Social Security and Medicare, the two largest entitlement programs. Some officials argue that a booming economy will generate the bushels of money needed to pay for these and other priorities, that current deficits are relatively small compared with an $11 trillion economy, and that various entitlement reforms will reduce the price tag for these programs. Still, analysts remain concerned about deficits. "The deficit is a hard thing to see the effects of. It's not the wolf at the door. . . . [I]t's termites in the woodwork, a constant drag, gnawing away at the capital stock."[60]

Conclusion

Today, lawmakers are preoccupied with important policy questions: defense and homeland security in an age of terrorism, economic growth, and the condition of various domestic social programs. Rep. Barney Frank, D-Mass., posed a question that crystallizes the debate over these various concerns: "What is the appropriate level of public activity in our society?" [61] Democrats and Republicans often provide different answers to this question. Governing, however, means making choices. Future decisions about budgeting and national priorities will surely reflect the values, goals, and interests that result from the confrontations and accommodations inherent in America's pluralist policy-making system.

"Hard" and "soft" diplomacy. Preparing for assault in Iraq, a U.S. Army tank is unloaded from a navy cargo ship (above). Food supplies go to needy countries under the State Department's foreign aid program and the Agriculture Department's P.L. 480 program, which distributes surplus agricultural products abroad. Below, angry at the Bush administration's go-it-alone policies, thousands march in Paris in 2003 to protest the U.S.-led war on Iraq.

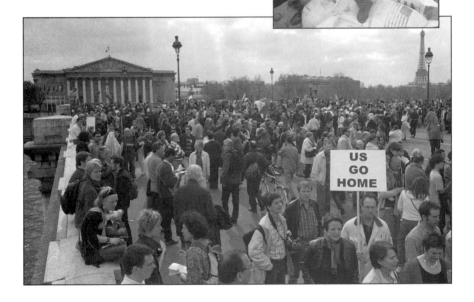

15

Congress and National Security Policies

On September 11, 2001, one of the authors of this book was traveling in China. After a day hiking along China's Great Wall and attending the Beijing Opera, he flipped on the TV in his hotel room to witness the scene then unfolding twelve time-zones away. The other author was on Capitol Hill, giving a talk to federal executives, when word came to evacuate the building. The members of the group were mystified until they saw the television footage of smoke rising from the Pentagon, across the Potomac River. It was the prelude to a day of terror and uncertainty. The Capitol itself was a possible target, and so he made his way home on the Metro, which was jammed with people worried that it, too, might be hit.

Not that violence is a stranger to the continent. Nineteenth-century wars were fought on American soil; and some sixty-odd years ago the U.S. military forces stationed at Pearl Harbor, Hawaii, were attacked—the trigger for World War II. Violent acts against innocent or random victims—riots, lynchings, and even massacres—are part of U.S. history. As for recent terrorist acts, think of schoolyard and workplace shootings and of Timothy McVeigh's bombing of the Oklahoma City federal building in 1995. Few countries in the world have been free of terrorism within any American's living memory.

But Americans cling to the myth that they are a special people set apart from the world's conflicts. Having abandoned old-world conflicts and rivalries, its citizens—protected by two oceans—historically resolved to maintain an aloofness toward other nations' struggles. The most famous passage of President George Washington's 1796 Farewell Address, read dutifully in the chambers of Congress every year on his birthday, counsels that

> [t]he great rule of conduct for us, in regard to foreign nations is in extending our commercial relations to have with them as little political connection as possible. . . . 'Tis our true policy to steer clear of permanent alliances, with any portion of the foreign world. . . . Taking care to keep ourselves, by suitable establishments, on a respectable defensive posture, we may safely trust to temporary alliances for extraordinary emergencies.[1]

This American dream was never fulfilled, but it was shattered irrevocably by the attacks of 9/11.

Such events are a reminder that forming U.S. foreign and national security policies is not an episodic activity but an ongoing responsibility. Congress and the president share in these duties just as they do in domestic and budgetary matters. Congress has broad constitutional authority to participate in making foreign and defense decisions. Even the most decisive chief executives can find themselves constrained by active, informed, and determined policy makers on Capitol Hill.

Constitutional Powers

The Constitution is "an invitation to struggle for the privilege of directing American foreign policy." [2] In other words, foreign and military powers are divided between the branches. "While the president is usually in a position to *propose,* the Senate and Congress are often in a technical position at least to *dispose.*" [3] The struggle over the proper role of each branch in shaping foreign policy typically focuses on two broad issues: conflict over policy and conflict over process.

The president commands formidable constitutional powers. He manages day-to-day relations with foreign governments, nominates ambassadors and other emissaries, receives other nations' representatives, and negotiates treaties and other agreements. Of mounting importance, moreover, he is commander in chief of the nation's armed forces.

Presidential leadership in conducting diplomacy has led some observers to presume that foreign affairs are the president's exclusive domain. Two historical sources are cited by advocates of presidential supremacy in foreign affairs. One is a statement by John Marshall in 1800, before he became chief justice: "The president is the sole organ of the nation in its external relations, and its sole representative with foreign nations." [4] Marshall was correct in a formal sense. But far from claiming that the president makes foreign policy single-handedly, he merely was noting that the president executes foreign policy. It is formulated jointly.

Second is a misleading statement by Justice George Sutherland in *United States v. Curtiss-Wright Export Corp.* (1936). Legislation dealing with foreign affairs "must often accord to the president a degree of discretion and freedom from statutory restriction which would not be admissible were domestic affairs alone involved." [5] Because this decision dealt with a president's implementation of a congressional enactment, Justice Sutherland's expansive language was beside the point (an obiter dictum, in legal usage), and it certainly does not support a claim of exclusive presidential domain in foreign affairs. The most that can be said, as Justice Robert Jackson later noted in *Youngstown Sheet and Tube Co. v. Sawyer* (1952), is that "the president might act in external affairs without congressional authority, but not that he might act contrary to an act of Congress." [6]

Congress has an impressive arsenal of explicit constitutional duties, such as the power to declare war, to regulate foreign commerce, and to raise and support military forces. The president's explicit international powers are to serve as commander in chief, to negotiate treaties and appoint ambassadors (powers shared with the Senate), and to receive ambassadors and other emissaries. Throughout U.S. history, presidents have claimed not only these powers but also others not spelled out in the Constitution. Whether they are called implied, inherent, or emergency powers, they are often invoked by presidents in conducting foreign policy.

Chief executives, in truth, enjoy certain innate advantages in dealing with foreign affairs. As John Jay wrote in *The Federalist Papers,* No. 64, the office's unity, its superior information sources, and its capacity for secrecy and dispatch give the president daily charge of foreign intercourse.[7] In Jay's time Congress was not in session the whole year, whereas the president was always on hand to make decisions.

The president's advantages are magnified in times of warfare or crisis. The legislature's clumsy management of affairs during the Revolutionary War led the founders to champion an independent, energetic executive and to designate the president as commander in chief. Because wars and conflicts tend to centralize authority, presidential powers have been at their zenith during armed conflict. This held true during the cold war—hostilities between the United States and the Soviet Union—and the hot wars that ignited in Korea (1950–1953) and Vietnam (1965–1974). Throughout this period, from the late 1940s through the 1980s, presidents vigorously exploited their powers as commander in chief—buttressed by the nation's place as a world leader and by a military and intelligence establishment that was, by historical standards, enormous for a period in which there were no declared wars.

After hostilities cease, presidential powers tend to dissipate. As bipolar tensions lessened after the collapse of the Soviet Union in 1991, for example, the U.S. president's ability to rally the nation behind foreign commitments was curtailed.

The pendulum swung back decisively after the terrorist attacks of September 2001. Heightened security fears, the assault against terrorism, and wars launched against Afghanistan and Iraq brought new and sometimes unprecedented assertions of executive authority. Meanwhile, Congress's voice was muted—noticeably, and perhaps temporarily.

Who Speaks for Congress?

In the spring of 1999, after a House select committee found that China had used U.S. technology to build powerful long-range weapons, a number of House and Senate panels scrambled to claim jurisdiction over various aspects of the scandal—from intelligence and law enforcement to currency transfers and weapons research. The wide-ranging subjects of foreign policy and military affairs fall within the purview of twenty-three committees (see Table 15-1). In addition, other House panels and Senate panels consider matters related to foreign and military policy.

The foreign affairs and national security panels are among the most visible on Capitol Hill. The Senate Foreign Relations and House International Relations Committees get more time on the nightly television newscasts than do

Table 15-1 Selected Congressional Committees Dealing with
International Affairs

House	Senate	Jurisdiction
Agriculture	Agriculture, Nutrition, and Forestry	Agricultural marketing and food in foreign countries
Appropriations	Appropriations	Funding of foreign policy agencies and programs
Armed Services	Armed Services	National defense and security
Budget	Budget	Functional allotment for International affairs
Energy and Commerce	Commerce, Science, and Transportation	Foreign commerce; environmental issues
Financial Services	Banking, Housing, and Urban Affairs	International finance
Government Reform	Governmental Affairs	Executive branch reorganizations affecting international affairs
Homeland Security (Select)	—	Department of Homeland Security
Intelligence (Select)	Intelligence (Select)	Intelligence agencies
International Relations	Foreign Relations	State Department and other foreign affairs agencies; foreign aid program; foreign relations
Judiciary	Judiciary	Immigration
Ways and Means	Finance	Tariffs and trade agreements

other committees.[8] The Senate and House Armed Services Committees rank fourth, which still means relatively high TV exposure.

The Senate Foreign Relations Committee considers treaties and nominations of many foreign policy officials. It has normally seen itself as a working partner and adviser to the president. But, during the height of dispute over the Vietnam War in the late 1960s and early 1970s, the committee became a forum for antiwar debate under the leadership of Chairman J. William Fulbright, D-Ark. (1959–1974). Jesse Helms, R-N.C. (1995–2001), attacked international agencies and repeatedly locked horns with the Clinton administration. Despite the committee's prestige, its subject matter is sometimes hazardous for its members. Not a few of them, Fulbright included, were defeated for reelection in part because their work was portrayed as irrelevant to constituents' concerns. Richard G. Lugar, R-Ind., who became chairman in 2003, observed of a more recent issue, "There's almost no political sex appeal to issues like Bosnia. For those who get involved it's strictly a pro bono service." [9] The panel's stock fell so low during Helms's regime that the Republican Conference talked about downgrading its status.

For most of its history the House International Relations (formerly Foreign Affairs) Committee worked in the shadow of its Senate counterpart. This situation changed after World War II, when foreign aid programs thrust the House—with its special powers of the purse—into virtual parity with the Senate.[10] Today the House committee addresses nearly as wide a range of issues as does the Senate committee. It tends, however, to attract members who are more liberal and internationalist in outlook than the House as a whole. Consequently, its reports sometimes encounter skepticism on the House floor.

The Senate and House Armed Services Committees oversee the nation's military establishment. Annually, they authorize Pentagon spending for research, development, and procurement of weapons systems; construction of military facilities; and civilian and uniformed personnel. This last-mentioned jurisdiction includes the Uniform Code of Military Conduct, which governs the lives of men and women in uniform—and which has attracted congressional scrutiny of such diverse matters as sexual harassment and the right of Jewish officers to wear yarmulkes with military headgear. Although global strategy may intrigue some of the committees' members, what rivets their attention is structural policy making; that is, force levels, military installations, and defense contracts—issues closer to home. Thus constituency politics often drives military policy.

Because defense spending is the single largest controllable segment of the yearly federal budget, Appropriations subcommittees exert detailed control over foreign and defense policies. Senate and House oversight committees review intelligence activities. Tariffs and other trade regulations are the province of the taxing committees (House Ways and Means, Senate Finance). Committees involved with banking handle international, financial, and monetary policies; the commerce committees have jurisdiction over foreign commerce generally. With the creation of the Homeland Security Department, nearly every other panel asserts jurisdiction linked in some way to national security. Congress's organization for policy making is far from tidy. The profusion of congressional power centers leads chief executives to complain that they do not know whom to consult when crises arise and that leaks of sensitive information are inevitable with so many players. But the notion that the president, executive strategists, or even a few congressional experts know best is no longer an acceptable notion on Capitol Hill. Chief executives are free to consult with as few or as many lawmakers as they like—in some cases with only the joint party leaders, in others with chairmen of the relevant committees (Armed Services, Foreign Relations, International Relations, Select Intelligence).

Types of Foreign and National Security Policies

Foreign policy is the sum total of decisions and actions governing a nation's relations with other nations. The major foreign policy ingredients are national goals to be achieved and resources for achieving them. Statecraft is the art of formulating realistic goals and marshaling appropriate resources to attain them.

Ascertaining a nation's goals is no simple matter. Many of the great congressional debates have been over divergent and even incompatible foreign policy goals—over ties to such old-world powers as England and France during the nation's first decades, over high versus low tariffs, over American expansionism and industrialization abroad, over involvement in foreign wars, and over strategies for combating terrorists. Among a nation's resources for achieving its goals are its military strength and preparedness (national security policies), but other assets (for example, wealth, productivity, and cultural values) are even more potent in the long run.

In balancing national goals and national resources, policy makers must manipulate several different types of foreign and national security policies. Structural policies involve deploying resources or personnel; strategic policies advance the nation's interests militarily or diplomatically; and crisis policies protect the nation's vital interests against specific foreign threats.

Structural Policies

National security programs combined involve millions of workers and expend billions of dollars annually. Decisions about deploying such vast resources are called structural policy decisions. Examples include choices of specific weapons systems, contracts with private suppliers, location of military installations, sales of weapons and surplus goods to foreign countries, and trade policies that affect domestic industries and workers. Structural policy making on foreign and defense issues is virtually the same as distributive policy making in the domestic realm.

The last sixty years have seen a growing imbalance in the weight of military versus nonmilitary elements of foreign policies. The nation's singular military machine—it spends more on defense than the next fifteen nations combined—is, historically speaking, a fairly recent phenomenon. After each of its earlier wars, the United States quickly "sent the boys home" and, under congressional pressure, shrank its armed forces—though each time to somewhat higher plateaus.[11] Following World War II, the nation's global burdens (and the cold war threat) led to unprecedented levels of peacetime preparedness. By 1960, when retiring president Dwight D. Eisenhower, himself a career officer, warned against the "military-industrial complex," the new militarism was already embedded in the nation's political and economic system.

Department of Defense (DOD) spending—some $400 billion annually—is the largest controllable portion of the federal budget. As the nation's largest employer, its largest customer, and its largest procurer of equipment and services, DOD controls a huge number of structural outlays, which attract a wide swath of political interests.

By contrast, the State Department makes relatively few such decisions. In contrast to the 17 cents of every federal dollar spent on the military, the nation spends only half a penny on international affairs—which includes military assistance as well as diplomatic representation, foreign development, and humanitarian assistance.[12] The State Department's services and achievements are largely intangible, and in any event it spends much of its energy and money overseas. Little surprise, then, that it has few strong domestic clients and relatively few champions on Capitol Hill.

The Congressional–Military-Industrial Complex

Defense dollars—for projects, contracts, and bases, for example—are pursued by business firms, labor unions, and local communities, not to mention their representatives on Capitol Hill. Lobbying for military projects comes naturally to members of Congress who are expected to champion local interests. The impulse is bipartisan. Historically, southern Democrats relied upon defense dollars to lift their economically depressed communities. Republicans, many of whom now represent those areas, tend to favor military expansion even as they want other federal programs scaled back.

Pentagon procurement officers have learned to anticipate congressional needs in planning and designing projects. The perfect weapons system, it is said, is one with a component manufactured in every congressional district in the nation. Many weapons are made by widely scattered subcontractors. The Air Force's F/A-22 Raptor jet fighter, each costing $200 million, is assembled at a Georgia factory from parts made in forty-three states. "What it means to the company is the technology and the jobs," explained the factory's manager.[13]

Even when military planners decide to phase out a weapon, they may be pressured by lawmakers into keeping the item in production. The result can be both wasteful and expensive. Consider the Marines' V-22 Osprey, a tilt-rotor aircraft that flies like a conventional plane but takes off and lands like a helicopter. The project was conceived during the cold war, but the Pentagon later decided that the planes—at some $80 million apiece—were too costly to be continued. The planes had design problems; several of them were lost in crashes that claimed the lives of two dozen Marines. But the Osprey lives on. At full production, the project would involve some twenty-three thousand workers in forty-three states. A coalition of representatives from regions in which the plane was manufactured—especially from Pennsylvania, Texas, and New York—worked with contractors to keep the project alive.[14] "It is the hardest thing to do, to take a weapon out of the budget," a defense undersecretary noted. "It is just so easy to put one in." [15]

Lawmakers and lobbyists exploit divisions among the military services, which persist despite efforts of civilian managers over several presidencies, Republican and Democratic alike. The Air Force's projects include the F/A-22, the Marines want the Osprey, the Navy covets new aircraft carriers, and the Army has new artillery and combat vehicles. President George W. Bush more than once advocated military reform that would exceed "marginal improvements" and "skip a generation of technology." [16] His defense secretary, Donald H. Rumsfeld, pushed these novel ideas on Capitol Hill. Lawmakers' reactions ranged from worried to angry. In the end Rumsfeld capitulated on many conventional weapons programs, but his perceived success in the Iraqi war could buttress his long-range reform efforts.

The proliferation and geographic dispersion of military installations are another example of distributive military policy making. L. Mendel Rivers, D-S.C., chairman of the House Armed Services Committee from 1965 to 1971, kept defense money flowing to bases in Charleston, South Carolina, campaigning on the slogan "Rivers Delivers!" More recently, Sen. Trent Lott, R-Miss., described a Pascagoula, Mississippi, firm that keeps busy building ships for the navy: "It's one of the most important shipyards in the country, and if I were not supportive of my hometown, that shipyard and the workers in that shipyard, I wouldn't deserve to be in Congress, now would I?" [17]

In the post–cold war era, Congress tried to cut back military spending and confront the politically unpalatable problem of reducing military installations. In 1988 Congress passed a law intended to insulate decisions on base closures from congressional pressure by delegating them to a bipartisan Base Realignment and Closing Commission (BRAC). This agency would draw up a list of installations targeted for closure. To make the decisions hard to overturn, the list had to be accepted or rejected as a whole by the president and Congress.

Four rounds of BRACs (between 1989 and 1995) reduced or eliminated nearly a hundred defense installations. Each round was more contentious than the last. The third one "cast its net so broadly that it snared bases in areas represented by some of the most ardent budget-cutters in Congress as well as by critics of meddling in military affairs." [18] Political pressures were intense. The last commission chair, former senator Alan J. Dixon, D-Ill., was greeted at base entrances by parents holding children who, they said, would starve if the base closed.[19] Senators and representatives from affected areas fought the closure lists and nearly succeeded in overturning them. Everyone seemed relieved when the agency closed its doors at the end of 1995, having succeeded in shutting some one hundred major facilities at home and more than six hundred abroad.

The base-closing issue has not gone away. DOD argues that it still has 25 percent more bases than it needs. The Clinton administration called for two additional BRAC rounds in 1999 and 2001. "Over my dead body!" exclaimed Joel Hefley, R-Colo., a member of the House Armed Services Committee whose Colorado Springs district bristles with military installations (some of them obsolete).[20] Secretary Rumsfeld renewed the appeal to Congress for a base closing in 2003—but finally had to settle for one in 2005. It will not be easy. Members want changes in BRAC procedures and, over the years, have pumped money into facilities likely to be targeted. A former Senate Armed Services staff aide, now a base-closing consultant, claims that "virtually every addition to the legislation that is not sought by the administration is connected to helping save a base." [21]

Structural decisions, like distributive ones in the domestic realm, are typically reached in congressional subcommittees. Legislators from areas containing major military installations or defense contractors lobby with executive agencies for continued support, and subcommittee decisions are reached with local needs in mind. Referring to military bases, Rep. Tom Allen, D-Maine, explained how constituency interests attracted him to the Armed Services Committee as a freshman: "There are enough jobs dependent [on defense] that I believed it was important to be present when those issues are discussed." [22] Rarely do these issues spill out on the House or Senate floor. Interested members can usually craft agreements at the subcommittee or committee stage on how to allocate defense resources.

Trade Politics

Another obvious arena for distributive politics is foreign trade. Since the First Congress, the power "to regulate commerce with foreign nations" has been used to protect and enhance the competitive position of domestic goods and industries—whether cotton or wheat or textiles or computer software. From 1789 through the early 1930s, tariff legislation was fiercely contested on Capitol Hill by political parties and economic regions. Increasingly, however, Congress delegated the details of tariff negotiations to the executive branch, starting with the Reciprocal Trade Agreements Act of 1934.

Protectionist impulses have not waned, however. Myriad trade interests are represented on Capitol Hill. Republicans—reflecting the business community—tend to favor lowering trade barriers at home and combating them abroad, to open world markets for U.S. goods. Democrats from areas of union strength want barriers to slow the loss of jobs to low-wage countries. Specific commodity concerns—steel, textiles, and farm products, for example—may be voiced by representatives of either party. Free trade is more popular in the Senate, where export-minded agricultural interests are overrepresented; the House, with its patchwork of local interests, has stronger protectionist leanings.

Most battles over trade bills call forth variations of the above lineups. In the thirteen months preceding completion of the North American Free Trade Agreement (NAFTA) negotiations in 1992, U.S. trade representative Carla A. Hills logged forty consultations with individual lawmakers and no fewer than 199 meetings with congressional groups, from the House Ways and Means and Senate Finance Committees to the Northeast-Midwest Coalition and the Senate Textile Group.[23]

When the bill implementing NAFTA reached Capitol Hill the next year, a bipartisan effort was needed to approve it. Opposing the treaty were many Democrats, including the House majority leader and chief whip. President Bill Clinton launched a high-profile public relations campaign, trumpeted the bill's job-creation benefits, welcomed support from Republican leaders, and cut deals to meet individual legislators' objections. In the end, only 40 percent of House Democrats supported the president, but their 102 votes along with those of 132 Republicans were enough to gain House passage. NAFTA then easily passed the Senate. The legislation was a huge patchwork of provisions aimed at placating disparate interests. It included a $140 million job retraining program to help U.S. workers who lost their jobs because of competition with Mexico.[24]

Still other foreign policy concerns can fragment these lines even further. In the debate over U.S.-China trade status, for example, representatives splintered across the political spectrum. The lure of China's vast potential market for U.S. goods vied with doubts over China's unpredictable government and its poor human rights, worker safety, and environmental record. Trade policy and negotiations, asserts Rep. Sander M. Levin, D-Mich., "now involve virtually every area of what used to be considered U.S. domestic law—from antitrust and food safety to telecommunications." [25]

Congress, however, confronts a dilemma in dealing with trade. Members understand that trading partners need assurances that agreements can be ratified quickly and as a package. But having delegated most decisions to the executive, lawmakers who want to review specific trade deals must struggle to get back in the game. The Trade Act of 1974 addressed this dilemma. The president, it said, must actively consult, notify, and involve Congress as he negotiates trade agreements. These agreements take effect only after an implementing bill is enacted. Such legislation would be handled under an expedited fast-track procedure, including required steps and deadlines, limits on debate, and prohibition of amendments. Congress's involvement in trade decisions continued with passage of the Omnibus Trade and Competitiveness Act of 1988, which strengthened its oversight of trade agreements.[26]

Most presidents since 1974 have been awarded so-called fast-track (or trade promotion) authority to negotiate trade pacts subject to up-or-down votes in both houses within ninety days. (The authority lapsed during Clinton's presidency and was not renewed by the Republican-controlled Congress.) After a vigorous lobbying effort, President George W. Bush in August 2002 won a five-year renewal of the fast-track procedure. Even so, the House vote was close—215–212 (the Senate margin was 64–34). To gain the needed House votes, numerous concessions were made. For example, to cope with textile workers (Rep. Jim DeMint, R-S.C.) and citrus growers (Rep. Mark Foley, R-Fla.), "I told the president that we are not going to support anything that leaves us bare on citrus," Foley declared.[27] The measure also featured a Democratic-sponsored expansion of the Trade Adjustment Assistance fund for workers whose jobs are lost to foreign competition.[28]

Distributive politics infuse many other foreign and defense programs. For example, P.L. 480 dispenses agricultural surpluses to needy nations. This law not only serves humanitarian purposes but also provides outlets for subsidized farm products at home. Selling arms to other countries profits the U.S. government and private firms (some $53 billion in the four-year period ending in 1999) and affects civil and military affairs in every corner of the globe.[29]

Strategic Policies

To protect the nation's interests, decision makers design strategies for dealing with other countries. Strategic policies are concerned with spending levels for international and defense programs; total military force levels; the basic mix of military forces and weapons systems; arms sales to foreign powers; foreign trade inducements or restrictions; allocation of economic, military, and technical aid to developing nations; treaty obligations to other nations; U.S. responses to human rights abuses abroad; and America's basic stance toward international bodies such as the United Nations (UN), the North Atlantic Treaty Organization (NATO), and world financial agencies.

Strategic policies embrace most major foreign policy questions. They engage not only top-level executive decision makers but also congressional committees and midlevel executive officers. The key agencies for strategic decision making include the State Department, the Office of the Secretary of Defense, and the National Security Council—all advisory to the president. Although such issues usually draw less attention from the public and the media than crisis situations, they can capture citizens' ideological, ethnic, racial, or economic interests.[30] Despite their obvious distributive elements, strategic issues typically involve broader themes and invoke policy makers' long-term attitudes and beliefs.

The Power of the Purse

The spending power gives Congress the leverage to establish overall appropriation levels for foreign and defense purposes. Within these ceilings, priorities must be assigned—among military services, among weapons systems, between uniformed personnel and military hardware, and on economic, cultural, or military aid, to name just a few of the choices. The president exerts leadership by presenting an annual budget, lobbying for the administration's priorities, and threatening to veto options deemed unacceptable. Yet Congress, too, is equipped to write its own budgets down to the smallest detail. And the omnibus character of appropriations measures places pressure on the president to accede to the outcome of legislative bargaining on expenditures. To get the 95 percent of the budget the administration wants, the president may have to swallow the 5 percent he opposes. For example, to support his ambitious post–9/11 military goals, President George W. Bush was obliged to sign military spending bills that included projects he and his defense advisers had resisted.[31]

Congress responds both to perceived levels of international tension and to shifting public views about the salience of global engagement. Following the collapse of the Soviet Union, both Republican and Democratic strategists agreed to a gradual reduction of defense spending—from either the belief that a sizable "peace dividend" could be realized or the hope that savings could be gained from smarter planning and trimming waste, fraud, and abuse. However, downsizing the military establishment is politically and economically disruptive. Defense planners still envision military forces that are slimmer, more nimble, and better coordinated. But the post–9/11 threats give lawmakers new ammunition for fattening traditional military programs.

Congressional stakes in the defense budget showed up early in Bush's presidency. Everyone expected the administration to lavish support on defense, so the Pentagon's allies were upset when Defense Secretary Rumsfeld insisted on launching a thorough and mostly secret strategic review before he would make specific budget requests. The president came down on the side of military reform and promised to "skip a generation" of weapons to modernize. "[G]ood appropriations will really only occur if there is a strategic vision," the president explained to Republican House members.[32] But soon then Senate GOP leader Trent Lott was telling Rumsfeld that he felt "in the dark" about the Pentagon review. Failure to consult with Capitol Hill leaders, Lott said, would impede acceptance of the administration's policies and budget. Senators received assurances of access to Rumsfeld's review. "If they think we'll take hook, line and sinker whatever the administration asks for, they're crazy," one GOP Senate aide said.[33]

Footing the bills for combat operations, however, poses dilemmas for Congress. How much money is really needed, and how much freedom should the president have in spending it? Lyndon B. Johnson gradually deepened U.S. involvement in Vietnam, but he hesitated to ask Congress to appropriate the needed funds. Thus the first supplemental funding bill was passed in February 1966, even though Congress had signed onto the war as early as August 1964 (with the Gulf of Tonkin Resolution). Johnson's effort to hide the escalating war costs while maintaining domestic programs elevated both inflation and the federal debt.

Figure 15-1   Defense and Foreign Policy Spending as Percentage of Total Budget Outlays, 1940–2002

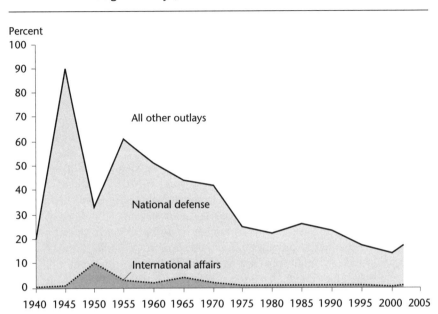

Source: Office of Management and Budget, *Budget of the United States Government, Fiscal Year 2003, Historical Tables* (Washington, D.C.: Government Printing Office, 2002), Table 5-1.

Note: Figures are fiscal year outlays, according to current statistical conventions for treating off-budget items. The total budget in billions of dollars was $9.5 in 1940, $42.6 in 1950, $92.2 in 1960, $195.6 in 1970, $590.9 in 1980, $1,253.2 in 1990, $1,825.0 in 2000, and $2,085 in 2002.

After the September 2001 assaults, Congress acted swiftly to pass a supplemental appropriations package of $40 billion—one-fourth of which was under the president's near-total control. The following summer Congress approved another $30 billion, again featuring flexibility. However, a number of lawmakers, especially on the funding committees, began to have second thoughts. "All presidents want unlimited authority. In any time of conflict, there's a tendency to allow a little more leeway," said Rep. David L. Hobson, R-Ohio, an appropriations subcommittee chair. "We have a responsibility to maintain a balance . . . and we're struggling with that." [34]

Unlike national defense, international affairs funding represents a relatively small expenditure (see Figure 15-1). Historically, the nation's foreign operations required relatively small outlays. In the immediate post–World War II years, 1947–1951, however, programs to rebuild devastated Europe and Japan consumed as much as 16 percent of U.S. annual spending. Throughout the cold war, the United States was a major provider of economic, military, and technical aid throughout the world.

In recent years, such spending—for Department of State operations, the diplomatic service, and foreign aid—has accounted for less than 1 percent of all expenditures. U.S. economic assistance to promote democracy, address poverty, and improve health and education amounts to only about one-third of 1 percent. And most of this aid goes to a handful of frontline states (Israel and Egypt, most prominently). U.S. foreign aid, although high in pure dollar terms, ranks dead last among the world's wealthiest nations as a proportion of gross domestic product.[35] (Opinion surveys show that citizens indicate lukewarm support for foreign aid spending but grossly overestimate how much is actually spent.) President George W. Bush announced support for increased economic aid and requested $15 billion to combat AIDS (acquired immune deficiency syndrome) worldwide. But Congress will set the eventual funding levels and write conditions for dispensing the money.

In the final analysis, no major foreign or military enterprise can be sustained unless Congress provides money and support. A president can conduct an operation for a time using existing funds and supplies, as Lyndon B. Johnson did at first in Vietnam, but sooner or later he must ask Congress for funding. The United States' role in South Vietnam ended belatedly in 1974, when Congress simply refused to provide emergency aid funds. Many of the Reagan administration's clashes with Congress took the form of fights over funding; for example, for aid to anticommunist "freedom fighters" in Nicaragua and Angola and for arms to Saudi Arabia and Jordan.

The dependence of foreign and defense policies on economic resources heightens Congress's leverage. It also has made the House more of an equal partner with the Senate. Because the House traditionally originates taxing and funding legislation, its key panels (especially Ways and Means and the Appropriations subcommittees on defense and foreign operations) usually set forth the detailed specifications and dollar amounts. The Senate serves as the court of appeals, ratifying or modifying the House committees' products.

Treaties and Executive Agreements

The Constitution makes Congress an active partner with the president in a key element of strategic policy: treaties with foreign powers. Although initiated by the president, treaties are made "by and with the advice and consent of the Senate." The Senate's consent is signified by the concurrence of two-thirds of the senators present and voting.

Congress may or may not be taken into the president's confidence when treaties and executive agreements are negotiated. To avoid President Woodrow Wilson's humiliation when the Senate rejected the Versailles treaty after World War I, modern chief executives typically inform key senators during the negotiation process. After the pact is sent to the Senate, several courses of action may follow, above and beyond a simple up-or-down vote.

Rarely does the Senate reject a treaty outright. It has turned down only twenty treaties since 1789. One study found that the Senate had approved without change 944 treaties, or 69 percent of those submitted to it.[36] Such was the case in March 2003, when the Senate unanimously approved a U.S.-Russian treaty requiring cuts in the two nations' arsenals of long-range missiles. Despite critics' charges that the deal was "flimsy," senators opted to send a positive signal to Russia during the run-up to the Iraqi war. Citing "many reservations," Sen. Joseph R. Biden Jr., D-Del., ranking minority member on the Foreign Relations Committee, explained that "the reason I'm for this treaty is, failure to ratify [it] would be read as bad faith." [37]

The Senate may attach reservations to a treaty, which, if serious enough, may oblige the president to renegotiate the document. Formal reservations are employed to change policy, according to two scholars who examined the process. "Ratification reservations can dictate how the U.S. will interpret and implement a treaty, how the U.S. will behave on unrelated foreign policy issues, and in some instances can even change the actual text of a treaty." [38]

The Senate may simply decline to act at all. Some fifty treaties negotiated and signed by various presidents now languish without Senate approval, including pacts dealing with the oceans, women's and children's rights, nuclear weapons testing, global warming, and biological diversity.[39]

The Chemical Weapons Agreement, negotiated during President George Bush's administration and signed by 161 nations, illustrates the Senate's active role in ratification. Although the treaty had broad bipartisan support, a group of hawkish advocates argued that the agreement was filled with loopholes and would not prevent such rogue states as Iraq or Libya from making and using chemical weapons. Simply to get the measure to the Senate floor required arcane negotiations with the treaty's archenemy, Foreign Relations chairman Helms. Negotiations were spearheaded during the Clinton administration by Secretary of State Madeleine K. Albright and mediated by GOP leader Lott. The administration not only agreed to twenty-eight clarifications demanded by the conservatives, but it also made other major concessions—including a State Department reorganization, UN reform, and submission of other arms control treaties to the Senate—aimed at strengthening the Senate's role in future bargaining. During the floor debate, President Clinton and his aides worked the phones, trumpeted support from such Republican luminaries as retired general Colin Powell and former senator Bob Dole, and sent a last-minute letter to Lott promising to withdraw from the treaty if it subverted U.S. interests in any way. The multiple offensive paid off when Lott brought in enough skeptical Republicans to ratify the treaty in April 1997. Five days later it went into effect.[40]

A different fate befell another major multilateral pact, the Comprehensive Test Ban Treaty (CTBT) in autumn 1999. From the moment it reached the Senate two years earlier, the pact met widespread resistance from conservatives who held that it would jeopardize the nation's nuclear superiority and weaken deterrence against would-be nuclear powers. From their private discussions, Senate Republicans realized they had the votes to kill the treaty. Normally the Senate would have simply taken no action. But when pressed by President Clinton and Democratic leaders to bring the treaty to the floor, Republican leaders suddenly scheduled a flurry of hearings quickly followed by floor debate. By the time the treaty's advocates realized they had fallen into a trap (partially of their own making) it was too late to turn back. After debate described as "nasty, brutish, and short," the treaty failed by a 48–51 vote—short of a majority, much less the required two-thirds.[41]

The defeat of the CTBT was a misadventure for all concerned. Although the United States had spearheaded the delicate multilateral talks that led to the pact, the Bush and Clinton administrations had failed to involve senators in the process. Nor was the treaty a White House priority until the last moment. Even then, the effort fell short of a full-court press—not even the usual public relations tactics were employed of enlisting expert endorsements or creating advisory task forces. No bargaining was evident in the brief committee and floor treatment of the matter.[42] For their part, the treaty's foes seemed bent on humiliating the president and signaling a unilateralist approach to future arms control efforts. "While there was nothing improper or illegal in their parliamentary tactics," one commentator wrote, "it was nonetheless a nasty and contemptuous way of doing business quite out of character with the stately, sometimes ponderous way of doing business." [43]

The hurdle of obtaining a two-thirds Senate vote has led many presidents to rely increasingly on executive agreements—international accords that are not submitted to the Senate for its advice and consent. Of the more than fifty-six hundred U.S. international accords signed between 1981 and 1996, 96 percent were executive agreements.[44] Such agreements are enforceable under international law, which regards a treaty as any binding agreement among nations.

Executive agreements should be regarded as congressional-executive instruments. In theory all of them are signed pursuant to some grant of legislative authority, though the laws cited are often outdated and only vaguely linked. Many agreements are subsequently approved by Congress. Kikki Caruson describes the agreements' subject matter:

> The vast majority of executive agreements concern routine procedural matters such as postal agreements, mutual legal assistance, cooperation in the fields of science and technology, conservation, civil aviation agreements, and other relatively non-controversial issues. But the executive agreement has also been used to address important foreign policy issues, such as security and defense matters.[45]

According to the Case-Zablocki Act of 1972, copies of all executive agreements must be transmitted to Congress within sixty days of their going into effect.

From time to time a constitutional amendment requiring Senate ratification of executive agreements has been proposed.

Other Policy-Making Powers of Congress

In addition to controlling the purse strings, Congress employs an array of techniques to shape or influence strategic policies. Sometimes the techniques are used to support presidential initiatives. Often, however, Congress ventures on its own and challenges the president to respond. The most common tools of congressional policy leadership are informal advice, legislative prodding through nonbinding resolutions or policy statements, policy oversight, legislative directives or restrictions, and structural or procedural changes.[46]

Congressional leaders and key members routinely provide the president and other executive officials with informal advice. Sometimes this advice proves decisive. In 1954 President Eisenhower dispatched Secretary of State John Foster Dulles to meet with a small bipartisan group of congressional leaders to determine whether the United States should intervene militarily in Indochina (Vietnam). The leaders unanimously declined to sponsor a resolution favoring involvement until other nations indicated their support of military action. Lacking assurances from either Congress or foreign allies, Eisenhower decided against intervening.[47]

Congress engages in legislative prodding by passing nonbinding resolutions that set forth positions or give advice about foreign policy. Recent Congresses have each approved, on average, more than fifty simple or concurrent resolutions that are not legally binding or enforceable. Such pronouncements may lend support to the executive branch, advance certain policies, or signal assurances or warnings to other nations. Occasionally, nonbinding resolutions put forward fresh policy ideas; at other times they are little more than posturing. Some of both were embedded in the House resolution backing troops for the Kosovo crisis in 1999. The resolution—supported by 174 Democrats, 44 Republicans, and 1 independent—authorized the president to deploy troops with the NATO peacekeeping force, but it also instructed the president to explain to Congress an exit strategy from the area and to ensure that U.S. troops would answer only to American commanders.[48]

Congress shapes foreign policy through oversight of the executive branch's performance. Hearings and investigations often focus on foreign policy issues. Recurrent hearings on authorizing and funding State Department and Defense Department programs offer many opportunities for lawmakers to voice their concerns, large and small. Another oversight technique is requiring that certain decisions or international agreements be submitted to Congress before they go into effect. Or Congress and its committees can require reports from the executive that "provide not only information for oversight but also a handle for action." [49] Some six hundred foreign policy reporting requirements are embedded in current statutes.

Oversight in time of war or crisis is especially hazardous. The president resists intrusions, and lawmakers are reluctant to impede the action. "The trick is to rein in the White House but not seem unpatriotic," writes historian Bruce J. Schulman.[50] The boldest legislative foray into wartime oversight occurred during the Civil War. As confederate guns threatened Washington, D.C., the Joint Committee on the Conduct of the War (1861–1865), controlled by Radical Republicans, held hearings on Capitol Hill and published reports that questioned President Abraham Lincoln's war policies, criticized military operations, berated generals who failed to pursue the enemy, and exposed waste and fraud in military procurements. During World War II, Missouri senator Harry S. Truman's Special Committee to Investigate the National Defense Program (1941–1948) uncovered profiteering, contract abuses, and shoddy workmanship in wartime projects. It saved taxpayers billions of dollars and, not incidentally, boosted the career of its chairman ("Truman Committee," its letterheads proclaimed). Senate Foreign Relations Committee hearings, launched in 1966, raised doubts in the public's mind about the Vietnam War.

In the wake of the 2001 terrorist attacks, a joint House-Senate panel probing intelligence failures met stiff White House resistance. The White House accused the committee of security leaks and later delayed its bipartisan report, which found missteps by the CIA and FBI prior to September 11. Congress subsequently authorized an independent commission to expand on its own inquiries. Sen. John McCain, R-Ariz., who had pushed for the commission along with Sen. Joseph I. Lieberman, D-Conn., called for a "full and frank accounting" and said that administration delays in providing access to materials "creates the appearance of bureaucratic stonewalling." [51]

Congress sometimes makes foreign policy by legislative directives—to launch new programs, to authorize certain actions, or to set guidelines. A cornerstone enactment of the cold war era was the Jackson-Vanik amendment to the Trade Act of 1974 (named for Sen. Henry M. "Scoop" Jackson, D-Wash., and Rep. Charles Vanik, D-Ohio). Prompted by concern over the Soviet Union's treatment of its Jewish minority, the amendment denied government credits and most-favored-nation (now called "normal trade relations") trade status to any communist country that restricted free emigration of its citizens.

Foreign policy statutes may include explicit legislative restrictions—perhaps Congress's most effective weapon. Often they are embedded in authorization or appropriation bills that the president is unlikely to veto. Throughout the Reagan years, for example, Congress passed many limits on military aid to Central American countries. Most notable were the Boland amendments (named for House Intelligence Committee chairman Edward P. Boland, D-Mass.) that were attached to various bills after 1982 to forbid nonhumanitarian aid to the contra rebels in Nicaragua. In the 1987 Iran-contra scandal, President Ronald Reagan and his National Security Council staff were accused of violating this prohibition.

Even the threat of passing legislation may bring about the desired result. Dissatisfied with the Reagan administration's weak "constructive engagement" policy toward South African apartheid (a brutal form of racial separation), a

pro-civil rights coalition on Capitol Hill threatened to pass legislation imposing economic and other sanctions. Just before a sanctions bill was to be approved in 1985, President Reagan issued an executive order imposing limited
sanctions. (The next year, over Reagan's veto, Congress enacted tougher restrictions.)

Legislation also shapes the structures and procedures through which policies are carried out. "Congress changes the structure and procedures of decision making in the executive branch in order to influence the content of policy," writes James M. Lindsay.[52] When lawmakers wanted to reform military
procurement, they restructured the Defense Department to clarify and stream-
line the process; when they wanted more say in trade negotiations, they wrote
themselves into the process with the 1974 and 1988 trade laws.

Crisis Policies: The War Powers

When the nation is directly threatened, national self-preservation pushes
aside other foreign policy goals. One definition of an international crisis is a
sudden challenge to the nation's safety and security. Examples range from
Japan's attack on the U.S. naval fleet in Pearl Harbor in 1941 to the terrorist
attacks of September 11, 2001.

Crisis policies engage decision makers at the very highest levels: the president, the secretaries of state and defense, the National Security Council, and
the Joint Chiefs of Staff. Congressional leaders are sometimes brought into the
picture. More rarely, congressional advice is sought and heeded—as in President Eisenhower's 1954 decision against military intervention in Indochina.
Often when executive decision makers fear congressional opposition, they
simply neglect to inform Capitol Hill until the planned action is under way. A
failed 1980 attempt to rescue American hostages in Iran, for example, was
planned in strictest secrecy, and no consultations were undertaken.

As long as a crisis lingers, policy makers keep a tight rein on information
flowing upward from line officers. The attention of the media and the public
is riveted upon crisis events. Patriotism runs high. Citizens hasten to "rally
round the flag" and support whatever course their leaders choose.[53]

United States as Empire? Underlying current debates over the global role
of U.S. power is the issue of the nation's imperial prerogative. To what degree
can or should the United States act alone in the international arena?[54]

On the one side, unilateralists advocate using the nation's vast military
and economic power to reshape the global environment to its advantage. They
argue that the nation can and should act alone and even preemptively to further its interests, regardless of objections of allies and international organizations. They promoted the 2003 Iraq war, for instance, as an easy first step in
recasting the Middle East in ways that would favor U.S. interests (for example,
oil, Israel, antiterrorism). Unilateralists—who are prominent in Congress, the
Bush administration, and neoconservative think tanks—dismiss international
organizations (the UN in particular) and shun multilateral pacts (for example,

the International Criminal Court, the Kyoto Protocol on Climate Change, and such arms control agreements as the Biological Weapons Convention and the Comprehensive Test Ban Treaty).

Globalists, in contrast, maintain that U.S. power, however awesome, is by no means unchecked. Other powers compete with the United States (the European Union, for example), and their cooperation is deemed essential for defending common interests, especially combating such destabilizing elements as hunger, disease, poverty, terrorism, and environmental degradation. Globalists—who include senior members of the Senate and House foreign policy committees as well as analysts in academia, peace organizations, and foreign policy think tanks—argue that superpowers are ironically most in danger when they spurn allies. Their arrogance may spur other nations to unite against them. The United States, in this view, should collaborate with other nations and nurture the international network of alliances it sponsored after World War II. Political theorist Benjamin R. Barber has called for a new "declaration of interdependence" whereby the United States will fully join "the world to which it is ever more seamlessly bound. . . . It involves strengthening international law, reinforcing multilateralism and spreading equality." [55]

Constitutional Powers. War powers are shared by the president and Congress. The president is the commander in chief (Article II, Section 2), but Congress has the power to declare war (Article I, Section 8). Congress has declared war only five times: the War of 1812 (1812–1814), the Mexican War (1846-1848), the Spanish-American War (1898), World War I (1917–1918), and World War II (1941–1945). In four instances, Congress readily assented to the president's call for war, acknowledging in the declaration that a state of war already existed. Only once did Congress delve into the merits of waging war, and that was in 1812, when the vote was close. In two cases—the Mexican and Spanish-American conflicts—lawmakers later had reason to regret their haste.

More problematic than formal declarations of war are the almost three hundred instances when U.S. military forces have been deployed abroad. The examples range from an undeclared naval war with France (1798–1800) to deployment of military forces to Iraq (2003). [56] (The number is uncertain because of quasi engagements involving military or intelligence advisers.) Since the end of the last declared war—World War II—in 1945, numerous military interventions have taken place abroad. Some of them were massive prolonged wars (Korea, 1950–1953; Vietnam, 1964–1975). Others were full-scale but brief wars: Afghanistan (2001) and Iraq (1991, 2003). Still others were short-lived actions (for example, military coordination of medical and disaster relief after U.S. embassies in Kenya and Tanzania were bombed in 1998) and rescue or peacekeeping missions, some of which involved casualties (Lebanon, 1983; Somalia, 1992–1993).

Most of these interventions were authorized by the president as commander in chief on the pretext of protecting American lives, property, or interests abroad. Some were justified on the grounds of treaty obligations or inherent powers derived from a broad reading of executive prerogatives. Others were peacekeeping efforts under UN or NATO sponsorship. In virtually every armed intervention in U.S. history, constitutional questions have generated "lively disagreement among the president, Congress, and the Supreme Court, and between the central government and the states." [57]

Members of Congress, though wary of armed interventions, are reluctant to halt them: "No one actually wants to cut off funds when American troops are in harm's way," in the words of a House leadership aide. "The preferred stand is to let the president make the decisions and, if it goes well, praise him, and if it doesn't, criticize him," observed Lee H. Hamilton, D-Ind., former chairman of the House Foreign Affairs Committee (1993–1995). [58] Interventions go well if they come to a swift, successful conclusion with few American lives lost. Actions that drag on without a satisfactory resolution or that cost many lives will eventually tax lawmakers' patience. As the sense of urgency subsides, competing information appears that may challenge the president's version of the event. Congressional critics thus are emboldened to voice their reservations. This reaction occurred as the undeclared wars in Korea and Vietnam dragged on and after U.S. troops suffered casualties in Lebanon and Somalia.

The War Powers Resolution. Backlash against the Vietnam War made lawmakers skeptical of presidential initiatives abroad. In 1973 Congress passed the War Powers Resolution (WPR, P.L. 93–148) over President Richard M. Nixon's veto. This law requires the president to consult with Congress before introducing U.S. troops into hostilities; report any commitment of forces to Congress within forty-eight hours; and terminate the use of forces within sixty days if Congress does not declare war, does not extend the period by law, or is unable to meet. (The president may extend the period to ninety days, if necessary.)

Through 2002, presidents had submitted a hundred reports to Congress that troops had been deployed abroad. [59] In several other cases the military action was brief, and no report was filed. In still other cases the executive branch claimed that reports were not required because U.S. personnel were not confronting hostilities or imminent hostilities. Thus the Reagan administration declined to comply with congressional reporting requirements when it sent military advisers to El Salvador in 1981 or when it provided protection for oil tankers in the Persian Gulf in 1987 and 1988.

The WPR is an awkward compromise of executive and legislative authority, and presidents still intervene as they see fit. Members of Congress tend to sit on the sidelines, only later questioning presidential initiatives. Sometimes deployments are heatedly debated. President Reagan dispatched two thousand Marines to Lebanon in 1982, but it was not until the troops came under hostile fire in 1983 that Congress seriously debated invoking the War Powers Resolution. Finally, a compromise was reached. The president signed congressional legislation invoking the WPR, and Congress authorized U.S. troops to remain in Lebanon for eighteen months (P.L. 98–119). Shortly afterward, 241 Marines were killed by a suicide truck bombing, raising new complaints from Congress and the public. The president withdrew the troops early in 1984.

The law figured prominently in the Persian Gulf War of 1991, a real war involving forces from the United States and the United Nations. A week after Iraqi troops invaded Kuwait in August 1990, President George Bush notified Congress that he had deployed troops to the region. Although the president did not consult with congressional leaders before acting, both chambers later adopted measures supporting the deployment and urging Iraqi withdrawal from Kuwait. Urged by congressional leaders, President Bush later asked for a resolution supporting the use of all necessary means to implement the UN decrees. After a lively, high-minded debate, both houses passed a statutory authorization of military action (P.L. 102–1) under the WPR.

Wars against Terrorism. Post–9/11 authorizations under the WPR found Congress in a reactive posture. Three days after the terrorist attacks, with smoke still lingering above the damaged Pentagon building, both chambers passed S. J. Res. 23, authorizing the president "to use all necessary and appropriate force against those nations, organizations, or persons he determines planned, authorized, committed, or aided the terrorist attacks." The single dissenter was Rep. Barbara Lee, D-Calif. The measure included the declaration that "[n]othing in this resolution supercedes any requirement of the War Powers Resolution." Some three weeks later, President Bush notified Congress that he had launched an assault "designed to disrupt the use of Afghanistan as a terrorist base of operations."

After the Afghanistan war ended and its Taliban regime was toppled, the White House resumed its drumbeat of war threats against the Iraqi regime of Saddam Hussein, which had survived the 1991 war. The rationale was elusive: perhaps Iraq's weapons of mass destruction, or its ties to terrorist organizations, or simply the regime's cruelty to its people. (Probably none of the above, to be honest.) Elite and public opinion agreed that regime change in Iraq would be desirable, but it sharply clashed over whether the United States should act unilaterally or work through the UN and a broad coalition of allies, as in 1991. These battles were waged more on media talk shows and editorial pages than in the halls of Congress.

The president's advisers initially asserted that the president could launch a preemptory attack without further approval. But as his father had done before in the Gulf War, President Bush bowed to demands that he obtain congressional approval to act. By the standards set in 1991, however, debate in the two chambers was muted and desultory. Sen. Chuck Hagel, R-Neb., voted for the resolution but cautioned against using the military option. "America must understand that it cannot alone win a war against terrorism," he said. "It will require allies, friends and partners." [60] Sen. Bob Graham, D-Fla., chair of the

Intelligence Committee, opposed the resolution because, he explained, Iraq posed a less urgent threat than terrorist networks: "There are many evils out there, a number of which are substantially more competent, particularly in their ability to attack America here at home, than Iraq is likely to be in the foreseeable future." [61] Sen. Robert C. Byrd, D-W.Va., railed against what he termed the president's unique demand for "power to launch this nation into war without provocation and without clear evidence of an imminent attack on the United States. And we are going to be foolish enough to give it to him." [62] Lopsided majorities backed the resolution: 296–133 in the House, 77–23 in the Senate, (Democrats provided most of the no votes: 126 in the House and 21 in the Senate.) In March 2003 the president began the war. Even lawmakers with misgivings signed onto resolutions of "support for the troops."

The final Iraqi authorization (H. J. Res. 114) preserved at least a fig leaf of congressional prerogatives. The original White House proposal—reminiscent of the infamous Tonkin Gulf Resolution of 1964 and the panicky post–9/11 action—was narrowed somewhat. First, the action made clear that the UN must have time to act before force could be employed. Second, the president had to declare promptly that "diplomatic and other peaceful means" failed and that U.S. action was "consistent with" continuing actions against terrorism by the nation and its allies. Finally, such action would fall under the WPR, requiring reports to Congress at least every sixty days.

Congress's War Powers in Today's World. With each new crisis the War Powers Resolution is attacked or defended, depending on the view held of the proposed intervention. Although presidents are encouraged to pause and consult before acting, experience since 1973 shows that the WPR has not prevented them from boldly exercising military powers, including military responses to sudden threats.

Champions of executive authority—reportedly including Vice President Dick Cheney—think that WPR and other post-Vietnam enactments limit executive flexibility, but recent history belies such a claim. In the case of the war powers, Louis Fisher's careful study of the historical record reveals that a combination of presidential hubris and congressional abdication has caused an "unmistakable . . . drift" away from Capitol Hill. "Congress had made repeated efforts since the 1970s to restore legislative prerogatives, with only moderate success," he concludes. "Presidents continue to wield military power single-handedly, agreeing only to consult with legislators and notify them of completed actions. This is not the framers' model." [63]

For the record, every post–1973 president has denied WPR's legality, but no one is willing to have the courts resolve the question. Lawmakers strive vainly to be consulted. They support the action as long as it is politically feasible. If the crisis persists and the president's actions backfire, however, Congress moves in and sometimes curtails the action by refusing funds.

Although the resolution has few outright defenders, members of Congress are not ready to repeal or replace it. Leaders in the last Democratic Congress

(1993–1995) vowed to rewrite the statute but fell short. In 1995 Republican leaders in both chambers introduced repeal bills. The House measure, authored by Judiciary chairman Henry J. Hyde, R-Ill., was brought to the floor. Closing the debate, Speaker Newt Gingrich, R-Ga., argued for passage. But in a rare rebuff to the leadership, the measure was rejected, 217–201. Forty-four Republicans joined 172 Democrats to retain the War Powers Resolution. "The power of the purse is not equivalent to Congress sharing the critical decision, up front, to send troops or not," argued Rep. Hamilton, then ranking Democrat on the International Relations Committee. "Congress should hold tenaciously to the power of sharing the decision." Rep. Fred Upton of Michigan, one of three Republicans who spoke against repeal, contended that the resolution, even when not invoked, forces presidents to work with Congress. "The biggest vote that I ever cast was to give President Bush the authority to go into the Gulf War," he said. "I'm not so certain he would have done that [consulted Congress] if there had not been a war powers act." [64]

Although it compromises Congress's constitutional power of declaring war, the WPR has some practical virtues. It accommodates the rapid use of armed force without the traditional but awkward step of formally declaring war on a nation-state and its people—especially when the real target may be, say, a rogue regime or a shadowy terrorist network. "[Y]ou can't just go off and declare war when you don't know who you are declaring war against," Sen. John B. Breaux, D-La., after the 9/11 attacks. "It is beneath our dignity to declare war against Osama bin-Laden," stated Sen. John W. Warner, R-Va.[65]

Moreover, the WPR bids at least a nodding respect for the framers' belief that Congress, the branch most representative of the people, is the sole source of legal and moral authority for major military enterprises. Presidents may succeed at short-lived actions. But, lacking a legislative mandate, longer and more costly engagements will surely falter—as the Korean and Vietnam wars did. For the time being, then, the War Powers Resolution stands as a reminder of the ultimate need to gain congressional acquiescence, if not approval, for major military deployments.

Conclusion

Some politicians still believe that their constituents are preoccupied with domestic concerns and thus uninterested in world affairs. This seems to be a misreading of public sentiment. A strong majority of citizens endorses an active role for the United States in world affairs. Although people are reluctant to use U.S. troops overseas, they support fights against international terrorism, nuclear proliferation, and drug trafficking.[66]

Scant evidence of isolationism among constituents was found by Steven Kull and I. M. Destler in an ingenious study comparing national surveys with opinions in four House districts whose members had anti-internationalist public records. In every district the citizens supported the UN, foreign aid, and an active role in world trouble spots. Their findings undermined such assumptions that "members necessarily mirror their districts" or that "the aggregate behavior of Congress, in particular its move away from international engagement, is a good indicator of American public opinion as a whole." [67]

Unfolding developments ought to enhance Congress's role in foreign policy. First, the United States, as the world's remaining superpower, continues to exert influence in every corner of the globe through its actions—and its inactions. Second, the post–cold war conditions may mean that the public will expect more legislative dissent in foreign affairs than was previously the case. Legislators are more likely to oppose the president if they believe the voters will not punish them for doing so. Third, global interdependence blurs the line that once demarked domestic policy from foreign policy. Insofar as the resulting issues trespass upon traditional domestic matters, such questions are bound to encourage congressional intervention and influence. Finally, the question of whether the nation is able or willing to underwrite its costly international projects may lead Congress to curtail the nation's global commitments. [68]

Members of Congress dare not abandon their interest in foreign and national security policies. As the world grows ever more interdependent, these policies impinge upon every citizen and every local community. An internationally minded electorate—sensitive to famines and plagues in Africa, deforestation in the Amazon, foreign competition for jobs and trade, and anti-Americanism and terrorism in various regions—may well draw fewer distinctions between domestic and global matters than in the past.

Far more than their predecessors, today's legislators do seem to care about world issues. They realize that global developments touch their local constituencies, and they believe (rightly or wrongly) that they will be judged to some degree on their mastery of those subjects. "In Lyndon Johnson's age, you just had to be able to say [Soviet premier Nikita] Khrushchev," remarked Sen. Bob Kerrey, D-Neb. (1989–2001). Now, "you need to know the leaders in sixteen former Soviet Union States." Nebraska's exports, mostly farm-related, go to foreign customers. As Senator Hagel, a Nebraska Republican, told college students in Kearney: "We are living in a global village, undergirded by a global economy." [69]

Paradoxically, however, the militarization of U.S. foreign policy—an imbalance between the nation's military hegemony and its diplomatic resources—works to Congress's detriment. Hot (and cold) wars inevitably tend to elevate the presidency and mute legislative voices. To the extent that U.S. policy is defined in military rather than diplomatic or cultural terms, the impulse on Capitol Hill is to defer to the commander in chief and, at all costs, to "support the troops." The following warning by Senate Foreign Relations chair Richard Lugar was aimed at policy makers at both ends of Pennsylvania Avenue:

Military action will be necessary to deal with serious and immediate threats to our national security, but the war on terrorism will not be won through attrition—particularly because military action will often breed more terrorism. To win this war, the United States must assign to economic and diplomatic capabilities the same strategic priority we assign to military capabilities. What is still missing from the American political discourse is support for the painstaking work of foreign policy and the commitment of resources to vital foreign policy objectives that lack a direct political constituency.[70]

Prelude to the 21st century. Members of Congress take part in a prayer vigil in the Capitol Rotunda on September 12, 2001, for victims of the previous day's terrorist attacks.

16

The Two Congresses
and the American People

On the morning of September 11, 2001, the president of the United States was whisked aboard *Air Force One,* where for most of the day he was flown to various military installations, while receiving nonstop status reports from around the world. By nightfall he was back in the White House, where he delivered a brief message to the American people.

Meanwhile, members and staff aides on Capitol Hill were told to evacuate their offices. The Capitol building, like the White House, was a potential terrorist target, and smoke could already be seen above the Pentagon, across the Potomac River. "I remember so vividly racing through this hallway . . . as we departed the building as quickly as we could, having been told that we may be under attack," recalled Senate majority leader Tom Daschle, D-S.D.[1] A month later a staff aide in the Hart Senate Office Building opened a letter addressed to Daschle, and a cloud of fine white dust billowed out. Infected with anthrax, Capitol Hill was virtually shut down for several weeks.

The initial images of the post-9/11 government were starkly symbolic: The president in charge and in touch, Congress scattered and for the moment out of the loop.

Granted, the threats were palpable. Capitol Hill was at risk, and a local postal handler died after contact with anthrax-contaminated mail. But the impression remained of a proactive president and a reactive legislature. The deliberative processes of legislatures (and courts) are sorely tested in times of warfare or emergency. Yet the authors of the Constitution—who were under no illusions about the need for a strong commander in chief or the flaws of legislative bodies, especially in fighting wars—nonetheless envisioned the legislative branch as a preeminent maker of public policy in war as well as peace.

The United States is not, as some have claimed, a "presidential nation"; it is a "separated system" marked by the ebb and flow of power among the policy-making branches of government.[2] As Speaker Newt Gingrich, R-Ga. (1995–1999), said about the nation's complex and frustrating governing arrangements:

> We have to get the country to understand that at the heart of the process of freedom is not the presidential press conference. It is the legislative process; it is the give and take of independently elected, free people coming together

to try to create a better product by the friction of their passions and the friction of their ideas.[3]

Anxious or fearful citizens, in particular, need to recall the American system's deliberate, and all too fragile, give-and-take among institutions.

Citizens' ambivalent feelings toward the popular branch of government are yet another reminder of the dual character of Congress—the theme that has pervaded our explanations of how Congress and its members work. This notion of the two Congresses manifests itself in public perceptions and assessments. Citizens look at Congress in Washington, D.C., through lenses different from those with which they view their individual senators and representatives.[4] This same dualism appears in media coverage. The two Congresses are covered by different kinds of reporters working for different kinds of media organizations.

Congress-as-Politicians

Lawmakers' working conditions and schedules are far from ideal and beg for periodic examination.[5] The hours are killing, the pay comparatively modest, the toll on family life heavy, and the psychic rewards fleeting. "Your schedule is not your own," remarked Sen. Fred Thompson, R-Tenn. (1994–2003), on announcing his retirement.[6] For Rep. Joe Scarborough, R-Fla. (1995–2001), "The conflict between being a good congressman and full-time father has grown even greater in recent years."[7]

In addition to the frantic pace and damage to family life, many congressional retirees cite a decline in comity and an erosion of the arts of bargaining and compromise. Incivility became so rife in the House that a bipartisan group of lawmakers sponsored a series of retreats aimed at helping members get along with one another. The decline of comity is no doubt a product of frictions caused by the demographic and ideological party realignment over the past decade.

Despite their job pressures, elected representatives are by no means an endangered species. Diligence and attentive home styles yield dividends at the polls. If voters regard elected officials as a class as rascals, they tend to be more charitable toward their own elected officials. Nor do they seem eager to "throw the rascals out." Since World War II, 93 percent of all incumbent representatives and 80 percent of incumbent senators running for reelection have been returned to office. However, members of Congress scan reelection rates less calmly than do scholars or reporters sitting on the sidelines. They rarely feel wholly secure. Bent on maintaining their vote margins, members see themselves as "unsafe at any margin."[8]

Members' Bonds with Constituents

Lawmakers forge bonds with voters out of perceived mutual agreement on important issues facing the constituency and the nation. The recruitment process yields lawmakers who reflect local views and prejudices. Contacts with voters throughout the campaign and while in office reinforce this convergence of views, as do representational norms adopted by most members. Citizens tend to regard their own legislators as agents of personal or localized interests. Legislators are judged on their service to the state or district, their communication with constituents, and their home style—that is, the way they deal with the home folks.

Members' unique visibility in their states or districts helps explain their support from potential voters. A majority of citizens report contacts with their House members by receiving mail from them, reading about them in a newspaper or magazine, or seeing them on television. Incumbents, for their part, lose few opportunities to do favors for constituents—gestures that are remembered or at least appreciated by recipients.

Individual senators and representatives present themselves to their constituents largely on their own terms, through advertising, self-promotion, and uncritical coverage by local or regional news media. House Rules chairman David Dreier, R-Calif., explains, for example, that "member web pages serve not only as a basic informational resource [for constituents], but as a tool *advocating,* in the member's own words, their work." [9]

Members and their staffs devote constant attention to generating publicity and local press. "I am never too busy to talk to local TV," said a prominent House member. "Period. Exclamation point." [10] A survey of House press secretaries showed virtually unanimous agreement: "We'd rather get in [the hometown paper] than on the front page of the *New York Times* any day." [11]

Individual lawmakers tend to bask in favorable light cast by their local media. Hometown reporters, especially for the electronic media, usually work on general assignment and are ill prepared to question the lawmaker in detail about issues or events. Often their primary goal is simply to get the legislator on tape or film. For politicians this is an ideal situation. They can express their views in their own words with a minimum of editing and few challenges from reporters.

Questions of Ethics

One question mark in assessing individual lawmakers is the recurrence of doubts about members' personal ethics. Only 25 percent of the respondents in a recent survey ranked the ethics of members of Congress as "high" or "very high"—in the same league with journalists, business executives, and auto mechanics. (Firefighters and pharmacists are among those seen as most ethical.) [12]

In fact, "Members of Congress behave better than people think," confides former representative Lee H. Hamilton, D-Ind. (1965–1999). [13] The vast majority of lawmakers are dedicated and ethical in their behavior. There is no reason to think that overall ethical standards are not as high as, or higher than, at any time in history. As Norman J. Ornstein points out, "Most observers would suggest that real corruption on the Hill has in fact *declined* significantly over the past 20 or 30 years, whether the misbehavior is licentiousness or bribery or financial chicanery." [14] Among the reasons he cites are the rising quality of members, broader scrutiny by the public, and reforms in campaign finance, disclosure, and ethics procedures.

Why, then, do ethical questions continue to loom so large in public and media commentary about members of Congress? First, organized interests and lobbies of all kinds are no less eager than in past eras to manipulate lawmakers and bend public policy to their wishes. The public policy stakes are now higher as government reaches into more sectors of Americans' economic and social lives. Huge sums of money find their way to Capitol Hill in the form of political contributions and other perquisites. Fearful of raising their own salaries because of expected backlash from voters, some members can fall prey to the blandishments of money and favors.

Many of the most blatant financial abuses, however, have been curtailed or subjected to disclosure requirements. Direct gifts and honoraria have been virtually eliminated, and lobbying by former members or staff has been restricted. Money used to flow under the table. "Back in the old days, it was a common occurrence that you walked around with envelopes of cash in your pocket" to hand out to powerful lawmakers, recalled a Washington lobbyist.[15] Today, most contributions—campaign contributions and direct lobbying expenses, for example—are reported and subject to scrutiny by reporters and civic groups. Although loopholes remain, contemporary financial practices unquestionably are tame by the standards common before, say, the 1970s.

Second, changing standards of behavior have cast new light upon issues of personal habits and conduct. Sexual misconduct and substance abuse, for example, are less tolerated today than they were a generation ago. Colleagues and journalists are less inclined to look the other way. An adulterous affair led would-be House Speaker Bob Livingston, R-La. (1977–1999), to resign from the House. Rep. Gary A. Condit, D-Calif. (1989–2003), was dogged by reporters and defeated in the 2002 primary after disclosures that he had an affair with a Capitol Hill intern who disappeared and was later found dead (he was never linked to the crime). Allegations of adultery against earlier public figures—for example, Presidents John F. Kennedy and Lyndon B. Johnson—were kept largely out of public view.

Third, ethical lapses and scandals are the glaring exceptions to the rule that the media exert little enterprise or energy in covering individual senators and representatives. The rise of investigative journalism has increased the odds that ethics violations—or even allegations—will be headline news. For example, the House bank (a disbursing office that offered check-writing and check-cashing services) had been around since the 1830s. Not until 1991 did it become a front-page story with unsavory implications.

Finally, intensified regulation of public life has itself opened windows for press coverage and citizens' reaction. Elected officials are scrutinized by the Federal Election Commission, the House and Senate ethics committees, and occasionally by the Justice Department and federal prosecutors (see box on

Congressional Ethics

Members of Congress are bound by the Constitution, federal laws, party provisions, and House and Senate rules and conduct codes. Although many observers criticize loopholes, the panoply of regulations is extensive.

Constitution. Each chamber has the power to punish its members for "disorderly behavior" and, by a two-thirds vote, to expel a member. Members are immune from arrest during attendance at congressional sessions (except for treason, felony, or breach of peace), and "for any speech or debate in either house, they shall not be questioned in any other place" (Article I, Section 6). This latter provision protects lawmakers from any reprisals for expressing their legislative views.

Criminal Laws. Federal laws make it a crime to solicit or accept a bribe; to solicit or receive "anything of value" for performing any official act or service, or for using influence in any proceeding involving the federal government; to enter into or benefit from any contracts with the government; or to commit any fraud against the United States. Lawmakers involved in the so-called Abscam affair were convicted in 1981 for violating these statutes.

Ethics Codes. Adopted in 1968 and substantially tightened in 1977, 1989, and 1995, the House and Senate ethics codes apply to members and key staff aides. The codes require extensive financial disclosure; restrict members' outside earned income (to 15 percent of salaries); prohibit unofficial office accounts that many members used to supplement official allowances; impose stricter standards for using the frank; and ban lawmakers from accepting most meals and gifts from lobbyists. The House Committee on Standards of Official Conduct and the Senate Select Ethics Committee implement the codes, hear charges against members, issue advisory opinions, and recommend disciplinary actions.

Party Rules. Congressional parties can discipline members who run afoul of ethics requirements. House Democratic and Republican rules require a committee leader who is indicted to step aside temporarily; a leader who is censured or convicted is automatically replaced.

Federal Election Campaign Act Amendments of 1974. As amended again in 1976 and 1979, the Federal Election Campaign Act imposes extensive requirements on congressional incumbents as well as challengers. Additional rules and penalties are set in the Bipartisan Campaign Reform Act of 2002, whose constitutionality is under review.

---

congressional ethics). Reports, investigations, hearings, and even court proceedings are not uncommon. So many rules govern the public activities of lawmakers that they can unintentionally run afoul of them. As law professor Cass Sunstein puts it:

> If the law books were taken entirely seriously and every American were fully investigated with an unlimited budget for crimes committed within the past two decades, we could probably manage to put a high percentage of Americans behind bars and bring the economy to a grinding halt. High-level public officials are particularly good targets for investigation, if only because of the complex network of statutes that regulate their behavior.[16]

Some of these inquiries uncover genuine wrongdoing that warrants legal punishment or defeat at the polls. Other cases are politically motivated—by electoral foes, by regulators seeking partisan advantage, or by ambitious prosecutors hoping to bag a high-profile trophy. In his study of the impact of what he calls "the ethics culture" on federal appointments, G. Calvin Mackenzie writes that

> [i]nstead of getting out of the way so the winners can govern, the losers begin guerrilla operations that never cease, using every weapon and every opportunity to attack, harass, embarrass, and otherwise weaken those who hold office. If you cannot beat them in an election, current practice now suggests, then do everything in your power to keep the winners from governing and implementing their policy priorities.[17]

In other words, ethics charges and countercharges can become another means of waging political warfare.

Do these hazards of public life deter "the best and the brightest" from seeking elective office? It is hard to answer that question. Young people, despite their professed altruism, show lamentably scant interest in federal government careers.[18] Although most congressional seats have no shortage of claimants, who knows how many of the ablest individuals decide to sit on the sidelines—especially in one-party areas?

The rising demands and costs of congressional life may well lie beyond the reach of average men and women. Reflecting on the multiplicity of presidential duties, Woodrow Wilson once remarked that Americans might be forced to pick their leaders from among "wise and prudent athletes"—a small class of people.[19] The same might now be said of senators and representatives. And if the job specifications exceed reasonable dimensions, can even the most qualified citizens be expected to perform these tasks successfully?

Congress-as-Institution

The American public expects much from Congress. Surveys over the years have consistently found that people prefer that Congress exert a strong, independent policy-making role. People want Congress to check the president's initiatives and to examine the president's proposals carefully.[20] They often express support for the notion of divided government: the White House controlled by one party but checked by another party controlling Capitol Hill.

Congress's institutional performance deserves at least qualified praise. In an intriguing experiment, Paul C. Light of the Brookings Institution set out to identify the federal government's most influential actions over a fifty-year period.[21] A survey of historians and political scientists served to winnow a preliminary roster of 588 items to a list of fifty "greatest achievements." For the record, the top three successes were judged to be rebuilding Europe after World War II (the Marshall Plan, 1947), expanding the right to vote (Voting

Rights Act of 1965), and promoting equal access to public accommodations (Civil Rights Act of 1964).

In every case Light uncovered, Congress played a vital role at the policy's inception, ratification, or implementation stages. Although Congress was not always the initiator, many programs associated with given presidents—for example, Medicare (Lyndon B. Johnson) and the Marshall Plan (Harry S. Truman)—had antecedents on Capitol Hill. "No one party, Congress, or president can be credited with any single achievement. . . . Rather, achievement appears to be the direct product of endurance, consensus, and patience." [22]

Congress continues to affect Americans' daily lives. Former representative Hamilton tells the following story:

> [A] group of [young people] visiting my Indiana office told me that Congress was irrelevant. So I asked them a few questions. How had they gotten to my office? On the interstate highway, they said. Had any of them gone to the local university? Yes, they said, admitting they'd got some help from federal student loans. Did any of them have grandparents on Social Security and Medicare? Well sure they replied, picking up on where I was headed. Their lives had been profoundly affected by Congress. They just hadn't focused on all of the connections before. [23]

Congress's institutional shortcomings, at the same time, are numerous and often all too obvious. Beyond the structural and procedural complexities (recounted in the vast congressional reform literature), the quality of its deliberations often falls short of democratic ideals. The bottom-line question for citizens probably is: Do the two chambers respond promptly and debate thoroughly the issues upon which the nation needs leadership and resolution? Most Americans could compile a must-do legislative agenda—many of whose items have been left unattended by recent Congresses. Even routine matters such as annual appropriations bills are often postponed by the passage of continuing resolutions (fiscal year 2003 funding, for example, was not completed until four months after the fiscal year began). Authorizing bills—required mandates for agencies and programs before they are funded—are also routinely neglected. In fiscal year 2002, for example, Congress appropriated $91.5 billion for some 356 programs whose authorizations had expired. [24]

Reforming Congress is often touted as a solution to its organizational or procedural faults. The two chambers themselves periodically engage in self-examination (although the last broad-scale inquiry took place more than a decade ago). The historical record, however, shows that major innovations flow from numerous and sometimes conflicting goals—enhancing legislative power and efficiency, to be sure, but also gaining partisan or policy advantage or augmenting individual lawmakers' perquisites. In his careful survey of forty-two major institutional innovations of the past century, Eric Schickler explains that "preexisting institutions create constituencies for their preservation that typically force reformers with new goals to build upon, rather than dismantle, these structures." [25] Thus reforms fall short of their sponsors' objectives. Instead of achieving stable, effective arrangements, what results is "a set of institutions that often work at cross-purposes." [26]

Media Coverage

The most open and accessible of the branches of government, Congress is covered by a large press corps containing many of the nation's most skilled journalists. (As CBS News reporter Bob Schieffer notes, Capitol Hill is the best news beat in Washington.)[27] But neither reporters nor their editors are able to convey in the mass media the internal subtleties or the external pressures that shape lawmaking.

The problem is compounded because the major mass media outlets have curtailed their coverage of Congress and national politics in general. Stephen Hess, who has been studying the press since the 1970s, contends that "the most obvious change in governmental and political news . . . is that a lot less of it reaches the mainstream press." [28] Even prestige daily papers and newsmagazines have de-emphasized public affairs coverage in favor of stories about celebrities, entertainment, and lifestyle issues. The very first cover of *Time* magazine in 1926 portrayed former House Speaker Joseph G. Cannon, R-Ill. (1903–1911). Today, national political figures—aside from the president—are rarely seen on the covers of *Time* and its competitors.

The decline has been especially drastic in television (including the so-called all-news channels), where most Americans receive their news about government and politics. "Apart from technology," observes journalist Bill Moyers, "the biggest change in my thirty years in broadcasting has been the shift of content from news about government to consumer-driven information and celebrity features." [29] Radio and TV talk shows are chronic offenders. Although they spend much airtime on issues of one kind or another, their content and style are typically ill informed, combative, and contemptuous of politicians and their work.[30]

The focus of this shrinking coverage has shifted. Fewer stories appear on policy issues and more on scandal, wrongdoing, or corruption. Following the canons of investigative journalism, reporters play the role of suspicious adversaries on the lookout for good guys and bad guys, winners and losers. Ethical problems, congressional pay and perquisites, campaign war chests, and foreign junkets are frequent targets of their investigations. Their stories reinforce popular negative stereotypes about Congress as an institution.

Former Speaker Thomas S. Foley, D-Wash. (1989–1995), tells a story about how his remarks to a new-member orientation session were covered by the press. Foley advised the freshmen to avoid the mistake of some former members who had promised perfect attendance for floor votes. He told them to expect to miss a procedural vote someday. Get it over with, he said, and do not drive yourself crazy trying to make every vote. The Speaker also counseled that foreign travel, though a cheap political target, was a good way to learn about world conditions and, incidentally, to get acquainted with colleagues

Table 16-1   High Approval for Members, Low Approval
for Congress

Individual members	Congress as institution
Serve constituents	Resolves national issues only with difficulty or not at all
Run against Congress	Has few defenders
Emphasize personal style and outreach to constituents	Operates as collegial body that is difficult for citizens to understand
Covered by local media in generally positive terms	Covered by national media, often negatively (with focus on scandals and conflicts)
Respond quickly to most constituent needs and inquiries	Moves slowly with cumbersome processes that inhibit rapid responses
Are able to highlight personal goals and accomplishments	Has many voices but none can speak clearly for Congress as a whole

Sources: Timothy E. Cook, "Legislature vs. Legislator: A Note on the Paradox of Congressional Support," *Legislative Studies Quarterly* (February 1979): 43–52; Glenn R. Parker and Roger H. Davidson, "Why Do Americans Love Their Congressmen So Much More Than Their Congress?" *Legislative Studies Quarterly* (February 1979): 53–61; and Richard Born, "The Shared Fortunes of Congress and Congressmen: Members May Run from Congress but They Can't Hide," *Journal of Politics* (November 1990): 1223–1241.

from the opposing party. The next day's headline proclaimed: "Foley tells freshmen: Take a junket, miss a vote." [31]

Divergent press coverage—local versus national media—widens the gap between the two Congresses' distinct images: more positive for individual members than for the institution. It is still true that "Americans love their congressmen much more than they love their Congress." [32] Individual lawmakers tend to be well known, sympathetically judged, respectfully covered by the local media, and—most important—reelected. Congress the institution, in contrast, is covered by the national press with considerable skepticism and cynicism. In short, the two Congresses are viewed through different lenses, reported by different channels of communication, and judged by different criteria.

Citizens' Attitudes toward Congress

If individual members get respectable marks, people often seem ready to flunk Congress as a whole (see Table 16-1). The institutional Congress usually ranks well below respondents' own representatives in public esteem. Citizens'

Figure 16-1   Public Assessments of the Two Congresses, 1974–2003

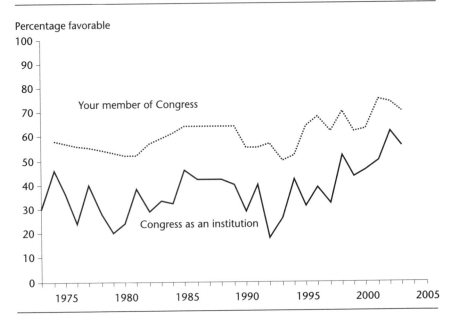

Percentage favorable

Source: Authors' interpolations of surveys of the Gallup Organization and the Harris Survey for the years 1974 to 1992 as summarized in "Public Opinion and Demographic Report," *American Enterprise,* November-December 1992, 86–87. Recent figures are from *National Journal,* May 13, 1995, 1180; April 26, 1997, 842; March 21, 1998, 642; October 31, 1998, 2559; *Roll Call,* May 25, 2000, 16; February 13, 2003, 4; washingtonpost.com...tics/polls/result/stories/data.

Note: The Gallup Organization's questions are "Do you approve of the way the U.S. Congress is handling its job? Do you approve or disapprove of the way the representative from your own congressional district is handling his/her job?" The Harris Survey's questions are "How would you rate the job done this past year by [Congress] [your member of Congress]—excellent, pretty good, only fair, or poor?" Responses are dichotomized as favorable ("excellent," "pretty good") or unfavorable ("only fair," "poor"). The plotted points in the figures indicate respondents having opinions who approve of or are favorable toward congressional performance.

ratings of the job Congress is doing fluctuate with economic conditions, wars and crises, scandals, and waves of satisfaction or cynicism (see Figure 16-1). Approval of Congress surged briefly after it handled the Watergate affair in 1974, after the Republican takeover twenty years later, before the Clinton scandal of 1998, and after the terrorist attacks of 2001. These surges eventually subsided.

After global terrorism intruded upon U.S. citizens' consciousness, positive appraisals of Congress soared to 62 percent and individual members to

75 percent—matching a surge in President George W. Bush's popularity.[33] This reflected the well-known "rally around the flag" phenomenon observed by students of public opinion following nearly every national crisis. Approval levels fell somewhat as the attacks' immediacy faded.

Citizens' overall "trust and confidence" in the branches of the federal government has, however, remained fairly robust since the 2001 attacks. Sixty-seven percent of the respondents in a late 2002 survey expressed high confidence in the legislative branch, which was only slightly below the 71 percent who gave the same response in 1971.[34] Unfolding events clearly will determine levels of citizen support in the years to come.

Although extensively reported in the media, Congress is not well understood by the average American. Partly to blame are the institution's size and complexity, not to mention the arcane twists and turns of the legislative process. What many citizens find distasteful are the core attributes of lawmaking: controversy, messiness, and compromise. In truth, this same messiness is found in the other branches of government. The president speaks with one voice, but fierce competition for the president's ear is unending. President George W. Bush's administration, despite its stress on secrecy and loyalty, witnessed public debates on military reform, the preemptive war doctrine, relations with the United Nations, and even the Iraqi war. As for the judiciary, opinions are frequently divided or unclear, and they seldom resolve or even clarify great national controversies.

The public's ambivalence toward Congress, however, goes far deeper than unhappiness with specific policies or disgust with scandals, if the sobering conclusions of John R. Hibbing and Elizabeth Theiss-Morse are to be believed.

> People do not wish to see uncertainty, conflicting opinions, long debate, competing interests, confusion, bargaining, and compromised, imperfect solutions. They want government to do its job quietly and efficiently, sans conflict and sans fuss. In short . . . they often seek a patently unrealistic form of democracy.[35]

In other words, people abhor the very attributes that are the hallmarks of robust representative assemblies such as Congress. As Hibbing and Theiss-Morse observe, Congress "is structured to embody what we dislike about modern democratic government, which is almost everything." [36]

Twenty-first Century Challenges

The U.S. Congress is now in its third century. Survival for more than two centuries is no mean feat. Perhaps like Dr. Johnson's dog (noted not for its skill at standing on hind legs but for doing so at all), Congress's longevity is proof enough of its worth. Congress has withstood repeated stress and turbulence including a civil war, political assassinations, terrorist attacks, domestic scandals, and contentious foreign involvement. It is sobering to realize that the U.S. constitutional system is far older than most of the world's governments.

Global Threats and Alarms

The physical setting of the U.S. Capitol now mirrors the status of security worldwide. Only a few short years ago, visitors and Hill personnel moved freely in and out of the Capitol and surrounding office buildings. Members of the public may still visit most Capitol Hill facilities, but they will encounter the now-common elements of security: uniformed officers, metal detectors, and mostly ugly concrete barriers. One welcome development, however, is a long-needed Capitol Visitors' Center—constructed underground on the East Front—that will not only enhance the building's safety but also serve to inform visitors about Congress and its work.

The possibility of future terrorist attacks forces people to think the unthinkable about the physical continuity of Congress. If the Capitol were attacked, how could deceased House members be quickly replaced? Nearly every state empowers governors to fill Senate seats temporarily, but House seats constitutionally could be filled only by time-consuming special elections. What could be done about incapacitated members? What would happen if the nation's capital were destroyed or uninhabitable? Could lawmakers continue to conduct business by teleconferencing from remote locations?

Under a constitutional amendment sponsored by Rep. Brian Baird, D-Wash., if more than a quarter of House members were killed, governors could appoint new ones to serve ninety-day terms while their states arranged special elections. A bipartisan Continuity of Government Commission recommended a simpler amendment empowering Congress to enact legislation addressing a range of continuity questions.[37] Given the difficulty of making constitutional changes, however, others have suggested rules changes to, for example, permit expedited special elections or lower House quorum requirements.[38]

Mere survival, though, may be the least of Congress's challenges. In a world of uncertain global challenges, Congress continues to face divisive domestic issues, such as energy, health care, economic inequality, and care for aging baby boomers (who reach retirement age beginning in 2008). Such issues are played out in "a narrowly divided House and Senate in which every move by congressional leaders is driven by the desire to win control of both chambers."[39] "Everyone is less secure about what the hell they're doing," remarked former representative Leon Panetta, D-Calif. (1977–1993). "They're basically playing the politics and issues on a day-to-day basis."[40]

On top of these continuing domestic issues are global challenges linked to an ongoing war on terror plus targeted warfare against such states as Afghanistan and Iraq. Among the collateral damages inflicted by wartime conditions is the quality of deliberation—and deliberateness—essential to legislative processes. In its haste to respond to terrorist attacks, Congress gave only fleeting attention to details of the vast grants of power it ceded to the president and the executive branch—for example, in approving open-ended military action, the problematic U.S.A. Patriot Act, and the 170,000-employee Homeland Security Department—all emergency actions whose implications were unknown to the lawmakers who voted for them.

A year later, Congress seemed to shy away from a grand debate in approving the Iraqi war resolution. "We have left the field," confessed Sen. Richard J. Durbin, D-Ill. "This is the largest grant of presidential authority ever given by a Congress." [41] Sen. Robert C. Byrd, D-W.Va., whose Senate career began in 1959, put it this way on the eve of the Iraq war, in an eloquent speech to an almost empty chamber:

> We stand passively mute in the Senate today, paralyzed by our own uncertainty, seemingly stunned by the sheer turmoil of events. Only on the editorial pages of some of our newspapers is there much substantive discussion concerning the prudence or the imprudence of engaging in this particular war. . . . But today we hear nothing, almost nothing, by way of debate. . . .
>
> The rafters should ring. The press galleries should be filled. Senators should be at their seats listening to questions being asked about this war, questions to which the American people out there have a right to expect answers. The American people are longing for information and they are not getting it. This chamber is silent. . . . We are truly sleepwalking through history.[42]

Congress nonetheless showed signs of regaining its equilibrium once the initial shock waves had subsided from the terrorist attacks and the Afghan and Iraqi wars. Issues of costs, personnel deployments, and foreign policy implications began to be explored. Following the military success in Iraq, for example, congressional committees moved to scrutinize the slow pace and mounting costs of reconstruction and nation-building efforts there. Thwarted by what House International Relations chair Henry J. Hyde, R-Ill., called a "lack of transparency" on the part of the administration, the chairmen and ranking minority members of both House and Senate foreign policy committees requested the General Accounting Office to undertake a thorough study.[43] As a staff aide explained, "The members gave up on getting the administration to share information so they asked for this full investigation." [44] No doubt other aspects of the changed security environment will receive legislative scrutiny and action.

Checks and Imbalances?

The constitutional system of divided powers and competing branches rarely yields a perfect equilibrium. Powers ebb and flow among the branches. National security crises tend to elevate the presidency, whereas peaceful times are friendlier to congressional power. Activist judges with an agenda can pull the judiciary into the political thickets of policy debate; passivist judges are more inclined to defer to the other branches.

Even before the 9/11 threats, some members of the Bush administration tended to undervalue or dismiss congressional prerogatives. Despite the flimsiest electoral victory in U.S. history, the president's strategists opted for an aggressive reading of executive powers. The rationale seemed to echo Vice President Dick Cheney's argument that "we are weaker today as an institution because of the unwise compromises" on the part of past presidents. Cheney thus vowed "to pass on our offices in better shape than we found them." [45]

Although events from the immediate post–Vietnam War and post–Watergate years lent some credence to Cheney's assumption, the underlying trends have mostly gone in the opposite direction—toward broader White House prerogatives and narrower legislative involvement. This pattern is clearest in war powers questions.

Through September 10, 2001, White House claims met with considerable resistance on Capitol Hill. The next day, what had up to then been a modestly successful presidency was transformed into a wartime one. The stakes and resources in the ongoing constitutional struggle were profoundly altered—at least for the duration of the crisis.

Executive branch encroachments upon legislative priorities are, in truth, a phenomenon that is neither new nor confined to crisis periods. President George W. Bush had precedent on his side when he used rulemaking powers to install policies Congress was unlikely to approve. Many of the new rules were written to overturn those instituted by his predecessor, Bill Clinton. Nor was Bush the first president to abandon treaties without legislative consultation. Most presidents, moreover, fight for broader leeway in spending appropriated funds and freedom to reorganize agencies and redeploy their personnel. To the extent that lawmakers acquiesce, they have only themselves to blame.

The Bush administration's very success in implementing timeworn practices has tended to impede the work of Congress—especially what Woodrow Wilson called the "informing function." Presidents and their appointees naturally seek to control information about what they are up to. But the Bush administration made secrecy a watchword. A first-ever lawsuit was lodged against the White House—and later abandoned under pressure—by Congress's investigative arm, the General Accounting Office, in an effort to obtain information on White House consultations leading to the administration's energy plans. Regarding a range of inquiries, such staunch GOP committee chairmen as Charles E. Grassley of Iowa (Senate Finance), Henry J. Hyde of Illinois (House International Relations), and F. James Sensenbrenner Jr. of Wisconsin (House Judiciary) protested repeatedly about the executive's failure to provide information. (Sensenbrenner threatened at one point to subpoena information from the Justice Department.) [46]

Congress at the same time faces attacks upon its powers from an activist federal judiciary, which has invalidated federal enactments in some thirty cases since 1995. For the first time since the late 1930s, the courts challenged federal laws in such areas as interstate commerce and civil rights, often in the name of guarding states' rights. By narrow majorities, for example, the Supreme Court curbed the 1990 Americans with Disabilities Act on grounds it had not dared to apply to earlier civil rights statutes.

Federal circuit court judge John T. Noonan Jr., a Reagan appointee, argues that the court's elevation of states' rights over congressional power has "invented criteria for Congress that invaded the legislative domain." [47] Whatever the constitutional arguments, future activist-controlled courts could constrict legislative powers in much the same way that late-nineteenth-century courts gutted the Civil War constitutional amendments. As Noonan explains, "If five members of the Supreme Court are in agreement on an agenda, they are mightier than five hundred members of Congress with unmobilized or warring constituencies." [48]

We cite such views out of a strong belief in traditional U.S. constitutional values and representative democracy—not from a partisanship that is intentionally liberal or conservative, Democrat or Republican. Historically, it is true, leaders driven by partisan policy agendas have favored one branch over another. Early-twentieth-century liberals, who generally preferred national power over states' rights, made common cause with activist presidents such as Franklin D. Roosevelt or John F. Kennedy. Conservatives tended to favor state and local power and, on Capitol Hill, that era's conservative coalition leaders. More recently, the situation has often been reversed, as conservative presidents (such as Ronald Reagan or George W. Bush) faced Democratic or closely divided Congresses.

Partisans of all stripes, however, have a long-term stake in an active, robust legislative branch. Executive initiatives, however popular, need critical review. Executive programs must be overseen and evaluated. That is why leaders and members of both parties have expressed concern over recent developments. What will the future hold? Much depends on how long the wartime ethos continues and whether Republicans will consolidate their gains to reestablish one-party government in the nation's capital. Answers to such questions must await the unfolding of future events.

"The Fundamental Things Apply"

Congress must help America succeed in a world where all countries increasingly face similar or interrelated problems.[49] National borders and the authority of national governments are becoming less potent than in the past. "The real problem [members of Congress] face," wrote a political observer, "is that local and national politics have now become irretrievably global because their economies are locked into the global system." [50]

Representative assemblies, however, rest on the principle of geographic representation—an idea that made sense when land was the basic productive resource. Political divisions over most of U.S. history followed local and regional fissures. Today, America's divisions tend to be more economic, social, intellectual, or ideological than geographic. States and even districts now tend to be microcosms of the nation as a whole in terms of the diversity of interests they embrace.

Some contend that too much is expected of members of Congress. How can elected generalists render intelligent judgments on the dizzyingly complex problems of governance? "People shouldn't expect those in office to be at the forefront of new developments," observed Rep. Barney Frank, D-Mass. "The best we can do is to be adapters. No one has the intellectual energy to be an elected official and simultaneously break new intellectual ground." [51]

When the First Congress convened, the United States had a tiny population, mostly rural and uneducated. Its social and industrial structure was simple. Changes occurred slowly, and the government's tasks were few. Nothing could be farther from the contemporary situation. "Today," reflected Sen. Nancy Landon Kassebaum, R-Kan. (1978–1997), "there's an almost information overload, a bombardment by news, by faxes. Everything is instantaneous with too little time for thoughtful reflection." [52]

In light of all this buzzing confusion, a single national assembly of generalists elected by plurality votes from geographical areas may seem anomalous. Perhaps Congress imperfectly mirrors the real-world "democracy of . . . complex, multiple, and transient minorities." [53] Far from retreating from participation or civic involvement, people may simply be moving away from traditional forms—elections, mass political parties, and adversarial courts—and toward more varied, personal, and adaptable modes of participation. Perhaps the movement is away from government itself and toward more fluid, decentralized nongovernmental entities. One thoughtful observer even suggests that "Congress is so unpleasantly noisy these days not because it has too much to do but because it has too little." [54]

We have no confident solutions to these dilemmas, and so we end our discourse with questions for the twenty-first century. Are the two Congresses ultimately compatible? Or are they diverging, each detrimental to the other? Even if the federal government were to be downsized (a doubtful prospect), the burden placed on both Congresses would remain heavy by historical standards. Congress-as-institution is expected to resolve all kinds of problems, not only by processing legislation but also by monitoring programs and serving as an all-purpose watchdog. Legislators struggle to keep abreast of these demands. The question is whether it will be a winning or losing effort.

At the same moment, Congress-as-politicians seems busier than ever. In part because of the sheer scope of modern government, in part because of citizens' empowerment, constituents are insisting that senators and representatives communicate with them more often, serve their states or districts materially, play the role of ombudsmen, and adhere to stricter standards of personal conduct. Legislators have accepted and profited electorally from these functions, but not without misgivings and not without detriment to their legislative tasks.

To maintain its vitality, Congress needs not fewer politicians, but more of them—officeholders who are willing to learn their craft and who will stay around long enough to master it. "To avoid coming apart at the seams," former representative Hamilton declares, "our country needs people who know how to practice the art of politics. That is what good politicians do: they make democratic government possible in a nation alive with competing factions." [55]

If Congress is to fulfill its promise, citizens also must be engaged in politics—learning about issues that concern them and participating by conveying their views. Again former representative Hamilton's assessment is on the mark. Citizens, he says,

> must understand that they need to get involved if they want our system to improve. They need to know that the nature of this relationship between the representative and the represented—and the honesty of the exchange between the two—shapes the strength of our representative democracy.[56]

In the longer view the question is whether an institution embracing so many disparate motives and careers can continue to function as a coherent whole. Can policies patched together from many discrete interests guide the nation on its course? Ever since 1787 people have wondered about this question. History is only mildly reassuring, and the future poses new and delicate challenges for which the margin of error may be narrower than ever before. And yet representative democracy itself is a gamble. The proposition that representation can yield wise policy making remains a daring one. As always, it is an article of faith whose proof lies inevitably in the future.

Reference Materials

Appendix A   Party Control: Presidency, Senate, House, 1901-2003

Congress	Years	President	Senate			House		
			D	R	Other	D	R	Other
57th	1901-1903	McKinley/T. Roosevelt	31	55	4	151	197	9
58th	1903-1905	T. Roosevelt	33	57	—	178	208	—
59th	1905-1907	T. Roosevelt	33	57	—	136	250	—
60th	1907-1909	T. Roosevelt	31	61	—	164	222	—
61st	1909-1911	Taft	32	61	—	172	219	—
62d	1911-1913	Taft	41	51	—	228	161	1
63d	1913-1915	Wilson	51	44	1	291	127	17
64th	1915-1917	Wilson	56	40	—	230	196	9
65th	1917-1919	Wilson	53	42	—	216	210	6
66th	1919-1921	Wilson	47	49	—	190	240	3
67th	1921-1923	Harding	37	59	—	131	301	1
68th	1923-1925	Coolidge	43	51	2	205	225	5
69th	1925-1927	Coolidge	39	56	1	183	247	4
70th	1927-1929	Coolidge	46	49	1	195	237	3
71st	1929-1931	Hoover	39	56	1	167	267	1
72d	1931-1933	Hoover	47	48	1	220	214	1
73d	1933-1935	F. Roosevelt	60	35	1	313	117	5
74th	1935-1937	F. Roosevelt	69	25	2	319	103	10
75th	1937-1939	F. Roosevelt	76	16	4	331	89	13
76th	1939-1941	F. Roosevelt	69	23	4	261	164	4
77th	1941-1943	F. Roosevelt	66	28	2	268	162	5
78th	1943-1945	F. Roosevelt	58	37	1	218	208	4
79th	1945-1947	Truman	56	38	1	242	190	2
80th	1947-1949	Truman	45	51	—	188	245	1
81st	1949-1951	Truman	54	42	—	263	171	1
82d	1951-1953	Truman	49	47	—	234	199	1
83d	1953-1955	Eisenhower	47	48	1	211	221	1
84th	1955-1957	Eisenhower	48	47	1	232	203	—
85th	1957-1959	Eisenhower	49	47	—	233	200	—
86th[a]	1959-1961	Eisenhower	65	35	—	284	153	—

Appendix A   (continued)

Congress	Years	President	Senate D	Senate R	Senate Other[a]	House D	House R	House Other
86th[a]	1959-1961	Eisenhower	65	35	—	284	153	—
87th[a]	1961-1963	Kennedy	65	35	—	263	174	—
88th	1961-1963	Kennedy/Johnson	67	33	—	258	177	—
89th	1965-1967	Johnson	68	32	—	295	140	—
90th	1967-1969	Johnson	64	36	—	247	187	—
91st	1969-1971	Nixon	57	43	—	243	192	—
92d	1971-1973	Nixon	54	44	2	254	180	—
93d	1973-1975	Nixon/Ford	56	42	2	239	192	1
94th	1975-1977	Ford	60	37	2	291	144	—
95th	1977-1979	Carter	61	38	1	292	143	—
96th	1979-1981	Carter	58	41	1	276	157	—
97th	1981-1983	Reagan	46	53	1	243	192	—
98th	1983-1985	Reagan	45	55	—	267	168	—
99th	1985-1987	Reagan	47	53	—	252	183	—
100th	1987-1989	Reagan	55	45	—	258	177	—
101st	1989-1991	Bush	55	45	—	260	175	—
102d	1991-1993	Bush	57	43	—	268	166	1
103d	1993-1995	Clinton	56	44	—	258	176	1
104th	1995-1997	Clinton	47	53	—	204	230	1
105th	1997-1999	Clinton	45	55	—	207	227	1
106th	1999-2001	Clinton	45	55	—	211	223	1
107th	2001-2003	Bush	50	49	1	210	222	3
108th	2003-2005	Bush	48	51	1	205	229	1

☐ Republican control   ▨ Democratic control

Source: Encyclopedia of the United States Congress, ed. Donald C. Bacon, Roger H. Davidson, and Morton Keller (New York: Simon and Schuster, 1995), 1556–1558.

Note: Figures are for the beginning of the first session of each Congress and do not include vacancies, subsequent shifts, or changes in party affiliation.

Note: Data for the 107th Congress are current as of June 30, 2001. The "other" category for the House includes 2 independents and 1 vacancy.

[a] The House in the 86th and 87th Congress had 437 members because of an at-large representative given to both Alaska (January 3, 1959) and Hawaii (August 21, 1959) prior to redistricting in 1962.

Appendix B

Internships: Getting Experience on Capitol Hill

Capitol Hill is an excellent place to obtain first-hand experience with the U.S. government. With 540 lawmakers (representatives, senators, delegates, and resident commissioners); hundreds of committees and subcommittees; scores of informal caucuses; and three congressional support agencies (the Congressional Research Service, General Accounting Office, and Congressional Budget Office), intern opportunities abound for students interested in experiencing Congress and its members "up close and personal."

Undergraduates will find useful information about landing an internship on Capitol Hill in several sources. One of the best is published under the auspices of the American Political Science Association and is titled *Storming Washington: An Intern's Guide to National Government*. Political scientist Stephen E. Frantzich discusses how to get a good internship, make the most of the experience, and find a place to live in Washington, D.C.

From our own years of "soaking and poking" on Capitol Hill, we offer five observations about getting congressional experience. First, there is no central clearinghouse for internships. Every congressional office, committee, caucus, and support agency manages its own internship program. You must be persistent, patient, and determined to find a position that will be a rewarding learning experience. Not only should you determine what duties and functions will be assigned to you as a volunteer intern (it is sometimes possible to find paid internships), but you need to remember that you have something useful to offer. Most congressional offices and committees are understaffed and subject to high staff turnover. Although the market for interns is competitive, congressional lawmakers, committees, and staffers want and need your talent.

Second, develop some notion as to where you would like to intern. Do research on the committee, lawmaker, support agency, or caucus that you would like to intern with. Remember that every office has its own personality. Senate offices, for instance, are often large enterprises with many staff aides, while House offices generally are smaller. Interns thus will have more opportunities for personal, day-to-day contact with House members than with senators. The best way to determine the office environment is by interviewing people who have worked in a particular office, talking with intern coordinators at your college or university, or visiting the office yourself.

Third, target your own representative and senators. Many congressional members prefer interns from their own state or district who are likely to be familiar with the geography and concerns of that area. In addition, potential interns probably will have family and friends who are constituents of the law-maker. Don't hesitate to use your contacts. You might also volunteer to work in a state or district office of the lawmaker. Before accepting an internship, consider your own views and ideals. If your views are conservative, working for a lawmaker who espouses liberal causes may be difficult. On the other hand, if you are tactful and open-minded, working for someone whose views differ from yours may be instructive. Because you are a student, an internship with someone who holds divergent ideological views probably will not be held against you later in landing a position.

Fourth, intern placement opportunities are plentiful. Many colleges and universities sponsor semester programs in Washington. Several schools, in-cluding the American University, Boston University, Hamilton College, the State University of New York, the University of Southern California, and sev-eral University of California campuses run programs in Washington; some ac-cept students from other accredited colleges and universities. The Washington Center for Internships and Academic Seminars, in existence since 1975, has placed thousands of students from hundreds of colleges.

Finally, Congress needs and welcomes the influx of new ideas and experi-ences that interns bring with them. The work at times may be drudgery— answering mail and telephones, entering information into computers, and run-ning errands—but the opportunity to learn about Congress and to pick up "po-litical smarts" not easily available from textbooks is nearly without equal. You may even want to keep a private journal of your experiences: what you have done and what you have learned. In sum, a volunteer job on Capitol Hill is likely to be rewarding intellectually and in other ways that are impossible to predict.

Resources

The Congressional Intern Handbook. Washington, D.C.: Congressional Management Foundation, 2001.

Frantzich, Stephen E. *Storming Washington: An Intern's Guide to National Government.* 4th ed. Washington, D.C.: American Political Science Association, 1994.

Jimenez, Rita. *Internships and Fellowships: Congressional, Federal, and Other Work Experience Opportunities.* Congressional Research Service, Library of Congress. Report No. 98-654C. August 5, 1998. Provides extensive listings and bibliographies of internships.

Maxwell, Bruce. *Insider's Guide to Finding a Job in Washington: Contacts and Strategies to Build Your Career in Public Policy.* Washington, D.C.: CQ Press, 1999.

Oldman, Mark. *Student Advantage Guide to America's Top Internships, 1998.* New York: Random House, 1997.

Peterson's Internships. Princeton, N.J.: Peterson's Guides. Annual.

The Washington Center for Internships and Academic Seminars, 2000 M Street, N.W., Suite 750, Washington, D.C. 20036. Telephone: (202) 336-7600 or (800) 486-8921; Fax: (202) 336-7609; e-mail: info@twc.edu and Internet: http://www.twc.edu.

Washington Information Directory. Washington, D.C.: Congressional Quarterly. Annual publication that provides information about governmental and nongovernmental groups as well as addresses and phone numbers for congressional offices and committees.

Notes

Chapter 1 (pages 3–11)

1. Ben Pershing, "Tragedy Hits Home for New York-Area Members," *Roll Call,* September 13, 2001, 3.
2. Pershing, "Tragedy Hits Home for New York-Area Members."
3. Congressional Quarterly, *CQ's Politics in America 2002* (Washington, D.C.: CQ Press, 2001), 684–685.
4. Paul S. Herrnson, *Congressional Elections: Campaigning at Home and in Washington,* 3d ed. (Washington, D.C.: CQ Press, 2000), 249.
5. Alexander Hamilton, James Madison, and John Jay, *The Federalist Papers,* ed. Clinton Rossiter, No. 51 (New York: Mentor, 1961), 322.
6. *The Federalist Papers,* No. 52, 327.
7. Sam Rayburn, *Speak, Mr. Speaker,* ed. H. G. Dulaney and Edward Hake Phillips (Bonham, Texas: Sam Rayburn Foundation, 1978), 263–264. Rayburn was Speaker from 1940 to 1947, 1949 to 1953, and 1955 to 1961.
8. Glenn R. Parker, *Homeward Bound: Explaining Campaign Changes in Congressional Behavior* (Pittsburgh: University of Pittsburgh Press, 1986), 18.
9. U.S. Congress, House Committee on Administrative Review, *Administrative Management and Legislative Management,* 2 vols., H. Doc. 95–232, 95th Cong., 1st sess., September 28, 1977, 2:18–19.
10. Alan Abramowitz, "A Comparison of Voting for U.S. Senator and Representative in 1978," *American Political Science Review* 74 (September 1980): 633–640; and Richard F. Fenno Jr., *The United States Senate: A Bicameral Perspective* (Washington, D.C.: American Enterprise Institute, 1982), 29ff.
11. U.S. Congress, Joint Committee on the Organization of Congress, *Organization of the Congress, Final Report,* 2 vols., H. Rept. 103–14, 103d Cong., 1st sess., December 1993, 2:275–287. See Table 5-2 in this book.
12. Glenn R. Parker and Roger H. Davidson, "Why Do Americans Love Their Congressmen So Much More Than Their Congress?" *Legislative Studies Quarterly* 4 (February 1979): 53–61; Kelly D. Patterson and David B. Magleby, "Public Support for Congress," *Public Opinion Quarterly* 56 (winter 1992): 539–540; and Randall B. Ripley, Samuel C. Patterson, Lynn M. Mauer, and Stephen V. Quinlan, "Constituents' Evaluations of U.S. House Members," *American Politics Quarterly* 20 (October 1992): 442–456.
13. Edmund Burke, "Speech to Electors at Bristol," in *Burke's Politics,* ed. Ross J. S. Hoffman and Paul Levack (New York: Knopf, 1949), 116.
14. Burke, "Speech to Electors at Bristol."
15. Quoted in *Roll Call,* September 9, 1993, 16.
16. Frank E. Smith, *Congressman from Mississippi* (New York: Random House, 1964), 127.
17. David R. Mayhew, *Congress: The Electoral Connection* (New Haven: Yale University Press, 1974), 16.
18. *U.S. Term Limits v. Thornton,* 115 S. Ct. 1842 (1995).
19. Quoted in Mark Carl Rom, "Why Not Assume That Public Officials Seek to Promote the Public Interest?" *Public Affairs Report* 37 (July 1996): 12.
20. Woodrow Wilson, *Congressional Government* (1885; reprint, Baltimore: Johns Hopkins University Press, 1981), 210.
21. Richard F. Fenno Jr., *Home Style: House Members in Their Districts* (Boston: Little, Brown, 1978), 168.

22. Quoted in Ilan Graff and Mary Lynn F. Jones, "Lessons about Congress Not Taught in School," *The Hill*, August 7, 2002, 13.

Chapter 2 (pages 13–37)

1. Alvin M. Josephy Jr., *On the Hill: A History of the American Congress* (New York: Simon and Schuster, 1980), 41–48.
2. Charles A. Beard and John P. Lewis, "Representative Government in Evolution," *American Political Science Review* (April 1932): 223–240.
3. Beard and Lewis, "Representative Government in Evolution."
4. Jock P. Green, ed., *Great Britain and the American Colonies, 1606–1763* (New York: Harper TorchBooks, 1970), xxxix.
5. Edmund C. Burnett, *Continental Congress* (New York: Norton, 1964).
6. *Congressional Quarterly's Guide to Congress*, 5th ed., vol. I (Washington, D.C.: CQ Press, 2000), 9.
7. Burnett, *Continental Congress*, 171. When quoting the Constitution in this volume, the authors used modern capitalization.
8. Jack N. Rakove, *The Beginnings of National Politics: An Interpretive History of the Continental Congress* (New York: Knopf, 1979), 43.
9. Charles C. Thach Jr., *The Creation of the Presidency, 1775–1789: A Study in Constitutional History* (Baltimore: Johns Hopkins University Press, 1969), 34.
10. James Sterling Young, "America's First Hundred Days," *Miller Center Journal* 1 (winter 1994): 57.
11. John Locke, *Two Tracts on Government*, ed. Philip Abrams (New York: Cambridge University Press, 1967), 374.
12. Alexander Hamilton, James Madison, and John Jay, *The Federalist Papers*, ed. Clinton Rossiter, No. 48 (New York: Mentor, 1961), 308.
13. Joseph Story, *Commentaries on the Constitution of the United States*, 5th ed., vol. 1 (Boston: Little, Brown, 1905), 396. For Justice Robert Jackson's comments, see *Youngstown Sheet and Tube Co. v. Sawyer*, 343 U.S. 579, 635 (1952).
14. *Nixon v. United States*, 506 U.S. 224 (1993).
15. *The Federalist Papers*, No. 65, 396.
16. Van Tassel, Emily Field, and Paul Finkelman, *Impeachable Offenses: A Documentary History from 1787 to the Present* (Washington, D.C.: Congressional Quarterly, 1999).
17. *Marbury v. Madison*, 1 Cranch 137 (1803).
18. *The Constitution of the United States of America: Analysis and Interpretation*, S. Doc. 92–80, 92d Cong., 2d sess., 1973, 1597–1619. Recent figures are courtesy of George Costello, specialist in American law, Congressional Research Service.
19. Larry D. Kramer, "The Supreme Court v. Balance of Powers," *New York Times*, March 3, 2001, A17. See also Erwin Chemerinsky, "Disabled Feel the Sting of an Arbitrary Court," *Los Angeles Times*, February 26, 2001, B7; and Cass Sunstein, "A Narrowed Right to Challenge the States, *New York Times*, May 31, 2002, A25.
20. *Board of Trustees of the University of Alabama v. Garrett*, No. 99–1240 (2001).
21. The U.S. Supreme Court majority contended, in this and similar rulings, that the Eleventh Amendment granted the states "sovereign immunity" from legal suits. But the Amendment's plain language protects states only from suits by citizens of other states or of foreign nations, not those from its own citizens. Moreover, it is hard to escape the supposition that, whatever the protections afforded by the Eleventh Amendment (ratified in 1798), they were superseded—at least in the realm of civil rights—by the Fourteenth Amendment (ratified in 1868), which not only nationalized basic civil rights but also expressly granted Congress the power of enforcement. For a detailed critique of the Court's activism in such cases, see John T. Noonan Jr., *Narrowing the Nation's Power: The Supreme Court Sides with the States* (Berkeley: University of California Press, 2002).

22. Quotes from the opinions of Chief Justice William H. Rehnquist and Justice Stephen G. Breyer are drawn from "Excerpts from Supreme Court Opinions on Limits of Disabilities Act," *New York Times*, February 22, 2001, A21.
23. William N. Eskridge Jr., "Overriding Supreme Court Statutory Interpretation Decisions," *Yale Law Journal* 101 (November 1991): 331–455. See also R. Shep Melnick, *Between the Lines: Interpreting Welfare Rights* (Washington, D.C.: Brookings Institution, 1994).
24. Louis Fisher, *Constitutional Dialogues: Interpretation as Political Process* (Princeton: Princeton University Press, 1988), 275.
25. Quoted in Charles Warren, *The Making of the Constitution* (Boston: Little, Brown, 1928), 162.
26. Quoted in Charles Warren, *The Supreme Court in United States History* (Boston: Little, Brown, 1919), 195.
27. Lindsay Rogers, *The American Senate* (New York: Knopf, 1926).
28. *The Federalist Papers*, No. 55, 343.
29. Charles A. Kromkowski and John A. Kromkowski, "Why 435? A Question of Political Arithmetic," *Polity* 24 (fall 1991): 129–145; and David C. Huckabee, *House of Representatives: Setting the Size at 435*, Congressional Research Service Report No. 95–791GOV, July 11, 1995.
30. *The Federalist Papers*, No. 27, 168.
31. Joe Martin as told to Robert J. Donovan, *My First Fifty Years in Politics* (New York: McGraw-Hill, 1960), 49–50.
32. Norman J. Ornstein, Thomas E. Mann, and Michael J. Malbin, *Vital Statistics on Congress, 2001–2002* (Washington, D.C.: American Enterprise Institute Press, 2002), 149.
33. Ornstein, Mann, and Malbin, *Vital Statistics on Congress*, 146–147.
34. U.S. Congress, House Commission on Administrative Review, *Administrative Reorganization and Legislative Management*, 2 vols., H. Doc. 95–232, 95th Cong., 1st sess., September 28, 1977, 2:17; and U.S. Congress, Senate Commission on the Operation of the Senate, *Senators: Offices, Ethics, and Pressures*, 94th Cong., 2d sess., 1977, Committee Print, xi.
35. See Jefferson's Manual, Section XI; House, *Rules of the House of Representatives*, H. Doc. 105–358, 105th Cong., 2d sess., 1999, 145–148.
36. George B. Galloway, *History of the House of Representatives* (New York: Crowell, 1961), 67.
37. Barbara Sinclair, *Legislators, Leaders, and Lawmaking* (Baltimore: Johns Hopkins University Press, 1995), 75.
38. Neil MacNeil, *Forge of Democracy: The House of Representatives* (New York: McKay, 1963), 306.
39. Elaine K. Swift, *The Making of an American Senate* (Ann Arbor: University of Michigan Press, 1996), 5.
40. David C. King, *Turf Wars: How Congressional Committees Claim Jurisdiction* (Chicago: University of Chicago Press, 1997).
41. Noble Cunningham Jr., ed., *Circular Letters of Congressmen, 1789–1839*, 3 vols. (Chapel Hill: University of North Carolina Press, 1978).
42. Quoted in Galloway, *History of the House*, 122.
43. Quoted in Anthony Champagne, "John Nance Garner," in *Masters of the House: Congressional Leaders over Two Centuries*, ed. Roger H. Davidson, Susan Webb Hammond, and Raymond W. Smock (Boulder: Westview Press, 1998), 148.
44. Martin, *My First Fifty Years*, 101.
45. James Sterling Young, *The Washington Community, 1800–1828* (New York: Harcourt Brace Jovanovich, 1966), 89.
46. Cunningham, *Circular Letters of Congressmen*, 57.
47. Roy Swanstrom, *The United States Senate, 1787–1801*, S. Doc. 99–19, 99th Cong., 1st sess., 1985, 80.
48. Nelson W. Polsby, "The Institutionalization of the House of Representatives," *American Political Science Review* 62 (March 1968): 146–147; and Randall B. Ripley, *Power in the Senate* (New York: St. Martin's, 1969), 42–43.
49. Peter Swenson, "The Influence of Recruitment on the Structure of Power in the U.S. House, 1870–1940," *Legislative Studies Quarterly* 7 (February 1982): 7–36.

50. Woodrow Wilson, *Congressional Government* (1885; reprint, Baltimore: Johns Hopkins University Press, 1981).

51. Martin, *My First Fifty Years*, 49.

52. Ripley, *Power in the Senate,* 43–44.

53. David W. Brady, "After the Big Bang House Battles Focused on Committee Issues," *Public Affairs Report* 32 (March 1991): 8. See also Samuel Kernell, "Toward Understanding the Nineteenth Century Congressional Career Patterns: Ambition, Competition, and Rotation," *American Journal of Political Science* 21 (November 1977): 669–693; and Nelson W. Polsby, Miriam Gallagher, and Barry S. Rundquist, "The Growth of the Seniority System in the U.S. House of Representatives," *American Political Science Review* 63 (September 1969): 794.

54. Swanstrom, *The United States Senate,* 283.

55. Young, *The Washington Community,* 126–127.

56. Ornstein, Mann, and Malbin, *Vital Statistics on Congress,* 126–127.

Chapter 3 *(pages 39–79)*

1. *U.S. Term Limits v. Thornton,* 115 S. Ct. 1842 (1995).

2. Quoted in David S. Broder, "Escape from the Term-Limits Trap," *Washington Post,* February 19, 1997, A21. The authors of *The Federalist Papers* discuss election qualifications and arrangements in detail. See Nos. 53, 56, 57, 58, 59, 60, and 61 of Alexander Hamilton, James Madison, and John Jay, *The Federalist Papers,* ed. Clinton Rossiter (New York: Mentor, 1961).

3. Arend Lijphart, *Democracies: Patterns of Majoritarian and Consensus Government in Twenty-one Countries* (New Haven: Yale University Press, 1984), 174.

4. Quoted in Judith Havemann, "Moynihan Poses Questions of Balance," *Washington Post,* August 14, 1995, A15.

5. This method is only one of several mathematical formulas that could be employed. Another, the major fractions method, was used from 1911 until 1940. The methods yield slightly different results. For example, in 1992 Montana faced the prospect of losing its second House seat. The state challenged the apportionment formula in the courts but was rejected by the Supreme Court, which found no conclusive answer to the question of "what is the better measure of inequality." *Department of Commerce v. Montana,* 503 U.S. 442 (1992). See also Linda Greenhouse, "Supreme Court Upholds Method Used in Apportionment of House," *New York Times,* April 1, 1992, B8. The methods are examined in David C. Huckabee, *House Apportionment Following the 1990 Census: Using the Official Counts,* Congressional Research Service Report No. 91–130, February 4, 1991.

6. Jonathan Tilove, "Pandora's Box: The Pitfalls of Census 2000," *American Prospect* 11 (April 24, 2000): 39–42.

7. Tilove, "Pandora's Box," 39.

8. Genaro C. Armas, "Census Must Show Adjusted Estimates," *Santa Barbara News-Press,* November 23, 2002, B5.

9. Robin Fields, "State Census Sampling Shows Huge Undercount," *Los Angeles Times,* December 7, 2002, B10.

10. Eric Schmitt, "U.S. Census Bureau Rejects Revision to Nation's Tally," *New York Times,* March 3, 2001, A1. The bureau has continued its strategic retreat from statistical adjustments. Reexamining its numbers three years later, the bureau pronounced its original count a success and claimed it had overcounted the U.S. population by 1.3 million people. However, accuracy varied from state to state, and blacks and Latinos were still undercounted. "Census Bureau Issues Data on Accuracy of 2000 Count," *New York Times,* April 16, 2003, A13.

11. Mark Z. Barabak, "Democrats Rule the Redistricting Roost in California," *Los Angeles Times,* July 25, 2001, A15; and Susan F. Rasky, "Redistricting Defanged by Energy Crisis," *Los Angeles Times,* April 22, 2001, M6.

12. Quoted in Raymond Hernandez, "Lobbying in Albany, New York's Representatives Fight for Their Seats," *New York Times,* February 19, 2001, A16.

13. Mark Z. Barabak, "Redistricting Fuels Partisan Frenzy," *Los Angeles Times*, A1, A14; and Gregory L. Giroux, "GOP in Position to Have Its Say When States Redraw Congressional Districts," *CQ Weekly*, January 6, 2001, 39.
14. Eric Schmitt, "New Census Shows Hispanics Now Even with Blacks in U.S.," *New York Times*, March 8, 2001, A1, A15.
15. *Growe v. Emerson*, 507 U.S. 25 (1993). See Susan B. Glasser, "Supreme Court Voids Minnesota Redistricting," *Roll Call*, February 25, 1993, 1.
16. The classic study is still Gordon E. Baker, *The Reapportionment Revolution: Representation, Political Power, and the Supreme Court* (New York: Random House, 1966).
17. Alan Ehrenhalt, "Redistricting and the Erosion of Community," *Governing*, June 1992, 10.
18. Chris Cillizza, "Republicans Score Big in Pa.," *Roll Call*, January 7, 2002, 9.
19. Bruce E. Cain and David Butler, "Redistricting Myths Are at Odds with Evidence," *Public Affairs Report* 32 (September 1991): 6. See also Bruce E. Cain, "Assessing the Partisan Effects of Redistricting," *American Political Science Review* 79 (June 1985): 320–333.
20. *Davis v. Bandemer*, 478 U.S. 109 (1986).
21. *Hunt v. Cromartie*, 526 U.S. 541 (1999).
22. Rhodes Cook, "Do the Math, and the Result Is: Not Much of a Contest," *Washington Post*, October 6, 2002, B3.
23. Cain and Butler, "Redistricting Myths Are at Odds with Evidence," 7.
24. *Thornburg v. Gingles*, 478 U.S. 30 (1986).
25. Charles S. Bullock, "Affirmative Action Districts: In Whose Faces Will They Blow Up?" *Campaigns and Elections* (April 1995): 22.
26. Bullock, "Affirmative Action Districts," 23.
27. David Lublin, *The Paradox of Representation: Racial Gerrymandering and Minority Interests in Congress* (Princeton: Princeton University Press, 1997).
28. Lani Guinier, "What Color Is Your Gerrymander?" *Washington Post*, March 27, 1994, C3.
29. Abigail M. Thernstrom, "A Republican–Civil Rights Conspiracy," *Washington Post*, September 23, 1991, A11. See also Abigail M. Thernstrom, *Whose Votes Count? Affirmative Action and Minority Voting Rights* (Cambridge: Harvard University Press, 1987).
30. *Shaw v. Reno*, 509 U.S. 630 (1993).
31. Ehrenhalt, "Redistricting and the Erosion of Community," 10.
32. Carol M. Swain, "The Voting Rights Act: Some Unintended Consequences," *Brookings Review* 10 (winter 1992): 51. See also Lublin, *The Paradox of Representation*.
33. Alexander Bolton, "Dems Seek to 'Unpack' Minority Districts," *The Hill*, May 9, 2001, 4.
34. *Gomillion v. Lightfoot*, 364 U.S. 339 (1960).
35. *Shaw v. Reno*.
36. *Miller v. Johnson*, 115 S. Ct. 2475 (1995).
37. Research by Charles S. Bullock and Richard E. Dunn, cited in Adam Clymer, "Shaping the New Math of Racial Redistricting," *New York Times*, July 15, 2001, D16.
38. *Easley v. Cromartie* 121 S. Ct. (2001). The decision was described by Linda Greenhouse in "Court Gives Wiggle Room to Racially Drawn Districts," *New York Times*, May 18, 1999, A12; and in "Justices Reconsider Race and Redistricting," *New York Times*, November 28, 2000, A25.
39. Linda Greenhouse, "Justices Permit Race as a Factor in Redistricting," *New York Times*, April 19, 2001, A1, A16.
40. Mara Caputo and Ragan Narash, "Despite Series of Court Rulings, State Officials Are Left Guessing," *CQ Weekly*, August 11, 2001, 1970.
41. *DeWitt v. Wilson*, 515 U.S. 1170 (1995).
42. Louis Sandy Maisel, *From Obscurity to Oblivion: Running in the Congressional Primary* (Knoxville: University of Tennessee Press, 1982), 34.
43. Quoted in Jon Margolis, "The Disappearing Candidates," *American Prospect* 11 (January 31, 2000): 32.
44. Alan Ehrenhalt, *The United States of Ambition* (New York: Random House, 1991), 17.

45. The four Capitol Hill campaign committees are the National Republican Senatorial Committee (NRSC), the Democratic Senatorial Campaign Committee (DSCC), the National Republican Congressional Committee (NRCC), and the Democratic Congressional Campaign Committee (DCCC). See Paul S. Herrnson, *Congressional Elections: Campaigning at Home and in Washington*, 2d ed. (Washington, D.C.: CQ Press, 1998), especially chaps. 4–5.

46. Edward Walsh, "To Every Campaign, There Is a Recruiting Season," *Washington Post*, November 12, 1985, A1.

47. Connie Bruck, "The Politics of Perception," *New Yorker*, October 9, 1995, 61.

48. Bruck, "The Politics of Perception," 63.

49. David S. Broder, "A New Democrat Revival," *Washington Post*, July 22, 2001, B7.

50. Alice A. Love, "Small Business Group Helps Grow Its Own Grassroots Candidates at Meeting Next Week," *Roll Call*, October 16, 1995, 22.

51. David T. Canon, *Actors, Athletes, and Astronauts: Political Amateurs in the United States Congress* (Chicago: University of Chicago Press, 1990), 2–3, 25–31.

52. Maisel, *From Obscurity to Oblivion*, 23.

53. Michael Janofsky, "Two Congressional Candidates Know They'll Lose, But It's Still Fun," *New York Times*, October 31, 1992, 27.

54. The seminal work on strategic politician theory is Gary C. Jacobson and Samuel Kernell, *Strategy and Choice in Congressional Elections*, 2d ed. (New Haven: Yale University Press), 1983.

55. Gary C. Jacobson, *The Politics of Congressional Elections*, 5th ed. (New York: Longman, 2000), 20.

56. Gary C. Jacobson, "The Marginals Never Vanished: Incumbency and Competition in Elections to the U.S. House of Representatives, 1952–1982," *American Journal of Political Science* 31 (February 1987): 126–141.

57. Norman J. Ornstein, Thomas E. Mann, and Michael J. Malbin, *Vital Statistics on Congress, 1999–2000* (Washington, D.C.: American Enterprise Institute, 2000), 57.

58. Donald Gross and David Breaux, "Historical Trends in U.S. Senate Elections: 1912–1988," *American Politics Quarterly* 19 (July 1991): 284–309.

59. Frances E. Lee and Bruce I. Oppenheimer, *Sizing Up the Senate: The Unequal Consequences of Equal Representation* (Chicago: University of Chicago Press, 1999), 95.

60. On the first view mentioned in this paragraph, see Morris P. Fiorina, *Congress: Keystone of the Washington Establishment*, 2d ed. (New Haven: Yale University Press, 1989); and Bruce Cain, John Ferejohn, and Morris Fiorina, *The Personal Vote: Constituency Service and Electoral Independence* (Cambridge: Harvard University Press, 1987), especially chaps. 6–7. For more on the second view, see Glenn R. Parker and Roger H. Davidson, "Why Do Americans Love Their Congressmen So Much More Than Their Congress?" *Legislative Studies Quarterly* 4 (February 1979): 53–61. On the question of whether incumbents' resources are directly tied to votes, see John R. Johannes, *To Serve the People: Congress and Constituency Service* (Lincoln: University of Nebraska Press, 1984), especially chap. 8.

61. Jacobson, *Politics of Congressional Elections*, 43.

62. Jacobson and Kernell, *Strategy and Choice in Congressional Elections*, chap. 3.

63. Quoted in John Mercurio, "Dickey on Defense," *Roll Call*, June 7, 1999, 16.

64. Quoted in Jim VanderHei and Tim Curran, "Parties Pushing for Early Money," *Roll Call*, June 14, 1999, 34.

65. Peverill Squire, "Challengers in U.S. Senate Elections," *Legislative Studies Quarterly* 14 (November 1989): 531–547.

66. William Claiborne, "In Neb., a Gridiron Hero Scores in Political Arena," *Washington Post*, June 14, 2000, A3.

67. Gary C. Jacobson, "The 105th Congress: Unprecedented and Unsurprising," in *The Elections of 1996*, ed. Michael Nelson (Washington, D.C.: CQ Press, 1997), 154.

68. Rachel Van Dongen, "Ripken Helped Dems Break Streak," *Roll Call*, November 19, 1998, 13.

69. Linda L. Fowler and Robert D. McClure, *Political Ambition: Who Decides to Run for Congress* (New Haven: Yale University Press, 1989).

70. Quoted in Burt Solomon, "A Daunting Task: Running for House," *National Journal*, March 21, 1992, 712.
71. Cited in Robin Toner, "Willing Contenders at a Premium in Fierce Fight to Rule Congress," *New York Times*, January 3, 2000, A14.
72. Maisel, *From Obscurity to Oblivion*, 23.
73. L. Sandy Maisel, Cary T. Gibson, and Elizabeth J. Ivry, "The Continuing Importance of the Rules of the Game: Subpresidential Nominations in 1994 and 1996," in *The Parties Respond*, 3d ed., ed. L. Sandy Maisel (Boulder: Westview Press, 1998), 148–151.
74. Quoted in Linda Greenhouse, "Court Rejects One-Ballot Primary as Limit on Party's Right to Shape Its Identity," *New York Times*, June 27, 2000, A19.
75. *California Democratic Party et. al. v. Jones*, 99–401 (2000).
76. Maisel, Gibson, and Ivry, "The Continuing Importance of the Rules of the Game," 162–164.
77. Harvey L. Schantz, "Contested and Uncontested Primaries for the U.S. House," *Legislative Studies Quarterly* 5 (November 1980): 559. The linkage between interparty and intraparty competition is sometimes referred to as Key's Law. See V. O. Key Jr., *Parties, Politics and Pressure Groups*, 5th ed. (New York: Crowell, 1964), 438, 447.
78. Allison Stevens, "Primaries Point to Low Turnout in November, *The Hill*, June 26, 2002, 23.
79. Kirk Victor, "Meddling in Minnesota," *National Journal*, May 12, 2001, 1422.
80. Quoted in Jodi Wilgoren, "Illinois Senator Announces He Won't Seek Reelection," *New York Times*, April 16, 2003, A10.
81. Richard A. Oppel, Jr., "Despite Big Issues, Primaries Prompted Only 17% to Vote," *New York Times*, September 28, 2002, A12.
82. Austin Ranney, "Parties in State Politics," in *Politics in the American States*, ed. Herbert Jacob and Kenneth Vines (Boston: Little, Brown, 1976), 61–99.
83. Herrnson, *Congressional Elections*, 128.
84. Figures for 2001–2002 are derived from Federal Election Commission (FEC) reports, available at fec.gov, and analyses prepared from those data by the Center for Responsive Politics (CRP), available at crp.org. The figures sometimes differ due to CRP's statistical breakdowns of FEC data.
85. See Ornstein, Mann, and Malbin, *Vital Statistics on Congress*, 87–98.
86. Gary C. Jacobson, "Money in the 1980 and 1982 Congressional Elections," in *Money and Politics in the United States*, ed. Michael J. Malbin (Chatham, N.J.: Chatham House, 1984), 58.
87. Christopher Buchanan, "Candidates' Campaign Costs for Congressional Contests Have Gone Up at a Fast Pace," *Congressional Quarterly Weekly Report*, September 29, 1979, 2154–2155.
88. Jacobson, "Money in the 1980 and 1982 Congressional Elections," 57.
89. Quoted in Andy Plattner, "The High Cost of Holding—and Keeping—Public Office," *U.S. News and World Report*, June 22, 1997, 30.
90. See James M. Snyder, Jr., "The Market for Campaign Contributions: Evidence for the U.S. Senate, 1980–1996," *Economics and Politics*, 5: 219–250.
91. Federal Election Commission, "Party Fundraising Escalates," news release, January 12, 2001.
92. Jacobson, "Money in the 1980 and 1982 Congressional Elections," 58–59.
93. Committee for Responsive Politics, based on FEC data as of February 25, 2002.
94. Case studies of political action committees are found in Robert Biersack, Paul Herrnson, and Clyde Wilcox, *Risky Business? PAC Decisionmaking and Congressional Elections* (Armonk, N.Y.: M. E. Sharpe, 1994).
95. Jim VanderHei, "Hastert Starting to Raise Big Bucks," *Roll Call*, June 7, 1999, 1.
96. Quoted in Leslie Wayne, "Business Is Biggest Campaign Spender, Study Says," *New York Times*, October 18, 1996, A1, A26.
97. Quoted in Jonathan D. Salant, "Business PACs Pick Their Cause," *Congressional Quarterly Weekly Report*, May 6, 1995, 1234.
98. Quoted in Diana F. Dwyer and Victoria A. Farrar-Myers, *Legislative Labyrinth: Congress and Campaign Finance Reform* (Washington, D.C.: CQ Press, 2001), 233.
99. Scott Turow, "The High Court's 20-Year-Old Mistake," *New York Times*, October 12, 1997, E15.

100. E. J. Dionne Jr., "Politics as Public Auction," *Washington Post,* June 19, 1998, A25.
101. Gary C. Jacobson, *Money in Congressional Elections* (New Haven: Yale University Press, 1980).
102. Quoted in Brooks Jackson, "Loopholes Allow Flood of Campaign Giving by Business, Fat Cats," *Wall Street Journal,* July 5, 1984, 1.
103. Dan Balz, "In Long Battle, Small Victories Add Up," *Washington Post,* March 21, 2002, A1.
104. David G. Savage and Nick Anderson, " 'Soft Money' Ad Ban Upheld," *Los Angeles Times,* May 3, 2001, A1; and Linda Greenhouse, "1,638 Pages, but Little Weight in Supreme Court," *New York Times,* May 3, 2001, A14.
105. Chuck Alston, "A Field Guide to Election Spending Limits," *CQ Weekly,* May 22, 1990, 1621–1626.

Chapter 4 (pages 81–117)

1. The Jon Corzine campaign was chronicled by David Beiler, "Jon Corzine and the Power of Money," *Campaigns and Elections* 22 (April 2001): 22–36; Clifford J. Levy, "History's Richest Senate Bid Began in a Grass Roots Flood," *New York Times,* May 27, 2000, A1, A13; and Don Van Natta Jr., "In Politics, It's Only Money: Yours or Theirs," *New York Times,* June 11, 2000, D4.
2. Quoted in Beiler, "Jon Corzine and the Power of Money," 29.
3. Ibid., 24.
4. Ibid., 27.
5. Ibid., 36.
6. See Richard G. Niemi, Lynda W. Powell, and Patricia L. Bickell, "The Effects of Congruity between Community and District on Salience of U.S. House Candidates," *Legislative Studies Quarterly* 11 (May 1986): 187–201; and James E. Campbell, John R. Alford, and Keith Henry, "Television Markets and Congressional Elections," *Legislative Studies Quarterly* 9 (November 1984): 665–678.
7. Theodore E. Jackson Jr., "Brand Marketing in Today's Cluttered Political Marketplace," *Campaigns and Elections* 24 (April 2003): 30.
8. Quoted material in this paragraph is from Allison Stevens, "House Candidates in Maryland Striving to Hone Their Messages," *The Hill,* May 8, 2002, 31–32.
9. Quoted in Robin Toner, "In a Cynical Election Season, the Ads Tell an Angry Tale," *New York Times,* October 24, 1994, A1.
10. Kristin Brainerd, "Three Davids, No Goliath, and Plenty of Slingshots," *Campaigns and Elections* 20 (September 1999): 35–47.
11. Kevin McNeill and Cheryl Klock, "Connecticut Upset," *Campaign and Elections* 22 (May 2001): 39, 43.
12. Parke Skelton, quoted in Mary Clare Jalonick, "How to 'Primary' an Incumbent," *Campaigns and Elections* 22 (May 2001): 35.
13. EMILY's List Web site (emilyslist.org).
14. Thomas B. Edsall, "In Tight Races, Early Cash Means Staying Competitive," *Washington Post,* July 14, 1998, A6.
15. Robin Toner, "In Final Rounds, Both Sides Whip Out Bare-Knuckle Ads," *New York Times,* October 21, 1996, B7.
16. Sara Fritz and Dwight Morris, *Gold-Plated Politics: Running for Congress in the 1990s* (Washington, D.C.: Congressional Quarterly, 1992), 28.
17. Statistics on spending in the 2001–2002 electoral cycle are taken from Federal Election Commission (FEC), "Median Activity of House Candidates," available from the Web sites of the FEC (fec.gov.press.hsemed) and the Committee for Responsive Politics (opensecrets.org).
18. Gary C. Jacobson, *The Politics of Congressional Elections,* 5th ed. (New York: Longman, 2000), 81.
19. Gary C. Jacobson, "The Effects of Campaign Spending on Congressional Elections," *American Political Science Review* 72 (June 1978): 469–491.

20. "Total Congressional Campaign Spending," *New York Times*, November 6, 2002, B2.
21. Quoted in Herbert E. Alexander and Brian A. Haggarty, "Misinformation on Media Money," *Public Opinion* 11 (May–June 1988): 7.
22. Paul Houston, "TV and High Tech Send Campaign Costs Soaring," *Los Angeles Times*, October 2, 1986, 121.
23. Jamie Stiehm, "Ben and Jerry's State Offers a Choice of Three Flavors," *The Hill*, November 22, 1995, 26.
24. Glenn R. Simpson, "In Rhode Island, Everyone Goes to Bristol Parade," *Roll Call*, July 9, 1990, 1; and Glenn R. Simpson, "Judging from July 4th Bristol Parade in R.I., Chafee Looks Well-Positioned for November," *Roll Call*, July 11, 1994, 21.
25. Edie N. Goldberg and Michael W. Traugott, *Campaigning for Congress* (Washington, D.C.: CQ Press, 1984), 93.
26. Craig Karmin, "Campaign Funds Used for Private Expenses," *The Hill*, September 6, 1995, 1.
27. Larry J. Sabato and Glenn R. Simpson, *Dirty Little Secrets: The Persistence of Corruption in American Politics* (New York: Times Books, 1996), 156.
28. "The Living-Room Campaign," *New York Times*, November 6, 2002, B2.
29. Pew Research Center for the People and the Press, *The Tough Job of Communicating with Voters* (February 5, 2000), 1.
30. Peter Clarke and Susan H. Evans, *Covering Campaigns: Journalism in Congressional Elections* (Stanford: Stanford University Press, 1983).
31. "Media Mix," *Campaigns and Elections* (May 1998): 44.
32. Burdett A. Loomis, "Kansas's Third District: 'Pros from Dover' Set Up Shop," in *The Battle for Congress*, ed. James A. Thurber (Washington, D.C.: Brookings Institution, 1999), 148.
33. Michael Barone and Grant Ujifusa, *The Almanac of American Politics, 1996* (Washington, D.C.: National Journal, 1995), 1445–1446.
34. David T. Canon, "The Wisconsin Second District: History in the Making," in *The Battle for Congress*, ed. James A. Thurber (Washington, D.C.: Brookings Institution, 1999), 230.
35. Loomis, "Kansas's Third District," 147–148.
36. Stephen Ansolabehere and Shanto Iyengar, *Going Negative: How Attack Ads Shrink and Polarize the Electorate* (New York: Free Press, 1996), 128.
37. Quoted in David S. Broder, "Death by Negative Ads," *Washington Post*, November 3, 2002, B7.
38. Richard R. Lau and Gerald M. Pomper, "Effects of Negative Campaigning on Turnout in U.S. Senate Elections, 1988–1998," *Journal of Politics* 63 (August 2001): 817.
39. See Howard Kurtz, "Hearing 'Foul,' Stations Pull Political Ads," *Washington Post*, September 20, 2002, A14.
40. Benjamin Sheffner, "Minn. Candidate Can't Be Charged for Misleading Ad," *Roll Call*, March 7, 1996, 13; and John E. Yang, "Oregon Rep. Cooley Indicted for Lying about Military Service," *Washington Post*, December 12, 1996, A3.
41. Norman J. Ornstein, "Should Liars Be Seated? It's Not Up to Congress," *Roll Call*, May 17, 1993, 12.
42. Quoted in Adam Nagourney, "Politicians Turn to Alternatives to TV Advertising," *New York Times*, October 5, 2002, A1.
43. Figures from the Wisconsin Advertising Project, cited in "The Living-Room Campaign." See also Lizette Alverez, "In Political Din, South Dakotans Long for 'Mute,'" *New York Times*, October 19, 2002, A1.
44. Quoted in Nagourney, "Politicians Turn to Alternatives to TV Advertising," A1, 15.
45. David S. Broder, "Shoe Leather Politicking," *Washington Post*, June 13, 2001, A29.
46. Merle Miller, *Lyndon: An Oral Biography* (New York: Putnam, 1980), 120.
47. Robert G. Kaiser, "The Smiling Majority," *Washington Post*, June 6, 2001, C1.
48. Ron Faucheux, "Candidate Canvassing," *Campaigns and Elections* (May 1997): 43.
49. Donald Green, quoted in Broder, "Shoe Leather Politicking."
50. See E. J. Dionne Jr., "Radical," *Washington Post Magazine*, January 19, 1997, 8ff.

51. David T. Canon, "The Wisconsin Second Congressional District: History in the Making," in *The Battle for Congress*, ed. James A. Thurber (Washington, D.C.: Brookings Institution, 1999), 230.
52. Jonathan E. Kaplan, "Large Voter Turnout Was Key to GOP Victory," *The Hill*, November 7, 2002, 17.
53. David M. Halbfinger, "Improved Ground Game Is Seen as Important Factor in G.O.P. Victories," *New York Times*, November 10, 2002, A24.
54. Quoted in Halbfinger, "Improved Ground Game Is Seen as Important Factor in G.O.P. Victories."
55. Thomas B. Edsall, "Issues Coalitions Take On Political Party Functions," *Washington Post*, August 9, 1996, A1.
56. Louis Jacobson, "Fighting the Political 'Ground War,'" *National Journal*, October 12, 2002, 2983–2985.
57. Quoted in David S. Broder and Thomas B. Edsall, "Amid Election Apathy, Parties Bet On Core Voters," *Washington Post*, September 7, 1998, A12.
58. Edsall, "Issues Coalitions Take On Political Party Functions," A1.
59. Kaplan, "Large Voter Turnout Was Key to GOP Victory."
60. Leslie Wayne, "A Back Door for the Conservative Donor," *New York Times*, May 22, 1997, A24.
61. Figures from the Committee for the Study of the American Electorate (Web site: gspn.org/csae/). See Edward Walsh, "Election Turnout Rose Slightly, to 39.3%" *Washington Post*, November 8, 2002, A10.
62. A sensible review of the question is found in Martin P. Wattenberg, *Where Have All the Voters Gone?* (Cambridge: Harvard University Press, 2002).
63. Raymond E. Wolfinger and Steven J. Rosenstone, *Who Votes?* (New Haven: Yale University Press, 1980), 18ff.
64. Data on the results of the act are distressingly incomplete. See Raymond E. Wolfinger and Jonathan Hoffman, "Registering and Voting with Motor Voter," *P.S.* 34 (March 2001): 85–92.
65. B. Drummond Ayres Jr., "Easier Voter Registration Doesn't Raise Participation," *New York Times*, December 3, 1995, 22. Registration data from Committee for the Study of the American Electorate, news release, November 6, 1998.
66. Richard Morin and Claudia Deane, "As Turnout Falls, Apathy Emerges as Driving Force," *Washington Post*, November 4, 2000, A1.
67. Lyn Ragsdale and Jerrold G. Rusk, "Who Are Nonvoters? Profiles from the 1990 Senate Elections," *American Journal of Political Science* 37 (August 1993): 721–746; and Associated Press, "Many More Non-Voters in '96 Were 'Too Busy,'" *Washington Post*, August 17, 1998, A4.
68. Samuel L. Popkin and Michael P. McDonald, "Turnout's Not as Bad as You Think," *Washington Post*, November 5, 2000, B1.
69. Wolfinger and Rosenstone, *Who Votes?* See also Steven J. Rosenstone and John Mark Hansen, *Mobilization, Participation, and Democracy* (New York: Macmillan, 1993); and Ruy Teixeira, *The Disappearing Voter* (Washington, D.C.: Brookings Institution, 1992).
70. Sidney Verba, Kay Lehman Schlozman, and Henry E. Brady, *Voice and Equality: Civic Voluntarism in American Politics* (Cambridge: Harvard University Press, 1995).
71. M. Margaret Conway, "Political Participation in Midterm Congressional Elections," *American Politics Quarterly* 9 (April 1981): 221–244.
72. Samuel L. Popkin, *The Reasoning Voter* (Chicago: University of Chicago Press, 1991), 7.
73. Marjorie Connelly, "Who Voted: A Portrait of American Politics, 1976–2000," *New York Times*, November 12, 2000, D4.
74. *Washington Post*-ABC News Poll (July 2002). See Richard Morin and Claudia Deane, "How Independent Are Independents?" *Washington Post*, August 2, 2002, A1.
75. Quoted in Morin and Deane, "How Independent Are Independents?"
76. Warren E. Miller, Donald R. Kinder, Steven J. Rosenstone, and the National Election Studies, *American National Election Study, 1990: Post-Election Survey*, 2d ed. (Ann Arbor, Mich.: Inter-University Consortium for Political and Social Research, January 1992), 193–194.

77. Gary C. Jacobson, *The Electoral Origins of Divided Government: Competition in U.S. House Elections, 1946–1988* (Boulder: Westview Press, 1990), 20.

78. Martin P. Wattenberg, *The Rise of Candidate-Centered Politics* (Cambridge: Harvard University Press, 1991), 36–39.

79. Gregory L. Giroux, "Split-Ticket Voting Lowest in 48 Years," *CQ Weekly*, May 12, 2001, 1052.

80. See Bernard Grofman, William Koetzle, Michael P. McDonald, and Thomas L. Brunell, "A New Look at Split-Ticket Outcomes for House and President: The Comparative Midpoints Model," *Journal of Politics* 62 (February 2000): 34–50.

81. Jacobson, *The Politics of Congressional Elections*, 132–133.

82. Angus Campbell, "Surge and Decline: A Study of Electoral Change," in *Elections and the Political Order*, ed. Angus Campbell, Phillip E. Converse, Warren E. Miller, and Donald E. Stokes (New York: Wiley, 1966), 40–62; and Raymond E. Wolfinger, Steven J. Rosenstone, and Richard A. McIntosh, "Presidential and Congressional Voters Compared," *American Politics Quarterly* 9 (April 1981): 245–255.

83. Eric M. Uslaner and Margaret Conway, "The Responsible Electorate: Watergate, the Economy, and Vote Choice in 1974," *American Political Science Review* 79 (September 1985): 788–803; and Samuel Kernell, "Presidential Popularity and Negative Voting: An Alternative Explanation of the Midterm Congressional Decline of the President's Party," *American Political Science Review* 71 (March 1977): 44–46.

84. Ceci Connolly and Howard Kurtz, "Gingrich Orchestrated Lewinsky Ads," *Washington Post*, October 30, 1998, A18.

85. Thomas B. Edsall and Claudia Deane, "Poll Shows Democratic Gains with Key Voters," *Washington Post*, November 4, 1998, A27.

86. "The Bush Effect," *New York Times*, November 8, 2002, chart, A20.

87. Committee for the Study of the American Electorate, news release, November 6, 1998, 2.

88. Thomas B. Edsall and Claudia Deane, "Poll Shows Democratic Gains with Key Voters," *Washington Post*, November 4, 1998, A27.

89. Quoted in Dale Russakoff, "In Tight Arkansas Senate Race, Family Matters," *Washington Post*, August 3, 2002, A1.

90. David Brady, Brian Gaines, and Douglas Rivers, "The Incumbency Advantage in the House and Senate: A Comparative Institutional Analysis," unpublished paper, Stanford University, August 1994; Robert S. Erikson, "The Advantage of Incumbency in Congressional Elections," *Polity* 3 (spring 1971): 395–405; and Robert S. Erikson, "Malapportionment, Gerrymandering, and Party Fortunes in Congressional Elections," *American Political Science Review* 66 (December 1972): 1234–1245.

91. Jacobson, *The Electoral Origins of Divided Government*, 28–29.

92. Warren Lee Kostroski, "Party and Incumbency in Postwar Senate Elections: Trends, Patterns, and Models," *American Political Science Review* 67 (December 1974): 1233.

93. Mark C. Westlye, "Competitiveness of Senate Seats and Voting Behavior in Senate Elections," *American Journal of Political Science* 27 (May 1983): 253–283.

94. Thomas E. Mann and Raymond E. Wolfinger, "Candidates and Parties in Congressional Elections," *American Political Science Review* 74 (September 1980): 623; Alan I. Abramowitz, "Name Familiarity, Reputation, and the Incumbency Effect in a Congressional Election," *Western Political Quarterly* 28 (December 1975): 668–684; Abramowitz, "A Comparison of Voting for U.S. Senate and Representative in 1978," 633–650; and Thomas E. Mann, *Unsafe at Any Margin: Interpreting Congressional Elections* (Washington, D.C.: American Enterprise Institute, 1978).

95. David R. Mayhew, *Congress: The Electoral Connection* (New Haven: Yale University Press, 1974).

96. Michael J. Robinson, "Three Faces of Congressional Media," in *The New Congress*, ed. Thomas E. Mann and Norman J. Ornstein (Washington, D.C.: American Enterprise Institute, 1981), 91.

97. Frances E. Lee and Bruce I. Oppenheimer, *Sizing Up the Senate: The Unequal Consequences of Equal Representation* (Chicago: University of Chicago Press, 1999), chap. 4.
98. Gary C. Jacobson, "Incumbents' Advantages in the 1978 U.S. Congressional Elections," *Legislative Studies Quarterly* 6 (May 1981): 198.
99. Mann, *Unsafe at Any Margin*.
100. Donald E. Stokes and Warren E. Miller, "Party Government and the Saliency of Congress," *Public Opinion Quarterly* 26 (winter 1962): 531–546.
101. Patricia A. Hurley and Kim Quaile Hill, "The Prospects for Issue Voting in Contemporary Congressional Elections," *American Politics Quarterly* 8 (October 1980): 425–448; and Lynda W. Powell, "Analyzing Misinformation: Perceptions of Congressional Candidates' Ideologies," *American Journal of Political Science* 33 (May 1989): 272–293.
102. Miller and others, *American National Election Study,* 126–129, 171.
103. Abramowitz, "A Comparison of Voting for U.S. Senator and Representative in 1978," 635.
104. Gerald C. Wright Jr. and Michael B. Berkman, "Candidates and Policy in United States Senate Elections," *American Political Science Review* 80 (June 1986): 567–588.
105. John B. Bader, *Taking the Initiative: Leadership Agendas in Congress and the "Contract with America"* (Washington, D.C.: Georgetown University Press, 1996).
106. These quotes are from James G. Gimpel, *Fulfilling the Contract: The First 100 Days* (Boston: Allyn and Bacon, 1996), 28, 29. Gimpel presents a balanced insider's view of the origin, development, and effects of the Contract with America.
107. Frank Bruni, "G.O.P. Is Trying to Counter Erosion of Women's Support," *New York Times,* August 1, 2001, A1.
108. Quoted in Judy Newman, "Do Women Vote for Women?" *Public Perspective* 7 (February– March 1996): 10.
109. See Felicia Pratto, Stanford University, and Jim Sidanius, University of California at Los Angeles, e-mail news release, December 2, 1996.
110. Quoted in Barbara Vobejda, "Fragmentation of Society Formidable Challenge to Candidates, Report Says," *Washington Post,* March 7, 1996, A15.
111. Richard F. Fenno Jr., *Home Style: House Members in Their Districts* (Boston: Little, Brown, 1978).
112. Mann and Wolfinger, "Candidates and Parties in Congressional Elections," 630.
113. David W. Brady, "Electoral Realignments in the U.S. House of Representatives," in *Congress and Policy Change,* ed. Gerald C. Wright Jr., Leroy N. Reiselbach, and Lawrence C. Dodd (New York: Agathon Press, 1986), 46–69.
114. Stephen Earl Bennet and Linda L. M. Bennet, "Out of Sight, Out of Mind: Americans' Knowledge of Party Control of the House of Representatives, 1960–1984," *Political Research Quarterly* 46 (March 1993): 67ff.
115. Gary C. Jacobson, "Meager Patrimony: The Reagan Era and Republican Representation in Congress," in *Looking Back on the Reagan Presidency,* ed. Larry Berman (Baltimore: Johns Hopkins University Press, 1990), 288–316; and Jacobson, *The Electoral Origins of Divided Government,* 105ff.
116. Warren E. Miller and Donald E. Stokes, "Constituency Influence in Congress," *American Political Science Review* 57 (March 1963): 45–57.
117. John L. Sullivan and Robert E. O'Connor, "Electoral Choice and Popular Control of Public Policy: The Case of the 1966 House Elections," *American Political Science Review* 66 (December 1972): 1256–1268.
118. Mann and Wolfinger, "Candidates and Parties in Congressional Elections," 629.

Chapter 5 (pages 119–149)

1. John Lancaster, "Daschle's Low-Key Style Helps Keep Party United," *Washington Post,* April 7, 2001, A1.
2. Richard F. Fenno Jr., *The Making of a Senator: Dan Quayle* (Washington, D.C.: CQ Press, 1989), 119.

3. Commission on Executive, Legislative, and Judicial Salaries, *Fairness for Our Public Servants* (Washington, D.C.: U.S. Government Printing Office, 1988), 23.
4. Data on characteristics of the 108th Congress are found in Mildred L. Amer, *Membership of the 108th Congress: A Profile,* Congressional Research Service Report No. RS21379, January 7, 2003.
5. Joseph Schlesinger, "Lawyers and American Politics: A Clarified View," *Midwest Journal of Political Science* 1 (May 1957): 26–39; and Allen G. Bogue, Jerome M. Clubb, Caroll R. McKibbin, and Santa A. Tarugott, "Members of the House of Representatives and the Processes of Modernization, 1789–1960," *Journal of American History* 63 (September 1976): 284.
6. George Gallup Jr., "Religion in America," *Public Perspective,* October–November 1995, 4–5.
7. The pioneering study of this subject is Irwin N. Gertzog, *Congressional Women: Their Recruitment, Treatment, and Behavior* (New York: Praeger, 1984). Two more recent studies are Barbara C. Burrell, *A Women's Place Is in the House* (Ann Arbor: University of Michigan Press, 1994); and Richard Logan Fox, *Gender Dynamics in Congressional Elections* (Thousand Oaks, Calif.: Sage Publications, 1997).
8. Betsy Rothstein, "Congresswomen Press Women's Health Issues," *The Hill,* February 24, 1999, 19; and Maureen Dowd, "Growing Sorority in Congress Edges into the Ol' Boys' Club," *New York Times,* March 5, 1993, A1, A18.
9. Jamie Stiehm, "In Senate, Sisterhood Can Override Party," *The Hill,* November 22, 1995, 16.
10. Quoted in Erika Niedowski, "Four Walk Out of the Closet and toward the House," *CQ Weekly,* April 25, 1998, 1051.
11. Amer, *Membership of the 108th Congress,* 1.
12. Amer, *Membership of the 108th Congress,* 4.
13. Charles S. Bullock and Burdett A. Loomis, "The Changing Congressional Career," in *Congress Reconsidered,* 3d ed., ed. Lawrence C. Dodd and Bruce I. Oppenheimer (Washington, D.C.: CQ Press, 1985), 66–69, 80–82.
14. Quoted in Adam Clymer, "G.O.P. Revolution Hits Speed Bumps on Capitol Hill," *New York Times,* January 21, 1996, 14.
15. Quoted in Lizette Alvarez, "Lawmaker Hedging on Term Limit Vow," *New York Times,* February 22, 1998, 16.
16. Allison Stevens, "As More Promises Are Broken, 2004 Election Could Spell Death of the Term Limit Movement," *The Hill,* April 2, 2003, 23.
17. Hannah Finichel Pitkin, *The Concept of Representation* (Berkeley: University of California Press, 1967), 166.
18. Susan Welch and John R. Hibbing, "Hispanic Representation in the U.S. Congress," *Social Science Quarterly* 64 (June 1984): 328–335; and Charles Tien and Deny Levy, "Asian-American and Hispanic Representation in the U.S. House of Representatives," paper presented at the Midwest Political Science Association, 1998.
19. L. Marvin Overby and Kenneth Cosgrove, cited in Carol Swain, "The Future of Black Representation," *American Prospect* 23 (fall 1995): 81.
20. Roger H. Davidson, *The Role of the Congressman* (Indianapolis: Bobbs-Merrill, 1969), 199.
21. Katherine Tate, "The Political Representation of Blacks in Congress: Does Race Matter?" *Legislative Studies Quarterly* 26 (November 2001), 631.
22. Arturo Vega and Juanita Firestone, "The Effects of Gender on Congressional Behavior and the Substantive Representation of Women," *Legislative Studies Quarterly* 20 (May 1995): 213–222.
23. Quoted in Adam Nagourney, "Upbeat Schumer Battles Polls, Turnouts, and His Image," *New York Times,* May 16, 1998, A14.
24. Frank E. Smith, *Congressman from Mississippi* (New York: Pantheon, 1964), 129–130.
25. Donald R. Matthews, *U.S. Senators and Their World* (Chapel Hill: University of North Carolina Press, 1960), chap. 5; and Ross K. Baker, *House and Senate,* 3d ed. (New York: Norton, 2001), chap. 2.
26. Herbert B. Asher, "The Learning of Legislative Norms," *American Political Science Review* 67 (June 1973): 499–513.

27. Eric M. Uslaner, *The Decline of Comity in Congress* (Ann Arbor: University of Michigan Press, 1993), 5.

28. Quoted from an interview with Jake Tapper, "Retiring, Not Shy," *New York Times Magazine*, September 1, 2002, 25.

29. Thomas E. Cavanagh, "The Two Arenas of Congress," in *The House at Work*, ed. Joseph Cooper and G. Calvin Mackenzie (Austin: University of Texas Press, 1981), 65.

30. Quoted in *New York Times*, August 14, 1980, B9.

31. Damon Chappie, "The New Look of Pork in the 104th," *Roll Call*, January 22, 1996, B19.

32. Quoted in Louis Jacobson, "For Arkansas, No Abundance of Clout," *National Journal*, February 20, 1999, 475.

33. James S. Fleming, "The House Member as Teacher: An Analysis of the Newsletters of Barber B. Conable, Jr.," *Congress and the Presidency* 20 (spring 1993): 53–74.

34. Smith, *Congressman from Mississippi*, 127. See also David Mayhew, *Congress: The Electoral Connection* (New Haven: Yale University Press, 1974).

35. Davidson, *The Role of the Congressman*, 98; Senate Commission on the Operation of the Senate, *Toward a Modern Senate*, S. Doc. 94-278, 94th Cong., 2d sess., committee print, 1997, 27; and House Commission on Administrative Review, *Final Report*, 2 vols., H. Doc. 95-272, 95th Cong., 1st sess., December 31, 1977, 2:874–875.

36. Joint Committee on the Organization of Congress, *Organization of Congress, Final Report*, H. Rept. 103-413, 103d Congress, 1st sess., December 1993, 2:231–232.

37. Ross A. Webber, "U.S. Senators: See How They Run," *Wharton Magazine* (winter 1980–1981): 38.

38. Senate Commission on the Operation of the Senate, *Toward a Modern Senate*.

39. Quoted in Lindsay Sobel, "Former Lawmakers Find Trade Association Gold," *The Hill*, November 26, 1997, 14.

40. Webber, "U.S. Senators," 37.

41. Center for Responsive Politics, *Congressional Operations: Congress Speaks—A Survey of the 100th Congress* (Washington, D.C.: Center for Responsive Politics, 1988), 47–49.

42. Quoted in *Washington Post*, October 18, 1994, B3.

43. Center for Responsive Politics, *Congressional Operations*, 62–64.

44. Joint Committee on the Organization of Congress, *Organization of Congress*, 2: 281–287.

45. Quoted in Vernon Louviere, "For Retiring Congressmen, Enough Is Enough," *Nation's Business*, May 1980, 32.

46. John R. Hibbing, *Congressional Careers: Contours of Life in the U.S. House of Representatives* (Chapel Hill: University of North Carolina Press, 1991), 117 (italics in original).

47. Hibbing, *Congressional Careers*, 126, 128.

48. William H. Riker, *The Theory of Political Coalitions* (New Haven: Yale University Press, 1962), 24–38.

49. Pitkin, *The Concept of Representation*, 166.

50. Davidson, *The Role of the Congressman*, 80.

51. Ross J. S. Hoffman and Paul Levack, eds., *Burke's Politics* (New York: Knopf, 1949), 114–116.

52. Henry J. Hyde, "Advice to Freshmen: 'There Are Things Worth Losing For,' " *Roll Call*, December 3, 1990, 5.

53. Quoted in Jamie Stiehm, "Ex-Rep Mike Synar, Who Fought Lobbyists, Succumbs to Brain Tumor," *The Hill*, January 10, 1996, 5.

54. Cited in Richard Morin, "Unconventional Wisdom," *Washington Post*, February 28, 1999, B5.

55. Thomas E. Cavanagh, "The Calculus of Representation: A Congressional Perspective," *Western Political Quarterly* 35 (March 1982): 120–129.

56. John W. Kingdon, *Congressmen's Voting Decisions*, 3d ed. (Ann Arbor: University of Michigan Press, 1989), 47–54.

57. Lawrence N. Hansen, *Our Turn: Politicians Talk about Themselves, Politics, the Public, the Press, and Reform*, part 2 (Washington, D.C.: Centel Public Accountability Project, 1992), 9.

58. Richard F. Fenno Jr., *Home Style: House Members in Their Districts* (Boston: Little, Brown, 1978), 1.
59. See the discussion of senators' varied constituencies in Frances E. Lee and Bruce I. Oppenheimer, *Sizing Up the Senate* (Chicago: University of Chicago Press, 1999), chap. 3.
60. David C. Huckabee, *Districts of the 103d Congress: Income Data and Rankings,* Congressional Research Service Report No. 93–285GOV, March 1, 1993.
61. Fenno, *Home Style,* 4–8.
62. John F. Bibby and Thomas M. Holbrook, "Parties and Elections," in *Politics in the American States: A Comparative Analysis,* 7th ed., ed. Virginia Gray, Russell L. Hanson, and Herbert Jacob (Washington, D.C.: CQ Press, 1999), 66–112.
63. James L. Payne, "The Personal Electoral Advantage of House Incumbents, 1936–1976," *American Politics Quarterly* 8 (October 1980): 465–482; and Robert S. Erikson, "Is There Such a Thing as a Safe Seat?" *Polity* 8 (summer 1976): 623–632.
64. Thomas E. Mann, *Unsafe at Any Margin: Interpreting Congressional Elections* (Washington, D.C.: American Enterprise Institute, 1978).
65. Fenno, *Home Style,* 8–27.
66. Thomas P. O'Neill Jr., with William Novak, *Man of the House* (New York: St. Martin's, 1987), 25.
67. Nancy Bocskor, "Fundraising Lessons Candidates Can Learn from Tom Sawyer . . . and Other Great American Salesmen," *Campaigns and Elections* 24 (April 2003): 33.
68. Richard F. Fenno Jr., *Senators on the Campaign Trail* (Norman: University of Oklahoma Press, 1996), 131–132.
69. David E. Price, *The Congressional Experience,* 2d ed. (Boulder: Westview Press, 2000), 10.
70. Fenno, *Home Style,* 153.
71. Ibid., 56.
72. Anthony Champagne, *Congressman Sam Rayburn* (New Brunswick: Rutgers University Press, 1984), 28.
73. Kingdon, *Congressmen's Voting Decisions.*
74. Fenno, *Home Style,* 153.
75. Rhodes Cook, "The Safe and the Vulnerable: A Look Behind the Numbers," *Congressional Quarterly Weekly Report,* January 9, 1982, 35–38.
76. Quoted in Lloyd Grove, "For Bill Cohen, a Midlife Correction," *Washington Post,* January 26, 1996, F2.
77. E. Michael Myers, "Millions of Miles from Home," *The Hill,* June 14, 1995, 8.
78. Fenno, *Home Style,* 36, 209; and Myers, "Millions of Miles from Home."
79. Hibbing, *Congressional Careers,* 139.
80. Quoted in Jim Wright, *You and Your Congressman* (New York: Coward-McCann, 1965), 35.
81. John R. Johannes, *To Serve the People: Congress and Constituency Service* (Lincoln: University of Nebraska Press, 1984), chap. 5.
82. Quoted in Richard E. Cohen, "Assertive Freshmen," *National Journal,* May 2, 1987, 1061.
83. Amy Keller and Ben Pershing, "Study Faults Hill on E-Mail," *Roll Call,* March 19, 2001, 1.
84. House Commission on Administrative Review, *Final Report,* 1:655; and Janet Breslin, "Constituent Service," in U.S. Senate, Senate Commission on the Operation of the Senate, *Senators: Offices, Ethics, and Pressures,* 94th Cong., 2d sess., committee print, 1977, 21.
85. Lee and Oppenheimer, *Sizing Up the Senate,* 56.
86. Ibid., 58.
87. Warren E. Miller, Donald R. Kinder, Steven J. Rosenstone, and the National Election Studies, *American National Election Study, 1990: Post-Election Survey,* 2d ed. (Ann Arbor, Mich.: Inter-University Consortium for Political and Social Research, January 1992), 166–170.
88. Morris P. Fiorina, *Congress: Keystone of the Washington Establishment,* 2d ed. (New Haven: Yale University Press, 1989), 45; and Miller and others, *American National Election Study,* 171.
89. George Serra and David Moon, "Casework, Issue Positions, and Voting in Congressional Elections: A District Analysis," *Journal of Politics* 56 (February 1994): 211.

90. Paul E. Dwyer, *Congressional Salaries and Allowances,* Congressional Research Service Report No. RL30064, October 30, 2002. See also Congressional Management Foundation, *1999 Senate Staff Employment Study* (Washington, D.C.: Congressional Management Foundation, 1999), 82ff; and Congressional Management Foundation, *2000 House Staff Employment Study* (Washington, D.C.: Congressional Management Foundation, 2000), 48–49.

91. Congressional Management Foundation, *1999 Senate Staff Employment Study,* 88–89; and Congressional Management Foundation, *2000 House Staff Employment Study,* 1–2.

92. Amy Keller, "Senate Salaries Lag Behind," *Roll Call,* September 5, 2002, 1, 34; and Congressional Management Foundation, *2000 House Staff Employment Study,* 34–35.

93. Charles R. Babcock, "Frankly, an Election-Year Avalanche," *Washington Post,* September 19, 1988, A19.

94. John Pontius, *Congressional Official Mail Costs,* Congressional Research Service Report No. RS20671, March 24, 2003, 5.

95. Quoted in David Burnham, "Congress's Computer Subsidy," *New York Times Magazine,* November 2, 1980, 98.

96. U.S. Congress, Committee on Administration, *Campaign Reform and Election Integrity Act of 1999* H. Rept. 106-295, 106th Congress, 1st sess., 22.

97. Editor and Publisher, *International Yearbook 2002* (New York: Editor and Publisher, 2002), I: vi, II: vi; and *Broadcasting and Cable Yearbook 2002* (New York: Reed Elsevier, 2002), xxxii.

98. Charles Bosley, "Senate Communications with the Public," in U.S. Senate, Commission on the Operation of the Senate, *Senate Communications with the Public,* 94th Cong., 2d sess., 1977, 17.

99. For descriptions of the studios, see Michael J. Robinson, "Three Faces of Congressional Media," in *The New Congress,* ed. Thomas E. Mann and Norman J. Ornstein (Washington, D.C.: American Enterprise Institute, 1981), 62–63; and Martin Tolchin, "TV Studio Serves Congress," *New York Times,* March 7, 1984, C22.

100. Jeffrey L. Katz, "Studios Beam Members from Hill to Hometown," *Congressional Quarterly Weekly Report,* November 29, 1997, 2946.

101. Marcia Gelbert, "Call-in Show: Hoosiers 'Bark at Mark,' " *The Hill,* February 1, 1995, 41.

102. Tolchin, "TV Studio Serves Congress."

103. Robinson, "Three Faces of Congressional Media," 80–81.

104. John F. Bibby and Roger H. Davidson, *On Capitol Hill: Studies in the Legislative Process,* 2d ed. (Hinsdale, Ill.: Dryden Press, 1972), 72.

105. Peter Clarke and Susan H. Evans, *Covering Campaigns: Journalism in Congressional Elections* (Stanford: Stanford University Press, 1983). See also Charles M. Tidmarch and Brad S. Karp, "The Missing Beat: Press Coverage of Congressional Elections in Eight Metropolitan Areas," *Congress and the Presidency* 10 (spring 1983): 47–61.

106. Robinson, "Three Faces of Congressional Media," 84.

107. Katz, "Studios Beam Members from Hill to Hometown."

108. Cokie Roberts, "Leadership and the Media in the 101st Congress," in *Leading Congress: New Styles, New Strategies,* ed. John J. Kornacki (Washington, D.C.: CQ Press, 1990), 94.

109. Quoted in Katz, "Studios Beam Members from Hill to Hometown."

110. Fenno, *Home Style,* 99.

Chapter 6 *(pages 151–191)*

1. A. B. Stoddard, "Rejuvenated Gingrich Mounts Media Offensive," *The Hill,* July 10, 1996, 24.

2. See, for example, Bob Gravely and Lori Nitschke, "Shell-Shocked GOP Settles on Hastert as a Source of Calm," *CQ Monitor,* December 21, 1998, 3; Ceci Connolly, "Plain-Talking Hastert Poised to Be Speaker," *Washington Post,* December 21, 1998, A1; and Art Pine, "It's Official: GOP Picks Hastert as New Speaker," *Los Angeles Times,* January 6, 1999, A10.

3. Juliet Eilperin, "Speaker-to-Be Hastert Vows Civility and Unity for House," *Washington Post,* January 6, 1999, A8.

4. Susan Crabtree, "Hastert Foresees Net Gain of '2 or 3' Seats," *Roll Call,* September 23, 2002, 1.

5. Gebe Martinez, "The Seasoned Speaker: Still Hastert, But Harder," *CQ Weekly,* September 14, 2002, 2362.

6. *Wall Street Journal,* January 30, 1985, 56.

7. The seminal work on the collective action problem is Mancur Olson, *The Logic of Collective Action, Public Goods, and the Theory of Groups* (Boston: Harvard University Press, 1965).

8. Barbara Sinclair, *Legislators, Leaders, and Lawmaking* (Baltimore: Johns Hopkins University Press, 1995), 9.

9. Kerry Kantin, "Rep. Rob Portman," *The Hill,* April 10, 2002, 12.

10. Ethan Wallison, "Conyers as Kingmaker?" *Roll Call,* July 11, 2002, 1.

11. Eric Pianin and Helen Dewar, "GOP Leaders on Hill Find Unity Elusive," *Washington Post,* September 30, 2000, A10.

12. Ceci Connolly and Juliet Eilperin, "Hastert Steps Up to Leading Role," *Washington Post,* January 5, 1999, A4.

13. See Graeme Browning, "The Steward," *National Journal,* August 5, 1995, 2004–2007.

14. *U.S. News and World Report,* October 13, 1950, 30.

15. See, for example, Barbara Sinclair, *Majority Leadership in the U.S. House* (Baltimore: Johns Hopkins University Press, 1983).

16. John M. Barry, *The Ambition and the Power: The Fall of Jim Wright* (New York: Viking Penguin, 1989), 4.

17. Tom Kenworthy, "House GOP Signals It's in a Fighting Mood," *Washington Post,* December 26, 1988, A8.

18. Barry, *The Ambition and the Power,* 6.

19. Newt Gingrich, *Lessons Learned the Hard Way* (New York: HarperCollins, 1998), 37.

20. David Rogers, "Gingrich's New Style as Speaker Has a Few Hitches," *Wall Street Journal,* June 2, 1997, A24.

21. Peter King, "Why I Oppose Newt," *Weekly Standard,* March 31, 1997, 23.

22. See, for example, Ceci Connolly, David Broder, and Dan Balz, "GOP's House Divided," *Washington Post,* July 28, 1997, A1; Sandy Hume, "Gingrich Foils Coup by Deputies," *The Hill,* July 16, 1997, 1; and Jackie Koszczuk, "Party Stalwarts Will Determine Gingrich's Long-Term Survival," *Congressional Quarterly Weekly Report,* July 26, 1997, 1751–1755.

23. See Robert Pear, Pam Belluck, and Lizette Alvarez, "Humble Man at the Helm: John Dennis Hastert," *New York Times,* January 7, 1999, A20.

24. Kathy Kiely, " 'Listener' of the House Takes Reins," *USA Today,* June 8, 2001, 11A.

25. Jim VandeHei, "Hastert Takes Gavel, Promises Cooperation," *Roll Call,* January 7, 1999, 22.

26. Ben Pershing, "Smith Spars with Leaders," *Roll Call,* March 26, 2003, 13.

27. Jonathan Allen, "Effective House Leadership Makes the Most of Majority," *CQ Weekly,* March 29, 2003, 748.

28. Daniel Parks and Andrew Taylor, "House GOP Discord Prompts Fiscal Showdown," *CQ Daily Monitor,* September 13, 2002, 2.

29. John Bresnahan, "Portman Named Chairman of House GOP Leadership," *Roll Call,* January 8, 2001, 8.

30. See, for example, Ronald M. Peters Jr., *The American Speakership: The Office in Historical Perspective,* 2d ed. (Baltimore: Johns Hopkins University Press, 1997); and D. B. Hardeman and Donald C. Bacon, *Rayburn: A Biography* (Austin, Texas: Texas Monthly Press, 1987).

31. Michael Barone, "Slender Is the Newt," *National Review,* November 24, 1997, 28. This quotation leads off David R. Mayhew's *America's Congress: Actions in the Public Sphere, James Madison through Newt Gingrich* (New Haven: Yale University Press, 2000), ix.

32. See, for example, Joseph Cooper and David Brady, "Institutional Context and Leadership Style: The House from Cannon to Rayburn," *American Political Science Review* 75 (June 1981): 411–425; David Rohde, *Parties and Leaders in the Postreform House* (Chicago: University of Chicago Press, 1991); and Sinclair, *Legislators, Leaders, and Lawmaking.*

33. John Aldrich and David Rohde, "The Logic of Conditional Party Government: Revisiting the Electoral Connection," in *Congress Reconsidered,* 7th ed. , ed. Lawrence Dodd and Bruce Oppenheimer (Washington, D.C.: CQ Press, 2001), 275–276.
34. Erin Billings and Susan Crabtree, "The Greening of Tom DeLay," *Roll Call,* September 9, 2002, B18.
35. Douglas Waller, "House Whips Pelosi and DeLay, Battling Each Other for Control of Congress, Turn Out to Be Two of a Kind," *Time,* May 13, 2002, 51.
36. Janet Hook, "Conservatives Make Gains in GOP Congress," *Los Angeles Times,* November 11, 2002, A9.
37. Jim VandeHei, "DeLay Nears Top of House He Reshaped," *Washington Post,* November 13, 2002, A4.
38. Christopher Madison, "Message Bearer," *National Journal,* December 1, 1990, 2906.
39. Floyd M. Riddick, *Congressional Procedure* (Boston: Chapman and Grimes, 1941), 345–346.
40. *CQ Weekly,* December 30, 2000, 24.
41. See Gebe Martinez, "Solidly Backed By Her Colleagues, Pelosi Faces GOP's Sharpened Barbs," *CQ Weekly,* November 16, 2002, 3008–3013.
42. Susan Ferrechio, "Rep. Nancy Pelosi," *CQ Weekly,* December 28, 2002, 55.
43. "Nancy Pelosi," *Newsweek,* December 30, 2002–January 6, 2003, 7.
44. Jonathan Kaplan, "New GOP Whip, Roy Blunt Offers Different Style," *The Hill,* November 20, 2002, 4.
45. Juliet Eilperin, "From Freshman to Deputy Whip," *Washington Post,* December 16, 2002, A23.
46. Jim VandeHei, "Blunt Takes Place among Potential Leaders," *Washington Post,* November 18, 2002, A19.
47. Susan Ferrechio, "His Star Once Again Ascendant, Hoyer Has Big Plans for Whip's Role," *CQ Weekly,* November 16, 2002, 3010.
48. Peter Brand, "Hoyer Says He and Pelosi Will Work Well Together," *The Hill,* November 20, 2002, 33.
49. Mark Preston, "Cheney to Help Craft Legislation," *Roll Call,* January 22, 2001, 1. See also Eric Schmitt, "Cheney Assembles Formidable Team," *New York Times,* February 3, 2001, A1.
50. Susan Crabtree, "Cheney Gets Liaison Team," *Roll Call,* February 26, 2001, 1.
51. Woodrow Wilson, *Congressional Government* (Boston: Houghton Mifflin, 1885), 223.
52. David J. Rothman, *Politics and Power: The United States Senate, 1869–1901* (Cambridge: Harvard University Press, 1966), 5–7.
53. Margaret Munk, "Origin and Development of the Party Floor Leadership in the United States Senate," *Capital Studies* 2 (winter 1974): 23–41; and Richard A. Baker and Roger H. Davidson, eds., *First among Equals: Outstanding Senate Leaders of the Twentieth Century* (Washington, D.C.: Congressional Quarterly, 1991).
54. See Robert Caro, *Master of the Senate* (New York: Random House, 2002).
55. Rowland Evans and Robert Novak, *Lyndon B. Johnson: The Exercise of Power* (New York: New American Library, 1966), 104.
56. See John G. Stewart, "Two Strategies of Leadership: Johnson and Mansfield," in *Congressional Behavior,* ed. Nelson W. Polsby (New York: Random House, 1971), 61–92; William S. White, *Citadel: The Story of the United States Senate* (New York: Harper and Bros., 1956); Joseph S. Clark, *The Senate Establishment* (New York: Hill and Wang, 1963); and Randall B. Ripley, *Power in the Senate* (New York: St. Martin's, 1969).
57. U.S. Congress, *Congressional Record,* daily ed., 96th Cong., 2d sess., April 18, 1980, S3294.
58. David S. Broder, "Don't Bet on Bipartisan Niceties," *Washington Post,* January 1, 2003, A19.
59. Kathy Kiely and Wendy Koch, "Committee Shaped by Party Ties," *USA Today,* October 5, 1998, 2A.
60. Kiely and Koch, "Committee Shaped by Party Ties."
61. Kirk Victor, "Deconstructing Daschle," *National Journal,* June 1, 2002, 610.
62. To review all the provisions of the power-sharing agreement, see U.S. Congress, *Congressional Record,* daily ed., 107th Cong., 1st sess., January 5, 2001, S32–S44; and *U.S. Congress, Congressional Record,* daily ed., 107th Cong., 1st sess., January 8, 2001, S53–S54.

63. U.S. Congress, *Congressional Record*, daily ed., 107th Cong., 1st sess., June 6, 2001, S5844.
64. Dave Boyer, "Lott Rails on Radio against Jeffords' 'Coup of One,'" *Washington Times*, May 31, 2001, A1.
65. Kirk Victor, "Bill Frist, In His Own Words," *National Journal*, January 4, 2003, 37.
66. Karen Tumulty, "A One-Man Political Earthquake," *Time*, June 4, 2001, 34.
67. Hendrik Hertzberg, "Dakota Demon," *New Yorker*, January 21, 2002, 23.
68. John Cochran and David Nather, "Fast-Moving Events Challenge Frist's Debut at Senate Helm," *CQ Weekly*, January 4, 2003, 17.
69. *CQ Weekly*, December 30, 2000, 44.
70. *New York Times*, December 6, 1988, B13.
71. Barbara Sinclair, *Majority Leadership in the U.S. House* (Baltimore: Johns Hopkins University Press, 1983).
72. David S. Broder, "Expect to Hear from Hastert," *Washington Post*, January 15, 2003, A19.
73. Helen Dewar, "Senate Resolves Fight Over Money," *Washington Post*, January 16, 2003, A4.
74. U.S. Congress, *Congressional Record*, daily ed., 98th Cong., 1st sess., November 15, 1983, H9856.
75. Thomas B. Rosenstiel and Edith Stanley, "For Gingrich, It's 'Mr. Speaker!'" *Los Angeles Times*, November 9, 1994, A2.
76. U.S. Congress, *Congressional Record*, daily ed., 94th Cong., 1st sess., January 26, 1973, S2301.
77. Christopher Madison, "The Heir Presumptive," *National Journal*, April 29, 1989, 1036.
78. Sidney Waldman, "Majority Leadership in the House of Representatives," *Political Science Quarterly* 95 (fall 1980): 377.
79. Edward Epstein, "Colorful Congressman a Backer of Property Rights," *Washington Times*, January 12, 2003, A3.
80. Neil MacNeil, *Dirksen: Portrait of a Public Man* (New York: World, 1970), 168–169.
81. Mark Preston, "Daschle May Write Book Chronicling His Times as Leader," *Roll Call Daily Issue E-newsletter*, May 20, 2002, 3.
82. *New York Times*, June 7, 1984, B16.
83. Noelle Straub and Melanie Fonder, "GOP Shifts Strategy for New Minority Status," *The Hill*, July 18, 2001, 6.
84. Mark Preston, "Lott Showcases Senators Facing Re-election," *Roll Call*, March 15, 2001, 3.
85. Stephen Gettinger, "Potential Senate Leaders Flex Money Muscles," *Congressional Quarterly Weekly Report*, October 8, 1988, 2776.
86. Sinclair, *Majority Leadership in the U.S. House*, 96–97.
87. Marc Lacey, "Bush to Attend Democratic Caucuses," *New York Times*, January 27, 2001, A9.
88. Erin Billings, "Pelosi Revamps the Steering Committee," *Roll Call*, March 13, 2003, 3.
89. Alan Ota, "Moderates Anticipate Added Clout in 108th Congress," *CQ Daily Monitor*, November 25, 2002, 12.
90. Robin Kolodny, *Pursuing Majorities: Congressional Campaign Committees in American Politics* (Norman: University of Oklahoma Press, 1998).
91. See Paul S. Herrnson, "National Party Organizations and the Postreform Congress," in *The Postreform Congress*, ed. Roger H. Davidson (New York: St. Martin's, 1992), 48–70.
92. John J. Pitney Jr., "War on the Floor," *Extension of Remarks*, January 2001, 8.
93. Lars-Erik Nelson, "The Republicans' War," *New York Review of Books*, February 4, 1999, 7.
94. David Rogers and Jeannie Cummings, "Democrats Aim to Stir Public as Impeachment Nears," *Wall Street Journal*, December 14, 1998, A20.
95. Alexander Bolton, "House Leaders Tighten Grip, Anger Centrists," *The Hill*, January 15, 2003, 23.
96. Elizabeth Shogren, "Will Welfare Go Way of Health Reform?" *Los Angeles Times*, August 10, 1995, A18.
97. "Sen. Mitch McConnell (R-Ky.)," *The Hill*, January 17, 2001, 24.
98. David Nather and Adriel Bettelheim, "Moderates and Mavericks Hold Key to 107th Congress," *CQ Weekly*, January 6, 2001, 50.

99. Fred Barnes, "Raging Representatives," *New Republic,* June 3, 1985, 9.

100. See David Rohde, *Parties and Leaders in the Postreform Congress* (Chicago: University of Chicago Press, 1991), 27–47.

101. See V. O. Key Jr., *Politics, Parties, and Pressure Groups,* 5th ed. (New York: Crowell, 1964); and Austin Ranney and Willmoore Kendall, *Democracy and the American Party System* (New York: Harcourt Brace, 1956).

102. See Harold Stanley and Richard Niemi, *Vital Statistics on American Politics, 2001–2002* (Washington, D.C.: CQ Press, 2001), 38–39.

103. "Ralph Nader," *The Hill,* June 12, 2002, 28. See Ralph Nader, *Crashing the Party* (New York: St. Martin's, 2002); and Micah Sifry, *Spoiling for a Fight: Third Party Politics in America* (New York: Routledge, 2002).

104. Susan Crabtree, "House GOP Plans Parliamentary Counterattack," *Roll Call,* June 13, 2002, 3.

105. Mark Preston and Paul Kane, "Democrats Won't Bow to Bush, GOP," *Roll Call,* November 21, 2002, 18.

106. U.S. Congress, *Congressional Record,* daily ed., 104th Cong., 1st sess., October 11, 1995, E1926. Rep. Lee Hamilton, D-Ind., who made the comment, strongly opposed the overuse of omnibus bills.

107. Lee H. Hamilton with Jordan Tama, *A Creative Tension: The Foreign Policy Roles of the President and Congress* (Washington, D.C.: Woodrow Wilson Center Press, 2002), 33.

108. Nick Anderson, "In Shift, GOP Proposes Easing Immigration Rules," *Los Angeles Times,* October 26, 2000, A6.

109. Ralph Hallow, "House Likely to Remain Bush's Base," *Washington Times,* January 6, 2003, A4.

110. Jonathan Kaplan, "Bidding Up the Senate and Bush," *The Hill,* January 15, 2003, 1.

111. Richard E. Cohen, "Byrd of West Virginia: A New Job, a New Image," *National Journal,* August 20, 1977, 1294.

Chapter 7 *(pages 193–227)*

1. *Washington Post,* May 14, 1987, A23.

2. U.S. Congress, *Congressional Record,* daily ed., 100th Cong., 1st sess., June 25, 1987, H5564.

3. *Little legislatures* was a term coined by Woodrow Wilson in *Congressional Government* (Boston: Houghton Mifflin, 1885), 79.

4. *New York Times,* July 11, 1988, A14.

5. See, for example, Kenneth A. Shepsle and Barry R. Weingast, "The Institutional Foundations of Committee Power," *American Political Science Review* (March 1987): 85–104.

6. See Keith Krehbiel, *Information and Legislative Organization* (Ann Arbor: University of Michigan Press, 1991); and Bruce Bimber, "Information as a Factor in Congressional Politics," *Legislative Studies Quarterly* (1991): 585–606.

7. John W. Ellwood, "The Great Exception: The Congressional Budget Process in an Age of Decentralization," in *Congress Reconsidered,* 3d ed., ed. Lawrence C. Dodd and Bruce I. Oppenheimer (Washington, D.C.: CQ Press, 1985), 329. For the classic discussion of committee and member roles, see Richard F. Fenno Jr., *Congressmen in Committees* (Boston: Little, Brown, 1973).

8. Roy Swanstrom, *The United States Senate, 1787–1801,* S. Doc. 64, 87th Cong., 1st sess., 1962, 224.

9. Lauros G. McConachie, *Congressional Committees* (New York: Crowell, 1898), 124.

10. DeAlva Stanwood Alexander, *History and Procedure of the House of Representatives* (Boston: Houghton Mifflin, 1916), 228; George H. Haynes, *The Senate of the United States: Its History and Practice,* vol. 1 (Boston: Houghton Mifflin, 1938), 272; and Ralph V. Harlow, *The History of Legislative Methods in the Period before 1825* (New Haven: Yale University Press, 1917), 157–158.

11. *Cannon's Procedures in the House of Representatives,* H. Doc. 122, 80th Cong., 1st sess., 1959, 83.

12. *Wall Street Journal*, May 3, 1979, 1.
13. Susan Crabtree, "House to Maintain Ratios at Status Quo," *Roll Call*, January 6, 2003, p. 1.
14. "Chairman Young Announces Homeland Security Reorganization," press release, January 29, 2003, House Committee on Appropriations Web site (house.gov/appropriations).
15. Andrew Taylor, "Sen. Stevens Calls House Appropriators' Reorganization Decision Premature," *CQ Today*, January 30, 2003, 4.
16. Niels Sorrellis, "Armed Services," *CQ Weekly*, January 11, 2003, 93.
17. U.S. Congress, *Congressional Record*, daily ed., 104th Cong., 1st sess., January 4, 1995, H33.
18. Alan Ota, "Chairman Tauzin Charts a Bold Course for Commerce," *CQ Weekly*, February 3, 2001, 261.
19. Martin Kady, "Select Homeland Security," *CQ Weekly*, January 11, 2003, 95.
20. U.S. Congress, *Congressional Record*, daily ed., 108th Cong., 1st sess., January 7, 2003, H12.
21. Charles L. Clapp, *The Congressman: His Job as He Sees It* (Washington, D.C.: Brookings Institution, 1963), 245.
22. Lawrence D. Longley and Walter J. Oleszek, *Bicameral Politics: Conference Committees in Congress* (New Haven: Yale University Press, 1989), 196.
23. Keith Krehbiel, Kenneth A. Shepsle, and Barry R. Weingast, "Why Are Congressional Committees Powerful?" *American Political Science Review* 81 (September 1987): 935.
24. Roderick Kiewiet and Mathew McCubbins, *The Logic of Delegation: Congressional Parties and the Appropriations Process* (Chicago: University of Chicago Press, 1991).
25. James Bornemeier, "Berman Accepts Seat on House Ethics Panel," *Los Angeles Times*, February 5, 1997, B1; and *CQ Daily Monitor*, December 11, 1999, 1.
26. Sonni Efron and Janet Hook, "Lugar Now the Man in the Middle," *Los Angeles Times*, December 23, 2002, A7.
27. Fenno, *Congressmen in Committees*. See also Heinz Eulau, "Legislative Committee Assignments," *Legislative Studies Quarterly* (November 1984): 587–633.
28. Christopher J. Deering and Steven S. Smith, *Committees in Congress*, 3d ed. (Washington, D.C.: CQ Press, 1997), 61–62, 78.
29. Nancy Roman, "Freshman Nets Prized Panel by Seeking Leader's Support," *Washington Times*, December 3, 1996, A4. See also Greg Hitt, "Ways and Means: An Illinois Republican Staged Hard Campaign for Key House Panel," *Wall Street Journal*, January 3, 1997, A1.
30. Office of Rep. Jennifer Dunn, R-Wash., Washington, D.C.
31. Shirley Chisholm, *Unbought and Unbossed* (Boston: Houghton Mifflin, 1970), 84, 86.
32. Susan Ferrechio, "House Democrats Back New Leader as She Spreads Committee Plums Wider," *CQ Today*, January 29, 2003, 15.
33. See Kirk Victor and Eliza Carney, "Lights, Camera, History!" *National Journal*, October 10, 1998, 2375; and T. R. Goldman, "Anatomy of a Committee," *Legal Times*, September 14, 1998, 19.
34. Ethan Wallison, "Freshman Democrats Get Panel Waivers," *Roll Call*, June 21, 1999, 20.
35. Andrew Beadle, "First Lady's Résumé Won't Impress Seniority System," *CQ Daily Monitor*, November 20, 2000, 9.
36. Peter Kaplan and David Mark, "With Election Day Over, the Campaigns Begin in the House," *CQ Daily Monitor*, November 20, 2000, 3.
37. Jim VandeHei, "Would-Be Chairmen Hit Money Trail," *Roll Call*, July 12, 1999, 1.
38. Paul Gigot, "Mack Uses Knife on Old Senate Order," *Wall Street Journal*, July 14, 1995, A12.
39. Matthew Tully and Emily Pierce, "Senate Republicans Adjust Their Committee Term-Limits Rule," *CQ Daily Monitor*, June 26, 2002, 4.
40. Paul Kane, "Republican Conference Clarifies Term-Limit Rules," *The Hill*, June 27, 2002, 23.
41. *Washington Post*, November 20, 1983, A9.
42. See David King, *Turf Wars* (Chicago: University of Chicago Press, 1997).
43. *CQ Daily Monitor*, March 1, 2000, 8.
44. U.S. Congress, *Congressional Record*, daily ed., 108th Cong., 1st sess., January 7, 2003, H11.
45. Elizabeth Kastor, "The Capital Star System," *Washington Post*, May 9, 1986, D8.

46. Bob Pool, "Survivors Take Stock of Gains against Cancer," *Los Angeles Times*, May 30, 1997, B1.

47. Ralph Vartabedian, "Senate Panel Is Ready to Take IRS to Task," *Los Angeles Times*, September 22, 1997, A1.

48. Sean Piccoli, "Hill Samples 'Third Wave,' " *Washington Times*, June 13, 1995, A8.

49. *Washington Post*, September 23, 1998, A23.

50. Jill Barshay, "Democrats Will Try to Shift the Debate on Stimulus Legislation," *CQ Daily Monitor,* January 21, 2003, 3.

51. U.S. Congress, *Congressional Record,* daily ed., 107th Cong., 2d sess., July 16, 2002, S6849.

52. *Washington Post*, November 25, 1985, A4. See also Richard L. Hall, *Participation in Congress* (New Haven: Yale University Press, 1997).

53. Eric Redman, *The Dance of Legislation* (New York: Simon and Schuster, 1973), 140.

54. Hugh Heclo, "Issue Networks in the Executive Establishment," in *The New American Political System*, ed. Anthony King (Washington, D.C.: American Enterprise Institute, 1978), 87–124. See also David E. Price, "Policy Making in Congressional Committees: The Impact of 'Environmental Factors,' " *American Political Science Review* (fall 1978): 548–574.

55. David Hosansky and Andrew Taylor, "Judiciary's 'Fateful Leap,' " *CQ Weekly*, December 12, 1998, 3290–3294.

56. Norris Cotton, *In the Senate* (New York: Dodd, Mead, 1978), 65.

57. *2002 House Staff Employment Study,* produced for the chief administrative officer, U.S. House of Representatives, by the Congressional Management Foundation, 2003, 2.

58. Telephone interview with a staff person at the Congressional Management Foundation (CMF), Washington, D.C., January 27, 2003. CMF is a nonpartisan research organization with expertise in, among other things, congressional office manaanalyses of House and Senate staff, and enhancing the productivity of lawmakers.

59. *Washington Post*, March 20, 1977, E9.

60. David Whiteman, *Communication in Congress: Members, Staff, and the Search for Information* (Lawrence: University Press of Kansas, 1995).

61. *Washington Post*, November 20, 1983, A13.

62. See Eliza Newlin Carney, "Losing Support," *National Journal*, September 23, 1995, 2353–2357.

63. Brett Pulley, "Black Clerics Criticize Torricelli on Minority Hiring for His Staff," *New York Times*, March 21, 1997, A25.

64. See C. Lawrence Evans and Walter J. Oleszek, *Congress under Fire: Reform Politics and the Republican Majority* (Boston: Houghton Mifflin, 1997).

65. Quoted in Roger H. Davidson and Walter J. Oleszek, *Congress against Itself* (Bloomington: Indiana University Press, 1977), 263.

66. E. Scott Adler, *Why Congressional Reforms Fail* (Chicago: University of Chicago Press, 2002), 11.

67. Richard Cohen and Marilyn Serafina, "Taxing Times," *National Journal,* December 23, 2000, 3961.

68. Cohen and Serfina, "Taxing Times," 3963.

69. David Firestone, "G.O.P.'s 'Cardinals of Spending' Are Reined In by House Leaders," *New York Times,* December 2, 2002, A16.

70. David Nather, "Daschle's Soft Touch Lost in Tough Senate Arena," *CQ Weekly,* July 20, 2002, 1922.

71. Noelle Straub, "Senate Finance Panel Faces July 15 Deadline," *The Hill,* July 3, 2002, 6.

72. Norman J. Ornstein, "The Perils of Misunderestimation," *Roll Call,* January 27, 2003, 4.

73. U.S. Congress, *Congressional Record,* daily ed., 108th Cong., 1st sess., January 7, 2003, H18.

74. U.S. Congress, *Congressional Record,* daily ed., 107th Cong., 1st sess., March 22, 2001, S2718.

75. U.S. Congress, *Congressional Record,* daily ed., 107th Cong., 2d sess., October 2, 2002, S9837.

76. U.S. Congress, *Congressional Record,* daily ed., 107th Cong., 1st sess., March 22, 2001, H1070.

77. Nather, "Daschle's Soft Touch Lost in Tough Senate Arena," 1922.
78. *Committee Structure*, hearings before the Joint Committee on the Organization of Congress (Washington, D.C.: U.S. Government Printing Office, 1993), 779.
79. Curt Suplee, "The Science Chairman's Unpredictable Approach," *Washington Post*, October 15, 1991, A21.80. 81.

Chapter 8 (pages 229–259)

1. *Constitution, Jefferson's Manual, and Rules of the House of Representatives*, House Doc. 106–320, 106th Cong., 2d sess., 2001, 123–124. The rules of the Senate are contained in *Senate Manual*, Senate Doc. 106-1, 106th Cong., 1st sess., 2000.
2. Donald R. Matthews, *U.S. Senators and Their World* (Chapel Hill: University of North Carolina Press, 1960), chap. 5.
3. *Wall Street Journal*, October 2, 1987, 1.
4. John Solomon, "Family Crisis Shifts Politics," *USA Today*, August 16, 2001, 15A.
5. Deborah Sontag, "When Politics Is Personal," *New York Times Magazine*, September 15, 2002, 92.
6. *National Journal*, April 10, 1982, 632.
7. Julie Rovner, "Senate Committee Approves Health Warnings on Alcohol," *Congressional Quarterly Weekly Report*, May 24, 1986, 1175.
8. Woodrow Wilson, *Congressional Government* (Boston: Houghton Mifflin, 1885), 320.
9. Theodore Sorensen, *Kennedy* (New York: Harper and Row, 1965), 184.
10. *Wall Street Journal*, June 2, 1988, 56.
11. U.S. Congress, *Congressional Record*, daily ed., 95th Cong., 1st sess., May 17, 1977, E3076.
12. Chuck Todd, "So Many Bills of Rights, So Little Time," *National Journal, CongressDaily/PM*, August 1, 2001, 1.
13. Peter Baker, "White House Finds 'Fast Track' Too Slippery," *Washington Post*, September 14, 1997, A4. See also U.S. Congress, *Congressional Record*, daily ed., 105th Cong., 2d sess., Sept. 29, 1998, S11133 (the McGwire bill); U.S. Congress, *Congressional Record*, daily ed., 106th Cong., 1st sess., January 25, 1999, S979 (the Ali measure); and Ceci Connolly, "Consultant Offers GOP a Language for the Future," *Washington Post*, September 4, 1997, A1.
14. For information on the drafting process, see Lawrence E. Filson, *The Legislative Drafter's Desk Reference* (Washington, D.C.: Congressional Quarterly, 1992).
15. *CQ Monitor*, July 24, 1998, 5.
16. Lawrence J. Haas, "Unauthorized Action," *National Journal*, January 2, 1988, 20.
17. T. R. Reid, *Congressional Odyssey: The Saga of a Senate Bill* (San Francisco: W. H. Freeman, 1980), 17.
18. Carroll J. Doherty, "Lots of Inertia, Little Lawmaking as Election '98 Approaches," *CQ Weekly*, July 18, 1998, 1925.
19. Margaret Kriz, "Still Charging," *National Journal*, December 6, 1997, 2462.
20. Donald R. Wolfensberger, "Suspended Partisanship in the House: How Most Laws Are Really Made," paper prepared for the 2002 annual meeting of the American Political Science Association, Boston, Mass., August 29–September 1, 2002, 11.
21. U.S. Congress, *Congressional Record*, daily ed., 108th Cong., 1st sess., January 7, 2003, H22.
22. Jonathan Salant, "Under Open Rules, Discord Rules," *Congressional Quarterly Weekly Report*, January 28, 1995, 277.
23. *National Journal*, January 21, 1995, 183.
24. Lizette Alvarez, "Campaign Finance Measure Soundly Rejected by House," *New York Times*, June 18, 1998, A26.
25. Stanley Bach and Steven Smith, *Managing Uncertainty in the House of Representatives: Adaptation and Innovation in Special Rules* (Washington, D.C.: Brookings Institution, 1988), 87.
26. Alfred Steinberg, *Sam Rayburn* (New York: Hawthorn, 1975), 313.
27. Neil MacNeil, *The Forge of Democracy* (New York: McKay, 1963), 411.

28. Lindsay Sobel, "Democrats Weight Discharge Petition Barrage," *The Hill*, July 1, 1998, 2.
29. Alexander Bolton, "House Leaders Tighten Grip, Anger Centrists," *The Hill*, January 15, 2003, 23.
30. Information courtesy of Richard Beth, specialist in legislative process, Congressional Research Service, Library of Congress.
31. *National Journal's Congress Daily/P.M.*, January 13, 1995, 4.
32. *Mt. Vernon* [Ohio] *News*, September 20, 1980, 2.
33. Robert S. Walker, "Why House Republicans Need a Watchdog," *Roll Call*, January 19, 1987, 10.
34. John F. Bibby, ed., *Congress off the Record* (Washington, D.C.: American Enterprise Institute, 1983), 23.
35. Sen. J. Bennett Johnston, D-La. (1972–1997), quoted in *New York Times*, November 22, 1985, B8.
36. "Democrats to Forgo Control in Brief Edge," *Washington Times*, November 29, 2000, A4.
37. U.S. Congress, *Congressional Record*, daily ed., 101st Cong., 2d sess., July 20, 1990, S10183.
38. Susan F. Rasky, "With Few Bills Passed or Ready for Action, Congress Seems Sluggish," *New York Times*, May 14, 1989, 24.
39. U.S. Congress, *Congressional Record*, daily ed., 98th Cong., 2d sess., January 27, 1984, S328–S329.
40. Walter J. Oleszek, *Congressional Procedures and the Policy Process*, 5th ed. (Washington, D.C.: CQ Press, 2001), 236–241. See also Lewis A. Froman Jr., *The Congressional Process* (Boston: Little, Brown, 1967); and Terry Sullivan, *Procedural Structure: Success and Influence in Congress* (New York: Praeger, 1984).
41. Elizabeth Drew, *Senator* (New York: Simon and Schuster, 1979), 158.
42. U.S. Congress, *Congressional Record*, daily ed., 97th Cong., 2d sess., May 20, 1982, S5648.
43. Mary Dalrymple, "Democrats Say They Are Unified in Opposition Platform," *CQ Today*, January 29, 2002, 5.
44. U.S. Congress, *Congressional Record*, daily ed., 107th Cong., 2d sess., April 17, 2002, S2850.
45. Helen Dewar, " 'Hold' Likely for IRS Pick, Daschle Says," *Washington Post*, October 30, 1997, A11.
46. See, for example, U.S. Congress, *Congressional Record*, daily ed., 107th Cong., 2d sess., April 17, 2002, S2850.
47. See comments by Alan Cranston of California, then Senate Democratic whip, in *New York Times*, July 17, 1986, A3.
48. Sean Piccoli, "Byrd Still Senate Caesar Despite GOP Takeover," *Washington Times*, February 14, 1995, A11.
49. U.S. Congress, *Operations of the Congress: Testimony of House and Senate Leaders*, hearing before the Joint Committee on the Organization of Congress (Washington, D.C.: U.S. Government Printing Office, 1993), 50.
50. David Baumann, "The Collapse of the Senate," *National Journal*, June 3, 2000, 1759.
51. U.S. Congress, *Congressional Record*, daily ed., 106th Cong., 2d sess., April 11, 2000, S2516.
52. U.S. Congress, *Congressional Record*, daily ed., 106th Cong., 2d sess., March 28, 2000, S1832.
53. Testimony of Steven S. Smith, University of Minnesota, before the Joint Committee on the Organization of Congress, 103d Cong., 1st sess., May 20, 1993, 14.
54. U.S. Congress, *Congressional Record*, daily ed., 106th Cong., 2d sess., October 13, 2000, S10520.
55. Philip Shenon, "Democrat Would Appoint McCain to Campaign Finance Panel," *New York Times*, April 2, 2001, A12.
56. Randall B. Ripley, *Power in the Senate* (New York: St. Martin's, 1969), 128.
57. Janet Hook, "In Conference: New Hurdles, Hard Bargaining," *Congressional Quarterly Weekly Report*, September 6, 1986, 2081.
58. U.S. Congress, *Congressional Record*, daily ed., 99th Cong., 2d sess., February 20, 1986, S1463.

59. Barbara Sinclair, *Unorthodox Lawmaking: New Legislative Processes in the U.S. Congress,* 2d ed. (Washington, D.C.: CQ Press, 2000).
60. Barber B. Conable, "Weaving Webs: Lobbying by Charities," *Tax Notes,* November 10, 1975, 27–28.

Chapter 9 (pages 261–289)

1. Jeffrey L. Katz, "Politically Charged Vote Sets Tone for Impeachment Inquiry," *CQ Weekly,* October 10, 1998, 2712.
2. Katz, "Politically Charged Vote Sets Tone for Impeachment Inquiry."
3. Richard L. Hall, *Participation in Congress* (New Haven: Yale University Press, 1996), 27–30.
4. Quoted in Janet Hook, "Moderates on Outside of GOP Big Tent," *Los Angeles Times,* May 24, 2001, A22.
5. Norman J. Ornstein, "After Shelby Precedent, Bush Had Better Be Careful with Jeffords," *Roll Call,* May 14, 2001, 10.
6. Richard Simon, "Holdout Senators Provide Key Votes on Cut in Dividend Taxes," *Los Angeles Times,* May 16, 2003, A22.
7. Craig Winneker and Glenn R. Simpson, "Obscure Caucus, Year Five," *Roll Call,* September 12, 1994, A25–26. The listing omits senators: "senators are by definition not obscure, although there are several who seem to strive for it." To be listed in the Obscure Caucus, House members must have served at least three terms.
8. Quoted in *The Hill,* November 15, 2000, 16.
9. David Price, *Who Makes the Laws?* (Cambridge, Mass.: Schenkman Publishing, 1972), 297; and David Price *The Congressional Experience,* 2d ed. (Boulder: Westview Press, 2000), chap. 6.
10. Quoted in Laura Blumenfeld, "When Politics Becomes Personal," *Washington Post,* June 19, 1996, C1, 2. See also Sarah Pekkanen, "From Drunk Driving to Health Care, Lawmakers' Bills Have Personal Roots," *The Hill,* April 17, 1996, 10.
11. Guy Gugliotta, "On the Hill, Ex-Wrestlers Go to the Mat for the Sport," *Washington Post,* April 30, 1998, A19.
12. Bernard Asbell, *The Senate Nobody Knows* (Garden City, N.Y.: Doubleday, 1978), 210.
13. Richard F. Fenno Jr., "Observation, Context, and Sequence in the Study of Politics," *American Political Science Review* 80 (March 1976): 3–15.
14. Lindsay Sobel, "Early Fast-Track Support Cost Members Leverage," *The Hill,* November 12, 1997, 33.
15. Quoted in Betsy Rothstein, "GOP Leaders Must Cope with Pesky Chafee and Jeffords," *The Hill,* May 16, 2001, 28.
16. Quoted by Joshua Michael Maarshall, "Let's (Not) Make a Deal," *American Prospect* 12 (February 26, 2001): 12.
17. Cited in Philippe Shepnick, "Moynihan Is Champion Bill Writer," *The Hill,* March 10, 1999, 6.
18. Rick K. Wilson and Cheryl D. Young, "Cosponsorship in the U.S. Congress," *Legislative Studies Quarterly* 22 (February 1997): 25–43.
19. The study was released by Congressional Connection, an online database. Reported in *Roll Call,* June 16, 1994, 4.
20. Richard F. Fenno Jr., *The Making of a Senator: Dan Quayle* (Washington, D.C.: CQ Press, 1989), 43–45.
21. T. R. Reid, *Congressional Odyssey: The Saga of a Senate Bill* (San Francisco: W. H. Freeman, 1980), 15.
22. Quoted in Hall, *Participation in Congress,* 139; see also 119.
23. Hall, *Participation in Congress,* 126–127.
24. Mike Sherry, "Vote Participation Still High," *CQ Weekly,* December 14, 2002, 3243–3244.
25. U.S. Congress, *Congressional Record,* daily ed., 103d Cong., 1st sess., June 23, 1993, H3941–3973.

26. Allan Freedman, "Elimination of NEA Squeaks By as House Passes Interior Rule," *Congressional Quarterly Weekly Report,* July 12, 1997, 1615–1618.

27. John D. Wilkerson, " 'Killer' Amendments in Congress," *American Political Science Review* 93 (September 1999): 535–552.

28. Quoted in Eric Schmitt, "House Votes to Bar Religious Abuse Abroad," *New York Times,* May 15, 1998, A1.

29. Albert R. Hunt, "Balanced-Budget Measure Is Likely to Pass Senate Next Week, Faces Battle in House," *Wall Street Journal,* July 30, 1982, 2.

30. Norman J. Ornstein, Thomas E. Mann, and Michael J. Malbin, *Vital Statistics on Congress, 1999–2000* (Washington, D.C.: American Enterprise Institute, 2000), 194.

31. Glenn R. Parker and Suzanne L. Parker, "Factions in Committees: The U.S. House of Representatives," *American Political Science Review* 73 (March 1979): 85–102.

32. For an authoritative analysis of the decline and resurgence of congressional partisanship, see David W. Rohde, *Parties and Leaders in the Postreform House* (Chicago: University of Chicago Press, 1991), esp. 3–11.

33. David W. Rohde, "Electoral Forces, Political Agendas, and Partisanship in the House and Senate," in *The Postreform Congress,* ed. Roger H. Davidson (New York: St. Martin's, 1992), esp. 34–40.

34. Helmut Norpoth, "Explaining Party Cohesion in Congress: The Case of Shared Policy Attitudes," *American Political Science Review* 70 (December 1976): 1171.

35. Morton Kondracke, "Who's Running the House? GOP Freshmen or Newt?" *Roll Call,* December 18, 1995, 5.

36. Rohde, "Electoral Forces," 28.

37. Jerrold E. Schneider, *Ideological Coalitions in Congress* (Westport, Conn.: Greenwood Press, 1979); Keith T. Poole and Howard Rosenthal, "Patterns of Congressional Voting," *American Journal of Political Science* 35 (February 1991): 228–278; and Keith T. Poole and Howard Rosenthal, *Congress: A Political-Economic History of Roll-Call Voting* (New York: Oxford University Press, 1997).

38. John F. Manley, "The Conservative Coalition in Congress," *American Behavioral Scientist* 17 (December 1973): 223–247; Barbara Sinclair, *Congressional Realignment: 1925–1978* (Austin: University of Texas Press, 1982); and Mack C. Shelley, *The Permanent Majority: The Conservative Coalition in the United States Congress* (University: University of Alabama Press, 1983).

39. Robert J. Donovan, "For America, a New Coalition?" *Los Angeles Times,* July 6, 1981, 4.

40. Stephen Gettinger, "R.I.P. to a Conservative Force," *CQ Weekly,* January 9, 1999, 82–83.

41. Sarah A. Binder, "The Disappearing Political Center," *Brookings Review* 15 (fall 1996): 36–39.

42. Binder, "The Disappearing Political Center," 37.

43. Numbers computed from *CQ Weekly,* December 14, 2002, 3281–3285.

44. Sean M. Theriault, "The Case of the Vanishing Moderates: Party Polarization in the Modern Congress," paper presented at the Western Political Science Association, Denver, Colorado, March 27, 2003, Figure 1.

45. James G. Gimpel, *Fulfilling the Contract: The First 100 Days* (Boston: Allyn and Bacon, 1996), 120.

46. R. Douglas Arnold, *The Logic of Congressional Action* (New Haven: Yale University Press, 1990), 64–65. This section draws heavily upon Arnold's work. The original reference to attentive and inattentive publics is from V. O. Key Jr., *Public Opinion and American Democracy* (New York: Knopf, 1961), 265, 282–285.

47. Arnold, *The Logic of Congressional Action,* 68.

48. Ibid., 84.

49. Sen. James M. Jeffords, R-Vt., statement, Burlington, Vermont, May 24, 2001. See Jeffords Web site at Ussenate.gov/Jeffords.

50. Mark A. Peterson, "The President and Congress," in *The Presidency and the Political System,* 5th ed., ed. Michael Nelson (Washington, D.C.: CQ Press, 1998), 486–487; recent figures are from *CQ Weekly,* December 14, 2002, 3275.

51. See Charles O. Jones, *The Trusteeship Presidency: Jimmy Carter and the United States Congress* (Baton Rouge: Louisiana State University Press, 1988).

52. Jon Healey, "Clinton Success Rate Declined to a Record Low in 1995," *Congressional Quarterly Weekly Report,* January 27, 1996, 193; and David Nather, "Clinton's Floor Vote Victories Yielded Few Accomplishments," *CQ Weekly,* January 6, 2001, 52ff.

53. Ornstein, Mann, and Malbin, *Vital Statistics on Congress,* 168–169. Recent figures are reported by John Cochran, "Bush Readies Strategies for Legislative Success in 2003," *CQ Weekly,* December 14, 2002, 3235–3238.

54. Roger H. Davidson, *The Role of the Congressman* (Indianapolis: Bobbs-Merrill, 1969), 22–23.

55. Robert L. Peabody, "Organization Theory and Legislative Behavior: Bargaining, Hierarchy, and Change in the U.S. House of Representatives," paper presented at the annual meeting of the American Political Science Association, New York, September 4–7, 1963.

56. Carl J. Friedrich, *Constitutional Government and Democracy,* 4th ed. (Waltham, Mass.: Blaisdell Publishing, 1967), 269–270.

57. Ben Pershing, "Boehlert Holding Bush's Feet to Fire," *Roll Call,* April 30, 2001, 28.

58. Mark Preston, "Chafee Remembered as War Hero, Political Giant," *Roll Call,* October 28, 1999, 36.

59. John W. Kingdon, *Congressmen's Voting Decisions,* 3d ed. (Ann Arbor: University of Michigan Press, 1989).

60. Quoted in John F. Bibby, ed., *Congress Off the Record* (Washington, D.C.: American Enterprise Institute, 1983), 22.

61. Quoted in Claudia Dreifus, "Exit Reasonable Right," *New York Times Magazine,* June 2, 1996, 26.

62. Edward J. Derwinski, "The Art of Negotiation within the Congress," in *International Negotiation: Art and Science,* ed. Diane B. Bendahmane and John W. McDonald Jr. (Washington, D.C.: U.S. Department of State, Foreign Service Institute, 1984), 11.

63. Quoted in Paul Bluestein, "Who Really Pays to Help U.S. Farmers?" *International Herald-Tribune,* May 6, 2002, 1, 5.

64. Lizette Alvarez, "In Slap at GOP Leadership, House Stops Move to Deny Food Stamps to Immigrants," *New York Times,* May 23, 1998, A9. For background, see John Ferejohn, "Logrolling in an Institutional Context: A Case Study of Food Stamp Legislation," in *Congress and Policy Change,* ed. Gerald C. Wright Jr., Leroy N. Rieselbach, and Lawrence C. Dodd (New York: Agathon Press, 1986), 223–253.

65. Elliott Abrams, "Unforgettable Scoop Jackson," *Reader's Digest,* February 1985. Quotation cited in U.S. Congress, *Congressional Record,* daily ed., 99th Cong., 1st sess., February 20, 1985, E478.

66. David E. Rosenbaum, "The Favors of Rostenkowski: Tax Revision's Quid Pro Quo," *New York Times,* November 27, 1985, B6.

67. Dale Tate, "Use of Omnibus Bills Burgeons Despite Members' Misgivings," *Congressional Quarterly Weekly Report,* September 25, 1982, 2379.

68. The politics of blame avoidance is outlined in R. Kent Weaver, "The Politics of Blame," *Brookings Review* 5 (spring 1987): 43–47. The term *credit claiming* originated with David R. Mayhew, *Congress: The Electoral Connection* (New Haven: Yale University Press, 1974), 52–61.

69. R. Douglas Arnold, "The Local Roots of Domestic Policy," in *The New Congress,* ed. Thomas E. Mann and Norman J. Ornstein (Washington, D.C.: American Enterprise Institute, 1981), 286.

70. Steve Waldman, *The Bill* (New York: Viking, 1994), 94–95.

71. Quoted in Lindsay Sobel, "NAFTA Supporters Desert Clinton on Fast-Track," *The Hill,* November 12, 1997, 8.

72. Quoted in "In Defense of Political Logrolling," *The Hill,* November 12, 1997, 28.

73. Quotes from Jonathan Allen, "Effective House Leadership Makes the Most of Majority," *CQ Weekly,* March 29, 2003, 751.

74. Quoted in Kirk Victor, "Kennedy the Pragmatist," *National Journal,* December 8, 2001, 3791.

75. John B. Gilmour, *Strategic Disagreement: Stalemate in American Politics* (Pittsburgh: University of Pittsburgh Press, 1995), 4.

76. Quoted by Sarah A. Binder in "Going Nowhere: A Gridlocked Congress," *Brookings Review* 18 (winter 2000): 19.

77. See William H. Riker, *The Theory of Political Coalitions* (New Haven: Yale University Press, 1962), 32. Theorists define legislative bargaining situations formally as *n*-person, zero-sum games where side payments are permitted. That is, a sizable number of participants are involved; when some participants win, others must lose; and participants can trade items outside the substantive issues under consideration.

78. John G. Stewart, "Two Strategies of Leadership: Johnson and Mansfield," in *Congressional Behavior,* ed. Nelson W. Polsby (New York: Random House, 1971), 67.

79. Russell Hardin, "Hollow Victory: The Minimum Winning Coalition," *American Political Science Review* 79 (December 1976): 1202–1214.

80. Robert J. Dole, remarks to the Senate, March 29, 2000, quoted in *The Hill,* April 5, 2000, 32.

Chapter 10   (pages 291–317)

1. Amy Goldstein and Dana Milbank, "Hill GOP, Bush Split On Tax Cuts, Medicare," *Washington Post,* February 14, 2003, A9.

2. Jonathan Kaplan, "Speaker Veers From Bush Line," *The Hill,* February 19, 2003, 8.

3. See Stephen Wayne, *The Legislative Presidency* (New York: Harper and Row, 1978).

4. Charles O. Jones, *Separate But Equal Branches: Congress and the Presidency* (Chatham, N.J.: Chatham House, 1995), 138–157.

5. Michael Nelson, "Evaluating the President," in *The Presidency and the Political System, 7th ed.,* ed. Michael Nelson (Washington, D.C.: CQ Press, 2003), 21.

6. See Norman J. Ornstein, "Theories of the Presidency," in *Encyclopedia of the American Presidency,* vol. 4, ed. Leonard Levy and Louis Fisher (New York: Simon and Schuster, 1994), 1458–1462.

7. Richard E. Neustadt, *Presidential Power* (New York: John Wiley and Sons, 1960), 23.

8. Neustadt, *Presidential Power,* 16.

9. Leonard D. White, *The Federalist* (New York: McMillan, 1948), 55.

10. Leonard D. White, *The Jeffersonians* (New York: Macmillan, 1951), 35.

11. John A. Farrell, *Tip O'Neill and the Democratic Century* (Boston: Little, Brown, and Co., 2001), 553.

12. Paul C. Light, *The President's Agenda* (Baltimore: Johns Hopkins University Press, 1982), 230–231.

13. Lyndon Johnson, *The Vantage Point* (New York: Popular Library, 1971), 448.

14. Jack Valenti, "Some Advice on the Care and Feeding of Congressional Egos," *Los Angeles Times,* April 23, 1978, 3.

15. Richard Berke, "Courting Congress Nonstop, Clinton Looks for an Alliance," *New York Times,* March 8, 1993, A1.

16. Roy P. Basler, ed., *The Collected Works of Abraham Lincoln,* vol. 3 (New Brunswick: Rutgers University Press, 1953), 27.

17. Samuel Kernell, *Going Public: New Strategies of Presidential Leadership,* 3rd ed. (Washington, D.C.: CQ Press, 1997), 2. Also see James Ceaser and others, "The Rise of the Rhetorical Presidency," *Presidential Studies Quarterly* 21 (spring 1981): 158–171.

18. Richard M. Pious, *The American Presidency* (New York: Basic Books, 1979), 194. See also George C. Edwards III, *The Public Presidency* (New York: St. Martin's, 1983).

19. *Wall Street Journal,* December 4, 1987, 8D.

20. Tom Rosenstiel and James Gerstenzang, "Bush Team Rejects Public Relations Techniques of Reagan White House," *Los Angeles Times,* April 30, 1989, 1.

21. George Hager, "For GOP, a New Song—Same Ending," *Congressional Quarterly Weekly Report,* June 14, 1997, 1406.

22. Paul Bedard, "Living, Dying by the Polls," *Washington Times*, April 30, 1993, A1.
23. David S. Broder, "The Reticent President," *Washington Post*, April 22, 2001, B7. See also Mike Allen, "Bush on Stage: Deft or Just Lacking Depth?" *Washington Post*, February 19, 2001, A8–A9.
24. Elisabeth Bumiller, "Keepers of Bush Image Lift Stagecraft to New Heights," *New York Times*, May 16, 2003, A1.
25. Bumiller, "Keepers of Bush Image Lift Stagecraft to New Heights," A20.
26. See, for example, Richard P. Nathan, *The Administrative Presidency* (New York: John Wiley and Sons, 1983); and Robert R. Durant, *The Administrative Presidency Revisited* (Albany: State University of New York Press, 1992).
27. See Kenneth Mayer, *With the Stroke of a Pen: Executive Orders and Presidential Power* (Princeton: Princeton University Press, 2001).
28. Elizabeth Shogren, "President Plans Blitz of Executive Orders Soon," *Los Angeles Times*, July 5, 1998, A11.
29. Susan Page, "When a Law Is Unlikely, Often an Order Will Do," *USA Today*, August 11, 1997, 7A.
30. Dana Milbank and Ellen Nakashima, "Bush Team Has 'Right' Credentials," *Washington Post*, March 25, 2001, A1.
31. Linda Feldmann, "Faith-Based Initiatives Quietly Lunge Forward," *Christian Science Monitor*, February 6, 2003, 2.
32. James Gerstenzang, "Bush Circumventing Congress," *Los Angeles Times*, December 15, 2002, A10.
33. John Stanton, "Daschle Building 'Special Interest' Watchdog Group in Senate," *National Journal, CongressDaily/AM*, January 17, 2003, 8.
34. For a critique of electoral realignments, see David R. Mayhew, *Electoral Realignments: A Critique of an American Genre* (New Haven: Yale University Press, 2002).
35. Stephen Skowronek, "Presidential Leadership in Political Time," in *The Presidency and the Political System*, 7th ed., ed. Michael Nelson (Washington, D.C.: CQ Press, 2003), 112.
36. Skowronek, "Presidential Leadership in Political Time," 112.
37. David Maraniss and Michael Wiesskopf, *"Tell Newt to Shut Up!"* (New York: Simon & Schuster, 1996), 146.
38. U.S. Congress, *Congressional Record*, daily ed., 108th Cong., 1st sess., February 13, 2003, E260.
39. Gary Jacobson, "Party Polarization in National Politics: The Electoral Connection," in *Polarized Politics: Congress and the President in a Partisan Era*, ed. Jon R. Bond and Richard Fleisher (Washington, D.C.: CQ Press, 2000), 14. The 98 percent party unity score for Democrats and Republicans is also taken from the Jacobson study (see page 10).
40. Ron Faucheux, "Presidential Popularity: A History of Highs and Lows," *CQ Daily Monitor*, February 7, 2002, 14.
41. Aaron Wildavsky, "The Two Presidencies," in *The Beleaguered Presidency*, ed. Aaron Wildavsky (Brunswick, N.J.: Transaction Publishers, 1991), 29. Wildavsky's article originally appeared in the December 1966 issue of *Transaction* magazine.
42. Aaron Wildavsky, "The Two Presidencies Thesis Revisited at a Time of Political Dissensus," in *The Beleaguered Presidency*, ed. Aaron Wildavsky (Brunswick, N.J.: Transaction Publishers, 1991), 47–65.
43. Dan Balz, "Bush Lays Out Ambitious Plan for Long Term," *Washington Post*, May 6, 2001, A10.
44. Dana Milbank, "Bush Signs Tax Bill Into Law," *Washington Post*, June 8, 2001, A19.
45. "Bush's Tax-Cut Hardball Seems to Have Paid Off," *USA Today*, May 29, 2001, 9A.
46. Milbank, "Bush Signs Tax Bill Into Law," A19.
47. Norman J. Ornstein,"Bush Faces Strategic Fork in the Road," *Roll Call*, November 14, 2002, 9.
48. Ornstein, "Bush Faces Strategic Fork in the Road," 9.
49. Ronald Brownstein, "Strategies Shift as Bush Drops in Polls," *Los Angeles Times*, July 5, 2001, A9.

50. Ronald Brownstein, "Bush Is a Surprise Hard Liner," *Los Angeles Times,* March 2, 2003, A14.
51. John Harwood and Jeanne Cummings, "Bush's Approval Rating Slips to 50%, a 5-Year Presidential Low," *Wall Street Journal,* June 28, 2001, A18.
52. Faucheux, "Presidential Popularity," 14.
53. Judy Keen, William Welch, and Andrea Stone, "Tension with Republicans Ties Up Bush's Legislation," *USA Today,* May 13, 2002, 2A.
54. E. J. Dionne Jr., "A Wartime Leader Can't Be Partisan as Usual," *Washington Post,* January 26, 2003, B5.
55. Ronald Brownstein, "Home Front Still Key to Bush's Reelection," *Los Angeles Times,* April 8, 2003, A13.
56. Woodrow Wilson, *Congressional Government* (Boston: Houghton Mifflin, 1885), 52.
57. Frank B. Cross, "The Constitutional Legitimacy and Significance of Presidential 'Signing Statements,' " *Administrative Law Review* 40 (spring 1988): 209–238.
58. Mike Allen, "Bush Signs Corporate Reforms Into Law," *Washington Post,* July 31, 2002, A4. Also see Elizabeth Bumiller, "When Bush Picks Up a Pen, He Drops Names," *New York Times,* December 2, 2002, A16.
59. *Los Angeles Times,* March 18, 1988, part I, 4.
60. Erika Niedowski, "GOP to Skirt Line Item Veto," *The Hill,* February 12, 1997, 24.
61. Andrew Taylor, "Lawmakers File Challenge to Line-Item Veto Law," *Congressional Quarterly Weekly Report,* January 4, 1997, 24.
62. John F. Harris, "Clinton Wields New Authority, Vetoing Three Items," *Washington Post,* August 12, 1997, A1.
63. John Broder, "Clinton Vetoes Eight Projects, Two in States of Leadership," *New York Times,* October 18, 1997, A10.
64. Helen Dewar and Joan Biskupic, "Line-Item Vote Struck Down: Backers Push for Alternative," *Washington Post,* June 26, 1998, A1.
65. U.S. Congress, *Congressional Record,* daily ed., 106th Cong., 1st sess., February 23, 1999, E265.
66. *Analytical Perspectives, Budget of the United States Government, Fiscal Year 2004* (Washington, D.C.: Government Printing Office, 2003), 318.
67. Richard Neustadt, *Presidential Power* (New York: Wiley, 1960), 187.
68. *National Journal, CongressDaily/AM,* February 27, 2001, 8.
69. *National Journal, CongressDaily/AM,* February 27, 2001.
70. *National Journal, CongressDaily/AM,* February 27, 2001, 8.
71. Johnson, *The Vantage Point,* 448.
72. Ethan Wallison, "Adding DeLay Makes It a 'Gang of Five,' " *Roll Call,* March 6, 2003, 3.
73. George C. Edwards, *At the Margins* (New Haven: Yale University Press, 1989).
74. See Joseph P. Harris, *The Advice and Consent of the Senate* (Berkeley: University of California Press, 1953); and G. Calvin Mackenzie, *The Politics of Presidential Appointments* (New York: Free Press, 1981).
75. James MacGregor Burns, *Presidential Government* (Boston: Houghton Mifflin, 1966), 284.
76. See, for example, Stephen J. Wayne, "Great Expectations: What People Want from Presidents," in *Rethinking the Presidency,* ed. Thomas E. Cronin (Boston: Little, Brown, 1982), 185–199.
77. David Broder, "Midterm Jitters in the House," *Washington Post,* May 16, 2001, A23.
78. Arthur M. Schlesinger Jr. and Alfred De Grazia, *Congress and the Presidency: Their Role in Modern Times* (Washington, D.C.: American Enterprise Institute, 1967), 1.
79. Wilson, *Congressional Government;* and Burns, *Presidential Government.*
80. See Joseph S. Clark, *Congress: The Sapless Branch* (New York: Harper and Row, 1964); and Arthur M. Schlesinger Jr., *The Imperial Presidency* (Boston: Houghton Mifflin, 1973).
81. David Mayhew, *Divided We Govern* (New Haven: Yale University Press, 1991), 198.
82. See Wilfred E. Binkley, *President and Congress* (New York: Knopf, 1947); Jones, *Separate But Equal Branches: Congress and the Presidency;* and Richard E. Neustadt, *Presidential Power and the Modern Presidents* (New York: Free Press, 1990).

83. Susan Page, "GAO Chief, Cheney Barreling toward Showdown," *USA Today,* February 18, 2002, 6A.
84. Alexander Bolton, "Members Hit White House Over Secrecy," *The Hill,* August 7, 2002, 1.
85. J. William Fulbright, "The Legislator as Educator," *Foreign Affairs* (spring 1979): 726.

Chapter 11 (pages 319–343)

1. Walter Shapiro, "Bush Suddenly Has the Energy for Big Government," *USA Today,* May 18, 2001, 6A.
2. Christopher Lee, "Uncertainty at Homeland Security," *Washington Post,* March 1, 2003, A10.
3. David S. Broder, "So, Now Bigger Is Better?" *Washington Post,* January 12, 2003, B1.
4. Quoted in E. J. Dionne Jr., "Back from the Dead: Neoprogressivism in the 90s," *American Prospect* (September–October 1996): 25.
5. David Hosansky, "GOP Confounds Expectations, Expands Federal Authority," *Congressional Quarterly Weekly Report,* November 2, 1996, 3117.
6. Sam Howe Verhovek, "Legislators Meet, Surprised at Limit on Shift of Powers," *New York Times,* January 12, 1997, 1.
7. Eliza Newlin Carney, "Power Grab," *National Journal,* April 11, 1998, 799. See also Timothy Conlan, *From New Federalism to Devolution* (Washington, D.C.: Brookings Institution, 1998).
8. U.S. Congress, *Congressional Record,* 105th Cong., 1st sess., November 5, 1997, S11737.
9. Richard E. Neustadt, "Politicians and Bureaucrats," in *The Congress and America's Future,* 2d ed., ed. David B. Truman (Englewood Cliffs, N.J.: Prentice-Hall, 1973), 199. See also Louis Fisher, *The Politics of Shared Power: Congress and the Executive,* 3d ed. (Washington, D.C.: CQ Press, 1993).
10. See Dave Boyer, "Ridge Reluctant to Testify in Senate," *Washington Times,* February 27, 2002, A4.
11. George Archibald, "Panel Ties Funding to Ridge Testimony," *Washington Times,* March 22, 2002, A1; and George Archibald, "Ridge Attends Private Meetings on Hill," *Washington Times,* April 11, 2002, A4.
12. See Harold C. Relyea, "Homeland Security: Department Organization and Management—Legislative Phase," Congressional Research Service Report, February 25, 2003.
13. U.S. Congress, *Congressional Record,* daily ed., June 18, 2002, H3639–H3641. Under forms of reorganization noted in this chapter on page 323, DHS is a statutory creation.
14. Adriel Bettelheim, "Personnel Issues Have Senate Stumbling on Homeland Security," *CQ Weekly,* September 28, 2002, 2515.
15. U.S. Congress, *Congressional Record,* daily ed., 100th Cong., 1st sess., May 1, 1987, S5848.
16. Steven V. Roberts, "In Confirmation Process, Hearings Offer a Stage," *New York Times,* February 8, 1989, B7.
17. Kirk Victor, "Executive Branch End Run," *National Journal,* May 16, 1998, 1112. See also David Byrd, "Affirmatively Acting," *National Journal,* March 6, 1999, 612–616.
18. William Schneider, "New Rules for the Game of Politics," *National Journal,* April 1, 1989, 830.
19. See Dennis Thompson, *Ethics in Congress* (Washington, D.C.: Brookings Institution, 1995).
20. G. Calvin McKenzie, "Hung Out to Dry," *Washington Post,* April 1, 2001, B5.
21. Paul Light, "The Glacial Pace of Presidential Appointments," *Wall Street Journal,* April 4, 2001, A20.
22. Al Kamen, "Confirmation Delays Hobble Administration," *Washington Post,* May 20, 2001, A1. See also Laurence McQuillan, "Complex Process Slows Hiring," *USA Today,* May 30, 2001, 10A.
23. Light, "The Glacial Pace of Presidential Appointments," A20.
24. Nancy Kassebaum Baker and Franklin Raines, "Uncle Sam Wants a Few Good Appointees," *Los Angeles Times,* April 5, 2001, A17. Baker and Raines are cochairs of the Presidential Appointee Initiative Advisory Board, which is a project of the Brookings Institution. Its basic goal is to propose improvements in the presidential appointments process.

25. G. Calvin MacKenzie, ed., *Innocent until Nominated* (Washington, D.C.: Brookings Institution, 2001), 30.
26. Doyle McManus and Robert Shogun, "Acrid Tone Reflects Long-Term Trend for Nominations," *Los Angeles Times*, March 9, 1997, A6.
27. Peter Grier, "Why Senate Roughs Up Some Cabinet Nominees," *Christian Science Monitor*, March 19, 1997, 3.
28. James Dao, "In Protest, Republican Senators Hold Up Defense Confirmations," *New York Times*, May 10, 2001, A20.
29. Paul C. Light, *Thickening Government* (Washington, D.C.: Brookings Institution and Governance Institute, 1995), esp. 111–116.
30. Paul Light, "Big Bureaucracy," *Washington Times*, May 10, 2001, A17.
31. Light, "Big Bureaucracy."
32. Stephen Barr, "Title Creep Reported at Agencies," *Washington Post*, March 8, 1999, A17.
33. Paul Light, "Pressure to Grow," *Government Executive*, October 2000, 24.
34. David M. Cohen, "Amateur Government," *Journal of Public Administration Research and Theory* (October 1998): 451.
35. U.S. Congress, *Congressional Record*, daily ed., 106th Cong., 1st sess., January 19, 1999, S554.
36. U.S. Congress, *Congressional Record*, daily ed., 105th Cong., 1st sess., September 12, 1996, S10367.
37. *Federal Times*, December 12, 1988, 6; and *Washington Post*, August 6, 1987, A2.
38. Robert Maranto and Robert Mofifit, "Keep 'Em Coming," *Washington Times*, May 2, 2001, A17.
39. *Roll Call*, March 11, 1999, 4. See also Amy Keller, "English Targets Members' COLA, Tax Break," *Roll Call*, March 11, 1999, 3.
40. Laura Michaelis, "Judge Upholds Hill Pay Raise; Old, New Congresses Benefit," *Congressional Quarterly Weekly Report*, December 19, 1992, 3880.
41. David Francis, "Government Size: Don't Buy the Hype," *Christian Science Monitor*, February 8, 1999, 17; and "How Big the Government?" *Christian Science Monitor*, February 5, 1998, 20.
42. Ellen Nakashima, "Pentagon Hires Out More Than In," *Washington Post*, April 3, 2001, A19.
43. Joel Brinkley, "Energy Dept. Contractors Due for More Scrutiny," *New York Times*, November 24, 2002, 21.
44. Richard Stevenson, "Government Plan May Make Private Up to 850,000 Jobs," *New York Times*, November 15, 2002, A1.
45. Nakashima, "Pentagon Hires Out More Than In."
46. Paul C. Light, "The True Size of Government," *Government Executive*, January 1999, 20.
47. Peter Zimmerman, "Not So Big," *Government Executive*, February 1999, 39, 42.
48. U.S. Congress, *Congressional Record*, daily ed., 96th Cong., 2d sess., July 1, 1980, E3320.
49. Rebecca Fairley Raney, "Move to Open Government Electronically," *New York Times*, December 23, 2002, nytimes.com/2002.
50. Cornelius Kerwin, *Rulemaking: How Government Agencies Write Law and Make Policy*, 2d ed. (Washington, D.C.: CQ Press, 1999), 8–9. See also Jeffrey Lubbers, *A Guide to Federal Agency Rulemaking*, 3d ed. (Chicago: ABA Publishing, 1998).
51. U.S. Congress, *Congressional Record*, daily ed., 100th Cong., 1st sess., July 29, 1987, S10850.
52. Matthew Wald, "Court Overturns Air Quality Rules," *New York Times*, May 15, 1999, A1.
53. Charles Lane, "Clean-Air Authority of EPA Is Upheld," *Washington Post*, February 28, 2001, A1.
54. *Roll Call*, December 4, 1995, 15.
55. Rebecca Adams, "Regulating the Rule-Makers: John Graham at OIRA," *CQ Weekly*, February 23, 2002, 520.
56. Cyril Zaneski, "Escape Artist," *Government Executive*, March 2001, 29. See also Amy Goldstein, " 'Last-Minute' Spin on Regulatory Rite," *Washington Post*, June 9, 2000, A1.
57. Zaneski, "Escape Artist," 28.

58. Edmund Andrews, "New Scale for Toting Up Lost Freedom vs. Security Would Measure in Dollars," *New York Times*, March 11, 2003, A11.
59. See Helen Dewar and Cindy Skrzycki, "Workplace Health Initiative Rejected," *Washington Post*, March 7, 2001, A1; and Helen Dewar and Cindy Skrzycki, "House Scraps Ergonomics Regulation," *Washington Post*, March 8, 2001, A1.
60. U.S. Congress, *Congressional Record*, daily ed., 104th Cong., 1st sess., July 11, 1995, S9705.
61. U.S. Congress, *Congressional Record*, daily ed., 104th Cong., 1st sess., July 11, 1995, S9697.
62. Morris P. Fiorina, *Congress: Keystone of the Washington Establishment* (New Haven: Yale University Press, 1977), 48.
63. R. Douglas Arnold, "The Local Roots of Domestic Policy," in *The New Congress*, ed. Thomas E. Mann and Norman J. Ornstein (Washington, D.C.: American Enterprise Institute, 1981), 284.
64. *CQ Monitor*, July 15, 1998, 5; and Donald L. Barlett and James B. Steele, "Special Report: Corporate Welfare," *Time*, November 16, 1998, 79–93.
65. Joseph S. Clark, *Congress: The Sapless Branch* (New York: Harper and Row, 1964), 63–64.
66. David B. Frohnmayer, "The Separation of Powers: An Essay on the Vitality of a Constitutional Idea," *Oregon Law Review* (spring 1973): 330.
67. David B. Truman, *The Governmental Process*, rev. ed. (New York: Knopf, 1971), 439.
68. Woodrow Wilson, *Congressional Government* (Boston: Houghton Mifflin, 1885), 297.
69. *Washington Times*, December 29, 1986, A1; and David Rogers, "Sen. Lott Becomes GOP's New Standard-bearer, but His Style Will Be Tested in the Next Congress," *Wall Street Journal*, November 15, 1996, A16.
70. Jackie Koszczuk, "House GOP Is Closing the Door on an Era of Aggressive Inquiry," *CQ Weekly*, February 6, 1999, 328.
71. Rochelle Stanfield, "Plotting Every Move," *National Journal*, March 26, 1988, 796.
72. *Watkins v. United States*, 354 U.S. 178 (1957). See also James Hamilton, *The Power to Probe* (New York: Vantage Books, 1976).
73. William S. Cohen and George J. Mitchell, *Men of Zeal: A Candid Inside Story of the Iran-Contra Hearings* (New York: Viking Penguin, 1988), 305.
74. *Immigration and Naturalization Service v. Chadha*, 462 U.S. 919 (1983).
75. Louis Fisher, in *Extensions*, Carl Albert Congressional Research and Studies Center newsletter (spring 1984): 2.
76. John R. Johannes, "Study and Recommend: Statutory Reporting Requirements as a Technique of Legislative Initiative—A Research Note," *Western Political Quarterly* (December 1976): 589–596.
77. Guy Gugliotta, "Reporting on a Practice That's Ripe for Reform," *Washington Post*, February 11, 1997, A19.
78. Walter Pincus, "Congress Cracks Down on Overdue CIA Reports," *Washington Post*, December 1, 2002, A5.
79. Cindy Skrzycki, "The Regulators," *Washington Post*, January 8, 1999, F7. See also *CQ Monitor*, March 25, 1996, 7.
80. Michael W. Kirst, *Government without Passing Laws* (Chapel Hill: University of North Carolina Press, 1969).
81. Joseph A. Davis, "War Declared Over Report-Language Issue," *Congressional Quarterly Weekly Report*, June 25, 1988, 1752–1753; and David Rapp, "OMB's Miller Backs Away from Report-Language Battle," *Congressional Quarterly Weekly Report*, July 9, 1988, 1928.
82. George Archibald, "Hill Panel Examines Fraud at Education," *Washington Times*, April 4, 2001, A6.
83. "The Inspector General Act: Twenty Years Later," hearing before the Senate Governmental Affairs Committee, September 9, 1998, 32. See also Paul C. Light, *Monitoring Government: Inspectors General and the Search for Accountability* (Washington, D.C.: Brookings Institution, 1993).
84. Steven Holmes, "Amendment Would Strip a Top Official of His Powers," *New York Times*, October 6, 2000, A20.

85. Slade Gorton and Larry Craig, "Congress's Call to Accounting," *Washington Post*, July 27, 1998, A23.

86. U.S. Congress, *Congressional Record*, daily ed., 95th Cong., 1st sess., April 30, 1975, E2080.

87. One of the three federal judges impeached during the 1980s, Alcee L. Hastings, was elected in November 1992 as a Democrat to the U.S. House of Representatives from Florida. David Huckabee, "Impeachment: Days and Dates of Consideration in the House and Senate," *Congressional Research Service Report*, January 13, 1999, 1.

88. See Peter Baker, *The Breach: Inside the Impeachment and Trial of William Jefferson Clinton* (New York: Scribner, 2000).

89. See Joel D. Aberbach, *Keeping a Watchful Eye: The Politics of Congressional Oversight* (Washington, D.C.: Brookings Institution, 1990); and James Q. Wilson, *Bureaucracy: What Governmental Agencies Do and Why They Do It* (New York: Basic Books, 1991).

90. Richard Cohen, "King of Oversight," *Government Executive*, September 1988, 17.

91. Paul Bedard, "White House Fumes at Probes," *Washington Times*, April 7, 1995, A1. See also Charles Tiefer, "Congressional Oversight of the Clinton Administration and Congressional Procedure," *Administrative Law Review* (winter 1998): 199–216; Robert Weissman, "Hearings Loss: Oversight in the Republican Congress," *American Prospect* (November–December 1998): 50–55; and William West, "Oversight Subcommittees in the House of Representatives," *Congress and the Presidency* (autumn 1998): 147–160.

92. Ethan Wallison, "Burton Closes In on His 1,000th Subpoena," *Roll Call*, April 2, 2001, 1.

93. Audrey Hudson, " 'Tough but Fair' Judiciary Leader Maps Oversight," *Washington Times*, March 19, 2001, A4.

94. Stephen Barr, "GOP Seeking More Control of Programs and Spending," *Washington Post*, February 5, 1997, A25. See also Beryl Radin, "Searching for Performance: The Government Performance and Results Act," *PS*, September 1998, 553–555.

95. Jennifer Kabbany, "Armey Targets Waste in Federal Agencies," *Washington Times*, February 12, 1999, A6.

96. Joel D. Aberbach, "The Congressional Committee Intelligence System: Information, Oversight, and Change," *Congress and the Presidency* 14 (spring 1987): 51–76; and Mathew McCubbins and Thomas Schwartz, "Congressional Oversight Overlooked: Police Patrol versus Fire Alarm," *American Journal of Political Science* (February 1984): 165–177.

97. Louis Fisher, "Micromanagement by Congress: Reality and Mythology," paper presented at a conference sponsored by the American Enterprise Institute, Washington, D.C., April 8–9, 1988, 8. See also David S. Broder and Stephen Barr, "Hill's Micromanagement of Cabinet Blurs Separation of Powers," *Washington Post*, July 25, 1993, A1.

Chapter 12 *(pages 345–365)*

1. Alexis de Tocqueville, *Democracy in America* (New York: American Library, 1956), 72.

2. Richard L. Pacelle Jr., *The Role of the Supreme Court in American Politics: The Least Dangerous Branch?* (Boulder, Colo.: Westview Press, 2001).

3. Alexander Bickel, *The Least Dangerous Branch* (Indianapolis, Ind.: Bobbs-Merrill, 1962), 1.

4. See Dexter Perkins and Glyndon Van Deusen, *The United States of America: A History*, vol. II (New York: Macmillan Co., 1962), 560–566.

5. Joan Biskupic, "Justices Defer to 'Congress' Power to Extend Copyright," *USA Today*, January 16, 2003, 4A.

6. Jamin Raskin, "Courts v. Citizens," *American Prospect* 14 (March 2003), A25.

7. Colton C. Campbell and John F. Stack Jr., "Diverging Perspectives on Lawmaking: The Delicate Balance between Congress and the Court," in *Congress Confronts the Court*, ed. Colton C. Campbell and John F. Stack Jr. (Lanham, Md.: Rowman and Littlefield, 2001), 2.

8. Charles Warren, *The Supreme Court in United States History*, vol. I (Boston: Little, Brown, and Co., 1926), 759.

9. Cass Sunstein, "The Right-Wing Assault," *American Prospect* 14 (March 2003), A2.

10. Linda Greenhouse, "High Court Faces Moment of Truth in Federalism Cases," *New York Times,* March 28, 1999, 3.
11. Louis Fisher, *American Constitutional Law,* 5th ed. (Durham, N.C.: Carolina Academic Press, 2003), 365.
12. Louis Fisher, "*The Law:* Litigating the War Power with *Campbell v. Clinton,*" *Presidential Studies Quarterly* (September 2000), 568.
13. Richard Briffault, "A Fickle Federalism," *American Prospect* 14 (March 2003), A26.
14. Donald F. Kettl, "Dusting Off 'Dignity,' " *Governing,* August 2002, 14.
15. Edward Walsh, "Justices Extend Family Act's Reach," *Washington Post,* May 28, 2003, A1.
16. Linda Greenhouse, "Steady Rationale at Court Despite Apparent Bend," *New York Times,* May 29, 2003, A23.
17. Linda Greenhouse, "Will the Court Reassert National Authority?" *New York Times,* September 30, 2001, E14.
18. Linda Greenhouse, "The Imperial Presidency vs. the Imperial Judiciary," *New York Times,* September 8, 2002, E5.
19. Gail Russell Chaddock, "Congress Watches Its Power Ebb," *Christian Science Monitor,* May 21, 2003, 4.
20. See Robert A. Katzmann, ed., *Judges and Legislators* (Washington, D.C.: Brookings Institution, 1988); and Robert A. Katzmann, *Courts and Congress* (Washington, D.C.: Brookings Institution, 1997).
21. *New York Times,* May 12, 1983, B8.
22. See, for example, Antonin Scalia, *A Matter of Interpretation* (Princeton: Princeton University Press, 1997).
23. Jonathan Kaplan, "High Court to Congress: Say What You Mean," *The Hill,* February 5, 2003, 21.
24. Ruth Marcus, "Lawmakers Override High Court," *Washington Post,* October 31, 1991, A1.
25. U.S. Congress, *Congressional Record,* daily ed., 102d Cong., 1st sess., October 29, 1991, S15324–15325.
26. Joan Biskupic, "Scalia Sees No Justice in Trying to Judge Intent of Congress on a Law," *Washington Post,* May 11, 1993, A4.
27. Kaplan, "High Court to Congress," 21.
28. The First Amendment to the Constitution is shaped by court opinion as well as congressional action. In 1986 the Supreme Court upheld, in *Goldman v. Weinberger,* the constitutionality of a U.S. Air Force regulation that prohibited an Air Force captain from wearing his yarmulke indoors while on duty. The next year, Congress passed legislation telling the Air Force to change its regulation to permit military personnel to wear unobtrusive religious apparel indoors so long as it did not interfere with their military duties. See Fisher, *American Constitutional Law,* 593, 599–602.
29. U.S. Congress, *Congressional Record,* daily ed., 106th Cong., 1st sess., January 19, 1999, S702.
30. Joan Biskupic and Elder Witt, *Guide to the U.S. Supreme Court,* 3d ed., vol. II (Washington, D.C.: CQ Press, 1997), 720.
31. William H. Rehnquist, *Grand Inquests: The Historic Impeachment of Justice Samuel Chase and President Andrew Johnson* (New York: William Morrow, 1992), 132.
32. U.S. Congress, *Expressing the Sense of the House of Representatives That the Ninth Circuit Court of Appeals Ruling in NEWDOW V. UNITED STATES CONGRESS Is Inconsistent with the Supreme Court's Interpretation of the First Amendment and Should Be Overturned, and for Other Purposes,* H. Rept. 108-41, Committee on the Judiciary, 108th Cong., 1st sess., March 18, 2003, 2.
33. Stephen Dinan, "DeLay Threatens to Curb Courts' Jurisdiction," *Washington Times,* March 6, 2003, A4.
34. William Rehnquist, *Grand Inquests: The Historic Impeachments of Justice Samuel Chase and President Andrew Johnson* (New York: William Morrow, 1992), 114.
35. Louis Fisher, "Congressional Checks on the Judiciary," *CRS Report for Congress,* 97–497, April 29, 1997, 4.

36. Biskupic and Witt, *Guide to the U.S. Supreme Court,* 717.

37. Ibid., 718.

38. Seth Stern, "A Career as Federal Judge Isn't What It Used to Be," *Christian Science Monitor,* January 22, 2002, 1.

39. Edward Walsh, "Federal Judicial Pay Called Too Low," *Washington Post,* May 29, 2003, A23.

40. See Fisher, *American Constitutional Law,* 1072.

41. Jennifer Dlouhy, "Congress Reluctant to Change Constitution," *CQ Today,* February 11, 2003, 9.

42. Brannon Denning, "The 'Blue Slip': Enforcing the Norms of the Judicial Confirmation Process," *William and Mary Bill of Rights Journal* 10 (December 2001), 92.

43. "GOP Move Would Help Nominees," *Washington Post,* January 24, 2003, A25.

44. Janet Hook, "Democrats Spoiling for Estrada Fight," *Los Angeles Times,* February 6, 2003, A10.

45. Michael J. Gerhardt, "Here's What Less Experience Gets You," *Washington Post,* March 2, 2003, B1, B4.

46. Ralph Neas, "United States Needs More Discussion of Judicial Philosophy," *Roll Call,* May 9, 2002, 10.

47. Richard Baker, "Senate Historical Minute," *The Hill,* October 2, 2002, 12.

48. Helen Dewar, "Confirmed Frustration with Judicial Nominations Process," *Washington Post,* March 10, 2003, A19.

49. Helen Dewar, "Polarized Politics, Confirmation Chaos," *Washington Post,* May 11, 2003, A5.

50. James Robertson, "A Cure for What Ails the Judiciary," *Washington Post,* May 27, 2003, A19.

51. Elizabeth Palmer, "Appellate Courts at Center of Fight for Control of Judiciary," *CQ Weekly,* February 23, 2002, 534.

52. Quoted in *Christian Science Monitor,* May 12, 2003, 2.

53. Robin Toner and Neil Lewis, "Lobbying Starts as Groups Foresee Vacancy on Court," *New York Times,* June 8, 2003, 1.

54. R. Jeffrey Smith, "Judge's Fate Could Turn On 1994 Case," *Washington Post,* May 27, 2003, A8.

55. E. J. Dionne Jr., "They Started It," *Washington Post,* February 21, 2003, A27.

56. Jennifer Diouhy and Keith Perine, "Judiciary Committee Agenda Disrupted by Partisan Acrimony," *CQ Weekly,* April 19, 2003, 945.

57. Dewar, "Confirmed Frustration with Judicial Nomination Process," A19.

58. Amy Goldstein and Helen Dewar, "President Criticizes Filibusters," *Washington Post,* May 10, 2003, A6.

59. Lauren Cohen Bell, "Senatorial Discourtesy: The Senate's Use of Delay to Shape the Federal Judiciary," *Political Research Quarterly* 56 (September 2002), 593.

60. Recent Senate debates on judicial nominations are often filled with each party's analysis of the delays and obstructionism aimed at its president's judicial selections. See, for example, U.S. Congress, *Congressional Record,* 107th Cong., 2d sess., August 1, 2002, S7856–S7857; 108th Cong., 1st sess., February 26, 2003, S2724–S2730, and March 3, 2003, S2996–S2997.

61. Sheldon Goldman, "Assessing the Senate Judicial Confirmation Process: The Index of Obstruction and Delay," *Judicature* 86 (March-April 2003), 252.

62. See Sarah Binder, "The Senate as a Black Hole: Lessons Learned from the Judicial Appointment Experience," *Brookings Review* 19 (spring 2001), 37–40.

63. Mike Allen and Amy Goldstein, "Bush Has Plan to Speed Judicial Confirmations," *Washington Post,* October 31, 2002, A21.

64. E. J. Dionne Jr., "Order and the Courts," *Washington Post,* May 9, 2003, A35.

65. Janet Hook, "Democrats Spoiling for Estrada Fight," *Los Angeles Times,* February 6, 2003, A10. Nominees who are the first to serve on the Supreme Court may spark controversy or provoke special attention by senators, such as the 1916 nomination of the first Jewish member (Louis Brandeis) of the high court; the 1967 confirmation of Thurgood Marshall as the first African American to serve on the Supreme Court; and the Senate's unanimous approval in 1981 of Sandra Day O'Connor to be the first female Supreme Court justice.

66. U.S. Congress, *Congressional Record,* 108th Cong., 1st sess., February 25, 2003, S2621.
67. Charles Hurt, "Feminists Criticize Female Court Picks," *Washington Times,* April 28, 2003, A5. See also Jonathan Groner, "Air Wars: Spinning the Estrada Showdown," *Legal Times,* March 17, 2003, 1.
68. Louis Fisher, "Congressional Checks on the Judiciary," in *Congress Confronts the Court,* ed. Colton C. Campbell and John F. Stack Jr. (Lanham, Md.: Rowman and Littlefield, 2001), 35.

Chapter 13 (pages 367–389)

1. Stephen Labaton, "House Panel Starts Work on Bank Bill," *New York Times,* May 22, 1991, D3.
2. Francis Clines, "Among the Not So Well Heeled of Gucci Gulch," *New York Times,* June 22, 1997, A28. See also David Rosenbaum, "At $500 an Hour, Lobbyist's Influence Rises with G.O.P.," *New York Times,* April 3, 2002, A1.
3. *Washington Post,* August 19, 2002, A11. The 2002 average monthly figure was in *National Journal, CongressDaily/PM,* February 20, 2003, 7–8.
4. *Washington Post,* August 19, 2002, A11.
5. Alexis de Tocqueville, *Democracy in America,* ed. Phillips Bradley (New York: Knopf, 1951), 119. See also Richard A. Smith, "Interest Group Influence in the U.S. Congress," *Legislative Studies Quarterly* 20 (February 1995): 89-139.
6. Robert D. Putnam, "The Strange Disappearance of Civic America," *American Prospect* (winter 1996): 35.
7. Roy Rivenburg, "There Is No Such Thing as the Odd Man Out," *Los Angeles Times,* October 1, 1997, B9.
8. Janny Scott, "Medicine's Big Dose of Politics," *Los Angeles Times,* September 25, 1991, A15.
9. Andrea Petersen, "Episodic Illnesses: How Rare Ailments Get on Prime Time," *Wall Street Journal,* April 14, 1998, A1.
10. Putnam, "The Strange Disappearance of Civic America."
11. Suzi Parker, "Civic Clubs: Elks, Lions May Go Way of the Dodo," *Christian Science Monitor,* August 24, 1998, 1.
12. Everett Carll Ladd, "The American Way—Civic Engagement—Thrives," *Christian Science Monitor,* March 1, 1999, 9.
13. Sidney Verba, Kay Lehman Schlozman, and Henry Brady, "The Big Tilt: Participatory Inequality in America," *American Prospect* (May-June 1997): 78.
14. Elise D. Garcia, "Money in Politics," *Common Cause,* February 1981, 11.
15. Jeffrey H. Birnbaum, "Lobbyists: Why the Bad Rap?" *American Enterprise,* November-December 1992, 74. See also Jeffrey H. Birnbaum, *The Lobbyists* (New York: Times Books, 1992).
16. Norman J. Ornstein and Shirley Elder, *Interest Groups, Lobbying, and Policymaking* (Washington, D.C.: Congressional Quarterly, 1978), 224.
17. Jeffrey Birnbaum, "The Thursday Group," *Time,* March 27, 1995, 30-31.
18. Mark Preston, "Daschle Starts Monday Meetings," *Roll Call,* February 13, 2003, 1.
19. Preston, "Daschle Starts Monday Meetings," 22.
20. Hedrick Smith, *The Power Game* (New York: Random House, 1988), 232.
21. See, for example, David Ottaway and Dan Morgan, "Former Top U.S. Aides Seek Caspian Gusher," *Washington Post,* July 6, 1997, A1.
22. Ronald J. Hrebenar and Ruth K. Scott, *Interest Group Politics in America* (Englewood Cliffs, N.J.: Prentice-Hall, 1982), 63.
23. Mark Preston, "Ex-GOP Senators Get Special Access," *Roll Call,* April 3, 2003, 1, 24.
24. Janet Hook, "Ex-Members Have Access, but Not Always Clout," *Congressional Quarterly Weekly Report,* June 18, 1988, 1651-1653. See also Alan Ota, "Top-Tier Lobbyists: Ex-Members' Special Access Becomes an Issue," *CQ Weekly,* February 16, 2002, 455-462; and Melanie Fonder, "Resolution Would Deny Privileges for Lobbyists," *The Hill,* December 12, 2001, 4.
25. *Wall Street Journal,* October 5, 1987, 54.
26. Thomas Hale Boggs Jr., "All Interests Are Special," *New York Times,* February 16, 1993, A17.

27. Sam Walker, "Who's In and Who's Out among Capitol Lobbyists," *Christian Science Monitor,* November 8, 1995, 3.

28. Quoted in *National Journal, CongressDaily/PM,* March 15, 2002, 8.

29. *New York Times,* January 20, 1981, B3.

30. Sam Walker, "Gift Ban Shows New Ethics on Hill," *Christian Science Monitor,* September 19, 1995, 1.

31. Bill McAllister, "Free Liquor Still Flows on Capitol Hill," *Washington Post,* January 17, 1999, A6.

32. Juliet Eilperin, "House Ethics Panel Limits Gifts," *Washington Post,* April 15, 2003, A7.

33. Jim VandeHei and Juliet Eilperin, "House GOP Erodes Its Gift Ban," *Washington Post,* January 21, 2003, A6.

34. Carol Matlack, "Getting around the Rules," *National Journal,* May 12, 1990, 1139.

35. Juliet Eilperin, "Travel by Lawmakers Scrutinized," *Washington Post,* March 11, 2003, A9.

36. Nancy E. Roman, "Who Should Pick Up Travel Tab?" *Washington Times,* March 31, 1997, A10. See also Tyler Marshall, "As 'Junket' Becomes Dirty Word, Congress Loses Overseas Interest," *Los Angeles Times,* February 10, 1997, A8.

37. Leslie Wayne, "A Special Deal for Lobbyists: A Getaway with Lawmakers," *New York Times,* January 26, 1997, 1.

38. Al Kamen, "PAC-ed on the Slippery Slopes," *Washington Post,* January 17, 1997, A19.

39. Ernest Wittenberg, "How Lobbying Helps Make Democracy Work," *Vital Speeches of the Day,* November 1, 1982, 47.

40. Audrey Hudson, "Diverse Coalition Joins Fight against McCain-Feingold Bill," *Washington Times,* March 2, 2001, A5.

41. Lori Nitschke, "Coalitions Make a Comeback," *CQ Weekly,* March 3, 2001, 470.

42. Eric Schmitt, "How a Fierce Backlash Saved the 'Made in U.S.A.' Label," *New York Times,* December 6, 1997, A1.

43. *Washington Star,* December 31, 1980, C2.

44. John T. Tierney and Kay Lehman Schlozman, "Congress and Organized Interests," in *Congressional Politics,* ed. Christopher J. Deering (Chicago: Dorsey, 1989), 212.

45. Scott Shepard, " 'Grass-roots' or 'Astroturf'?" *Washington Times,* December 20, 1994, A2.

46. Juliet Eilperin, "Police Track Down Telecom Telegraphs," *Roll Call,* August 7, 1995, 1.

47. Alison Mitchell, "A New Form of Lobbying Puts Public Face on Private Interest," *New York Times,* September 30, 1998, A14. See also Ken Kollman, *Outside Lobbying: Public Opinion and Interest Group Strategies* (Princeton: Princeton University Press, 1998).

48. Sara Fritz and Dan Morain, "Stealth Lobby Drives Fuel-Additive War," *Los Angeles Times,* June 16, 1997, A6.

49. *New York Times,* January 24, 1980, A16.

50. *The Economist,* June 17, 1995, 22.

51. Mitchell, "A New Form of Lobbying Puts Public Face on Private Interest."

52. Craig Karmin, " 'Third Wave' Lobbyists Battle On-line over Smut Ban Proposal," *The Hill,* December 20, 1995, 7.

53. "Trends in Grassroots Lobbying: Consultant Q&A," *Campaigns and Elections,* February 1999, 22.

54. Mary Lynn Jones, "How to Lobby from Home or Office," *The Hill,* January 7, 1998, 7; and " 'Billion Byte March' Trips over E-mail Surge from Trial," *CQ Monitor,* January 20, 1999, 1.

55. *CQ Today,* February 24, 2003, 7.

56. Ethan Wallison, "Jackson Spins Web to Make His Point," *Roll Call,* March 25, 1999, 1.

57. Alice Love, "Small Business Group Helps Grow Its Own Grassroots Candidates at Meeting Next Week," *Roll Call,* October 16, 1995, 22.

58. Juliet Eilperin and Dan Morgan, "Something Borrowed, Something Blue," *Washington Post,* March 9, 2001, A16.

59. Philip M. Stern, "The Tin Cup Congress," *Washington Monthly,* May 1988, 24.

60. U.S. Congress, *Congressional Record,* daily ed., 107th Cong., 1st sess., March 26, 2001, S2853.

61. U.S. Congress, *Congressional Record,* daily ed., 100th Cong., 1st sess., August 5, 1987, S11292.

62. "Fundamentals of Fund-raising," *Washington Post,* December 5, 1990, A23.

63. Jeanne Cummings, "Candidates Learn to Defuse Outside Groups' Attack Ads," *Wall Street Journal,* July 20, 1998, A20.

64. Sarah Pekkanen, "How Lobbyists Are Changing the Lobbying Game," *The Hill,* February 12, 1997, 21.

65. *National Journal, CongressDaily/PM,* May 30, 1997, 6.

66. Eric Pianin, "How Business Found Benefits in Wage Bill," *Washington Post,* February 11, 1997, A8.

67. John Bresnahan, "GOP Congressional Leaders Continue to Prod Lobbying Firms to Hire More Republicans," *Roll Call,* September 10, 2001, B26. See also Kathleen Day and Jim VandeHei, "Congressman Urges Republican Lobbyist," *Washington Post,* February 15, 2003, A3.

68. Leslie Wayne, "Lobbyists' Gift to Politicians Reap Benefits, Study Shows," *New York Times,* January 23, 1997, B11.

69. Jim Drinkard, "Report: Interests Are Running Congress," *USA Today,* September 10, 1998, 7A.

70. Kirk Victor, "Making a Leap in Logic," *National Journal,* July 16, 1988, 1904.

71. Claudia Dreifus, "And Then There Was Frank," *New York Times Magazine,* February 4, 1996, 25.

72. Don Van Natta Jr., "$250,000 Buys Donors 'Best Access to Congress,' " *New York Times,* January 27, 1997, A1.

73. *Roll Call,* June 19, 1988, 12. See also Brooks Jackson, *Honest Graft: Big Money and the American Political Process* (New York: Knopf, 1988).

74. John Brinkley, "Members of Congress Perform under Judging Eyes of Lobbyists," *Washington Times,* March 16, 1994, A16.

75. Bill Whalen, "Rating Lawmakers' Politics by Looking into Their Eyes," *Insight,* October 20, 1986, 21. See John Cochran, "Interest Groups Make Sure Lawmakers Know the 'Score,' " *CQ Weekly,* April 19, 2003.

76. *New York Times,* May 13, 1986, A24.

77. *CQ Monitor,* April 13, 1998, 4.

78. U.S. Congress, *Oversight of the 1946 Federal Regulation of Lobbying Act,* Hearings before the Senate Committee on Governmental Affairs, 98th Cong., 1st sess., November 15 and 16, 1983, 228.

79. Kirk Victor, "New Kids on the Block," *National Journal,* October 31, 1987, 2727.

80. Mary Lynn Jones, "Survey Says Lobbyists Find Information Rules the Hill," *The Hill,* November 18, 1998, 8. See also Allan J. Cigler and Burdett Loomis, *Interest Group Politics,* 5th ed. (Washington, D.C.: CQ Press, 1998).

81. Dan Morgan and Juliet Eilperin, "A House GOP Reform Boomerangs," *Washington Post,* January 12, 2001, A8.

82. Scott, "Medicine's Big Dose of Politics," A12.

83. Alexander Bolton, "House Partisan Conflict Roils Enron Reform," *The Hill,* February 27, 2002, 7.

84. *New York Times,* May 31, 1985, D16.

85. *Roll Call,* March 19, 1998, 1.

86. Amy Goldstein, "Patients' Rights: A Prescription for Lobbyists," *Washington Post,* June 23, 2001, A7.

87. Nina Bernstein, "Deletion of Word in Welfare Bill Opens Foster Care to Big Business," *New York Times,* May 4, 1997, 1.

88. *CQ Monitor,* January 26, 1998, 3.

89. For a detailed listing of the informal congressional groups active in the 105th Congress, see *Congressional Yellow Book* (Washington, D.C.: Leadership Directories, spring 1997), section VI.

90. *Washington Star,* May 22, 1978, A1.

91. U.S. Congress, *Congressional Record,* daily ed., 96th Cong., 1st sess., April 3, 1979, 7065.
92. JoAnn Kelly, "Rural Members Lead Internet Drive," *The Hill,* February 3, 1999, 10.
93. See Susan Webb Hammond, *Congressional Caucuses in National Policy Making* (Baltimore: Johns Hopkins University Press, 1998).
94. U.S. Congress, *Organization of the Congress,* H. Rept. 1675, 79th Cong., 2d sess., 1946, 26.
95. Francesca Contiguaglia, "GAO Finds That Lobbyist Registration Has Soared," *Roll Call,* May 14, 1998, 14.
96. Sam Fulwood, "Lobbying Reform Passes House on Unanimous Vote," *Los Angeles Times,* November 30, 1995, A9.
97. Eierdre Shesgreen, "Shining a Dim Light," *Legal Times,* December 21 and 28, 1998, 26, 27.
98. Brody Mullins, "Talking Turkey," *Roll Call,* April 2, 2003, 9.
99. Steven Erlanger, "For Forty-seven Years, a Lobby with Muscle Has Tirelessly Tended U.S.-Israeli Ties," *New York Times,* April 26, 1998, 6.
100. Katharine Seelye, "National Rifle Association Is Turning to World Stage to Fight Gun Control," *New York Times,* April 2, 1997, A12.
101. Sam Loewenberg, "Tobacco Lights Into WHO," *Legal Times,* September 11, 2000, 1.
102. See Adam Hochschild, "Into the Light from the Heart of Darkness," *Los Angeles Times,* December 6, 1998, M1.
103. Steven Pearlstein and John Mintz, "Too Big to Fly?" *Washington Post,* May 4, 1997, H7.
104. Sara Fritz, "Big Firms Plant Seeds of 'Grass-roots' China Lobby," *Los Angeles Times,* May 12, 1997, A8.
105. Edgar Lane, *Lobbying and the Law* (Berkeley: University of California Press, 1964), 18.

Chapter 14 (pages 391–417)

1. Mike Allen, "Administration Launches Tax Blitz," *Washington Post,* April 19, 2003, A2.
2. Geoff Earle and Hans Nichols, "Sen. Voinovich," *The Hill,* April 16, 2003, 3.
3. E. J. Dionne Jr., "Now, How Do We Pay for It?" *Washington Post,* February 1, 2002, A25. The italics were in the original, and the quote from Bush is from this article.
4. See David Easton, *The Political System* (New York: Knopf, 1963); Harold D. Lasswell, *Politics: Who Gets What, When, How* (New York: Meridian Books, 1958); and Randall B. Ripley and Grace A. Franklin, *Congress, the Bureaucracy, and Public Policy,* 5th ed. (Pacific Grove, Calif.: Brooks/Cole, 1991).
5. Theodore R. Marmor, *The Politics of Medicare* (Chicago: Aldine Publishing, 1973).
6. John W. Kingdon, *Agendas, Alternatives, and Public Policies* (Boston: Little, Brown, 1984), 3.
7. Kingdon, *Agendas, Alternatives, and Public Policies,* 17–19.
8. Kingdon, *Agendas, Alternatives, and Public Policies,* chap. 2.
9. Nelson W. Polsby, "Strengthening Congress in National Policymaking," *Yale Review* (summer 1970): 481–497.
10. James L. Sundquist, *Politics and Policy: The Eisenhower, Kennedy, and Johnson Years* (Washington, D.C.: Brookings Institution, 1968).
11. Elizabeth Wehr, "Numerous Factors Favoring Good Relationship between Reagan and New Congress," *Congressional Quarterly Weekly Report,* January 24, 1981, 173.
12. Kingdon, *Agendas, Alternatives, and Public Policies,* 148–149.
13. American Enterprise Institute, *The State of the Congress: Tomorrow's Challenges?* (Washington, D.C.: 1981), 8.
14. Theodore Lowi, "American Business, Public Policy, Case Studies, and Political Theory," *World Politics* (July 1964): 677–715; Theodore Lowi, "Four Systems of Policy, Politics and Choice," *Public Administration Review* (July–August 1972): 298–310; Samuel P. Huntington, *The Common Defense* (New York: Columbia University Press, 1961); and Ripley and Franklin, *Congress, the Bureaucracy, and Public Policy.*
15. *Wall Street Journal,* May 13, 1988, 17R.
16. Mary Russell, " 'Park-Barrel Bill' Clears House Panel," *Washington Post,* June 22, 1978, A3.

17. Ben Pershing, "Want a Highway Project Next Year? The Road Starts Here," *Roll Call,* April 3, 2003, 3.

18. Lewis Lord, "Grand Old Pork," *U.S. News and World Report,* March 23, 1998, 7.

19. Edwin Chen, "Senate Fattens Its 'Ice Tea' with Porky Politics," *Los Angeles Times,* March 10, 1998, A6.

20. See, for example, Margaret Kriz, "Heavy Breathing," *National Journal,* January 4, 1997, 8–12.

21. Joby Warrick, "White House Taking a Hands-on Role in Writing New Clean Air Standards," *Washington Post,* May 22, 1997, A10.

22. Marmor, *The Politics of Medicare,* 108–109.

23. Donald Lambro, "Steady GOP Rebound Strategy," *Washington Times,* June 7, 2001, A17.

24. Benjamin I. Page, "Cooling the Legislative Tea," in *American Politics and Public Policy,* ed. Walter Dean Burnham and Martha Wagner Weinberg (Cambridge: MIT Press, 1978), 171–187.

25. Judy Sarasohn, "Money for Lat. 40 N, Long. 73 W," *Congressional Quarterly Weekly Report,* May 12, 1979, 916.

26. Paula Drummond, "Unfunded Mandates Bill Becomes Law," *Kansas Government Journal,* May 1995, 122.

27. "Mandates—With Money," *Christian Science Monitor,* February 27, 2003, 8.

28. "Don't Just Do Something, Sit There," *Economist,* December 23, 1995–January 5, 1996, 11–12.

29. Barber Conable, "Government Is Working," *Roll Call,* April 19, 1984, 3. Congress has initiated change many times. A classic example is the 37th Congress (1861–1863), which drafted "the blueprint for modern America" by enacting measures to finance the Civil War, build the transcontinental railroad, eradicate slavery, promote the land-grant college movement, provide settlers with homesteaded land, and create the Department of Agriculture. See James M. McPherson, *Battle Cry of Freedom: The Civil War Era* (New York: Ballantine, 1988), 452.

30. Robert Luce, *Legislative Problems* (Boston: Houghton Mifflin, 1935), 426. See also Louis Fisher, "The Authorization-Appropriation Process in Congress: Formal Rules and Informal Practices," *Catholic University Law Review* (fall 1979): 51–105; and Richard F. Fenno Jr., *The Power of the Purse* (Boston: Little, Brown, 1966).

31. See Louis Fisher, "Annual Authorizations: Durable Roadblocks to Biennial Budgeting," *Public Budgeting and Finance* (spring 1983): 23–40.

32. David Baumann, "Shirking Duties on the Hill," *National Journal, CongressDaily/AM,* March 27, 2003, 5.

33. *National Journal, CongressDaily/PM* May 12, 2003, 3.

34. Erik Eckholm, "Payments to the Retired Loom Ever Larger," *New York Times,* August 30, 1992, E1, E4.

35. Jason DeParle, "U.S. Welfare System Dies as State Programs Emerge," *New York Times,* June 30, 1997, A1.

36. Julie Rovner, "The Real Budget Buster," *National Journal, CongressDaily/AM,* April 5, 2001, 5.

37. Rovner, "The Real Budget Buster."

38. Matthew Miller, "The Big Federal Freeze," *New York Times Magazine,* October 15, 2000, 94.

39. Maya MacGuineas, "The Real State of the Budget," *Atlantic Monthly,* January/February 2003, 81.

40. Andrew Taylor and Alan Ota, "GOP to Seek Budget Deal Now, Tax Cut Decision Later," *CQ Today,* April 10, 2003, 6.

41. " 'You Know What? Democracy Is a Tough Business,' " *The Hill,* April 8, 2003, 3.

42. U.S. Congress, *Congressional Record,* daily ed., 106th Cong., 2d sess., March 2, 2000, S1050.

43. Mark Preston, " 'Vote-a-Rama' Keeps Wearing Senate Down," *Roll Call,* March 26, 2003, 1.

44. U.S. Congress, *Congressional Record,* daily ed., 107th Cong., 1st sess., February 15, 2001, S1532.

45. John Ellwood, "Budget Control in a Redistributive Environment," in *Making Economic Policy in Congress,* ed. Allen Schick (Washington, D.C.: American Enterprise Institute, 1983), 93.

46. David Rosenbaum, "Negotiators Reach Rare Deal on Tax Cut," *New York Times*, April 10, 2003, A18.
47. Stephen Dinan and Bill Sammon, "Frist Apologizes for Tax Deal," *Washington Times*, April 30, 2003, A12.
48. David Rosenbaum, "Democratic Filibuster Hopes Fade," *New York Times*, November 18, 2002, A15.
49. Mollie Ziegle and Tim Kaufman, "Lawmaker Strikers Deal to Save Worker Benefits," *Federal Times*, April 7, 2003, 4.
50. William Dauster, "Budget Process Issues for 1993," *Journal of Law and Politics* 9, no. 9 (1992), 26.
51. Dauster, "Budget Process Issues for 1993," A7.
52. U.S. Congress, *Congressional Record,* daily ed., 107th Cong., 1st sess., January 4, 2001, S19.
53. U.S. Congress, *Congressional Record,* daily ed., 108th Cong., 1st sess., February 26, 2003, H1370.
54. Dana Milbank and Dan Balz, "GOP Eyes Tax Cuts as Annual Events," *Washington Post*, May 11, 2003, A1.
55. John Maggs and David Baumann, "Speaking His Mind," *National Journal*, July 6, 2002, 2004.
56. David Firestone, "Conservatives Now See Deficits as a Tool to Fight Spending," *New York Times*, February 11, 2003, A22.
57. Robin Toner, "For Republicans, Deficits Are Nothing to Be Ashamed Of," *New York Times*, February 9, 2003, E3.
58. Alan Ota, "Rise of the 'Growth Hawks,' " *CQ Weekly*, November 16, 2002, 2999.
59. U.S. Congress, *Congressional Record,* daily ed., 107th Cong., 2d sess., June 20, 2002, S5810.
60. Sue Kirchhoff, "Deficit Warnings Increase in Urgency," *USA Today*, February 27, 2003, 5B.
61. U.S. Congress, *Congressional Record,* daily ed., 107th Cong., 2d sess., July 16, 2002, H4749.

Chapter 15 (pages 419-445)

1. Quoted in Samuel Eliot Morison, *The Oxford History of the American People* (New York: Oxford University Press, 1965), 346.
2. Edward S. Corwin, *The President: Office and Powers, 1787–1957*, 4th ed. (New York: New York University Press, 1957), 171. See also Cecil V. Crabb Jr. and Pat M. Holt, *Invitation to Struggle: Congress, the President, and Foreign Policy,* 4th ed. (Washington, D.C.: CQ Press, 1992).
3. Corwin, *The President*, 171; italics are in the original.
4. U.S. Congress, *Annals of Congress*, 6th Cong., 1800, 613.
5. *United States v. Curtiss-Wright Export Corp.*, 299 U.S. 304 (1936).
6. *Youngstown Sheet and Tube Co. v. Sawyer*, 343 U.S. 636 (1952).
7. Alexander Hamilton, James Madison, and John Jay, *The Federalist Papers*, ed. Clinton Rossiter, No. 64 (New York: Mentor Books, 1961), 391–393.
8. Christopher J. Deering and Steven S. Smith, *Committees in Congress*, 3d ed. (Washington, D.C.: CQ Press, 1997), 92.
9. Quoted in Helen Dewar, "Clinton, Congress at Brink of Foreign Policy Dispute," *Washington Post*, May 16, 1994, A10.
10. Holbert N. Carroll, *The House of Representatives and Foreign Affairs*, rev. ed. (Boston: Little, Brown, 1966), 20.
11. Christopher J. Deering, "Congress, the President, and Military Policy," in *Congress and the Presidency: Invitation to Struggle*, ed. Roger H. Davidson, *The Annals* 499 (September 1988): 136–147.
12. *Budget of the United States Government, Fiscal 2003, Historical Tables* (Washington, D.C.: Government Printing Office, 2002), Tables 4.2, 5.1.
13. Tim Smart, "Getting the F-22 Off the Ground," *Washington Post*, April 20, 1998, 12.
14. Tim Weiner, "For Military Plane in Crash, A History of Political Conflict," *New York Times*, April 11, 2000, A1.

15. Quoted in Vernon Loeb, "Weapon Systems Die Hard, Especially on Capitol Hill," *Washington Post*, May 6, 2002, A4.
16. Thomas E. Ricks, "For Rumsfeld, Many Roadblocks," *Washington Post*, August 7, 2001, A1.
17. Quoted in Kevin Sack, "For the South, GOP Secures Defense Bounty," *New York Times*, November 18, 1997, A1.
18. Helen Dewar and Kevin Merida, "When Defense Cuts Hit Home," *Washington Post*, March 22, 1993, A1.
19. Karl Viox, "It's Closing Time for Base Commission," *Washington Post*, December 29, 1995, A21. Scholars regard this as an intriguing example of blame-avoidance politics. See, for example, Christopher J. Deering, "Congress, the President, and Automatic Government: The Case of Military Base Closures," in *Rivals for Power: Presidential-Congressional Relations*, ed. James A. Thurber (Washington, D.C.: CQ Press, 1996).
20. Rep. Joel Hefley, "Base Closings? 'Over My Dead Body,'" *The Hill*, May 2, 1997, 24.
21. Chuck McCutcheon, with Donna Casata, "Lawmakers Seek to Avoid Closures by Pumping Money into Military Bases," *CQ Weekly*, August 10, 2002, 2190.
22. Quoted in Robert Schlesinger, "Defense Downsizing Also Impacts Hill Committees," *The Hill*, May 21, 1997, 17.
23. U.S. Congress, *Congressional Record*, daily ed., 102d Cong., 2d sess., August 6, 1992, H7701–7703.
24. Keith Bradsher, "NAFTA: Something to Offend Everyone," *New York Times*, November 14, 1993. See also I. M. Destler, "Protecting Congress or Protecting Trade?" *Foreign Policy* 62 (spring 1986): 96–107.
25. Sander Levin, "Derailing a Consensus on Trade," *Washington Post*, December 5, 2001, A29.
26. Vladimir Pregelj, *Fast-Track Implementation of Trade Agreements: History, Status, and Other Options*, Congressional Research Service Report No. 97–41E, December 27, 1996.
27. Quoted in Joseph Kahn, "As Vote Nears, Bush Presses for New Trade Powers," *New York Times*, December 5, 2001, A18.
28. Richard Simon and Nancy Cleeland, "Senate OKs Fast-Track Trade Bill," *Los Angeles Times*, August 2, 2002, A1.
29. William A. Orme Jr., "Israeli Armorer in Global Arena," *New York Times*, June 30, 2000, C1.
30. Charles McC. Mathias Jr., "Ethnic Groups and Foreign Policy," *Foreign Affairs* 59 (summer 1981): 975–998.
31. Leslie Wayne, "So Much for the Plan to Scrap Old Weapons," *New York Times*, December 22, 2002, D1.
32. Quoted in James Dao and Steven Lee Myers, "Bush Warning on Spending Cools a Wishful Pentagon," *New York Times*, February 5, 2001, A14.
33. Quoted in James Dao, "In Protest, Senators Hold Up Defense Confirmations," *New York Times*, May 10, 2001, A20.
34. Joseph J. Schatz, "Has Congress Given Bush Too Free a Spending Hand?" *CQ Weekly*, April 12, 2002, 859.
35. Robin Wright, "Don't Just Fund the War, Shell Out for Peace," *Washington Post*, March 10, 2002, B5; and Stephen Kinzer, "Why They Don't Know Us," *New York Times*, November 11, 2001, D5.
36. Loch Johnson and James M. McCormick, "Foreign Policy by Executive Fiat," *Foreign Policy* 28 (fall 1977): 118–124.
37. Quoted in Paul Richter, "Senate Approves U.S.-Russian Treaty to Cut Some Nuclear Weapons," *Los Angeles Times*, March 7, 2003, A18.
38. David Auerswald and Forrest Maltzman, "Shaping Foreign Policy through Ratification: The Senate and Treaties," paper delivered at the American Political Science Association, Boston, Massachusetts, August 2002, 6.
39. Peter Grier, "Why 48 Treaties Languish in the Senate," *Christian Science Monitor*, March 20, 1997, 3.

40. Thomas W. Lippman and Peter Baker, "Bipartisanship, But at a Price," *Washington Post*, April 25, 1997, A1.

41. David Silverberg, "Nasty, Brutish and Short: The CTBT Debates," *The Hill*, December 8, 1999, 16.

42. Roger H. Davidson, "Senate Floor Deliberation: A Preliminary Inquiry," in *The Contentious Senate*, ed. Colton C. Campbell and Nicol C. Rae (Lanham, Md.: Rowman and Littlefield, 2001), 22–29.

43. Silverberg, "Nasty, Brutish and Short," 16.

44. Kiki Caruson, "International Agreement-Making and the Executive-Legislative Relationship," *Presidential Research Group Report* 25 (fall 2002): 22.

45. Caruson, "International Agreement-Making and the Executive-Legislative Relationship," 21.

46. This section draws upon the invaluable summary of congressional policy initiation in Ellen C. Collier, *Foreign Policy Roles of the President and Congress*, Congressional Research Service Report No. 93–20F, January 6, 1993, 11–17.

47. The classic account of this incident is Chalmers M. Roberts, "The Day We Didn't Go to War," *The Reporter*, September 14, 1954, 31–35.

48. Alison Mitchell, "In Vote Clinton Sought to Avoid, House Backs a Force for Kosovo," *New York Times*, March 12, 1999, A1.

49. Ellen C. Collier, "Foreign Policy by Reporting Requirement," *Washington Quarterly* 11 (winter 1988): 75.

50. Bruce J. Schulman, "Congress' Wartime Quandary," *Los Angeles Times*, April 27, 2003, M2.

51. Quoted in Dan Eggen, "Lawmakers Urge More Aggressive Sept. 11 Probe," *Washington Post*, May 22, 2002, A1.

52. James M. Lindsay, "Congress, Foreign Policy, and the New Institutionalism," *International Studies Quarterly* 38 (June 1994): 281–304.

53. An early, influential analysis of this phenomenon is John E. Mueller, *War, Presidents, and Public Opinion* (New York: Wiley, 1973), 208–213.

54. A thoughtful survey of the debate between unilateralists and globalists is presented by Ivo H. Daalder and James M. Lindsay, "The Globalization of Politics: American Foreign Policy for the New Century," *Brookings Review* 23 (winter 2003): 12–17.

55. Benjamin R. Barber, "Mutual Aid Society on a Grand Scale," *Los Angeles Times*, November 17, 2002, M2.

56. Richard F. Grimmett, *War Powers Resolution: Presidential Compliance*, Congressional Research Service Issue Brief 81050, May 9, 2003.

57. Harold M. Hyman, *Quiet Past and Stormy Present: War Powers in American History* (Washington, D.C.: American Historical Association Bicentennial Essays on the Constitution, 1986).

58. Quotes from Helen Dewar, "Congress's Reaction to TV Coverage Shows Ambivalence on Foreign Policy," *Washington Post*, October 9, 1993, A14; and Dewar, "Clinton, Congress at Brink of Foreign Policy Dispute," A1.

59. Grimmett, *War Powers Resolution*.

60. U.S. Congress, *Congressional Record*, daily ed., 107th Cong., 2d sess., October 9, 2002, S10175.

61. U.S. Congress, *Congressional Record*, daily ed., 107th Cong., 2d sess., October 9, 2002, S10161.

62. U.S. Congress, *Congressional Record*, daily ed., 107th Cong., 2d sess., October 10, 2002, S10247.

63. Louis Fisher, *Presidential War Power* (Lawrence: University Press of Kansas, 1995), 185.

64. Quotes from Gabriel Kahn, "House Saves Its War Power," *Roll Call*, June 8, 1995, 21.

65. Both these quotes are from "Congress Backs Bush on Emergency Aid," *International Herald-Tribune*, September 15, 2001, 5.

66. John E. Reilly, *Public Opinion and Foreign Policy* (Chicago: Chicago Council on Foreign Relations, April 25, 1999).

67. Steven Kull and I. M. Destler, *Misreading the Public: The Myth of a New Isolationism* (Washington, D.C.: Brookings Institution, 1999), 204.
68. James M. Lindsay, "Congress and Foreign Policy: Why the Hill Matters," *Political Science Quarterly* 107 (winter 1992–1993): 626–627.
69. Quotes from Lindsay Sobel, "Hill Profile: Sen. Bob Kerrey," *The Hill*, October 29, 1997, 24; and Helen Dewar, "Farming Locally, Thinking Globally," *Washington Post*, April 21, 1998, A1.
70. Richard G. Lugar, "Beating Terror," *Washington Post*, January 27, 2003, A19.

Chapter 16 (pages 447–464)

1. Quoted in David Nather, "For Congress, A New World—And Business as Usual, *CQ Weekly*, September 7, 2002, 2276.
2. See Charles O. Jones, *The Presidency in a Separated System* (Washington, D.C.: Brookings Institution, 1994).
3. U.S. Congress, *Congressional Record*, daily ed., 105th Cong., 1st sess., May 21, 1997, H3072.
4. Glenn R. Parker and Roger H. Davidson, "Why Do Americans Love Their Congressmen So Much More Than Their Congress?" *Legislative Studies Quarterly* 4 (February 1979): 53–61.
5. See Roger H. Davidson, "The House of Representatives: Managing Legislative Complexity," in *Workways of Governance: Monitoring the Government's Health,* ed. Roger H. Davidson (Washington, D.C.: Governance Institute and Brookings Institution Press, 2003), 24–46; and Sarah A. Binder, "The Senate: Does It Deliberate? Can It Act?" in *Workways of Governance: Monitoring the Government's Health,* ed. Roger H. Davidson (Washington, D.C.: Governance Institute and Brookings Institution Press, 2003), 47–64.
6. Quoted in Mary Lynn F. Jones, "Family Concerns Prompt Early Hill Retirements," *The Hill,* March 20, 2002, 12.
7. Jones, "Family Concerns Prompt Early Hill Retirements."
8. Thomas E. Mann, *Unsafe at Any Margin: Interpreting Congressional Elections* (Washington, D.C.: American Enterprise Institute, 1978).
9. David Dreier, "We've Come a Long Way . . . Maybe," in *Congress and the Internet,* ed. James A. Thurber and Colton C. Campbell (Upper Saddle River, N.J.: Prentice Hall, 2003), 58.
10. Bob Benenson, "Savvy 'Stars' Making Local TV a Potent Tool," *Congressional Quarterly Weekly Report,* July 18, 1987, 1551–1555.
11. Timothy Cook, *Making Laws and Making News: Media Strategies in the U.S. House of Representatives* (Washington, D.C.: Brookings Institution, 1989), 82–83.
12. Gallup-CNN-*USA Today* survey, reported in Karlyn Bowman, "Quarter Polled Rank Congress' Honesty High," *Roll Call,* December 13, 2001, 14.
13. Lee H. Hamilton, "Ten Things I Wish Political Scientists Would Teach about Congress," Pi Sigma Alpha Lecture, American Political Science Association, August 31, 2000, 7.
14. Norman J. Ornstein, "Prosecutors Must End Their Big Game Hunt of Politicians," *Roll Call,* April 26, 1993, 16; italics are in the original.
15. Quoted in T. R. Goldman, "The Influence Industry's Senior Class," *Legal Times,* June 16, 1997, 4.
16. Cass R. Sunstein, "Unchecked and Unbalanced," *American Prospect* 38 (May–June 1998): 23.
17. G. Calvin Mackenzie with Michael Hafken, *Scandal Proof: Do Ethics Laws Make Government Ethical?* (Washington, DC: Brookings Institution Press, 2002), 158.
18. Paul C. Light, "Measuring the Health of the Public Service," in *Workways of Governance: Monitoring the Government's Health,* ed. Roger H. Davidson (Washington, DC: Governance Institute and Brookings Institution Press, 2003), 96–97.
19. Woodrow Wilson, *Constitutional Government in the United States* (New York: Columbia University Press, 1908), 79–80.
20. Diane Hollern Harvey, "Who Should Govern? Public Preferences for Congressional and Presidential Power," Ph.D. dissertation, University of Maryland, 1998.
21. Paul C. Light, *Government's Greatest Achievements: From Civil Rights to Homeland Security* (Washington, D.C.: Brookings Institution Press, 2002).

22. Light, *Government's Greatest Achievements*, 63.
23. Hamilton, "Ten Things I Wish Political Scientists Would Teach about Congress," 3.
24. Sandy Davis, Congressional Budget Office, *Unauthorized Appropriations and Expiring Authorizations*, Appendix A, cbo.gov/byclasscat.cfm?class=0&cat=6.
25. Eric Schickler, *Disjointed Pluralism: Institutional Innovation and the Development of the U.S. Congress* (Princeton University Press, 2001), 268.
26. Schickler, *Disjointed Pluralism*, 267.
27. Bob Schieffer, *This Just In: What I Couldn't Tell You on TV* (New York: Putnam, 2003).
28. Stephen Hess, "Media to Government: Drop Dead," *Brookings Review* 18 (winter 2000): 28.
29. Bill Moyers, "Journalism and Democracy," *Nation*, May 7, 2001, 12.
30. Media critic Neal Gabler's commentaries are especially incisive. See his "The Media Bias Myth," *Los Angeles Times*, December 22, 2002, M1.
31. Quoted in Bernard Aronson, "Tired of 'Gotcha' Journalism," *Washington Post*, March 6, 1997, A21.
32. Parker and Davidson, "Why Do Americans Love Their Congressmen So Much More Than Their Congress?"
33. *Washington Post* survey archives: washingtonpost.com.politics/polls/vault/stories/data.
34. Gallup Poll, reported by Karlyn Bowman, "POLLitics," *Roll Call*, December 5, 2002, 8.
35. John R. Hibbing and Elizabeth Theiss-Morse, *Congress as Public Enemy* (Cambridge, England: Cambridge University Press, 1995), 147.
36. Hibbing and Theiss-Morse, *Congress as Public Enemy*, 158.
37. Christopher Lee, "Amendment to Be Recommended on Continuity of Congress," *Washington Post*, May 25, 2003, A11.
38. See Kerry Kantin, "House Weighs Response to a Terror Attack," *The Hill*, July 17, 2002, 1.
39. Nather, "For Congress, a New World," 2274.
40. Ibid., 2274.
41. Quoted in Kirk Victor, "Congress in Eclipse," *National Journal*, April 5, 2003, 1067.
42. U.S. Congress, *Congressional Record*, daily ed., 108th Congress, 1st sess., February 12, 2002, S2268, S2271.
43. James Dao, "Congressman Seeks Review of U.S. Effort to Aid Iraq," *New York Times*, May 16, 2003, A15.
44. Quoted in Elizabeth Becker, "Bipartisan Call to Expand Inquiry Into Occupation," *New York Times*, May 24, 2003, A6.
45. Quoted in Victor, "Congress in Eclipse," 1068.
46. Quoted in Victor, "Congress in Eclipse," 1069.
47. John T. Noonan Jr., *Narrowing the Nation's Power* (Berkeley: University of California, 2002), 11.
48. Noonan, *Narrowing the Nation's Power*, 139.
49. The wording of the title of this section, "The Fundamental Things Apply," is from the Herman Hupfeld song "As Time Goes By," which was featured in the 1942 movie *Casablanca*.
50. E. J. Dionne Jr., "All Politics Is Now Global," *Washington Post*, July 13, 1993, A15.
51. "Lessons on Opposition," interview with Barney Frank, *Working Papers Magazine*, May–June 1982, 43.
52. Quoted in Francis X. Clines, "Weary of Political Noise, a Senator Sees a Peaceful Farm in Her Future," *New York Times*, December 3, 1995, 30.
53. Alvin Toffler, "Congress in the Year 2000," *GAO Review* (fall 1980): 44.
54. Alan Ehrenhalt, "Demanding the Right Size Government," *New York Times*, October 4, 1999, A31.
55. Hamilton, "Ten Things I Wish Political Scientists Would Teach about Congress," 7.
56. Ibid., 10.

Suggested Readings

This list of suggested readings is not intended to be exhaustive. We have listed those books we feel are most useful and accessible to students. In addition, we have listed Internet addresses that are good sources of information about Congress. Journal articles, papers delivered at meetings, doctoral dissertations, and individual essays in books are not included.

Reference Works

Bacon, Donald C., Roger H. Davidson, and Morton Keller, eds. *Encyclopedia of the United States Congress.* 4 vols. New York: Simon and Schuster, 1995.

Barone, Michael, with Richard E. Cohen and Grant Ujifusa. *The Almanac of American Politics, 2004.* Washington, D.C.: National Journal, 2003.

Byrd, Robert C. *The Senate, 1789–1989.* 4 vols. Washington, D.C.: U.S. Government Printing Office, 1988–1993.

Congressional Quarterly's *Guide to Congress.* 5th ed. 2 vols. Washington, D.C.: CQ Press, 2000.

CQ's Politics in America 2004: The 108th Congress. Ed. David Hawkings and Brian Nutting. Washington, D.C.: CQ Press, 2003.

Maxwell, Bruce. *How to Track Politics on the Internet.* Washington, D.C.: CQ Press, 2000.

Ornstein, Norman J., Thomas E. Mann, and Michael J. Malbin. *Vital Statistics on Congress, 2001–2002.* Washington, D.C.: AEI Press, 2002.

Internet Addresses

Architect of the Capitol: http://www.aoc.gov
Campaigns and Elections: http://www.camelect.com
Carl Albert Congressional Research and Studies Center, University of Oklahoma: www.ou.edu/special/albertctr/cachome.html
Center for Congress, Indiana University: http://www.congress.indiana.edu
Center for Legislative Archives (National Archives): http://www.nara.gov/nara/legislative
Center for Responsive Politics: http://www.opensecrets.org
CNN/*Time* Allpolitics: http://www.allpolitics.com
Committee for the Study of the American Electorate: http://www.gspm.org/csae
Congressional Quarterly: http://www.cq.com
C-SPAN: http://www.c-span.org
Democratic National Committee: http://www.democrats.org
Dirksen Center's Congresslink: http://www.congresslink.org
Federal Election Commission: http://www.fec.gov
Federal government information: http://www.firstgov.gov
Federal judiciary: http://www.uscourts.gov *or* http://www.fjc.gov
Federal statistics: http://www.fedstats.gov
Gallup Organization: http://www.gallup.com
Government Printing Office: http://www.access.gpo.gov
Green Party: www.greenparties.org
Library of Congress: http://www.lcweb.loc.gov *or* http://www.thomas.loc.gov
New York Times: http://www.nytimes.com

Project Vote Smart: http://www.vote-smart.org
Republican National Committee: http://www.rnc.org
Roll Call: http://www.rollcall.com
U.S. House of Representatives: http://www.house.gov *or* http://www.clerkweb.house.gov
U.S. Senate: http://www.senate.gov
Washington Post: http://www.washingtonpost.com
White House: http://www.whitehouse.gov

Chapter 1 The Two Congresses

Bianco, William, ed. *Congress on Display, Congress at Work.* Ann Arbor: University of Michigan Press, 2000.

Hibbing, John R., and Elizabeth Theiss-Morse. *Congress as Public Enemy.* Cambridge: Cambridge University Press, 1995.

Mayhew, David R. *Congress: The Electoral Connection.* New Haven: Yale University Press, 1974.

Chapter 2 Evolution of the Modern Congress

Binder, Sarah A. *Minority Rights, Majority Rule: Partisanship and the Development of Congress.* Cambridge: Cambridge University Press, 1997.

Currie, David P. *The Constitution Congress: The Federalist Period, 1789–1801.* Chicago: University of Chicago Press, 1997.

Galloway, George B. *History of the House of Representatives.* Rev. ed. Edited by Sidney Wise. New York: Crowell, 1976.

Haynes, George H. *The Senate of the United States: Its History and Practice.* 2 vols. Boston: Houghton Mifflin, 1938.

Josephy, Alvin M., Jr. *On the Hill: A History of the American Congress.* New York: Simon and Schuster, 1980.

MacNeil, Neil. *Forge of Democracy: The House of Representatives.* New York: McKay, 1963.

Miller, William Lee. *Arguing about Slavery: John Quincy Adams and the Great Battle in the United States Congress.* New York: Vintage, 1998.

Rakove, Jack N. *Original Meanings: Politics and Ideas in the Making of the Constitution.* New York: Vintage, 1997.

Schickler, Eric. *Disjointed Pluralism: Institutional Innovation and the Development of the U.S. Congress.* Princeton University Press, 2001.

Swift, Elaine K. *The Making of an American Senate: Reconstitutive Change in Congress, 1787–1841.* Ann Arbor: University of Michigan Press, 1996.

Young, James S. *The Washington Community, 1800–1828.* New York: Columbia University Press, 1966.

Chapter 3 Going for It: Recruitment and Candidacy

Canon, David T. *Race, Redistricting, and Representation.* University of Chicago Press, 1999.

Ehrenhalt, Alan. *The United States of Ambition.* New York: Random House, 1991.

Fowler, Linda L., and Robert D. McClure. *Political Ambition: Who Decides to Run for Congress.* New Haven: Yale University Press, 1989.

Kazee, Thomas A., ed.*Who Runs for Congress? Ambition, Context, and Candidate Emergence.* Washington, D.C.: Congressional Quarterly, 1994.

Loomis, Burdett. *The New American Politician.* New York: Basic Books, 1988.

Monmonier, Mark. *Bushmanders and Bullwinkles: How Politicians Manipulate Electronic Maps and Census Data to Win Elections.* Chicago: University of Chicago Press, 2001.

Chapter 4 Making It: The Electoral Game

Cain, Bruce, John Ferejohn, and Morris Fiorina. *The Personal Vote: Constituency Service and Electoral Independence.* Cambridge: Harvard University Press, 1987.

Herrnson, Paul S. *Congressional Elections: Campaigning at Home and in Washington.* 3d ed. Washington, D.C.: CQ Press, 2000.

Jacobson, Gary C. *The Politics of Congressional Elections.* 5th ed. New York: Longman, 2001.

Krasno, Jonathan S. *Challengers, Competition, and Reelection.* New Haven: Yale University Press, 1994.

Thurber, James A., ed. *The Battle for Congress: Consultants, Candidates, and Voters.* Washington, D.C.: Brookings Institution, 2001.

Chapter 5 Being There: Hill Styles and Home Styles

Baker, Ross K. *Friend and Foe in the U.S. Senate.* New York: Free Press, 1980.

_____. *House and Senate.* 3d ed. New York: Norton, 2001.

Davidson, Roger H. *The Role of the Congressman.* Indianapolis: Bobbs-Merrill, 1969.

Fenno, Richard F., Jr. *Home Style: House Members in Their Districts.* Boston: Little, Brown, 1978.

Fiorina, Morris P. *Congress: Keystone of the Washington Establishment.* 2d ed. New Haven: Yale University Press, 1989.

Hibbing, John R. *Congressional Careers: Contours of Life in the U.S. House of Representatives.* Chapel Hill: University of North Carolina Press, 1991.

Price, David E. *The Congressional Experience: A View from the Hill.* 2d ed. Boulder: Westview Press, 2000.

Chapter 6 Leaders and Parties in Congress

Aldrich, John H. *Why Parties? The Origins and Transformation of Party Politics in America.* Chicago: University of Chicago Press, 1995.

Baker, Richard A., and Roger H. Davidson, eds. *First Among Equals: Outstanding Senate Leaders of the Twentieth Century.* Washington, D.C.: Congressional Quarterly, 1991.

Cox, Gary W., and Mathew D. McCubbins. *Legislative Leviathan: Party Government in the House.* Berkeley: University of California Press, 1993.

Davidson, Roger H., Susan Webb Hammond, and Raymond W. Smock, eds. *Masters of the House: Congressional Leaders over Two Centuries.* Boulder: Westview Press, 1998.

Peters, Ronald M., Jr. *The American Speakership: The Office in Historical Perspective.* 2d ed. Baltimore: Johns Hopkins University Press, 1997.

Rohde, David W. *Parties and Leaders in the Postreform House.* Chicago: University of Chicago Press, 1991.

Sinclair, Barbara. *Legislators, Leaders, and Lawmaking: The U.S. House of Representatives in the Postreform Era.* Baltimore: Johns Hopkins University Press, 1995.

_____. *The Transformation of the U.S. Senate.* Baltimore: Johns Hopkins University Press, 1989.

Chapter 7 Committees: Workshops of Congress

Deering, Christopher J., and Steven S. Smith. *Committees in Congress.* 3d ed. Washington, D.C.: CQ Press, 1997.

Evans, C. Lawrence. *Leadership in Committee: A Comparative Analysis of Leadership Behavior in the U.S. Senate.* Ann Arbor: University of Michigan Press, 1991.

Fenno, Richard F., Jr. *Congressmen in Committees.* Boston: Little, Brown, 1973.

Hall, Richard L. *Participation in Congress.* New Haven: Yale University Press, 1996.

King, David C. *Turf Wars: How Congressional Committees Claim Jurisdiction.* Chicago: University of Chicago Press, 1997.

Krehbiel, Keith. *Information and Legislative Organization.* Ann Arbor: University of Michigan Press, 1991.

Maltzman, Forrest. *Competing Principals: Committees, Parties, and the Organization of Congress.* Ann Arbor: University of Michigan Press, 1997.

Wilson, Woodrow. *Congressional Government.* Reprint of 1885 ed. Baltimore: Johns Hopkins University Press, 1981.

Chapter 8 Congressional Rules and Procedures

Binder, Sarah A., and Steven S. Smith. *Politics or Principle? Filibustering in the United States Senate.* Washington, D.C.: Brookings Institution, 1997.

_____. *Stalemate: Causes and Consequences of Legislative Gridlock.* Washington, D.C.: Brookings Institution, 2003.

Evans, C. Lawrence, and Walter J. Oleszck. *Congress under Fire: Reform Politics and the Republican Majority.* Boston: Houghton Mifflin, 1997.

Krehbiel, Keith. *Pivotal Politics: A Theory of U.S. Lawmaking.* Chicago: University of Chicago Press, 1998.

Krutz, Glen. *Omnibus Legislating in the U.S. Congress.* Columbus: Ohio State University Press, 2001.

Longley, Lawrence D., and Walter J. Oleszek. *Bicameral Politics: Conference Committees in Congress.* New Haven: Yale University Press, 1989.

Loomis, Burdett ed. *Esteemed Colleagues: Civility and Deliberation in the U.S. Senate.* Washington, D.C.: Brookings Institution, 2000.

Oleszek, Walter J. *Congressional Procedures and the Policy Process.* 5th ed. Washington, D.C.: CQ Press, 2001.

Sinclair, Barbara. *Unorthodox Lawmaking: New Legislative Processes in the U.S. Congress.* 2d ed. Washington, D.C.: CQ Press, 2000.

Smith, Steven S. *Call to Order: Floor Politics in the House and Senate.* Washington, D.C.: Brookings Institution, 1989.

Chapter 9 Decision Making in Congress

Arnold, R. Douglas. *The Logic of Congressional Action.* New Haven: Yale University Press, 1990.

Baumgartner, Frank, and Bryan D. Jones. *Agendas and Instability in American Politics.* Chicago: University of Chicago Press, 1993.

Binder, Sarah A. *Stalemate: Causes and Consequences of Legislative Gridlock.* Washington, D.C.: Brookings Institution, 2003.

Edwards, George C. *At the Margins: Presidential Leadership of Congress.* New Haven: Yale University Press, 1989.

Kingdon, John W. *Congressmen's Voting Decisions.* 3d ed. Ann Arbor: University of Michigan Press, 1989.

Poole, Keith T., and Howard Rosenthal. *Congress: A Political-Economic History of Roll Call Voting.* New York: Oxford University Press, 1996.

Chapter 10 Congress and the President

Binkley, Wilfred. *President and Congress.* New York: Knopf, 1947.

Bond, Jon R., and Richard Fleisher, eds. *Polarized Politics: Congress and the President in a Partisan Era.* Washington, D.C.: CQ Press, 2000.

Fisher, Louis. *Constitutional Conflicts between Congress and the President.* 4th ed. Lawrence: University Press of Kansas, 1997.

Gilmour, John B. *Strategic Disagreement: Stalemate in American Politics.* Pittsburgh: University of Pittsburgh Press, 1995.

Jones, Charles O. *Separate but Equal Branches: Congress and the Presidency.* 2d ed. New York: Chatham House, 1999.

Mayhew, David R. *Divided We Govern: Party Control, Lawmaking, and Investigating, 1946–1990.* New Haven: Yale University Press, 1991.

Chapter 11 Congress and the Bureaucracy

Aberbach, Joel D. *Keeping a Watchful Eye: The Politics of Congressional Oversight.* Washington, D.C.: Brookings Institution, 1990.

Arnold, R. Douglas. *Congress and the Bureaucracy: A Theory of Influence.* New Haven: Yale University Press, 1979.

Foreman, Christopher J., Jr. *Signals from the Hill: Congressional Oversight and the Challenge of Social Regulation.* New Haven: Yale University Press, 1988.

Light, Paul C. *The New Public Service.* Washington, D.C.: Brookings Institution, 1999.

———. *The True Size of Government.* Washington, D.C.: Brookings Institution, 1999.

Rosenbloom, David. *Building a Legislative-Centered Public Administration: Congress and the Administrative State, 1946–1999.* Tuscaloosa: University of Alabama Press, 2000.

Chapter 12 Congress and the Courts

Berger, Raoul. *Congress v. The Supreme Court.* Cambridge: Harvard University Press, 1969.

Campbell, Colton and John Stack, eds. *Congress Confronts the Court.* Lanham, Md.: Rowan and Littlefield, 2001.

Fisher, Louis. *Constitutional Dialogues.* Princeton: Princeton University Press, 1988.

Katzmann, Robert A. *Courts and Congress.* Washington, D.C.: Brookings Institution, 1997.

Morgan, Donald. *Congress and the Constitution.* Cambridge: Harvard University Press, 1966.

Noonan, John T., Jr. *Narrowing the Nation's Power: The Supreme Court Sides with the States.* Berkeley: University of California Press, 2002.

Chapter 13 Congress and Organized Interests

Birnbaum, Jeffrey H., and Alan S. Murray. *Showdown at Gucci Gulch: Lawmakers, Lobbyists, and the Unlikely Triumph of Tax Reform.* New York: Random House, 1987.

Cigler, Allan J., and Burdett A. Loomis, eds. *Interest Group Politics.* 6th ed. Washington, D.C.: CQ Press, 2002.

Rauch, Jonathan. *Demosclerosis: The Silent Killer of American Government.* New York: Times Books, 1994.

Rozell, Mark, and Clyde Wilcox. *Interest Groups in American Campaigns.* Washington, D.C.: CQ Press, 1999.

Truman, David B. *The Governmental Process, Political Interests, and Public Opinion.* 2d ed. New York: Knopf, 1971.

Chapter 14 Congress, Budgets, and Domestic Policy Making

Elving, Ronald D. *Conflict and Compromise: How Congress Makes the Law.* New York: Simon and Schuster, 1995.

Kerwin, Cornelius M. *Rulemaking: How Government Agencies Write Laws and Make Policy.* 3d ed. Washington, D.C.: CQ Press, 2003.

Kingdon, John W. *Agendas, Alternatives, and Public Policies.* Boston: Little, Brown, 1984.

Rubin, Irene S. *Balancing the Federal Budget.* New York: Chatham House, 2003.

Schick, Allen. *The Federal Budget: Politics, Policy, Process.* Rev. ed. Washington, D.C.: Brookings Institution, 2000.

Chapter 15 Congress and National Security Policies

Crabb, Cecil V., Jr., Glenn, J. Antizzo, and Leila E. Sarieddine. *Congress and the Foreign Policy Process.* Baton Rouge, Lousiana State University Press, 2000.

Fisher, Louis. *Congressional Abdication on War and Spending.* College Station: Texas A&M University Press, 2000.

Hinckley, Barbara. *Less Than Meets the Eye: Foreign Policy Making and the Myth of the Assertive Congress.* University of Chicago Press, 1994.

Lindsay, James. *Congress and the Politics of U.S. Foreign Policy.* Baltimore: Johns Hopkins University Press, 1994.

Mann, Thomas E., ed. *A Question of Balance: The President, the Congress, and Foreign Policy*. Washington, D.C.: Brookings Institution, 1990.

Chapter 16 The Two Congresses and the American People

Bessette, Joseph M. *The Mild Voice of Reason: Deliberative Democracy and American National Government*. Chicago: University of Chicago Press, 1994.

Bok, Derek. *The Trouble with Government*. Cambridge: Harvard University Press, 2001.

Cook, Timothy E. *Making Laws and Making News: Media Strategies in the U.S. House of Representatives*. Washington, D.C.: Brookings Institution, 1989.

Dodd, Lawrence C., and Bruce I. Oppenheimer, eds. *Congress Reconsidered*. 7th ed. Washington, D.C.: CQ Press, 2001.

Mackenzie, G. Calvin, with Michael Hafken. *Scandal Proof: Do Ethics Laws Make Government Ethical?* Washington, D.C.: Brookings Institution, 2002.

Mann, Thomas E., and Norman J. Ornstein, eds. *Congress, the Press, and the Public*. Washington, D.C.: Brookings Institution, 1994.

Schickler, Eric. *Disjointed Pluralism: Institutional Innovation and the Development of the U.S. Congress*. Princeton: Princeton University Press, 2001.

Wolfensberger, Donald. *Congress and the People: Deliberative Democracy on Trial*. Washington, D.C.: Woodrow Wilson Center Press, 2000.

Index

Congressional Time Line: Nineteenth Century

	1790	1800	1810	1820	1830
Size of House of Representatives	65	142	186	213	242
Size of Senate	26	34	36	48	48

Parties

Federalist Era (1789–1800)   Jeffersonian Era (1800–1828)   Jacksonian Era (1828–1856)

1st Congress Antifederalists (1792) ▲

Congressional Nominating Caucus (1804–1828)

J. Q. Adams elected (1824) ▼

Presidential nominating conventions (1832) ▲

Internal

Jefferson's *Manual* (1801)

Congress convenes; Ways and Means Committee (1789) ▲▼

Procedural rules, standing committees (1790s) ▼▲

Speaker Henry Clay (1811) ▲

Committees control legislation (1820s)

Unlimited debate in Senate (1828) ▼ ▼

Major Court Cases

Judicial review *Marbury v. Madison* (1803)

Marshall Court (1801–1835)

Alien and Sedition Acts (1798) ▲ ▼

McCulloch v. Maryland (1819) ▼▼

Major Laws/ Investigations

St. Clair Investigation (1792)

Slave importation halted (1807)

Rivers and Harbors Act (1823)

Bill of Rights (1791) ▲▲

Louisiana Purchase (1803) ▲ ▲

Missouri Compromise (1820) ▲ ▲

Science/ Technology/ Communications

"National Road" (Wheeling-Cumberland) (1806)

Lewis and Clark Expedition (1803–1806) ▼ ▼▲

Rotary printing press (1814) ▲

Commercial railroads (1830s) ▼

Wars/ World Events

Barbary pirates (1801–1805) ▼ ▼

War of 1812 (1812–1814) ▼ ▼

Monroe Doctrine (1823) ▲

Presidents

Washington (1789–1797) ▼ ▼

Jefferson (1801–1809) ▼ ▼▼

"Jeffersonians" (Madison; Monroe) (1809–1825)

Jackson (1829–1837) ▼ ▼

	1790	1800	1810	1820	1830